THE HUMAN RIGHTS COVENANTS AT 50

The Human Rights Covenants at 50

Their Past, Present, and Future

Edited by
DANIEL MOECKLI
HELEN KELLER

Assistant Editor
CORINA HERI

OXFORD
UNIVERSITY PRESS

OXFORD
UNIVERSITY PRESS

Great Clarendon Street, Oxford, OX2 6DP,
United Kingdom

Oxford University Press is a department of the University of Oxford.
It furthers the University's objective of excellence in research, scholarship,
and education by publishing worldwide. Oxford is a registered trade mark of
Oxford University Press in the UK and in certain other countries

First Edition published in 2018

Published in the United States of America by Oxford University Press
198 Madison Avenue, New York, NY 10016, United States of America

British Library Cataloguing in Publication Data
Data available

Library of Congress Control Number: 2018930388

ISBN 978–0–19–882589–0

Acknowledgements

At the origin of this volume was the idea that the fiftieth anniversary of the two UN human rights Covenants was a cause for celebration and reflection. We therefore gathered a group of eminent scholars and invited them to a symposium co-organized by the University of Zurich's Institute for Public International Law and the European Society of International Law and held in Zurich on 14–15 April 2016. The symposium, as well as the book resulting from it, would not have been possible without the support of many people, to whom we would like to express our gratitude.

First and foremost, we would like to thank the contributors for agreeing to draft their respective papers, presenting them in Zurich, and then turning them into chapters for this book.

We would also like to thank the many people who helped make the 2016 symposium a success. Matthew Craven, Jürg Lindenmann, and Matthias Mahlmann generously agreed to provide comments that helped improve the papers. Oliver Diggelmann and Joseph HH Weiler introduced and chaired the symposium panels and provided insightful remarks. Unfortunately, two of the contributors were prevented from travelling to Zurich. We are extremely grateful to Leena Grover and Lorenz Langer for agreeing to present their papers at the symposium at very short notice. Many thanks also go to Natalie Balazs, Patrik Dudar, Christine Tramontano, and Reto Walther, who were instrumental in organizing the symposium. Finally, we would like to express our gratitude to all the participants in the symposium for their perceptive questions and comments and to the Swiss Federal Department of Foreign Affairs, which kindly sponsored the event.

Corina Heri played a key role in editing all the chapters for the book. We thank her for the admirable efficiency and diligence with which she carried out this role. At Oxford University Press, Merel Alstein, Emma Endean-Mills, Natasha Flemming, and Kimberly Marsh expertly steered us through the various editorial stages, and we are very grateful for their support.

We hope that this volume will inspire the work of the UN treaty bodies and of human rights scholars as they begin to give the Covenants the shape they will take for the coming fifty years.

Daniel Moeckli/Helen Keller
February 2018

Contents

II. THE PRESENT: WHAT IS THE INFLUENCE OF THE COVENANTS?

List of Tables

Table of Cases

INTERNATIONAL AND REGIONAL BODIES

African Commission on Human and Peoples' Rights

African Committee of Experts on the Rights and Welfare of the Child

African Court on Human and People's Rights (ACtHPR)

Committee on the Elimination of Racial Discrimination (CERD)

International Centre for Settlement of Investment Disputes (ICSID)

International Court of Justice (ICJ)

NATIONAL COURTS

List of Contributors

Samantha Besson is Professor of Public International Law and European Law at the University of Fribourg, Switzerland.

Başak Çali is Professor of International Law at Hertie School of Governance, Berlin, and Director of the Centre for Global Public Law at Koç University, Istanbul. She has published widely in many areas of international human rights law, including the influence of human rights law in domestic settings.

Felice D Gaer is the Director of the Jacob Blaustein Institute for the Advancement of Human Rights. She is also the Vice-Chair of the Committee against Torture, a United Nations-administered treaty monitoring body on which she has served since 2000.

Stephen Humphreys is an Associate Professor of International Law at the London School of Economics.

Christine Kaufmann is Professor of International and Constitutional Law and Chair of the Centre for Human Rights Studies at the University of Zurich. Her main research interests include the interactions between human rights, business and economic law, and the related implications on global governance.

Helen Keller serves as a Judge at the European Court of Human Rights and is Professor of Public Law, European Law. and Public International Law at the University of Zurich. She is also a former member of the UN Committee on Human Rights.

Daniel Moeckli is an Assistant Professor of Public International Law and Constitutional Law at the University of Zurich and a Fellow of the University of Nottingham Human Rights Law Centre.

Amrei Müller is a Leverhulme Trust Early Career Researcher in the Health and Human Rights Unit at the School of Law, Queen's University, Belfast. At present, she is conducting research for the project 'Healthcare in conflict: Do armed groups have obligations and responsibilities?', spanning human rights and international humanitarian law.

Patrick Mutzenberg holds a PhD in Human Rights from the University of Grenoble. He is currently the Director of the Centre for Civil and Political Rights, an NGO facilitating the participation of civil society in the work of the Human Rights Committee. He is also a lay-judge at the Criminal Tribunal in Geneva.

Gerald L Neuman is the J Sinclair Armstrong Professor of International, Foreign, and Comparative Law at Harvard Law School, and the Co-Director of its Human Rights Program. From 2011 to 2014, he was a member of the Human Rights Committee.

Mónica Pinto is Professor of International Law and International Human Rights Law, Director of the Master Program on International Human Rights Law, University of Buenos Aires Law School. She is a Member of the Committee of Experts on the Application of ILO Conventions and Recommendations, and President of the World Bank Administrative Tribunal.

Maya Hertig Randall (attorney at law, LLM Cambridge) is a tenured Professor of Constitutional Law at Geneva University. She is a member of the Swiss Federal Commission Against Racism and the ICRC, and co-directs the Certificate of Advanced Studies in Human Rights at the University of Geneva.

Martín Sigal is a Professor at the University of Buenos Aires Law School. He qualified as a lawyer at the University of Buenos Aires, and holds a Master in Laws (LLM) from Columbia University. He is a founder and former director of Asociación Civil por la Igualdad y la Justicia, and currently Director of the Center of Human Rights at UBA Law School, and a Member of the Board of Amnesty International, Argentina, and ACIJ.

Manisuli Ssenyonjo is Professor of International Law and Human Rights at Brunel University, London. He is the managing editor and co-editor-in-chief of the *International Human Rights Law Review*. His research and teaching interests are in areas of public international law and human rights law, including economic, social, and cultural rights.

Yogesh Tyagi is Vice Chancellor of the University of Delhi and a Member of the *Institut de Droit International.*

List of Abbreviations

AC	Appeal Cases
ACHPR	African Charter on Human and Peoples' Rights
ACHR	American Convention on Human Rights
ACIJ	Civil Association for Equality and Justice (*Asociación Civil por la Igualdad y la Justicia*)
ACtHPR	African Court on Human and Peoples' Rights
AD	Appellate Division (of the Bangladeshi Supreme Court)
AICHR	Intergovernmental Commission of Human Rights
AIR	All India Reporter
AJIL	American Journal of International Law
ALI	American Law Institute
ASEAN	Association of Southeast Asian Nations
AU	African Union
AWC	Allahabad Weekly Cases
BGBl	Bundesgesetzblatt (Germany)
BLC	Bangladesh Law Chronicles
BLD	Bangladesh Legal Decisions
BT	German Bundestag
BVerwG	Bundesverwaltungsgericht (German Federal Administrative Court)
BvR	*Verfassungsbeschwerde zum Bundesverfassungs-gericht* (constitutional complaint to the Federal Constitutional Court of Germany)
BwCA	Botswana Court of Appeal
BYIL	British Yearbook of International Law
Cal.	Calcutta
CAR	Central African Republic
CAT	United Nations Convention against Torture (also referred to as UNCAT)
CBDR	common but differentiated responsibilities
CEDAW	United Nations Convention on the Elimination of all Forms of Discrimination Against Women
CEDMHR	Commission for Eliminating Discrimination and Monitoring of Human Rights (Sri Lanka)
CELS	*Centro de Estudios Legales y Sociales* (Center for Legal and Social Studies)
CERD	Committee on the Elimination of Racial Discrimination
CESCR	Committee on Economic, Social and Cultural Rights
ch	chapter
CJEU	Court of Justice of the European Union
CMW	Committee on the Rights of Migrant Workers
CoE	Council of Europe
CPR	civil and political rights
CRC	Convention on the Rights of the Child
Cri LJ	Criminal Law Journal (India)
CRPD	Convention on the Rights of Persons with Disabilities

DLR	Dhaka Law Reports (Bangladesh)
DRC	Democratic Republic of the Congo
ECHR	European Convention on Human Rights
ECLAC	Economic Commission for Latin America and the Caribbean
ECOSOC	UN Economic and Social Council
ECSR	European Committee of Social Rights
ECtHR	European Court of Human Rights
EFSF	European Financial Stability Facility
EHRC	Equality and Human Rights Commission
EJIL	European Journal of International Law
eKLR	Kenya Law Reports
ESCh	European Social Charter
ESCR	economic, social and cultural rights
ESCR-Net	International Network for Economic, Social and Cultural Rights
ESIL	European Society of International Law
ESM	European Stability Mechanism
ETS	European Treaty Series
EU	European Union
EWCA	England and Wales Court of Appeal
EWHC	England and Wales High Court (Administrative Court)
F.Supp.2d	Federal Supplement, Second Series (US)
FAO	UN Food and Agriculture Organization
FCC	German Constitutional Court
FMSLR	Federated Malay States Law Report
GAOR	Official Records of the UN General Assembly
GATT	WTO General Agreement on Tariffs and Trade
GDP	Gross Domestic Product
GHG	greenhouse gas
Hague YIL	Hague Yearbook of International Law
HCD	High Court Division (of the Bangladeshi Supreme Court)
HCJ	Israeli High Court of Justice
HIV	human immunodeficiency virus
HL	House of Lords
HRC	Human Rights Committee
HRCSL	Human Rights Commission of Sri Lanka
HRTF	Human Rights Task Force (Sri Lanka)
IACHR	Inter-American Commission on Human Rights
IACtHR	Inter-American Court of Human Rights
IASHR	Inter-American System on Human Rights
ICC	International Criminal Court
ICCPR	International Covenant on Civil and Political Rights
ICERD	Convention on the Elimination of All Forms of Racial Discrimination
ICESCR	International Covenant on Economic, Social and Cultural Rights
ICJ	International Court of Justice
ICM	Inter-Committee Meeting
ICSID	International Centre for Settlement of Investment Disputes
ICT-BD	International Crimes Tribunal of Bangladesh
IFC	International Finance Corporation
IFIs	international financial institutions

IFOR	International Fellowship of Reconciliation
IHRL	international human rights law
IHRR	International Human Rights Reports
ILA	International Law Association
ILDC	Oxford Reports on International Law in Domestic Courts
ILO	International Labour Organization
IMF	International Monetary Fund
IPCC	Intergovernmental Panel on Climate Change
JCHR	the UK Parliament's Joint Committee on Human Rights
Ker.	Kerala
LeCA	Lesotho Court of Appeal
LNTS	League of Nations Treaty Series
LOIPR	List of Issues Prior to Reporting
LR	Law Review
MENA	Middle East and North Africa
MLJ	Malayan Law Journal
NASC	Namibian Supreme Court
NCHR	National Commission for Human Rights (Pakistan)
NCIIHRT	National Committee for the Implementation of International Human Rights Treaties (North Korea)
NDCs	nationally determined contributions
NGO(s)	non-governmental organization(s)
NHRC	National Human Rights Commission (India)
NHRIs	national human rights institutions
NIHRC	the Northern Ireland Human Rights Commission
NMRF	National Mechanism for Reporting and Follow-up
OAS	Organization of American States
OECD	Organization for Economic Co-operation and Development
OHCHR	Office of the United Nations High Commissioner for Human Rights
OP1-ICCPR	First Optional Protocol to the ICCPR
OP-ICESCR	Optional Protocol to the ICESCR
PACE	Parliamentary Assembly of the Council of Europe
PCIJ	Permanent Court of International Justice
PSNR	permanent sovereignty over natural resources
RCC	Russian Constitutional Court
(R)ESCh	(Revised) European Social Charter
RSC	Russian Supreme Court
SAR	Special Administrative Region
SC	Supreme Court
SCC	Supreme Court Cases (India)
SCGLR	Supreme Court of Ghana Law Reports
SCHR	the Scottish Human Rights Commission
ScotCS	Scottish Court of Session
SCR	Supreme Court Reports (India)
SeCC	Senegalese Court of Cassation
SLR	Sri Lankan Law Reports
SPR	Simplified Reporting Procedure
SUHAKAM	National Human Rights Commission of Malaysia (*Suruhanjaya Hak Asasi Manusia*)

UDHR	Universal Declaration of Human Rights
UgCC	Ugandan Constitutional Court
UK	United Kingdom
UKSC	Supreme Court of the United Kingdom of Great Britain and Northern Ireland
UNCAT	United Nations Convention against Torture (also referred to as CAT)
UNGA	United Nations General Assembly
UNGP	UN Guiding Principles on Business and Human Rights
UNTB	UN human rights treaty bodies
UNTC	United Nations Treaty Collection
UNTS	United Nations Treaty Series
UPR	Universal Periodic Review
VCLT	Vienna Convention on the Law of Treaties
WTO	World Trade Organization
ZACC	Constitutional Court of South Africa
ZASCA	Supreme Court of Appeal of South Africa
ZWHHC	Zimbabwe Harare High Court

1

Introduction

Helen Keller and Daniel Moeckli

Human rights protection today marks a cornerstone of international law and belongs to its most developed areas. Human rights are enshrined in international conventions, as well as national constitutions, and form the subject of innumerable treatises. As compared to many other subject areas of international law, human rights have a considerable advantage: they can be asserted before international adjudicative bodies or courts. Their recognition is 'the foundation of freedom, justice and peace in the world', as the preambles of the International Covenant on Economic, Social and Cultural Rights (ICESCR)[1] and the International Covenant on Civil and Political Rights (ICCPR)[2] proclaim. However, the international system of human rights protection has been facing a number of major challenges, such as how to deal with the distinction between different categories of rights or how to design effective monitoring mechanisms. The system is very likely to continue to attract a great deal of attention over the next few years, as it is faced with the question of how to guarantee human rights in times of globalization, financial crises, environmental disasters, and climate change, war, and terrorism. The reader will find some answers to these questions in the present book, which contains papers that were presented during a symposium held in Zurich, Switzerland, in 2016 on the occasion of the fiftieth anniversary of the adoption of the ICESCR and the ICCPR.[3]

Half a century ago, on 16 December 1966, the UN General Assembly adopted the two UN human rights Covenants. While their adoption was celebrated all over the world, their fiftieth anniversary has received very little attention from the international community.[4] The present volume marks this anniversary by taking stock of the first half-century of the existence of what are probably the world's two most important human rights treaties. It does so by reflecting on what the Covenants have achieved (or failed to achieve) in the years that have passed, by determining

[1] International Covenant on Economic, Social and Cultural Rights (opened for signature 16 December 1966, entered into force 3 January 1976) 993 UNTS 3.

[2] International Covenant on Civil and Political Rights (opened for signature 16 December 1966, entered into force 23 March 1976) 999 UNTS 171.

[3] The Symposium was organized by the Institute for Public International Law of the University of Zurich together with the European Society of International Law (ESIL) and took place on 14–15 April 2016.

[4] See, for one of the rare exceptions, Eibe Riedel, 'Reflections on the UN Human Rights Covenants at Fifty' (2016) 54 Archiv des Völkerrechts, 132–54.

The Human Rights Covenants at 50: Their Past, Present, and Future. Daniel Moeckli, Helen Keller, and Corina Heri. Published 2018 by Oxford University Press.

and comparing their current influence in the various regions of the world, and by assessing their potential roles in the future.

Some fundamental issues that are addressed by the contributors to this book are as old as the two Covenants themselves. They concern, for example, the division of human rights into first- and second-generation rights, and the questions of whether there should be one central monitoring body—possibly a world court—or more than just one, and whether such a body or bodies should be able to issue legally binding decisions or 'only' recommendations. Other important questions dealt with in this book are how human rights treaties should be interpreted—in compliance with the Vienna Convention on the Law of Treaties or, rather, *sui generis*—and who is bound by the Covenants—only State actors or also private individuals. However, the contributors go beyond such questions, which have been explored before; they develop new answers to old questions and point to new challenges.

The book begins by looking back to the origins of the Covenants. The Covenants' story began with the ambitious goal of creating an International Bill of Human Rights. In 1945, the first milestone in this regard was reached with the proclamation of the Universal Declaration of Human Rights (UDHR).[5] The next step was to be the inclusion of the UDHR rights in a binding human rights treaty. After years of tough negotiations, the two binding UN human rights covenants were finally adopted on 16 December 1966. In her chapter entitled 'The History of the Covenants: Looking Back Half a Century and Beyond', MAYA HERTIG RANDALL gives a detailed account of that time and the political context of the negotiation process.

The ICCPR and the ICESCR have played an important role in the protection of human rights in the last decades. The fact that a large number of States have ratified the twin Covenants can certainly be regarded as a success.[6] Furthermore, the introduction of different monitoring and enforcement mechanisms—from the State reporting process to the individual application system—is another important achievement. With regard to the implementation of the Covenants, much depends on the actors involved, including the treaty bodies—the Committee on Economic, Social and Cultural Rights (CESCR) and the Human Rights Committee (HRC)—and non-governmental organizations (NGOs). In this context, GERALD L NEUMAN, in his chapter 'Giving Meaning and Effect to Human Rights: The Contributions of Human Rights Committee Members', presents and discusses the multiple roles that the members of the HRC play with regard to the implementation of the rights guaranteed in the ICCPR. He argues that the members' most important contribution is their credible and professional interpretation of the ICCPR rights, thereby providing an objective framework for criticizing States' failure to respect these rights. DANIEL MOECKLI, on the other hand, comments on the—disputed—techniques that the CESCR has developed in order to interpret the ICESCR. His chapter 'Interpretation of the ICESCR: Between Morality and State Consent' argues that,

[5] Universal Declaration of Human Rights (adopted 10 December 1948) UNGA Res 217 A(III).

[6] 165 States have ratified the ICESCR and 169 States have ratified the ICCPR. See Office of the High Commissioner for Human Rights, 'Ratification of 18 International Human Rights Treaties' <http://indicators.ohchr.org/> accessed 6 June 2017.

for its interpretive practice to be legitimate, the CESCR must adhere to a set of interpretive principles, apply these principles in a coherent manner, and lay bare how a particular interpretive outcome is reached. PATRICK MUTZENBERG, in his contribution on 'NGOs: Essential Actors for Embedding the Covenants in the National Context', illustrates the position and the tasks of NGOs within the work of the Committees, as well as their crucial role in the process of implementing the recommendations of the Committees at the national level.

Almost half of the chapters of this book are dedicated to the assessment of the current influence of either the ICCPR or the ICESCR in one of the world's regions. The authors—namely MANISULI SSENYONJO for Africa, BAŞAK ÇALI for the Middle East, MÓNICA PINTO and MARTÍN SIGAL for Latin America, YOGESH TYAGI for Asia, and AMREI MÜLLER for Europe—were provided with the same set of non-exhaustive questions as a starting point for their contributions. They were asked to identify broad trends and challenges within the respective regions, or rather within States parties belonging to these regions, by considering, inter alia, the impact of the Covenants on national legislation and on the jurisprudence of national and regional courts; the influence of the General Comments, concluding observations on State reports, and Views concerning individual communications issued by the HRC and the CESCR; the impact of the Universal Periodic Review process with regard to the Covenants; the impact of the Covenants' standing on legal scholarship; and the availability of the relevant UN documents in the respective local languages as well as the accessibility of these documents.

The differences between the methodological approaches adopted by the authors of the five regional reports and the results they reached are striking. This might already be taken as an indication of the different underlying perceptions of the Covenants within the various world regions. None of the reports is based strictly on empirical studies. In other words, it is not possible to scientifically establish what kind of impact the Covenants have—or rather have had in the past—on the relevant national societies or on individuals, or the extent of such an impact. However, each of these reports contains the appraisal of a human rights expert—or, in the case of the Latin American report, two experts—who knows the relevant region and gives professional insight into the situation. It goes without saying that these assessments are subjective. Nevertheless, in the words of SAMANTHA BESSON, 'the five reports ... provide the first opportunity for a global or universal comparison of the influence of the two Covenants in domestic law'.[7] BESSON accepted the challenge of comparing the regional reports. In her chapter, entitled 'The Influence of the Two Covenants on States Parties across Regions: Lessons for the Role of Comparative Law and of Regions in International Human Rights Law', she not only presents a study in comparative international human rights law, but also provides a contribution to its methodology. Furthermore, she explores a central and recurring issue, namely the legitimacy of the Committees' interpretations of their respective Covenants, from

[7] Samantha Besson, 'The Influence of the Two Covenants on States Parties Across Regions: Lessons for the Role of Comparative Law and of Regions in International Human Rights Law', Chapter 11 in this volume.

a comparative perspective. She argues that a comparison of regional approaches to human rights issues may provide the Committees with a fruitful avenue for identifying and consolidating an international consensus around Covenant rights, and that such a region-by-region approach may ease this process as compared to a purely State-by-State approach.

Finally, the book dares to take a look into the future. What challenges will the Covenants have to face? What role will they play in the years to come? Is there a need for institutional changes to ensure better implementation of the human rights enshrined in these treaties? Possible answers to these questions are found in STEPHEN HUMPHREYS's chapter, 'The Covenants in the Light of Anthropogenic Climate Change'. He predicts a rather bleak future for the Covenants given that climate change has a huge and growing impact on the human rights system. He claims that the gap between the nominal rights enshrined in the Covenants and the legal remedies available to assert their breach is widening and beginning to appear unbridgeable. Hence, in a warming world, the promise of the Covenants to protect human rights cannot be kept. CHRISTINE KAUFMANN, for her part, elaborates on the nature of financial crises, their impact on human rights, and the role(s) of the States bound by the Covenants. Her chapter, entitled 'The Covenants and Financial Crises', proposes three key elements for an effective implementation of the Covenants in times of financial crises: a people-oriented, rights-based perspective, a process to foster coherence, and a fresh paradigm which she calls 'translational human rights'. Finally, in 'The Institutional Future of the Covenants: A World Court for Human Rights?', FELICE GAER discusses and analyses the proposal by Manfred Nowak and Martin Scheinin to introduce a 'world court of human rights' to overcome the problem of the weak implementation system for Covenant rights. She advocates, instead of aiming at the creation of a 'world court' as a new 'big idea', a thorough analysis of the existing treaty body system in order to achieve the ultimate goal: providing greater human rights protection and enforcement of individual complaint decisions. In this analysis, one would, inter alia, need to consider the question of how to respond to the phenomenon that the human rights treaty bodies' reactions are notoriously late in many cases. Or, to put it differently: how can human rights bodies discuss imminent human rights violations in good time, in order to prevent them from taking place?

The added value of this book, we believe, lies in the diversity of its essays. Due to the different regional, theoretical, and professional backgrounds of the contributors, the volume gives the reader a unique, comprehensive, and practical insight into the multifaceted and contentious nature of human rights from different perspectives.

In times when the human rights system is constantly challenged, the international community would do well to pay (more) attention to the fiftieth anniversary of the two human rights treaties that are probably the most important and well-known instruments of their kind worldwide, to recall the—positive and negative—experiences made with them in the past half-century, and to learn from them. Today's challenges call for an effective human rights system. This book tells us that the ICESCR and the ICCPR undoubtedly contribute to the powerful protection of human rights throughout the world.

PART I

THE PAST

What Have the Covenants (Not) Achieved?

2

The History of the Covenants

Looking Back Half a Century and Beyond

Maya Hertig Randall

I. Introduction

The adoption of the Universal Declaration of Human Rights (UDHR)[1] on 10 December 1948 realized the first of the three limbs of an international bill of rights: (1) a declaration of rights, to be complemented at a later stage by (2) a binding human rights treaty and (3) international measures of implementation.[2] Whilst the adoption of the UDHR undoubtedly marked a milestone in the history of international human rights and has rightly been celebrated as a tremendous achievement,[3] the realization of the second and third prongs was no less important. Casting the rights contained in the UDHR into binding treaty law was a paradigm shift,[4] raising many intricate questions:[5] how precisely should the rights be worded? Under which circumstances and conditions should it be possible to limit or to suspend them at times of emergency? Should States be free to enter reservations to binding human rights provisions or would this undermine the universal aspiration of the

[1] Universal Declaration of Human Rights (adopted 10 December 1948) UNGA Res 217 A(III).

[2] See ECOSOC (UN Economic and Social Council) Res 1/5 (16 February 1946).

[3] As the UDHR did not provide for legal institutionalization, international lawyers' early reactions were, however, marked by scepticism. See Jochen von Bernstorff, 'The Changing Fortunes of the Universal Declaration of Human Rights: Genesis and Symbolic Dimensions of the Turn to Rights in International Law' (2008) 19 EJIL 903, 903–10.

[4] When the UDHR was adopted, many State representatives stressed the fact that it did not create any legal obligations. The representative of the United States, for instance, made the following statement before the General Assembly: '[i]n giving our approval to the Declaration today, it is of primary importance that we keep clearly in mind the basic character of the document. It is not a treaty; it is not an international agreement. It is not and does not purport to be a statement of law or of legal obligation' ('Remarks by Mrs Franklin D Roosevelt' (1948) Department of State Bulletin 19 751, as cited in Hersch Lauterpacht, 'The Universal Declaration of Human Rights' (1948) 25 BYIL 354, 358). The United States' insistence that the UDHR was not a treaty reflected its stance during the drafting process. Like the Soviet Union, it had been pushing for a nonbinding document (see Christopher NJ Roberts, *The Contentious History of the International Bill of Human Rights* (CUP 2015) 68.

[5] The negotiations on most of these questions are described in Roger Normand and Sarah Zaidi, *Human Rights at the UN: The Political History of Universal Justice* (University of Indiana Press 2008) 197–242.

International Bill of Human Rights?[6] What obligations would States precisely have under a binding human rights treaty? Should these obligations extend to all levels of government or should the federal structure of States be taken into account?[7] Should the human rights treaty to be drafted extend to dependent territories? Drafting a binding human rights treaty required agreement on these vexing legal issues.

Providing for international supervision and enforcement mechanisms for the rights enshrined in a binding treaty was even more challenging: it required 'States to submit to international supervision their relationship with their own citizens, something which has been traditionally regarded as an absolute prerogative of national sovereignty'.[8] Accepting international implementation signified 'a revolutionary change in the status of the individual',[9] based on the insight that the most fundamental rights of every human being are a matter of international concern transcending the interest of any single State.[10]

The members of the United Nations (UN) grappled with the tremendous obstacles entailed in completing the International Bill of Human Rights for almost two decades. The Commission on Human Rights (hereafter 'the Commission') finished its task in 1954. As is well known, its work resulted in two draft treaties, instead of one as originally envisaged.[11] The subsequent negotiation and review process of the two draft Covenants within the UN General Assembly (UNGA) (mainly within its Third Committee) lasted twelve years. By the time the UNGA adopted the International Covenant on Economic, Social and Cultural Rights (ICESCR),[12]

[6] As no agreement could be reached, the Covenants are silent on this issue. On the negotiations, see ibid 232–40.

[7] The United States, supported by other federal States, namely Canada and Australia, pressed for over a decade for a so-called federal clause, which would have enabled federal States to limit the applicability of the covenant to the federal government. Due to strong opposition, this view did not prevail. ICCPR art 50 and ICESCR art 28, as finally adopted, read: '[t]he provisions of the present Covenant shall extend to all parts of federal States without any limitations or exceptions.' On the controversy raised by the federal clause, see Normand and Zaidi, *Human Rights* (n 5) 224–32; AW Bryan Simpson, *Human Rights and the End of Empire: Britain and the Genesis of the European Convention* (paperback edn, OUP 2004) 470–71.

[8] Speech by John Humphrey (1 January 1952) UN Archives/Geneva, SOA 317/4/01 (C), quoted in Paul Gordon Lauren, *The Evolution of International Human Rights: Visions Seen* (3rd edn, University of Pennsylvania Press 2011) 232.

[9] Hersch Lauterpacht, *An International Bill of the Rights of Man* (OUP 2013) 194–95.

[10] ibid.

[11] For the decision to adopt two Covenants instead of one, see UNGA Res 543 (VI) (5 February 1952) UN Doc A/RES/543(VI). The General Assembly requested ECOSOC to instruct the Commission on Human Rights 'to draft two Covenants on Human Rights, to be submitted simultaneously for the consideration of the General Assembly at its seventh session, one to contain civil and political rights and the other to contain economic, social and cultural rights, in order that the General Assembly may approve the two Covenants simultaneously and open them at the same time for signature, the two Covenants to contain, in order to emphasize the unity of the aim in view and to ensure respect for and observance of human rights, as many similar provisions as possible, particularly in so far as the reports to be submitted by States on the implementation of those rights are concerned' (para 1). For a detailed analysis of the process leading to the split into two Covenants, see Daniel J Whelan, *Indivisible Human Rights: A History* (University of Pennsylvania Press 2010) 113–14 (ch 6).

[12] International Covenant on Economic, Social and Cultural Rights (ICESCR) (opened for signature 16 December 1966, entered into force 3 January 1976) 993 UNTS 3.

the International Covenant on Civil and Political Rights (ICCPR),[13] and the Optional Protocol to the ICCPR[14] on 16 December 1966,[15] eighteen years had elapsed since the adoption of the UDHR in 1948. It took another decade until both Covenants entered into force once the necessary thirty-five ratifications had been gained.[16]

The present chapter will not recount the various stages of the lengthy drafting process.[17] To provide a better sense of what the drafters of the Covenants achieved, Section II will outline the political context of the genesis of the two human rights treaties. Section III will cast a spotlight on three thorny and intertwined issues with which the drafters grappled, namely: what rights should be included in a binding human rights treaty (Section III.A)? What obligations should States have under the Covenants to ensure effective implementation of human rights on the domestic level (Section III.B)? What mechanisms of international supervision and enforcement should be established as ultimate safeguards against State failure to observe human rights (Section III.C)? These questions are closely related to the controversial and much-debated decision to split the proposed covenant into two.[18] This schism was not only of ideological, symbolic, and political significance. It also mattered for legal reasons, as the ICESCR and the ICCPR differ with respect to States' obligations and the measures of international oversight. In analysing these three issues, this chapter will also cast some light on the reasons for and implications of the decision to adopt two human rights instruments instead of one and on the relationship between the two sets of rights protected by the Covenants.

[13] International Covenant on Civil and Political Rights (ICCPR) (opened for signature 16 December 1966, entered into force 23 March 1976) 999 UNTS 171.

[14] First Optional Protocol to the ICCPR (opened for signature 16 December 1966, entered into force 23 March 1971) 999 UNTS 171.

[15] UNGA Res 2200A (XXI) (16 December 1966) UN Doc A/RES/21/2200. The ICESCR was adopted with a vote of 105 to zero, the ICCPR with a vote of 106 to zero, and the Optional Protocol to the ICCPR with 66 to 2 votes (with Togo and Niger voting against) and 38 abstentions, including all of the socialist States (see Christian Tomuschat, 'International Covenant on Civil and Political Rights (1966)' in Rüdiger Wolfrum (ed), *Max Planck Encyclopedia of Public International Law* (OUP 2012) vol V, 639).

[16] The ICESCR entered into force on 3 January 1976, in accordance with ICESCR art 27. It has been ratified by 165 States (as of May 2017). The ICCPR entered into force on 23 March 1976, in accordance with its art 49. It has been ratified by 169 States (as of May 2017).

[17] For a detailed account, see Whelan, *Indivisible* (n 11) chs 4–6, with an Appendix showing the timeline of the drafting process (217), and Normand and Zaidi, *Human Rights* (n 5) 197–98. Immensely valuable for tracing the genesis of the ICCPR is Marc J Bossuyt, *Guide to the 'Travaux Préparatoires' of the International Covenant on Civil and Political Rights* (Martinus Nijhoff 1986). For succinct overviews of the drafting process, see Dominic McGoldrick, *The Human Rights Committee: Its Role in the Development of the International Covenant on Civil and Political Rights* (OUP 1991) 3–18, and Tomuschat, 'ICCPR' (n 15) (both focusing on the ICCPR); Matthew CR Craven, *The International Covenant on Economic, Social, and Cultural Rights: A Perspective on its Development* (OUP 1995) 16–22 (focusing on the ICESCR).

[18] On the various reasons (ideological/political, pragmatic, and legal) underlying the split, see Craig Scott, 'The Interdependence and Permeability of Human Rights Norms: Towards a Partial Fusion of the International Covenants on Human Rights' (1989) 27 Osgoode Hall L J 794.

II. The Political Context

The aftermath of the Second World War was the 'constitutional moment'[19] of international society, leading to the creation of the UN and to work on an international catalogue of human rights.[20] The authors of the UDHR were, however, aware that the 'window of opportunity'[21] was closing fast,[22] and therefore pressed for a speedy adoption of the Declaration. Although the Commission on Human Rights had decided in 1947 to proceed first with the Declaration,[23] work on the second and third prongs of the International Bill of Human Rights had been going on in parallel.[24] The Commission officially resumed work on the covenant and international measures of implementation in 1949. Although tensions between West and East had already overshadowed the drafting process of the UDHR, Cold War antagonism left an even stronger imprint on the work on the covenant, both within the Commission and within the General Assembly. In 1950, for instance, the Soviet Union withdrew from the Commission's sessions as a sign of protest against the refusal of the UN to unseat the representative of the Kuomintang in favour of the representative of the People's Republic of China after the 1949 Revolution. As Samuel Moyn highlights, the Soviet absence enabled an agreement within the Commission on a first draft of a human rights covenant but came at the cost of labelling the UN human rights endeavour a Western, anti-communist project.[25]

Apart from the 'Deep Freeze',[26] another influential factor was the decolonization movement. Between 1948 and 1966, UN membership increased dramatically from 58 to 122 States,[27] many of which were newly independent African and Asian countries. Decolonization and the new African-Asian group shaped the evolution

[19] The term is borrowed from Bruce Ackerman, *The Future of Liberal Revolution* (Yale University Press 1992) 48.

[20] For the evolution of international human rights before the adoption of the UN Charter, see eg Jan Herman Burgers, 'The Road to San Francisco: The Revival of the Human Rights Idea in the Twentieth Century' (1992) 14 Human Rights Q 447.

[21] On the 'window of opportunity' for domestic constitution-making after revolutionary changes, see Ackerman, *Liberal Revolution* (n 19) 46–47.

[22] See Mary Ann Glendon, 'The Forgotten Crucible: The Latin American Influence on the Universal Human Rights Idea' (2003) 16 Harvard Human Rights J 27, 37 (recounting mainly John Humphrey's concerns).

[23] The United States and the Soviet Union were the main driving forces behind the move to put off work on a binding convention (see Simpson, *End of Empire* (n 7) 431).

[24] Three working groups, each dealing with one prong of the International Bill of Human Rights, were set up in 1947 (ibid 431–32).

[25] Samuel Moyn, *The Last Utopia: Human Rights in History* (Harvard University Press 2010) 69–70. Prominent human rights issues raised within the UN around the same time reinforced the impression that human rights went hand-in-hand with anticommunism (for more details, see 71).

[26] This expression is used by the title of ch 11 of Mary Ann Glendon, *A World Made New: Eleanor Roosevelt and the Universal Declaration of Human Rights* (Random House 2001).

[27] See the information available at UN, 'Growth in United Nations Membership, 1945–Present' <www.un.org/en/sections/member-states/growth-united-nations-membership-1945-present/index.html> accessed 7 April 2017.

of human rights and the work on the Covenants in manifold ways.[28] Firstly, they favoured the universal reach of international human rights law by dealing a deadly blow to the attempts of colonial powers to keep human rights out of dependent territories on the grounds that the colonial people lacked the necessary level of development.[29] Secondly, with the newly independent nations becoming the biggest voting bloc in the General Assembly,[30] the emphasis shifted towards their major concerns, namely the fight against racism and discrimination on the one hand and self-determination on the other. The influence of the former colonies favoured the inclusion of non-discrimination provisions in the Covenants.[31] African and Asian States' opposition to racial discrimination was epitomized by the struggle against apartheid in South Africa.[32] Supported by a transnational network of grass-roots movements,[33] the fight against racism and apartheid was also the driving force behind the first human rights treaty to be adopted after the UDHR, the International Convention on the Elimination of All Forms of Racial Discrimination (ICERD) of 21 December 1965.[34] Claims for self-determination were supported by the Soviet Union,[35] which was competing with the West for the support of the newly independent States. Backed by the General Assembly,[36] these claims resulted in the inclusion of a provision on the right to self-determination—a right that is absent from the UDHR—in both Covenants.[37]

[28] Several authors caution, however, against an understanding of the movement of decolonization as a human rights movement. See mainly Moyn, *Last Utopia* (n 25) 97–98; Simpson, *End of Empire* (n 7) 300.

[29] See Moyn, *Last Utopia* (n 25) 96; Lauren, *Evolution* (n 8) 234. During the negotiation of the Covenants, the United Kingdom pressed for a so-called colonial clause enabling ratifying States to limit or exclude the applicability of the Covenants to their dependent territories. These efforts were not backed by the General Assembly (see UNGA Res 422(V) (4 December 1950) UN Doc A/RES/422(V) instructing the Commission to include a provision specifying that the covenant should apply to all territories governed or administered by the metropolitan State) and were ultimately defeated. See Normand and Zaidi, *Human Rights* (n 5) 230–35; on the colonial clause, see also Roberts, *Contentious History* (n 4) 132–33; Simpson, *End of Empire* (n 7) also 288–89 and 476–77.

[30] See Jean H Quataert, *Advocating Dignity: Human Rights Mobilizations in Global Politics* (University of Pennsylvania Press 2009) 71–72, highlighting that in 1966, 64 out of the 117 member States of the UN were African and Asian States.

[31] For more details, see Moyn, *Last Utopia* (n 25) 97–98.

[32] For a detailed account of the struggle against apartheid and its impact on the human rights movement, see Quataert, *Advocating Dignity* (n 30) 69–70.

[33] See ibid 87–88. The same author's study stresses the more general importance of human rights advocacy groups for human rights policies within the UN system. On the contribution of social movements and social practices to fleshing out the content of human dignity, see Matthias Mahlmann, 'The Good Sense of Dignity: Six Antidotes to Dignity Fatigue in Ethics and Law' in Christopher McCrudden (ed), *Understanding Human Dignity* (OUP 2013) 593, 598–99.

[34] International Convention on the Elimination of All Forms of Racial Discrimination (opened for signature 7 March 1966, entered into force 4 January 1969) 666 UNTS 195. See also Quataert, *Advocating Dignity* (n 30) 77.

[35] For the Soviet Union's official anticolonial stance, see eg Moyn, *Last Utopia* (n 25) 79; Simpson, *End of Empire* (n 7) 290.

[36] UNGA Res 545 (VI) (5 February 1952) UN Doc A/RES/545(VI).

[37] On self-determination and the ICCPR, see Burak Cop and Doğan Eymirlioğlu, 'The Right of Self-Determination in International Law Towards the 40th Anniversary of the Adoption of the ICCPR and the ICESCR' [2005] Perceptions 115; Normand and Zaidi, *Human Rights* (n 5) 212–24; Moyn, *Last Utopia* (n 25) 97–98.

The movement emphasizing self-determination was not only beneficial to the development of human rights; it also had its drawbacks. Once former colonies had gained independence, there was a trend to conflate self-determination with national sovereignty and non-interference in domestic affairs.[38] This vision, also championed by the Soviet Union, was difficult to reconcile with the project for an international bill of rights aimed at providing effective protection to individuals against their own States. Coupled with development concerns, the focus on self-determination triggered Western fears that human rights were being transformed from individual rights claims into interstate claims to international assistance[39] and into an ideological tool of anti-colonialism.[40] The fact that newly independent States had become an important force within the General Assembly and its Third Committee exacerbated these concerns.

In the light of shifting power constellations and Cold War antagonism, the victorious powers of the Second World War showed little enthusiasm for a binding human rights treaty and international measures of implementation. They were also aware that their human rights record was not immune to criticism: 'the Soviet Union had domestic terror and the Gulag; England and France had colonies; and the United States had racism'.[41] The superpowers did not miss a chance to attack their political opponents, shaming them for their human rights violations whilst turning a blind eye to their own weaknesses.[42] In this context, the United Kingdom decided in 1951 on the 'prudent course ... to prolong the international discussions, to raise legal and practical difficulties, and to delay the conclusion of the Covenant as long as possible'.[43] The Soviet Union persisted in its strategy of being highly defensive of national sovereignty. It adamantly opposed any international supervision of human rights in the name of non-interference in domestic affairs.[44] The United States was facing domestic opposition to the UN and the international human rights project, as epitomized by McCarthyism, the proposed Bricker Amendment to the Constitution,[45] and opposition from the American Bar Association.[46] As a result,

[38] Moyn, *Last Utopia* (n 25) 98. [39] See Whelan, *Indivisible* (n 11) 108.

[40] ibid 86, recounting John Humphrey's and Eleanor Roosevelt's concerns.

[41] Wiktor Osiatynski, 'On the Universality of the Universal Declaration of Human Rights' in Andras Sajó (ed), *Human Rights with Modesty: The Problem with Universalism* (Springer 2004) 36.

[42] The federal and the anti-colonial clauses, championed by the United States and the United Kingdom, respectively, made both States subject to strong criticism from the Eastern bloc (see Normand and Zaidi, *Human Rights* (n 5) 228 and 231). Criticism levelled at the federal clause was linked to the broader charge that the United States failed to grapple with racial discrimination in the Southern states (on Soviet criticism of racial discrimination in the United States, see Glendon, *World Made New* (n 26) 203). Self-determination was an issue exploited by both camps to accuse each other of imperialism and hypocrisy (see Normand and Zaidi, *Human Rights* (n 5) 215–16).

[43] Memorandum by Foreign Secretary Herbert Morrison, as cited in Simpson, *End of Empire* (n 7) 815.

[44] See eg Simpson, *End of Empire* (n 7) 417, 478–79; Normand and Zaidi, *Human Rights* (n 5) 237.

[45] Senator John Bricker made several proposals to amend the US Constitution which would have severely restricted both the government's treaty-making power and the domestic incorporation of treaty law (for detailed studies, see Richard O Davies, *Defender of the Old Guard: John Bricker and American Politics* (Ohio State University Press 1993); Duane Tanabaum, *The Bricker Amendment Controversy: A Test of Eisenhower's Political Leadership* (Cornell University Press 1988).

[46] On the opposition within the United States, see Lauren, *Evolution* (n 8) 232–33.

President Eisenhower turned his back on the positivization of international human rights in 1953. The US government withdrew its support from Eleanor Roosevelt,[47] putting an end to her membership in the Commission, and announced its intention not to become part of any human rights treaty elaborated under the auspices of the UN.[48]

The drafters not only encountered the challenge of overcoming attitudes strongly defensive of national sovereignty and the ideological cleavages linked to the Cold War and decolonization. They were also faced with disagreement among allies.[49] The United Kingdom and the United States, for instance, fundamentally disagreed about the level of precision of the drafting language:[50] on the one hand, the United Kingdom favoured a 'fairly tightly drawn Covenant',[51] meaning a treaty with precisely drafted provisions and clearly spelled-out limitations, as a general policy. The United States, on the other hand, preferred rather general, inclusive wording.[52] As regards the limits of rights, the United States pressed for a general limitation clause modelled on UDHR article 29 instead of narrowly drawn qualifications specific to each right.[53] Whilst the United Kingdom suspected the United States of proposing a general limitation clause so as to arrive at a 'text which committed nobody to anything',[54] the American side retorted that it was 'impossible to avoid using general terms to express restrictions'[55] and that 'the more restrictions there were, the harder it would be to draw up a Covenant and the more hesitant certain States would be about ratifying it'.[56] The last part of that statement refers to the difficulties of securing the required two-thirds majority vote in the US Senate to pave the way for

47 See Lauren, *Evolution* (n 8) 233. Eleanor Roosevelt was replaced by Mary Lord, whose attitude to the human rights project was, according to René Cassin, marked by indifference (see René Cassin, *La pensée et l'action* (Editions F Lalou 1972) 83).

48 Whelan, *Indivisible* (n 11) 138.

49 An additional challenge was intra-State disagreement between different ministries. In the United Kingdom, for instance, there was persistent disagreement between the Foreign Office and the Colonial Office during the drafting process, as both departments pursued different policies (see Simpson, *End of Empire* (n 7) 296, 408–10, 493–98, 500–01, 512; Normand and Zaidi, *Human Rights* (n 5) 230–31, 238). With respect to the contentious issue of individual petition, AW Bryan Simpson (Simpson, *End of Empire* (n 7) 497) summarizes the opposition between both offices eloquently as follows: 'the real source of the disagreement was that the Foreign Office wanted an effective stick with which to beat the Soviets, whilst the Colonial Office feared the application of the same stick to its vulnerable posterior'.

50 See Simpson, *End of Empire* (n 7) 466–70, 512, 518–19, 532–33; Whelan, *Indivisible* (n 11) 71 and 85. A further issue of fundamental disagreement was the federal clause. See Normand and Zaidi, *Human Rights* (n 5) 225.

51 Simpson, *End of Empire* (n 7) 467.

52 On the conflict between the United States and the United Kingdom, see Simpson, *End of Empire* (n 7) 512, 518–19.

53 See Philip Alston and Gerard Quinn, 'The Nature and Scope of States Parties' Obligations under the International Covenant on Economic, Social and Cultural Rights' (1987) 9 Human Rights Q 156, 194; Simpson, *End of Empire* (n 7) 466–67.

54 Simpson, *End of Empire* (n 7) 467.

55 Statement by Herzel Plaine (US Department of Justice) as cited in Simpson, *End of Empire* (n 7) 469.

56 ibid.

ratification.[57] The domestic political context, marked by concerted opposition to international human rights treaties and controversies about racial discrimination, exacerbated concerns that the constitutional hurdles to ratification would be too high.[58] Nevertheless, these disputes over the level of precision and general versus specific limitations cannot be reduced exclusively to pragmatic reasons and to disagreement over a covenant 'with or without teeth'.[59] The opposing views also reflected different legal traditions. The US approach was in line with the provisions of the US Bill of Rights, which are phrased in succinct, general terms and do not spell out detailed limitations.[60] Some of the UK's proposals for detailed limitation clauses codified all of the existing qualifications in English law, and aimed to ensure that the status quo of domestic legislation would be in line with the covenant.[61] The controversy over the level of precision exemplifies the challenges the drafters faced to reach a consensus in the face of different legal traditions and more or less conscious attempts to 'export' domestic conceptions of human rights.[62]

III. Select Thorny Issues

A. The rights to be included

The purpose of the drafting process was to translate the rights protected in the UDHR into binding treaty law. The content of the Universal Declaration provided the point of reference for the substantive part of the future covenant. However, this did not prevent discussions aiming to add new rights to the list (including rights rejected during the drafting process of the UDHR, namely self-determination[63] and

[57] Simpson, *End of Empire* (n 7) 469; the United Kingdom's view on the matter was that the United States was 'determined to secure a Covenant sufficiently meaningless for Congress to ratify' (statement by JP Duffy, as cited in Simpson, *End of Empire* (n 7) 521).

[58] Simpson, *End of Empire* (n 7) 521.

[59] The General Assembly expressed its preference for precise drafting, instructing the Commission to consider the view that it is 'desirable to define the rights set forth in the Covenant and the limitations thereto with the greatest possible precision' (UNGA Res 421(V)B (4 December 1950), UN Doc A/RES/421(V)B, s 4(ii)).

[60] Some drafting proposals made by the United States closely resembled the text of the US Constitution. Compare the proposal for the following provision: '[n]o one shall be deprived of life, liberty or property without due process of law' (see Simpson, *End of Empire* (n 7) 505) with the fifth Amendment of the US Constitution.

[61] Simpson, *End of Empire* (n 7) 468.

[62] See ibid 468, referring to the 'export theory of human rights' in connection with the United Kingdom's position on limitations of human rights, and ibid 399, stressing that 'those involved in government are deeply reluctant to promote bills of rights unless they anticipate that this will make absolutely no difference to their own domestic situation. One technique for achieving this result, though not the only one, is to match the bill to the domestic *status quo*, treating human rights as primarily for export'. The final draft of the ICCPR is a compromise between diverging views. Unlike the UDHR, it does not contain a general limitation clause, but several human rights provisions incorporate a fairly broadly phrased limitation clause. See ibid 532–33. By contrast, the ICESCR contains a general limitation clause (art 4), the wording of which was, however, considerably tightened during the drafting process (see Alston and Quinn, 'Parties' Obligations' (n 53) 194–95).

[63] See Section II.

minority rights[64]), or, conversely, to reduce the number and scope of rights enshrined in the UDHR. The Covenants, as finally adopted, for instance do not include the right to seek asylum (UDHR article 14), the right to a nationality (UDHR article 15), or the right to own property (UDHR article 17). The latter right turned out to be intractable. In the context of the Cold War and decolonization, it raised highly sensitive issues, including the definition of the concept of property (as individual or collective)[65] and questions related to nationalization and just compensation.[66]

Fundamental disagreements extended well beyond the right to property to the whole class of economic, social, and cultural rights (ESCR). During the drafting of the UDHR, several factors had favoured an agreement on including so-called second-generation rights: in the direct aftermath of the Second World War, the insight that economic hardship paved the way for totalitarianism was still very present.[67] In the United States, supporters of second-generation rights invoked the experience of the New Deal, President Roosevelt's defence of the 'freedom from want',[68] and his proposal for a 'Second Bill of Rights'. The famous American Law Institute (ALI) Statements on Essential Human Rights,[69] which were an influential source of inspiration for the drafters of the UDHR,[70] also included second-generation rights. Moreover, the bloc of Latin American States (twenty out of the fifty-one founding members of the UN) were strong supporters of ESCR.[71] Their human rights traditions, influenced by Catholic social thought, synthesized

[64] See ICCPR art 27. Like self-determination, minority rights were championed by the Soviet Union but met with opposition from Western States (see Normand and Zaidi, *Human Rights* (n 5) 201; on minority protection during the drafting process of the UDHR, see Simpson, *End of Empire* (n 7) 435, 441–42, and 450).

[65] The UDHR accommodated both positions in asserting that '[e]veryone has the right to own property *alone as well as in association with others*' (art 17(1) UDHR, emphasis added).

[66] For a more detailed analysis, see Whelan, *Indivisible* (n 11) 93–94.

[67] See Moyn, *Last Utopia* (n 25) 64, stressing '[t]he powerful welfarist consensus in America and around the world' and the fact that it 'reflected a brief and unprecedented moment'.

[68] The extent to which 'the West' opposed second-generation rights is debated; see the controversy between Daniel J Whelan and Jack Donnelly on the one hand, and Alex Kirkup and Tony Evans and Susan L Kang on the other hand (Daniel J Whelan and Jack Donnelly, 'The West, Economic and Social Rights, and the Global Human Rights Regime: Setting the Record Straight' (2007) 29 Human Rights Q 908; Alex Kirkup and Tony Evans, 'The Myth of Western Opposition to Economic, Social, and Cultural Rights? A Reply to Whelan and Donnelly' (2009) 31 Human Rights Q 221; Daniel J Whelan and Jack Donnelly, 'Yes, a Myth: A Reply to Kirkup and Evans' (2009) 31 Human Rights Q 239; Susan L Kang, 'The Unsettled Relationship of Economic and Social Rights and the West: A Response to Whelan and Donnelly' (2009) 31 Human Rights Q 1006; Daniel J Whelan and Jack Donnelly, 'The Reality of Western Support for Economic and Social Rights: A Reply to Susan L. Kang' (2009) 31 Human Rights Q 1030).

[69] ALI, 'Statements on Essential Human Rights, with Commentary' (1946) 243 Annals of the American Academy of Political and Social Science 18 and (1995) 89 AJIL 550. On the ALI Statement, see eg Hanne Hagtvedt Vik, 'Taming the States: the American Law Institute and the "Statement of Essential Human Rights"' (2012) 7(3) J of Global History 461.

[70] See Thilo Rensmann, 'The Constitution as Normative Order of Values: The Influence of International Human Rights Law on the Evolution of Modern Constitutionalism' in Pierre-Marie Dupuy and others (eds), *Völkerrecht als Wertordnung: Festschrift für Christian Tomuschat* (NP Engel 2003) 259, 265.

[71] On the contribution of Latin American countries to international human rights, see Glendon, 'Forgotten Crucible' (n 22); Paolo G Carozza, 'From Conquest to Constitutions: Retrieving a Latin American Tradition of the Idea of Human Rights' (2003) 25 Human Rights Q 281.

'the individualistic with the social and economic dimensions of human dignity'[72] and helped to steer a middle course 'between the Scylla of brutally atomistic liberal capitalism and the Charybdis of excessive socialist collectivism'.[73] The drafters of the UDHR bridged the rift between West and East by stressing the ideological neutrality of ESCR, which were to be realized '*in accordance with the organization* and resources of each State'.[74] Another favourable factor for the inclusion of social and economic rights in the UDHR was the intensive and successful activity of the International Labour Organization (ILO). In the period between the two Wars, it had adopted nearly 100 conventions on labour standards.[75] Last but not least, the fact that the UDHR was a legally non-binding document and did not provide for international enforcement mechanisms also helped States to reach a consensus on second-generation rights.

It was a much bigger challenge to secure an agreement on incorporating ESCR into a legally binding instrument backed up by international implementation measures given the far more polarized political context.[76] After the adoption of the UDHR, the Commission started discussions on a binding international treaty based on a draft covenant, prepared by the United Kingdom, which was very limited in scope.[77] Reflecting the Anglo-American rights tradition,[78] it set out a list of civil rights but did not contain second-generation rights (nor did it protect political rights).[79] The proposal was in line with the United Kingdom's policy that a legally binding treaty should spell out clearly defined and enforceable provisions.[80] Second-generation rights were considered as not fulfilling these requirements, a view shared by the United States and other nations, namely India, the Netherlands, Canada, China, and Venezuela.[81]

The omission of ESCR triggered immediate concerns within the Commission and later within the Third Committee, where States defending the incorporation of ESCR outnumbered the opponents. Advocates of second-generation rights not only included Socialist nations, newly independent developing countries linking the issue to self-determination, and Latin American delegations, but also the representative of France, René Cassin, and the delegates of Australia and Denmark. According

[72] Carozza, 'Conquest to Constitutions' (n 71) 312.

[73] ibid 311 (referring to the Mexican Constitution of 1917).

[74] UDHR art 22 (emphasis added).

[75] Osiatynski, 'Universality' (n 41) 45.

[76] McCarthyism and the Bicker Amendments were miles away from President Roosevelt's four freedoms, the New Deal, and a Second Bill of Rights. The account given by Whelan and Donnelly (Whelan and Donnelly, 'The West' (n 68)), portraying the United States as a constant defender of second-generation rights, adopts an excessively monolithic view and does not account for the evolution of the political context.

[77] On the genesis and the content of the draft UK Bill of Rights, see Simpson, *End of Empire* (n 7) 390–91.

[78] Whelan, *Indivisible* (n 11) 65; Normand and Zaidi, *Human Rights* (n 5), 201; see also Simpson, *End of Empire* (n 7) 399, highlighting the minimalist character of the bill, the content of which was limited to guaranteeing existing common law rights.

[79] Political rights were opposed by the United Kingdom's Colonial Office (see Simpson, *End of Empire* (n 7) 374).

[80] Simpson, *End of Empire* (n 7) 511.

[81] Whelan, *Indivisible* (n 11) 74; for similar statements from other representatives, see 76.

to this view, expressed prominently by Cassin, a truncated covenant would be 'an unpardonable anachronism'.[82] The representative of Yugoslavia made a philosophical defence in favour of a comprehensive covenant before the Third Committee, arguing that the UDHR includes economic and social rights 'because it conceives of man as a integrated personality, which for its full expression and well-being requires the employment of economic and social as well as political and civil rights'.[83]

Once it had become obvious that a blanket 'no' would not be acceptable to the majority of States, the emphasis of the debates shifted from the fundamental question of inclusion or non-inclusion to other issues, namely whether provisions on ESCR should be worded in concise, general terms or spelled out in detail. The United States, for instance, favoured the first approach, whilst the USSR and Yugoslavia submitted proposals for extremely detailed provisions.[84] Despite the General Assembly's policy decision to include second-generation rights in the covenant,[85] discussions continued to centre around the question whether social and economic rights should be protected in the same instrument as civil or political rights, or in a different instrument to be adopted at the same time as the covenant, or in a later one. As is well known, the ultimate compromise that emerged was to protect each generation of rights in a separate Covenant, to be adopted simultaneously and containing as many similar provisions as possible.[86] The problematic issues of defining States' obligations and international enforcement were linked to this solution.

B. States' obligations under the Covenants

Legally binding human rights norms are meaningful only if they entail corresponding legal duties. It was thus essential to define what obligations States would have under the Covenants to provide for effective implementation on the domestic level. Spelling out States' duties, was, however, a highly sensitive issue. Firstly, States had, and continue to have, different constitutional traditions. For instance, a duty to incorporate international human rights treaties into domestic law is easier to satisfy for monist than for dualist States. Ensuring that international human rights prevail in cases of conflict with domestic law, including Acts of Parliament, raises difficulties for States attached to the United Kingdom's tradition of parliamentary sovereignty

[82] UNGA 'Draft First International Covenant on Human Rights and Measures of Implementation (continued)' (30 October 1950) UN Doc A/C.3/SR.298, 177 (Cassin, as quoted in Whelan, *Indivisible* (n 11) 74). Similarly worded claims were made by the Czechoslovak and the Yugoslav delegates, and by the representative of Mexico (see Normand and Zaidi, *Human Rights* (n 5) 203–04).

[83] UN Doc A/C.3/SR.298 (n 82) 178 (see Normand and Zaidi, *Human Rights* (n 5) 204).

[84] See Whelan, *Indivisible* (n 11) 73–74. A Soviet Union draft on trade union rights, for instance, contained thirteen sub-paragraphs (see Whelan and Donnelly, 'The West' (n 68) 929 fn 80).

[85] UNGA Res 421(V)E (4 December 1950) UN Doc A/RES/421(V)E. The resolution requested to include 'a clear *expression* of economic, social and cultural rights' (para 7(b), emphasis added). The chosen formulation is a compromise: the term 'expression' affords the drafters a wide margin of discretion and does not put second-generation rights exactly on the same level as civil and political rights.

[86] UNGA Res 543 (VI) (n 11).

or nations following the traditional French conception considering parliamentary statutes as the 'expression of the general will'.[87]

Secondly, the negotiations on States' obligations under an international bill of rights brought to the fore the divisive problem of the relationship between civil and political rights on the one hand, and ESCR on the other hand. The question of how the two sets of rights relate to each other—thus, their commonalities and their differences—had already been vigorously debated during the drafting process of the UDHR.[88] The United Kingdom, for instance, proposed introducing qualifications to some social rights so as to stress their dependence on resources.[89] Cassin, in turn, sought to tackle the question by proposing an 'umbrella' clause specifying how second-generation rights should be realized.[90] Neither of these proposals was accepted. As the Declaration was a legally non-binding document, it was possible to gloss over disagreement by leaving the question unspecified. The same approach could not be adopted when it came to drafting a legally binding human rights treaty.[91] During the negotiations, the dominant view was that both categories of rights called for different implementation measures, both on the domestic and on the international level. The question then was whether a differentiated approach should be realized within one covenant or whether it was preferable to adopt two different instruments. Whilst the Commission chose the first option in 1951 and prepared a single draft with two umbrella clauses introducing ESCR,[92] it was the second option which prevailed one year later. Opposition to uniform implementation provisions thus turned out to be a factor favouring the division of the covenant.[93]

Articles 2 of the ICESCR and the ICCPR, as finally adopted,[94] clearly express the drafters' choice for a differentiated approach with respect to States' obligations and domestic implementation. Under the ICESCR, each State party:

> undertakes to take steps, individually and through international assistance and co-operation, especially economic and technical, to the maximum of its available resources, with a view to achieving progressively the full realization of the rights recognized in the present Covenant by all appropriate means, including particularly the adoption of legislative measures.

[87] The United Kingdom, for instance, rejected a duty to incorporate the Covenants as superior domestic law on the grounds of parliamentary sovereignty (see Simpson, *End of Empire* (n 7) 405 and 417). The wording of ICCPR art 2(2) is a compromise that accommodates different constitutional traditions. It holds that 'each State Party ... undertakes to take the necessary steps, *in accordance with its constitutional processes*' with a view to giving effect to the rights recognized in the Covenant (emphasis added).

[88] See Roland Burke, 'Confronting "Indivisibility" in the History of Economic and Social Rights: From Parity to Priority and Back Again' (2012) 12 Human Rights & Human Welfare 53, 56–57.

[89] ibid 57. [90] ibid. [91] ibid 58.

[92] The result was, in Whelan's terms, 'a very odd looking Covenant', which also met with criticism at the time. See Whelan, *Indivisible* (n 11) 100–01 and 105.

[93] ibid 214.

[94] For an analysis of the arts 2 of the respective Covenants, including their drafting history, see, for the ICESCR, Alston and Quinn, 'Parties' Obligations' (n 53) 164–65, and for the ICCPR, Anja Seibert-Fohr, 'Domestic Implementation of the International Covenant on Civil and Political Rights Pursuant to its Article 2(2)' in *Max Planck Yearbook of United Nations Law* (Brill 2001) vol 5, 399; Bossuyt, *Guide to the Travaux* (n 17) 56–57.

References to the qualifying elements of 'progressive realization', 'available resources', and 'international assistance and co-operation' are absent in the ICCPR. Conversely, unlike the ICESCR, the ICCPR contains a clause obligating States to 'ensure that any person whose rights or freedoms as herein recognized are violated shall have an effective remedy'.[95]

The different wording of articles 2 of the Covenants did not merely express the view that both sets of rights had different characteristics. After the adoption of the Covenants, this difference served to justify and reinforce polarized visions, conceptualizing the two sets of rights in opposing terms: first-generation rights were 'negative', 'cost-free', and justiciable rights, to be realized immediately and giving rise to obligations of result. By contrast, second-generation rights were framed as 'positive', 'costly', and non-justiciable (ie merely programmatic) rights, to be realized over time, and generating obligations of means contingent on the available resources. Pushed one step further, these characteristics provided the ground for claims that the ICESCR did not really assert rights, but merely policy objectives. This view became widespread not only in the United States[96] and in the United Kingdom,[97] but also in other countries with a legal tradition viewing judicial enforceability as a necessary feature of legal rights.[98]

Mainly since the end of the Cold War, our understanding of both sets of rights has substantially evolved. Human rights bodies and academics have started tearing down the wall upholding a categorical distinction between civil and political rights on the one hand, and ESCR on the other.[99] Instead of operating on the basis of distinctions between different sets of rights, it has become common to distinguish between different types of obligations generated by human rights norms. Based on this approach, the realization of all human rights entails both negative duties (the duty to respect) as well as positive duties (the duty to protect and fulfil the rights in question).[100] The corollary of this approach is a more nuanced theory of justiciability.[101] Negative duties, independently of whether they pertain to a first- or

[95] ICCPR art 2(3)(a).

[96] See, on the American reluctance to view positive rights as fundamental rights, Mary Ann Glendon, 'Rights in Twentieth-Century Constitutions' (1992) 59 University of Chicago L Rev 519, 523–24.

[97] For a prominent academic view, see Maurice William Cranston, *What Are Human Rights?* (Taplinger Publishing Company 1973) 54–55; for a critical discussion, see Jack Donnelly, *Universal Human Rights in Theory and Practice* (3rd edn, Cornell University Press 2013) 40–41.

[98] For examples of continental jurisdictions adopting the opposite view and acknowledging so-called programmatic rights as fundamental rights, see Glendon, 'Rights' (n 96) 527–28.

[99] See eg the famous holding of the European Court of Human Rights that 'the mere fact that an interpretation of the Convention may extend into the sphere of social and economic rights should not be a decisive factor against such an interpretation; there is *no water-tight division* separating that sphere from the field covered by the Convention' (ECtHR, *Airey v Ireland*, App no 6289/73, 9 October 1979, para 26, emphasis added). For an academic study, drawing on political and social theory and comparative constitutional law, see eg Sandra Fredman, *Human Rights Transformed: Positive Rights and Positive Duties* (OUP 2008).

[100] For the duty to respect, protect, and fulfil, see the seminal work of Henry Shue, *Basic Rights: Subsistence, Affluence, and U.S. Foreign Policy* (first published 1980, 2nd edn, Princeton University Press 1996).

[101] For a comprehensive study, see Gregor T Chatton, *Vers la pleine reconnaissance des droits économiques, sociaux et culturels* (Schulthess 2014).

a second-generation right, can clearly be enforced by courts. To the extent that human rights bodies and many constitutional courts accept that the duty to protect is also capable of judicial enforcement, no principled reason justifies confining justiciability to first-generation rights.[102] To date, the question if and to what extent the duty to fulfil human rights is enforceable by the judiciary has not been clearly settled. This duty pertains to all human rights, but is generally of greater importance for the realization of second- rather than of first-generation rights. The difference between both sets of rights is, however, not one of kind, but one of degree.[103] The social rights jurisprudence which has emerged on the domestic level mainly as of the late 1980s[104] shows that the duty to fulfil ESCR can, to some extent, be enforced by the judiciary.[105] Some courts have, for instance, affirmed their power to enforce core obligations, holding States to their obligation to realize the essential minimal content of social rights.[106] Others have reviewed compliance with second-generation rights, applying a deferential 'reasonableness' standard.[107] The Committee on Economic, Social and Cultural Rights endeavours to spell out the normative content of ICESCR rights and States' duties under article 2, and has also helped to pave the way for a more sophisticated approach to the enforcement of ESCR.[108]

At the time when the Covenants were drafted, few voices advocated for a nuanced understanding of the characteristics and the justiciability of first- and second-generation rights. During the negotiations of what became ICESCR article 2, in 1952, the representative of Egypt suggested inserting the phrase 'if necessary' after 'progressively', arguing that some social rights, namely trade union rights, could be implemented immediately.[109] During the same year, the Israeli delegate questioned the artificial categorization of rights,[110] noting that effective implementation of civil and political rights required 'a highly developed judiciary organization, which could not be achieved at short notice'.[111] Contesting the simplistic equation of first-generation rights with immediate realization on the one hand, and that of second-generation rights with progressive realization on the other hand, he

[102] The case law of the European Court of Human Rights is a prominent example. See Dimitris Xenos, *The Positive Obligations of the State Under the European Convention of Human Rights* (Routledge 2012).

[103] Alston and Quinn, 'Parties' Obligations' (n 53) 184.

[104] See Malcolm Langford, 'The Justiciability of Social Rights: From Practice to Theory' in Malcolm Langford (ed), *Social Rights Jurisprudence: Emerging Trends in International and Comparative Law* (CUP 2008) 3.

[105] For a comparative study of social rights jurisprudence, see Malcolm Langford (ed), *Social Rights Jurisprudence: Emerging Trends in International and Comparative Law* (CUP 2008).

[106] The Swiss Supreme Court adopted this approach in a judgment of 27 October 1995 (BGE 121 I 367). Asserting the justiciability of the entitlement to have one's most basic needs covered, the Court recognized the right to assistance when in need as an unwritten constitutional right. The Swiss Constitution of 1999 provides for an explicit guarantee of this right in art 12.

[107] This approach has been adopted by the South African Supreme Court. See eg *Government of the Republic of South Africa & others v Grootboom & others* [2000] ZACC 19.

[108] See mainly CESCR, 'General Comment 3' and 'General Comment 9' in 'Note by the Secretariat, Compilation of General Comments and General Recommendations Adopted by Human Rights Treaty Bodies' (2003) UN Doc HRI/GEN/1/Rev.6 (mainly s A related to domestic remedies).

[109] Whelan, *Indivisible* (n 11) 99.

[110] See Alston and Quinn, 'Parties' Obligations' (n 53) 173.

[111] Quoted in ibid 123–24.

proposed a different approach. Depending on differences of development and structure, each government should divide human rights, 'whatever their nature', into two categories: one comprising rights capable of immediate implementation and enforcement, and another including the rights which necessitated 'the execution of programmes, including economic and social programmes', to become effective.[112] The insight that all human rights, including civil and political rights, require State action to afford protection against third-party interference and may necessitate adequate institutions and procedures was also reflected in the ALI Statement of Essential Human Rights.[113] Like the unsuccessful Egyptian and Israeli proposals, this vision also went far beyond the understanding of international human rights law that was common at the time.

Apart from ideological reasons and differences in the understanding of the characteristics and justiciability of first- and second-generation rights, the economic context favoured a cautious approach with respect to ESCR. Representatives of several States were concerned that unqualified social rights might raise hopes that would be impossible to fulfil considering the economic situation prevailing in their countries.[114] The delegates of India and Greece, for instance, both argued that most States' 'resources and state of economic development did not permit them to implement the economic and social rights at one stroke of the pen'.[115] In the context of decolonization, the debates on second-generation rights became intertwined with the larger issue of economic development.[116] As the drafting history shows, the wording of the reference to international cooperation and assistance in ICESCR article 2 was fiercely debated.[117] Western States had the impression that developing countries championed ESCR not so much as individual human rights but rather as interstate claims to development,[118] which made them suspicious with respect to second-generation rights.

Moreover, at the time of drafting, a minority of States had a constitutional framework combining two powerful features for effective enforcement of human rights: a constitutional bill of rights *and* a developed system of constitutional review. Thus, it comes as no surprise that it was the representative of Mexico, a country with a long tradition of judicial review as a means to enforce constitutional rights, who proposed the inclusion of the right to a domestic remedy in the UDHR.[119]

[112] Quoted in ibid 173–74. [113] See Rensman, 'Normative Order' (n 70) 264.

[114] The ECHR, which is limited to civil and political rights, and several constitutions adopted shortly after the Second World War reflect this cautious approach. Written against the backdrop of dire economic conditions, the German Basic Law of 23 May 1949, for instance, contains a commitment to a social State (art 20(1)), but does not protect social rights as fundamental rights (see Rensman, 'Normative Order' (n 70) 273). The Constitution of India, adopted on 26 January 1950, tackles social welfare not in Part III 'Fundamental Rights' but in Part IV 'Directive Principles of State Policy'.

[115] ECOSOC, 'Summary Record of the 248th Meeting of the Commission on Human Rights' (10 July 1951) UN Doc E/CN.4/SR.248, 6 (representative of India). In the words of the Greek representative, '[i]t was, however, clearly impossible to abolish want and illness by the stroke of a pen' (UN Doc A/C.3/SR.298 (n 82) 179, para 24).

[116] On the connection between including ESCR in the covenant and the anticolonial movement and wider development goals, see Whelan, *Indivisible* (n 11) 76–77.

[117] See Alston and Quinn, 'Parties' Obligations' (n 53) 186–87. [118] See Section II.

[119] See UDHR art 8; Glendon, 'Forgotten Crucible' (n 22) 38; Simpson, *End of Empire* (n 7) 450. More generally on the long tradition of judicial review in Latin America, see Axel Tschentscher and Caroline

However, the tradition of judicial enforcement was mainly limited to civil and political rights. As Daniel J Whelan argues, models of judicial review as applied to ESCR were lacking.[120] The socialist concept of human rights did nothing to fill this void. Although socialist constitutions contained extensive catalogues of social rights, welfare services were provided to the citizens on a discretionary basis and not in terms of rights—that is, entitlements enforceable in courts.[121] Put differently, social rights were conceived of as a way to 'enhance government's authority'[122] in the relevant areas 'rather than accepting State accountability to individual rights'.[123] Not surprisingly, meaningful social rights jurisprudence has emerged mainly in countries with a developed system of judicial or quasi-judicial enforcement of civil and political rights.[124] Soviet opposition to the division of the covenant and to the qualifying elements expressed in ICESCR article 2 was mainly based on ideological and not on legal grounds.[125]

Lastly, it is interesting to note that immediate realization of civil and political rights could not be taken for granted. During the drafting process of what became ICCPR article 2, States were divided.[126] One camp, including the United Kingdom, argued that States were bound to secure compliance with the ICCPR immediately upon ratification. If they had difficulties in doing so, they had the option to enter reservations. Another camp, led by the United States, favoured an approach that left States a reasonable time frame to bring their law and practise into line with the ICCPR. The concept of immediate realization was thus a contested issue. It may not have prevailed if the drafters had insisted on uniform treatment of civil and

Lehner, 'The Latin American Model of Constitutional Jurisdiction: Amparo and Judicial Review' (2013) SSRN Research Paper 2296004 <https://papers.ssrn.com/sol3/papers.cfm?abstract_id=2296004> accessed 7 April 2017; Norbert Lösing, *Die Verfassungsgerichtsbarkeit in Lateinamerika* (Nomos 2001); Francisco Fernández Segado, 'Les origines du contrôle juridictionnel de la constitutionnalité des lois en Amérique latine' <www.umk.ro/images/documente/publicatii/Buletin18/3_les_origines.pdf> accessed 19 October 2015.

[120] Whelan, *Indivisible* (n 11) 193.

[121] Andras Sajó, 'Rights in Post-Communism' in Andras Sajó (ed), *Western Rights? Post-communist Application* (Kluwer 1996) 139, 141–42.

[122] Normand and Zaidi, *Human Rights* (n 5) 201 (describing the Soviet stance during the drafting process).

[123] ibid. [124] Langford, 'Justiciability' (n 104) 10.

[125] In the General Assembly debate on 4 December 1950, the French delegate voiced criticism directed at the Soviet Union and its allies. He deplored their opposition to effective implementation mechanisms, holding that disregarding the legal consequences of implementing ESCR would render the covenant meaningless, unless one considered that the purpose of the covenant was 'to secure some political and propaganda advantage by means of oft-repeated democratic slogans. It could have a meaning if the only purpose were to use a phraseology savoring of progress as a cloak for continuing the old errors of the policy of the reason of State' (UNGA (4 December 1950) UN Doc A/PV.317, 559, para 90), as quoted in Whelan, *Indivisible* (n 11) 81. See also Whelan and Donnelly, 'The West' (n 68) 935, arguing that the Soviet Union viewed ESCR in terms no different from the West: as social policy goals and not as enforceable individual rights.

[126] See Bossuyt, *Guide to the Travaux* (n 17) 57–58; Seibert-Fohr, 'Domestic Implementation' (n 94) 407–08; Simpson, *End of Empire* (n 7) 528–29 (focusing on the positions of the United States and the United Kingdom).

political rights on the one hand, and ESCR on the other. The same risk of levelling down could not be denied out of hand when it came to defining international enforcement.

C. Measures of international supervision and enforcement

Providing for international supervision and enforcement of the human rights obligations undertaken by States turned out to be 'the most difficult and controversial aspect' of developing the International Bill of Human Rights,[127] raising difficult questions such as: which bodies were to be the guardians of the rights enshrined in the Covenants? What powers should they be invested with to improve compliance? It was a formidable challenge to tackle these issues in a context where the three superpowers were jealously guarding their sovereignty and reluctant to accept international enforcement mechanisms 'with teeth'.[128] The Commission took up negotiations on international enforcement based on drafts prepared by its Working Group on Implementation. A panoply of options had been discussed,[129] including the establishment of an international court of human rights, of a high commissioner, or of a permanent human rights body vested with the power to receive individual petitions, to initiate inquiries, and to carry out independent monitoring. The option to expel States from the UN in case of persistent human rights violations was also considered.[130] The Commission's draft submitted to the General Assembly in 1954 did not include any of these 'bold' proposals. The Third Committee only started working on implementation measures in 1963.[131]

The asymmetrical solution finally adopted in 1966, after protracted and tough negotiations, is well known: the ICCPR established a supervisory body consisting of independent experts, the Human Rights Committee. It provided for a mandatory reporting system and an optional interstate complaint procedure. An Optional Protocol complemented the ICCPR, enabling the Human Rights Committee to receive and consider communications from individuals claiming to be victims of a violation of any of the rights set forth in the Covenant. For the ICESCR, no body equivalent to the Human Rights Committee was created. The only available supervisory mechanism was a mandatory reporting procedure, as ECOSOC had been entrusted with examining the periodic reports submitted by States. It was only two decades after the adoption of the Covenants, once the initial monitoring system

[127] Quote by the Polish delegate, as cited in Philip Alston, 'The Committee on Economic, Social and Cultural Rights' in Philip Alston (ed), *The United Nations and Human Rights: A Critical Appraisal* (OUP 1992) 473, 476. For a detailed account of the drafting history of implementation measures, see Egon Schwelb, 'Notes on the Early Legislative History of the Measures of Implementation of the Human Rights Covenants' in *Mélanges offerts à Polys Modinos* (Editions Pedone 1968) 270; Egon Schwelb, 'Civil and Political Rights: The International Measures of Implementation' (1968) 62 AJIL 827.

[128] See Normand and Zaidi, *Human Rights* (n 5) 198.

[129] See Schwelb, 'Notes' (n 127) 274–75; Normand and Zaidi, *Human Rights* (n 5) 236.

[130] Schwelb, 'Notes' (n 127) 274.

[131] Schwelb, 'Civil and Political Rights' (n 127) 830–31.

had turned out to be highly ineffective, that an independent expert committee (the Committee on Economic, Social and Cultural Rights) was established.[132]

The difference between the monitoring provisions in both Covenants has received much attention and tends to be viewed through the lens of the ideological rift between the Soviet and the Western blocs. The drafting history reveals, however, a more complex picture: debates around the choice of supervisory body for the ICESCR, for instance, did not reflect a socialist–capitalist divide.[133] The Soviet Union and other socialist States opposed the creation of a Committee for the ICESCR throughout the drafting process. The position of other States varied over time. During the 1950s, Lebanon—a Western ally—and France submitted proposals for entrusting an independent expert body with the oversight of ESCR.[134] The States opposing the French and Lebanese proposals included China, the United Kingdom, and Australia. A decade later, during the final debates preceding the adoption of the Covenants, the United States proposed the establishment of an independent expert committee for the ICESCR. Italy made a more moderate proposal providing for an ad hoc body of experts that was supported by several Western States, including Canada, the Netherlands, Finland, and Norway.[135] Strong opposition stemmed from African States, disillusioned with international bodies after the International Court of Justice's decision in the *South West Africa* cases.[136]

As regards the choice of oversight mechanisms, negotiations occurred against the backdrop of many States' uneasiness about any implementation measures 'with teeth'.[137] In line with its opposition to any international enforcement, the Soviet Union and its allies initially rejected even the system of periodic reporting as contrary to the principle of non-intervention in domestic affairs, a position they reversed in 1963.[138] Whilst the reporting procedure was considered well-adapted for the implementation of ESCR, its suitability for ensuring the effectiveness of civil and political rights was controversial. The major sceptic of the reporting procedure for the ICCPR was the United Kingdom, which considered that State reporting would weaken the immediacy of States' obligations under the ICCPR.[139] Other States also voiced concerns that the provisions on reporting might introduce elements of progressive realization and reduce the effectiveness of civil and political rights.[140] Nevertheless, the Commission extended the reporting procedure to the

[132] See Alston, 'CESCR' (n 127) 473–74.

[133] Malcolm Langford and Jeff A King, 'Committee on Economic, Social and Cultural Rights: Past, Present and Future' in Malcolm Langford (ed), *Social Rights Jurisprudence: Emerging Trends in International and Comparative Law* (CUP 2008) 477, 478, fn 15.

[134] See Alston, 'CESCR' (n 127) 476–77; Langford and King, 'CESCR' (n 133) 478, fn 15; Whelan, *Indivisible* (n 11) 181. By contrast with Lebanon, France did not favour the establishment of a separate monitoring body, but instead sought a solution that extended the competence of the Human Rights Committee to examine State reports under the ICESCR.

[135] Langford and King, 'CESCR' (n 133) fn 15.

[136] *South West Africa (Ethiopia v South Africa; Liberia v South Africa)* (Preliminary Objections) [1962] ICJ Rep 319; see Whelan, *Indivisible* (n 11) 181.

[137] See Burke, 'Confronting Indivisibility' (n 88) 59.

[138] Schwelb, 'Notes' (n 127) 285.

[139] See Bossuyt, *Guide to the Travaux* (n 17) 617–18.

[140] Including New Zealand, Ireland, Uruguay, Madagascar, and Chile (see Schwelb, 'Civil and Political Rights' (n 127) 840–41).

ICCPR in 1954. Within the Third Committee, the draft provisions and subsequent amendments were subject to careful scrutiny, which led to the wording that became article 40 of the Covenant.[141]

Providing for complaint mechanisms was, without surprise, the subject of intense discussions. As Whelan convincingly demonstrates, the debates were, however, limited to the ICCPR. A violations approach for ESCR was not on the negotiating table,[142] for reasons similar to those discussed above in relation to States' obligations.[143] Individual or interstate complaints were not viewed as a suitable mechanism for giving effect to social, economic, and cultural rights. For civil and political rights, the Commission's draft as sent to ECOSOC and the General Assembly in 1954 provided for mandatory interstate complaints but did not propose an individual complaint procedure. Proposals to grant individuals or non-governmental organizations the right to petition the Human Rights Committee were met with strong opposition by the three superpowers.[144] These initiatives were ultimately either defeated, often by narrow margins, or withdrawn by their sponsors.[145]

Between 1963 and 1966, fundamental changes of the Commission's proposal on implementation measures were debated within the General Assembly. In 1966, supporters of the complaint mechanisms (including the United Kingdom, Canada, the Netherlands, and Australia) could point to the adoption of the ICERD on 7 March 1966. Adopted unanimously, with the support of the Soviet Union, the ICERD became the first human rights convention to provide for a mandatory interstate complaint mechanism, and, more importantly, for an optional individual complaint procedure. Not all States, however, were willing to consider the ICERD as a precedent for implementation measures under the ICCPR.[146] Despite its approval of the ICERD, the Soviet Union, for instance, reverted to its long-held opposition to international oversight (albeit having come to accept the reporting system[147]), arguing that the monitoring mechanisms for both Covenants should be identical.[148] Considering the 'no violation' approach agreed upon for the ICESCR, following

[141] Under ICCPR art 40(1), State parties 'undertake to submit reports on the measures they have adopted which give effect to the rights recognized herein and on the progress made in the enjoyment of those rights'. This wording differs from previous drafts, which provided for reporting on 'the progress made in giving effect to the rights' recognized in the Covenant, and could have been understood as meaning that States were only committed to giving effect to the rights progressively. To prevent such a reading, the final wording established a distinction between 'giving effect to rights' and reporting on the 'progress made in the enjoyment of those rights'. This approach limited the notion of progressiveness to the enjoyment of rights, 'i.e., to the results of the governmental action without implying that the governmental action might be taken progressively' (Schwelb, 'Civil and Political Rights' (n 127) 840; Schwelb, 'Notes' (n 127) 279).

[142] Whelan, *Indivisible* (n 11) 101 and 113–14; see also Normand and Zaidi, *Human Rights* (n 5) 240.

[143] See Section III.A.

[144] See Simpson, *End of Empire* (n 7) 453, 522, 535, and 539; in the United Kingdom, opposition to the right of individual petition was linked to the colonial question, leading to conflicts between the Foreign Office and the Colonial Office (see Normand and Zaidi, *Human Rights* (n 5) 238).

[145] See Schwelb, 'Notes' (n 127) 276–77; Schwelb, 'Civil and Political Rights' (n 127) 832.

[146] Schwelb, 'Civil and Political Rights' (n 127) 833.

[147] Schwelb, 'Notes' (n 127) 285.

[148] Many Afro-Asian States and France considered the ICERD approach to be too stringent for application to the ICCPR. See Schwelb, 'Civil and Political Rights' (n 127) 832–33.

the Soviet position would have left the ICCPR with weak implementing measures, privileging State sovereignty over effective monitoring.[149]

An African–Asian proposal, partially inspired by the ICERD, helped to reach an acceptable compromise.[150] Whilst the Commission's proposal had envisaged a mandatory interstate complaints procedure as the main monitoring mechanism for the ICCPR, the Third Committee made interstate complaints optional and subject to reciprocity. In line with the ICERD, an optional individual complaint mechanism was added in the form of the First Optional Protocol and submitted to the General Assembly together with the Covenants.

The results of the negotiations on the third prong of an international bill of rights—international measures of implementation—clearly stayed away from more bold and visionary projects, such as the establishment of a universal human rights court. Optional individual petitions (tellingly renamed, during the drafting process, as 'communications') were the maximum that States were willing to accept.

IV. Concluding Remarks

The Preamble of the UDHR asserts that 'it is essential, if man is not to be compelled to have recourse, as a last resort, to rebellion against tyranny and oppression, that human rights should be protected by the rule of law'. This recital expresses the framers' view that the Declaration was only 'a step forward in the great evolutionary process'.[151] To afford effective protection against tyranny and oppression, it was essential to translate the text of the Declaration into binding treaty law, backed up by international supervision and enforcement. Reaching a consensus on these issues was an 'acid test' for the international community. The volatile political context, marked by the interlocking challenges of the Cold War and decolonization, and thus changing power constellations within the UN, could have easily precluded an agreement.

These were, however, not the only difficulties the drafters were facing. They also had to overcome conflicts between nations belonging to the same ideological bloc (as the long-lasting disagreement between the United Kingdom and the United States on precise versus general drafting language and on the immediacy of States' obligations under the ICCPR shows). The framers also had to defeat attempts by States to 'export' their own fundamental rights traditions whilst resisting commitments going beyond the domestic status quo.

Another important challenge was the relative indifference of the three superpowers and their reluctance to enter into human rights commitments limiting their national sovereignty. In this context, the adoption of the Covenants is due largely

[149] ibid 833.

[150] Samuel Hoare, 'The United Nations and Human Rights: A Brief Survey of the Commission on Human Rights' in Yoram Dinstein (ed), *Israel Yearbook on Human Rights* (Israel Press 1971) vol 1, 29, 30; see also Schwelb, 'Civil and Political Rights' (n 127) 834.

[151] Verbatim Record of the General Assembly proceedings (GAOR 3rd Session (10 December 1948) UN Doc A/PV.183, 934) as quoted in Lauterpacht, 'The Universal Declaration' (n 4) 354.

to the efforts of other nations. The group of African and Asian States, for instance, favoured an agreement on the right to individual petition, both directly and indirectly: they submitted a compromise solution paving the way for an optional complaint procedure. This proposal was inspired by the ICERD, a convention which African–Asian States had championed, as it reflected one of their core concerns. The Latin American States, with their long tradition of judicial review and commitment to social rights, had already left a strong imprint on the UDHR. As the Declaration was the reference point for the Covenants, its content established a baseline below which a binding human rights treaty was expected not to fall. Unsurprisingly, attempts to exclude the whole set of ESCR met with strong resistance and did not succeed. However, the prevalent view at the time of drafting was that the two sets of rights called for differentiated measures of implementation, both at the domestic and at the international level. The opposing view, defended by the Soviet Union, was unconvincing: it was based on the premise of an extremely weak international implementation regime and on an understanding of rights as ideological tools rather than enforceable entitlements for holding the State accountable. Reinforcing the protection of ESCR remains a challenge to which the contemporary international community needs to live up. A milestone in this process was achieved in 2008, when the General Assembly adopted the Optional Protocol on individual complaints to the ICESCR,[152] adding a 'missing piece of the International Bill of Rights'.[153] This does not mean that the International Bill of Human Rights is complete or can be taken for granted. On the one hand, '[t]he human rights revolution is by definition ongoing'.[154] On the other, human rights, and the underlying vision of common humanity, are demanding ideals that will not prevail without firm support from both States and their people.

Bibliography

Ackerman, Bruce, *The Future of Liberal Revolution* (Yale University Press 1992)

ALI, 'Statements on Essential Human Rights, with Commentary' (1946) 243 Annals of the American Academy of Political and Social Science 18 and (1995) 89 AJIL 550

Alston, Philip, 'The Committee on Economic, Social and Cultural Rights' in Philip Alston (ed), *The United Nations and Human Rights: A Critical Appraisal* (OUP 1992)

Alston, Philip, and Quinn, Gerard, 'The Nature and Scope of States Parties' Obligations under the International Covenant on Economic, Social and Cultural Rights' (1987) 9 Human Rights Q 156

Bossuyt, Marc J, *Guide to the 'Travaux Préparatoires' of the International Covenant on Civil and Political Rights* (Martinus Nijhoff 1986)

152 UNGA Res 63/117 (10 December 2008) UN Doc A/RES/63/117.

153 Catarina de Albuquerque, 'Chronicle of an Announced Birth: The Coming into Life of the Optional Protocol to the International Covenant on Economic, Social and Cultural Rights, the Missing Piece of the International Bill of Human Rights' (2010) 32 Human Rights Q 144.

154 Lynn Hunt, *Inventing Human Rights: A History* (WW Norton 2007) 29.

Burgers, Jan Herman, 'The Road to San Francisco: The Revival of the Human Rights Idea in the Twentieth Century' (1992) 14 Human Rights Q 447

Burke, Roland, 'Confronting "Indivisibility" in the History of Economic and Social Rights: From Parity to Priority and Back Again' (2012) 12 Human Rights & Human Welfare 53

Carozza, Paolo G, 'From Conquest to Constitutions: Retrieving a Latin American Tradition of the Idea of Human Rights' (2003) 25 Human Rights Q 281

Cassin, René, *La pensée et l'action* (Editions F Lalou 1972)

Chatton, Gregor T, *Vers la pleine reconnaissance des droits économiques, sociaux et culturels* (Schulthess 2014)

Cop, Burak, and Eymirlioğlu, Doğan, 'The Right of Self-Determination in International Law Towards the 40th Anniversary of the Adoption of the ICCPR and the ICESCR' [2005] Perceptions 115

Cranston, Maurice William, *What are Human Rights?* (Taplinger Publishing Company 1973)

Craven, Matthew CR, *The International Covenant on Economic, Social, and Cultural Rights: A Perspective on its Development* (OUP 1995)

Davies, Richard O, *Defender of the Old Guard: John Bricker and American Politics* (Ohio State University Press 1993)

de Albuquerque, Catarina, 'Chronicle of an Announced Birth: The Coming into Life of the Optional Protocol to the International Covenant on Economic, Social and Cultural Rights, the Missing Piece of the International Bill of Human Rights' (2010) 32 Human Rights Q 144

Donnelly, Jack, *Universal Human Rights in Theory and Practice* (3rd edn, Cornell University Press 2013)

Fernández Segado, Francisco, 'Les origines du contrôle juridictionnel de la constitutionnalité des lois en Amérique latine' <www.umk.ro/images/documente/publicatii/Buletin18/3_les_origines.pdf> accessed 19 October 2015

Fredman, Sandra, *Human Rights Transformed: Positive Rights and Positive Duties* (OUP 2008)

Glendon, Mary Ann, 'Rights in Twentieth-Century Constitutions' (1992) 59 University of Chicago L Rev 519

Glendon, Mary Ann, *A World Made New: Eleanor Roosevelt and the Universal Declaration of Human Rights* (Random House 2001)

Glendon, Mary Ann, 'The Forgotten Crucible: The Latin American Influence on the Universal Human Rights Idea' (2003) 16 Harvard Human Rights J 27

Hoare, Samuel, 'The United Nations and Human Rights: A Brief Survey of the Commission on Human Rights' in Yoram Dinstein (ed), *Israel Yearbook on Human Rights* (Israel Press 1971), vol 1

Hunt, Lynn, *Inventing Human Rights: A History* (WW Norton 2007)

Kang, Susan L, 'The Unsettled Relationship of Economic and Social Rights and the West: A Response to Whelan and Donnelly' (2009) 31 Human Rights Q 1006

Kirkup, Alex, and Evans, Tony, 'The Myth of Western Opposition to Economic, Social, and Cultural Rights? A Reply to Whelan and Donnelly' (2009) 31 Human Rights Q 221

Langford, Malcolm (ed), *Social Rights Jurisprudence: Emerging Trends in International and Comparative Law* (CUP 2008)

Langford, Malcolm, 'The Justiciability of Social Rights: From Practice to Theory' in Malcolm Langford (ed), *Social Rights Jurisprudence: Emerging Trends in International and Comparative Law* (CUP 2008)

Langford, Malcolm, and King, Jeff A, 'Committee on Economic, Social and Cultural Rights: Past, Present and Future' in Malcolm Langford (ed), *Social Rights Jurisprudence: Emerging Trends in International and Comparative Law* (CUP 2008)

Lauren, Paul Gordon, *The Evolution of International Human Rights: Visions Seen* (3rd edn, University of Pennsylvania Press 2011)
Lauterpacht, Hersch, 'The Universal Declaration of Human Rights' (1948) 25 BYIL 354
Lauterpacht, Hersch, *An International Bill of the Rights of Man* (OUP 2013)
Lösing, Norbert, *Die Verfassungsgerichtsbarkeit in Lateinamerika* (Nomos 2001)
Mahlmann, Matthias, 'The Good Sense of Dignity: Six Antidotes to Dignity Fatigue in Ethics and Law' in Christopher McCrudden (ed), *Understanding Human Dignity* (OUP 2013)
McGoldrick, Dominic, *The Human Rights Committee: Its Role in the Development of the International Covenant on Civil and Political Rights* (OUP 1991)
Moyn, Samuel, *The Last Utopia: Human Rights in History* (Harvard University Press 2010)
Normand, Roger, and Zaidi, Sarah, *Human Rights at the UN: The Political History of Universal Justice* (University of Indiana Press 2008)
Osiatynski, Wiktor, 'On the Universality of the Universal Declaration of Human Rights' in Andras Sajó (ed), *Human Rights with Modesty: The Problem with Universalism* (Springer 2004)
Quataert, Jean H, *Advocating Dignity: Human Rights Mobilizations in Global Politics* (University of Pennsylvania Press 2009)
Rensmann, Thilo, 'The Constitution as Normative Order of Values: The Influence of International Human Rights Law on the Evolution of Modern Constitutionalism' in Pierre-Marie Dupuy and others (eds), *Völkerrecht als Wertordnung: Festschrift für Christian Tomuschat* (NP Engel 2003)
Roberts, Christopher NJ, *The Contentious History of the International Bill of Human Rights* (CUP 2015)
Sajó, Andras, 'Rights in Post-Communism' in Andras Sajó (ed), *Western Rights? Post-communist Application* (Kluwer 1996)
Schwelb, Egon, 'Civil and Political Rights: The International Measures of Implementation' (1968) 62 AJIL 827
Schwelb, Egon, 'Notes on the Early Legislative History of the Measures of Implementation of the Human Rights Covenants' in *Mélanges offerts à Polys Modinos* (Editions Pedone 1968)
Scott, Craig, 'The Interdependence and Permeability of Human Rights Norms: Towards a Partial Fusion of the International Covenants on Human Rights' (1989) 27 Osgoode Hall L J 794
Seibert-Fohr, Anja, 'Domestic Implementation of the International Covenant on Civil and Political Rights Pursuant to its Article 2(2)' in *Max Planck Yearbook of United Nations Law* (Brill 2001) vol 5
Shue, Henry, *Basic Rights: Subsistence, Affluence, and U.S. Foreign Policy* (first published 1980, 2nd edn, Princeton University Press 1996)
Simpson, AW Bryan, *Human Rights and the End of Empire: Britain and the Genesis of the European Convention* (paperback edn, OUP 2004)
Tanabaum, Duane, *The Bricker Amendment Controversy: A Test of Eisenhower's Political Leadership* (Cornell University Press 1988)
Tomuschat, Christian, 'International Covenant on Civil and Political Rights (1966)' in Rüdiger Wolfrum (ed), *Max Planck Encyclopedia of Public International Law* (OUP 2012) vol V
Tschentscher, Axel, and Lehner, Caroline, 'The Latin American Model of Constitutional Jurisdiction: Amparo and Judicial Review' (2013) SSRN Research Paper 2296004 <https://papers.ssrn.com/sol3/papers.cfm?abstract_id=2296004> accessed 7 April 2017

Vik, Hanne Hagtvedt, 'Taming the States: the American Law Institute and the "Statement of Essential Human Rights"' (2012) 7(3) J of Global History 461

von Bernstorff, Jochen, 'The Changing Fortunes of the Universal Declaration of Human Rights: Genesis and Symbolic Dimensions of the Turn to Rights in International Law' (2008) 19 EJIL 903

Whelan, Daniel J, *Indivisible Human Rights: A History* (University of Pennsylvania Press 2010)

Whelan, Daniel J, and Donnelly, Jack, 'The West, Economic and Social Rights, and the Global Human Rights Regime: Setting the Record Straight' (2007) 29 Human Rights Q 908

Whelan, Daniel J, and Donnelly, Jack, 'The Reality of Western Support for Economic and Social Rights: A Reply to Susan L. Kang' (2009) 31 Human Rights Q 1030

Whelan, Daniel J, and Donnelly, Jack, 'Yes, a Myth: A Reply to Kirkup and Evans' (2009) 31 Human Rights Q 239

Xenos, Dimitris, *The Positive Obligations of the State Under the European Convention of Human Rights* (Routledge 2012)

3

Giving Meaning and Effect to Human Rights

The Contributions of Human Rights Committee Members

*Gerald L Neuman**

I. Introduction

This chapter discusses the role of the members of the Human Rights Committee (HRC or Committee) in the implementation of the International Covenant on Civil and Political Rights (ICCPR),[1] and the human rights project as a whole. Initially, that requires a discussion of the functions of the Committee as an overall institution, and then the essay concentrates on the contributions of the members, individually and collectively. It emphasizes the collective activity of authoritatively interpreting the rights within their mandate as the members' most important contribution.

II. The Functions of the Human Rights Committee

The HRC is the independent expert body created by the ICCPR for monitoring compliance by States parties with their obligations under the treaty. Its overbroad name reflects a historical moment when no other treaty bodies were contemplated. Although some of the rights protected by the ICCPR are also addressed in other human rights treaties at the global level, certain key rights are substantively guaranteed to everyone only by the ICCPR, such as freedom from detention, freedom of expression, and political participation.

The HRC has three principal activities: the examination of States' reports, the decision of individual communications, and the writing of General Comments. Each of these activities has evolved over the lifetime of the Committee. This chapter will mostly address their operation from the perspective of 2011–14, my term on the HRC. The three activities have contrasting natures, in terms of how publicly

* Although the author was a member of the Human Rights Committee from 2011 to 2014, this essay does not speak on behalf of the Committee.

[1] International Covenant on Civil and Political Rights (opened for signature 16 December 1966, entered into force 23 March 1976) 999 UNTS 171.

they are performed and their generality or specificity. State reporting is a major public event for the HRC, although some preparatory and deliberative phases take place in closed meetings, and each dialogue covers a wide range of civil and political rights issues in the particular reporting State. Communications involve claims of violation by a specific individual or group of individuals against a particular State, and are processed in confidence; in fact, even the existence of the communication is generally unknown to the rest of the world until the case has been decided and published.[2] General Comments address recurring legal issues of substance or procedure under the ICCPR, without being focused on any particular State, and over the years the HRC has increased the transparency of its process for generating General Comments. It now receives several rounds of public input, and deliberates on the text in open session.

Like any other international body, the HRC has a variety of other auxiliary functions in support of the three main tasks. These functions include adopting procedural rules and practices, drafting an annual report, and maintaining relations with the United Nations (UN) and other human rights institutions. There is also one potentially significant task assigned by the ICCPR that actually lies dormant—the resolution of interstate disputes regarding violations of the treaty[3]—as no State has ever launched such a proceeding. Unlike some of the other treaty bodies, the HRC very rarely issues public statements about human rights crises unconnected to a pending State report or communication, and it does not operate an 'urgent action' procedure for self-initiated investigations.

The periodic reporting process is the primary mode of interaction between States and the HRC required by the ICCPR. States' written reports on their implementation of the treaty lead to a live and public dialogue between the States and Committee members. As the process has evolved, it has encompassed earlier written and oral input to the HRC from non-governmental organizations (NGOs), national human rights institutions, and various UN agencies. Increasingly, States agree to file written answers to a list of questions posed in advance by the HRC, instead of a comprehensive written report, as the foundation for the public dialogue.[4] The dialogue not only takes place before civil society observers and is documented, but (when resources permit) is webcast to reach a wide audience, particularly in the State's own territory. Since 1992, the dialogue has led to the HRC's collectively deliberated concluding observations, which welcome positive developments in the reporting period and then set forth a series of concerns about possible or definite noncompliance with the State's ICCPR obligations, and recommendations for how the State should address these problems. During the Cold War period, individual members were able to make observations at the end of the dialogue, but the members from the socialist States successfully blocked any collective evaluation of States'

[2] HRC, Rules of Procedure of the Human Rights Committee, Rule 102 UN Doc CCPR/C/3/Rev.10 (2012).

[3] ICCPR art 41.

[4] This optional substitute is known as the List of Issues Prior to Reporting (LOIPR), or more recently as the 'simplified reporting procedure'. See United Nations General Assembly (UNGA) Res 68/268 (9 April 2014) UN Doc A/RES/68/268, paras 1–2.

compliance.[5] The HRC now makes collective observations, and follows up on them, within one year for a few selected recommendations, and in connection with the next periodic report for the full set.

The reporting system currently serves a number of overlapping purposes, depending on the quality of the State's participation. The activity of generating the report should focus the attention of State organs on their ICCPR obligations and on the needs expressed by civil society; the constructive dialogue between the State and the HRC gives the State the opportunity to educate the Committee and the world at large on its efforts to comply, and to receive legal guidance and advice from the HRC; the transparency of the dialogue, especially if webcast, offers the State's populace a different perspective on their government; the HRC's welcoming and use of NGOs' information can bolster the legitimacy of their activities and their issues; the HRC's concluding observations offer a form of public accountability for human rights violations; the concluding observations give the HRC an opportunity to indicate its interpretation of the ICCPR; and the follow-up activities create a further forum for civil society engagement.

The HRC can consider individuals' communications only if the relevant State has ratified the (first) Optional Protocol to the ICCPR, as roughly two-thirds of the parties to the ICCPR proper have done thus far.[6] It has been suggested that the optional character of the procedure facilitated the HRC's ability to make findings of violations in its decisions (known as 'Views') during the Cold War years, because the members from socialist States did not seek to undermine a mechanism to which their States were not parties.[7] The communications process serves a variety of purposes—most obviously, extending a forum where individuals can seek vindication of their claims; but also bringing neglected issues to the HRC's attention; operating as an adjunct to the monitoring function of the State report; and giving the HRC the opportunity to expound its interpretation of the ICCPR in a more definite way than concluding observations on State reports usually allow. The HRC also engages in public follow-up on its Views, pressing for implementation of its recommendations.

A key limitation of the HRC's role is that its evaluation of State reports and its final decisions on communications do not produce legally binding outcomes.[8] Most of the concluding observations on State reports do not purport to express definitive

[5] See eg Christian Tomuschat, *Human Rights: Between Idealism and Realism* (OUP 2003), 147–49.

[6] First Optional Protocol to the ICCPR (opened for signature 16 December 1966, entered into force 23 March 1976) 999 UNTS 302.

[7] Nejib Bouziri, 'Problèmes particuliers rencontrés dans les premières années d'activité du Comité' in Nisuke Ando (ed), *Towards Implementing Universal Human Rights: Festschrift for the Twenty-Fifth Anniversary of the Human Rights Committee* (Brill 2004) 79, 98 (Mr Bouziri was an HRC member from 1979 to 1986).

[8] The HRC has held, however, that its requests to States to avoid inflicting irreparable harm on the author of a communication—such as execution or deportation to a country where the author fears torture—pending resolution of the communication are legally binding, because the State would be rendering the communications procedure futile by acting irreversibly before the Committee has expressed its Views on the State's obligations. See eg *Yuzepchuk v Belarus*, HRC Communication No 1906/2009 (24 October 2014) UN Doc 112/D/1906/2009, para 6.4.

conclusions. Each set of concluding observations includes a series of paired 'concern' paragraphs and 'recommendation' paragraphs; usually the concerns involve possible violations, or even regrets about matters that the HRC recognizes as suboptimal, such as reservations to the ICCPR that could be withdrawn. Occasionally the concern paragraph will forthrightly describe a legal rule or practice as incompatible with the treaty. The recommendations are ordinarily proposed measures for dealing with the concern, which are not necessarily the only measures that would suffice, although sometimes the recommendation may openly assert that a rule incompatible with the treaty must be amended. Whether tentative or certain in phrasing, the concluding observations are not legally binding under the ICCPR.

In Views on communications, the HRC's resolution of the dispute does include definite findings of violation or non-violation. The Views also point out the State's obligation to provide reparations for any violations, with details whose status as recommendations or legal conclusions is less clear.[9] Neither the findings of violation nor the remedial indications are legally binding under the Optional Protocol to the ICCPR authorizing the communications procedure.

Although the reporting procedure and the communications procedure do not result in legally binding outcomes for the State involved, they exert a softer normative force for compliance, and they also generate indirect effects on the implementation of the ICCPR. State authorities may be persuaded by the HRC's findings, and re-examine individual decisions or policies. Views and concluding observations can reinforce internal political forces and social movements arguing for reform. The HRC's follow-up processes call upon States to document and explain their measures of implementation. At the international level, a treaty body must be understood as an element in a broader network, where the outputs of the treaty body motivate or are utilized by other institutions that play different roles. The HRC's findings possess an authority and objectivity that can be combined with the political power or financial resources of other external actors to induce change. The HRC's legal interpretations of the ICCPR provide an objective framework for criticizing the State's failure to respect human rights.

The HRC has characterized its elaboration of the meaning of the ICCPR as 'authoritative', a term that is subtly different from 'binding'.[10] The International Court of Justice (ICJ) expressed its appreciation of the HRC's role in a well-known judgment applying the ICCPR:

[9] The HRC's lists of forms of reparation in its Views may be understood as conclusions on the exact remedy required by the violations found, or as recommended measures to remedy these violations, or as being sometimes one and sometimes the other. See eg HRC, 'Summary Record' (31 October 2014) UN Doc CCPR/C/SR.3134, 3 (for an abbreviated and approximate summary of the discussion); Martin Scheinin, 'The Human Rights Committee's Pronouncements on the Right to an Effective Remedy: An Illustration of the Legal Nature of the Committee's Work under the Optional Protocol' in Ando, *Implementing Universal Human Rights* (n 7) 101, 108–10; cf Gerald L Neuman, 'Bi-Level Remedies for Human Rights Violations' (2014) 55 Harvard Intl L J 323 (examining remedies from a theoretical perspective). Moreover, the Views rarely include reasons in their remedial paragraph.

[10] HRC, 'General Comment 33' (2008) UN Doc CCPR/C/GC/33, para 13.

Since it was created, the Human Rights Committee has built up a considerable body of interpretative case law, in particular through its findings in response to the individual communications which may be submitted to it in respect of States parties to the first Optional Protocol, and in the form of its 'General Comments'.

Although the Court is in no way obliged, in the exercise of its judicial functions, to model its own interpretation of the Covenant on that of the Committee, it believes that it should ascribe great weight to the interpretation adopted by this independent body that was established specifically to supervise the application of the treaty. The point here is to achieve the necessary clarity and the essential consistency of international law, as well as legal security, to which both the individuals with guaranteed rights and the States obliged to comply with treaty obligations are entitled.[11]

In other words, when the HRC performs its task properly, its consistent interpretations provide focal points around which interpretation of the ICCPR should coalesce.

From my own perspective, this interpretive function constitutes the most important contribution of the HRC to the implementation of the ICCPR. In saying this, I do not mean to minimize the value of the other functions, but rather to emphasize the need for authoritative elaboration. Covenant rights cannot be left to the chaos of self-serving interpretations by each indifferent or complacent State. The HRC's interpretations are foreshadowed in concluding observations, articulated in holdings on communications, and summarized in General Comments.

General Comments usually provide a synthesis or progressive codification of the HRC's interpretation of a particular substantive article of the ICCPR, based primarily on its past experience in communications and concluding observations. Some General Comments address cross-cutting issues, and others have addressed HRC procedures. In the past, General Comments often requested States to include particular information in their reports, but this function may be fading as advance lists of issues replace comprehensive reports. General Comments may include both passages that elaborate obligations and passages that set forth recommended means of avoiding violations; the use of the verb 'should' often, but not always, indicates a recommendation, in contrast with the mandatory 'must'. General Comments guide States and the HRC's own conduct in drafting concluding observations and Views. Nonetheless, the HRC may further develop its jurisprudence without first amending or replacing an older General Comment.[12]

[11] *Ahmadou Sadio Diallo (Republic of Guinea v Democratic Republic of the Congo)* (Merits) [2010] ICJ Rep 639, 664.

[12] eg in 1996 the HRC's General Comment 25 had identified 'established mental incapacity' as a permissible basis for denying the right to vote (HRC, 'General Comment 25' in 'Note by the Secretariat, Compilation of General Comments and General Recommendations Adopted by Human Rights Treaty Bodies' (2008) HRI/GEN/1/Rev.9 (vol I) para 4). This conclusion appeared problematic after the advent of the Convention on the Rights of Persons with Disabilities (CRPD) (opened for signature 13 December 2006, entered into force 3 May 2008) 2515 UNTS 3. In response, the HRC declined to amend or replace its old General Comment, but rather took into account some of the insights of the CRPD Committee and adopted concluding observations that articulated a stricter standard for (but not an absolute ban on) finding an inability to vote. See eg HRC, 'Concluding Observations on the Third

The importance of the HRC's interpretive function varies somewhat in the different regions. It is most crucial in regions that lack independent human rights tribunals, and for countries that are not parties to relevant regional treaties. In the Council of Europe, which has a thick set of human rights institutions and a well-established if overburdened court with mandatory jurisdiction, the HRC's role is supplementary. The HRC has filled in some gaps in the coverage of the European Convention on Human Rights,[13] and has occasionally led the way in the interpretation of particular rights, such as conscientious objection to military service as an element of religious freedom.[14] The HRC also provides a global corrective to certain region-specific interpretations, such as the excessive margin of appreciation that the European Court of Human Rights (ECtHR) affords to limitations on non-Christian religious practices.[15] In the Americas, where most States are now subject to the jurisdiction of a regional court that borrows freely from European and global sources and exercises considerable interpretive freedom of its own, the HRC's role may have become supplementary as well. Nonetheless, for non-parties to the American Convention on Human Rights, most prominently the United States of America, the ICCPR reporting system provides an essential impartial global forum for accountability.[16] In Africa, where the regional human rights convention expressly encourages use of global human rights instruments in its interpretation, the HRC influences the articulation of human rights standards both directly under the ICCPR and indirectly through the regional convention, although great challenges of implementation remain.[17] Moreover, the new African Court on Human and Peoples' Rights (ACtHPR) has already invoked the HRC's General Comments in some of its judgments,[18]

Periodic Report of Hong Kong, China' (29 April 2013) UN Doc CCPR/C/CHN-HKG/CO/3, para 24; HRC, 'Summary Record' (28 March 2013) UN Doc CCPR/C/SR.2978, para 14.

[13] eg there is a weakened version of the right to criminal appeal, with an exception that allows appeals to be restricted to pure issues of law, in the European human rights system (Protocol No 7 to the Convention for the Protection of Human Rights and Fundamental Freedoms (opened for signature 22 November 1984, entered into force 1 November 1988) ETS 117). HRC Views finding violations by Spain of the stronger provision in ICCPR art 14(5) led the legislature to adopt legal reforms broadening the right of appeal. See International Law Association, 'Final Report on the Impact of Findings of the United Nations Human Rights Treaty Bodies' (2004) 9–10.

[14] See *Bayatyan v Armenia* App no 23459/03 (ECtHR, 7 July 2011) paras 105–09 (changing the Court's interpretation of ECHR art 9 in relation to conscientious objection, in parallel to the HRC's change in interpretation of ICCPR art 18).

[15] Compare eg *Bikramjit Singh v France*, HRC Communication No 1852/2008 (1 November 2012) UN Doc CCPR/C/106/D/1852/2008 (protecting a male Sikh student's right to wear a religiously required head covering in public school), with *Jasvir Singh v France* App no 25463/08 (ECtHR, 30 June 2009) (finding that the denial of such a right was within France's margin of appreciation); see Gerald L Neuman, 'Human Rights and Constitutions in a Complex World' (2013) 50 Irish Jurist 1, 7–8.

[16] Perhaps it should be mentioned here that, in the HRC, members are recused from participation in examining the State report of their country of nationality, as well as communications brought against it, in contrast to the mandatory inclusion of national judges in cases before the ECtHR. See HRC, Rules of Procedure (n 2) Rules 71(4), 90(1)(a). The United States is not a party to the Optional Protocol.

[17] See Frans Viljoen, *International Human Rights in Africa* (OUP 2007) 345.

[18] *Konaté v Burkino Faso* App no 004/2013 (ACtHPR, 5 December 2014); *Mtikila v United Republic of Tanzania* App nos 009/2011 and 011/2011 (ACtHPR, 14 June 2013).

and has exercised its explicit authority to find a violation of the ICCPR in a case.[19]

III. The Committee and Its Members

According to the ICCPR, the Human Rights Committee 'shall consist of eighteen members'.[20] The Committee *is* its members, taken together. In addition, the ICCPR requires the UN Secretary-General to 'provide the necessary staff and facilities for the effective performance of the functions of the Committee under the present Covenant'.[21] The result of this arrangement is that personnel of the UN human rights bureaucracy (currently the Treaty Bodies Division of the Office of the High Commissioner for Human Rights (OHCHR)) furnish vital support and assistance to the work of the HRC, and the Conference Management division of the UN supplies other facilities, such as interpretation, translation, and publication services.

In a broad sense, the Committee could be said to include the members, the human rights officers, and the Conferences Services personnel, just as the ICJ could be said to include the judges and the entire Registry, from the legal officers to the security division and the medical unit.[22] Unlike the ICJ, however, the HRC does not have formal authority over any of the people who assist it—they are all part of the UN Secretariat.[23] The HRC proper is an independent treaty-based body outside the UN hierarchy, but dependent on the UN for financial and human resources. The Committee members have a close working relationship with their own Secretary and other helpful people from the Treaty Bodies Division, and a much more arms-length relationship with others, including Conference Services, whose translation and publication services actually consume the great majority of the treaty body budget.[24] This unfortunate structure weakens the HRC.

The Committee proper, then, consists of the members, nationals of eighteen different States that are parties to the ICCPR. They attend the HRC's three sessions per year, and they also perform preparatory work between sessions, in addition to the full-time jobs that support them. They are elected by the States parties for staggered four-year terms, with consideration given to 'equitable geographical distribution of membership and to the representation of the different forms of civilization and of the principal legal systems'.[25] The regional distribution is not fully proportional,

[19] See *Konaté* (n 18); *Thomas v United Republic of Tanzania* App no 005/2013 (ACtHPR, 20 November 2015).

[20] ICCPR art 28.

[21] ICCPR art 36.

[22] See ICJ 'Report of the International Court of Justice: 1 August 2013–31 July 2014' (2014) UN Doc A/69/4, 61.

[23] See Torkel Opsahl, 'The Human Rights Committee' in Philip Alston (ed), *The United Nations and Human Rights: A Critical Appraisal* (OUP 1992) 369, 388–91.

[24] See eg Navanethem Pillay, 'Strengthening the United Nations Treaty Body System: A Report by the United Nations High Commissioner for Human Rights' (OHCHR 2012) 26 (describing treaty body costs for 2010 and 2011 as $39.3 million for human rights personnel, including members' travel, and $72 million for conference services).

[25] ICCPR art 31(2).

but the HRC benefits from the existing diversity of its membership.[26] From recent experience I would report that the members interact as equals and without the factionalism that characterized the HRC's Cold War period. Nearly all the HRC members have been lawyers, though with different career paths, including academia, the judiciary, foreign ministries, and NGO service. Their legal experience, which the ICCPR encourages but does not require, contributes to the quality of the HRC's work; so do other skills, such as diplomacy, which academics often lack but which is helpful in dialogue with recalcitrant States or in sometimes awkward relations with UN structures. The HRC could benefit from greater gender diversity in its membership, an issue that the two Covenants do not expressly address.[27]

The members contribute through a division of labour within the Committee. Every two years since 1987, the HRC has elected a new Chairperson from a different region than the previous one, though not in a strictly regular rotation. Along with three Vice-Chairpersons and a Rapporteur (for the Annual Report), the Chairperson participates in the Bureau to handle certain administrative matters. Special Rapporteurs are appointed for two-year terms to perform certain specialized functions, such as the follow-up procedures. The heaviest load is carried by the Special Rapporteur for New Communications and Interim Measures, who is on call for urgent decisions year-round. An average member in an average session is likely to play multiple roles: as rapporteur for one State report, task force member on another, rapporteur for a few communications, and more generally by actively participating in deliberations on concluding observations, communications, the pending draft General Comment, and the HRC's working methods.

The HRC's Views, concluding observations, and General Comments are all the product of deliberations by the plenary Committee.[28] Concluding observations and General Comments are adopted by consensus. Views on individual communications, however, may be adopted by majority vote if consensus cannot be reached, and this is the one area where the HRC's rules provide for the publication of separate individual opinions (concurring or dissenting).[29]

Members write their individual opinions, alone or with others, for a variety of reasons. The HRC has a fairly restrained culture of dissent, and members do

[26] See eg UNGA 'Promotion of Equitable Geographical Distribution in the Membership of the Human Rights Treaty Bodies' (3 August 2015) UN Doc A/70/257 (providing statistics). Members with human rights expertise contribute understanding of the operation of their legal systems, including the defects; they should not serve as mere conduits for conveying national and regional preferences. For further discussion of regional representation, see Samantha Besson, 'The Influence of the Two Covenants on States Parties Across Regions: Lessons for the Role of Comparative Law and of Regions in International Human Rights Law', Chapter 11 in this volume.

[27] See eg Alice Edwards, 'Universal Suffrage and the International Human Rights Treaty Bodies: Where are the Women?' in M Cherif Bassiouni and William A Schabas (eds), *New Challenges for the UN Human Rights Machinery: What Future for the UN Treaty Body System and the Human Rights Council Procedures?* (Intersentia 2011) 151; UNGA Res 68/268, 9 April 2014, paras 12–13.

[28] Some of the inadmissibility decisions may be drafted by a Special Rapporteur or Working Group, and adopted by the Committee without discussion if no member raises a concern. See HRC, Rules of Procedure (n 2) Rule 93(3).

[29] ibid Rule 104.

not write every time they disagree with some aspect of the majority opinion.[30] Separate opinions may argue for a different evaluation of the facts, or may articulate a different legal approach with regard to substance, methodology, or procedure. Sometimes concurring opinions explain more fully reasoning that may be latent in a terse majority opinion, or emphasize one of the rationales that contributed to a compromise formulation. On a few occasions, concurring members have written in order to respond to the arguments of a dissenting opinion. Separate opinions bring internal debates into the open, which may prompt wider discussion, and they record arguments that may prove influential when a related issue arises in a later case. The individualized style of many separate opinions has potential to persuade a variety of audiences that the concise institutional style of HRC majority opinions may lack.

In the HRC, the members write the General Comments. They possess the legal expertise to draft, and they would not delegate the task to the Secretariat or to outside agencies or NGOs, as some other treaty bodies have done.[31] Serving as rapporteur on a General Comment is a huge time commitment, both during and between sessions. The rapporteur produces the initial draft, and shepherds the evolving text through the stages of discussion. The procedure for adopting General Comments has become highly consultative, and the HRC receives very useful suggestions from States and other stakeholders, but the members must be persuaded of their merit, and each paragraph of the text is adopted by consensus.

Members play diverse roles in another respect. One former member, Martin Scheinin, has emphasized three ideal types of the Committee member, which he and a co-author call the Captain, the Fire Brigade, and the Icebreaker.[32] The captain emphasizes maintaining stability on a forward course, as if the Committee were a massive vessel that could not make sharp turns or reduce speed quickly. The fire brigade responds to burning injustices, and rushes to extinguish them by any means that work. The icebreaker leads the way through blocked seas, creating the single

[30] During 2011–14, somewhat under 40 per cent of the Views included at least one separate opinion, concurring or dissenting (author's calculation). Far fewer inadmissibility decisions inspire separate opinions. The number of separate opinions on Views, written or joined, varied greatly among members during this period, from zero to forty-eight (an outlier). I do not distinguish here between concurring and dissenting opinions, because members may disagree sharply on issues of interpretation in cases where they agree that the provision at issue has been violated. The HRC's rate of separate opinions is much lower than that of the ECtHR, but far higher than that of the Committee on the Elimination of Racial Discrimination (CERD), which did not see its first separate opinion until 2013. See Robin CA White and Iris Boussiakou, 'Separate Opinions in the European Court of Human Rights' (2009) 9 Human Rights L Rev 37 (finding 80 per cent of Chamber and Grand Chamber judgments from 1999 to 2004 non-unanimous); Luzius Wildhaber, 'Opinions dissidentes et concordantes de juges individuels à la Cour Européenne des Droits de l'Homme' in René-Jean Dupuy (ed), *Mélanges en l'Honneur de Nicolas Valticos: Droit et justice* (A Pedone 1999) 529 (giving earlier statistics); *TBB Turkish Union in Berlin-Brandenburg v Germany* (2013), CERD Communication No 48/2010, UN Doc CERD/C/82/D/48/2010.

[31] See eg Jaap E Doek, 'The CRC: Dynamics and Directions of Monitoring its Implementation' in Antonella Invernizzi and Jane Williams (eds), *The Human Rights of Children: From Visions to Implementation* (Routledge 2011) 99, 106.

[32] See Pamela Slotte and Martin Scheinin, 'Captain, Fire Brigade or Icebreaker? Political Legitimacy as a Rationale in Human Rights Adjudication' in Tage Kurtén and Lars Hertzberg (eds), *Legitimacy: The Treasure of Politics* (Peter Lang 2011) 89.

channel that States must follow to reach the treaty's goal. Scheinin makes evident his sympathy with the fire brigade.

I agree that the HRC benefits from having members with diverse approaches and strategies, and I recognize the fire brigade type as making an essential contribution, challenging the others to perceive new problems and find new solutions. My own view is that the HRC also needs counterweights to the fire brigade, and I note Scheinin's observation that the fire brigade concentrates on putting out the fire, leaving it to civilians to clean up 'the mess left behind'.[33] If we depict the members' roles in such terms, then I would add here the need for Chess Players, who can listen to the fire brigade's suggestion, but who think several moves ahead, and consider the specific and systemic consequences of employing the proposed method and its alternatives.

Another useful type, who would also double in one of the other capacities, is the Historian: the HRC has been fortunate in having a few long-serving members who could shed light not only on past events, but on why they occurred. Regrettably, the Secretariat has not been in a position to perform that function. Historians are not necessarily resistant to change, but are knowledgeable about the Committee's past. The value of institutional memory provides an argument against rigid term limits for treaty bodies, which benefit from both infusion of new perspectives and an insider's understanding of a treaty body's history.

IV. The Interpretative Function of the Members

The HRC's members understand that their task is to apply the ICCPR. Unlike some other human rights tribunals,[34] they are not given competence to adjudicate claims brought under other human rights treaties, either global or regional. The doctrine of the indivisibility of human rights does not confer omnicompetence on treaty bodies. Neither does it imply that whatever violates a substantive provision of one human rights treaty should also be regarded as violating some substantive provision of every other human rights treaty.

At the same time, application of the ICCPR may require the Committee to give attention to other treaties, or even customary international law. For example, article 4 ICCPR authorizes and restricts derogations from certain provisions of the ICCPR in times of public emergency, while expressly specifying that derogating measures must remain consistent with the State's other obligations under international law. The Committee could not give proper effect to that restriction on derogation

[33] ibid 109.

[34] See the Protocol to the African Charter of Human and Peoples' Rights on the Establishment of an African Court on Human and Peoples' Rights (opened for signature 9 June 1998, entered into force 25 January 2004), art 3(1) (extending jurisdiction to disputes regarding either the Charter or 'any other relevant Human Rights instrument ratified by the States concerned'); *Konaté* (n 18) (applying both the ICCPR and the Charter).

without taking into account the State's obligations under treaty-based or customary international humanitarian law.[35]

More broadly, the HRC faces recurring questions about the relationship between rights guaranteed by the ICCPR and the obligations of States under other human rights treaties. In 2013–14, the Committee engaged in an explicit debate on the effect of other 'core' human rights treaties—either the texts of the treaties themselves or the interpretations by the respective treaty bodies—on the interpretation of the ICCPR.[36] Committee members were in general agreement that dialogue with other treaty bodies was important, and that the HRC should be open to learning from the insights of other treaty bodies. No member proposed that the HRC should automatically and unquestioningly adopt other treaty bodies' interpretations of their respective treaties as settling the meaning of the ICCPR.

The HRC's conversation took place in the context of the issues that arise repeatedly in its work, but also in the context of contemporary debates related to the OHCHR's report on 'strengthening the United Nations treaty body system'.[37] (It deserves notice that the OHCHR's self-interested formulation made the 'system' the object of the strengthening, rather than the treaty bodies.) The report insisted, for example, that treaty bodies 'need to ensure consistency among themselves on common issues in order to provide coherent treaty implementation advice and guidance to States'.[38] The calls for consistency and coherence could be read as seeking either absence of conflict or achievement of uniformity.

To my own understanding, direct contradiction between treaty bodies, in the sense of the HRC's concluding that the ICCPR obliges a State to perform an action that another treaty body regards as a violation of its respective treaty, or vice versa, amounts to a very serious problem to be avoided if possible. Avoiding such contradictions may not be possible, however, if the other treaty body does not take

35 See HRC, 'General Comment 29' in 'Compilation of General Comments' (vol I) (n 12) 234, paras 9–10.

36 The conversation included a discussion in open session on 28 March 2014 as part of the HRC's improvement of its working methods, and an earlier preliminary discussion by the ten HRC members who attended an informal retreat in the Hague in April 2013. The March 2014 meeting is summarized in abbreviated and approximate form in HRC, 'Summary Record' (28 March 2014) UN Doc CCPR/C/SR.3066; there is no public record of the April 2013 retreat, although its content was briefly discussed at the HRC's meeting with the States parties to the ICCPR in July 2013, as summarized in HRC, 'Summary Record' (22 July 2013) UN Doc CCPR/C/SR.3000, paras 32–48.

37 See Pillay, 'Strengthening' (n 24); UNGA Res 68/268 (9 April 2014) UN Doc A/RES/68/268 (adopting the outcome of the intergovernmental process).

38 See Pillay, 'Strengthening' (n 24) 25 and 68 ('ensuring consistency of jurisprudence among treaty bodies'). As another example, the so-called Poznan formula for uniformizing the procedural rules of treaty bodies by enhancing the role of joint meetings of the committees' chairpersons (see Pillay, 'Strengthening' (n 24) 31; UNGA Res 68/268, 9 April 2014, para 38) shifts power from the treaty bodies' members to the OHCHR. The Treaty Bodies Division drafts proposals for procedural changes and can present them—with insufficient prior notice—at the chairpersons' intersessional meetings, which are then under pressure to act. For example, at the 2014 meeting of chairs, the OHCHR put a series of texts on the agenda that had been made available only after the most recent sessions of the HRC and the Committee on the Elimination of Racial Discrimination had ended. See UNGA, 'Implementation of Human Rights Instruments' (11 August 2014) UN Doc A/69/285 (report of the meeting of chairs), paras 25–26.

ICCPR obligations adequately into account. Specialized treaty bodies may lack legal expertise, and they may pay insufficient attention to the rights of others that come into conflict with the rights within their specialized mandate. Of course, the HRC may also have misperceived empirical realities that the other treaty body understands better, or may have neglected the perspective of a disadvantaged group whose situation prompted the creation of the other treaty. The HRC needs to examine both possibilities, by means that may include actual dialogue with the other treaty body, but it cannot automatically yield to the expertise or choices of the other body.

'Consistency' in a stronger sense, however, is a different issue. Even with regard to civil and political rights listed in the ICCPR, other 'core' treaties (by text or interpretation) may impose stricter or more specific standards, more detailed implementing measures, or more extensive positive obligations. The Convention against Torture and Other Cruel, Inhuman or Degrading Treatment or Punishment (UNCAT)[39] provides an instructive example. The UNCAT could be considered as a kind of 'implementing treaty' for ICCPR article 7, which prohibits torture and cruel, inhuman, or degrading treatment or punishment. The UNCAT's preamble refers to ICCPR article 7 as one of its predecessors, and it emphasizes the States parties' desire to 'make more effective the struggle against torture and other cruel, inhuman or degrading treatment or punishment throughout the world'.[40] UNCAT article 1 provides a definition of torture for the purposes of the UNCAT—without prejudice to wider definitions elsewhere—and there follow a series of preventive, repressive, and remedial obligations, some quite detailed, to increase effectiveness. Cruel, inhuman, or degrading treatment is handled more succinctly in UNCAT article 16, without providing a definition and expressly imposing a subset of the obligations listed for torture, again without prejudice to other instruments.

The HRC has considered UNCAT as useful guidance with respect to the implementation of ICCPR article 7, but not as wholly determining the meaning of article 7 obligations within the framework of the ICCPR.[41] It would be excessive and formalistic to consider every detailed regulation listed in the UNCAT as a mandatory component of the State's duties of implementation under article 2 ICCPR in combination with article 7. The HRC also does not rely exclusively on the definition of torture in UNCAT article 1, or the scope given to other ill-treatment in UNCAT article 16, both of which restrict UNCAT obligations to acts committed 'by or at the instigation of or with the consent or acquiescence of a public official or other person acting in an official capacity.' That aspect of the definition is relevant to the range of detailed obligations in the UNCAT. In contrast, the HRC understands the rights in ICCPR article 7 as 'amenable to application between private persons' in a manner that generates positive obligations for the State to prevent and punish private torture

[39] Convention against Torture and Other Cruel, Inhuman or Degrading Treatment or Punishment (opened for signature 10 December 1984, entered into force 26 June 1987) 1465 UNTS 85.

[40] UNCAT Preamble.

[41] See eg *Giri v Nepal*, HRC Communication No 1761/2008 (24 March 2011) UN Doc CCPR/C/101/D/1761/2008, para 7.5.

or ill-treatment.[42] Thus, even a treaty as closely linked to the ICCPR as the UNCAT needs to be used with care in interpreting the ICCPR itself.[43]

It would admittedly simplify the work of the Secretariat and provide uniform advice to States if the HRC and other treaty bodies always gave identical answers to questions about the permissibility of particular practices. A State party to the ICCPR would have understandable objections, however, if the result were that it became bound de facto by the content of another treaty that it had not ratified, or if the HRC's communications procedure became the vehicle for bringing complaints under the other treaty when the State had not accepted the other treaty's optional procedure. And, as illustrated by the UNCAT, identical interpretation would sometimes reduce protection under the ICCPR.

Using the text of another 'core' treaty to shed light on provisions of the ICCPR differs from using other treaty bodies' *interpretations* of their treaties for that purpose. Generally speaking, States parties have agreed to be bound by the texts of treaties, and the wording of the texts is stable over time.[44] Interpretations by other treaty bodies, in contrast, are not formally binding, and they change over time, not necessarily in a predictable direction. The HRC has found the interpretations by other treaty bodies of their treaties informative,[45] but it has not tried to emulate all their innovations. To maintain dynamic consistency would not only be taxing; it would also mean abandoning the HRC's own credibility as authoritatively interpreting the ICCPR.

In the context of the present volume, particular interest attaches to the relationship between the two Covenants in light of the indivisibility of civil and political rights on the one hand from economic, social, and cultural rights on the other. The interplay between the ICCPR and the International Covenant on Economic, Social and Cultural Rights (ICESCR)[46] differs from the relationship between the two Covenants and later treaties. Neither Covenant can be understood as generally implementing the other. There are a variety of relationships among the rights in the

[42] See eg HRC, 'General Comment 31' in 'Compilation of General Comments' (vol I) (n 12) 244, para 8.

[43] Similarly, the HRC has not mechanically incorporated into its definition of the child's right to protection by the State under ICCPR arts 23 and 24 all the obligations set forth in the Convention on the Rights of the Child ((opened for signature 20 November 1989, entered into force 2 September 1990) 1577 UNTS 3). Instead, it has characterized that Convention as 'a valuable source informing the Committee's interpretation of the Covenant' (*Blessington and Elliot v Australia,* HRC Communication No 1968/2010 (22 October 2014) UN Doc CCPR/C/112/D/1968/2010, para 7.11).

[44] Qualifications to this proposition include the fact that not all States parties to the ICCPR may have ratified another treaty; that some ratifications are accompanied by reservations; and that different language versions of treaties exist. In fact, later translations of both Covenants into Chinese may have been substituted for the original ones: see Sun Shiyan, 'The International Covenant on Civil and Political Rights: One Covenant, Two Chinese Texts?' (2006) 75 Nordic J of Intl L 187; James D Seymour and Patrick Yuk-tung Wong, 'China and the International Human Rights Covenants' (2015) 47 Critical Asian Studies 514.

[45] See eg HRC, 'General Comment 35' (16 December 2014) UN Doc CCPR/C/GC/35 (citing General Comments of both the Committee on the Rights of the Child and the Committee Against Torture, among other sources, in construing ICCPR art 9).

[46] International Covenant on Economic, Social and Cultural Rights (opened for signature 16 December 1966, entered into force 3 January 1976) 993 UNTS 3.

two Covenants, and there are two conspicuous instances of overlapping rights: the right to form and join trade unions is mentioned in both ICCPR article 22 and ICESCR article 8(1)(a), and the generally phrased non-discrimination norm in ICCPR article 26 shares content with the ancillary norms of non-discrimination with regard to ICESCR rights expressed in ICESCR articles 2(2) and 3.[47] Nonetheless, considerable differences remain in the rights enumerated by the Covenants and their interpretations by the respective bodies.

One might usefully contrast the prohibition of arbitrary interference with the home under ICCPR article 17 and the right to adequate housing under ICESCR article 11(1). The Committee on Economic, Social and Cultural Rights (CESCR) has elaborated the right to adequate housing in its General Comment 4 (issued in 1991) as including obligations to take necessary steps toward ensuring shelter for everyone that is 'adequate' in numerous dimensions, including legal security of tenure; availability of services, materials, facilities, and infrastructure; affordability; habitability; accessibility; location 'which allows access to employment options, health-care services, schools, child-care centers and other social facilities'; and enabling the expression of cultural identity.[48] While fulfilling this ambitious conception of adequacy was subject to the ICESCR mandate for progressive achievement, some dimensions of the right had more immediate consequences. One such consequence, noted in General Comment 4 and more fully expounded in General Comment 7 (issued in 1997), involved protection against 'forced evictions'.[49] The CESCR pointed out that 'forced eviction' is a term of art, referring not to all compelled relinquishment of housing for any reason, but rather 'the permanent or temporary removal against their will of individuals, families and/or communities from the homes and/or land which they occupy, without the provision of, and access to, appropriate forms of legal or other protection', and does not include 'evictions carried out by force in accordance with the law and in conformity with the provisions of the International Covenants on Human Rights.'[50] That conformity implies both procedural and substantive limitations on the process of lawful eviction, and also:

> Evictions should not result in individuals being rendered homeless or vulnerable to the violation of other human rights. *Where those affected are unable to provide for themselves, the State party must take all appropriate measures, to the maximum of its available resources, to ensure that adequate alternative housing, resettlement or access to productive land, as the case may be, is available.*[51]

That is, under ICESCR article 11, a person may sometimes be lawfully evicted from a particular housing unit, but the State must then ensure that the person's right to adequate housing, as understood by CESCR, is respected.

[47] The HRC clarified in *Broeks v the Netherlands*, HRC Communication No 172/1984 (9 April 1987) UN Doc CCPR/C/29/D/172/1984, and a companion case that the prohibition of sex discrimination in ICCPR art 26 was autonomous rather than limited to discrimination with regard to other rights under the ICCPR, and that it applied to unemployment benefits.

[48] CESCR, 'General Comment 4' in 'Compilation of General Comments' (vol I) (n 12) 11.

[49] CESCR, 'General Comment 7' in 'Compilation of General Comments' (vol I) (n 12) 38.

[50] ibid para 3.

[51] ibid para 16 (emphasis added).

The HRC has examined the phenomenon of eviction from informal settlements in connection with several State reports, and has expressed concerns and made some recommendations.[52] The Committee did not make precise findings in Views on that subject until 2012. The authors in *Naidenova et al v Bulgaria* were Roma residents of a longstanding informal settlement constructed on municipal land, which the city sought to reclaim after acquiescing in its presence for several decades.[53] The NGOs that briefed their case raised claims of both arbitrary and unlawful interference with their homes under ICCPR article 17, as well as claims of discrimination based on their Roma ethnicity.[54] Among the arguments, counsel urged that the threatened evictions would violate the right to adequate housing under ICESCR article 11 and the CESCR's General Comments, and therefore were unlawful within the meaning of ICCPR article 17.[55] Counsel also argued that the right to adequate housing in the ICESCR was similar to the prohibition of arbitrary interference with the home in ICCPR article 17, and that the factors articulated in CESCR, General Comment 7 showed that the threatened eviction should be condemned as arbitrary.

The HRC unanimously concluded that carrying out the threatened evictions as planned would be arbitrary under ICCPR article 17, but did not endorse the strong form of the NGOs' arguments. The HRC wrote narrowly in its first Views on the subject of eviction from unlawfully occupied property. It agreed that the dwellings were the residents' 'homes' within the meaning of article 17, despite the fact that they did not own the land on which they had built. The HRC's own analysis avoided using the term 'forced eviction,' and did not equate the meaning of article 17 with the meaning of ICESCR article 11 or the CESCR General Comment. The analysis emphasized a series of factors that, taken together, rendered the city's conduct unreasonable, including the lengthy acquiescence in the presence of the settlement, the fact that the land was publicly owned, the absence of any pressing need to change the status quo, and the unavailability of satisfactory replacement housing. The HRC did not determine how it would rule if any of these factors had been different, but left those issues for analysis in future cases.[56] It also avoided saying that the residents were immediately entitled to 'adequate' housing as defined by CESCR.

The *Naidenova* case could be seen as the HRC's effort to independently explore the content of a prohibition of arbitrary interference with the home in the context

[52] See eg HRC, 'Concluding Observations on the Second Periodic Report of Kenya' (29 April 2005) UN Doc CCPR/CO/83/KEN, para 22.

[53] *Naidenova et al v Bulgaria*, HRC Communication No 2073/2011 (30 October 2012) UN Doc CCPR/C/106/D/2073/2011.

[54] The HRC found the discrimination claims inadmissible because the evidence submitted insufficiently substantiated them, and also observed that these claims seemed not to have been exhausted in the domestic proceedings (ibid para 13.6).

[55] ibid para 3.4. Article 5(4) of the Bulgarian Constitution gives duly ratified treaties force of law superior to statute. It does not expressly give the General Comments of treaty bodies force of law.

[56] In a later decision on another communication brought against Bulgaria by the same NGOs, the HRC found the claim inadmissible for lack of substantiation after the authors failed to provide information the Committee had requested regarding such factors as the length of the occupancy and the public or private ownership of the land. See *SID v Bulgaria*, HRC Communication No 1926/2010 (21 July 2014) UN Doc CCPR/C/111/D/1926/2010.

of unauthorized occupation of land. Counsel had called to the HRC's attention the CESCR's interpretation of the other Covenant, and the HRC took into account the insights expressed by the CESCR but also the difference in the two committees' mandates. For example, from the perspective of a treaty body monitoring progressive realization of the right to adequate housing, it might be appropriate to infer strict obligations on a State that has neglected implementation of the right and subsequently confronts the need to demolish unsanitary and dangerous structures, or seeks to protect the interests of private owners whose land has recently been occupied. At the same time, a treaty body that has a different monitoring task, focused on a prohibition of arbitrary interference with the home, may justifiably base its evaluation on a narrower view of the duties involved, within the framework of a different treaty. If the period of occupation has been short, or if the reason for removing the occupiers from the land is compelling, it may be reasonable within the framework of the ICCPR for a State with limited resources to expel them from their current home without prioritizing them for housing that meets the CESCR's standards of adequacy. Such divergence, if it occurred, would express no disrespect for the CESCR's interpretation of its own Covenant, but rather the HRC's respect for the limits of its own competence. The right to adequate housing and the right against arbitrary interference with the home may be interrelated, but they are not identical.

Some may regard the foregoing as an unduly modest vision of the task of the HRC and its members. Some authors have argued that the subsequent 'core' human rights treaties should be considered as incorporated into the ICCPR, or more comprehensively that States' obligations under relevant economic, social, and cultural rights should be enforced as part of compliance with an ICCPR right.[57] I do not believe that the HRC can implement this program. The HRC would require a large increase in financial and human resources to adequately perform the role contemplated by this comprehensive approach. If the HRC were perceived as arrogating that task to itself, the General Assembly would cut its resources, not increase them.

Even the current modest role, performed across the range of civil and political rights guaranteed by the ICCPR, constitutes a major contribution to the global human rights project. The HRC is known for its impartial, credible, professional exposition of the content of its Covenant. Among all the tasks that the members accomplish, that is their most important contribution.

Bibliography

Bouziri, Nejib, 'Problèmes particuliers rencontrés dans les premières années d'activité du Comité' in Nisuke Ando (ed), *Towards Implementing Universal Human Rights: Festschrift for the Twenty-Fifth Anniversary of the Human Rights Committee* (Brill 2004)

[57] See eg Eva Brems, 'Should Pluriform Human Rights Become One? Exploring the Benefits of Human Rights Integration' (2014) European J of Human Rights 447, 463–64. Given that ICCPR art 26 contains an autonomous guarantee of equality, it is likely that the requisite linkage could always be found.

Brems, Eva, 'Should Pluriform Human Rights Become One? Exploring the Benefits of Human Rights Integration' (2014) European J of Human Rights 447

Doek, Jaap E, 'The CRC: Dynamics and Directions of Monitoring its Implementation' in Antonella Invernizzi and Jane Williams (eds), *The Human Rights of Children: From Visions to Implementation* (Routledge 2011)

Edwards, Alice, 'Universal Suffrage and the International Human Rights Treaty Bodies: Where are the Women?' in M Cherif Bassiouni and William A Schabas (eds), *New Challenges for the UN Human Rights Machinery: What Future for the UN Treaty Body System and the Human Rights Council Procedures?* (Intersentia 2011)

Neuman, Gerald L, 'Bi-Level Remedies for Human Rights Violations' (2014) 55 Harvard Intl L J 323

Neuman, Gerald L, 'Human Rights and Constitutions in a Complex World' (2013) 50 Irish Jurist 1

Opsahl, Torkel, 'The Human Rights Committee' in Philip Alston (ed), *The United Nations and Human Rights: A Critical Appraisal* (OUP 1992)

Scheinin, Martin, 'The Human Rights Committee's Pronouncements on the Right to an Effective Remedy: An Illustration of the Legal Nature of the Committee's Work under the Optional Protocol' in Nisuke Ando (ed), *Towards Implementing Universal Human Rights: Festschrift for the Twenty-Fifth Anniversary of the Human Rights Committee* (Brill 2004)

Seymour, James D, and Wong, Patrick Yuk-tung, 'China and the International Human Rights Covenants' (2015) 47 Critical Asian Studies 514

Shiyan, Sun, 'The International Covenant on Civil and Political Rights: One Covenant, Two Chinese Texts?' (2006) 75 Nordic J of Intl L 187

Slotte, Pamela, and Scheinin, Martin, 'Captain, Fire Brigade or Icebreaker? Political Legitimacy as a Rationale in Human Rights Adjudication' in Tage Kurtén and Lars Hertzberg (eds), *Legitimacy: The Treasure of Politics* (Peter Lang 2011)

Tomuschat, Christian, *Human Rights: Between Idealism and Realism* (OUP 2003)

Viljoen, Frans, *International Human Rights in Africa* (OUP 2007)

White, Robin CA, and Boussiakou, Iris, 'Separate Opinions in the European Court of Human Rights' (2009) 9 Human Rights L Rev 37

Wildhaber, Luzius, 'Opinions dissidentes et concordantes de juges individuels à la Cour Européenne des Droits de l'Homme' in René-Jean Dupuy (ed), *Mélanges en l'Honneur de Nicolas Valticos: Droit et justice* (A Pedone 1999)

4

Interpretation of the ICESCR

Between Morality and State Consent

*Daniel Moeckli**

I. Introduction

In September 2015, the Committee on Economic, Social and Cultural Rights (CESCR or Committee) published its first Views on a communication brought under the Optional Protocol to the International Covenant on Economic, Social and Cultural Rights (ICESCR-OP).[1,2] The new complaint mechanism offers the CESCR the opportunity to enhance its standing by pronouncing, similarly to a court, on violations in individual cases. Consideration of particular cases, it has been hoped, will allow the Committee to provide greater clarity on the scope of the rights and obligations under the International Covenant on Economic, Social and Cultural Rights (ICESCR or Covenant)[3] than it has thus far been able to provide through its General Comments and concluding observations.[4] At the same time, given that the stakes are arguably higher for States parties in individual cases as compared to the State reporting procedure, they will start to scrutinize the Committee's work more critically.[5] Therefore, how the CESCR interprets the ICESCR will become more important than ever before. Whether the Committee's interpretations

* I am grateful to Matthew Craven for his detailed comments on an earlier draft of this chapter. Thanks are also due to Helen Keller, Stefan Schürer, Lea Raible, and Raffael Fasel for sharing their insights.

[1] Optional Protocol to the International Covenant on Economic, Social and Cultural Rights (opened for signature 10 December 2008, entered into force 5 May 2013) UN Doc A/RES/63/117, 48 ILM 256 (2009).

[2] *IDG v Spain* CESCR Communication No 2/2014 (13 October 2015) UN Doc E/C.12/55/D/2/2014.

[3] International Covenant on Economic, Social and Cultural Rights (opened for signature 16 December 1966, entered into force 3 January 1976) 993 UNTS 3.

[4] Philip Alston, 'No Right to Complain About Being Poor: The Need for an Optional Protocol to the Economic Rights Covenant' in Asbjørn Eide and Jan Helgesen (eds), *The Future of Human Rights Protection in a Changing World: Fifty Years Since the Four Freedoms Address (Essays in Honour of Torkel Opsahl)* (Norwegian University Press 1992) 79, 86–93.

[5] See ibid 92; David Marcus, 'The Normative Development of Socioeconomic Rights through Supranational Adjudication' (2006) 42 Stanford J of Intl L 53, 54.

are regarded as persuasive will determine how many States will ratify the Optional Protocol, how many complaints will be submitted, and what the influence of the Committee's Views will be.

The present chapter starts by setting out the role of the Committee in interpreting the ICESCR (Section II) and by giving an overview of the rules governing interpretation of the Covenant (Section III). Discussions concerning the Committee's interpretive practice have so far centred on the question as to the legality of the 'special' interpretive methods it has developed. Section IV shows that the framework provided by articles 31–33 of the Vienna Convention on the Law of Treaties (VCLT)[6] is broad enough to accommodate the CESCR's methods, which, on closer inspection, turn out not to be that special at all. The real problem with the Committee's interpretations is not (il)legality but (lack of) *legitimacy*. Section V demonstrates that its interpretive practice can be read as a constant oscillation between morality on the one hand and, on the other, State consent as the source from which legitimacy may be derived in international law. Yet, as is argued in Section VI, the legitimacy of a given interpretation depends on more than the extent of (pre-existing) State consensus it embodies. Interpreters, including the CESCR, can *generate* legitimacy by adhering to the agreed-upon interpretive principles and applying them in a coherent and transparent manner.

II. The CESCR as Interpreter

As the International Law Commission (ILC) acknowledged when drafting the VCLT, how rules of interpretation are applied inevitably depends on who it is who applies them.[7] The interpreter's approach, in turn, is influenced by the assumptions and categories of understanding shared by the community of actors engaged in the interpretation of a given text: 'meaning is produced by neither the text nor the reader but by the interpretive community in which both are situated'.[8]

As a treaty, the ICESCR is primarily to be interpreted by the States that are parties to it. However, as a *human rights* treaty, its implementation, and thereby interpretation, cannot be entrusted to States alone. Since the beneficiaries of the commitments contained in human rights treaties are third parties, States will tend to interpret them restrictively. In addition, because of the essentially non-reciprocal nature of these obligations, States parties have no obvious incentive to ensure

[6] Vienna Convention on the Law of Treaties (opened for signature 23 May 1969, entered into force 27 January 1980) 1155 UNTS 331.

[7] ILC, 'Yearbook of the International Law Commission 1966' (vol II, 1966) UN Doc A/CN.4/SER.A/1966/Add.1, 218.

[8] Ian Johnstone, 'Treaty Interpretation: The Authority of Interpretive Communities' (1991) 12 Michigan J of Intl L 371, 378 (building on Stanley Fish, *Is There a Text in This Class? The Authority of Interpretive Communities* (Harvard University Press 1980)).

compliance by other States.[9] This is why human rights treaties typically establish collective enforcement systems.

In the case of the ICESCR, the body that has been entrusted with monitoring compliance and must thus assume a central role in its interpretation is the CESCR: the parties to the ICESCR have charged the United Nations (UN) Economic and Social Council (ECOSOC) with supervising implementation of the Covenant;[10] ECOSOC, in turn, has established the CESCR to carry out this task.[11] In the perceptive characterization of Matthew Craven, the CESCR 'acts as a "clearing centre" for the divergent interpretations of the Covenant offered by States parties and is best placed for establishing the common agreement of States as to the interpretation of the Covenant'.[12] Due to its key role in the interpretive process, the chapter focuses on the interpretation of the ICESCR by the Committee.

The first and main means for the CESCR to define the normative content of the Covenant have been its *General Comments*. They allow it 'to announce its interpretations of different provisions of the Covenant in a form that bears some resemblance to the advisory opinion practice of international tribunals',[13] without having to address individual States.[14] The Committee's General Comments enjoy a considerable degree of acceptance by States parties and are often relied upon by national courts when they interpret the Covenant.[15] Second, the *concluding observations* on State reports offer the Committee a further opportunity to clarify the Covenant's content, although, due to the need to address a wide range of concerns with regard to a particular country, there is only very limited scope for it to go into any depth. Nevertheless, the CESCR has used, for example, its concluding observations on the State reports submitted by Israel to summarily clarify the territorial scope of the Covenant.[16] In its *Wall Advisory Opinion*, the International Court of Justice (ICJ) relied on the Committee's interpretation with regard to this point.[17] Third, the various *statements* and *open letters* issued by the CESCR 'to clarify and confirm its position with respect to major international developments and issues bearing upon the implementation of the Covenant'[18] may sometimes also touch upon questions

[9] Louis Henkin, 'The International Bill of Rights: The Universal Declaration and the Covenants' in Rudolf Bernhardt and John-Anthony Jolowicz (eds), *International Enforcement of Human Rights* (Springer 1987) 1, 8.

[10] ICESCR arts 16–22.

[11] ECOSOC Res 1985/17 (28 May 1985).

[12] Matthew CR Craven, *The International Covenant on Economic, Social, and Cultural Rights: A Perspective on its Development* (OUP 1995) 4.

[13] Thomas Buergenthal, 'The U.N. Human Rights Committee' in Jochen A. Frowein and Rüdiger Wolfrum, *Max Planck Yearbook of United Nations Law* vol 5 (Brill 2001) 341, 386 (the statement relates to the CESCR's 'sister committee', the Human Rights Committee).

[14] Craven, *The ICESCR* (n 12) 90–91.

[15] See International Law Association (ILA) Committee on International Human Rights Law and Practice, 'Final Report on the Impact of Findings of the United Nations Human Rights Treaty Bodies' (ILA Conference, Berlin, 2004) 24–25.

[16] CESCR, 'Concluding Observations on the Initial Periodic Report of Israel' (4 December 1998) UN Doc E/C.12/1/Add.27, para 8; CESCR, 'Concluding Observations on the Second Periodic Report of Israel' (26 June 2003) UN Doc E/C.12/1/Add.90, paras 15, 31.

[17] *Legal Consequences of the Construction of a Wall in the Occupied Palestinian Territory* (Advisory Opinion) [2004] ICJ Rep 136, 180–81.

[18] CESCR, 'Report on the Fiftieth and Fifty-first Sessions' (2014) UN Doc E/2014/22, para 62.

of interpretation. Fourth, as explained above, the new possibility to publish *Views* on complaints will allow the Committee to define the meaning of the Covenant's provisions more precisely.

What is the legal status of the interpretations put forward by the CESCR? Unlike judgments of the regional human rights courts,[19] the findings of the UN treaty bodies are not legally binding.[20] However, considering that the States parties created these bodies to monitor compliance with the respective treaties, which logically presupposes interpreting them, it would go against the good faith requirement of VCLT article 26 if States disregarded their findings simply because they disagree with them.[21] It is before this background that the ICJ held (with regard to the Human Rights Committee (HRC), charged with supervising implementation of the International Covenant on Civil and Political Rights (ICCPR))[22] that 'it should ascribe great weight to the interpretation adopted by this independent body that was established specifically to supervise the application of that treaty'.[23] Although the ICJ has not spelled out what exactly ascribing 'great weight' involves, it is certainly not far-fetched to conclude that, at the very least, there is a presumption that such findings are correct and that States would have to adduce good reasons for any conflicting view.[24]

III. Rules of Interpretation

According to the ICJ, a treaty must be interpreted 'in accordance with the intentions of its authors as reflected by the text of the treaty and the other relevant factors in terms of interpretation'.[25] The aim of treaty interpretation is thus to establish the common intention of the parties, understood in an 'objectivized'[26] sense as the result of the application of the admissible means of interpretation, rather than as a separately identifiable original will of the parties ('subjective intention').[27] The 'relevant

[19] See Convention for the Protection of Human Rights and Fundamental Freedoms (European Convention on Human Rights, as amended) art 46; American Convention on Human Rights (opened for signature 21 November 1969, entered into force 18 July 1978) 1144 UNTS 123, art 68; Protocol to the African Charter on Human and Peoples' Rights on the Establishment of an African Court on Human and Peoples' Rights (opened for signature 9 June 1998, entered into force 25 January 2004) OAU Doc OAU/LEG/EXP/AFCHPR/PROT (III), art 30.

[20] ILA, 'UN Treaty Bodies' (n 15) 5.

[21] See Office of the United Nations High Commissioner for Human Rights, 'Fact Sheet No 16 (Rev.1): The Committee on Economic, Social and Cultural Rights' (1991) <www.ohchr.org/Documents/Publications/FactSheet16rev.1en.pdf> accessed 30 May 2017, 17.

[22] On the differences regarding the establishment and composition of the CESCR as compared to the HRC and other UN treaty bodies, see Section VI.C.

[23] *Ahmadou Sadio Diallo (Republic of Guinea v Democratic Republic of the Congo)* (Merits) [2010] ICJ Rep 639, 664.

[24] Geir Ulfstein, 'Individual Complaints' in Helen Keller and Geir Ulfstein (eds), *UN Human Rights Treaty Bodies: Law and Legitimacy* (CUP 2012) 73, 100.

[25] *Dispute regarding Navigational and Related Rights (Costa Rica v Nicaragua)* (Merits) [2009] ICJ Rep 213, 237.

[26] Eirik Bjorge, *The Evolutionary Interpretation of Treaties* (OUP 2014) 2–3.

[27] Richard Gardiner, *Treaty Interpretation* (2nd edn, OUP 2015) 6–9 and 466.

factors' to be used to ascertain the intention of the parties to a treaty are those set out in, first, the respective treaty itself and, second, VCLT articles 31–33.

A. The ICESCR

Since the VCLT's rules of interpretation are dispositive,[28] the first port of call to look for guidance on how a treaty is to be interpreted is that treaty itself. The ICESCR contains a number of rules of interpretation, although the guidance they provide is rather limited. Accordingly, they have not played a significant role in the practice of the CESCR or other interpreters of the Covenant.

ICESCR article 5(1), which is derived from article 30 of the Universal Declaration of Human Rights (UDHR) and is identical to ICCPR article 5(1), makes it clear, first, that the Covenant rights may not be interpreted in such a way as to destroy another right, and, second, that the limitation clauses contained in the ICESCR are exhaustive. ICESCR article 5(2), which corresponds to ICCPR article 5(2), provides that the Covenant may not be used as a basis for restricting any human rights guaranteed by national law or other treaties, thus clarifying that the Covenant rights are meant as minimum standards. The CESCR has not paid much attention to article 5 in its work.[29] Further special rules of interpretation can be found in articles 24 and 25, prescribing that nothing in the ICESCR shall be interpreted as impairing the provisions of the UN Charter or, respectively, the right of all peoples to enjoy and utilize their natural wealth and resources. In the final analysis, all of these interpretive principles can be understood as specific expressions of the general rule of treaty interpretation requiring a treaty to be interpreted in the light of its object and purpose. Finally, ICESCR article 31(1) provides that the various language versions of the Covenant are equally authentic, restating the general rule of treaty interpretation now codified in VCLT article 33.

B. VCLT articles 31–33

The essential framework for the interpretation of all treaties is provided by the set of rules contained in VCLT articles 31–33. The ICJ and several other international courts and tribunals, as well as numerous national courts, have confirmed that the VCLT rules of interpretation reflect pre-existing customary international law.[30] They therefore also govern interpretation of the ICESCR, regardless of the facts that the Covenant was concluded before the entry into force of the VCLT in 1980 and that, according to its article 4, the VCLT is not retroactive.

As is highlighted by the provision's marginal note, the 'general rule of interpretation' in VCLT article 31 constitutes the core of these rules. According to article 31(1), '[a] treaty shall be interpreted in good faith in accordance with the ordinary

[28] ILC, 'Yearbook 1966' (n 7) 218.

[29] See Magdalena Sepúlveda, *The Nature of the Obligations under the International Covenant on Economic, Social and Cultural Rights* (Intersentia 2003) 303–04.

[30] See the references cited in Gardiner, *Treaty Interpretation* (n 27) 13–20.

meaning to be given to the terms of the treaty in their context and in the light of its object and purpose.' The three main means of interpretation are thus the *wording*, the *context*, and the *object and purpose*, with good faith serving as the guiding principle directing the whole process of interpreting a treaty.[31] Article 31(2) specifies what is meant by 'context'. Article 31(3) adds further elements that need to be taken into account, including '[a]ny subsequent practice in the application of the treaty which establishes the agreement of the parties regarding its interpretation' (subparagraph b) and '[a]ny relevant rules of international law applicable in the relations between the parties' (subparagraph c).

The various elements mentioned in article 31 are all of equal value; there is no hierarchy between them.[32] As the ILC explained in its Commentary on the draft articles on the law of treaties, it intended the application of the means of interpretation to be 'a single combined operation. All the various elements, as they were present in any given case, would be thrown in the crucible, and their interaction would give the legally relevant interpretation'.[33] Interpretation is not a mechanical process that would allow the interpreter to *find* the meaning, but instead, as is reflected in the wording of article 31(1), involves *giving* a meaning to a text.[34] In other words, 'the meaning of norms is a product of interpretative practice'.[35] Accordingly, the VCLT rules allow interpreters considerable leeway. They are more akin to principles or guidelines,[36] providing an 'intellectual checklist'[37] of the elements to be taken into account and some methodological direction on how to approach these elements. This flexible nature of the VCLT rules is perhaps captured best by the metaphor proposed by Hugh Thirlway, who characterized them as 'scaffolding for the reasoning on questions of treaty interpretation'.[38]

IV. A Special Regime of Treaty Interpretation?

The CESCR relies not only on the means of interpretation traditionally associated with VCLT articles 31–33, but also employs methods that are often described as 'special' or even as falling outside the VCLT framework.[39] These special interpretive methods include, in particular, the principle of effectiveness and evolutive

31 ibid 167–72.

32 Mark E Villiger, *Commentary on the 1969 Vienna Convention on the Law of Treaties* (Brill 2009) 435.

33 ILC, 'Yearbook 1966' (n 7) 219–20.

34 Harvard Law School, 'Research in International Law: Part III, Law of Treaties' (1935) 29 American J of Intl L Supplement 946.

35 Ingo Venzke, *How Interpretation Makes International Law: On Semantic Change and Normative Twists* (OUP 2012) 10.

36 ILC, 'Yearbook 1966' (n 7) 94.

37 Michael Waibel, 'Uniformity Versus Specialization (2): A Uniform Regime of Treaty Interpretation?' in Christian J Tams, Antonios Tzanakopoulos, and Andreas Zimmermann (eds), *Research Handbook on the Law of Treaties* (Edward Elgar 2014) 375, 381.

38 Hugh Thirlway, 'The Law and Procedure of the International Court of Justice 1960–1989, Supplement, 2006: Part Three' (2006) 77 British YB of Intl L 1, 19.

39 See eg Sepúlveda, *Nature of Obligations* (n 29) 87 (stating that the VCLT rules 'are not the only rules considered by the Committee' when interpreting the ICESCR).

interpretation (Section IV.A). It is especially this aspect of the Committee's interpretive practice that has been singled out for criticism, with concerns being raised about its legality. The most common response to this criticism is to invoke the special nature of the ICESCR as a human rights treaty, which, it is contended, justifies recourse to specialized methods of interpretation. I will argue that a special interpretive regime is neither warranted nor needed. The Committee's allegedly 'special' techniques are, in fact, quite common and fit well into the VCLT framework (Section IV.B).

A. 'Special' interpretive methods

1. Effectiveness

An interpretive approach that has become very influential in the practice of all human rights bodies—in fact, so influential that it is often exclusively associated with human rights—is that based on the principle of effectiveness.[40] This principle requires an interpretation that gives meaning and effect to all the terms of the treaty to be preferred over one that does not.[41] Since human rights treaties are, in the famous words of the European Court of Human Rights (ECtHR), 'intended to guarantee not rights that are theoretical or illusory but rights that are practical and effective,'[42] they must be read so that they have a real impact on the actual lives of individuals.

This basic notion underlies large parts of the CESCR's interpretive practice. Already very early on, the Committee explained that the obligation under ICESCR article 2(1) to realize the Covenant rights 'progressively' 'should not be misinterpreted as depriving the obligation of all meaningful content',[43] and it has since repeated this statement several times.[44] Similarly, it held that, '[i]n order not to render this provision devoid of any meaning', ICESCR article 15(1)(c) must be read in a way that affords authors of scientific, literary, or artistic productions 'effective' protection of their moral and material interests.[45] Finally, with regard to discrimination, the 'effective enjoyment of Covenant rights' in the CESCR's understanding requires elimination of not only formal but also substantive discrimination.[46]

[40] Birgit Schlütter, 'Aspects of Human Rights Interpretation by the UN Treaty Bodies' in Helen Keller and Geir Ulfstein (eds), *UN Human Rights Treaty Bodies: Law and Legitimacy* (CUP 2012) 261, 286–87; Başak Çali, 'Specialized Rules of Treaty Interpretation: Human Rights' in Duncan B Hollis (ed), *The Oxford Guide to Treaties* (OUP 2012) 525, 538–41.

[41] Gardiner, *Treaty Interpretation* (n 27) 179–81.

[42] *Airey v Ireland* App no 6289/73 (ECtHR, 9 October 1979) para 24.

[43] CESCR, 'General Comment 3' in 'Note by the Secretariat, Compilation of General Comments and General Recommendations Adopted by Human Rights Treaty Bodies' (2008) UN Doc HRI/GEN/1/Rev.9 (vol I) para 9.

[44] CESCR, 'General Comment 13' in 'Compilation of General Comments' (2008) (vol I) (n 43) para 44; CESCR, 'General Comment 14' in 'Compilation of General Comments' (2008) (vol I) (n 43) para 31.

[45] CESCR, 'General Comment 17' in 'Compilation of General Comments' (2008) (vol I) (n 43) para 10.

[46] CESCR, 'General Comment 20' (2 July 2009) UN Doc E/C.12/GC/20, para 8.

2. *Evolutive interpretation*

Another special interpretive method that is characteristic for the practice of courts and other bodies supervising the implementation of human rights treaties is the evolutive (often also called 'evolutionary' or 'dynamic') interpretation of treaties.[47] According to this method, the terms of a treaty must be interpreted not as understood at the time of its conclusion but 'in the light of present-day conditions'.[48] Hence, the meaning of treaty terms can 'evolve over time in view of existing circumstances'.[49] Most supervisory bodies, although not (yet) the CESCR, have invoked the 'living instrument' character of 'their' human rights treaties to justify an evolutive interpretation.[50] In scholarship, the evolutive approach is often presented as a method that is unique, or almost unique, to human rights treaties.[51] Magdalena Sepúlveda argues that it has particular relevance in the case of treaties guaranteeing economic, social, and cultural rights, as these are more dependent on changes in economic, social, and political conditions than civil and political rights.[52]

The CESCR has made it abundantly clear that the meaning of the ICESCR's terms can evolve over time. A good example is its General Comment on the right to health, wherein the Committee, referring to formerly unknown diseases such as HIV, observed that 'the world health situation has changed dramatically' since 1966 and concluded that the notion of 'health' in ICESCR article 12 must be interpreted in the light of these changes.[53] Similarly, it has pointed out that the reference to 'himself and his family' in article 11(1) 'reflects assumptions as to gender roles and economic activity patterns commonly accepted in 1966', but 'cannot be read today as implying any limitations upon the applicability of the right to individuals or to female-headed households or other such groups'.[54] With regard to the list of prohibited grounds for discrimination in article 2(2), finally, the Committee has held that '[a] flexible approach to the ground of "other status" is ... needed', since '[t]he nature of discrimination varies according to context and evolves over time'.[55]

[47] See Malgosia Fitzmaurice, 'Dynamic (Evolutive) Interpretation of Treaties, Part I' (2008) 21 Hague YB of Intl L (hereafter Hague YIL) 101; Malgosia Fitzmaurice, 'Dynamic (Evolutive) Interpretation of Treaties, Part II' (2009) 22 Hague YIL 3; Rudolf Bernhardt, 'Evolutive Treaty Interpretation, Especially of the European Convention on Human Rights' (1999) 42 German YB of Intl L 11.

[48] *Tyrer v the United Kingdom* App no 5856/72 (ECtHR, 25 April 1978) para 31.

[49] *'Street Children' (Villagrán Morales et al) v Guatemala,* Judgment (Merits) Inter-American Court of Human Rights Series C No 77 (19 November 1999) para 193 (slightly misquoting *The Right to Information on Consular Assistance in the Framework of Guarantees for Due Legal Process* (Advisory Opinion) Inter-American Court of Human Rights Series C No 16 (1 October 1999) para 114).

[50] Daniel Moeckli and Nigel D White, 'Treaties as "Living Instruments"' in Michael J Bowman and Dino Kritsiotis (eds), *Conceptual and Contextual Perspectives on the Modern Law of Treaties* (CUP 2018) 136, 143–54.

[51] Bernhardt, 'Evolutive Treaty Interpretation' (n 47) 12, 21; Schlütter, 'Human Rights Interpretation' (n 40) 295.

[52] Sepúlveda, *Nature of Obligations* (n 29) 83.

[53] CESCR, 'General Comment 14' (n 44) para 10.

[54] CESCR, 'General Comment 4' in 'Compilation of General Comments' (2008) (vol I) (n 43) para 6.

[55] CESCR, 'General Comment 20' (n 46) para 27.

B. Legality of 'special' interpretive methods

The special interpretive methods developed by human rights bodies, it has been argued, have 'drawn away from traditional treaty-reading'[56] and are 'hard to reconcile'[57] with VCLT articles 31–33. Does this mean that there is no legal basis for the use of the techniques described above? Or does the special nature of human rights treaties justify recourse to methods of interpretation that are not covered by the VCLT? This question has triggered an extensive debate,[58] which may be understood to form part of the wider debate as to whether human rights law constitutes a special (or even self-contained) regime exempt from the rules of general law.[59]

It is undoubtedly true that human rights treaties have certain characteristics that set them apart from other types of treaties. They do not merely create reciprocal obligations between States, but recognize pre-existing rights of third parties (individuals).[60] By establishing a system for the collective enforcement of these rights, they embody objective obligations and thus have a law-making or even 'constitutional' nature.[61] The HRC, the ECtHR, and the Inter-American Court of Human Rights (IACtHR) have all invoked the special nature of human rights treaties in the context of, for instance, reservations.[62]

More problematic is the claim that the 'high purposes'[63] or 'higher shared values'[64] pursued by human rights treaties necessitate a special approach to interpretation that prioritizes the teleological over the textual element. Rudolf Bernhardt, for example, maintains that the 'unique' object and purpose of human rights treaties must entail special principles of interpretation.[65] Magdalena Sepúlveda states that, since '[t]he specific object and purpose of human rights treaties is the protection of the individual human person', it should be given 'a central and crucial role' in their interpretation.[66] According to Judge Cançado Trindade, finally, 'keeping in mind that

[56] Detlef F Vagts, 'Treaty Interpretation and the New American Ways of Law Reading' (1993) 4 European J of Intl L 472, 497.

[57] Malgosia Fitzmaurice, 'Interpretation of Human Rights Treaties' in Dinah Shelton (ed), *The Oxford Handbook of International Human Rights Law* (OUP 2013) 739, 740.

[58] See ibid 740–44; Çali, 'Specialized Rules' (n 40) 526–33.

[59] ILC, 'Fragmentation of International Law: Difficulties Arising from the Diversification and Expansion of International Law, Report of the Study Group of the ILC, finalized by Martti Koskenniemi' (13 April 2006) UN Doc A/CN.4/L.682, 30–102.

[60] Matthew CR Craven, 'Legal Differentiation and the Concept of the Human Rights Treaty in International Law' (2000) 11 European J of Intl L 489.

[61] On the constitutional nature of human rights, see Stephen Gardbaum, 'Human Rights as International Constitutional Rights' (2008) 19 European J of Intl L 749.

[62] HRC, 'General Comment 24' in 'Compilation of General Comments' (2008) (vol I) (n 43) paras 8, 17; *Loizidou v Turkey* (Preliminary Objections) App no 15318/89 (ECtHR, 23 March 1995) paras 93, 96; *The Effect of Reservations on the Entry into Force of the American Convention on Human Rights* (Advisory Opinion) Inter-American Court of Human Rights Series A No 2 (24 September 1982) paras 29–35.

[63] *Reservations to the Convention on Genocide* (Advisory Opinion) [1951] ICJ Rep 15, 23.

[64] *Case of the 'Mapiripán Massacre' v Colombia*, Judgment (Merits) Inter-American Court of Human Rights Series C No 134 (15 September 2005) para 104.

[65] Rudolf Bernhardt, 'Thoughts on the Interpretation of Human-Rights Treaties' in Franz Matscher and Herbert Petzold (eds), *Protecting Human Rights: The European Dimension, Studies in Honour of Gérard J. Wiarda* (Heymanns 1988) 65, 65.

[66] Sepúlveda, *Nature of Obligations* (n 29) 79.

superior values . . . are at stake',[67] greater weight needs to be placed on the object and purpose element when it comes to human rights treaties, 'so as to secure protection to human beings'.[68]

In my view, this boils down to a *droit de l'hommiste* argument[69] that is not convincing. It is not clear why, simply because human rights treaties pursue an important objective, the teleological element should assume a greater importance than when it comes to, say, investment treaties.[70] The object and purpose of every treaty is, when compared to other treaties, special. The weight to be given to the teleological element must be determined not by comparing a treaty's object and purpose to that of *other treaties*, but by comparing it to the *other interpretive elements*. In fact, a look at the jurisprudence of international courts and tribunals reveals that the teleological element may play a crucial role in the interpretation not only of human rights treaties, but of any type of treaty.[71]

Hence, the nature of the object and purpose of a treaty is not determinative for the application of the interpretive rules. The VCLT rules were designed for all types of treaties,[72] without any distinction between law-making and other treaties.[73] By allowing for a variety of elements to be taken into account, they provide an interpretive framework that can be appropriately applied to any treaty. This is, of course, not to argue that interpretive practices do not, or should not, vary across different subfields of international law.[74] It is only to point out that the VCLT's 'scaffolding for the reasoning on questions of treaty interpretation'[75] is broad enough to also accommodate the 'special' methods used to interpret human rights treaties, including the ICESCR.

In fact, on closer inspection, these 'special' methods, including the two techniques described above, turn out not to be special at all. Far from being a unique interpretive technique restricted to human rights treaties, the *principle of effectiveness* has been characterized by the ILC as 'a true general rule of interpretation' that, even though not explicitly mentioned in the VCLT, is embodied in the 'good faith' and the 'object and purpose' elements of its article 31(1).[76] The principle plays a prominent role in the interpretive practice of the Appellate Body of the World Trade Organization (WTO)[77] and has also been relied upon, for example, to interpret treaty provisions fixing boundaries.[78]

[67] *Application of the International Convention on the Elimination of All Forms of Racial Discrimination* (*Georgia v Russian Federation*) (Preliminary Objections) [2011] ICJ Rep 70, Dissenting Opinion of Judge Cançado Trindade, 276.

[68] ibid 267.

[69] See Alain Pellet, '"Droits-de-l'hommisme" et droit international' (2001) 1 Droits fondamentaux 167.

[70] See also Bjorge, *Evolutionary Interpretation* (n 26) 36.

[71] See the references cited in ibid.

[72] James Crawford, *Brownlie's Principles of Public International Law* (OUP 2012) 370.

[73] ILC, 'Yearbook 1966' (n 7) 219.

[74] See Waibel, 'Uniformity' (n 37).

[75] Thirlway, 'ICJ' (n 38) 19.

[76] ILC, 'Yearbook 1966' (n 7) 219.

[77] See WTO, *Korea: Definitive Safeguard Measure on Imports of Certain Dairy Products—Report of the Appellate Body* (14 December 1999) WT/DS98/AB/R, paras 80–82.

[78] *Territorial Dispute* (*Libyan Arab Jamahiriya v Chad*) (Merits) [1994] ICJ Rep 6, 23, 25.

Similarly, the *evolutive interpretation* of treaties falls squarely under and, indeed, may be required by VCLT article 31, in particular its 'good faith', 'object and purpose', 'subsequent practice', and 'relevant rules of international law' elements. Evolutive interpretation has not only been embraced by human rights bodies, but also by the ICJ,[79] and the technique has been applied to a broad range of treaties, from the UN Charter to multilateral environmental agreements and the General Agreement on Tariffs and Trade (GATT).[80] Furthermore, contrary to a widely-held assumption,[81] it is not the case that deployment of evolutive interpretation will automatically result in an expansion of human rights and the correlating State duties. As pointed out by Eirik Bjorge,[82] the ECtHR's invocation of 'the growing and legitimate concern both in Europe and internationally in relation to environmental offences' in *Mangouras v Spain*, for instance, had exactly the opposite result, namely a lowering of the protection offered by article 5 of the European Convention on Human Rights (ECHR).[83]

In short, from the perspective of legality, the 'special' interpretive techniques employed by the CESCR are unproblematic; they fit well into the VCLT framework. There is neither a need nor a justification for a special interpretive regime. Instead, the real problem with these methods of interpretation is that they are, as will be shown in the following section, the product of the Committee's 'moral reading' of the Covenant and, as such, are regarded with suspicion by States. In other words, the problem is—as with the CESCR's interpretive practice in general—not (il)legality but (lack of) legitimacy.

V. Between Morality and State Consent

Studying the CESCR's interpretations of the ICESCR, one cannot help sensing a basic dilemma with which it is constantly struggling. On the one hand, one can often almost grasp the Committee's urge to give the Covenant's terms a 'moral reading'. On the other hand, it seems to be acutely aware that the interpretations it adopts must find the support of States parties. The Committee's interpretive practice, I submit, is a manifestation of its being torn between the poles of morality and State consent or, as some might call them, 'utopia' and 'apology'.[84]

The purpose of this section is to demonstrate that the gravitational force of morality has led the CESCR to emphasize one set of interpretive elements, and the pull towards State consent another. To be clear, this section merely aims to give

[79] *Dispute regarding Navigational and Related Rights* (n 25) 242–44.

[80] See Fitzmaurice, 'Part I' (n 47); Fitzmaurice, 'Part II' (n 47); Moeckli and White, 'Living Instruments' (n 50).

[81] See eg Çali, 'Specialized Rules' (n 40) 539–40.

[82] Bjorge, *Evolutionary Interpretation* (n 26) 78.

[83] *Mangouras v Spain* App no 12050/04 (ECtHR, 28 September 2010) paras 86–93 (as a result, the Court found that setting bail in the amount of EUR 3,000,000 was compatible with ECHR art 5(3)).

[84] Martti Koskenniemi, *From Apology to Utopia: The Structure of International Legal Argument* (CUP 2005).

an account of the Committee's interpretive practice; I do not claim that the interpretive elements listed below are *inherently* linked to morality and State consent, respectively.

A. Morality

One pole of the Committee's interpretive practice is constituted by the moral values or principles that underlie the ICESCR and which may thus serve as guidance for its interpretation. According to Ronald Dworkin's concept of a 'moral reading', legal norms must be interpreted 'on the understanding that they invoke moral principles about political decency and justice'.[85] In the case of the Covenant, these moral principles may be taken to be human survival,[86] human dignity,[87] and/or liberty.[88] Given that human rights are meant to protect minorities from the majority, it would seem to make sense that, in the interpretive process, more weight should be attached to the fundamental moral interests of individuals than to considerations such as State consent. In one view, moral reasons are even '[t]he only thing which can justify interpretive outcomes'.[89] The Committee's urge to give the Covenant a moral reading is apparent throughout its interpretive practice.

1. Object and purpose: Teleological interpretation

First and most obviously, the pole of morality pulls the Committee's interpretations towards an emphasis of the object and purpose element. While large parts of its interpretive practice are *implicitly* based on the teleological approach, the Committee has sometimes also *expressly* highlighted the central role that it accords to the object and purpose element. Already in its very first General Comment, it pointed out that the Covenant must be interpreted in accordance with its spirit.[90] Similarly, the CESCR has justified the establishment of its concept of minimum core obligations—specifying the obligations that States must satisfy as a matter of priority under the various ICESCR rights—on the basis that ICESCR article 2(1) 'must be read in the light of the overall objective, indeed the *raison d'être*, of the Covenant'.[91]

One of the central purposes of the Covenant is, in the CESCR's view, realization of the moral principle of human dignity mentioned in the preamble. Accordingly, it

[85] See Ronald Dworkin, *Freedom's Law: The Moral Reading of the American Constitution* (Harvard University Press 1996) 2.

[86] Henry Shue, *Basic Rights: Subsistence, Affluence and U.S. Foreign Policy* (2nd edn, Princeton University Press 1996); David Bilchitz, *Poverty and Fundamental Rights: The Justification and Enforcement of Socio-Economic Rights* (OUP 2007).

[87] Sandra Liebenberg, 'The Value of Human Dignity in Interpreting Socio-Economic Rights' (2005) 21 South African J on Human Rights 1.

[88] Jeremy Waldron, 'Homelessness and the Issue of Freedom' (1991) 39 UCLA L Rev 295.

[89] George Letsas, 'Strasbourg's Interpretive Ethic: Lessons for the International Lawyer' (2010) 21 European J of Intl L 509, 532.

[90] CESCR, 'General Comment 1' in 'Compilation of General Comments' (2008) (vol I) (n 43) para 1.

[91] CESCR, 'General Comment 3' (n 43) paras 9–10.

has repeatedly interpreted Covenant rights, including the rights to housing,[92] education,[93] work,[94] and social security,[95] in the light of this principle. Human survival is seen as another key purpose by the Committee. Although ICESCR article 11(1) does not mention a separate right to water, it has held that it must be understood to include one, explaining that such a right is 'one of the most fundamental conditions for survival'.[96] Finally, its practice concerning minimum core obligations is equally grounded in the moral values of human dignity and survival.[97]

2. *Rules of international law*

The Committee's urge to give the ICESCR a moral reading also explains its liberal approach to the invocation of other rules of international law to interpret the Covenant. VCLT article 31(3)(c) allows for the consideration of 'any relevant rules of international law applicable in the relations between the parties', which may include other treaties, customary international law, and general principles of law. According to the ICJ, rules that came into force after the conclusion of the treaty at issue can be taken into account where the respective treaty terms are open to evolution.[98] However, it would seem to be clear from the terms 'rules' and 'applicable' that non-binding instruments cannot be relied upon.[99] Furthermore, the wording of the provision suggests that, with regard to the consideration of another treaty, all parties to the treaty under interpretation (or, at the very least, the parties to the dispute over the interpretation) must also be parties to the other treaty.[100]

Nevertheless, the CESCR has frequently interpreted ICESCR rights in the light of other international standards, be they binding or not, and, in the case of treaties, regardless of the number of ratifications. With regard to the right to education, for example, the Committee referred to the World Declaration on Education for All, the Vienna Declaration and Programme of Action, and the Plan of Action for the UN Decade for Human Rights Education to read into ICESCR article 13 'elements which are not expressly provided for in article 13(1), such as specific references to gender equality and respect for the environment'.[101] In other contexts, it has

[92] CESCR, 'General Comment 4' (n 54) para 7.

[93] CESCR, 'General Comment 13' (n 44) para 41.

[94] CESCR, 'General Comment 18' in 'Compilation of General Comments' (2008) (vol I) (n 43) paras 1, 4, and 31.

[95] CESCR, 'General Comment 19' in 'Compilation of General Comments' (2008) (vol I) (n 43) paras 1, 22, and 41.

[96] CESCR, 'General Comment 15' in 'Compilation of General Comments' (2008) (vol I) (n 43) para 3.

[97] See Liebenberg, 'Human Dignity' (n 87) 17 (stressing the role of dignity for the concept); Bilchitz, *Poverty* (n 86) 178–235 (stressing the role of survival).

[98] *Legal Consequences for States of the Continued Presence of South Africa in Namibia (South West Africa), notwithstanding Security Council Resolution 276 (1970)* (Advisory Opinion) [1971] ICJ Rep 12, 31; *Gabčíkovo-Nagymaros Project (Hungary v Slovakia)* (Merits) [1997] ICJ Rep 7, 67–68.

[99] Villiger, *VCLT* (n 32) 433; Oliver Dörr, 'Article 31' in Oliver Dörr and Kirsten Schmalenbach (eds), *Vienna Convention on the Law of Treaties: A Commentary* (Springer 2012) 521, 564, 567.

[100] Dörr, 'Article 31' (n 99) 566; Ulf Linderfalk, *On the Interpretation of Treaties* (Springer 2007) 178.

[101] CESCR, 'General Comment 13' (n 44) para 5.

taken into account ILO (International Labour Organization) Conventions ratified by as few as eight,[102] eleven,[103] or sixteen States,[104] as well as non-treaty standards such as the Principles for the Protection of Persons with Mental Illness and the Improvement of Mental Health Care,[105] the Alma-Ata Declaration on Primary Health Care,[106] the Voluntary Guidelines on the Right to Food of the UN Food and Agriculture Organization (FAO),[107] and the World Programme of Action concerning Disabled Persons.[108]

The CESCR's extensive citation of various rules of international law that are not legally binding on (all) the parties to the ICESCR can be understood as forming part of its moral reading of the Covenant. Although other rules of international law could also be invoked to justify *restrictions* of human rights,[109] the Committee has only referred to rules that *support* the moral values underlying the ICESCR. Like the ECtHR,[110] it is not so much concerned with establishing State consensus in the sense of VCLT article 31(3)(c) as with identifying values shared across societies that help it make sense of the Covenant's terms.

3. *'Special' interpretive methods*

The pull towards the pole of morality also underlies the CESCR's 'special' interpretive techniques, analysed in more detail earlier in Section IV. The Committee's heavy reliance on the principle of effectiveness is intended to maximize the protection of the fundamental values underlying the Covenant and is thus clearly prompted by a moral reading of that instrument. The same holds true for the Committee's approach to evolutive interpretation. Despite the fact that, as explained above, evolutive interpretation must not necessarily result in an expansion of protection for the individual, the CESCR has employed it exclusively with this aim in mind.

[102] CESCR, 'General Comment 19' (n 95) para 24 (referring to ILO Convention No 168 on Employment Promotion and Protection against Unemployment (opened for signature 21 June 1988, entered into force 17 October 1991) 1654 UNTS 67).

[103] CESCR, 'General Comment 23' (27 April 2016) UN Doc E/C.12/GC/23, para 28 (referring to the ILO Protocol to the Occupational Safety and Health Convention, 1981 (opened for signature 20 June 2002, entered into force 9 February 2005) 2308 UNTS (Annex A) 112).

[104] CESCR, 'General Comment 6' in 'Compilation of General Comments' (2008) (vol I) (n 43) para 27 (referring to ILO Convention No 128 on Invalidity, Old-Age and Survivors' Benefits (opened for signature 29 June 1967, entered into force 1 November 1969) 699 UNTS 185).

[105] UNGA Res 46/119 (17 December 1991) A/RES/46/119, Annex, referred to in CESCR, 'General Comment 14' (n 44) para 34.

[106] World Health Organization and UN Children's Fund, 'Declaration of the Alma-Ata International Conference on Primary Health Care' (Alma-Ata, 6–12 September 1978), referred to in CESCR, 'General Comment 14' (n 44) para 38.

[107] FAO, *Voluntary Guidelines on the Right to Food* (FAO 2005), referred to in CESCR, 'Concluding Observations on the Fifth Periodic Report of Germany' (12 July 2011) UN Doc E/C.12/DEU/CO/5, para 9.

[108] UNGA Res 37/52 (3 December 1982) A/RES/37/52, referred to in CESCR, 'General Comment 5' in 'Compilation of General Comments' (2008) (vol I) para 7.

[109] See *Al-Adsani v the United Kingdom* App no 35763/97 (ECtHR, 21 November 2001) paras 55–56.

[110] See Letsas, 'Interpretive Ethic' (n 89) 521–23.

B. State consent

As opposed to the regional human rights courts, the CESCR cannot issue judgments—and thus propose interpretations—which would be legally binding on States parties. Arguably, it is in an even more precarious position than, say, the HRC, as its findings have—or are believed to have—a greater impact on matters that have traditionally been understood to belong to the core of a State's sovereignty, such as budgetary allocations.[111] Even more so than for other human rights bodies, it is therefore crucial for the Committee that its views on the correct reading of the Covenant are shared, or at least regarded as legitimate, by States. The CESCR simply cannot afford to engage in a purely moral reading of the Covenant. Hence, the CESCR's interpretive practice is pulled towards a search for common ground among the States parties. This pull towards State consent, which has exerted an especially strong influence on the Committee's early work, manifests itself, above all, in its reliance on the *travaux préparatoires*, a textual approach, and subsequent State practice.

1. Travaux *as supplementary means of interpretation*

According to VCLT article 32, recourse to the preparatory work of the treaty at issue and the circumstances of its conclusion may be had in order to confirm the meaning resulting from the application of article 31 or to determine the treaty's meaning when the interpretation according to article 31 leaves it ambiguous or obscure or leads to a manifestly unreasonable result. While article 32 requires the interpreter to first employ the means of interpretation provided for in the general rule under article 31, the elastic nature of the term 'ambiguous' provides considerable discretion to use the *travaux préparatoires*.[112]

The CESCR has made full use of this discretion to link its interpretations to the original intention of the States parties. For example, it has backed up its rejection of the notion that ICESCR rights are 'non-self-executing' by referring to the respective drafting debates,[113] it has drawn upon the drafting history of ICESCR article 12 to clarify that the right to health is not confined to the right to health care but 'embraces a wide range of socio-economic factors',[114] and it has explained that the term 'moral interests' contained in ICESCR article 15(1)(c) must be given a meaning that is in line with the intention of the drafters of the UDHR and the ICESCR.[115]

[111] Marcus, 'Normative Development' (n 5) 60, 66; Jeff A King, *Judging Social Rights* (CUP 2012) 117–18.

[112] Villiger, *VCLT* (n 32) 447; Oliver Dörr, 'Article 32' in Oliver Dörr and Kirsten Schmalenbach (eds), *Vienna Convention on the Law of Treaties: A Commentary* (Springer 2012) 571, 584.

[113] CESCR, 'General Comment 9' in 'Compilation of General Comments' (2008) (vol I) (n 43) para 11.

[114] CESCR, 'General Comment 14' (n 44) para 4.

[115] CESCR, 'General Comment 17' (n 45) paras 12–13.

2. Wording: Textual interpretation

The pull towards State consent may lead the Committee to focus on the terms used by the States parties in the treaty. Whereas the wording of the ICESCR is quite specific and clear in some parts, especially those concerning economic rights, in others, especially those concerning social rights, the Covenant contains terms that—even by the standards of a treaty guaranteeing economic, social, and cultural rights[116]—are extremely imprecise and obscure.[117] Since the 'ordinary meaning' of the Covenant terms is thus often ambiguous, the scope for textual interpretation is rather narrow. Nevertheless, the CESCR has repeatedly tried to demonstrate that its interpretations reflect State consensus by adopting a textual approach. For example, it has compared some of the different language versions of ICESCR article 2(1) to gauge the meaning of the phrase 'to take steps',[118] it has inferred from the inclusion of the term 'other status' in the list of prohibited grounds of discrimination in article 2(2) that the list is not exhaustive,[119] and it has stated that the (very broad) wording of article 9 indicates that the requisite measures for the provision of social security benefits cannot be defined narrowly.[120]

3. Subsequent practice

Another way of demonstrating that a given interpretation embodies the will of the States parties is by pointing to 'subsequent practice in the application of the treaty' in the sense of VCLT article 31(3)(b). Such practice may be taken into account provided it establishes the agreement of the parties regarding that interpretation. The practice must be actively shared by at least some States parties and acquiesced in by the others.[121]

It was the search for common ground among the States parties that led to the creation of the Committee's key interpretive instruments, concluding observations and General Comments, in the first place. The original idea behind these instruments was to clarify the normative content of ICESCR rights through a process of documenting State practice and distilling common standards from it. The State reporting procedure allows the Committee to collect information regarding implementation of the Covenant from States, engage them in 'a constructive and mutually rewarding dialogue',[122] and, based on this, offer suggestions and recommendations in its concluding observations. Its General Comments, in turn, serve 'to make the experience gained so far through the examination of [State] reports available for the benefit of all States parties'.[123] The whole process may be described as one in which

[116] See Craven, *The ICESCR* (n 12) 25.
[117] ibid 3, 353; Sepúlveda, *Nature of Obligations* (n 29) 131–33.
[118] CESCR, 'General Comment 3' (n 43) para 2.
[119] CESCR, 'General Comment 20' (n 46) para 15.
[120] CESCR, 'General Comment 19' (n 95) para 4.
[121] Report of the International Law Commission on the work of its sixty-eighth session (2 May–10 June and 4 July–12 August 2016) UN Doc A/71/10, Chapter VI, Draft Conclusion 10 [9]; Villiger, *VCLT* (n 32) 431; Linderfalk, *Interpretation* (n 100) 167.
[122] CESCR, 'Report on the Seventh Session' (1999) UN Doc E/1993/22, para 32.
[123] ibid para 49.

'[State] practice builds consensus and vice versa'.[124] As will be explained in Section VI.C below, in recent years, however, the Committee has increasingly invoked its own practice in support of its interpretations, which, from the perspective of VCLT article 31(3)(b), is problematic.

C. Morality or State consent?

Although, for the sake of illustration, they have been described here as 'poles', it is important to acknowledge that morality and State consent are not strict opposites: an interpretation that appears to be morally appropriate will often be one that finds the support of States, and vice versa. Nevertheless, sometimes morality and State consent do pull in different directions.

The best illustration of how the Committee may be torn between the two poles is its 'meandering course of logic'[125] as to what is meant by 'minimum core obligations'. The development of this concept by the CESCR may be summarized as: (1) pragmatic, context-sensitive formulation; (2) moralist expansion; (3) tracking back in search of State support.

The Committee introduced the concept in its General Comment 3, stating that ICESCR article 2(1) must be understood to impose on every State party 'a minimum core obligation to ensure the satisfaction of, at the very least, minimum essential levels of each of the rights'.[126] However, in this first step, it confined the content of minimum core obligations to true essentials, such as 'essential foodstuffs', 'essential primary health care', 'basic shelter and housing', and 'the most basic forms of education', and explicitly acknowledged that, under strict conditions, non-compliance could be justified by resource constraints.[127]

In a second step, the Committee began to considerably expand the minimum entitlements it saw as being required by the moral values underlying the Covenant.[128] Furthermore, it held that these core obligations had to be met regardless of available resources: in General Comment 14 on the right to health, it stressed, in clear contradiction to its observations in General Comment 3, 'that a State party cannot, under any circumstances whatsoever, justify its non-compliance with the core obligations . . . which are nonderogable'.[129]

However, States continued to justify failure to satisfy their minimum core obligations by a lack of resources,[130] and the South African Constitutional Court rejected the concept on the basis that it was impossible to define a minimum core without

[124] Katharine G Young, *Constituting Economic and Social Rights* (OUP 2012) 54.

[125] Katharine G Young, 'The Minimum Core of Economic and Social Rights: A Concept in Search of Content' (2008) 33 Yale J of Intl L 113, 154.

[126] CESCR, 'General Comment 3' (n 43) para 10. [127] ibid.

[128] See eg CESCR, 'General Comment 15' (n 96) para 37 (listing nine core obligations under the right to water, including, for instance, an obligation to adopt and implement a national water strategy and plan of action).

[129] CESCR, 'General Comment 14' (n 44) para 47.

[130] eg CESCR, 'Second Periodic Report by Nepal' (7 August 2006) UN Doc E/C.12/NPL/2, para 240.

taking into account the context and available resources.[131] As a reaction to the lack of support for an ambitious notion of minimum core obligations in State practice, the CESCR, in a third step, started to scale back the concept and returned to its original formulation: General Comment 19 on the right to social security restates word-for-word the formulation of General Comment 3, thus recognizing that a failure to fulfil minimum core obligations *can* be justified by resource constraints.[132]

VI. Generating Legitimacy

The tension between morality and State consent cannot be resolved. It is inevitable that the CESCR will sometimes have to choose between an interpretation that may follow from a moral reading of the ICESCR but lacks State support and one that may run counter to the moral values underlying the Covenant but is carried by the consensus of States. There is no third way. Given its lack of power to issue legally binding decisions, all the Committee can do is try to lend legitimacy to what it regards as the morally correct interpretations. Legitimacy has been defined by Thomas Franck as 'a property of a rule or rule-making institution which itself exerts a pull toward compliance on those addressed normatively because those addressed believe that the rule or institution has come into being and operates in accordance with generally accepted principles of right process'.[133] According to this conception, legitimacy is a social fact, not a normative standard: it is the *belief* of those addressed that counts.[134] As the Committee's constant attempts to link its interpretations to State consensus demonstrate, it has realized that the pull toward compliance exerted by findings that are believed to be legitimate can, to some extent, compensate for its lack of coercive authority.

However, the Committee seems to have a too narrow understanding of what constitutes the *basis* of the legitimacy of its interpretations. First, it concentrates on the views of *States* and appears to regard these views as a given fact. While it is true that the primary addressees of the Committee's interpretations are States, the interpretive community of the ICESCR extends far beyond them and their representatives: international organizations, non-governmental organizations, multinational corporations, trade unions, aid agencies, and a wide range of further international and domestic actors all have an interest in the meaning assigned to Covenant terms and will therefore evaluate the appropriateness of a given interpretation.[135] Under the ICESCR-OP, involvement of these non-State actors will be further enhanced.[136]

[131] *Government of the Republic of South Africa & others v Grootboom & others* [2000] ZACC 19, paras 33, 46. See also *Mazibuko & others v City of Johannesburg & others* [2009] ZACC 28, paras 56–59.

[132] CESCR, 'General Comment 19' (n 95) para 60.

[133] Thomas M Franck, *The Power of Legitimacy Among Nations* (OUP 1990) 24.

[134] Christopher A Thomas, 'The Uses and Abuses of Legitimacy in International Law' (2014) 34 Oxford J of Legal Studies 729, 741.

[135] See also John Tobin, 'Seeking to Persuade: A Constructive Approach to Human Rights Treaty Interpretation' (2010) 23 Harvard Human Rights J 1, 8–10.

[136] See ICESCR-OP arts 2, 8(1), 8(3), and 11(3).

Their views, in turn, have the potential, through various social processes such as persuasion and 'acculturation', to influence State behaviour: States are not unitary actors with predetermined interests but may be 'socialized'.[137] Therefore, it would be crucial for the CESCR to also persuade non-State actors with its interpretations. Second, by focusing on the extent of pre-existing State *consensus* that its interpretations embody, the Committee follows an exclusively *source*-based understanding of legitimacy. Yet legitimacy can derive not only from a source—in international law, State consent—but also from the *process* of decision-making.[138] In other words, legitimacy can be *generated* through following a process of interpretation that the interpretive community regards as adequate and fair.[139] The other players in 'the game of interpretation in international law'[140] will only be convinced by an interpretation if it is clear that the interpreter has followed the rules of the game.

What exactly does process-based legitimacy imply? Since legitimacy is understood here as a social fact, it is clear that the relevant requirements cannot be determined through moral reasoning or derived from some settled concept of justice. Instead, an empirical evaluation must be undertaken to identify the qualities of a decision-making process that lead the relevant actors to regard it as adequate and fair. This is not the place to draw up such a list of detailed requirements for the interpretive practice of human rights treaty bodies.[141]

Instead, I will simply point to three requirements that are so basic that virtually any member of the interpretive community would agree that a given interpretation must meet them in order to enjoy legitimacy. The first and most obvious is *adherence*. Since in legal decision-making 'there is a limited set of arguments which can acceptably be invoked to justify a solution',[142] an interpretation will only appear legitimate if it is reached by adhering to the principles agreed upon by the interpretive community for this very purpose.[143] The game must be played by the rules. Second, a legitimate or, in Jan Klabbers's terms, 'virtuous' interpretation is one that pays heed to past interpretations.[144] Hence, there must be a certain *coherence* to the practice

[137] Ryan Goodman and Derek Jinks, *Socializing States: Promoting Human Rights Through International Law* (OUP 2013).

[138] Daniel Bodansky, 'The Legitimacy of International Governance: A Coming Challenge for International Environmental Law?' (1999) 93 American J of Intl L 596, 612; Rüdiger Wolfrum, 'Legitimacy of International Law from a Legal Perspective: Some Introductory Considerations' in Rüdiger Wolfrum and Volker Röben (eds), *Legitimacy in International Law* (Springer 2008) 1, 6.

[139] See Franck, *Power of Legitimacy* (n 133) 17–19.

[140] Andrea Bianchi, 'The Game of Interpretation in International Law: The Players, the Cards, and Why the Game is Worth the Candle' in Andrea Bianchi, Daniel Peat, and Matthew Windsor (eds), *Interpretation in International Law* (OUP 2015) 34.

[141] For such attempts, see Sepúlveda, *Nature of Obligations* (n 29) 87–111 (with regard to the findings of the CESCR); Helen Keller and Leena Grover, 'General Comments of the Human Rights Committee and their Legitimacy' in Helen Keller and Geir Ulfstein (eds), *UN Human Rights Treaty Bodies: Law and Legitimacy* (CUP 2012) 116, 140–92 (with regard to the HRC's General Comments).

[142] Koskenniemi, *From Apology to Utopia* (n 84) 67.

[143] See Franck, *Power of Legitimacy* (n 133) 183–94; Keller and Grover, 'General Comments' (n 141) 162–67.

[144] Jan Klabbers, 'Virtuous Interpretation' in Malgosia Fitzmaurice, Olufemi Elias, and Panos Merkouris (eds), *Treaty Interpretation and the Vienna Convention on the Law of Treaties: 30 Years on* (Brill 2010) 17, 36.

of the interpreter in question.[145] The rules cannot be changed in the middle of the game. Third, the interpreter must explain the means of interpretation used to arrive at a particular result; that is, the set of interpretive principles must be applied in a *transparent* manner.[146] Those affected by a norm should be given reasons for how it is used.[147] Interpretation is a game that needs to be played with open cards.

The better a particular interpretation meets these requirements, the greater will be the support for it in the interpretive community and therefore the more difficult it will be for States not to comply with it.[148] Thus, although the Committee's interpretive practice may be trapped between the poles of morality and State consent, there are still interpretations that will generate more legitimacy than others because they follow the prescription for how a legal argument has to be crafted.

A. Adherence

The agreed-upon set of principles for interpreting the ICESCR can be found, as explained earlier, in the Covenant itself and, more importantly, in the VCLT. The Committee apparently recognizes that the VCLT is applicable to the ICESCR, as it has made reference to its article 27.[149] However, unlike, for example, the ECtHR,[150] it has so far not been prepared to explicitly state that it feels bound by VCLT articles 31–33. Given that the existing 'rules of the game' give interpreters considerable latitude, this failure to commit to them is surprising.

B. Coherence

It has already been pointed out in the previous section that the tension between morality and State consent has led the CESCR to adopt interpretations of the concept of minimum core obligations that are plainly contradictory. This is not the only incoherence in the Committee's interpretive practice: the Committee has at times suggested that international organizations have 'obligations' under the ICESCR, then again it has spoken of their 'responsibilities';[151] it has developed the concept of extraterritorial obligations in such a way that '[w]ith every new General Comment the scope of such obligations seems either to expand or to shrink again';[152] and its interpretation of the term 'other status' in ICESCR article 2(2) is tainted with 'startling inconsistencies'.[153] These criticisms by commentators who can hardly be

145 See Franck, *Power of Legitimacy* (n 133) 135–82; Keller and Grover, 'General Comments' (n 141) 150–59.

146 Klabbers, 'Virtuous Interpretation' (n 144) 36; Keller and Grover, 'General Comments' (n 141) 183–85.

147 Venzke, *Interpretation* (n 35) 13.

148 Tobin, 'Seeking to Persuade' (n 135) 11.

149 CESCR, 'General Comment 9' (n 113) para 3.

150 *Golder v the United Kingdom* App no 4451/70 (ECtHR, 21 February 1975) para 29.

151 eg CESCR, 'General Comment 18' (n 94) para 52. See Kerstin Mechlem, 'Treaty Bodies and the Interpretation of Human Rights' (2009) 42 Vanderbilt J of Transnational L 905, 934–35.

152 Mechlem, 'Treaty Bodies' (n 151) 938.

153 Malcolm Langford and Jeff A King, 'Committee on Economic, Social and Cultural Rights' in Malcolm Langford (ed), *Social Rights Jurisprudence: Emerging Trends in International and Comparative Law* (CUP 2008) 477, 491.

described as fundamental opponents of the Committee's work go a long way to show how its constant see-saw between morality and State consent may undermine the legitimacy of its interpretations and, ultimately, of the Committee itself.

C. Transparency

Although the Committee apparently takes guidance from the interpretive rules of the VCLT, it has never given any explanation as to how it proceeds in applying them. At best, the reader may guess that this or that element of VCLT articles 31–33 was at play, as with the examples mentioned in Section V earlier. Why other elements were regarded as irrelevant or less important remains unexplained.

For example, in its General Comment on the right to water, the pull towards morality led the CESCR to ignore the full range of interpretive means and to focus exclusively on the teleological element. Thus, it read a separate right to water into ICESCR article 11(1) on the basis that such a right was 'essential for securing an adequate standard of living' and, indeed, 'one of the most fundamental conditions for survival'.[154] Yet it failed to point out that one construction of the *travaux* concludes that the drafters deliberately omitted water as a separate right[155] and that a textual interpretation also leads to the conclusion that the Covenant does not guarantee such a right.[156] This is not to argue that the Committee's interpretation is wrong—there may be perfectly good reasons to give a teleological approach priority over a textual interpretation and, even more so, over an interpretation according to original intent. However, if an interpretation is to be regarded as legitimate, the various interpretive elements should at least be dealt with. Thus, it cannot come as a surprise that the Committee's expansive reading of ICESCR article 11(1) has attracted severe criticism from academic commentators[157] as well as governments.[158]

The CESCR frequently refers to its previous General Comments, concluding observations, Statements, and Open Letters. Of course, the requirement of coherence may make it necessary to consider previous findings. However, since its Views are not legally binding, it is not sufficient for the Committee—as it tends to do—to simply point to its preceding output to justify a particular interpretation of the ICESCR.[159] If it wants to *persuade* the interpretive community that its own findings are relevant

[154] CESCR, 'General Comment 15' (n 96) para 3.

[155] Stephen Tully, 'A Human Right to Access Water? A Critique of General Comment No. 15' (2005) 23 Netherlands Q of Human Rights 35, 37–38.

[156] See Matthew CR Craven, 'Some Thoughts on the Emergent Right to Water' in Eibe Riedel and Peter Rothen (eds), *The Human Right to Water* (Berliner Wissenschafts-Verlag 2006) 37, 40.

[157] Tully, 'A Human Right to Access Water?' (n 155); Michael J Dennis and David P Stewart, 'Justiciability of Economic, Social, and Cultural Rights: Should There Be an International Complaints Mechanism to Adjudge the Rights to Food, Water, Housing, and Health?' (2004) 98 American J of Intl L 462, 493–94.

[158] eg Commission on Human Rights, '59th Session: Summary Record of the 56th Meeting' (22 April 2003) UN Doc E/CN.4/2003/SR.56, para 49 (Canada).

[159] For recent examples, see CESCR, 'General Comment 23' (n 103) paras 22, 52; CESCR, 'Concluding Observations on the Second Periodic Report of Greece' (27 October 2015) UN Doc E/C.12/GRC/CO/2, para 8; CESCR, 'Concluding Observations on the Second Periodic Report of Slovenia' (15 December 2014) UN Doc E/C.12/SVN/CO/2, para 8 (all referring to the letter on

for purposes of interpretation, it needs to *explain* why they are to be regarded as 'subsequent practice . . . which establishes the agreement of the parties' in the sense of VCLT article 31(3)(b). After all, this conclusion is far from self-explanatory. It is true that the ILA Committee on International Human Rights Law and Practice has argued that the special character of human rights treaties requires article 31(3)(b) to be interpreted widely: with regard to this type of treaties, 'subsequent practice' was broader than subsequent *State* practice and included 'the considered views of the treaty bodies adopted in the performance of the functions conferred on them by the States parties'.[160] However, considering that the UN treaty bodies are composed of independent experts rather than State representatives, it seems questionable whether their findings amount to evidence of the agreement of the parties.[161] Such a broad reading of article 31(3)(b) is particularly problematic in the case of the CESCR. Unlike the other treaty bodies, the CESCR was not created in accordance with the provisions of the treaty it monitors, but by ECOSOC, and its members are elected by ECOSOC rather than the States parties.[162] Not all members of ECOSOC are, however, parties to the ICESCR,[163] and only 51 out of the 165 States that are parties to the ICESCR are currently represented on ECOSOC.[164] Hence, the work of the CESCR cannot be said to be carried by the will of the States parties to the same extent as that of the other UN treaty bodies.

If not the Committee's findings themselves, can the *reactions of States* to them be qualified as 'subsequent practice' in the sense of VCLT article 31(3)(b)? To answer this question, the Committee would have to examine whether States have acquiesced in, or endorsed, a given interpretation put forth in, for example, one of its General Comments. The Committee has so far failed to engage in such analysis of State reactions. Without linking its findings to the agreement of States, however, there is a risk that they will amount to nothing more than circular reasoning, with references from its General Comments to its concluding observations and back. This is all the more deplorable given that a convincing case *could* be made that many of its interpretations do reflect State consensus. As pointed out in Section II, States should ascribe great weight to interpretations adopted by human rights treaty bodies: they must be presumed to be correct, so that good reasons must be presented to contest them. In practice, States only very rarely express disagreement with the

austerity measures by the CESCR's Chairperson sent to States parties (CESCR, 'Letter to States Parties from the Chairperson of the CESCR, Ariranga G Pillay' (16 May 2012) UN Doc CESCR/48th/SP/MAB/SW), which, without any explanation, established a number of requirements that austerity measures must meet).

160 ILA, 'UN Treaty Bodies' (n 15) 6.

161 Report of the International Law Commission on the work of its sixty-eighth session (2 May–10 June and 4 July–12 August 2016) UN Doc A/71/10, Chapter VI, Draft Conclusion 13 [12], Commentary, paras 9–10; Ulfstein, 'Individual Complaints' (n 24) 97.

162 ECOSOC Res 1985/17 (28 May 1985).

163 Of the current ECOSOC members, Andorra, the United Arab Emirates, and the United States are not parties to the ICESCR.

164 See also Urfan Khaliq and Robin Churchill, 'The Protection of Economic and Social Rights: A Particular Challenge?' in Helen Keller and Geir Ulfstein (eds), *UN Human Rights Treaty Bodies: Law and Legitimacy* (CUP 2012) 199, 207.

CESCR's General Comments or concluding observations.[165] Although a few States have pointed out that its General Comments are not legally binding,[166] there have been—unlike in the case of the HRC[167]—no formal objections to them.[168] Quite to the contrary, States typically base their own submissions on the Committee's findings. This could be understood as acquiescence in, or even endorsement of, these findings, establishing the agreement of the parties regarding the respective interpretations.[169] Yet such an understanding can only be maintained as long as there is at least minimal engagement by States with the Committee's output. This makes the legitimacy, and thus transparency, of its work all the more important.

The CESCR should also reveal why it regards it as appropriate to interpret the Covenant in the light of other rules of international law. As explained above, it regularly takes into account all sorts of international standards, be they binding upon (all) the parties to the ICESCR or not. Very exceptionally, the Committee may give some hints suggesting that it regards the rules referred to as 'applicable in the relations between the parties' in the sense of VCLT article 31(3)(c).[170] In general, however, it fails to explain why the standards cited should have a bearing on the understanding of the Covenant. This lack of transparency leaves the Committee open to the criticism that it may be 'cherry-picking' those international standards that best support the intended outcome.[171] If, as suggested in Section V, the Committee takes international standards into account because it believes them to reflect moral values underlying the Covenant and thus to be relevant for a teleological interpretation, then it should say so.

The lack of transparency regarding the Committee's interpretive approach contrasts starkly with that of some national courts. To refer to one especially illustrative example, the German Federal Administrative Court, in a case concerning access to higher education, first observed that the ICESCR must be interpreted according to the rules of VCLT articles 31–33 as these form part of customary international law. It then systematically went through the interpretive elements of VCLT article 31 to make sense of ICESCR article 13(2)(c). It examined the wording of the provision in its different language versions, analysed its systematic context, interpreted it in light of its object and purpose, and surveyed the subsequent practice of States and the CESCR.[172]

[165] ILA, 'UN Treaty Bodies' (n 15) 6–7. For a rare example, see CESCR, 'Comments by States Parties on Concluding Observations: Japan' (29 November 2002) UN Doc E/C.12/2002/12.

[166] Eibe Riedel, 'Allgemeine Bemerkungen zu Bestimmungen des Internationalen Paktes über wirtschaftliche, soziale und kulturelle Rechte' in Deutsches Institut für Menschenrechte (ed), *Die "General Comments" zu den VN-Menschenrechtsverträgen* (Nomos 2005) 160, 164–65.

[167] See eg the responses of the United States and the United Kingdom to General Comment 24 relating to reservations (HRC, 'General Comment 24' (n 62)): HRC, 'Report of the Human Rights Committee' (3 October 1995) UN Doc A/50/40, Annex VI.

[168] Sepúlveda, *Nature of Obligations* (n 29), 42; Riedel, 'Allgemeine Bemerkungen' (n 166) 164–65.

[169] ILA, 'UN Treaty Bodies' (n 15) 7.

[170] For such a rare exception, see CESCR, 'General Comment 13' (n 44) para 5 (pointing out the widespread endorsement that the standards cited have received from all regions of the world).

[171] Schlütter, 'Human Rights Interpretation' (n 40) 302.

[172] Bundesverwaltungsgericht, judgment of 29 April 2009, BVerwG 6 C 16/08, paras 47–55.

Of course, invocation of the VCLT rules of interpretation is no guarantee of actual adherence to them.[173] However, proceeding according to these rules at least forces the interpreter to consider other interpretive elements that may lead to a different result and to provide an explanation of how the various elements are weighed. A minimum of transparency is a prerequisite for proper scrutiny—to be able to review an interpretation, the interpretive community must at least know what the interpreter *claims* to be doing. Otherwise, as the example of its General Comment on the right to water shows, the Committee's interpretations become an easy target for criticism.

VII. Conclusion

The broad framework constituted by the VCLT rules of interpretation allows for a wide range of interpretive means, including the allegedly special methods used by the CESCR. Due to their nature as mere guidelines, there are, at the same time, limits to what these rules can achieve: giving interpreters considerable leeway, they cannot prevent a treaty text from being approached and understood very differently by different readers or, indeed, from being misread.[174] Against this background, it is the guiding principle of good faith, rather than the various means of interpretation also referred to in VCLT article 31(1), that should be accorded the central role in the process of interpretation. The importance of this guiding principle was already highlighted by Hersch Lauterpacht, who observed that '[m]ost of the current rules of interpretation ... are no more than elaborations of the fundamental theme that contracts must be interpreted in good faith'.[175] What really matters is thus *how*—the spirit in which—the task of interpretation is undertaken. Interpreting a treaty in good faith implies that the interpreter adheres to a set of principles, applies these principles in a coherent manner, and lays bare how a particular interpretive outcome is reached by explaining which interpretive elements were used and how they were weighed.

In contrast, a large part of the CESCR's interpretations may be viewed as 'result-driven jurisprudence'.[176] While especially its early practice was characterized by attempts to adopt interpretations that would find the support of States, more recently the Committee has often advanced interpretations that appear to be designed to justify outcomes that it regards as morally right—without, however, acknowledging that it engages in a moral reading of the Covenant. Its constant oscillation between the two poles of morality and State consent has resulted in an interpretive practice that lacks coherence and transparency.

[173] Waibel, 'Uniformity' (n 37) 386–88.

[174] Klabbers, 'Virtuous Interpretation' (n 144) 37. See also Hersch Lauterpacht, 'Restrictive Interpretation and the Principle of Effectiveness in the Interpretation of Treaties' (1949) 26 British YB of Intl L 48, 53–55.

[175] Lauterpacht, 'Restrictive Interpretation' (n 174) 56.

[176] Jeremy Waldron, 'Judges as Moral Reasoners' (2009) 7 Intl J of Constitutional L 2, 17.

The CESCR's new power to rule on individual cases offers it the unique opportunity to enhance its standing as a quasi-judicial authority. Yet this will only be achieved if the Committee succeeds in persuading the interpretive community surrounding the Covenant of the interpretations it advances. In order to generate legitimacy for its interpretive practice, it will have to demonstrate its good faith by applying the VCLT principles in a coherent and transparent manner.

Bibliography

Alston, Philip, 'No Right to Complain About Being Poor: The Need for an Optional Protocol to the Economic Rights Covenant' in Asbjørn Eide and Jan Helgesen (eds), *The Future of Human Rights Protection in a Changing World: Fifty Years Since the Four Freedoms Address (Essays in Honour of Torkel Opsahl)* (Norwegian University Press 1992)

Bernhardt, Rudolf, 'Evolutive Treaty Interpretation, Especially of the European Convention on Human Rights' (1999) 42 German YB of Intl L 11

Bernhardt, Rudolf, 'Thoughts on the Interpretation of Human-Rights Treaties' in Franz Matscher and Herbert Petzold (eds), *Protecting Human Rights: The European Dimension, Studies in Honour of Gérard J. Wiarda* (Heymanns 1988)

Bianchi, Andrea, 'The Game of Interpretation in International Law: The Players, the Cards, and Why the Game is Worth the Candle' in Andrea Bianchi, Daniel Peat, and Matthew Windsor (eds), *Interpretation in International Law* (OUP 2015)

Bilchitz, David, *Poverty and Fundamental Rights: The Justification and Enforcement of Socio-Economic Rights* (OUP 2007)

Bjorge, Eirik, *The Evolutionary Interpretation of Treaties* (OUP 2014)

Bodansky, Daniel, 'The Legitimacy of International Governance: A Coming Challenge for International Environmental Law?' (1999) 93 American J of Intl L 596

Buergenthal, Thomas, 'The U.N. Human Rights Committee' in Jochen A. Frowein and Rüdiger Wolfrum, *Max Planck Yearbook of United Nations Law*, vol 5 (Brill 2001)

Çali, Başak, 'Specialized Rules of Treaty Interpretation: Human Rights' in Duncan B Hollis (ed), *The Oxford Guide to Treaties* (OUP 2012)

Craven, Matthew CR, 'Legal Differentiation and the Concept of the Human Rights Treaty in International Law' (2000) 11 European J of Intl L 489

Craven, Matthew CR, 'Some Thoughts on the Emergent Right to Water' in Eibe Riedel and Peter Rothen (eds), *The Human Right to Water* (Berliner Wissenschafts-Verlag 2006)

Craven, Matthew CR, *The International Covenant on Economic, Social, and Cultural Rights: A Perspective on its Development* (OUP 1995)

Crawford, James, *Brownlie's Principles of Public International Law* (OUP 2012)

Dennis, Michael J, and Stewart, David P, 'Justiciability of Economic, Social, and Cultural Rights: Should There Be an International Complaints Mechanism to Adjudge the Rights to Food, Water, Housing, and Health?' (2004) 98 American J of Intl L 462

Dörr, Oliver, 'Article 31' in Oliver Dörr and Kirsten Schmalenbach (eds), *Vienna Convention on the Law of Treaties: A Commentary* (Springer 2012)

Dörr, Oliver, 'Article 32' in Oliver Dörr and Kirsten Schmalenbach (eds), *Vienna Convention on the Law of Treaties: A Commentary* (Springer 2012)

Dworkin, Ronald, *Freedom's Law: The Moral Reading of the American Constitution* (Harvard University Press 1996)

Fish, Stanley, *Is There a Text in This Class? The Authority of Interpretive Communities* (Harvard University Press 1980)

Fitzmaurice, Malgosia, 'Dynamic (Evolutive) Interpretation of Treaties, Part I' (2008) 21 Hague YIL 101

Fitzmaurice, Malgosia, 'Dynamic (Evolutive) Interpretation of Treaties, Part II' (2009) 22 Hague YIL 3

Fitzmaurice, Malgosia, 'Interpretation of Human Rights Treaties' in Dinah Shelton (ed), *The Oxford Handbook of International Human Rights Law* (OUP 2013)

Franck, Thomas M, *The Power of Legitimacy Among Nations* (OUP 1990)

Gardbaum, Stephen, 'Human Rights as International Constitutional Rights' (2008) 19 European J of Intl L 749

Gardiner, Richard, *Treaty Interpretation* (2nd edn, OUP 2015)

Goodman, Ryan, and Jinks, Derek, *Socializing States: Promoting Human Rights Through International Law* (OUP 2013)

Harvard Law School, 'Research in International Law: Part III, Law of Treaties' (1935) 29 American J of Intl L Supplement 946

Henkin, Louis, 'The International Bill of Rights: The Universal Declaration and the Covenants' in Rudolf Bernhardt and John-Anthony Jolowicz (eds), *International Enforcement of Human Rights* (Springer 1987)

Johnstone, Ian, 'Treaty Interpretation: The Authority of Interpretive Communities' (1991) 12 Michigan J of Intl L 371

Keller, Helen, and Grover, Leena, 'General Comments of the Human Rights Committee and their Legitimacy' in Helen Keller and Geir Ulfstein (eds), *UN Human Rights Treaty Bodies: Law and Legitimacy* (CUP 2012)

Khaliq, Urfan, and Churchill, Robin, 'The Protection of Economic and Social Rights: A Particular Challenge?' in Helen Keller and Geir Ulfstein (eds), *UN Human Rights Treaty Bodies: Law and Legitimacy* (CUP 2012)

King, Jeff A, *Judging Social Rights* (CUP 2012)

Klabbers, Jan, 'Virtuous Interpretation' in Malgosia Fitzmaurice, Olufemi Elias, and Panos Merkouris (eds), *Treaty Interpretation and the Vienna Convention on the Law of Treaties: 30 Years on* (Brill 2010)

Koskenniemi, Martti, *From Apology to Utopia: The Structure of International Legal Argument* (CUP 2005)

Langford, Malcolm, and King, Jeff A, 'Committee on Economic, Social and Cultural Rights' in Malcolm Langford (ed), *Social Rights Jurisprudence: Emerging Trends in International and Comparative Law* (CUP 2008)

Lauterpacht, Hersch, 'Restrictive Interpretation and the Principle of Effectiveness in the Interpretation of Treaties' (1949) 26 British YB of Intl L 48

Letsas, George, 'Strasbourg's Interpretive Ethic: Lessons for the International Lawyer' (2010) 21 European J of Intl L 509

Liebenberg, Sandra, 'The Value of Human Dignity in Interpreting Socio-Economic Rights' (2005) 21 South African J on Human Rights 1

Linderfalk, Ulf, *On the Interpretation of Treaties* (Springer 2007)

Marcus, David, 'The Normative Development of Socioeconomic Rights through Supranational Adjudication' (2006) 42 Stanford J of Intl L 53

Mechlem, Kerstin, 'Treaty Bodies and the Interpretation of Human Rights' (2009) 42 Vanderbilt J of Transnational L 905

Moeckli, Daniel, and White, Nigel D, 'Treaties as "Living Instruments"' in Michael J Bowman and Dino Kritsiotis (eds), *Conceptual and Contextual Perspectives on the Modern Law of Treaties* (CUP 2018)

Pellet, Alain, '"Droits-de-l'hommisme" et droit international' (2001) 1 Droits fondamentaux 167

Riedel, Eibe, 'Allgemeine Bemerkungen zu Bestimmungen des Internationalen Paktes über wirtschaftliche, soziale und kulturelle Rechte' in Deutsches Institut für Menschenrechte (ed), *Die 'General Comments' zu den VN-Menschenrechtsverträgen* (Nomos 2005)

Schlütter, Birgit, 'Aspects of Human Rights Interpretation by the UN Treaty Bodies' in Helen Keller and Geir Ulfstein (eds), *UN Human Rights Treaty Bodies: Law and Legitimacy* (CUP 2012)

Sepúlveda, Magdalena, *The Nature of the Obligations under the International Covenant on Economic, Social and Cultural Rights* (Intersentia 2003)

Shue, Henry, *Basic Rights: Subsistence, Affluence and U.S. Foreign Policy* (2nd edn, Princeton University Press 1996)

Thirlway, Hugh, 'The Law and Procedure of the International Court of Justice 1960–1989, Supplement, 2006: Part Three' (2006) 77 British YB of Intl L 1

Thomas, Christopher A, 'The Uses and Abuses of Legitimacy in International Law' (2014) 34 Oxford J of Legal Studies 729

Tobin, John, 'Seeking to Persuade: A Constructive Approach to Human Rights Treaty Interpretation' (2010) 23 Harvard Human Rights J 1

Tully, Stephen, 'A Human Right to Access Water? A Critique of General Comment No. 15' (2005) 23 Netherlands Q of Human Rights 35

Ulfstein, Geir, 'Individual Complaints' in Helen Keller and Geir Ulfstein (eds), *UN Human Rights Treaty Bodies: Law and Legitimacy* (CUP 2012)

Vagts, Detlef F, 'Treaty Interpretation and the New American Ways of Law Reading' (1993) 4 European J of Intl L 472

Venzke, Ingo, *How Interpretation Makes International Law: On Semantic Change and Normative Twists* (OUP 2012)

Villiger, Mark E, *Commentary on the 1969 Vienna Convention on the Law of Treaties* (Brill 2009)

Waibel, Michael, 'Uniformity Versus Specialization (2): A Uniform Regime of Treaty Interpretation?' in Christian J Tams, Antonios Tzanakopoulos, and Andreas Zimmermann (eds), *Research Handbook on the Law of Treaties* (Edward Elgar 2014)

Waldron, Jeremy, 'Homelessness and the Issue of Freedom' (1991) 39 UCLA L Rev 295

Waldron, Jeremy, 'Judges as Moral Reasoners' (2009) 7 Intl J of Constitutional L 2

Wolfrum, Rüdiger, 'Legitimacy of International Law from a Legal Perspective: Some Introductory Considerations' in Rüdiger Wolfrum and Volker Röben (eds), *Legitimacy in International Law* (Springer 2008)

Young, Katharine G, 'The Minimum Core of Economic and Social Rights: A Concept in Search of Content' (2008) 33 Yale J of Intl L 113

Young, Katharine G, *Constituting Economic and Social Rights* (OUP 2012)

5

NGOs

Essential Actors for Embedding the Covenants in the National Context

*Patrick Mutzenberg**

I. Introduction

Non-governmental organizations (NGOs)[1] are essential to the work of the Human Rights Committee (HRC), the monitoring body established by the 1966 International Covenant on Civil and Political Rights (ICCPR).[2] This was recently reaffirmed by Fabian Salvioli, former Chairperson of the HRC, when he pointed out that:

> Through its observations and analysis, civil society has a fundamental role to play in assessing how States Parties implement the ICCPR. NGOs represent a crucial link between national concerns and international mechanisms in providing the Human Rights Committee with the required information during the examination of States parties' reports. They are also important partners when it comes to the implementation of the Concluding Observations, whether through advocacy with the authorities, or under their own monitoring activities.[3]

The same can be said of NGO participation in the work of the Committee on Economic, Social and Cultural Rights (CESCR),[4] the monitoring body set up under

* The author would like to thank Emile Kinley-Gauthier for his research assistance and Lucy McKernan, of Global Initiative for Economic, Social and Cultural Rights, for her very useful comments and suggestions.

[1] See the definition of NGOs in George E Edwards, 'Assessing the Effectiveness of the Human Rights Non-Governmental Organisations (NGOs) from the Birth of the United Nations to the 21st Century: Ten Attributes of Highly Successful Human Rights NGOs' (2009) 18 Michigan State Intl L Rev 171.

[2] International Covenant on Civil and Political Rights (ICCPR) (opened for signature 16 December 1966, entered into force 23 March 1976) 999 UNTS 171.

[3] Peggy Brett and Patrick Mutzenberg, 'UN Human Rights Committee, Participation in the Reporting Process: Guidelines for Non-Governmental Organisations (NGOs)' (2nd edn, Centre for Civil and Political Rights 2015) foreword.

[4] The CESCR 'attaches great importance to cooperation with all non-governmental organisations (NGOs) active in the field of economic, social and cultural rights—local, national and international' (in CESCR, 'Report on the Twenty-second, Twenty-third, and Twenty-fourth Sessions' (2000) UN Doc E/C.12/2000/21, *Official Records of the Economic and Social Council* 2001, Supplement No 2, Annex

the International Covenant on Economic, Social and Cultural Rights (ICESCR),[5] and more generally with respect to the various United Nations (UN) human rights treaty bodies (UNTB).[6]

However, the role of NGOs has changed since these Committees were first set up. As neither of the Covenants specifically refers to a possible interaction between the Committees and civil society,[7] this role has been gradually and progressively developed over the years, initially on an ad hoc basis and subsequently in the working methods of the relevant bodies. Both Committees have recently adopted specific documents clarifying the modalities of NGO participation in their work. These documents established the Committees' cooperation with NGOs in relation to their three main functions, namely the reporting procedure, the individual communications procedure, and the elaboration of General Comments.

The CESCR was the first Committee to formalize its cooperation with NGOs. A first reference to NGOs was made by the CESCR in its 1994 Annual Report,[8] and in November 2000 it adopted its 'Guidelines for NGOs', which review its modalities of interaction with civil society.[9] More than a decade later, in March 2012, the HRC adopted similar guidelines clarifying the relationship between the Committee

V: 'Non-Governmental Organisation Participation in the Activities of the Committee on Economic, Social and Cultural Rights' 149, para 1.

[5] International Covenant on Economic, Social and Cultural Rights (ICESCR) (opened for signature 16 December 1966, entered into force 3 January 1976) 993 UNTS 3.

[6] The essential role of NGOs is recognized by all of the UNTB and is regularly reaffirmed by the various Committees and at the annual meetings of the Chairs of the UNTB. See eg the Report of the 27th meeting of the Chairs of the UNTB in San Jose, Costa Rica, 22–26 June 2015, where the 'Chairs welcomed the indispensable contribution of civil society organizations to the work of the treaty bodies, whether through submissions, inputs, hearings or briefings. They called upon civil society organizations to continue to participate in State party reviews as well as in the follow-up to recommendations emanating from the treaty bodies' ('Report of the Chairs of the Human Rights Treaty Bodies on their Twenty-seventh Meeting' (7 August 2015) UN Doc A/70/302, para 77).

[7] Similarly, the other UNTB do not have specific provisions foreseeing cooperation with civil society, with the notable exception of those adopted recently: art 45(a) of the Convention on the Rights of the Child (CRC) (opened for signature 20 November 1989, entered into force 2 September 1990) 1577 UNTS 3 provides that '[t]he Committee may invite ... other competent bodies as it may consider appropriate to provide expert advice on the implementation of the Convention in areas falling within the scope of their respective mandates'. Similar provisions are included in: the International Convention on the Protection of the Rights of All Migrant Workers and Members of Their Families (opened for signature 18 December 1990, entered into force 1 July 2003) 2220 UNTS 3, art 74(4); the Convention on the Rights of Persons with Disabilities (opened for signature 13 December 2006, entered into force 3 May 2008) 2515 UNTS 3, art 38(a); and to a lesser extent in the International Convention for the Protection of All Persons from Enforced Disappearance (opened for signature 20 December 2006, entered into force 23 December 2010) 2716 UNTS 3, art 28(1). There is no reference to NGOs in the Optional Protocols to the ICCPR and to the ICESCR on individual communications (First Optional Protocol to the ICCPR (OP1-ICCPR) (opened for signature 16 December 1966, entered into force 23 March 1971) 999 UNTS 171; Optional Protocol to the ICESCR (OP-ICESCR) (opened for signature 10 December 2008, entered into force 5 May 2016) UN Doc A/RES/63/117, 48 ILM 256 2009. See Katarzyna Sękowska-Kozłowska, 'The Role of Non-governmental Organisations in Individual Communication Procedures before the UN Human Rights Treaty Bodies' in Alexander J Bělohlávek, Naděžda Rozehnalová, and Filip Černý (eds), *Czech Yearbook of International Law*, vol V (Juris 2014) 367, 370.

[8] See CESCR, 'Report on the Tenth and Eleventh Sessions' (1 January 1995), UN Doc E/C.12/1994/20, *Official Records of the Economic and Social Council* 1995, Supplement No 3, 14, para 27.

[9] See CESCR, 'Annex V' (n 4) 149.

and NGOs[10] and analysing at length the role of NGOs in the different areas of its work.

The objective of this chapter is to analyse the specific role of NGOs before the Committees and how this role been reinforced and clarified over time, in particular through the adoption of the above-mentioned documents. The focus of the chapter is on the reporting procedure, which is by far the most important aspect of the Committees' work for NGOs, although other aspects should not be underestimated (Section II). The chapter also envisages the implication of NGOs in a broader context, in particular regarding the contribution of civil society to the implementation of the Covenants at the national level. An examination of the impact of NGOs should not be limited to their interaction with the Committees during their sessions, but should also consider the implementation of the Committees' views and concluding observations (Section III).[11]

II. Cooperation with the Committees Primarily Related to the Reporting Procedure

A. The role of NGOs in the reporting procedure

The reporting procedure, as set out in ICCPR article 40 and ICESCR article 16, is premised on the idea that States parties should submit reports to the Covenants' respective monitoring bodies on a regular basis. Such reports are discussed with the States parties during public meetings. Following a 'constructive dialogue',[12] both Committees adopt concluding observations with recommendations addressed to the States parties and aimed at improved implementation of the ICCPR and the ICESCR. The Covenants do not foresee the intervention of third parties in this

[10] This document mainly covers the reporting procedure but also provides brief information on other ways to contribute to the work of the Committee, namely regarding the individual communications procedure under the OP1-ICCPR and the elaboration of General Comments. See HRC, 'The Relationship of the Human Rights Committee with Non-governmental Organizations' (4 June 2012) UN Doc CCPR/C/104/3.

[11] This chapter does not intend to cover the role of civil society in the drafting process of the Covenants and their protocols. There is limited information on the role played by civil society in the negotiation of the texts of the ICCPR and the ICESCR, as suggested in Ida Lintel and Cedric Ryngaert, 'The Interface between Non-governmental Organisations and the Human Rights Committee' (2013) 15 Intl Community L Rev 359, 361. However, NGOs played a more crucial role in the adoption process of the OP-ICESCR by the UN General Assembly (UNGA). Several NGOs established a coalition for the OP-ICESCR. This coalition, coordinated by ESCR-Net, was active during the drafting process of the Optional Protocol, although it had a more significant impact by pushing for a time frame for negotiating the text than on the text itself. The NGO Coalition for the OP-ICESCR continues to play an important role in promoting the instrument's ratification. See Gamze Erdem Türkelli, Wouter Vandenhole, and Arne Vandenbogaerde, 'NGO Impact on Law-making: The Case of a Complaints Procedure under the International Covenant on Economic, Social and Cultural Rights and the Convention on the Rights of the Child' (2013) 5 J of Human Rights Practice 1, and Claire Mahon, 'Progress at the Front: The Draft Optional Protocol to the International Covenant on Economic, Social and Cultural Rights' (2008) 8 Human Rights L Rev 617.

[12] See HRC, 'Working Methods' <www.ohchr.org/EN/HRBodies/CCPR/Pages/WorkingMethods.aspx> accessed 4 April 2017, s B.

reporting procedure. However, since the first reviews of State reports, the participation of NGOs has been increasingly endorsed, at first informally and subsequently with a formal role given to NGOs at all stages of the reporting procedure (before, during, and after the review of State reports). During its early days, the HRC debated at length on whether it was authorized to receive (and to solicit) NGO information. In 1997, the HRC formally decided that it 'should also seek information from NGOs'.[13] At that time, very few NGO reports were submitted to the Committees, and then mainly by international NGOs which were acquainted with their work and the subtleties of the reporting procedure. Nowadays, both Committees receive a high volume of NGO reports. Figures from 2015 show that the HRC received 290 NGO reports and that the CESCR received 212 NGO reports that year. In-depth analysis of these reports reveals interesting data. Of the 290 NGO reports received by the HRC, 112 were submitted before the adoption of the Lists of Issues[14] and 178 were submitted in the context of the review procedure. The average number of reports per country is high (15.2 NGO reports per country); however, the volume of output varies significantly between different States. Some generated a high volume of NGO reports, with the review of Venezuela entailing the highest number at a total of thirty-seven (six reports for the List of Issues and thirty-one reports for the review), followed by the United Kingdom (thirty-one reports), the Russian Federation (twenty-six reports), and the Republic of Korea (twenty-two reports). However, it is concerning to observe that other States, namely Monaco, Cyprus, Benin, and Suriname, received little attention from the NGO community, with very few NGO reports submitted regarding either their Lists of Issues or their reviews.

A similar analysis of the CESCR demonstrates that this Committee received significantly fewer reports in 2015, with figures indicating that a total of 212 NGO reports were submitted predominantly in the context of the State review procedure (140 reports), with only seventy-two reports submitted prior to the adoption of the Lists of Issues. Therefore, in the case of this Committee, only 12.6 NGO reports per country were submitted on average. As with the HRC, the

[13] See HRC, 'Report on the Informal Meeting on Procedures' (22 December 1997) UN Doc CCPR/C/133. For a full overview of the early debate on NGO participation at the HRC, see Patrice Gillibert, 'Le Comité des droits de l'homme et les organisations non gouvernementales' in Emmanuel Decaux and Fanny Martin (eds), *Le Pacte international relatif aux droits civils et politiques: commentaire article par article* (Economica 2011) 55. For the first example of interaction between the HRC and the civil society organizations, see also Yogesh K Tyagi, 'Cooperation between the Human Rights Committee and Nongovernmental Organizations: Permissibility and Propositions' (1983) 18 Texas Intl L J 273.

[14] All UNTB now adopt a 'List of Issues and Questions' on the basis of the State party report and other available information (including information from specialized UN agencies, NGO submissions, etc). This List of Issues is transmitted to the State party in advance of the session at which the UNTB will consider the report. The List of Issues provides the framework for a constructive dialogue with the State party's delegation. The delegation may respond to the issues orally during the session, but most of the Committees request the State party to submit written responses to the List of Issues in advance, allowing the dialogue to focus on specific issues more expediently (<www2.ohchr.org/english/bodies/treaty/glossary.htm> accessed 4 April 2017). Additionally, the States parties can opt for the 'Simplified Reporting Procedure' (SRP), wherein the List of Issues is adopted prior to the submission of the State report. In that situation, the State report has to focus on the issues included in the List of Issues and is therefore more focused on the concerns of the specific Committee (<www.ohchr.org/EN/HRBodies/CCPR/Pages/SimplifiedReportingProcedure.aspx> accessed 4 April 2017).

number of reports according to country ranges significantly, from thirty reports received on Ireland (sixteen reports for the List of Issues and fourteen reports for the review) and twenty-two reports on Uganda (ten reports for the List of Issues and twelve reports for the review) to very limited NGO contributions on countries such as Mongolia (five reports), Guyana (four reports), or the Gambia (three reports).

Moreover, several reports submitted to both Committees were drafted by NGO coalitions, and as such these reports could either cover only a few issues (thematic reports)[15] or else were more global, addressing several of the provisions set out in the Covenants.[16]

At this stage, it is important to highlight that only the HRC benefits from the support of a structure—the Centre for Civil and Political Rights—specifically dedicated to NGO engagement with the Committee. The Centre for Civil and Political Rights acts as a focal point for civil society organizations[17] with regard to the various activities of the HRC. No similar platform exists in the framework of the CESCR, although the Secretariat and several NGOs play an active role to ensure that civil society is engaged in a coordinated manner.

All NGOs and civil society groups may involve themselves in the reporting procedure (as well as the other activities of the Committees), regardless of whether they have been granted ECOSOC (UN Economic and Social Council) consultative status.[18] There is no process that monitors the independence or the credibility of the NGOs interacting with the Committees. All of the information provided by civil society is generally transmitted to the Committees as long as it is formally submitted to their secretariats within the specific deadlines. It is therefore the Committee members' task to monitor and assess the quality of the NGO information received. In practice, there have been relatively few instances wherein NGO information was considered biased and non-independent.[19]

[15] See eg the thematic report by ten NGOs submitted to the HRC at its 114th session in July 2015 and concerning Canadian oil, mining, and gas companies operating abroad, restrictions on freedom of expression and democratic participation, and the rights of first nations, inequality, and environmental policy (Franciscans International and others, 'Alternative Report on Canada's Compliance with the International Covenant on Civil and Political Rights' (2015) <http://tbinternet.ohchr.org/Treaties/CCPR/Shared%20Documents/CAN/INT_CCPR_CSS_CAN_20763_E.doc> accessed 4 April 2017).

[16] See eg the global report on Cambodia submitted by ten NGOs to the HRC at its 113th session in March 2015 concerning the main issues included in the List of Issues (Cambodian Human Rights Action Committee and others, 'Cambodia: Civil Society Report on the Implementation of the ICCPR' (20 February 2015) <http://tbinternet.ohchr.org/Treaties/CCPR/Shared%20Documents/KHM/INT_CCPR_CSS_KHM_19618_E.pdf> accessed 4 April 2017).

[17] The Centre for Civil and Political Rights was established in 2008 as a platform dedicated to national and international NGOs, with the mandate to reinforce the presence and improve the coordination of NGOs before the HRC (<www.ccprcentre.org> accessed 4 April 2017).

[18] See Brett and Mutzenberg, 'NGO Guidelines' (n 3) 13.

[19] See eg the report by a coalition of NGOs from Venezuela submitted to the HRC in June 2015 (FUNDALATIN and others, 'Informe ante el Consejo de Derechos Humanos' (1 June 2015) <http://tbinternet.ohchr.org/Treaties/CCPR/Shared%20Documents/VEN/INT_CCPR_CSS_VEN_20713_S.doc> accessed 4 April 2017).

1. NGO interaction prior to the review

Once the State party has submitted its (initial or periodic) report, the review is scheduled and commences with the adoption of the List of Issues. This is the first entry point for NGOs that would like to see their main subjects of concern taken into consideration. It is also a key opportunity for NGOs to share their views, since the List of Issues forms the framework for subsequent dialogue and is thoroughly addressed with the representatives of the State party during their dialogue with the Committees. Both Committees welcome written information at this initial stage,[20] and NGOs frequently submit information at this point. The communication of the countries selected for the adoption of Lists of Issues and the deadlines for NGOs to submit information prior to their adoption are, however, challenging. Meeting these deadlines requires the NGOs to have a clear understanding of the working methods and the calendar of the Committee concerned. Deadlines to submit information are not easily accessible (in particular on the OHCHR website) and can be changed at short notice. To guarantee that such information is widely disseminated, the Centre for Civil and Political Rights issues regular newsletters and alerts as soon as the information is made available.

Information submitted for the List of Issues[21] should ideally refer to previous reporting cycles, with a specific emphasis on information related to the implementation of the previous concluding observations.[22] In reality, however, most of the information submitted does not refer to the previous cycle and remains silent on the progress made regarding the specific subjects of concern raised at an earlier stage.

Even though, at this point, information is mainly submitted in written form, NGOs also have the opportunity to brief the Committees orally. The CESCR is the only one of the two Committees to organize a formal and private meeting held in the pre-sessions that is specifically devoted to the List of Issues.[23] Such a formal meeting does not take place at the HRC, although informal briefings may be organized prior to the adoption of the Lists of Issues. In practice, meetings are organized depending on the need for more information identified by the Committee members involved

[20] The HRC 'emphasizes that it is highly desirable to receive input from NGOs at an early stage of the reporting process' (HRC, 'Relationship with NGOs' (n 10) para 9). The CESCR provides similar guidance (CESCR, 'Annex V' (n 4) 153, para 14).

[21] Information submitted by NGOs is even more crucial when the States parties opt for the SRP, which foresees that the List of Issues is to be adopted prior to the drafting of the State reports. In that context, NGO concerns will be addressed in both the State report and during dialogue with the States parties. See more on the SRP and NGOs' contribution in Brett and Mutzenberg, 'NGO Guidelines' (n 3) 9.

[22] See Brett and Mutzenberg, 'NGO Guidelines' (n 3) 10.

[23] This approach follows the long-standing practice of the Committee of the Rights of the Child, which engages in a three-hour dialogue with NGOs regarding each country at this stage of the procedure. See the working methods of the Committee of the Rights of Child <www.ohchr.org/Documents/HRBodies/CRC/WorkingMethodsCRC.doc> accessed 4 April 2017, s A. See also the information provided by Child Rights Connect on the reporting procedure (Child Rights Connect, 'CRC Reporting' <www.childrightsconnect.org/connect-with-the-un-2/crc-reporting/> accessed 4 April 2017).

in the adoption of the List of Issues; however, these meetings, which are usually held via video-conference, are rare.[24]

NGO briefings scheduled a few hours or days prior to the adoption of the Lists of Issues help to ensure that the main concerns of civil society organizations are voiced and that the latest human rights developments are fully taken into account. However, the effectiveness of this practice can be questioned for two main reasons. First, the impact of the information provided by NGOs at this stage is certainly mitigated due to the fact that the drafts of the Lists of Issues are prepared several weeks beforehand and, in most cases, only minor changes can occur at this point. Secondly, the participation of NGOs at this stage remains weak, as representatives who travel to Geneva to participate in NGO briefings have to budget for a second journey in order to attend the review itself, when another NGO briefing takes place. Hence, as NGOs (particularly national ones) usually have very limited resources, they often choose to participate in the review only and do not attend the pre-session.

2. *NGO interaction during the State report review*

Once the List of Issues is adopted and the review of the State report is scheduled, NGOs are presented with a second opportunity to provide information to the Committees. The format of this participation remains similar to the previous phase, with NGOs receiving an opportunity to provide written information prior to the review and to participate in formal and/or informal briefings during the sessions of the Committees.

Regarding written information, NGOs are encouraged to submit their reports prior to the examination of the State reports.[25] At this stage, the Committees welcome reports that focus on topics included in the Lists of Issues, although additional information is also appreciated. Such information helps the Committees to shed light on inconsistencies and contradictions in the State reports and, more importantly, in the written replies to the Lists of Issues provided by the States parties.[26] In practice, more and more NGO reports focus on the issues included in the Lists; whilst some deal with only one or a few topics, others are more comprehensive and address most of the concerns listed.

NGOs are also presented with the opportunity to formally brief the Committees. They have been exercising this possibility since 1993 in the case of the CESCR,[27]

[24] In its paper on the relationship of the HRC with NGOs, the Committee 'welcomes the organization of NGO briefings prior to the adoption of Lists of Issues' (HRC, 'Relationship with NGOs' (n 10) para 6).

[25] For the CESCR, see CESCR, 'Annex V' (n 4), 154, para 21, and for the HRC, see HRC, 'Relationship with NGOs' (n 10) para 9.

[26] NGO information is particularly crucial when the procedure of review in absence of a report is triggered according to the Rules of Procedure of the HRC (Rule 70), as—absent a State report—the main information available to the Committee stems from NGOs (HRC, 'Rules of Procedure of the Human Rights Committee' (11 January 2015) CCPR/C/3/REV.10).

[27] CESCR, 'NGO Participation in Activities of the Committee on Economic, Social and Cultural Rights' (12 May 1993) UN Doc E/C.12/1993/WP.14. See also Wouter Vandenhole, *The Procedures before the UN Human Rights Treaty Bodies: Divergence or Convergence?* (Intersentia 2004) 128.

which officialized this activity in its Guidelines for NGOs.[28] Such formal briefings are public and usually held on each Monday for the countries to be reviewed during the week ahead. The briefings are limited to NGO statements on ICESCR issues and strictly address the countries scheduled for review at the session. The process is similar for the HRC, although this is a more recent practice,[29] and meetings are private. This is certainly a key advantage compared to the NGO briefing practice of the CESCR, as it is thus ensured that human rights defenders participating in such meetings can raise their concerns freely without any fear of reprisals from their governments. This is particularly true since July 2016, when the public sessions of the UNTB started to be webcast live,[30] allowing anyone to follow the meetings of the Committees, including the formal NGO briefings.[31]

In addition to formal briefings, NGOs also have the opportunity to attend informal briefings. These are usually scheduled immediately before the examination of the relevant State report commences. Whilst the formal briefings allow NGO representatives to deliver statements, the informal briefings are usually viewed as an additional opportunity for members of the Committees to raise questions and seek clarification on issues mentioned in NGO reports.

NGOs tend to coordinate with each other in order to avoid duplication in their written submissions and subsequent oral presentations. This is possible with the support of third parties such as the Centre for Civil and Political Rights[32] or a national NGO working to correlate the efforts of the different stakeholders.[33] This greatly facilitates the organization of formal NGO briefings from an early stage, allowing NGOs to speak with one voice. In practice, the majority of NGOs that have submitted written information for the reporting procedure attend the sessions to brief the Committees' members. According to the internal figures of the Centre for Civil and Political Rights, 120 NGO representatives participated in the HRC's sessions in 2014, and 174 representatives attended the 2015 sessions.

In the context of the HRC, the Centre for Civil and Political Rights acts as the facilitator for the coordination of formal NGO briefings, aiming to avoid overlap in NGO statements and ensure a fair allocation of speaking time amongst the NGOs wishing to take the floor. The Centre also coordinates all of the informal briefings.

[28] See CESCR, 'Annex V' (n 4) 155, para 23.

[29] The formal briefings have been taking place since the 103rd session (October 2011). Their aim is to engage with the HRC 'during a formal closed meeting preceding the examination of the State party's report' (HRC, 'Relationship with NGOs' (n 10) para 10).

[30] See <www.webtv.un.org> accessed 4 April 2017.

[31] The review of Burundi by the Committee on the Elimination of Discrimination against Women (in October 2016) is a recent example wherein several national NGOs refused to participate in the formal briefing (which is also held in public and webcast) for fear of reprisals.

[32] The Centre for Civil and Political Rights organizes several national consultations prior to the review for the purpose of encouraging NGOs to participate in a joint consolidated NGO report. See eg the NGO report on Burundi (Actions des Chrétiens pour l'Abolition de la Torture and others, 'Rapport Alternatif de la société civile sur la mise en œuvre du Pacte International relatif aux Droits Civils et Politiques' (October 2014) <http://tbinternet.ohchr.org/_layouts/treatybodyexternal/Download.aspx?symbolno=INT%2fCCPR%2fCSS%2fBDI%2f18220&Lang=en> accessed 4 April 2017).

[33] See eg the testimony of Alex Neve, Secretary-General of Amnesty International Canada, in Brett and Mutzenberg, 'NGO Guidelines' (n 3) 15.

At this stage, it is prudent to address the extent to which the information contained in the NGO reports is taken into consideration by the Committees, and more specifically how this information is incorporated into and reflected in the outcome of the review, particularly in the concluding observations. For the purpose of this chapter, the Centre reviewed the NGO material received by the HRC at its 113th session (in March 2015)[34] and by the CESCR at its 56th session (in September 2015).[35] Figures indicate that, when NGOs submit global reports (covering several provisions of the ICESCR or the ICCPR), the majority of issues are taken into consideration and both the Lists of Issues and the concluding observations reflect the concerns highlighted by the NGOs. In cases where several global reports are submitted, the correlation of NGO concerns with Committee concerns can be very high. For instance, in the review of Cambodia, 87.5 per cent of the concerns raised in the List of Issues[36] were also mentioned in the four global NGO reports submitted, and 100 per cent of the concerns included in the concluding observations[37] were also reflected in the material submitted by civil society organizations (via five global NGO reports).

Also in the case of thematic reports, most of the concerns raised are fully reflected in the Lists of Issues and subsequently in the concluding observations. This is true also for very specific issues that are included in the NGO reports.[38] The analysis of NGO submissions for the Lists of Issues and for the reviews shows that thematic civil society groups cooperating with the Committees on a limited number of issues are usually well-organized and engage strategically with the members. They manage to submit information at this early stage, prior to the List of Issues, and then, at a later stage, for the dialogue with the State party. These NGOs comprehend how important it is to submit timely information to ensure that their issues remain high on the agenda, and these issues are usually well-reflected in the Lists of Issues and subsequently in the concluding observations.[39] This strategy of advocacy is sometimes

[34] The countries reviewed at the 113th session were Cambodia, Ivory Coast, Cyprus, Monaco, Croatia, and Russia.

[35] The countries reviewed at the 56th session were Burundi, Greece, Guyana, Iraq, Italy, Morocco, and Sudan.

[36] HRC, 'List of Issues in Relation to the Second Periodic Report of Cambodia' (19 August 2014) UN Doc CCPR/C/KHM/Q/2. A list of the written NGO replies to the List of Issues is available at <http://ccprcentre.org/doc/2015/03/CCPRCKHMQ2Add.1.pdf> accessed 4 April 2017.

[37] HRC, 'Concluding Observations on the Second Periodic Report of Cambodia' (27 April 2015) UN Doc CCPR/C/KHM/CO/2. A list of the NGO reports submitted for the review is available at <http://ccprcentre.org/country/cambodia> accessed 4 April 2017.

[38] See eg the NGO report from the European Association of Jehovah's Christian Witnesses on the violations against the Jehovah's Christian Witnesses in Russia (The European Association of Jehovah's Christian Witnesses, 'Complementary Submission to the UN Human Rights Committee Subsequent to the Adoption of the List of Issues' (18 February 2015) <http://tbinternet.ohchr.org/Treaties/CCPR/Shared%20Documents/RUS/INT_CCPR_CSS_RUS_19636_E.pdf> accessed 4 April 2017) and the related concluding observations on the Russian Federation (HRC, 'Concluding Observations on the Seventh Periodic Report of Russia' (28 April 2015) UN Doc CCPR/C/RUS/CO/7, para 20).

[39] See eg the specific contribution of the NGO coalition 'Cotton Campaign' in Uzbekistan. Their report (Cotton Campaign, 'Pre-Sessional Report on Forced Labour in Uzbekistan to the Country Report Task Force for the Adoption of the List of Issues' <http://tbinternet.ohchr.org/Treaties/CCPR/Shared%20Documents/UZB/INT_CCPR_ICO_UZB_17835_E.pdf> accessed 4 April 2017) was extensively taken into consideration in the List of Issues on Uzbekistan (HRC, 'List of Issues in Relation

conducted in a more systematic way by one specific NGO. If this systematic approach is successful, the same issue will therefore be addressed in the context of several countries' reviews and will be routinely discussed by the Committee. This is, for instance, the case for the regular submissions by the NGO International Fellowship of Reconciliation (IFOR) on the right to conscientious objection to military service. As a result of these submissions, this issue is now regularly taken into consideration in the Lists of Issues as well as in the concluding observations.[40]

Finally, from 2010 to 2016, a group of NGOs took the initiative to webcast the sessions of the UNTB, allowing video transmission of States parties' reviews. This process was carried out systematically for all the countries reviewed by the HRC,[41] but less so for the CESCR.[42] Since 2016, the OHCHR has taken over the webcasting of all of the sessions of all UNTB, acknowledging the precursor and leading role played by civil society in improving the outreach of the work of these bodies.

B. The role of NGOs in the elaboration of General Comments

The role of NGOs in the adoption of General Comments[43] is now well-established, and similar before both Committees. The CESCR's Guidelines for NGOs acknowledge the role of civil society organizations, which are granted permission to submit information to the Committee in writing 'during the stages of the drafting and discussion of a general comment'.[44] However, in practice, NGOs can only intervene

to the Fourth Periodic Report of Uzbekistan' (21 November 2014) UN Doc CCPR/C/UZB/Q/4, para 15) and in the concluding observations (HRC, 'Concluding Observations on the Fourth Periodic Report of Uzbekistan' (17 August 2015) CCPR/C/UZB/CO/4, para 19). See also the NGO reports on discrimination against lesbian, gay, bisexual, and transgender (LGBT) persons in Cambodia (Kaleidoscope Human Rights Foundation, 'Shadow Report to the UN Human Rights Committee Regarding Cambodia's Protection of the Rights of LGBTI Persons' <http://tbinternet.ohchr.org/Treaties/CCPR/Shared%20Documents/KHM/INT_CCPR_ICO_KHM_17317_E.pdf> accessed 4 April 2017) and how the issue is reflected in the List of Issues (HRC, 'List of Issues: Second Report of Cambodia' (n 36) para 5) and the concluding observations (HRC, 'Concluding Observations: Second Report of Cambodia' (n 37) para 9).

[40] See eg Cyprus, where an NGO report (IFOR and Conscience and Peace Tax International, 'Submission to the 111th Session of the Human Rights Committee for the attention of the Country Report Task Force on Cyprus' (April 2014) <http://tbinternet.ohchr.org/Treaties/CCPR/Shared%20Documents/CYP/INT_CCPR_ICO_CYP_17198_E.doc> accessed 4 April 2017) is reflected in the List of Issues (HRC, 'List of Issues in Relation to the Fourth Periodic Report of Cyprus' (19 August 2014) CCPR/C/CYP/Q/4, para 24) or Austria, where the List of Issues (HRC, 'List of Issues in Relation to the Fifth Periodic Report of Austria' (28 April 2015) CCPR/C/AUT/Q/5, para 18) and the concluding observations (HRC, 'Concluding Observations on the Fifth Periodic Report of Austria' (3 December 2015) CCPR/C/AUT/CO/5, paras 33–34) adequately take into consideration the report submitted by IFOR (IFOR, 'Submission to the 113th Session of the Human Rights Committee for the Attention of the Country Report Task Force on Austria' (December 2014) <http://tbinternet.ohchr.org/Treaties/CCPR/Shared%20Documents/AUT/INT_CCPR_ICO_AUT_19177_E.doc> accessed 4 April 2017).

[41] From 2010 to 2016, the webcasting of the sessions of the HRC was carried out by the Centre for Civil and Political Rights. The archive of the session is available at <www.treatybodywebcast.org> accessed 4 April 2017.

[42] This irregularity can be attributed to the fact that no NGOs are specifically dedicated to the CESCR.

[43] ICCPR art 40(4) and ICESCR art 19.

[44] CESCR, 'Annex V' (n 4), 157, para 34.

before the Committee initiates its drafting process, at the occasion of the regular '(half-)days of general discussion'. The objective of such general discussion, which allows NGOs to submit written information prior to the meeting and to deliver oral statements, is to 'help the Committee to lay the basis for a future general comment'.[45]

The HRC has taken much longer to accept the idea of a 'day of general discussion',[46] although since its early days NGOs have submitted informal written material at every stage of the drafting of General Comments.[47] In 2012, the HRC finally decided to host 'half-days of general discussion' prior to the beginning of the drafting process of the General Comment on article 9.[48] In July 2015, a similar set-up was established for the drafting of the General Comment on article 6. These general discussions were held in public and well-attended, with several dozen NGOs participating in the dialogue and providing 117 written submissions.[49] In addition, as opposed to those of the CESCR, the HRC's meetings devoted to the actual drafting of the General Comments are open to the public. Although NGOs cannot directly intervene in the drafting process, the publicity that surrounds the debate before the HRC ensures a certain level of transparency. In addition, NGOs have the possibility to comment on the draft of the General Comment once the first reading is completed. This opportunity is given to all stakeholders (including the States parties) and is not limited to NGOs.[50]

Given the fact that the introduction of the HRC's 'half-days of general discussion' is a recent development, it is difficult to assess the impact of NGOs on the drafting process of General Comments. Preliminary analysis shows, however, that information submitted by NGOs on the occasion of the July 2015 'half-day of general discussion' had a limited influence on the original draft prepared by the Rapporteurs. This is mainly due to the nature of a General Comment, which 'usually codifies the Committee's practice'[51] and therefore focuses primarily on the HRC's findings (either in its Views or its concluding observations). In that context, the contributions have a limited impact, as the HRC will not be inclined to follow new positions

45 CESCR, 'Working Methods' <www.ohchr.org/EN/HRBodies/CESCR/Pages/WorkingMethods.aspx> accessed 4 April 2017, part G, para 49. The first 'day of general discussion' took place in 1989 and concerned the right to food. See the list of the previous days of general discussion held by the CESCR at CESCR 'General Discussion Days' <www.ohchr.org/EN/HRBodies/CESCR/Pages/DiscussionDays.aspx> accessed 4 April 2017.

46 NGOs called for a better participation of civil society in the drafting process of the General Comments. A similar proposal was made by academics; see Helen Keller and Leena Grover, 'General Comments of the Human Rights Committee and their Legitimacy' in Helen Keller and Geir Ulfstein (eds), *UN Human Rights Treaty Bodies: Law and Legitimacy* (CUP 2012) 115, 190.

47 ibid.

48 HRC, 'Issues for Consideration During the Half-day General Discussion in Preparation for a General Comment on Article 9 (Liberty and Security of Person) of the ICCPR' (17 August 2012) UN Doc CCPR/C/105/3, para 2. The organization of a (half)-day of general discussion is also formally mentioned in the Guidelines for NGOs of the HRC (HRC, 'Relationship with NGOs' (n 10) para 14).

49 HRC, 'Written Contributions for the Half Day of Discussion' (2015) <www.ohchr.org/EN/HRBodies/CCPR/Pages/WCRightToLife.aspx> accessed 20 May 2017.

50 HRC, 'Summary record of the 3154th meeting' (27 March 2015) UN Doc CCPR/C/SR.3154, para 20.

51 HRC, 'Summary record of the 3185th meeting' (14 July 2015) UN Doc CCPR/C/SR.3185, para 2.

suggested by NGOs that are not strictly corroborated by its own findings. This situation is even truer when the NGOs' contributions reflect positions that are not in line with the HRC's position.[52]

C. The role of NGOs in the individual communications procedure under the Optional Protocols

NGO interaction with the Committees is not limited to the reporting procedure and the drafting of General Comments. NGOs also have an important role to play—albeit a more discrete one—in the individual communications procedure under the Optional Protocols. This is particularly true regarding the individual communications submitted to the HRC, which has a long history of NGO engagement with victims of ICCPR rights violations by assisting them and providing them with support to file their complaints. This is acknowledged by the HRC, which has stated that 'NGOs play an important role in providing assistance to alleged victims of human rights violations under the Covenant in submitting individual communications to the Committee under the Optional Protocol'.[53] The most common form of NGO engagement occurs when an NGO represents a petitioner, whilst in other instances NGOs can act on behalf of victims.[54] Several NGOs regularly submit cases before the HRC with the specific objective to develop strategic litigation. This may refer to particular issues not yet addressed by the Committee or be related to States parties where the relevant jurisprudence is still embryonic. This strategic litigation has led to the emergence of key HRC jurisprudence. One of the most remarkable examples is the recent development of the jurisprudence on enforced disappearances and its consequences for ICCPR article 6. In 2013–15, the Committee received several cases from the same NGO, 'Trial International', on cases of enforced disappearance in Bosnia and Herzegovina[55] and in Nepal.[56] Those cases have allowed the HRC to develop a clear jurisprudence clarifying—after much debate—how cases of enforced disappearance violate ICCPR article 6. NGO engagement also encouraged

[52] Amongst 117 NGOs contributions submitted to the July 2015 'day of general discussion' on the General Comment on art 6, 49 contributions emanated from 'Pro Life' organizations advocating for the application of art 6 to unborn children.

[53] HRC, 'Relationship with NGOs' (n 10) para 8.

[54] Sękowska-Kozłowska, 'Individual Communications' (n 7) 370. In contrast, NGOs face difficulties when they aim to submit a petition in their own name: art 1 of the OP1-ICCPR clearly limits the possibility of submitting a communication to individuals. The HRC remains particularly restrictive in its interpretation of art 1, considering most of the cases submitted by NGOs as petitioners inadmissible.

[55] Eight cases submitted by Trial International against Bosnia Herzegovina were decided by the HRC between 2014 and 2015. A list of the cases is available online (Centre for Civil and Political Rights, 'Bosnia and Herzegovina' <http://ccprcentre.org/country/bosnia_and_herzegovina> accessed 15 May 2017).

[56] Four cases submitted by Trial International against Nepal were decided by the HRC between 2014 and 2015: *JM Basnet and TB Basnet v Nepal*, HRC Communication No 2051/2011 (29 October 2014) UN Doc CCPR/C/112/D/2051/2011; *Bhandari v Nepal*, HRC Communication No 2031/2011 (29 October 2014) UN Doc CCPR/C/112/D/2031/2011; *Katwal v Nepal*, HRC Communication No 2000/2010 (1 April 2015) UN Doc CCPR/C/113/D/2000/2010; *AS v Nepal*, HRC Communication No 2077/2011 (6 November 2015) UN Doc CCPR/C/115/D/2077/2011.

the development of country-specific jurisprudence where the engagement of one particular NGO was at the origin of the submission of several cases against a particular State.[57]

In an interesting development, NGOs can now submit third-party interventions, such as *amicus curiae* briefs, regarding cases currently pending before the CESCR. This approach, taken on the grounds that third-party interventions are permissible under OP-ICESCR article 8(3), was confirmed in June 2015.[58] At that time, a first submission from the International Network for Economic, Social and Cultural Rights (ESCR-Net) was admitted by the CESCR.[59] Of course, such interventions are possible only with the consent of the complainant. After a similar request was made to the HRC by the NGOs,[60] the Committee is also considering the possibility of receiving third-party interventions, although no formal decisions have been made yet.

III. The Emerging Role of NGOs in the Implementation of Concluding Observations and Views

For several years, the role of NGOs was limited to the reporting procedure and, to a lesser extent, the individual complaints procedure. With the development of the follow-up procedure on the implementation of the concluding observations and the Views adopted under the OP1-ICCPR and OP-ICESCR, NGOs have started to play a greater role in promoting full implementation of the Committees' recommendations, not only at the national level but also as actors in the follow-up procedure. However, this role mainly reflects the procedure before the HRC, as the CESCR follow-up procedure remains embryonic.

A. At the national level

1. Raising awareness at the national level

Both Committees acknowledge that NGOs have a crucial role to play at the national level once the concluding observations have been adopted at the end of the reporting procedure. The primary role of NGOs, as suggested by both Committees, is to 'give publicity to the Concluding Observations locally and nationally'.[61] Regarding the

[57] See eg the five cases submitted by the NGO Kazakhstan International Bureau for Human Rights and Rule of Law against Kazakhstan between 2010 and 2012 (Centre for Civil and Political Rights, 'Kazakhstan' <http://ccprcentre.org/country/kazakhstan> accessed 18 May 2017).

[58] See *IDG v Spain* (2015) CESCR Communication No 2/2014 (13 October 2015) UN Doc E/C.12/55/D/2/2014, para 6.1.

[59] See ESCR-Net, 'Intervención de tercero' <www.escr-net.org/es/recursos/red-desc-intervencion-tercero-comite-desc-comunicacion-22014> accessed March 2016.

[60] See eg the 'Pretoria Statement on the Strengthening and Reform of the UN Human Rights Treaty Body System' (20–21 June 2011) <www2.ohchr.org/english/bodies/HRTD/docs/PretoriaStatement.doc> accessed 4 April 2017, which was signed by twelve NGOs.

[61] CESCR, 'Non-governmental Organization Participation in the Activities of the Committee on Economic, Social and Cultural Rights' (7 July 2000) UN Doc E/C.12/2000/6, para 26.

ICCPR, the Centre for Civil and Political Rights, which is involved in the follow-up phase, suggests several activities that may be carried out by national NGOs in order to raise awareness of the Committee's recommendations.[62] These activities include translating the concluding observations into national languages,[63] organizing press conferences,[64] or writing op-ed pieces,[65] all with the same goal in mind: to ensure that the different stakeholders, and more broadly the public, are aware of the Committees' recommendations.

2. *Engaging with national stakeholders*

Too often, NGOs limit their activities to lobbying the Committees whilst their country is under review, since they want to make sure that their main subjects of concern are considered seriously. They tend to forget that similar if not greater effort should be made to ensure that national authorities take the concluding observations seriously and initiate concrete action to implement them. It is therefore strongly recommended that NGOs initiate a medium- or long-term dialogue with national authorities, firstly to ensure that the latter are aware of the concluding observations, and secondly to learn more about any action taken by governments to implement the recommendations.

In order to initiate this dialogue with national authorities, the Centre for Civil and Political Rights, jointly with national NGOs, organizes regular in-country visits with members of the HRC.[66] These visits, though unofficial, are nonetheless organized in full cooperation with national authorities.[67] The various follow-up visits have shown that the authorities take these visits seriously and appreciate the possibility to continue the dialogue initiated during the review of the State report. Experience has shown that these visits are crucial for disseminating information about what is required of the State, as most of the stakeholders concerned are not aware of the concluding observations. This is also true for the members of Parliament, who are usually not part of the State delegation and do not participate in the review. They are often not aware of the recommendations made by the Committees, which raises

[62] Brett and Mutzenberg, 'NGO Guidelines' (n 3) 18.

[63] See eg the translation of the concluding observations on the second periodic report of Cambodia (HRC, 'Concluding Observations: Second Report of Cambodia' (n 37)) into Khmer (<http://ccprcentre.org/files/documents/CO-cambodia.pdf> accessed 4 April 2017).

[64] See eg the press conference organized in Abidjan by the NGO coalition in Ivory Coast on the review of the State report ('La situation des droits de l'Homme en Côte d'Ivoire examinée mercredi à Genève' (13 March 2015) <http://news.abidjan.net/h/528710.html> accessed 4 April 2017).

[65] See eg the op-ed written after the review of South Korea in October 2015 (Jung Hwan-bong and Choi Hyun-june, 'UN review finds regression on human rights in S. Korea' (7 November 2015) <http://english.hani.co.kr/arti/english_edition/e_national/716404.html> accessed 4 April 2017).

[66] The Centre for Civil and Political Rights has carried out several follow-up visits since 2010. See the 2014 annual report for an overview of the follow-up visits carried out recently (Centre for Civil and Political Rights, '2014 Annual Report' <http://ccprcentre.org/doc/2015/07/annual-rep-Online-View.pdf> accessed 4 April 2017).

[67] The follow-up visits are always discussed with national authorities and the agenda as well as the date of such visits are agreed with the Permanent Missions to the United Nations Office at Geneva.

concerns about their role in the implementation of these recommendations in relation to new legislation or amendments to existing laws.

In a few countries, national NGOs have been encouraged to adopt plans in order to better monitor the action taken by the authorities to implement recommendations. Such plans of action include regular meetings with authorities and in particular with the governmental bodies in charge of cooperation with the UNTB.[68] The possibility of organizing such activities depends very much on the national context and the willingness of the State authorities to cooperate with civil society. It is clear that follow-up activities are not possible in countries where civil society cannot work freely or is reduced to silence. For instance, recent reviews by the HRC of Uzbekistan, Turkmenistan, Yemen, or Sudan offered no opportunity for follow-up activities, either because of the absence of national NGOs or because of the States' refusal to initiate a dialogue with civil society.

B. Participation in the committees' follow-up procedure

1. *The embryonic follow-up procedure of the CESCR*

The follow-up procedure to the concluding observations was initially developed by the CESCR back in 1999.[69] This procedure authorizes the Committee to 'ask the State party to respond to any pressing specific issue identified in the concluding observations prior to the date that the next report is due to be submitted'.[70] NGOs can submit written information to the Committee, providing that it is specifically related to the recommendations selected for the follow-up procedure. As stated in its working methods, the Committee will 'consider and act upon the information received from sources other than a State party only in cases where such information has been specifically requested in its Concluding Observations'.[71] It is also specified that, with regard to other information (ie information not related to the recommendations selected for the follow-up procedure), the Committee is not 'in a position to consider and act upon such information without reopening its dialogue with a State party'[72] and will only consider this information in the subsequent review.

Analysis of the work of the CESCR shows that this procedure was not applied until very recently, and that the Committee was more inclined to request follow-up information to be reviewed at the occasion of the subsequent review. After a long debate, the CESCR finally decided in June 2017 to use its follow-up procedure in a more comprehensive way and to systematically identify up to three follow-up recommendations. In that regard, the Committee updated its working methods on

68 In many countries, there is a specific body in charge of the implementation of the recommendations, namely the National Mechanism for Reporting and Follow-up (NMRF). This body is a key partner for NGOs willing to engage with the government on follow-up to the UNTBs' recommendations. For more on the role of the NMRF, see OHCHR, 'A Practical Guide to Effective State Engagement with International Human Rights Mechanisms' (2016) <www.ohchr.org/Documents/Publications/HR_PUB_16_1_NMRF_PracticalGuide.pdf> accessed 4 April 2017.

69 CESCR, 'Report on the Twentieth and Twenty-first Sessions' (1999) UN Doc E/C.12/1999/11, *Official Records of the Economic and Social Council* 2000, Supplement No 2, 19, para 38.

70 ibid. 71 CESCR, 'Working Methods' (n 45) para 44. 72 ibid.

follow-up and formally adopted a note[73] which reaffirms that information from NGOs is welcome. This information has to be sent 'within 18 months after the adoption of the concluding observations or, at the latest, one month after the State party's follow-up report is made public'.[74] The note also clarifies that information submitted to the CESCR is made public.[75]

During the same June 2017 session, the CESCR decided to initiate a follow-up procedure to the Views adopted under the OP-ICESCR.[76] The working methods for this new procedure also provide the possibility for NGOs to engage with the CESCR, although this engagement is limited to the submission of information 'concerning the implementation of general recommendations'.[77] Moreover, the CESCR decided that the State party concerned will be able to comment upon the information provided by NGOs.[78]

At this stage, the opportunity for NGOs to participate in the follow-up procedure remains rather limited, although these recent developments will certainly prompt a stronger engagement from the NGO community.

2. *The key role of NGOs in the follow-up procedure of the HRC*

The practice adopted by the HRC is different from that of the CESCR, and allows for better interaction with civil society. Initiated in 2001[79] and further developed in 2013, the procedure foresees a specific role for NGOs. According to this follow-up procedure,[80] the HRC systematically selects between two and four recommendations as priorities and requests that States parties provide follow-up information within a one-year timeframe.[81] In his report, the Special Rapporteur responsible for the follow-up to concluding observations assesses the measures taken by the national authorities to implement the recommendations, with specific criteria on this adopted by the HRC in October 2011.[82] The HRC welcomes NGO submissions

[73] CESCR, 'Note on the Procedure for Follow-up to Concluding Observations' (2017) <www.ohchr.org/Documents/HRBodies/CESCR/Follow-upConcludingObservations.docx> accessed 21 July 2017.

[74] ibid para 4. [75] ibid para 4.

[76] CESCR, 'Working Methods Concerning the Committee's Follow-up to Views under the Optional Protocol to the International Covenant on Economic, Social and Cultural Rights' (2017) <www.escr-net.org/node/389644> accessed 21 July 2017.

[77] ibid para 4. [78] ibid para 4.

[79] HRC, 'Note by the HRC on the Procedure for Follow-up to the Concluding Observations' (21 October 2013) UN Doc CCPR/C/108/2. For the history of the procedure, see Patrick Mutzenberg, 'Agir pour la mise en œuvre des droits civils et politiques: l'apport du Comité des droits de l'homme' (l'Harmattan 2014) 193.

[80] For a complete overview of the follow-up procedure of the HRC, see HRC, 'Note on Follow-up' (n 79).

[81] ibid para 7.

[82] The replies received by the States parties are assessed against the following criteria: category A: Reply largely satisfactory; category B: Reply/action partially satisfactory; category C: Reply/action not satisfactory; category D: No cooperation with the Committee; and category E: The information or measures taken are contrary to or reflect rejection of the recommendation. See HRC, 'New Assessment of Follow-up replies' <http://tbinternet.ohchr.org/Treaties/CCPR/Shared%20Documents/1_Global/INT_CCPR_FGD_8108_E.pdf> accessed 10 February 2018.

as long as they focus on the recommendations selected for the follow-up procedure. These reports allow NGOs to indicate to the Committee the extent to which the recommendations have been effectively implemented.[83] Despite some suggestions to this end made by NGOs, the follow-up procedure does not allow NGOs to orally brief the HRC.[84]

The majority of States parties submit their follow-up reports to the HRC,[85] which in turn routinely analyses the measures taken to implement the recommendations and assesses the States parties based on the criteria mentioned above.[86] Similarly, civil society organizations are now generally familiar with the follow-up procedure, and the HRC receives numerous NGO follow-up reports each year. NGO feedback is systematically integrated into the reports of the Follow-up Rapporteur and usually taken into account in the follow-up assessment, although in some instances the HRC puts forth an alternative evaluation to that suggested by NGOs.[87]

The HRC has also reinforced its follow-up procedure regarding the Views adopted under the OP1-ICCPR, endorsing a similar approach to that developed regarding the concluding observations.[88] In its Guidelines for NGOs, the HRC has 'encouraged [NGOs] to submit follow-up information on the implementation of the Committee's Views'.[89] As in the follow-up to the concluding observations, the Committee's follow-up progress report on individual communications includes all of the information received from NGOs regarding measures taken to provide

[83] In order to support the work of NGOs in effectively reporting to the HRC, the Centre for Civil and Political Rights developed a template for the NGO follow-up report. It focuses on the measures taken by the authorities to ensure the implementation of recommendations and suggests additional action to fully implement them. It also includes similar categories of assessment to those adopted by the HRC. See Brett and Mutzenberg, 'NGO Guidelines' (n 3) 18 and HRC, 'Note on Follow-up' (n 79).

[84] The Committee Against Torture is the only UNTB that allocates a specific time to a formal NGO briefing dedicated to the follow-up to the concluding observations (see Committee against Torture, 'Working Methods' <www.ohchr.org/EN/HRBodies/CAT/Pages/WorkingMethods.aspx> accessed 4 April 2017, Part VIII: 'Participation of NGOs and NHRIs [national human rights institutions] in the activities of the Committee').

[85] The HRC has a specific webpage on the follow-up procedure where all the follow-up State reports are available (<http://tbinternet.ohchr.org/_layouts/TreatyBodyExternal/FollowUp.aspx?Treaty=CCPR&Lang=en> accessed 4 April 2017).

[86] One meeting per session is devoted to the follow-up to the concluding observations and to the Views, wherein the report of the Follow-up Rapporteur is adopted in a public meeting and posted on the relevant webpage of the session. See eg the HRC, 'Report on Follow-up to the Concluding Observations of October 2015' (21 December 2015) UN Doc CCPR/C/115/2 <http://tbinternet.ohchr.org/_layouts/treatybodyexternal/Download.aspx?symbolno=CCPR%2fC%2f115%2f2&Lang=en> accessed 4 April 2017.

[87] See eg the assessment of the follow-up report of Guatemala, in particular recommendation 7 (HRC, 'Report of the Special Rapporteur for Follow-up to Concluding Observations' (8 December 2014) UN Doc CCPR/C/112/2).

[88] The follow-up procedure on individual communications was established in July 1990 (39th session) according the HRC's Rules of Procedure, Rule 101 (HRC, 'Rules of Procedure' (n 26)). The adoption of categories of assessment to monitor the implementation of Views was initiated in October 2013 (109th session). See the introduction of HRC, 'Follow-up Progress Report on Individual Communications' (29 June 2015) UN Doc CCPR/C/113/3, para 3: '[a]t its 109th session [in October 2013], the Committee decided to include in its reports on follow-up to Views an assessment of the replies received from and action taken by States parties. The assessment is based on the criteria applied by the Committee in the procedure for follow-up to its concluding observations'.

[89] See HRC, 'Relationship with NGOs' (n 10) part B, para 13.

support and solutions for victims of human rights violations.[90] This information is systematically taken into consideration when the HRC assesses the implementation of its recommendations.[91]

C. Difficulties for NGOs in engaging systematically with the UN treaty body system

Despite a certain rigidity of the process of NGO engagement at the CESCR and the HRC, the level of NGO engagement is remarkably high. It is not only limited to the review itself, but also includes a strong involvement of civil society in the follow-up phase, at least as far as the HRC is concerned. The main challenge for NGOs is, rather, related to the capacity to consider the UNTB as a global and coherent system wherein the findings of the Committees should echo each other. So far, very few NGOs have managed to obtain such a global picture of the work of all of the UNTB on one given country. It is, in fact, difficult to find examples of NGOs that have engaged several UNTB on the same issues, thereby trying to establish links between the findings made by two or more Committees. This 'silo' approach undermines the efficiency of the advocacy strategy of civil society organizations that do not take the opportunity to address the same issue through various channels, and thus before various UNTB. The lack of a concerted approach on how NGOs address the issue of torture and cruel, inhuman, and degrading treatment and punishment in their advocacy work before the HRC and the Committee Against Torture (CAT) is illustrative. Indeed, in most of the recent appearances of particular States before the two bodies, none of the NGO submissions made direct reference to the review (and the findings) of the other Committee, therefore missing an opportunity to further advocate for specific measures to address the issue.[92]

The same 'silo' approach can be observed regarding advocacy efforts in the context of the Universal Periodic Review (UPR) procedure established by the Human Rights Council. Observers admit that the level of NGO engagement is important and that it represents one of the positive outcomes of this process.[93] However, analysis of the

[90] Information is also frequently submitted by the representatives of the author of a complaint.

[91] The HRC's follow-up progress reports on individual communications are available online (<www.ohchr.org/EN/HRBodies/CCPR/Pages/CCPRIndex.aspx> accessed January 2016).

[92] See eg the review of Colombia by the CAT in May 2015 (CAT, 'Concluding Observations on the Fifth Periodic Report of Colombia' (29 May 2015) CAT/C/COL/CO/5) and by the HRC in July 2016 (HRC, 'Concluding Observations on the Seventh Periodic Report of Colombia' (17 November 2016) CCPR/C/COL/CO/7). None of the NGOs that engaged with the CAT submitted information to the HRC. Similarly, there was no NGO report submitted to the HRC that refers to the previous CAT review. See also the review of the former Yugoslav Republic of Macedonia before the CAT in May 2015 (CAT, 'Concluding Observations on the Third Periodic Report of the Former Yugoslav Republic of Macedonia' (5 June 2015) CAT/C/MKD/CO/3) and the HRC in July 2015 (HRC, 'Concluding Observations on the Third Periodic Report of the former Yugoslav Republic of Macedonia' (16 August 2015) CCPR/C/MKD/CO/3), where none of the NGOs were in a position to submit a report to both Committees.

[93] See Ben Shokman and Phil Lynch, 'Effective NGO Engagement with the Universal Periodic Review' in Hilary Charlesworth and Emma Larking (eds), *Human Rights and the Universal Periodic Review: Rituals and Ritualism* (CUP 2015) 126.

submissions of NGOs to the UPR shows that most of the written information refers neither to the findings of the UNTB nor to the State implementation measures taken in response.[94] This is also the case when the same NGOs engage first with one specific Committee and then later on with the UPR.

The difficulties facing NGOs in streamlining their engagement before the UNTB echoes the struggle of the UNTB themselves to work in a more coherent and systematic manner and to create links amongst themselves and vis-à-vis the UPR. This can be explained by the variety of procedures available before the Committees and by the absence of a fixed and harmonized calendar of Committee reviews. It is also linked to difficulties in accessing the documents related to the UNTB reporting procedures and in extracting the relevant information from the various Committees' reports.

The capacity to digest all of the relevant information and to develop advocacy strategies that include a systematic and coordinated engagement before the different UN human rights mechanisms is certainly one of the main challenges ahead for NGOs.

IV. Conclusion

The purpose of this chapter has been to present the ways in which the HRC and the CESCR have developed a space for NGOs in their regular activities. Whilst the role of NGOs was not explicitly mentioned in the ICCPR or the ICESCR, both Committees have developed their practices over the years and have since established clear proceedings to ensure the meaningful participation of NGOs in all areas of work carried out by them. In practice, NGOs are more active in the context of the reporting procedure, submitting dozens of reports for each session prior to the List of Issues or for the review itself. Despite having to undergo a quite technical procedure, NGOs attend the Committees' sessions in large numbers, especially when there are specific meetings devoted to direct interaction between NGOs and Committee members. There is strong evidence to support the conclusion that concerns highlighted by NGOs are taken into serious consideration by the Committees, both in the case of global reports covering several provisions as well as thematic reports, which are usually fully reflected in the Committees' findings. However, NGO participation varies widely from one country to another, and in some instances there has been a complete lack of civil society involvement in the review process. This is of

[94] See eg the UPR review of Mongolia that took place May 2015 (UNGA, 'Report of the Working Group on the Universal Periodic Review: Mongolia' (13 July 2015) A/HRC/30/6), four years after the HRC's review in March 2011 (HRC, 'Concluding Observations on the Fifth Periodic Report of Mongolia' (2 May 2011) CCPR/C/MNG/CO/5). The submissions of NGOs to the UPR procedure hardly reflected the findings and recommendations of the HRC (only two out of sixteen NGO reports made such a link). Moreover, no information was provided about the measures taken by the State party to implement these recommendations. See the compilation of the reports of NGOs on the UPR of Mongolia (<www.upr-info.org/en/review/Mongolia/Session-22---May-2015/Civil-society-and-other-submissions#top> accessed 4 April 2017).

particular concern, as consequently the voice of civil society remains unheard and unrepresented in the Committees' findings.

Nonetheless, the role of NGOs is not limited to direct interaction with the HRC and the CESCR. Indeed, NGOs are taking an increasingly active role to ensure that the Committees' recommendations are actually implemented at the national level. This is a significant and recent trend demonstrated especially by the broad range of activities undertaken by NGOs, including lobbying governments to ensure that recommendations are taken seriously as well as monitoring the measures taken to implement them.

The outcome of these developments is that NGOs are now engaged in a more long-term process, whereby the reporting procedure is considered as part of a cycle that includes activities prior to and after the review. Ultimately, this long-term engagement between the Committees and civil society is key to ensuring that change actually occurs at the national level. These developments will hopefully coincide with and catalyse a process that will serve to further improve and harmonize the Committees' methods of work, with the ultimate objective being to see the UNTB working in a more coherent and coordinated way.

Bibliography

'La situation des droits de l'Homme en Côte d'Ivoire examinée mercredi à Genève' (13 March 2015) <http://news.abidjan.net/h/528710.html> accessed 4 April 2017

Brett, Peggy, and Mutzenberg, Patrick, 'UN Human Rights Committee, Participation in the Reporting Process: Guidelines for Non-Governmental Organisations (NGOs)' (2nd edn, Centre for Civil and Political Rights 2015)

Edwards, George E, 'Assessing the Effectiveness of the Human Rights Non-Governmental Organisations (NGOs) from the Birth of the United Nations to the 21st Century: Ten Attributes of Highly Successful Human Rights NGOs' (2009) 18 Michigan State Intl L Rev 171

Erdem Türkelli Gamze, Vandenhole, Wouter, and Vandenbogaerde, Arne, 'NGO Impact on Law-making: The Case of a Complaints Procedure under the International Covenant on Economic, Social and Cultural Rights and the Convention on the Rights of the Child' (2013) 5 J of Human Rights Practice 1

Gillibert, Patrice, 'Le Comité des droits de l'homme et les organisations non gouvernementales' in Emmanuel Decaux and Fanny Martin (eds), *Le Pacte international relatif aux droits civils et politiques: commentaire article par article* (Economica 2011)

Hwan-bong, Jung, and Hyun-june, Choi, 'UN review finds regression on human rights in S. Korea' (7 November 2015) <http://english.hani.co.kr/arti/english_edition/e_national/716404.html> accessed 4 April 2017

Keller, Helen, and Grover, Leena, 'General Comments of the Human Rights Committee and their Legitimacy' in Helen Keller and Geir Ulfstein (eds), *UN Human Rights Treaty Bodies: Law and Legitimacy* (CUP 2012)

Lintel, Ida, and Ryngaert, Cedric, 'The Interface between Non-governmental Organisations and the Human Rights Committee' (2013) 15 Intl Community L Rev 359

Mahon, Claire, 'Progress at the Front: The Draft Optional Protocol to the International Covenant on Economic, Social and Cultural Rights' (2008) 8 Human Rights L Rev 617

Mutzenberg, Patrick, 'Agir pour la mise en œuvre des droits civils et politiques: l'apport du Comité des droits de l'homme' (l'Harmattan 2014)

Sękowska-Kozłowska, Katarzyna, 'The Role of Non-governmental Organisations in Individual Communication Procedures before the UN Human Rights Treaty Bodies' in Alexander J Bělohlávek, Naděžda Rozehnalová, and Filip Černý (eds), *Czech Yearbook of International Law*, vol V (Juris 2014)

Shokman, Ben, and Lynch, Phil, 'Effective NGO Engagement with the Universal Periodic Review' in Hilary Charlesworth and Emma Larking (eds), *Human Rights and the Universal Periodic Review: Rituals and Ritualism* (CUP 2015)

Tyagi, Yogesh K, 'Cooperation between the Human Rights Committee and Nongovernmental Organizations: Permissibility and Propositions' (1983) 18 Texas Intl L J 273

Vandenhole, Wouter, *The Procedures before the UN Human Rights Treaty Bodies: Divergence or Convergence?* (Intersentia 2004)

PART II

THE PRESENT

What Is the Influence of the Covenants?

6

Influence of the ICESCR in Africa

Manisuli Ssenyonjo

I. Introduction

16 December 2016 marked fifty years since the United Nations (UN) General Assembly adopted the International Covenant on Economic, Social and Cultural Rights (the ICESCR or the Covenant),[1] the most comprehensive international treaty protecting economic, social, and cultural rights (ESCR), in 1966. Despite the ratification of the ICESCR by the vast majority (90 per cent) of African States,[2] there are no studies evaluating the 'influence' (effect) of the Covenant in Africa. As of May 2017, with the exception of only six states (Botswana, Comoros, Mozambique, the Sahrawi Arab Democratic Republic, São Tomé and Príncipe, and South Sudan), all other African states were parties to the ICESCR. Out of these, only eight States—Algeria, Egypt, Guinea, Kenya, Libya, Madagascar, South Africa, and Zambia—had entered reservations or made declarations to the ICESCR, in particular to article 13(2)(a) relating to the provision of 'compulsory and free' primary education.[3] It should be noted that, by the time the ICESCR entered into force on 3 January 1976, only seven African States had ratified the Covenant.[4] Eighteen more African States ratified the Covenant between 1976 and 1989.[5] The remaining twenty-three African States ratified the Covenant beginning in 1990, following increased global attention

[1] International Covenant on Economic, Social and Cultural Rights (opened for signature 16 December 1966, entered into force 3 January 1976) 993 UNTS 3.

[2] By December 2016, the following forty-nine African States were States parties to the ICESCR: Algeria, Angola, Benin, Burkina Faso, Burundi, Cape (Cabo) Verde, Cameroon, the Central African Republic (CAR), Chad, Congo, Côte d'Ivoire (Ivory Coast), the Democratic Republic of the Congo (DRC), Djibouti, Egypt, Equatorial Guinea, Eritrea, Ethiopia, Gabon, the Gambia, Ghana, Guinea, Guinea-Bissau, Kenya, Lesotho, Liberia, Libya, Madagascar, Malawi, Mali, Mauritania, Mauritius, Morocco, Namibia, Niger, Nigeria, Rwanda, Senegal, Seychelles, Sierra Leone, Somalia, South Africa, Sudan, Swaziland, Togo, Tunisia, Uganda, the United Republic of Tanzania, Zambia, and Zimbabwe. Comoros and São Tomé and Príncipe had signed the Covenant but had not ratified it. See United Nations Treaty Collection (UNTC), 'ICESCR' <https://treaties.un.org/doc/Publication/MTDSG/Volume%20I/Chapter%20IV/IV-3.en.pdf> accessed 20 June 2016.

[3] ibid.

[4] These were Kenya, Libya, Madagascar, Mali, Mauritania, Rwanda, and Tunisia.

[5] These were Algeria, the CAR, Cameroon, Congo, the DRC, Egypt, Gabon, the Gambia, Guinea, Equatorial Guinea, Morocco, Niger, Sudan, Senegal, Togo, Uganda, the United Republic of Tanzania, and Zambia.

The Human Rights Covenants at 50: Their Past, Present, and Future. Daniel Moeckli, Helen Keller, and Corina Heri. Published 2018 by Oxford University Press.

to the principles of universality, indivisibility, interdependence, and interrelatedness of *all* human rights[6] and the adoption of new (democratic and liberal) constitutions in Africa[7] protecting (some) ESCR alongside civil and political rights.[8] In addition, thirteen African States had signed the Optional Protocol to the ICESCR by December 2016,[9] though only four of these (Cape Verde, the CAR, Gabon, and Niger) had ratified it. The Covenant, therefore, enjoys widespread support in Africa, at least viewed in terms of ratification. What has been the influence of the Covenant on the protection of human rights in Africa at both regional and domestic levels? The term 'influence' is used in this chapter to refer to the Covenant's effect upon laws, policies, and practices in Africa that directly or indirectly contribute to the respect, protection, and fulfilment of ESCR. Key indicators of the Covenant's influence include: changes in laws and policies protecting ESCR at regional and national levels, including constitutional provisions and courts' jurisprudence; the domestic enforcement of such laws, including the availability and accessibility of effective remedies in instances in which ESCR are violated; and the practical enjoyment of ESCR. Has the Covenant had any influence on the African regional human rights instruments? What has been the influence of the Covenant, if any, on the constitutional protection of human rights and on national courts' jurisprudence in Africa?

It is widely accepted that the ratification of international human rights treaties is meaningful if the rights guaranteed in the relevant treaties have an effect upon domestic (national or municipal) protection of human rights, and effective remedies for violations of the protected rights are available and accessible at the domestic level.[10] Although the mere ratification of international treaties by States with poor human rights records without translating them into domestic law and policy does not necessarily result in improved outcomes in terms of human rights realization and redress of violations,[11] it might represent 'the initiation, culmination, or reconfiguration of a domestic political struggle' for better human rights practices.[12]

On the occasion of the fiftieth anniversary of the ICESCR in 2016, this chapter considers the influence of the ICESCR in Africa. To place the Covenant in the

[6] 'Vienna Declaration and Programme of Action' UN World Conference on Human Rights (Vienna, 14–25 June 1993) (25 June 1993) UN Doc A/CONF.157/24 (Part I) 20, para 5.

[7] See Henry Kwasi Prempeh, 'Africa's "Constitutionalism Revival": False Start or New Dawn?' (2007) 5 Intl J of Constitutional L 469.

[8] Christof H Heyns and Waruguru Kaguongo, 'Constitutional Human Rights Law in Africa: Current Developments' (2006) 22 South African J on Human Rights 673. See also the Constitutions of the fifty-four African Union member States (African Law Library, 'African Constitutions Collection' <www.africanlawlibrary.net/web/constitutions/overview> accessed 20 June 2016 and African Legal Centre, 'Constitutions of African Countries' <http://africanlegalcentre.org/constitutions-african-countries/> accessed 20 June 2016.

[9] These were Angola, Benin, Burkina Faso, Cape (Cabo) Verde, Congo, the DRC, Gabon, Ghana, Guinea-Bissau, Mali, Niger, Senegal, and Togo. See UNTC, Optional Protocol to the ICESCR <https://treaties.un.org/doc/Publication/MTDSG/Volume%20I/Chapter%20IV/IV-3-a.en.pdf> accessed 20 June 2016.

[10] See African Commission on Human and Peoples' Rights (the African Commission), *Anuak Justice Council v Ethiopia*, Communication No 299/05, 25 May 2006, AHRLR 97 (ACHPR 2006) paras 47–48.

[11] Oona A Hathaway, 'Do Human Rights Treaties Make a Difference?' (2002) 111 Yale L J 1870.

[12] Ryan Goodman and Derek Jinks, 'Measuring the Effects of Human Rights Treaties' (2003) 14 European J of Intl L 171, 174.

African regional human rights context, the analysis begins by discussing, in Section II, the influence of the ICESCR on the African regional human rights system. It then goes on to examine, in Section III, the influence of the ICESCR upon constitutional protection of human rights in Africa, drawing on examples from former British colonies in Africa (which apply a 'dualist' approach to the ICESCR) and former French and Portuguese colonies (which apply a 'monist' approach). It considers whether the rights protected in the ICESCR are part of national ('municipal', 'domestic', or 'internal') constitutional law in African States and, if so, where these rights feature in the hierarchy of the domestic legal order. The focus is primarily on the influence of the ICESCR on the constitutional protection of ESCR, because this is the most effective means of protecting human rights in Africa. All African States have, as their supreme law, national constitutions that protect human rights. The analysis examines whether the rights in the ICESCR have been invoked before, or 'applied' by, national courts in Africa. The chapter ends, in Section IV, with some concluding remarks about the influence of the Covenant in Africa on the occasion of its fiftieth anniversary, and comments on what needs to be done to maximize the influence of the ICESCR in the future.

II. Influence of the ICESCR on the African Regional Human Rights System

At the outset, it must be noted that the ICESCR influenced the drafting, legal protection, and development of ESCR in the African Charter on Human and Peoples' Rights (African Charter),[13] the African Union's primary human rights treaty, which was adopted on 27 June 1981, fifteen years after the adoption of the ICESCR. The African Charter, in articles 15–19, explicitly recognizes the following rights, which are also protected in the ICESCR: the right to self-determination, the right to work under equitable and satisfactory conditions, the right to enjoy the best attainable state of physical and mental health, the right to education, the protection of the family, and cultural rights. Although the formulation of the rights in the Charter is narrower than in the ICESCR, the Charter empowers the African Commission on Human and Peoples' Rights (the African Commission) to 'draw inspiration from international law on human and peoples' rights',[14] particularly from UN instruments such as the ICESCR, when interpreting the Charter. On this basis, the African Commission has relied on the ICESCR to develop the scope and content of ESCR as well as the corresponding State obligations.

For instance, in its 2016 Resolution on the Right to Education in Africa, the Commission specifically considered article 13 of the ICESCR and urged African States to 'guarantee the full scope of the right to education', including the 'provision of

[13] African Charter on Human and Peoples' Rights (opened for signature 27 June 1981, entered into force 21 October 1986) (1982) 21 ILM 58, ratified by fifty-three member States of the African Union (AU).

[14] ibid art 60.

pre-school, primary, secondary, tertiary, adult education and vocational training'.[15] Using the wording in ICESCR article 2, it called on States to adopt all necessary and 'appropriate' measures to the 'maximum of available resources' to promote, provide, and facilitate access to education for all in Africa.[16] Moreover, in 2010, the Commission adopted principles and guidelines on ESCR in Africa,[17] largely drawing inspiration from the ICESCR and the General Comments of the UN Committee on Economic, Social and Cultural Rights (CESCR), which have developed the normative content of ESCR and State obligations since the 1990s.[18] For example, in a decision adopted in 2009, the *Sudan Human Rights Organisation and Centre on Housing Rights and Evictions v the Sudan* (the *COHRE* case),[19] the Commission elaborated on the scope of the right to health under article 16 of the African Charter by relying on the interpretation of the right to health under the ICESCR. In this communication, the complainants alleged gross, massive, and systematic violations of human rights by the Republic of Sudan (involving the destruction of homes, livestock, and farms as well as the poisoning of water sources) against the indigenous Black African tribes in the Darfur region of Western Sudan, in particular members of the Fur, Marsalit, and Zaghawa tribes. It was claimed that the Republic of Sudan was complicit in looting and destroying foodstuffs, crops, and livestock as well as poisoning wells and denying access to water sources in the Darfur region, in violation of article 16. The Commission gave the right to health meaningful content by relying on the normative definition of that right as spelt out by the CESCR in its General Comment 14 on the 'right to the highest attainable standard of health'.[20] The Commission stated that:

> In its General Comment No. 14 on the right to health adopted in 2000, the UN Committee on Economic, Social and Cultural Rights sets out that, 'the right to health extends not only to timely and appropriate health care but also to the underlying determinants of health, such as, access to safe and portable water, an adequate supply of safe food, nutrition, and housing . . . '. In terms of the General Comment, the right to health contains four elements: availability, accessibility, acceptability and quality, and impose three types of obligations on States—to respect, fulfil and protect the right. In terms of the duty to protect, the State must ensure that third parties (non-state actors) do not infringe upon the enjoyment of the right to health.

[15] AU 'Resolution on the Right to Education in Africa' (20 April 2016) ACHPR/Res.346 (LVIII) 2016.

[16] ibid.

[17] See African Commission, 'Principles and Guidelines on the Implementation of Economic, Social and Cultural Rights in the African Charter on Human and Peoples' Rights' (47th Ordinary Session of the African Commission, Banjul, 12–26 May 2010) <www.achpr.org/files/instruments/economic-social-cultural/achpr_instr_guide_draft_esc_rights_eng.pdf> accessed 20 June 2016.

[18] The General Comments of the CESCR have been published in 'Note by the Secretariat, Compilation of General Comments and General Recommendations Adopted by Human Rights Treaty Bodies' (27 May 2008) HRI/GEN/1/Rev.9 (vol I) and at <http://tbinternet.ohchr.org/_layouts/treatybodyexternal/TBSearch.aspx?Lang=en&TreatyID=9&DocTypeID=11> accessed 20 June 2016.

[19] *Sudan Human Rights Organisation and Centre on Housing Rights and Evictions v the Sudan*, Communication Nos 279/03 and 296/05 (27 May 2009) EX.CL/600(XVII), Annex V (hereafter the *COHRE* case).

[20] CESCR, 'General Comment 14' in 'Compilation of General Comments' (2008) (vol I) (n 18).

> ... Violations of the right to health can occur through the direct action of States or other entities insufficiently regulated by States. According to General Comment 14, 'states should also refrain from unlawfully polluting air, water and soil ... during armed conflicts in violation of international humanitarian law ... States should also ensure that third parties do not limit people's access to health-related information and services, and the failure to enact or enforce laws to prevent the pollution of water ... [violates the right to health]'.[21]

Applying this understanding of the right to health—as extending to healthcare and the underlying determinants of health—to the facts, the Commission found that 'the destruction of homes, livestock and farms as well as the poisoning of water sources, such as wells exposed the victims to serious health risks and amounts to a violation of article 16 of the Charter'.[22] It is likely that in appropriate future communications the Commission will continue to rely on the General Comments of the CESCR to interpret ESCR rights under the Charter, as it did in the *Centre for Minority Rights Development (Kenya) and Minority Rights Group International on behalf of Endorois Welfare Council v Kenya*[23] and in *SERAC and CESR v Nigeria*.[24]

Accordingly, the Commission has interpreted the Charter as implicitly recognizing other ESCR which are protected by the ICESCR but not explicitly restated in the Charter, for example the right to an adequate standard of living (adequate food, clothing, housing, water, and sanitation), the right to social security, the right to rest and leisure, and the right to form and join trade unions.[25] This is so despite the fact that these rights were deliberately omitted from explicit protection in the African Charter so as to 'spare young states too many but important obligations'.[26] The African Court on Human and Peoples' Rights (ACtHPR or the Court) has also confirmed in *African Commission on Human and Peoples' Rights v Republic of Kenya* that, by virtue of articles 60 and 61 of the African Charter, it will draw inspiration

[21] The *COHRE* case (n 19) paras 209 and 210, emphasis removed.

[22] ibid para 212.

[23] *Centre for Minority Rights Development (Kenya) and Minority Rights Group International on behalf of Endorois Welfare Council v Kenya*, Communication No 276/2003 (25 November 2009) 27th Activity Report of the African Commission on Human and Peoples' Rights, para 200 (hereafter the *Endorois case*), citing with approval CESCR, 'General Comment 4' in 'Compilation of General Comments' (2008) (vol I) (n 18) para 18; and CESCR, 'General Comment 7' in 'Compilation of General Comments' (2008) (vol I) (n 18) para 14.

[24] African Commission, *Social and Economic Rights Action Center and Center for Economic and Social Rights v Nigeria*, Communication No 155/96, 27 October 2001, AHRLR 60 (ACHPR 2001) (hereafter *SERAC and CESR v Nigeria*).

[25] See eg *SERAC and CESR v Nigeria* (n 24), paras 60 and 65 (the Commission implied that the rights to housing or shelter and food are protected by the African Charter (n 13)); African Commission, *Sudan Human Rights Organisation and Another v Sudan*, Communication Nos 279/03 & 296/05, 27 May 2009, AHRLR 153 (ACHPR 2009), para 212 (the Commission stated that art 16 of the African Charter, which protects the right to health, implicitly protects the rights to adequate food and housing, including the prohibition on forced evictions, and also guarantees the right to water); African Commission, 'Guidelines for National Periodic Reports 1989' <www.achpr.org/instruments/guidelines_national_periodic_reports/> accessed 20 June 2016, paras II.A.31–34, para II.18, paras 9, 10, and 17; African Commission on Human and Peoples' Rights 'Resolution on Economic, Social and Cultural Rights in Africa' (7 December 2004) ACHPR/Res.73(XXXVI)04(2004), adopting the 'Statement on Social, Economic and Cultural Rights in Africa' (17 September 2004) (2005) 5 African Human Rights LJ 182, para 10.

[26] See Rapporteur's Report on the Draft African Charter on Human and Peoples' Rights, OAU Doc CAB/LEG/67/Draft Rapt Rpt (II) rev 4, para 13.

from 'other human rights instruments' including the ICESCR and the CESCR's General Comments to interpret the rights protected by the Charter.[27] In this case the Court found, inter alia, that the Republic of Kenya interfered with the enjoyment of the right to culture of the Ogiek population by evicting them from the Mau Forest, thereby restricting them from exercising their cultural activities and practices, in violation of article 17(2) and (3) of the African Charter. In arriving at this conclusion, the Court specifically relied on the CESCR's General Comment 21 to interpret the right to take part in cultural life under article 17 of the African Charter, observing that:

> The UN Committee on Economic, Social and Cultural Rights, in its General Comment on Article 15 (1)(a) also observed that 'the strong communal dimension of indigenous peoples' cultural life is indispensable to their existence, well-being and full-development, and includes the right to the lands, territories and resources which they have traditionally owned, occupied or otherwise used or acquired'.[28]

As a result, the Court accepted that the Ogiek population, as indigenous peoples, had the right to occupy their ancestral lands in the Mau Forest, as well as use and enjoy the said lands.

In addition, the African Commission's interpretation of the right to development under article 22 of the African Charter has been influenced by the ICESCR. The Commission has thus interpreted this right as 'an inalienable, individual or collective right, to participate in all forms of development, through the *full realisation of all fundamental rights*, and to enjoy them without unjustifiable restrictions'.[29] It follows that the right to development imposes obligations on States to respect, protect, and fulfil 'all fundamental rights', including civil and political rights as well as all ESCR. In this respect, the Commission has confirmed that '[t]he right to development will be violated when the development in question decreases the *well-being* of the community'.[30] Such well-being entails all ESCR protected in the ICESCR, such the right to housing, including the freedom 'to choose where to live',[31] the right to water and sanitation,[32] the right to adequate food,[33] and the right to economic self-determination, that is, the right of all peoples to 'freely dispose of their wealth and natural resources'.[34]

The content of some treaty provisions protecting ESCR in other, later African Union regional human rights treaties protecting specific vulnerable groups such as children, women, the youth, internally displaced persons, persons with disabilities, and older persons—in particular, the African Charter on the Rights and Welfare

[27] *African Commission on Human and Peoples' Rights v Republic of Kenya* App no 006/2012 (ACtHPR, 26 May 2017) para 108.

[28] ibid para 181, referring to CESCR, 'General Comment 21' (21 December 2009) UN Doc E/C.12/GC/21, paras 36–37.

[29] *Open Society Justice Initiative v Côte d'Ivoire*, Communication No 318/06 (27 May 2016), 38th Activity Report of the African Commission on Human and Peoples' Rights, para 183 (emphasis added).

[30] The *Endorois* case (n 23) para 294 (emphasis added).

[31] ibid para 278.

[32] ibid paras 87–92.

[33] *SERAC and CESR v Nigeria* (n 24).

[34] *Democratic Republic of the Congo v Burundi, Rwanda and Uganda*, Communication No 227/99 (29 May 2003) EX.CL/279 (IX), para 95; African Charter (n 13) art 21.

of the Child;[35] the Protocol to the African Charter on Human and Peoples' Rights on the Rights of Women in Africa;[36] the African Youth Charter;[37] the Convention for the Protection and Assistance of Internally Displaced Persons;[38] the Draft Protocol to the African Charter on Human and Peoples' Rights on the Rights of Persons with Disabilities in Africa;[39] and the Protocol to the African Charter on Human and Peoples' Rights on the Rights of Older Persons in Africa[40]—were heavily influenced, at least in part, by the ICESCR. The ACtHPR (or any other court that replaces it in the future) will enforce the ESCR protected in the ICESCR given that the Protocol to the African Charter on the Establishment of an African Court on Human and Peoples' Rights empowers the African Court to consider 'all cases and disputes submitted to it concerning the interpretation and application of the Charter, this Protocol and any other relevant Human Rights instrument ratified by the States concerned'.[41] This means that the Court will interpret relevant provisions of the African Charter in light of the provisions of any applicable international human rights instrument to which a participating State is a party, including the International Covenant on Civil and Political Rights (ICCPR),[42] the ICESCR, and the relevant jurisprudence of human rights bodies.[43]

[35] African Charter on the Rights and Welfare of the Child (opened for signature 11 July 1990, entered into force 29 November 1999) OAU Doc CAB/LEG/24.9/49 (1990) art 11 (right to education), art 12 (leisure, recreation and cultural activities), art 14 (right to health), art 15 (protection against child labour), art 18 (protection of the family), and art 21 (protection from harmful social and cultural practices). See also African Committee of Experts on the Rights and Welfare of the Child, *Institute for Human Rights and Development in Africa (IHRDA) and Open Society Justice Initiative on Behalf of Children of Nubian Descent in Kenya v the Government of Kenya*, Decision No 002/Com/002/2009 (22 March 2011) para 65.

[36] See Protocol to the African Charter on Human and Peoples' Rights on the Rights of Women in Africa (opened for signature 11 July 2003, entered into force 25 November 2005) Second Ordinary Session of the AU Assembly, Maputo <www.au.int/en/treaties/protocol-african-charter-human-and-peoples-rights-rights-women-africa> accessed 20 June 2016, arts 12–17, 22–24.

[37] See the African Youth Charter (opened for signature 2 July 2006, entered into force 8 August 2009), arts 13–16, 20, and 25.

[38] African Union Convention for the Protection and Assistance of Internally Displaced Persons in Africa (Kampala Convention) (opened for signature 22 October 2009, entered into force 6 December 2012), art 3(b) requires States to '[p]revent political, social, cultural and economic exclusion and marginalisation, that are likely to cause displacement of populations or persons by virtue of their social identity, religion or political opinion'.

[39] Draft Protocol to the African Charter on Human and Peoples' Rights on the Rights of Persons with Disabilities in Africa (adopted at the 19th Extra-Ordinary Session of the African Commission on Human and Peoples' Rights, held from 16–25 February 2016, not yet adopted by the Assembly of Heads of State) arts 12–21.

[40] Protocol to the African Charter on Human and Peoples' Rights on the Rights of Older Persons in Africa (opened for signature 31 January 2016, not yet entered into force) arts 2–19.

[41] Protocol to the African Charter on Human and Peoples' Rights on the Establishment of an African Court on Human and Peoples' Rights (opened for signature 10 June 1998, entered into force 25 January 2004) AU Doc OAU/LEG/EXP/AFCHPR/PROT(III) arts 3 and 7. See also the Protocol on the Statute of the African Court of Justice and Human Rights (opened for signature 1 July 2008, not yet entered into force) art 28(c).

[42] International Covenant on Civil and Political Rights (opened for signature 16 December 1966, entered into force 23 March 1976) 999 UNTS 171.

[43] See eg *In the Matter of Alex Thomas v United Republic of Tanzania* App No 005/2013 (ACtHPR, 12 November 2015) paras 88, 95–98, 114–121, 124, 130, 146, and 158, in which the Court relied on art 14(3)(d) of the ICCPR, decisions of the African Commission, judgments of the European Court of

The African Charter, which entered into force on 21 October 1986, five years after the entry into force of the ICESCR, places legally binding obligations on States parties and obliges them to 'recognize the rights, duties and freedoms' enshrined in the Charter and 'undertake to adopt legislative or other measures to give effect to them'.[44] This entails obligations to 'respect', 'protect', and 'fulfil' all rights protected by the African Charter, including ESCR.[45] As the Charter reaffirms in its preamble, 'civil and political rights cannot be dissociated from economic, social and cultural rights in their conception as well as universality and . . . the satisfaction of economic, social and cultural rights is a guarantee for the enjoyment of civil and political rights'.[46]

The African Commission has thus interpreted civil and political rights broadly to include ESCR. For example, the right to life under article 4 of the African Charter[47] has been understood to entail a 'dignified life'.[48] This includes State obligations to take 'preventive steps to preserve and protect the natural environment and humanitarian responses to natural disasters, famines, outbreaks of infectious diseases, or other emergencies'.[49] In addition, the Commission has interpreted the right to life as entailing State obligations 'to address more chronic yet pervasive threats to life, for example with respect to preventable maternal mortality, by establishing functioning health systems and eliminating discriminatory laws and practices which impact on individuals' and groups' ability to seek healthcare.'[50] Thus, the Commission has noted that violations of ESCR may, in certain circumstances, also entail violations of the right to life.[51] It is crucially important to note that the African Commission has strongly recommended that African States 'harmonize' domestic legislation with 'international human rights obligations'.[52] Have the African State parties to the ICESCR indeed harmonized their domestic laws with the ICESCR? The next section examines the influence of the ICESCR on domestic legal regimes in Africa with particular emphasis on whether the Covenant has influenced the constitutional protection of human rights.

Human Rights and the Inter-American Court of Human Rights, as well as Views of the Human Rights Committee. See also *Wilfred Onyango Nganyi and Nine others v United Republic of Tanzania* App No 006/2013 (ACtHPR, 18 March 2016) paras 165–79.

44 African Charter (n 13) art 1.

45 See eg African Commission, *Abdel Hadi, Ali Radi and others v Sudan,* Communication No 368/09, 5 November 2013, para 92: '[t]he Commission considers that if a State Party fails to respect, protect, promote or fulfil any of the rights guaranteed in the Charter, this constitutes a violation of Article 1 of African Charter.' See also *SERAC and CESR v Nigeria* (n 24) paras 44–47; African Commission, *Zimbabwe Human Rights NGO Forum v Zimbabwe*, Communication No 245/2002, Annex III, 15 May 2006, AHRLR 128 (ACHPR 2006) para 152.

46 African Charter (n 13) preamble, para 8.

47 ibid art 4 reads: 'Human beings are inviolable. Every human being shall be entitled to respect for his life and the integrity of his person. No one may be arbitrarily deprived of this right.'

48 See African Commission, 'General Comment 3' (2015) <www.achpr.org/files/instruments/general-comments-right-to-life/general_comment_no_3_english.pdf> accessed 20 June 2016, 3 and 43.

49 ibid para 41.

50 ibid para 42.

51 ibid para 43.

52 See eg African Commission, *Groupe de Travail sur les Dossiers Judiciaires Stratégiques v Democratic Republic of Congo*, Communication No 259/2002, 24 July 2011, para 92(i).

III. Influence of the ICESCR on the Domestic Protection of Human Rights in Africa

A. Are the rights protected in the ICESCR part of domestic constitutions in Africa?

State parties to the ICESCR are obliged to 'take steps' to the maximum of 'available resources' with a view to 'achieving progressively' the full realization of the rights recognized in the Covenant.[53] This must be done by all 'appropriate means, including particularly the adoption of legislative measures'.[54] While it is recognized that the ICESCR 'does not formally oblige States to incorporate its provisions in domestic law' and thus there is no obligation to adopt or incorporate the Covenant in national constitutions or other domestic laws, direct incorporation is highly desirable since it 'avoids problems that might arise in the translation of treaty obligations into national law, and provides a basis for the direct invocation of the Covenant rights by individuals in national courts.'[55]

The Covenant has influenced the domestic protection of human rights in Africa in several ways. Some African States have adopted constitutional provisions according priority to the provisions of international human rights treaties, including the ICESCR, over any inconsistent domestic laws, while others have transformed some rights protected in the Covenant into domestic law by supplementing or amending existing national constitutions and ordinary legislation, without invoking the specific terms of the Covenant. It is crucial to note that the CESCR has made important recommendations on the implementation of ESCR in several African States.[56] However, the influence of these recommendations generally remains limited since several African States still consider most ESCR (particularly the rights to adequate housing, food, water, and sanitation) to be merely non-justiciable 'directive principles' ('needs' or 'services') rather than fully justiciable human rights ('entitlements').[57] Thus, some national constitutions relegate the rights to health and education to the status of non-justiciable 'Principles of State Policy'.[58] Moreover, even a few of the States that have expressly given domestic effect to the African

[53] ICESCR art 2(1); CESCR, 'General Comment 3' in 'Compilation of General Comments and General Recommendations Adopted by Human Rights Treaty Bodies' (2003) UN Doc HRI/GEN/1/Rev.6, 14.

[54] ICESCR art 2(1).

[55] CESCR, 'General Comment 9' in 'Compilation of General Comments' (2003) (n 53) 54, para 8.

[56] See eg for a recent example, CESCR, 'Concluding Observations on the Third Periodic Report of Tunisia' (14 November 2016) UN Doc E/C.12/TUN/CO/3.

[57] See eg the constitutions of Nigeria (1999), Lesotho (1993), Sierra Leone (1991), Ghana (1992), Ethiopia (1994), Uganda (1995), and the Gambia (1996). See also *Khathang Tema Baitsokoli and Another v Maseru City Council and others*, Case (CIV) 4/05, CONST/C/1/2004, 20 April 2004, (2004) AHRLR 195 (LeCA 2004); High Court of Ghana, *Issa Iddi Abass & Ors v Accra Metropolitan Assembly and Anor*, Suit No Misc 1203/2002, 24 July 2002, unreported; Supreme Court of Ghana, *New Patriotic Party v Attorney-General* [1996–97] SCGLR 729.

[58] See eg Constitution of Lesotho, 1993, arts 27–28.

Charter (Nigeria and Benin)[59] consider most ESCR, including the right to free and compulsory primary education, to represent non-justiciable directive principles of State policy.[60] As a result, domestic courts in several States have been unwilling to enforce ESCR, claiming that they involve (non-justiciable) questions of 'a political nature'.[61]

In contrast, as a matter of international law, every State party to a treaty that has not submitted reservations is legally obliged to perform its obligations in 'good faith'.[62] Thus, a State party to the ICESCR may not invoke the provisions of its domestic law as a 'justification for its failure to perform a treaty'.[63] Rather, a State that has contracted valid international obligations, including those arising under the ICESCR, is 'bound to make in its legislation such modifications as may be necessary to ensure the fulfilment of the obligations undertaken'.[64] The ICESCR does not specify the specific means by which it is to be given effect or implemented in the national legal order.[65] As a result, every State enjoys a 'margin of discretion'[66] in adopting 'all appropriate means' to comply with its Covenant obligations. Nevertheless, 'legislative measures'[67] (eg the repeal or reform of laws that nullify or impair certain individuals' and groups' right to realize their ESCR, including where sexual and reproductive health, the legal prohibition of harmful practices, and the legal prohibition of harassment at work are concerned)[68] are in many instances 'highly desirable' and in some cases may even be 'indispensable'.[69] Such measures should provide for appropriate means of redress, or 'accessible, affordable, timely and effective' remedies, to ensure accountability.[70]

[59] See the African Charter on Human and Peoples' Rights (Ratification and Enforcement) Act, Cap 10, Laws of the Federation of Nigeria 1990 (Nigerian ACHPR Act); and Constitution of the People's Republic of Benin, 1990, art 7.

[60] See Constitution of the Federal Republic of Nigeria, 1999, ss 6(6)(c) and 18; ECOWAS Community Court, *Registered Trustees of Socio-Economic Rights and Accountability Project (SERAP) v Federal Republic of Nigeria and Universal Basic Education Commission* (30 November 2010) ECW/CCJ/APP/12/07 and ECW/CCJ/JUD/07/10; African Commission, *Socio-Economic Rights and Accountability Project v Nigeria*, Communication No 300/2005, 29 July 2008, AHRLR 108 (ACHPR 2008) paras 28, 29, 62–69.

[61] See eg Constitutional Court of Uganda, *Centre for Health, Human Rights and Development and three others v Attorney General*, Constitutional Petition No 16 of 2011, [2012] UGCC 4 (5 June 2012). But see Supreme Court of Uganda, *Centre for Health, Human Rights and Development & three others v Attorney General*, Constitutional Appeal No 1 of 2013 (30 October 2015), directing the Constitutional Court to hear the case on its merits before deciding whether it raised a 'political question'.

[62] Vienna Convention on the Law of Treaties (VCLT) (opened for signature 23 May 1969, entered into force 27 January 1980) 1155 UNTS 331, art 26.

[63] ibid art 27. The International Court of Justice (ICJ) has stated that VCLT art 27 reflects 'customary law' which binds all States (*Questions Relating to the Obligation to Prosecute or Extradite* (*Belgium v Senegal*) (Merits) [1949] ICJ Rep 422, 460).

[64] See *Exchange of Greek and Turkish Populations* (Advisory Opinion) PCIJ Rep Series B No 10, 20.

[65] CESCR, 'General Comment 9' (n 55) para 5.

[66] CESCR, 'General Comment 16' in 'Compilation of General Comments' (2008) (vol I) (n 18) para 32.

[67] ICESCR art 2(1).

[68] CESCR, 'General Comment 22' (4 March 2016) UN Doc E/C.12/GC/22, paras 34 and 49(a) and (b); CESCR, 'General Comment 23' (8 March 2016) UN Doc E/C.12/GC/23, paras 50 and 65(e).

[69] CESCR, 'General Comment 3' (n 53) para 3.

[70] CESCR, 'General Comment 9' (n 55) paras 2 and 9.

The ICESCR has influenced the legal protection of ESCR in African States in other ways. First, it has been applied as a guide for interpretation in some court judgments. Second, it has influenced the content of ESCR in national constitutions.[71] Third, it has specifically been referred to as a source of law in some national constitutions, and this has in turn influenced the adoption of certain ordinary legislation and policies essential to ESCR. All African States have constitutions containing provisions regulating the relationship between international treaties and national law and/or protecting human rights, including the right to life, human dignity, equality and non-discrimination, freedom from torture, inhuman, and degrading treatment, and some ESCR.[72] Although there is no uniform approach to treaties across Africa, African States generally apply either the 'dualist' or 'monist' approach to international treaties,[73] following the practice of domesticating international treaties applied by the former colonial powers in Africa, mainly Britain, France, and Portugal, though many constitutions embody both 'dualist' and 'monist' elements.

B. Dualist approaches to the ICESCR in Africa and their influence on human rights

The influence of the ICESCR in African States applying a 'dualist' approach to international treaties has depended on whether or not a particular State has adopted relevant domestic law (constitutional provisions or ordinary legislation) to give effect to its obligations under the Covenant. Generally, a dualist theoretical approach to the relationship between international and national law takes the view that international law regulates the relations between States whereas national law regulates the rights and obligations of individuals within a State.[74] In 'dualist' African States, mainly former colonies of the United Kingdom following the constitutional law tradition of that nation,[75] the principle is generally that international courts apply international law while domestic courts are obliged to apply domestic law and not international treaties, or at least that it is for the national court to decide which rule to apply.[76] Thus, international treaties such as the ICESCR, in whole or in part, are not applicable (and thus not ordinarily enforceable by the courts) unless they have been incorporated into national law (through incorporation or reception) by

[71] All African States have bills of rights in their constitutions. See African Legal Centre, 'Constitutions of African Countries' (n 8).

[72] ibid.

[73] For a discussion of the relationship between international treaties and domestic law, see Anthony Aust, *Modern Treaty Law and Practice* (3rd edn, CUP 2013) 159–77; James Crawford, *Brownlie's Principles of Public International Law* (8th edn, OUP 2012) 48–111; Malcolm N Shaw, *International Law* (7th edn, CUP 2014) 92–141; and David J Harris and Sandesh Sivakumaran, *Cases and Materials on International Law* (8th edn, Sweet & Maxwell 2015) 59–84.

[74] Crawford, *Brownlie's Principles* (n 73) 48.

[75] Lord Oliver, in *Maclaine Watson & Co v Dept of Trade and Industry* [1989] UKHL [1990] 2 AC 418, 500 (House of Lords), explained that 'a treaty is not part of English law unless and until it has been incorporated into the [domestic] law by legislation'. The former British colonies in Africa are: Botswana, Cameroon, the Gambia, Ghana, Kenya, Lesotho, Malawi, Mauritius, Mozambique, Namibia, Nigeria, Seychelles, Sierra Leone, South Africa, Swaziland, Tanzania, Uganda, Zambia, and Zimbabwe.

[76] Crawford, *Brownlie's Principles* (n 73) 48.

legislation in force to give effect to them.[77] The rationale for the dualist theory is to prevent the executive from being able to create law without observing the domestic constitutional requirements necessary for law-making (ie to prevent law creation by the executive without an Act of Parliament).[78] In States applying a 'dualist' approach to the ICESCR, domestic courts apply the Covenant as mediated by national legislation, and national legislation will prevail unless the issue can be resolved by interpretation. This means that, in 'dualist' States in Africa, the rights protected under the ICESCR and the jurisprudence developed by the CESCR are generally regarded as not directly enforceable unless incorporated into domestic law by legislation.

Furthermore, the influence of the Covenant has also depended on judicial attitudes towards the application of international treaties by domestic courts. Domestic judges are still reluctant to rely on the ICESCR and other international human rights treaties in the absence of domestic implementing legislation. Some constitutions of 'dualist' States have adopted in essence a monist approach regarding the relationship between international law and national law. For example, although the Constitution of Namibia provides that 'the general rules of public international law and international agreements' are binding and form part of domestic law unless otherwise provided by the Constitution or an Act of Parliament,[79] domestic courts have shown unwillingness to invoke international human rights treaties, including the ICESCR.[80] This has led to the absence of jurisprudence invoking Covenant rights and reluctance to apply other human rights treaties.

For example, the Supreme Court of Namibia stated that an international treaty ratified by Namibia (in this case the Convention on the Elimination of All Forms of Discrimination against Women,[81] which had not been implemented by domestic legislation) was 'subject to the Constitution and cannot change the situation'[82]

[77] See eg the Constitution of the Kingdom of Swaziland, 2005, s 238(4), which provides that: '[u]nless it is self-executing, an international agreement becomes law in Swaziland only when enacted into law by Parliament'. The Constitution of the Republic of South Africa, 1996, s 231(4), provides that: '[a]ny international agreement becomes law in the Republic when it is enacted into law by national legislation; but a self-executing provision of an agreement that has been approved by Parliament is law in the Republic unless it is inconsistent with the Constitution or an Act of Parliament' (see also *Glenister v President of the Republic of South Africa and others* (CCT 48/10) [2011] ZACC (Constitutional Court of South Africa) 6, para 92, and *Azanian Peoples Organization (AZAPO) and others v President of the Republic of South Africa and others* (CCT 17/96) [1996] ZACC 16, para 26).

[78] See eg *Re McKerr* [2004] UKHL 12, [2004] 1 WLR 807, Lord Steyn; *R v Jones* [2006] UKHL 16, [2006] 2 WLR 772, Lord Bingham; *R (Bancoult) v Secretary of State for Foreign and Commonwealth Affairs (No 2)* [2009] AC 453, para 44, Lord Hoffmann; Albert Venn Dicey, *Introduction to the Study of the Law of the Constitution* (8th edn, Macmillan 1915) 38, stating that Parliament has 'the right to make or unmake any law whatsoever; and further, no person or body is recognised by the law as having a right to override or set aside the legislation of Parliament'.

[79] Constitution of the Republic of Namibia, 1990, art 144.

[80] See CESCR, 'Concluding Observations on the Initial Periodic Report of Namibia' (23 March 2016) UN Doc E/C.12/NAM/CO/1, para 6. See also *Michael Andreas Müller and Imke Engelhard v Namibia*, CESCR Communication No 919/2000 (26 March 2002) UN Doc CCPR/C/74/D/919/2000.

[81] Convention on the Elimination of All Forms of Discrimination against Women (CEDAW) (opened for signature 18 December 1979, entered into force 3 September 1981) 1249 UNTS 13.

[82] Supreme Court of Namibia, *Michael Andreas Müller v President of Namibia* (SA 2/98) [1999] NASC 2.

relating to Namibia's legislation, which discriminated on the basis of sex in relation to the right to assume the surname of one's spouse on marriage.[83] This led the UN Human Rights Committee to find a violation of the right to equal protection of the law without discrimination under article 26 of the ICCPR.[84]

At the time of writing, in 2017, although most African States applying a 'dualist' approach to international treaties had adopted some policy and legislative measures (constitutional provisions and/or ordinary domestic legislation) protecting some aspects of ESCR, they had not enacted domestic legislation to explicitly and fully incorporate or give full effect to the ICESCR in national laws so as to ensure the applicability of all Covenant rights in domestic courts.[85] This non-domestication approach is also generally applied to other international and regional human rights treaties.[86] As noted above, Nigeria explicitly incorporated the African Charter into Nigerian law in 1990 by providing that the African Charter's provisions 'have force of law in Nigeria and shall be given full recognition and effect and be applied by all authorities and persons exercising legislative, executive or judicial powers in Nigeria'.[87] More than twenty-five years later, it had not extended the same treatment to the ICESCR. It remains unclear why the Nigerian authorities deemed it 'necessary and expedient'[88] to incorporate the African Charter, thereby making it possible for domestic courts to directly 'apply' the Charter and allowing individuals and groups to 'resort to its provisions to obtain redress in [the Nigerian] domestic courts',[89] but have not extended this approach to the ICESCR.

It is well known that, as a precondition to independence, most 'dualist' African States adopted constitutions that drew heavily from the European Convention on Human Rights.[90] Their bills of rights therefore provide exclusive protection of civil and political rights and the right to property of nationals of the former colonial power.[91] Thus, historically, some domestic courts in 'dualist' African States have referred to international treaties protecting civil and political rights, such as the ICCPR, rather than to the ICESCR when applying and interpreting relevant

[83] Aliens Act No 1 of 1937, as amended by Proclamation AG No 15 of 1989, s 9.

[84] *Müller v Namibia* (n 80) para 6.8.

[85] See eg CESCR, 'Concluding Observations on the Initial Periodic Report of Uganda' (24 June 2015) UN Doc E/C.12/UGA/CO/1, paras 4–5; CESCR, 'Concluding Observations on the Combined Second to Fifth Periodic Reports of Kenya' (4 March 2016) UN Doc E/C.12/KEN/CO/2-5, paras 5–6; Nana Tawiah Okyir, 'Toward a Progressive Realisation of Socio-Economic Rights in Ghana: A Socio-Legal Analysis' (2017) 51 African J of Intl and Comparative L 91; Howard Chitimira, 'An Analysis of Socio-Economic and Cultural Rights Protection under the Zimbabwe Constitution of 2013' (2017) 61 J of African L.

[86] As evidenced by a number of domestic constitutions (n 57). See also Bonita Meyersfeld, 'Domesticating International Standards: The Direction of International Human Rights Law in South Africa' (2015) 8 Constitutional Court Review 399.

[87] The Nigerian ACHPR Act (n 59) art 1.

[88] ibid preamble.

[89] Supreme Court of Nigeria, *Sanni Abacha and others v Gani Fawehinmi* (2001) AHLRR 172, [2002] 3 LRC 296.

[90] Convention for the Protection of Human Rights and Fundamental Freedoms (European Convention on Human Rights, as amended) (ECHR).

[91] See eg the bills of rights contained in the following constitutions: Constitution of Nigeria, 1960; Constitution of Uganda, 1962; Constitution of Kenya, 1969.

domestic law.[92] Given increased attention to the need to address widespread poverty, the inequitable distribution of resources, and systematic or widespread violations of ESCR (eg the rights to education, health, adequate food, housing, water, and sanitation) in many African States, several States have adopted new constitutions and other domestic legislation protecting at least some ESCR, particularly the rights of vulnerable and marginalized groups, since the 1990s.[93] This process was influenced in part (although not explicitly) by the ICESCR.

To date, in many African States, there have been no cases in which the ICESCR has been applied before domestic courts. Although domestic courts in Africa have handed down significant judgments concerning some aspects of ESCR, such as the protection of pregnant school girls and women in higher education against discrimination in education[94] and the protection of individuals from sterilization or compulsory testing on account of their Human Immunodeficiency Virus (HIV) positive status without informed consent,[95] most domestic courts do not regularly take into account the ICESCR when interpreting and applying domestic law.

For example, the Constitution of the Kingdom of Swaziland, 2005, in its section 29(6), protects the right to free primary education by providing that '[e]very Swazi child shall within three years of the commencement of this Constitution have the right to free education in public schools at least up to the end of primary school, beginning with the first grade.' The Supreme Court of Swaziland, contrary to the ICESCR,[96] held that the right to education, including primary education, could only be progressively realized subject to the availability of resources.[97] Thus, schools continued to levy compulsory parental contributions (indirect costs) for primary education, such as payment for school uniforms, which restrict access to primary education for children from families with high levels of poverty, particularly for girls.

[92] See eg High Court of Tanzania, *Ephraim v Pastory* [1990] Civil Appeal No 70 of 1989, (2001) AHRLR 236, para 10; Zimbabwe Supreme Court, *Kachingwe and others v Minister of Home Affairs and Another* [2005] ZWSC 134, (2005) AHRLR 288, paras 50–72.

[93] Constitution of Kenya, 2010, art 21(3). See also the Constitution of Zimbabwe, 2013, arts 63–65, 71–75, and 80–83; Constitution of Mozambique, 2004, arts 82–95; Constitution of the Republic of Seychelles, 1993, arts 26–39; Constitution of Malawi, 1994, s 30.

[94] See eg *Head of Dept, Dept of Education, Free State Province v Welkom High School and Another; Head of Dept, Dept of Education, Free State Province v Harmony High School and Another* (CCT 103/12) [2013] ZACC 25; Botswana Court of Appeal, *Student Representative Council of Molepolole College of Education v Attorney General* [1995] (3) LRC 447; Zimbabwe Supreme Court, *Lloyd Chaduka and Morgenster College v Enita Mandizvidza*, Judgment No SC 114/2001, Civil Appeal No 298/2000.

[95] *Government of the Republic of Namibia v LM and others* (SA 49/2012) [2014] NASC 19; *Kenya Legal and Ethical Network on HIV & AIDS (KELIN) & Three Others v Cabinet Secretary Ministry of Health & Four Others*, Petition No 250 of 2015 [2016] eKLR.

[96] The minimum core obligation of the State includes the obligation to provide primary education which is 'compulsory' and 'available free to all'. See ICESCR art 13(2)(a); CESCR, 'General Comment 11' in 'Compilation of General Comments' (2008) (vol I) (n 18) paras 6–7; CESCR, 'General Comment 13' in 'Compilation of General Comments' (2008) (vol I) (n 18) para 57; CESCR, 'Concluding Observations on the Initial Periodic Report by Cameroon' (8 December 1999) UN Doc E/C.12/1/Add.40, paras 27 and 47; CEDAW Committee 'Concluding Observations on the Combined Initial and Second Periodic Reports of Swaziland' (24 July 2014) UN Doc CEDAW/C/SWZ/CO/1-2, paras 30–31.

[97] Supreme Court of Swaziland, *Swaziland National Ex-Miners Workers Association v The Minister of Education & others* (2010) Civil Appeal Case No 2/10, [2010] SZSC 35, paras 16–21.

However, some domestic courts in Africa have relied on provisions of the ICESCR and other regional and international human rights instruments[98] to interpret and apply relevant domestic law even before ratification of the ICESCR.[99] For example, the Covenant has specifically been referred to as a source of interpretation in court judgments in Kenya 'for the purpose of removing ambiguity or uncertainty from national constitutions, legislation or common law'.[100] This general approach involving the use of international treaties to interpret ambiguous domestic law has also been used by other domestic courts in Africa. Thus, in August 2015 the Supreme Court of Uganda relied on the CEDAW[101] to interpret article 33(6) of the country's Constitution, 1995, which prohibits 'laws, cultures, customs or traditions which are against the dignity, welfare or interest of women or which undermine their status'.[102]

It is particularly instructive to note that the ICESCR influenced the protection of human rights in the South African Constitution, 1996, which entrenches both civil and political rights and ESCR (eg the right of 'everyone' to have access to adequate housing;[103] access to health care services, sufficient food and water, and social security;[104] and the right to education[105]) as 'inter-related and mutually supporting'.[106] The Constitution contains two important international law-friendly interpretive provisions. First, it provides that, in interpreting the bill of rights, courts or tribunals '*must consider* international law'.[107] While this provision indicates that it is possible for South African courts to use international law (treaties and the jurisprudence of relevant international bodies), the obligation—not a choice—is to simply 'consider'—and not to apply—international law. Second, the Constitution provides that 'when interpreting *any legislation*, every court must prefer any reasonable interpretation of the legislation that is consistent with international law over any alternative interpretation that is inconsistent with international law'.[108] This applies to the interpretation of 'any legislation', even in the absence of any ambiguity. On the basis

98 Universal Declaration of Human Rights (adopted 10 December 1948) UNGA Res 217 A(III) (UDHR) art 26; Convention on the Rights of the Child (CRC) (opened for signature 20 November 1989, entered into force 2 September 1990) 1577 UNTS 3, art 28(1)(a) and (b) and 29(1); African Charter (n 13) art 17; African Charter on the Rights and Welfare of the Child (n 35) art 11(2) and (3).

99 See eg *Governing Body of the Juma Musjid Primary School & others v Essay NO & others (Centre for Child Law & another as Amici Curiae)* [2011] ZACC 13 (hereafter *Juma Musjid*), paras 40–43; Botswana Court of Appeal, *Attorney General v Unity Dow* (2001) AHRLR 99 (BwCA 1992) paras 106–09, referring to UDHR art 2 and art 2 African Charter (n 13).

100 See eg High Court of Kenya, *Republic v Minister for Home Affairs & two others Ex Parte Sitamze*, Misc Civil Case No 1652 of 2004, [2008] eKLR. The Court extensively relied on arts 6 and 2 of the ICESCR to interpret the right of a non-national to work in Kenya.

101 CEDAW arts 2(f) and 16(1)(b) and (c).

102 See Supreme Court of Uganda, *Mifumi (U) Ltd and 12 others v Attorney General and Kenneth Kakuru* [2010] UGCC 2, noting at 59–60 that 'Uganda is a signatory [State party] to all major human rights Conventions [including the ICESCR] which require it to put in place laws and measures that prevent discrimination and perpetuate inequality (sic)'.

103 Constitution of the Republic of South Africa, 1996, s 26.

104 ibid s 27.

105 ibid s 29.

106 See *Government of the Republic of South Africa & others v Grootboom & others* [2000] ZACC 19 (hereafter *Grootboom*), para 23.

107 Constitution of the Republic of South Africa, 1996, sec 39(1)(b), emphasis is added.

108 ibid s 233, emphasis added.

of the relevant constitutional provisions, the South African Constitutional Court has developed useful jurisprudence on the justiciability of ESCR with particular reference to the rights of access to health care, adequate housing, water, electricity, basic sanitation, and education.[109] It is evident from the Court's jurisprudence that domestic courts will enforce the positive constitutional obligations imposed upon the government with respect to ESCR in at least the following ways. First, if the government fails to take steps to ensure that ESCR are progressively realized, 'the courts will require government to take steps'.[110] Second, if steps or measures taken by the government are unreasonable (eg by failing to provide for those most desperately in need), the courts will 'require that they be reviewed so as to meet the constitutional standard of reasonableness'.[111] Third, if the government adopts a policy with unreasonable limitations or exclusions, the court may order that those unreasonable limitations or exclusions 'are removed'.[112]

While the Court's jurisprudence shows how the State and specific aspects of public policy can be held accountable for failure to respect, protect, and fulfil ESCR via a constitutional culture of justification and accountability through litigation, it has signalled that the Court does not intend to adopt and apply the notion developed by the CESCR that ESCR contain a minimum core (or 'minimum essential levels') which the State is obliged to ensure.[113] The Committee's minimum core approach, recently reaffirmed in two General Comments adopted in March 2016,[114] has thus not been applied by the South African Constitutional Court. Instead, the Court has preferred a high level of deference to the legislature and executive.

Thus, in the *Mazibuko* case, the applicants alleged, inter alia, that a Free Basic Water policy to supply 6 kilolitres of free water per month to every account holder (regardless of household size) in the City of Johannesburg violated the right to have access to 'sufficient water' under section 27 of the South African Constitution 1996.[115]

[109] See eg *Thiagraj Soobramoney v Minister of Health (KwaZulu-Natal)* [1997] ZACC 17 (hereafter *Soobramoney*); *Grootboom* (n 106); *Minister of Health and others v Treatment Action Campaign* [2002] ZACC 16 (hereafter *Treatment Action Campaign*); *Khosa & others v Minister of Social Development* [2004] ZACC 11; *Abahlali Basemjondolo Movement SA and Another v Premier of the Province of Kwazulu-Natal & others* [2009] ZACC 31; *Mazibuko & others v City of Johannesburg & others* [2009] ZACC 28; *City of Johannesburg Metropolitan Municipality v Blue Moonlight Properties 39 (Pty) Ltd and Another* [2011] ZACC 33; and *Juma Musjid* (n 99).

[110] *Mazibuko* (n 109) para 67. [111] ibid. [112] ibid.

[113] CESCR, 'General Comment 3' (n 53) para 10: 'the Committee is of the view that a minimum core obligation to ensure the satisfaction of, at the very least, minimum essential levels of each of the rights is incumbent upon every State party. Thus, for example, a State party in which any significant number of individuals is deprived of essential foodstuffs, of essential primary health care, of basic shelter and housing, or of the most basic forms of education is, prima facie, failing to discharge its obligations under the Covenant'.

[114] CESCR, 'General Comment 22' (n 68) para 49; and CESCR, 'General Comment 23' (n 68) para 65.

[115] Section 27 provides: '(1) Everyone has the right to have access to—

(a) health care services, including reproductive health care;
(b) sufficient food and water; and
(c) social security, including, if they are unable to support themselves and their dependents, appropriate social assistance.

The Constitutional Court had to consider whether the City of Johannesburg's Free Basic Water policy was 'reasonable' in terms of section 27(1)(b) of the Constitution, which guarantees everyone's right of access to sufficient water. The applicants contended, inter alia, that the Court should determine a quantified amount of water as 'sufficient water' within the meaning of section 27, and that this amount is 50 litres per person per day.[116] The Court (contrary to the High Court[117] and the Supreme Court of Appeal[118]) refrained from defining the minimum core content of the right of access to 'sufficient water' and held that the 'applicants have not persuaded this Court to specify what quantity of water is "sufficient water" within the meaning of section 27 of the Constitution'.[119] According to the Court, the right to 'sufficient water' does not as such require the State to provide every person with sufficient water on demand, but rather 'it requires the state to take reasonable legislative and other measures progressively to realize the achievement of the right of access to sufficient water, within available resources'.[120] Without giving contextual meaning to the constitutional standard of 'reasonableness' and the minimum core content of the right to 'sufficient water', the Court found the City's Free Basic Water policy to fall 'within the bounds of reasonableness'. According to the Court,

> ordinarily it is institutionally inappropriate for a court to determine precisely what the achievement of any particular social and economic right entails and what steps government should take to ensure the progressive realisation of the right. This is a matter, in the first place, for the legislature and executive, the institutions of government best placed to investigate social conditions in the light of available budgets and to determine what targets are achievable in relation to social and economic rights. Indeed, it is desirable as a matter of democratic accountability that they should do so for it is their programmes and promises that are subjected to democratic popular choice.[121]

Therefore, the 'reasonableness' review for assessing State compliance with ESCR obligations has been applied to allow governments a wide margin of discretion, inter alia, to determine 'what the achievement of any particular social and economic right entails'. Thus, the normative core content of the right to 'sufficient water' has remained ambiguous. This means that there is no clear guidance regarding State obligations and entitlements for individuals and groups.

The influence of the ICESCR in South Africa can also be discerned from the constitutional protection of the right to education and how this right has been enforced by courts. In 2011 (before the ratification of the ICESCR by South Africa on 18 January 2015, and its entry into force for the State on 12 April 2015), in the case of *Juma Musjid*,[122] the Constitutional Court relied on articles 13 and 14 of the

(2) The state must take reasonable legislative and other measures, within its available resources, to achieve the progressive realisation of each of these rights.
(3) No one may be refused emergency medical treatment.'

116 *Mazibuko* (n 109) paras 44(a) and 51.

117 *Mazibuko and others v City of Johannesburg and others* (06/13865) [2008] 4 All SA 471 (W) (30 April 2008), Tsoka J (holding that a basic minimum of 50 litres per person per day should be provided).

118 *City of Johannesburg and others v Mazibuko and others* (489/08) [2009] 3 All SA 202 (SCA) (25 March 2009) (holding that a basic minimum of 42 litres per person per day should be provided).

119 *Mazibuko* (n 109) para 159.

120 ibid para 50.

121 ibid para 61, O'Regan J.

122 *Juma Musjid* (n 99).

ICESCR to interpret and apply section 29(1) of the Constitution, which states that '[e]veryone has the right ... to a basic education, including adult basic education; and ... to further education, which the state, through reasonable measures, must make progressively available and accessible.'

The Court held that, unlike some of the other 'socio-economic rights' under the South African Constitution,[123] the right to a basic education under article 29(1)(a) is 'immediately realisable' since there is no internal limitation requiring that the right be 'progressively realised' within 'available resources' subject to 'reasonable legislative measures'.[124] The Court distinguished the right to a 'basic education' from the right to 'further education' provided for in section 29(1)(b), which obliges the State, through reasonable measures, to make further education 'progressively available and accessible.'[125] The Court further relied on the CESCR's General Comment 13 to stress the importance of the right to education[126] and concluded that:

> Indeed, basic education is an important socio-economic right directed, among other things, at promoting and developing a child's personality, talents and mental and physical abilities to his or her fullest potential.[127] Basic education also provides a foundation for a child's lifetime learning and work opportunities. To this end, access to school—an important component of the right to a basic education guaranteed to everyone by section 29(1)(a) of the Constitution—is a necessary condition for the achievement of this right.[128]

The South African example of the constitutional protection of ESCR and judicial enforcement of these rights has been followed in other African States, in particular in Kenya.[129] Influenced by the ICESCR, the Constitution of Kenya, 2010 protects what used to be considered solely as 'needs' and 'services' as fully justiciable entitlements at par with civil and political rights.[130] The Constitution guarantees every person a right to the highest attainable standard of health, accessible and adequate housing, reasonable standards of sanitation, freedom from hunger, adequate food of acceptable quality, clean and safe water in adequate quantities, social security, and education.[131] The State is obliged to 'observe, respect, protect, promote and fulfil' all rights in the Bill of Rights and to 'take legislative, policy and other measures, including the setting of standards, to achieve the progressive realisation of the rights guaranteed under Article 43',[132] subject to available

[123] ibid referring to arts 26 (right to have access to adequate housing) and 27 (right to have access to health care services, sufficient food and water, and social security) of the Constitution of South Africa, 1996.

[124] *Juma Musjid* (n 99) para 37. See also *Minister of Basic Education v Basic Education for All* (20793/2014) [2015] ZASCA (Supreme Court of Appeal of South Africa) 198 (2 December 2015).

[125] *Juma Musjid* (n 99) para 37.

[126] CESCR, 'General Comment 13' (n 96) para 1.

[127] The Court cited CRC (n 98) art 29(1).

[128] *Juma Musjid* (n 99) para 43.

[129] Constitution of Kenya, 2010, arts 43–44, 53. In art 165(3)(b), the High Court is empowered to 'determine the question whether a right or fundamental freedom in the Bill of Rights has been denied, violated, infringed or threatened'.

[130] High Court of Kenya, *Michael Mutinda Mutemi v Permanent Secretary, Ministry of Education & two others*, Petition No 133 of 2013, [2013] eKLR, para 13.

[131] Constitution of Kenya, 2010, art 43.

[132] ibid arts 21(1) and (2). In High Court of Kenya, *Mitu-Bell Welfare Society v Attorney General & two others*, Petition No 164 of 2011, [2013] eKLR, para 53, Judge Mumbi Ngugi held that 'progressive

resources.[133] This provides a strong legal basis for courts to consider whether the measures or policies taken by the State or its organs, if any, with respect to ESCR (eg access to healthcare, housing, food, water, and sanitation) meet constitutional standards.[134] In several cases, the High Court has applied the standard of whether policies or measures are 'reasonable in the circumstances'.[135] Since the adoption of Kenya's 2010 Constitution, domestic courts have increasingly relied directly on the ICESCR and General Comments of the CESCR to interpret ESCR protected in the Constitution.[136]

C. Monist approaches to the ICESCR in Africa and their influence on human rights

Monism emphasizes that national and international law form one single legal order, or at least a number of interlocking orders that should be presumed to be coherent and consistent.[137] Accordingly, in States applying monism to international treaties, a treaty such as the ICESCR may, without legislation, become part of domestic law and can be applied directly within the national legal order once it has been concluded in accordance with the constitution and has entered into force for the State.[138] Nevertheless, in practice, legal institutions of a 'monist' State, such as its legislature and judiciary, should ensure that national law conforms to international law and that international law can be relied on in national courts. In cases of conflict, national courts should give effect to international law. In 'monist' African States (following the civil law tradition based on the Constitution of France, 1958),[139] international treaties in force for the State can be applied directly within the national legal order, without legislation. Some constitutions of a number of 'Francophone'[140]

realisation' implies that 'the state must begin to take steps, and I might add *be seen* to take steps, towards realization of these rights' (emphasis in the original).

133 Constitution of Kenya, 2010, art 43(5); art 2(1) ICESCR.

134 See eg High Court of Kenya, *Mathew Okwanda v Minister of Health and Medical Services & three others*, Petition No 94 of 2012, [2013] eKLR, para 24; High Court of Kenya, *Kenya Society for the Mentally Handicapped v Attorney General and seven others*, Petition No 155A of 2011, [2012] eKLR, para 18.

135 See eg High Court of Kenya, *Luco Njagi & 21 others v Ministry of Health & two others*, Petition No 218 of 2013, [2015] eKLR, paras 85 and 90, concluding that 'the measures taken by the respondents to ensure access to haemodialysis by the petitioner are reasonable in the circumstances' due to limited available resources. See also High Court of Kenya, *Consumer Federation of Kenya (COFEK) v Attorney General & 4 others*, Petition No 88 of 2011, [2012] eKLR, para 39.

136 See eg High Court of Kenya, *John Kabui Mwai & three others v Kenya National Examination Council & two others*, Petition No 15 of 2011, [2011] eKLR, 6–7, where the Court directly relied on arts 13 and 14 of the ICESCR after observing that under article 2(6) of the Constitution of Kenya, 2010, the ICESCR 'forms part of our [Kenyan] laws' since Kenya is a State party to the Covenant. See also High Court of Kenya, *PAO & two others v Attorney General*, Petition No 409 of 2009 [2012] eKLR, paras 58–64, 86; *Luco Njagi* (n 135) paras 63–64.

137 Crawford, *Brownlie's Principles* (n 73) 48.

138 Aust, *Modern Treaty Law* (n 73) 163.

139 The Constitution of France, 1958, art 55, reads: '[t]reaties or agreements duly ratified or approved shall, upon publication, prevail over Acts of Parliament, subject, with respect to each agreement or treaty, to its application by the other party'.

140 See the Constitutions of the following former French colonies in Africa: Algeria, 1989, art 132; Benin, 1990, preamble and art 147; Burkina Faso, 1991, preamble; Burundi, 2004, art 292; Cameroon,

and 'Lusophone'[141] African States expressly provide (in their preambles or elsewhere) that treaties that have duly been signed and ratified in accordance with constitutional processes are part of or take precedence over national legislation, or that human rights protected in the Constitution shall be interpreted in harmony with the relevant international instruments.[142] Treaties in such States are, in theory, superior to (and thus supersede) ordinary legislation, but subject to the constitution.[143] However, in practice, 'monist' States in Africa require international treaties to be officially published before becoming part of domestic law.[144] Courts may also need to determine the extent to which rights protected by the ICESCR are 'justiciable' or 'self-executing'; that is, whether they may be directly applied by courts without further specification or definition by the legislature. Thus, enforcement of the ICESCR in 'monist' African States may require a State to 'take prior legislative measures' to make provisions of the ICESCR applicable in domestic law.[145] It must be acknowledged that, generally, most courts in 'monist' African States have not given full effect to the provisions of the ICESCR in the domestic legal order, especially not by providing for judicial and other remedies for violations of ESCR.[146] As a result, the influence of the ICESCR on domestic legislation, policies, and national courts' jurisprudence in most 'monist' African States has been very limited partly because, historically, judicial training has not paid adequate attention to international human rights, including the justiciability of ESCR.[147] In this context, the ICESCR has not been used as a source of directly enforceable rights or a source of inspiration in the interpretation of relevant domestic law in court judgments, as judges tend to rely on domestic legislation (which is inadequate to implement the rights

1996, art 45; the CAR, 1995, preamble; Chad, 1996, preamble and art 221; the DRC, 2005, art 215; Congo, 2001, art 184; Guinea, 1990, preamble; Madagascar, 1992, preamble; Mali, 1992, preamble and art 116; Niger, 1999, preamble and art 132; Rwanda, 2003, art 190; Senegal, 2001, art 98; Seychelles, 1993, art 48; Togo, 1992, preamble; and Tunisia, 2014, art 20.

[141] See the Constitutions of the following six former colonies of the Portuguese Empire in Africa: Angola, 2010, art 13; Cape Verde, 1992, art 11; Guinea-Bissau, 1984, art 28; Mozambique, 2004, art 18; São Tomé and Príncipe, 1975, arts 12 and 17; and Equatorial Guinea, 1991, preamble and art 14.

[142] See eg the Constitutions of São Tomé and Príncipe, 1975, arts 12 and 17; Equatorial Guinea, 1991, preamble and art 14; Guinea-Bissau, 1984, art 28; and Mozambique, 2004, art 43. The latter states that '[t]he constitutional principles in respect of fundamental rights shall be interpreted and integrated in harmony with the Universal Declaration of Human Rights and with the African Charter of Human and Peoples' Rights.'

[143] See eg Constitution of the CAR, 2013, art 97, stating that '[a]greements or Treaties properly ratified or approved, take precedence, once published, over laws, on the condition, for each Agreement or Treaty, of its application by the other parties.' See also the Constitution of Cape Verde, 1992, art 11, and the Constitution of Tunisia, 2014, art 20.

[144] See eg Constitution of Senegal (2001) art 98, stating that '[t]reaties or agreements duly ratified shall, *upon their publication*, have an authority superior to that of the laws, subject, for each treaty and agreement, to its application by the other party' (emphasis added). See also Constitutions of Angola, 2010, art 13(1), and Benin, 1990, art 147.

[145] See *Souleymane Guengueng and others v Hissène Habré* (2002) AHRLR 183 (SeCC 2001), para 38.

[146] See CESCR, 'Concluding Observations on the Combined Second to Fourth Periodic Reports of the Democratic Republic of the Congo' (16 December 2009) UN Doc E/C.12/COD/CO/4, para 8.

[147] USAID, 'Democracy, Human Rights and Governance: Assessment of Senegal: Final Report' (2013) <http://pdf.usaid.gov/pdf_docs/pnaec828.pdf> accessed 16 June 2017, 28.

guaranteed under the ICESCR) with which they are more familiar.[148] Therefore, it is imperative to ensure that national human rights institutions do not concentrate solely on civil and political rights, but accord equal weight and attention to ESCR.

For example, the Constitution of Rwanda, 2003 protects several ESCR, including the rights to free choice of employment, equal pay for equal work, form trade unions, strike, education, and health.[149] It further provides that international treaties and agreements have precedence over domestic laws[150] and can thus be applied directly in the domestic legal order. In addition, it reaffirms 'adherence to the principles of human rights' enshrined in various treaties, namely the UN Charter,[151] the Convention on the Prevention and Punishment of the Crime of Genocide,[152] the Universal Declaration of Human Rights,[153] the International Convention on the Elimination of All Forms of Racial Discrimination,[154] the ICCPR, the ICESCR, the CEDAW, the African Charter, and the CRC.[155]

However, the influence of the ICESCR in Rwanda has been limited by the absence of cases of invocation before, or direct or indirect application of the Covenant by, domestic courts or tribunals.[156] This is also true in other African States giving primacy to international treaties, or making ratified international treaties part of domestic law,[157] or providing that the Bill of Rights 'shall be interpreted in such a way as not to be inconsistent with any international obligations',[158] including human rights obligations under the ICESCR. There has also been a lack of compliance with timely reporting obligations by several States. For instance, Seychelles acceded to the ICESCR on 5 May 1992, but had not submitted even a single report to the CESCR by May 2017, more than twenty-five years after its accession.

[148] See eg Case No 501 of 27 July 1984, Dakar Court of Appeal, Senegal. Although the case raised an issue concerning the right of access to good quality public health facilities, it was determined on the basis of relevant domestic law (article 142 of the Code of the Obligations of the Administration, Act No 65-61 of 19 July 1965) without any reference to article 12 ICESCR.

[149] Constitution of the Republic of Rwanda, 2003, arts 37–41.

[150] ibid art 190, provides: '[u]pon their publication in the official gazette, international treaties and agreements which have been conclusively adopted in accordance with the provisions of law shall be more binding than organic laws and ordinary laws except in the case of non-compliance by one of the parties'.

[151] Charter of the United Nations (opened for signature 26 June 1945, entered into force 24 October 1945) 1 UNTS 1.

[152] Convention on the Prevention and Punishment of the Crime of Genocide (opened for signature 9 December 1948, entered into force 12 January 1951) 78 UNTS 277.

[153] Universal Declaration of Human Rights (adopted 10 December 1948) UNGA Res 217 A(III).

[154] Convention on the Elimination of All Forms of Racial Discrimination (opened for signature 7 March 1966, entered into force 4 January 1969) 666 UNTS 195.

[155] ibid preamble para 9.

[156] CESCR, 'Concluding Observations on the Combined Second to Fourth Periodic Reports of Rwanda' (10 June 2013) UN Doc E/C.12/RWA/CO/2-4, para 6.

[157] See eg Constitution of the Federal Democratic Republic of Ethiopia, 1994, art 9(4), which provides: '[a]ll international agreements ratified by Ethiopia are an integral part of the law of the land'. See also the Constitution of the Republic of Namibia, 1990 (as amended), art 144; CESCR, 'Concluding Observations on the Combined Initial, Second, and Third Periodic Reports of Ethiopia' (31 May 2012) UN Doc E/C.12/ETH/CO/1-3, para 5.

[158] Constitution of the Republic of Seychelles, 1993, art 48.

As a further example, article 132 of the Constitution of the People's Democratic Republic of Algeria, 1989 (amended by the constitutional revision of 1996)[159] provides that '[t]reaties ratified by the President of the Republic in accordance with the conditions provided for by the Constitution are superior to [national] law.' Nevertheless, in 2010 the CESCR was concerned that there was 'an absence of jurisprudence invoking the Covenant provisions, despite the primacy of the Covenant over national law established by article 132 of the Constitution'.[160] The Committee recommended that Algeria 'take effective measures to increase awareness of Covenant rights among the judiciary and the public at large, and to ensure that judicial training take full account of the justiciability of Covenant rights'.[161] To date, jurisprudence invoking the ICESCR is still non-existent.

The observation above (concerning the failure to invoke the ICESCR before or to apply it by national courts) and the recommendation above (concerning the direct applicability of the ICESCR by promoting it, inter alia, among judges and the general population at large) appear in several other CESCR concluding observations on African State reports,[162] as most recently exemplified by the following observations with respect to Burundi:

> 5. The Committee finds it regrettable that, despite the constitutional standing of the Covenant, its provisions have never been invoked before or applied by national courts.
>
> 6. The Committee recommends that the State party ensure the direct applicability of the Covenant by promoting among judges, attorneys, public officials and other officials responsible for application of the Covenant, as well as among rights holders, an awareness of the content of the Covenant and of the possibility of invoking it in the justice system ...[163]

It follows from the foregoing that, while constitutional provisions providing for the direct applicability of the ICESCR provide a strong legal basis for the enforcement of ESCR before domestic courts and tribunals, they do not per se necessarily give rise to the application of the Covenant by national courts and tribunals. More needs to be done by non-governmental organizations (NGOs) to pursue cases involving systematic violations of ESCR in the public interest in order to protect the

159 Constitution of the People's Democratic Republic of Algeria, 1996.

160 CESCR, 'Concluding Observations on the Combined Third and Fourth Periodic Reports of Algeria' (7 June 2010) UN Doc E/C.12/DZA/CO/4, para 5.

161 ibid.

162 See eg CESCR, 'Concluding Observations on the Combined Initial, Second, and Third Periodic Reports of Angola' (1 December 2008) UN Doc E/C.12/AGO/CO/3, para 9; CESCR, 'Concluding Observations on the Second Periodic Report of Benin' (9 June 2008) UN Doc E/C.12/BEN/CO/2, paras 9 and 30; CESCR, 'Concluding Observations on the Combined Initial, Second, and Third Periodic Reports of Chad' (16 December 2009) UN Doc E/C.12/TCD/CO/3, para 9; CESCR, 'Concluding Observations on the Combined Initial, Second, and Third Periodic Reports of Ethiopia' (31 May 2012) UN Doc E/C.12/ETH/CO/1-3, para 5; CESCR, 'Concluding Observations on the Fourth Periodic Report of Morocco' (22 October 2015) UN Doc E/C.12/MAR/CO/4, paras 9–10; CESCR, 'Concluding Observations on the Second Periodic Report of Sudan' (27 October 15) UN Doc E/C.12/SDN/CO/2, paras 5–6; CESCR, 'Concluding Observations: Rwanda' (n 156) para 6; CESCR, 'Concluding Observations: Uganda' (n 85) para 5.

163 CESCR, 'Concluding Observations on the Initial Periodic Report of Burundi' (16 October 2015) UN Doc E/C.12/BDI/CO/1, paras 5–6. See also CESCR, 'Concluding Observations: Chad' (n 162) para 7.

underprivileged and marginalized populations in society. In addition, this will help national courts to apply the ICESCR when interpreting domestic law in order to develop the content of ESCR and to define the nature of obligations of both States and non-State actors.[164]

IV. Conclusion

The ICESCR has significantly influenced the regional and, to some extent, domestic legal protection of ESCR in Africa. As noted above, the Covenant influenced the explicit protection of ESCR in the African Charter and in several constitutions in Africa. It has also influenced the development of the jurisprudence of the African Commission on ESCR. While there is no consistent practice among African States, there is an increasing trend towards more constitutional protection of many ESCR in African States' constitutions, either as justiciable human rights or at least as 'directive principles' of State policy. Nevertheless, ESCR have still not attained the same level of protection and enforcement extended to civil and political rights in the constitutions of many African States. Besides, the influence of the Covenant on national courts' jurisprudence in most African States remains limited. There are still several factors limiting the realization of ESCR in Africa, including non-compliance with domestic court rulings in favour of ESCR,[165] political authoritarianism, high levels of corruption,[166] poverty,[167] armed conflicts, limited engagement of NGOs and civil society, and a lack of respect for the rule of law[168] including a lack of respect for international judicial bodies.[169] In order to enhance the influence of the

164 See Redson E Kapindu, 'Courts and the Enforcement of Socio-Economic Rights in Malawi: Jurisprudential Trends, Challenges and Opportunities' (2013) 13 African Human Rights LJ 125.

165 See eg High Court of Kenya, *Ibrahim Sangor Osman v Minister of State for Provincial Administration and Internal Security*, Constitutional Petition No 2 of 2011, [2011] eKLR; CESCR, 'Concluding Observations: Kenya' (n 85) paras 7–8.

166 See CESCR, 'Concluding Observations: Kenya' (n 85) paras 17–18 and Kolawole Olaniyan, *Corruption and Human Rights Law in Africa* (Hart 2014).

167 The Fund for Peace, 'Fragile States Index 2015: Fragility in the World 2015' <http://fsi.fundforpeace.org/rankings-2015> accessed 20 June 2016. The Index is based on several indicators including uneven economic development, poverty, and human rights.

168 See eg East African Court of Justice, *Matia Katabazi and 21 others v Secretary General of the East African Community and the Attorney General of the Republic of Uganda*, Reference No 1 of 2007; *Gramara (Private) Limited and Another v the Government of the Republic of Zimbabwe* (HC 33/09) [2010] ZWHHC (Zimbabwe Harare High Court) 1 (26 January 2010); *Government of the Republic of Zimbabwe v Fick & others* (657/11) [2012] ZASCA 122 (20 September 2012); *Government of the Republic of Zimbabwe v Fick and others* (CCT 101/12) [2013] ZACC 22.

169 eg although Uganda is a State party to the Rome Statute of the International Criminal Court (ICC) (opened for signature 17 July 1998, entered into force 1 July 2002) 2187 UNTS 90), on 12 May 2016, during his swearing-in speech extending his thirty-year rule, Ugandan President Yoweri Museveni told visiting heads of State and representatives of the US and EU member States in Uganda that '[w]e lost interest in the ICC. … ICC is none of our business. It is a useless body. We had supported the ICC initially thinking they were serious … but it is a bunch of useless people.' See Peter Clottey, 'International Court Urges Uganda to Arrest Sudan President Bashir' (*Voice of America*, 13 May 2016) <www.voanews.com/content/sudanese-president-bashir-defies-international-arrest-warrant-with-trip-to-uganda/3327216.html> accessed 20 June 2016.

ICESCR in Africa, these factors must be addressed by implementing a wider range of comprehensive, necessary, appropriate, and effective legal, economic, and educational measures, plans of action, and policies by States, including: (i) enacting and implementing domestic legislation to give effect to the ICESCR; (ii) providing extensive training and conducting awareness-raising campaigns on the ICESCR and the justiciability of ESCR to politicians, law-makers, national and local civil servants, law enforcement officers, and students at all levels of education; (iii) training members of all professions and sectors that have a direct role in the promotion and protection of human rights, including judges, lawyers, prosecutors, civil servants, teachers, immigration officers, the military, the police, and other law enforcement officers, on the domestic application of international human rights treaties, including through specific training programmes on the ICESCR; (iv) adopting and effectively implementing poverty reduction strategies, in cooperation with relevant (non-governmental or civil society, regional, and international) organizations and institutions, which should fully integrate ESCR; (v) ensuring the transparency of the conduct of public authorities and the allocation of available resources to relevant sectors, especially those addressed to the most disadvantaged and marginalized social groups and individuals, in law and in practice; (vi) signing and ratifying, without delay, the Optional Protocol to the ICESCR, which offers a complementary and accessible forum for accountability concerning neglected ESCR;[170] and (vii) timely submission of periodic reports to the CESCR, including a compilation of case summaries and decisions adopted by domestic courts and tribunals on the justiciability of ESCR.

Bibliography

Aust, Anthony, *Modern Treaty Law and Practice* (3rd edn, CUP 2013)

Chitimira, Howard, 'An Analysis of Socio-Economic and Cultural Rights Protection under the Zimbabwe Constitution of 2013' (2017) 61 J of African L 171

Clottey, Peter, 'International Court Urges Uganda to Arrest Sudan President Bashir' (*Voice of America*, 13 May 2016) <www.voanews.com/content/sudanese-president-bashir-defies-international-arrest-warrant-with-trip-to-uganda/3327216.html> accessed 20 June 2016

Crawford, James, *Brownlie's Principles of Public International Law* (8th edn, OUP 2012)

Dicey, Albert Venn, *Introduction to the Study of the Law of the Constitution* (8th edn, Macmillan 1915)

Goodman, Ryan, and Jinks, Derek, 'Measuring the Effects of Human Rights Treaties' (2003) 14 European J of Intl L 171

Harris, David J, and Sivakumaran, Sandesh, *Cases and Materials on International Law* (8th edn, Sweet & Maxwell 2015)

Hathaway, Oona A, 'Do Human Rights Treaties Make a Difference?' (2002) 111 Yale L J 1870

170 See eg *IDG v Spain* (2015) CESCR Communication No 2/2014 (13 October 2015) UN Doc E/C.12/55/D/2/2014.

Heyns, Christof H, and Kaguongo, Waruguru, 'Constitutional Human Rights Law in Africa: Current Developments' (2006) 22 South African J on Human Rights 673

Kapindu, Redson E, 'Courts and the Enforcement of Socio-Economic Rights in Malawi: Jurisprudential Trends, Challenges and Opportunities' (2013) 13 African Human Rights L J 125

Kwasi Prempeh, Henry, 'Africa's "Constitutionalism Revival": False Start or New Dawn?' (2007) 5 Intl J of Constitutional L 469

Meyersfeld, Bonita, 'Domesticating International Standards: The Direction of International Human Rights Law in South Africa' (2015) 8 Constitutional Court Review 399

Okyir, Nana Tawiah, 'Toward a Progressive Realisation of Socio-Economic Rights in Ghana: A Socio-Legal Analysis' (2017) 51 African J of Intl and Comparative L 91

Olaniyan, Kolawole, *Corruption and Human Rights Law in Africa* (Hart 2014)

Shaw, Malcolm N, *International Law* (7th edn, CUP 2014)

7

Influence of the ICCPR in the Middle East

Başak Çali

I. Introduction

This chapter aims to survey the influence of the International Covenant on Civil and Political Rights (ICCPR)[1] on the domestic laws of States in the Middle East region. The chapter approaches influence from the perspective of its legal features. It conceives of influence as the presence of an enabling domestic legal environment by way of the enactment, application, and interpretation of domestic laws compatible with the ICCPR and the subsequent interpretations of the ICCPR by the Human Rights Committee (HRC).[2] The chapter confines the region-level investigation to interactions between the ICCPR and the ten countries that are located in the geographical space of the Middle East and that are States parties to the ICCPR. These States are Bahrain, Egypt, Iraq, Iran, Israel, Kuwait, Lebanon, Turkey, Syria, and Yemen. The analysis excludes countries that are located in the region but are not States parties to the ICCPR. These are Oman, Qatar, Saudi Arabia, and the United Arab Emirates. It further excludes countries that share a common language and religion with most States in the region but are located solely in North Africa.

The primary sources used to identify region-level trends of influence are the ratification and reservation practices of States, the periodic reports of States to the HRC, shadow reports of non-governmental organizations, and the concluding observations of the HRC. Given the ever-increasing overlap between the ICCPR and other UN human rights treaties, the chapter will be confined to what will be delimited as the six core domains of the ICCPR: states of emergency and counter-terrorism legislation, the death penalty, the administration of justice, democratic rights, the protection of minorities and indigenous peoples, and equality and non-discrimination. These six core domains, together, make up the ICCPR's vision of what an enabling domestic legal environment for the protection of civil and political rights must feature. They together reflect a commitment for the entrenchment of a

[1] International Covenant on Civil and Political Rights (opened for signature 16 December 1966, entered into force 23 March 1976) 999 UNTS 171 (ICCPR or the Covenant).

[2] See Samantha Besson, 'The Influence of the Two Covenants on States Parties across Regions', Chapter 11 in this volume.

The Human Rights Covenants at 50: Their Past, Present, and Future. Daniel Moeckli, Helen Keller, and Corina Heri. © Daniel Moeckli, Helen Keller, and Corina Heri 2018. Published 2018 by Oxford University Press.

liberal, democratic, and multicultural domestic legal order based on the rule of law. The ICCPR is the only UN treaty that regulates derogation in cases of emergency and the death penalty. The remaining domains find further echoes in other UN human rights treaties that offer issue-specific protections (ie the Convention against Torture (UNCAT)[3] and the Convention on the Elimination of All Forms of Racial Discrimination (CERD)[4]) or group-specific protections (ie the Convention on the Elimination of Discrimination against Women (CEDAW),[5] the Convention on the Rights of the Child (CRC),[6] and the Convention on the Rights of Persons with Disabilities (CRPD)[7]).

The central argument of this chapter is two-fold. First, it is argued that the pathways of the ICCPR's influence on domestic law enactment, application, and interpretation are structurally hampered in the Middle East region due to how the ICCPR enters into domestic legal orders in the first place. The ICCPR's entry into domestic law is mired with reservations, the ambiguity of the ICCPR *qua* domestic law in the region, and the irregular relationship between the HRC and the States post-ratification. This amounts to the presence of limited legal opportunity structures in the region that would allow the ICCPR and the concluding observations of the HRC to have a bearing on domestic law.[8]

Second, the chapter argues that the interactions between the HRC and the States in the Middle East are governed primarily by defensive domestic legalism. The domestic laws and their interpretation post-ratification, for the most part, fall significantly short of the expectations of the HRC as formulated in the concluding observations. Instead, States in the region hold that their already existing domestic constitutional arrangements and laws offer adequate protection of civil and political rights and point out that the HRC's concluding observations are not 'fit' for a region marked by conflicts and internal and external national security concerns. Cases of the ICCPR operating as a mechanism for boosting existing constitutional civil and political rights, as it does, for example, in Israel, Turkey, and Kuwait, are thus limited and few and far between in the region.

Overall, this chapter's granular empirical investigation confirms existing political science wisdom that long-standing international human rights law (IHRL) influences are conditional on domestic legal and political opportunity structures[9] and

[3] Convention against Torture and Other Cruel, Inhuman or Degrading Treatment or Punishment (opened for signature 10 December 1984, entered into force 26 June 1987) 1465 UNTS 85.

[4] Convention on the Elimination of All Forms of Racial Discrimination (opened for signature 7 March 1966, entered into force 4 January 1969) 666 UNTS 195.

[5] Convention on the Elimination of All Forms of Discrimination against Women (opened for signature 18 December 1979, entered into force 3 September 1981) 1249 UNTS 13.

[6] Convention on the Rights of the Child (opened for signature 20 November 1989, entered into force 2 September 1990) 1577 UNTS 3.

[7] Convention on the Rights of Persons with Disabilities (opened for signature 13 December 2006, entered into force 3 May 2008) 2515 UNTS 3.

[8] On legal opportunity structures, see Chris Hilson, 'New Social Movements: The Role of Legal Opportunity' (2002) 9 J of European Public Policy 238, and Ellen Ann Andersen, *Out of the Closets and Into the Courts: Legal Opportunity Structure and Gay Rights Litigation* (University of Michigan Press 2005).

[9] Beth A Simmons, *Mobilizing for Human Rights: International Law in Domestic Politics* (CUP 2009).

that the conditions that would create receptive domestic partners for the ICCPR, allowing it to have a widespread positive influence, are not yet present in the Middle East region.[10]

This chapter has three parts. Section II addresses the methodological challenges in surveying the influence of the ICCPR in the Middle East as a geographical region. Section III investigates how the ICCPR enters into domestic law and how the States in the region interact with the HRC through reporting requirements. Section IV turns to the HRC's framing of the (in)compatibility of domestic laws with the ICCPR in the six core domains outlined above and discusses the limitations of the influence of the ICCPR in light of the logic of counterclaims by Middle Eastern States.[11]

II. Challenges to Surveying the Influence of the ICCPR in the Middle East

Investigating the influence of the ICCPR on the domestic laws of the Middle Eastern countries poses three central challenges.

The first is geographic. How do we delimit the Middle East as a region for comparative analysis? The term 'Middle East' was first introduced in 1890. Over time and in its various reiterations, it has encompassed an uncertain number of countries.[12] Which countries are to be included in the Middle East for the purposes of surveying the influence of the ICCPR? Is the Middle East a geographical space, a political space, a cultural space, or a space imagined, defined, and redefined by the West? Should the Middle East only cover States with Arabic culture and history?[13] Does it also incorporate Iran and Turkey? Does it include Afghanistan or Pakistan to the east or the States of North Africa to the west? This chapter employs a common sense understanding of the region, rather than a linguistic or a political one. Doing so permits inclusion of countries that are in more than one region, namely Turkey

[10] One exception to this is Turkey, where the shadow of the European Court of Human Rights (ECtHR), supported by the prospect of European Union membership, has indirectly influenced ICCPR-respecting practices. See also Başak Çalı, 'The Logics of Supranational Human Rights Litigation, Official Acknowledgment and Human Rights Reform: The Southeast Turkey Cases before the European Court of Human Rights, 1996–2006' (2010) 35 Law and Social Inquiry 311.

[11] See Stanley Cohen, 'Government Responses to Human Rights Reports: Claims, Denials, and Counterclaims' (1996) 18 Human Rights Q 517.

[12] On the history of the term 'Middle East', see Roderic H Davison, 'Where is the Middle East?' (1960) 38 Foreign Affairs 665. On the delimitation of the Middle East, see George Etzel Pearcy, 'The Middle East: An Indefinable Region' (1959) 40 Department of State Bulletin 407.

[13] eg Mehran Kamrava focuses on Arabic commonalities in his treatment of the Middle East and defines Iran as outside of the Middle East imaginary. See Mehran Kamrava, *The Modern Middle East: A Political History since World War I* (3rd edn, University of California Press 2013). Turkey has long contested its place in the Middle East space and wishes to be seen as part of Europe. The Arab League, by contrast, operates with a definition that includes all Arabic-speaking countries, regardless of whether they are included in the standard Middle East space, and the Office of the High Commissioner for Human Rights (OHCHR) operates with a definition of the Middle East and North Africa (MENA) that includes Arab States, but excludes Turkey.

and Egypt, a cross-section of countries that are also part of the sub-regional system of the Arab Charter on Human Rights,[14] and Israel, which is geographically in the region, but is not politically affiliated to it. This selection allows an assessment of whether a hybrid regional identity or a sub-regional identity makes a difference for the influence of the ICCPR in the Middle East.

The second challenge is motivational. For those familiar with the political science literature on the effects of human rights treaties, the proposed investigation is not likely to yield interesting results when focusing on a political space called the Middle East due to the prevalence of authoritarian States in the region for whom the ratification of treaties is best conceived as a low-cost reputational signal.[15] In fact, the central finding of any research into the influence of the ICCPR in the Middle East can be stated with little granular analysis: the ICCPR has had a negligible positive influence on the corpus of domestic law, encompassing domestic legislation, administration, and adjudication, in the vast majority of Middle Eastern countries. This is because most political and legal regimes in the Middle East are either unable or unwilling to be responsive to the demands of the HRC's interpretation of the ICCPR as a living instrument.

The central explanation for this is the sizeable discrepancy between the HRC's domestic legal–institutional vision for the protection of ICCPR rights and the legal–institutional arrangements prevalent across the Middle East. For the HRC, the protection of ICCPR rights depends on political and legal regimes that are committed to a pluralist democracy and the rule of law supported by strong independent judiciaries. Substantively, domestic institutions must be committed to equality, non-discrimination, and the protection of cultural, religious, and ethnic differences and vulnerabilities. In contrast to this vision, the Middle Eastern space is comprised of authoritarian or semi-authoritarian States and weak judiciaries, with the exception of Israel.[16] The region is—or at least has been—plagued by civil war, international armed conflict, military intervention, and invasion.[17] The security paradigm—in relation to internal and external threats—is in the foreground of domestic political agendas in Middle Eastern countries. Domestic attitudes towards

[14] The Arab Charter on Human Rights (opened for signature 22 May 2004, entered into force 15 March 2008) 12 IHRR 893 (2005) (the Arab Charter).

[15] On the limited effects of international human rights treaties in authoritarian political regimes, see generally: James Raymond Vreeland, 'Political Institutions and Human Rights: Why Dictatorships Enter into the United Nations Convention against Torture' (2008) 62 International Organization 65; Christine Min Wotipka and Kiyoteru Tsutsui, 'Global Human Rights and State Sovereignty: State Ratification of Human Rights Treaties, 1965–2001' (2008) 23 Sociological Forum 724; Simmons, *Mobilizing* (n 9); Thomas Risse, Stephen C Ropp, and Kathryn Sikkink (eds), *The Persistent Power of Human Rights: From Commitment to Compliance* (CUP 2013).

[16] Of all the region's countries, the Freedom House 2017 report rates Israel as 'free', Turkey, Kuwait, and Lebanon as 'partly free', and the rest of the countries studied as 'not free' (Freedom House, *Freedom in the World* (2017) <https://freedomhouse.org/report/freedom-world/freedom-world-2017> accessed 29 May 2017).

[17] Quintan Wiktorowicz, 'The Limits of Democracy in the Middle East: The Case of Jordan' (1999) 53 The Middle East J 606; Eva Bellin, 'The Robustness of Authoritarianism in the Middle East: Exceptionalism in Comparative Perspective' (2004) 36 Comparative Politics 139; Mehran Kamrava, 'The Arab Spring and the Saudi-Led Counterrevolution' (2012) 561 Orbis 96.

ethnic, religious, and cultural differences are infused with preferences hostile to non-majority groups and discourses[18] and religion-grounded defences of patriarchal structures.[19] Given the strong link between the enjoyment of civil and political rights and the absence of political repression and conflict, and the worsening effects of the latter on the former,[20] expecting positive influences of the ICCPR on domestic laws in the Middle East is unrealistic, and even, perhaps, uninteresting as a path of research inquiry. Ratification of the ICCPR in the region is more likely to amount to empty promises in the absence of domestic incentives to reform existing legal and political structures.

The third challenge is the difficulty of isolating the influence of the ICCPR on domestic laws from the influence of other United Nations (UN) human rights treaties or from the effects of a global human rights culture more generally. The latter is not only generated by UN treaty mechanisms, but also by the UN Charter mechanisms.[21] This includes the inter-State peer-to-peer review mechanism of Universal Periodic Review (UPR) and bilateral interactions between the States of the Middle East and those Western States that are human rights-promoting.[22] It is often the case that other UN treaty bodies, UN Charter mechanisms, or recommending States under the auspices of UPR make similar recommendations to those made by the HRC in the context of the ICCPR.[23] The HRC, too, is open to influences from other UN bodies. It allows for the permeability of rights[24] and employs the living instrument and the implied rights doctrines, resorting to quasi-judicial borrowing to bring concerns not addressed in earlier concluding observations under review.[25] The heightened emphasis on fighting gender stereotypes, concerns around child soldiers, and the rights of migrant workers are some examples of this. This is a two-way interaction. Other treaty bodies also take up points raised by the HRC in their concluding observations.[26] Given that countries in the Middle East are multiple

[18] Joshua Castellino and Kathleen A Cavanaugh, *Minority Rights in the Middle East* (OUP 2013).

[19] Fatma Müge Göcek and Shiva Balaghi (eds), *Reconstructing Gender in the Middle East: Tradition, Identity, Power* (Columbia University Press 1994); Ann Elizabeth Mayer, *Islam and Human Rights: Tradition and Politics* (4th edn, Westview Press 2007).

[20] M Rodwan Abouharb, Book Review (2008) 70 J of Politics 563.

[21] As envisaged in the Charter of the United Nations (opened for signature 26 June 1945, entered into force 24 October 1945) 1 UNTS 1.

[22] eg the fifth Yemeni periodic report makes references to the technical co-operation between Yemen, the OHCHR, and the Danish Institute for Human Rights as contributors to the Yemeni human rights reform agenda. See HRC, 'Fifth Periodic Report of Yemen' (8 January 2010) CCPR/C/YEM/5, para 45.

[23] eg all UN treaty bodies recommend the ratification of UN treaties that have not yet been ratified by a State and support the establishment of action plans on human rights as well as of National Human Rights Institutions. Such recommendations yield positive results; see Sonia Cardenas and Andrew Flibbert, 'National Human Rights Institutions in the Middle East' (2005) 59 The Middle East J 411.

[24] See eg the recommendation of the HRC to Israel with respect to discrimination in access to water (HRC, 'Concluding Observations on the Third Periodic Report of Israel' (3 September 2010) CCPR/C/ISR/CO/3, para 8).

[25] This includes eg the emphasis that the HRC places on gender stereotyping, the duty to combat gender prejudices, domestic and sexual violence including marital rape, concerns about the stigmatization of homosexuality, and migrant workers' rights.

[26] eg the recommendation of the CRC Committee to Bahrain with respect to the protection of the civil rights and freedoms of children (CRC Committee, 'Concluding Observations on the Second and Third Reports of Israel' (3 August 2011) CRC/C/BHR/Co/2-3, paras 38–46).

ratifiers of UN treaties,[27] it is therefore, empirically, more accurate to talk about the influence of IHRL through the ICCPR rather than the influence of the ICCPR per se on the domestic laws of States in the Middle East.

In addition, with respect to a sub-set of Middle Eastern countries, there is also a regional human rights treaty, the Arab Charter on Human Rights, with its own treaty monitoring mechanism, the Arab Human Rights Committee.[28] The Arab Charter, in its preamble, reaffirms the principles of the ICCPR. In article 43, it stipulates that the Charter should not be interpreted as impairing the rights in the treaties that have already been ratified by Arab States. Article 44 requires States to take legislative measures to give effect to the rights protected in the Charter. On the one hand, it may, therefore, operate as a regional vehicle for the influence of the ICCPR amongst its States parties, provided that the Arab Human Rights Committee interprets the Charter in sync with the ICCPR. On the other hand, the text of the Arab Charter on Human Rights does not fully mirror the ICCPR. Significantly, it does not prohibit cruel, inhuman, and degrading punishment, it allows for the imposition of the death penalty on juveniles, it subjugates women's rights in favour of Islamic Sharia, and it allows limitations on freedom of religion solely in accordance with domestic law.[29] In the absence of a harmonious interpretation between the ICCPR and the Arab Charter, the latter may thus offer a competing vision for sub-regional protection of civil and political rights. What we may view as the influence of the ICCPR and the HRC's recommendations, therefore, may in effect be the influences of a broad culture of human rights law generated through these multi-actor processes, globally and regionally, which may be both amplifying or undermining the influence of the ICCPR.

Given this cautious framing of the merits of analysing the influence of the ICCPR on domestic laws in the Middle East region, what can be usefully discussed with regard to the influence of the ICCPR *qua* ICCPR and the Middle East? The central contention of this chapter is that this inquiry is meaningful in order to investigate the region-specific reasons for the limited legal influence of the ICCPR in the Middle East and to better understand the terms of resistance to the concluding observations of the HRC. In order to do this, this chapter comparatively surveys (a) how the ICCPR enters into the domestic law realm in the first place in the region by way of ratification, reservations, and administrative engagement with the HRC, along with an assessment of the status of the ICCPR within the domestic legal orders (Section III), and (b) how the Covenant operates as a resource for framing the human rights law reform agenda in Middle Eastern countries with a specific focus

[27] See Table 7.2.

[28] The Arab Charter has currently been ratified by thirteen of the twenty-two member States of the Arab League situated in the wider geography of the Middle East and North Africa. These States are Algeria, Bahrain, Iraq, Kuwait, Lebanon, Jordan, Libya, Palestine, Qatar, Saudi Arabia, Syria, the United Arab Emirates, and Yemen. Egypt, Morocco, Sudan, and Tunisia have signed but not yet ratified the Charter. Collated from Center for Not-for-Profit Law, 'Civic Freedom Monitor: League of Arab States' <www.icnl.org/research/monitor/las.html> accessed 17 June 2016.

[29] See also Mervat Rishmawi, 'The Arab Charter on Human Rights and the League of Arab States: An Update' (2010) 10 Human Rights L Rev 169, 171.

on civil and political rights and how this is resisted by States in the region (Section IV). When seen in this more encompassing framework, despite the justified low expectations of influence on domestic laws, it is argued that we are able to obtain a more detailed picture of the potential of a long-term influence of IHRL through the lens of the ICCPR in the Middle East.

III. Pathways for Influence: Ratification, Reservations, Engagement, and Legal Status

The initial component of the ICCPR's pathway to influence on domestic laws in the Middle East are the terms on which the ICCPR enters into the domestic realm in the first place. The extent and scope of legal support that the ICCPR receives in the region through ratifications (including those of the Optional Protocols) and reservations is the starting point for this assessment. The Middle East stands out as a region from the perspective of support by way of ratification, given that four significant Middle Eastern countries are not States parties to the ICCPR. These are Oman, Qatar, Saudi Arabia, and the United Arab Emirates.[30] Given that, globally, most of the States that have not yet ratified the ICCPR are small island States, the concentration of four non-States parties to the ICCPR in one region is significant. What is more, three of the non-ICCPR ratifiers (Qatar, Saudi Arabia, and the United Arab Emirates) are States parties to the Arab Charter on Human Rights, signalling a preference for a sub-regional alternative to civil and political rights protection rather than the ICCPR. Middle Eastern countries are otherwise highly integrated into the UN human rights treaty system. All States in the region are States parties to the ICESCR,[31] CERD, CRC, UNCAT, and CRPD. With the exception of Iran, all States have also ratified CEDAW. Ratifications of the MWC[32] and CPED,[33] however, are not common.[34] Table 7.1 sets out ratifications of human rights treaties by States in the Middle East.

Countries in the Middle East acceded to the ICCPR at very different times. This can be distilled into five waves of ratification. The first wave consisted of the early

[30] The ICCPR has 168 States parties. There are only seven countries that have signed and not ratified the ICCPR (China, Comoros, Cuba, Nauru, Palau, St Lucia, and São Tomé and Principe) and twenty-four countries that have taken no action with respect to the ICCPR (Bhutan, Brunei Darussalam, the Cook Islands, Fiji, the Holy See, Kiribati, Malaysia, the Marshall Islands, Micronesia, Myanmar, Niue, Qatar, Oman, St Kitts and Nevis, Saudi Arabia, South Sudan, the Solomon Islands, Singapore, Tonga, Tuvalu, and the United Arab Emirates). The four Middle Eastern non-parties to the ICCPR—Saudi Arabia, Qatar, the United Arab Emirates, and Oman—are also not States parties to the ICESCR. They have, however, all acceded to CERD, CEDAW, and the CRC.

[31] International Covenant on Economic, Social and Cultural Rights (ICESCR) (opened for signature 16 December 1966, entered into force 3 January 1976) 993 UNTS 3.

[32] International Convention on the Protection of the Rights of All Migrant Workers and Members of their Families (opened for signature 18 December 1990, entered into force 1 July 2003) 2220 UNTS 3 (MWC).

[33] International Convention for the Protection of All Persons from Enforced Disappearance (CPED) (opened for signature 20 December 2006, entered into force 23 December 2010) 2716 UNTS 3.

[34] See Table 7.2.

Table 7.1 UN human rights treaty commitment in the Middle East

	ICCPR	ICESCR	CERD	CEDAW	CRC	CAT	CRPD	CPED	MWC
Bahrain	Yes	Yes	Yes	Yes	Yes	Yes	Yes	No	No
Iraq	Yes	Yes	Yes	Yes	Yes	Yes	Yes	Yes	No
Iran	Yes	Yes	Yes	No	Yes	No	Yes	No	No
Israel	Yes	Yes	Yes	Yes	Yes	Yes	Yes	No	No
Jordan	Yes	Yes	Yes	Yes	Yes	Yes	Yes	No	No
Lebanon	Yes	Yes	Yes	Yes	Yes	Yes	No	No	No
Syria	Yes	Yes	Yes	Yes	Yes	Yes	Yes	No	Yes
Turkey	Yes	Yes	Yes	Yes	Yes	Yes	Yes	No	Yes
Egypt	Yes	Yes	Yes	Yes	Yes	Yes	Yes	No	Yes
Kuwait	Yes	Yes	Yes	Yes	Yes	Yes	Yes	No	No
Yemen	Yes	Yes	Yes	Yes	Yes	Yes	Yes	No	No

ratifiers, namely Syria, Iraq, and Lebanon, in the late 1960s and early 1970s. The second wave, or the mid-1970s accessions, consisted of Iran and Jordan. The third wave, or the 1980s ratifications, included Egypt and Yemen. The fourth wave, or the ratifications that came about at the end of the Cold War, consisted of Israel and Kuwait. The fifth wave, or the new millennium ratifications, was made up of Turkey and Bahrain. Table 7.2 lists the dates of accession of Middle Eastern States to the ICCPR.

The underlying motivations for ratifying the ICCPR vary in the region.[35] In particular, they point to the lack of region-level political dynamics and highlight the importance of State-level considerations, tied to the low cost of ratification of human rights treaties and international political incentives for ratification. Early ratifications all came about when there was some domestic political stability in the ratifying countries. Thus, the ratifications by Syria, Iraq, and Lebanon came about in periods of relative calm in all three States and predate the more recent coups and civil wars.[36] The same is true for the 1970s ratifications by Jordan and Iran. In Egypt and Yemen, the decision by domestic actors not to remain isolated from the international system motivated ratifications in the 1980s. The Israeli ratification of the ICCPR took place in the context of the ongoing peace talks with the Palestinians and was part of a larger ratification package that also included the UNCAT and the ICESCR. Kuwait's ratification of the ICCPR was part of a ratification surge in the aftermath of the invasion and the country's attempts to signal deeper integration

[35] This argument, originally advanced by Andrew Moravcsick in the context of the European Convention on Human Rights ratifications is viewed as one domestic reason (Andrew Moravsick, 'The Origins of Human Rights Regimes: The Post War Delegation in Post War Europe' (2000) 54 International Organization 217).

[36] The Syrian ratification came before Assad's bloodless coup of 1970. In Lebanon, it predates the Lebanese civil war. In Iran, the ICCPR was ratified by Shah Pahlavi without any reservations.

Table 7.2 Accession to the ICCPR in chronological order

State	Date of Accession
Syria	21 April 1969
Iraq	25 January 1971
Lebanon	3 November 1972
Jordan	28 May 1975
Iran	24 June 1975
Egypt	14 January 1982
Yemen	9 February 1987
Israel	3 October 1991
Kuwait	21 May 1996
Turkey	23 September 2003
Bahrain	20 September 2006
Qatar	Has not ratified
UAE	Has not ratified
Oman	Has not ratified
Saudi Arabia	Has not ratified

with the international community.[37] In the case of Turkey, the late ratification is best explained by the dominant role of the European Convention on Human Rights (ECHR)[38] as the leading civil and political rights treaty with respect to that State and the European Union membership efforts in the early 2000s. In Bahrain, the recent ratification of the ICCPR is best explained as a concession to rising opposition to the King of Bahrain.[39]

Whilst heterogeneity is present at the level of the ratification of the ICCPR, States in the region converge with respect to their lack of interest in the Optional Protocols to the Covenant. With the exception of Turkey,[40] none of the other ten States have ratified the First Optional Protocol on the right to individual petition[41] or the Second Optional Protocol on the abolition of the death penalty.[42] The lack of ratifications of the First Optional Protocol limits the engagement of the HRC to

[37] cf Başak Çalı, Nazila Ghanea, and Benjamin Jones, 'Domestic Effects of Human Rights Treaty Ratification in the Member States of the Gulf Cooperation Council' (2016) 38 Human Rights Q 21, 39.

[38] Convention for the Protection of Human Rights and Fundamental Freedoms (European Convention on Human Rights, as amended) (ECHR).

[39] ibid 40.

[40] Turkey acceded to the Second Optional Protocol on 2 March 2006 and to the First Optional Protocol on 24 November 2006.

[41] First Optional Protocol to the ICCPR (opened for signature 16 December 1966, entered into force 23 March 1971) 999 UNTS 171.

[42] Second Optional Protocol to the ICCPR, aiming at the Abolition of the Death Penalty (opened for signature 15 December 1989, entered into force 11 July 1991) 1642 UNTS 414.

Table 7.3 Reservations to the ICCPR in the Middle East region

Syria	Article 48(1) and diplomatic relations with Israel
Iraq	Diplomatic relations with Israel
Lebanon	None
Jordan	None
Iran	None
Egypt	General reservation (Islamic Sharia)
Yemen	Diplomatic relations with Israel
Israel	Article 23
Kuwait	Articles 2(1), 3, 23, and 25(b)
Turkey	General reservation (territorial application) and article 27
Bahrain	General reservation, articles 3, 18, 23, 9(5), and 14(7)

recommendations for legal, institutional, and policy change without giving it the chance to interact with the specific decisions of the domestic courts in the region. As most of the countries in the Middle East also give either no or few examples of how the ICCPR is judicially implemented domestically,[43] the absence of ratifications of the First Optional Protocol seriously hampers the HRC's chances of having any impact on the judicial internalization of the ICCPR through individual case-based interaction. As will be discussed in the following section, the lack of ratifications of the Second Optional Protocol further means that ICCPR article 6, which delineates careful and limited exceptions to the death penalty, becomes a central site through which the ICCPR engages with and faces resistance in the Middle East.

A. Reservations to the ICCPR

The ICCPR is the most reserved-against UN human rights treaty. The ratifications from the Middle East, shown in Table 7.3, reflect this.[44] However, Middle Eastern States show important divergences in their reservation practices with respect to the Covenant. In this regard, two observations can be made.

First, despite the presence of large Muslim majorities and the constitutional status of Islamic Sharia in Egypt, Yemen, Jordan, and Iran, not all Middle Eastern States

[43] There are no examples of how the ICCPR is implemented by judges in the reports of Lebanon, Jordan, and Egypt. See, respectively, HRC, 'Concluding Observations on the Initial Periodic Report of Lebanon' (22 November 1996) CCPR/C/42/Add.14; HRC, 'Concluding Observations on the Fourth Periodic Report of Jordan' (18 November 2010) CCPR/C/JOR/CO/4 (HRC, 'Concluding Observations: Fourth Report of Jordan'); HRC, 'Combined Third and Fourth Periodic Reports of Egypt' (15 April 2002) CCPR/C/EGY/2001/3.

[44] Universal Rights Group, 'UN Human Rights Treaties Reservations Database', on file with author. See also Başak Çalı and Mariana Montoya, *The March to Universality? Religion-based Reservations to Core Human Rights Treaties* (Universal Rights Group 2017) <www.universal-rights.org/urg-policy-reports/march-universality-religion-based-reservations-core-un-human-rights-treaties-tell-us-human-rights-religion-universality-21st-century/> accessed 26 May 2017.

have made reservations to the ICCPR concerning Islamic Sharia. Significantly, this is true despite the fact that Sharia-based reservations are a common staple of reservations to the CEDAW and the CRC in the Middle East.[45] Thus, for example, Jordan, Lebanon, Iran, Iraq, Syria, and Yemen have not made any reservations to the ICCPR. This is best explained by the lack of a 'Sharia-based reservation' trend in the 1970s, when these States were ratifying the ICCPR, and the introduction of this type of reservation for the first time by Egypt in 1982. In contrast, post-1980 ratifications of other treaties both by the very same States[46] and by other States in the Middle East featured prevalent references to Sharia.

The Egyptian reservation to the ICCPR is a statement indicating that Egypt would comply with the ICCPR 'to the extent that it does not conflict with Sharia', and is a classic example of a 1980s general reservation of this kind.[47] Following this, similar reservations have been made by other Middle Eastern States when acceding to human rights treaties.[48] The reservations of Bahrain to articles 3 (equality between men and women), 18 (freedom of thought, conscience, and religion), and 23 (equality in family life) of the ICCPR continue this practice and make direct references to Sharia law. With respect to article 23, Kuwait also indicated that its personal status law based on Islamic law governs family relations.[49] In contrast, reservations by Kuwait to article 2(1) (non-discrimination) and article 3 only indicated that Kuwait would implement these provisions in so far as they are compatible with domestic law. Israel shares similarities to these three countries with respect to its article 23 reservation. Therein, it limits the scope of the ICCPR by making reference to personal status laws governed by the religious laws of the individuals concerned.

Second, the Middle Eastern ICCPR reservations reflect the legacies of the Arab-Israeli War of 1948. The early accessions by Iraq and Syria in the 1970s, as well as the Yemeni accession in 1987, were made under the indication that accession to the ICCPR does not signal any diplomatic relations with Israel. Turkey's reservation to the ICCPR stands out in the region, as it seeks to limit the definition and the scope of protection of minorities as laid out in the post-World War One Treaty

[45] cf United Nations General Assembly (UNGA), 'Report of the Committee on the Elimination of Discrimination against Women' (14 May 1998) A/53/38/Rev.1, pt II, ch 1, 'Statements on the Reservations to the Convention on the Elimination of All Forms of Discrimination against Women'.

[46] Iran started to formulate Sharia-based reservations in its post-1979 Iranian revolution ratifications. See eg its reservation to the CRC (cf United Nations Treaty Collection (UNTC) ch IV.11 <https://treaties.un.org/Pages/ViewDetails.aspx?src=IND&mtdsg_no=IV-11&chapter=4&clang=_en#EndDec> accessed 28 March 2017).

[47] See Egypt's reservation to the CESCR and ICCPR (UNTC, ch IV.3 <https://treaties.un.org/pages/ViewDetails.aspx?src=TREATY&mtdsg_no=IV-3&chapter=4&lang=en#EndDec> accessed 5 November 2015).

[48] Interviews carried out by the author with officials from Saudi Arabia indicated that, after the Egyptian reservation, it has become unthinkable for the Saudi authorities to accede to UN human rights treaties without a similar reservation since the 1980s (interviews conducted at Doha, May 2013).

[49] Kuwait's reservation to art 25(b) on the grounds that only male candidates can run for election has become obsolete after 2005 with the adoption of Act No 17 giving women the right to stand for election. The reservation still does not allow members of the armed forces and the police to benefit from the rights under art 25(b).

of Lausanne signed in 1923.[50] Turkey, in light of its unresolved territorial dispute with Cyprus, also seeks to limit the application of the ICCPR to the territory of the Turkish Republic.

Third, all reservations that seek to limit the legal effect of the ICCPR made by Middle Eastern States have attracted concern from the HRC. In its 2002 concluding observations on Egypt, the HRC took issue with the State's general reservation to the ICCPR as a whole, and concluded that:

> while observing that the State Party considers the provisions of the Islamic Shariah to be compatible with the Covenant, the Committee notes the general and ambiguous nature of the declaration made by the State party upon ratifying the Covenant. The State party should either clarify the scope of its declaration or withdraw it.[51]

The Committee has also shown concern for Turkey's general reservation on territoriality and its reservation to article 27.[52] The Committee has also been concerned about reservations making reference to religious laws governing personal status, as such laws can have discriminatory aspects and can strip individuals of their substantive rights guaranteed by the Covenant.[53] In the case of Iran, a country that made no reservations to the ICCPR when it ratified the Covenant in 1975, the HRC expressed concern with 'stealth reservations' made through constant references to religious norms as primary tenets in State reports.[54] The Committee has taken a clear stance on Kuwait's interpretative declaration subjecting ICCPR articles 2(1), 3, and 23 to limitations in Kuwaiti law and declared that the declaration 'contravenes the State party's essential obligations under the Covenant and is therefore without legal effect and does not affect the powers of the Committee'.[55] In the light of this de facto severance of the reservation, Kuwait was formally asked to withdraw the interpretive declaration.[56]

B. Engagement with the Human Rights Committee

In the region, the engagement of States with the HRC shows important discrepancies both through delays in regular reporting to the HRC and in the lack of follow-up with its concluding observations and recommendations in previous reports.[57] Delays

[50] Treaty of Peace between the British Empire, France, Italy, Japan, Greece, Romania, and the Serb-Croat-Slovene State and Turkey (signed 24 July 1923 at Lausanne) 28 LNTS 1–4 (1924).

[51] HRC, 'Concluding Observations on the Third and Fourth Periodic Reports of Egypt' (28 November 2002) CCPR/CO/76/EGY, para 5.

[52] HRC, 'Concluding Observations on the Initial Periodic Report of Turkey' (13 November 2012) CCPR/C/TUR/CO/1, para 9.

[53] cf HRC, 'Concluding Observations on the Fourth Periodic Report of Israel' (21 November 2014) CCPR/C/ISR/CO/4.

[54] HRC, 'Concluding Observations on the Third Periodic Report of Iran' (29 November 2011) CCPR/C/IRN/CO/3, para 5.

[55] HRC, 'Concluding Observations on the Initial Periodic Report of Kuwait' (27 July 2000) CCPR/CO/69/KWT, para 4.

[56] ibid. This is also repeated in HRC, 'Concluding Observations on the Second Periodic Report of Kuwait' (18 November 2011) CCPR/C/KWT/CO/2, para 7.

[57] It must be noted that delays in reporting are not a region-specific issue in the case of the ICCPR.

in reporting limit both the quality and the quantity of interactions between the HRC and member States by not offering any opportunity to follow up on how the State is progressing in implementing the ICCPR and the recommendations of the HRC and bringing its legislation and practice into line with those requirements.

With regard to some Middle Eastern States, there has been close to no continuous interaction between the HRC and the State concerned. Bahrain has not submitted any reports to the HRC since its accession to the ICCPR in 2006.[58] The last report by Lebanon was submitted in 1996[59] and was reviewed in 1997. There has been no meaningful assessment of the ICCPR's influence in Lebanon since then. In the case of Egypt, there have been three delayed reports to the HRC since 1987.[60] The fifth report has been pending since 2004. Jordan submitted its fourth periodic report twelve years late, in 2009, and has not submitted its fifth.[61] In the case of Iraq and Iran, engagement with the HRC resumed after a two-decade long break. The fifth Iraqi periodic report was submitted thirteen years late, in 2013 (twenty years after the fourth report in 1993). Iran's third periodic report arrived eighteen years after the second. Syria submitted its second report in 2000—twenty-four years after the first. Its fourth report has been pending since 2009. Ten years elapsed between the first and the second reports of Kuwait (which were submitted in 1999 and 2009, respectively), but a third report arrived in 2014. Israel's initial report was five years late, but since then Israel has continued its engagement with the HRC on a regular basis.[62] Yemen is the only country in the region that has not had a seriously interrupted exchange with the HRC.

When the reports have been submitted, a commonplace criticism of the region by the HRC has been that Middle Eastern States do not offer sufficient information on the implementation of the Covenant in practice and on the factors and difficulties restraining its effective implementation.[63] Instead, States offer ample information on the prevailing legislation and other domestic legal frameworks.[64] Significantly, States provide little or no information as to how the domestic judiciaries interact with the ICCPR in their case law[65] and how the ICCPR *qua* ICCPR has had an influence on legislative changes and human rights policy-making.[66] A common

[58] For this reason, further discussion of Bahrain is omitted after this section.

[59] HRC, 'Second Periodic Report of Lebanon' (22 November 1996) CCPR/C/42/Add.14.

[60] Egypt submitted a joint third and fourth report to the HRC and was asked to avoid this in the future (HRC, 'Concluding Observations: Third and Fourth Reports of Egypt' (n 51) para 2.

[61] HRC, 'Fourth Periodic Report of Jordan' (30 March 2009) CCPR/C/JOR/4.

[62] HRC, 'Initial Periodic Report of Israel' (2 June 1998) CCPR/C/81/Add.13.

[63] See HRC, 'Concluding Observations: Initial Report of Kuwait' (n 55) para 2; HRC, 'Concluding Observations on the Second Periodic Report of Egypt (9 August 1993) CCPR/C/79/Add.23, para 2; HRC, 'Second Periodic Report of Yemen' (12 October 1993) CCPR/C/82/Add.1, para 243; HRC, 'Concluding Observations on the Second Periodic Report of Lebanon' (5 May 1997) CCPR/C/79/Add.78, para 2; HRC, 'Concluding Observations on the Initial Periodic Report of Israel' (18 August 1998) CCPR/C/79/Add.93.

[64] eg Lebanon's 1996 Report is particularly telling, as it simply states regarding most of the ICCPR's provisions that 'there is nothing to report.' See HRC, 'Second Report of Lebanon' (n 59) para 81.

[65] See eg the List of Issues (CCPR/C/IRN/Q/3) to be taken up in connection with the consideration of the third Iranian periodic report (HRC, 'Third Periodic Report of Iran' (31 May 2010) CCPR/C/IRN/3, para 1).

[66] eg Iraq, in its second periodic report in 1987, indicated that all Iraqi law was fully compliant with the ICCPR (See HRC, 'Second Periodic Report of Iraq' (18 July 1986) CCPR/C/37/Add.3).

lacuna in the reports concerns information about the involvement of all relevant ministerial stakeholders and civil society organizations in their compilation.[67]

A qualitative mark of the engagement between Middle Eastern States and the HRC is that these States constantly reference extra-territorial circumstances, civil wars, and terrorist activities affecting the enjoyment of Covenant rights. Such circumstances include, inter alia, the ten-year war between Iraq and Iran, the Lebanese civil war, the Yemeni civil war, and the UN Security Council sanctions in Iraq. The HRC regularly makes note of these circumstances as allowing for legitimate limitations of the enjoyment of rights,[68] but also vents its frustrations as to the lack of concrete examples of how these justifications absolve countries of the responsibility to protect ICCPR rights. During its consideration of Iraq's third periodic report, in 1991, the HRC took a step forward from the otherwise diplomatic language requiring meaningful, concrete engagement, as habitually prevalent in its concluding observations. It stated that 'the representative of the state party had engaged in a kind of monologue or 'stonewalling' and sought constantly to evade certain issues and avoid responding to legitimate questions'.[69] In addition, there is often a 'fatigued' tone in HRC reports, showing disappointment in the lack of any follow-up to its previous concluding observations. There is also often a resigned repetition of the same recommendations and statements. An example of such language can be seen in the recommendation that Kuwait 'should officially recognize ethnic, religious or linguistic minorities as such and ensure the protection and promotion of their rights in compliance with article 27 of the Covenant'.[70]

Interactions between the HRC and the Middle Eastern States, therefore, offer a general pattern wherein States foreground the domestic political circumstances, in particular the existence or threat of violence (be this due to armed conflict or terrorism) as a blanket defence of the prevailing domestic laws against the demands of the ICCPR. Middle Eastern States also mobilize arguments with respect to the feasibility of the HRC's vision of the protection of civil and political rights, making frequent references to broadly conceived contextual constraints.

C. Domestic legal status of the ICCPR

The domestic legal status of the ICCPR in Middle Eastern countries exhibits varying degrees of ambiguity. All countries in the Middle East (with the exception

[67] One exception to this is represented by the Israeli reports, in reaction to which the HRC has commended the dissemination of the State reports to non-governmental organizations prior to consideration by the Committee (see HRC, 'Concluding Observations: Initial Report of Israel' (n 63) para 3).

[68] On the recognition of the ten-year Iran-Iraqi war, see HRC, 'Concluding Observations on the Fourth Periodic Report of Iraq' (19 November 1997) CCPR/C/79/Add.84, para 2 (HRC, 'Concluding Observations: Fourth Report of Iraq'). On the recognition of the Yemeni civil war, see HRC, 'Concluding Observations on the Second Periodic Report of Yemen' (30 March 1995) A/50/40, para 245.

[69] HRC, 'Concluding Observations on the Third Periodic Report of Iraq' (10 October 1991) A/46/40, para 651. The post-Saddam regime report of 2013 has indicated that Iraq concurs with the concluding observations adopted by the HRC following its Saddam-era reports (cf HRC, 'Fifth Periodic Report of Iraq' (12 December 2013) CCPR/C/IRQ/5, para 3).

[70] HRC, 'Concluding Observations: Initial Report of Kuwait' (n 55) para 31.

of Iran) allow for a formal legal status of the Covenant in the domestic legal system. International treaties, once ratified and promulgated in the official gazettes, have the power of domestic law. In Iran, the ICCPR enjoys no formal status in the domestic legal system.[71] In Israel, the ICCPR has not yet been incorporated into national law. However, it may enjoy persuasive authority if and when invoked by domestic courts, or may be made authoritative if conceived of as customary international law.[72]

There are two central regional commonalities concerning the domestic legal status of the ICCPR: the prevalence of domestic constitutionalism and the prevalence of open conflict between the ICCPR and domestic law. Middle Eastern countries view their own constitutions and the interpretation of those constitutions by constitutional courts (where they exist) as offering adequate protection of the ICCPR domestically. In Egypt, for example, the government defines the 1971 Constitution as the fundamental legal instrument that defines rights and freedoms.[73] In Kuwait, the Kuwaiti Constitution of 1962 is described as a document that highlights human rights and ascribes to them 'the elevated status they deserve'.[74] The ICCPR, therefore, is protected by the mere existence of constitutional provisions on civil and political rights[75] and the presence of domestic courts.[76] States hold on to this 'formal' argument even when there are discrepancies between the texts of their own constitutions and the ICCPR.[77]

The States of the Middle East are often silent on the legal value of the HRC's interpretation of the ICCPR as a method for interpreting constitutional rights. The widespread lack of acceptance of the right to individual petition before the HRC means that domestic courts have no opportunities to engage with the case law of the HRC directly. Even if courts do openly engage with the HRC's case law and guidance in other contexts, as in the case of Israel, thus far such engagement has been part of a comparative law exercise rather than an exercise in harmonious interpretation.[78]

Turkey, the only State that has accepted the right to individual petition before the HRC, also does not engage with the HRC's guidance on a regular basis. References to the HRC are few and far between. In the case of Turkey, however, the European regional system's influence on domestic constitutionalism, rather than domestic constitutionalism per se, may offer an explanation for the lack of engagement with

[71] HRC, 'Concluding Observations: Third Report of Iran' (n 54) para 5.

[72] Ruth Lapidoth, Orna Ben-Naftali, and Yuval Shani, *The Obligation to Incorporate Human Rights Conventions into Israeli Law*, position paper (Rishon LeZion 2004).

[73] HRC, 'Third and Fourth Reports of Egypt' (n 43) para 46 and 54.

[74] HRC, 'Initial Report of Kuwait' (3 December 1999) CCPR/C/120/Add.1, para 20.

[75] ibid paras 16–20.

[76] See also Egypt's written response to the HRC's Questions in HRC, 'Third and Fourth Reports of Egypt' (n 43) para 640.

[77] ibid para 49. In the case of Yemen, the HRC found that the human rights protections in the Yemeni Constitution offer less protection than the ICCPR, which puts the idea of protecting ICCPR rights via the Constitution at risk. See HRC, 'Concluding Observations: Second Report of Yemen' (n 68) para 251.

[78] Israeli High Court of Justice, HCJ 7146/12 *Adam et al v the Parliament* (16 September 2013) para 93. See also Yaël Ronen, 'The Use of International Jurisprudence in Domestic Courts: The Israeli Experience' (April 2015) The Hebrew University of Jerusalem Research Paper <http://ssrn.com/abstract=2599016> accessed 21 June 2016.

the HRC. Turkey boosted the effect of the ECHR and the corresponding case law in the domestic system through the introduction of the right to individual petition before the Turkish Constitutional Court for rights at the intersection of the ECHR and the Turkish Constitution in 2012, after which citations of the case law of the European Court of Human Rights have become common place in the case law of the Constitutional Court.[79]

Second is the prevalence of domestic laws that contradict the ICCPR and its interpretation by the HRC. Whilst it is generally acknowledged that the ICCPR has the status of law, can prevail over legislation, and can (at least) theoretically be invoked before domestic courts, there is scarce evidence of its active employment in domestic courts.[80] There is further ambiguity with respect to the relationship between the ICCPR and legislation that postdates its ratification.[81] Despite assurances by States in their reports, the HRC often raises concerns about the lack of clarity on the primacy of the Covenant over conflicting or contradictory national legislation, as States fail to provide consistent evidence of this theoretical position and, often, most evidence is contradictory evidence. States further tend to hold that existing legislation is compatible with the ICCPR.[82]

In the case of conflicts between Sharia-based domestic law and the ICCPR, the ambiguity of the legal status of the ICCPR becomes even more pronounced.[83] States also push back against the necessity of the ICCPR's domestic legal effects if its provisions are deemed to conflict with Sharia law. Iran holds the most uncompromising position in this regard. The Arab Charter further echoes the centrality of Sharia law in giving effect to civil and political rights.

In the face of both the formal and the practical ambiguity of the place of the ICCPR in domestic legal systems, the HRC sticks to its repetitive position that States have a duty to give legal effect to the ICCPR and, if necessary, amend legislation and constitutional provisions to ensure the compatibility of the legal order with the ICCPR.[84] Despite the long history of ICCPR ratifications in the Middle East, therefore, domestic legal systems across the region are significantly closed to the domestic legal influence of the ICCPR through courts. In practice, domestic constitutionalism and legalism emerge as forces of resistance to the influence of the ICCPR in domestic legal systems. Significantly, Middle Eastern States posit the ICCPR as interpreted by domestic legal orders as an alternative to the ICCPR as interpreted by

[79] See Başak Çalı, 'Third Time Lucky: The Turkish Constitutional Court and a Woman's Right to Identity' (*EJIL Talk!*, 29 January 2014) <www.ejiltalk.org/third-time-lucky-the-dynamics-of-the-internationalisation-of-domestic-courts-the-turkish-constitutional-court-and-womens-right-to-identity-in-international-law/> accessed 19 June 2016.

[80] The two exceptions to this, where there are examples of domestic courts making reference to the ICCPR, are Kuwait and Israel. See eg HRC, 'Initial Report of Israel' (n 62) para 42.

[81] HRC, 'Second Periodic Report of Syria' (25 August 2000) CCPR/S/SYR/2000/2, para 29.

[82] HRC, 'Third Periodic Report of Jordan' (26 May 1992) CCPR/C/76/Add.1, para 4.

[83] On the ambiguity of the ICCPR's place in the Kuwaiti domestic system with respect to Sharia, see HRC, 'Concluding Observations: Second Report of Kuwait' (n 56) para 6.

[84] eg the HRC asked for the amendment of Israeli Basic Laws to include the principle of non-discrimination. See HRC, 'Concluding Observations: Third Report of Israel' (n 24) para 6.

the HRC. As discussed below, this is a recurrent theme in the six core domains of the HRC's interpretation of the ICCPR.

IV. Resistance to HRC's Concluding Observations in the Middle East Region

The tension between the HRC's interpretation of the ICCPR and domestic visions for the protection of human rights is a prevalent theme in State reports and responses to the HRC's concluding observations. Here, the analysis will highlight six central areas of interconnected and independent contention that are within the core competencies of the ICCPR.

A. States of emergency, counter-terrorism, and extraordinary judicial practices

States in the Middle East stand out because they live under quasi-permanent forms of states of emergency—be these *de jure* or *de facto*—or suffer from non-international armed conflicts. Three States (Egypt,[85] Israel,[86] and Syria[87]) have been ruled by long-term *de jure* state of emergency laws throughout their interaction with the HRC. Emergency rule has been declared, lifted, and reintroduced in Iraq, Yemen, Lebanon, Jordan, Turkey, Egypt, and Bahrain.[88] There has been a recurrent non-international armed conflict in the territories of Turkey. At the time of writing, there are ongoing non-international armed conflicts in Yemen, Iraq, and Syria,[89] alongside the fifty-year occupation of Palestine by Israel.[90] Vis-à-vis all countries in this

[85] Egypt's state of emergency was declared in 1981. It was lifted in 2012 after thirty-one years. Since then, a state of emergency has been declared again multiple times. More recently, a three-month state of emergency was declared in April 2017. See also Nathan Brown, 'Egypt is in a State of Emergency and Here is What It Means for Its Government' *Washington Post* (Washington, DC, 13 April 2017).

[86] Israel has remained under a state of emergency from 19 May 1948 until the present day. See also HRC, 'Concluding Observations: Third Report of Israel' (n 24) para 11.

[87] Syria was under a *de jure* state of emergency between 1963 and 2011. The formal lifting of the state of emergency, however, coincided with the start of the Syrian conflict in 2011. See 'Syria Protests: Assad to Lift State of Emergency' *BBC News* (20 April 2011) <www.bbc.com/news/world-middle-east-13134322> accessed 26 May 2017.

[88] More recently, having lifted its states of emergency in 2002, Turkey reintroduced state of emergency laws in 2016 in reaction to a failed coup attempt. See Martin Scheinin, 'Turkey's Derogation from Human Rights Treaties: An Update' (*EJIL Talk!*, 18 August 2016) <www.ejiltalk.org/turkeys-derogation-from-human-rights-treaties-an-update/> accessed 26 May 2017. Iraq reintroduced a state of emergency in 2016 after protesters stormed into Parliament (Dominic Smith, 'Baghdad State of Emergency Declared after Protesters Storm Parliament' *The Guardian* (30 April 2016) <www.theguardian.com/world/2016/apr/30/moqtada-al-sadr-supporters-enter-baghdad-parliament-building-green-zone> accessed 26 May 2016).

[89] On the classification of conflicts in the Middle East region depending on their intensity, use of weapons, and the level of command and control of opposing armed forces, see 'Rule of Law' in 'The Rule of Law in Armed Conflicts' project of the Geneva Academy of International Humanitarian Law and Human Rights <www.rulac.org/browse/countries> accessed 26 May 2017.

[90] UN Security Council Res 2334 (23 December 2016) S/RES/2334 (2016).

study, the HRC has continuously raised concerns about the ambiguity of the scope of state of emergency powers, a lack of judicial safeguards against the application of state of emergency laws, and a lack of official notification to the HRC with respect to any derogations from the ICCPR.[91] In times when States in the Middle East are not governed by states of emergency, existing counter-terrorism legislation and practices often lead to *de facto* state of emergency practices undermining both the derogable and non-derogable rights protections envisaged by the HRC's autonomous interpretation of the ICCPR.[92]

The HRC, in this domain, constantly reiterates the incompatibility of such domestic practices with the ICCPR. This framing often focuses on the effects of state of emergency legislation and counter-terrorism laws and practices on the effective enjoyment of rights. With respect to Israel's state of emergency rules, for example, the HRC has insisted that derogation from ICCPR article 9 leads to the frequent use of administrative detention—thus failing to respect the proportionality test for derogable rights. The HRC has also held that Israeli state of emergency laws have practical effects on non-derogable fair trial rights (ICCPR articles 4, 14, and 24) and that the State's de facto derogation goes beyond the permissible for article 9 derogations.[93] Vis-à-vis Syria, the HRC has highlighted the lack of clarity of state of emergency laws and the lack of judicial remedies to challenge treatment under them.[94] The HRC has also raised concerns about the fact that state of emergency domestic frameworks often lack the clear distinction between derogable and non-derogable rights required by the ICCPR.[95]

In the Middle East, the HRC has also been intensely preoccupied with the broad scope of counter-terrorism laws in force. It has criticized Egypt,[96] Jordan,[97] Israel,[98] and Yemen[99] for their broad definitions of 'terrorist activities' in terrorism legislation and for the knock-on effects of domestic legal ambiguity for the enjoyment of the full range of civil and political rights, as well as for systemic values underlying the Covenant, such as the requirements of the principle of legality with regard to accessibility, equality, precision, and non-retroactivity. The HRC points to how counter-terrorism legislation undermines the non-derogable rights of fair trial and equality of arms.[100] In the face of this, Middle Eastern States defend their state of

[91] See eg HRC, 'Concluding Observations: Second Report of Lebanon' (n 63) para 10; HRC, 'Concluding Observations on the Second Periodic Report of Israel' (21 August 2003) CCPR/CO/78/ISR, para 13.

[92] cf HRC, 'General Comment 29' in 'Note by the Secretariat, Compilation of General Comments and General Recommendations Adopted by Human Rights Treaty Bodies' (2008) HRI/GEN/1/Rev.9 (vol 1) 234.

[93] HRC, 'Concluding Observations: Third Report of Israel' (n 24) para 7.

[94] HRC, 'Concluding Observations on the Second Periodic Report of Syria' (24 April 2001) CCPR/CO/71/SYR, para 7.

[95] HRC, 'Concluding Observations on the Fifth Periodic Report of Yemen' (23 April 2012) CCPR/C/YEM/CO/5.

[96] HRC, 'Third and Fourth Reports of Egypt' (n 43) para 16.

[97] HRC, 'Concluding Observations: Fourth Report of Jordan' (n 43) para 6.

[98] HRC, 'Concluding Observations: Second Report of Israel' (n 91) para 14; HRC, 'Concluding Observations: Fourth Report of Israel' (n 53) para 13.

[99] HRC, 'Concluding Observations: Fifth Report of Yemen' (n 95) para 8.

[100] ibid.

emergency legal frameworks and counter-terrorism laws through the prism of domestic legalism and formal constitutional or legal safeguards, with no engagement with the ICCPR's requirements on derogation clauses.

In Israel, the pushing back of the HRC's framing further extends to the applicability of the ICCPR in the occupied Palestinian Territories. The HRC has held that the applicability of international humanitarian law in the territories does not, of itself, impede the application of the ICCPR.[101] Israel, on the other hand, argues that the ICCPR is a 'territorially bound treaty and does not apply with respect to individuals under its jurisdiction, but outside its territory' and that the ICCPR does not apply when international humanitarian law is applicable.[102] This standoff has, thus far, continued in the interactions between the HRC and Israel.

B. Death penalty

In the States in the Middle East, many crimes are punishable by death—thereby leaving the region outside global norms. This includes some States where the death penalty is applicable to certain crimes committed by those under the age of eighteen.[103] The resistance to ICCPR article 6 standards on the death penalty is reflected in article 7 of the Arab Charter. This provision bans the imposition of the death sentence on those under the age of eighteen 'unless otherwise stipulated in the laws in force at the time of the commission of the crime'.

The HRC's view on the obligations of States with respect to article 6 has long been that they must take steps to limit the imposition of the death penalty with a view to it being abolished. They must also respect the ICCPR standard of not imposing the death penalty on juveniles and pregnant women. The HRC often finds that most domestic laws on the death penalty are vague and do not meet the strict scrutiny required under the 'most serious crimes' clause under article 6.[104] In Iran, the HRC is concerned with the extremely high number of death sentences imposed as well as the large number of crimes for which capital punishment is applicable and used.[105] With regard to Kuwait, the HRC has noted that the crimes for which the death penalty is applicable are vague and include references to internal and external security and drug-related crimes.[106]

With the exception of Israel and Turkey, which have abolished or strictly limited the use of the death penalty, the general trend in the Middle East contradicts the HRC's interpretation of article 6. Retrogressive measures have also been introduced in the region by the expansion of the category of crimes for which the death penalty

[101] HRC, 'Concluding Observations: Initial Report of Israel' (n 63) para 10.

[102] HRC, 'Concluding Observations: Fourth Report of Israel' (n 53) para 5.

[103] HRC, 'Concluding Observations: Fourth Report of Iraq' (n 68) para 10.

[104] HRC, 'Third and Fourth Reports of Egypt' (n 43) para 12; HRC, 'Concluding Observations: Second Report of Syria' (n 94) para 9; HRC, 'Second Report of Yemen' (n 63) para 256; HRC, 'Concluding Observations on the Third Periodic Report of Yemen' (12 August 2002) CCPR/CO/75/YEM, para 15.

[105] HRC, 'Concluding Observations: Third Report of Iran' (n 54) para 12.

[106] HRC, 'Concluding Observations: Initial Report of Kuwait' (n 55) para 8.

is applicable[107] and by imposing the death penalty on juveniles.[108] A further exception here is Jordan. It is the only country that has moved away from the regional trend of domestic autonomous interpretation of article 6. Following a call by the HRC, initially in 1994, Jordan placed a moratorium on the death penalty in 2007 and reduced the number of offences that are punishable by death.[109]

C. Extraordinary administration of justice systems

The HRC regularly finds discrepancies concerning the judicial protection of freedom from torture, security and liberty of person, and fair trial guarantees in the countries under study here. Such discrepancies are made all the more significant due to the prevalence of extraordinary justice systems, including military justice systems,[110] state security courts,[111] special courts,[112] and revolutionary courts.[113] Such extraordinary justice systems rely on the logic of states of emergency or have special powers under counter-terrorism legislation. The broad powers of extraordinary justice systems span arresting, detaining, interrogating, and trying civilians, including children.[114] These extraordinary judicial institutions raise a range of fair trial concerns,[115] both in terms of the independence and impartiality of such institutions and of their inability to meet equality of arms standards.[116] The forty-eight hour pre-trial detention limit established by the HRC also means that the HRC finds most practices of lengthy detentions by these judicial institutions to represent structurally arbitrary detention practices that also create a risk of disappearances.[117] The judicial prevention of torture is also undermined in these situations, as there is no positive protection against torturers by way of the criminalization of torture[118]

[107] cf the HRC's concerns with respect to the extension of the range of crimes carrying the death penalty in Lebanon. See HRC, 'Concluding Observations: Second Report of Lebanon' (n 63) para 20.

[108] cf Committee on the Rights of the Child 'Concluding Observations on the Third and Fourth Periodic Reports of Egypt' (20 June 2011) CRC/C/EGY/Co/3-4, para 39.

[109] HRC, 'Third Periodic Report of Jordan' (30 March 2009) CCPR/C/JOR/3, para 5.

[110] HRC, 'Concluding Observations: Fourth Report of Israel' (n 53) para 7; HRC, 'Concluding Observations: Second Report of Lebanon' (n 63) para 13.

[111] HRC, 'Concluding Observations: Second Report of Lebanon' (n 63) para 14; HRC, 'Concluding Observations: Third Periodic Report of Syria' (9 August 2005) CCPR/CO/84/SYR, para 9.

[112] HRC, 'Concluding Observations: Fourth Report of Jordan' (n 43) para 12.

[113] HRC, 'Concluding Observations: Third Report of Iran' (n 54) para 21.

[114] Cf HRC, 'Concluding Observations: Second Report of Lebanon' (n 63) para 14.

[115] eg in Egypt the President had powers to refer cases to State security courts and the right to ratify judgments and to grant pardons until State security courts were abolished in 2008. (HRC, 'Third and Fourth Reports of Egypt' (n 43) para 9). After the promulgation of the 2014 Constitution, the President, however, continues to have the power to refer cases to state of emergency courts ('Egypt's Emergency Law Explained' *Al Jazeera* (April 2017) <www.aljazeera.com/indepth/features/2017/04/egypt-emergency-law-explained-170410093859268.html> accessed 29 May 2017).

[116] HRC, 'Concluding Observations: Fourth Report of Israel' (n 53) para 7; HRC, 'Concluding Observations: Initial Report of Kuwait' (n 55) para 10.

[117] HRC, 'Concluding Observations: Initial Report of Kuwait' (n 55) para 12. The HRC has, in the past, made direct use of the Report of the Working Group on Enforced or Involuntary Disappearances (21 December 1999) E/CN.4/2000/64 (HRC, 'Concluding Observations: Initial Report of Kuwait' (n 55) para 11; HRC, 'Concluding Observations: Third Report of Iraq' (n 69) para 590).

[118] HRC, 'Concluding Observations: Initial Report of Kuwait' (n 55) para 16.

(for example in Israel,[119] Kuwait,[120] or Egypt[121]), despite nearly region-wide ratification of the UNCAT.

D. Non-discrimination and equal citizenship agenda

A common point of resistance between the HRC and Middle Eastern States in their interactions is either the States' refusal to view a legal practice as discriminatory or their tendency to take a largely positive view on whether de facto discrimination exists in society.

In the first sense, countries in the Middle East argue both for the primacy of their national laws and for the lack of discriminatory intent in them. Here, three points of contention on the adequacy of national laws emerge. First, in countries where Sharia law or other religion-based laws form the basis of legislation (be it in a wide sense or only for personal status laws), governments defend domestic law as lacking discriminatory intent. Instead, counter-arguments by States to concluding observations concern the unquestionability of such laws. Second, when the law in place does not have a religious basis, governments point to the illegality of the claims made by groups under the banner of discrimination. Bedouins in Kuwait, for example, are illegal residents.[122] A Bedouin in Israel cannot hold a title to land,[123] and the extension of nationality is framed as a sovereign prerogative.[124] Third, States in the Middle East employ public order or security clauses too easily to restrict the rights of minority groups.[125]

The reiterated interactions between the HRC and the States of the Middle East on the points of the legality of discriminatory measures, therefore, often finish at a dead end, with both the State in question and the HRC holding their positions. With respect to the Yemeni argument that it is impossible to fulfil HRC recommendations that contradict Sharia law, for example, the HRC stresses the duty of all States 'regardless of their political, economic and cultural systems to protect all human rights and fundamental freedoms'.[126]

[119] As concerns Israel, the HRC has raised concerns that the 'defence of necessity' may be allowed by domestic courts with respect to torture practices (HRC, 'Concluding Observations: Third Report of Israel' (n 24) para 11).

[120] HRC, 'Concluding Observations on the Third Periodic Report of Kuwait' (11 August 2016) CCPR/C/KWT/CO/3, para 24.

[121] HRC, 'Concluding Observations: Second Report of Egypt' (n 63) para 13. See also Amnesty International, 'Egypt: Officially You Do Not Exist—Disappeared and Tortured in the Name of Counter-Terrorism' (13 July 2016) <www.amnesty.org/en/documents/mde12/4368/2016/en/> accessed 29 May 2017.

[122] HRC, 'Concluding Observations: Initial Report of Kuwait' (n 55) para 15.

[123] HRC, 'Concluding Observations: Fourth Report of Israel' (n 53) para 24.

[124] In Egypt, Kuwait, Lebanon, Iran, Jordan, and Bahrain, women cannot pass citizenship on to their children. Yemen amended its laws in this respect, granting women the right to confer nationality in 2010.

[125] HRC, 'Concluding Observations: Third Report of Iran' (n 54) para 24 (on the arrests of Baha'is and Muslims who had converted to other religions).

[126] HRC, 'Concluding Observations on the Fourth Periodic Report of Yemen' (9 August 2005) CCPR/CO/84/YEM, para 5.

A second common source of resistance is that Middle Eastern States are complacent about discriminatory practices in their societies based on gender, ethnicity, and religious difference, and do not have a policy agenda to actively fight such discrimination. It is the absence of legislation and policies rather than their presence that forms part of the problem. The HRC often makes the point that there is no domestic legal framework or active policy to positively combat gender-based, ethnic, or religious discrimination or violence against women.[127] The HRC further makes reference to the duty to alter stereotypes and prejudices.[128]

E. Minorities and indigenous peoples

In the States of the Middle East, the European post-First World War definition of ethnic, linguistic, and religious historic minorities and the subsequent, more expansive interpretation by the HRC covering non-historic minorities[129] does not cohere with prevalent homogenizing historical nation-building discourses. Countries in the region follow the French Republican concept of citizenship and refuse to approach combatting non-discrimination within a minority rights paradigm *de jure* or de facto. This contrasts with the HRC's interpretation of article 27 protections.[130] The formalism of the citizenship project fights for the ideal of equal citizenship and relegates differences in identity to the private sphere. Furthermore, a concern for indigenous peoples is missing in the region, as Middle Eastern countries regard their nations as a continuation of indigenous peoples. Egypt, for example, states that 'the Egyptian people enjoy (sic) complete homogeneity between all groups and communities in society, since it is unified by single language and by the Arab culture'.[131] In Israel, the Bedouin population's right to their ancestral land[132] does not find support, as the Israeli State views Jews as the authentic indigenous people of the land.

In Middle Eastern States, the citizenship bond is viewed as an equalizer for all communities regardless of ethnic, religious, and linguistic differences. Syria reports that it 'has never known any discrimination on grounds of race, origin, religion or nationality'.[133] In Yemen, minorities enjoy their rights by virtue of Yemeni citizenship.[134] Kuwait holds that it has no minorities.[135] Egypt confirms that people belonging to the Baha'i faith have a freedom to have this belief in their homes. If individuals belonging to different identities seek to organize publicly, however, then they become suspect. For example, Egypt views the right of the Baha'i to form

[127] See eg HRC, 'Concluding Observations: Fourth Report of Jordan' (n 43); HRC, 'Concluding Observations: Initial Report of Kuwait' (n 55) para 5; HRC, 'Concluding Observations: Fourth Report of Israel' (n 53) para 6.

[128] See n 27. Cf HRC, 'Concluding Observations: Initial Report of Kuwait' (n 55) para 8.

[129] HRC, 'General Comment 23' in 'Compilation of General Comments' (2008) (vol 1) (n 92) 207.

[130] ibid.

[131] HRC, 'Third and Fourth Reports of Egypt' (n 43) para 628.

[132] HRC, 'Concluding Observations: Fourth Report of Israel' (n 53) para 24.

[133] HRC, 'Second Periodic Report of Syria' (25 August 2000) CCPR/C/SYR/2000/2, para 364.

[134] HRC, 'Second Report of Yemen' (n 63) para 113.

[135] HRC, 'Concluding Observations: Initial Report of Kuwait' (n 55) para 14.

associations to advance their faith in community with others as contrary to public order considerations under domestic law.[136]

Iran remains an exception to this, as the Iranian Constitution recognizes ethnic and tribal groups *qua* groups and affords them the right to use their own languages in the press, in mass media, and in school education.[137] Whilst Iranian constitutional precepts do make room for the legal protection of minorities *qua* minorities, official domestic recognition of minority groups is a necessary condition for their constitutional protection. Groups that fall outside of the official paradigm of minorities (eg Baha'i or Sunni Muslims) face a significant denial of their rights as well as repression.[138]

The only significant move from a unified vision of citizenship to a diverse construction thereof before the eyes of the law took place in the post-2005 Iraqi Constitution. Whilst Iraq, in 1987, held that the 'Iraqi constitution spoke of the "national" generation and not the "Arab" generation',[139] in the 2013 Report of Iraq to the HRC, Iraq is named as a State that experiences 'unity in diversity'.[140] This 2013 report lists Christians, Sabian-Mandaens, Yazidis, and Turkmen, Shabak, and Feyli Kurds as Iraqi minorities, and moves beyond the HRC's requirements by affording proportionate representation to minorities in governorates.[141] The Iraqi government is also the only State in the Middle East that has used the discourse of 'indigenous inhabitants' in its report to the HRC.

Whilst protections of the cultural heritage of linguistic, religious, and ethnic minorities are rejected, Middle Eastern States continue traditions of legal pluralism with respect to the regulation of personal status laws based on the religious identities of their inhabitants. As a legacy of the pre-nation state Ottoman *millet* regime, personal status (including marriage, divorce, child custody, and inheritance) is governed by the religions to which the affected individuals belong in Lebanon, Israel, Jordan, Egypt, and Iraq. In Yemen, the personal status laws of the majority are governed by Sharia. In Lebanon and Jordan, the *millet* paradigm is also the source of confessionalist political participation, with reserved seats for certain minorities in the parliament. According to the HRC, the application of personal status laws falls short of providing non-discriminatory safeguards, in particular for women. The HRC view, also echoed by CEDAW, is that personal status laws must exist within a unified framework of non-discrimination, and that the individual's right to opt out of religion-based personal status laws as well as their ability to legally challenge the discriminatory effects of such laws must be secured. The HRC further challenges the confessionalist paradigm as an adequate basis for political participation.

[136] cf the Egyptian Constitutional Court Judgment of 1 March 1975 (Case No 2, Judicial Year 2) finding the activities of Baha'i associations to be 'inimical to social security and public order', cited in HRC, 'Third and Fourth Reports of Egypt' (n 43) para 677.

[137] HRC, 'Third Report of Iran' (n 65) paras 1001–11.

[138] ibid para 24.

[139] UNGA, 'Report of the Human Rights Committee' GAOR 42nd Session Supp No 40 UN Doc A/42/40 (1987–1988) para 386.

[140] HRC, 'Fifth Report of Iraq' (n 69) para 225.

[141] ibid para 234.

F. Democratic expression of political pluralism

In a significant number of political regimes in the Middle East, protection of the standard democratic participation rights—freedom of expression, freedom of assembly and association, and the right to participate in the political process—falls below ICCPR standards. There are significant restrictions on the freedom of the media and the rights to assembly and association (both in law and in practice),[142] and amendments to domestic laws continue to reify such restrictions.[143]

In Syria and Kuwait, there are no opposition political parties. In Lebanon, a citizen must belong to a religious denomination officially recognized by the government to be eligible to run for public office.[144] In Egypt, the HRC has found that there are *de jure* and de facto impediments to the establishment and running of political parties.[145] In Iran, the Guardian Council has the power to reject parliamentary candidates, and political parties face the risk of dissolution with no clear legal safeguards.[146] Such requirements are so central to the regime's existing identities and political hold on power that calls by the HRC for the establishment of opposition political parties[147] or the abolishment of confessionalism[148] have no influence.

V. Conclusion

This survey of the influence of the ICCPR on domestic laws in the Middle East region shows a legal history of interrupted engagement due to conflicts and coups and of defensive engagement dominated by domestic legalism. Defensive domestic legalism is both a structural and an interactional feature of the region's engagement with the ICCPR. The former is reflected in the formulation of reservations (and the lack of interest in their lifting) and the unresolved ambiguity of the status of the ICCPR in domestic legal orders. The latter is prevalent in the post-ratification dialogues between the countries in the Middle East and the HRC. Countries in the region approach the influence of the ICCPR on domestic law primarily through the prism of pre-existing domestic laws. To borrow from Beth Simmons, the countries of the Middle East are, for the most part, 'insincere ratifiers'.[149]

There are three significant background explanations for the primacy of the domestic legal frameworks in the Middle East region as reflected in their resistance to HRC concluding observations. First, the region's authoritarian or majoritarian

142 HRC, 'Concluding Observations: Fourth Report of Jordan' (n 43) para 14.

143 cf Egyptian Law No 107/2013 of November 2013 regulating public meetings and peaceful assemblies.

144 For a most recent restatement of the denominational system in Lebanon, see CERD Committee, 'Combined Eighteenth to Twenty-Second Reports of Lebanon' (5 August 2015) CERD/C/LBN/18-22, para 51.

145 HRC, 'Concluding Observations: Third and Fourth Reports of Egypt' (n 51) para 22.

146 HRC, 'Concluding Observations: Third Report of Iran' (n 54) para 29.

147 HRC, 'Concluding Observations: Initial Report of Kuwait' (n 55).

148 HRC, 'Concluding Observations: Second Report of Lebanon' (n 63) para 23.

149 Simmons, *Mobilizing* (n 9) 77ff.

political structures, with their markedly patriarchal and robust religious establishment attributes, exhibit strong hostile preferences against minority identities and political views. This is demonstrated by de facto and *de jure* discrimination and blanket justifications in favour of public order and security when limiting rights and oppressing minority views. The second explanation is the prevalence of instability (de facto or perceived) and the existence of conflicts and violence in the region. The 'realities on the ground' narrative emerges as a predominant defence of domestic laws at the expense of the ICCPR, in particular when striking the balance between security concerns and human rights. The third explanation is the lack of independent and impartial judicial institutions and instead the prevalence of domestic administration of justice systems that are unable to produce civil and political rights-respecting outputs. Given the absence of strong domestic and international pro-reform partners, the HRC (and the rest of the UN human rights machinery for that matter) is unable to offer leverage for structural reform in the region.

There remains a significant gap between the HRC's vision of civil and political rights protection grounded in a liberal, democratic, and multicultural vision, and the domestic laws of the Middle East region. Some exceptions to this regional trend are found in Israel, Kuwait, and Turkey, in particular with respect to the engagement of high courts with the ICCPR as an aid to interpretation. In Israel, the ICCPR remains unincorporated into domestic law, but has the potential to act as a persuasive authority through the State's independent judiciary.[150] In Kuwait, the ICCPR has had some limited success in boosting the 1962 Constitution's protection of civil and political rights through the Kuwaiti Constitutional Court.[151] In both of these countries, the ICCPR pairs with the domestic constitutions and willing courts to have influence on domestic laws. In Turkey, the ICCPR plays a peripheral role thanks to the European Convention of Human Rights, the leverage of the EU on Turkey, and the Turkish Constitutional Court's explicit mandate to provide domestic remedies for rights protected at the intersection of the Turkish Constitution and the ECHR. The legal influence of the ICCPR here is achieved through the influence of a regional human rights mechanism in the constitutional legal order. Given that ECHR and ICCPR do not have identical provisions, however, the influence of the ICCPR in Turkey is limited to overlapping domains of protection. These exceptions show that the ICCPR and the concluding observations of the HRC need stronger pro-ICCPR domestic, regional, and international judicial and institutional partners in the region for sustainable and continuous legal influence to offset the prevalent regional culture of domestic legalism. Whether the Arab human rights monitoring mechanism, and the recently proposed Arab Court for Human Rights, may boost the influence of the ICCPR for some States in the region remains to be seen. The

[150] Israeli High Court of Justice, HCJ 3239/02 *Marab et al v Israeli Defence Force Commander* (5 February 2003) ILDC 15 (IL 2003).

[151] See eg the Kuwaiti Constitutional Court Judgment of 22 October 2009 <http://jurist.org/paperchase/2009/10/kuwait-constitutional-court-rules-women.php> accessed 28 March 2017.

influence of the ICCPR on domestic laws remains a long-term battle in the Middle East region, where small gains under limited existing legal opportunity structures remain the overarching norm.

Bibliography

Abouharb, M Rodwan, Book Review (2008) 70 J of Politics 563

Amnesty International, 'Egypt: Officially You Do Not Exist—Disappeared and Tortured in the Name of Counter-Terrorism' (13 July 2016) <www.amnesty.org/en/documents/mde12/4368/2016/en/> accessed 29 May 2017

Andersen, Ellen Ann, *Out of the Closets and Into the Courts: Legal Opportunity Structure and Gay Rights Litigation* (University of Michigan Press 2005)

Bellin, Eva, 'The Robustness of Authoritarianism in the Middle East: Exceptionalism in Comparative Perspective' (2004) 36 Comparative Politics 139

Brown, Nathan, 'Egypt is in a State of Emergency and Here is What It Means for Its Government' *Washington Post* (Washington, DC, 13 April 2017)

Çalı, Başak, 'The Logics of Supranational Human Rights Litigation, Official Acknowledgment and Human Rights Reform: The Southeast Turkey Cases before the European Court of Human Rights, 1996–2006' (2010) 35 Law and Social Inquiry 311

Çalı, Başak, 'Third Time Lucky: The Turkish Constitutional Court and a Woman's Right to Identity' (*EJIL Talk!*, 29 January 2014) <www.ejiltalk.org/third-time-lucky-the-dynamics-of-the-internationalisation-of-domestic-courts-the-turkish-constitutional-court-and-womens-right-to-identity-in-international-law/> accessed 19 June 2016

Çalı, Başak, Ghanea, Nazila, and Jones, Benjamin, 'Domestic Effects of Human Rights Treaty Ratification in the Member States of the Gulf Cooperation Council' (2016) 38 Human Rights Q 21

Çalı, Başak, and Montoya, Mariana, *The March to Universality? Religion-based Reservations to Core Human Rights Treaties* (Universal Rights Group 2017) <http://www.universal-rights.org/urg-policy-reports/march-universality-religion-based-reservations-core-un-human-rights-treaties-tell-us-human-rights-religion-universality-21st-century/> accessed on 26 May 2017

Cardenas, Sonia, and Flibbert, Andrew, 'National Human Rights Institutions in the Middle East' (2005) 59 The Middle East J 411

Castellino, Joshua, and Cavanaugh, Kathleen A, *Minority Rights in the Middle East* (OUP 2013)

Cohen, Stanley, 'Government Responses to Human Rights Reports: Claims, Denials, and Counterclaims' (1996) 18 Human Rights Q 517

Davison, Roderic H, 'Where is the Middle East?' (1960) 38 Foreign Affairs 665

'Egypt's Emergency Law Explained' *Al Jazeera* (April 2017) <www.aljazeera.com/indepth/features/2017/04/egypt-emergency-law-explained-170410093859268.html> accessed 29 May 2017

Göcek, Fatma Müge, and Balaghi, Shiva (eds), *Reconstructing Gender in the Middle East: Tradition, Identity, Power* (Columbia University Press 1994)

Hilson, Chris, 'New Social Movements: The Role of Legal Opportunity' (2002) 9 J of European Public Policy 238

Kamrava, Mehran, 'The Arab Spring and the Saudi-Led Counterrevolution' (2012) 561 Orbis 96

Kamrava, Mehran, *The Modern Middle East: A Political History since World War I* (3rd edn, University of California Press 2013)

Lapidoth, Ruth, Ben-Naftali, Orna, and Shani, Yuval, *The Obligation to Incorporate Human Rights Conventions into Israeli Law*, position paper (Rishon LeZion 2004)

Mayer, Ann Elizabeth, *Islam and Human Rights: Tradition and Politics* (4th edn, Westview Press 2007)

Moravsick, Andrew, 'The Origins of Human Rights Regimes: The Post War Delegation in Post War Europe' (2000) 54 International Organization 217

Pearcy, George Etzel, 'The Middle East: An Indefinable Region' (1959) 40 Department of State Bulletin 407

Rishmawi, Mervat, 'The Arab Charter on Human Rights and the League of Arab States: An Update' (2010) 10 Human Rights L Rev 169

Risse, Thomas, Ropp, Stephen C, and Sikkink, Kathryn (eds), *The Persistent Power of Human Rights: From Commitment to Compliance* (CUP 2013)

Ronen, Yaël, 'The Use of International Jurisprudence in Domestic Courts: The Israeli Experience' (April 2015) The Hebrew University of Jerusalem Research Paper <http://ssrn.com/abstract=2599016> accessed 21 June 2016

Scheinin, Martin, 'Turkey's Derogation from Human Rights Treaties: An Update' (*EJIL Talk!*, 18 August 2016) <www.ejiltalk.org/turkeys-derogation-from-human-rights-treaties-an-update/> accessed 26 May 2017

Simmons, Beth A, *Mobilizing for Human Rights: International Law in Domestic Politics* (CUP 2009)

Smith, Dominic, 'Baghdad State of Emergency Declared after Protesters Storm Parliament' *The Guardian* (30 April 2016) <www.theguardian.com/world/2016/apr/30/moqtada-al-sadr-supporters-enter-baghdad-parliament-building-green-zone> accessed 26 May 2016

Vreeland, James Raymond, 'Political Institutions and Human Rights: Why Dictatorships Enter into the United Nations Convention against Torture' (2008) 62 International Organization 65

Wiktorowicz, Quintan, 'The Limits of Democracy in the Middle East: The Case of Jordan' (1999) 53 The Middle East J 606

Wotipka, Christine Min, and Tsutsui, Kiyoteru, 'Global Human Rights and State Sovereignty: State Ratification of Human Rights Treaties, 1965–2001' (2008) 23 Sociological Forum 724

8

Influence of the ICESCR in Latin America

*Mónica Pinto and Martín Sigal**

I. Introduction

164 States from all over the world have ratified the International Covenant on Economic, Social and Cultural Rights (ICESCR or Covenant).[1] Among them are nearly all of the Latin American States,[2] with the exception of Cuba and three Caribbean States—Antigua and Barbuda, St. Kitts and Nevis, and St. Lucia. In the course of the following pages, we will assess the influence of the ICESCR's ratification in the Latin American region. For the purpose of our analysis, we will measure this influence by tracking the ICESCR's imprint on the different States at different levels; for example, the prevalence of references to the Covenant by political authorities, adjudicative bodies, and regional systems, as well as the institutional changes required by the incorporation of economic, social, and cultural rights (ESCR).

In assessing the influence of the ICESCR in Latin America, our main arguments are the following: (a) there is a constitutional framework shared by nearly all Latin American States according to which ESCR have found their place in constitutional provisions; (b) at the same time, while the great majority of Latin American States have adopted a regional instrument dealing with ESCR, namely the Pact of San Salvador, the gap in time between its adoption and its entry into force allowed the Covenant to exert a decisive impact in the countries of the region; (c) regarding justiciability, the great majority of courts in the region receive complaints concerning ESCR and adjudicate these complaints. However, this judicial activity is not reflected in an official public policy allowing citizens to avail themselves of those rights, and coexists with a regional situation of deep inequality and a lack of access to ESCR. At the same time, there is a need to incorporate a collective rights approach

* The authors thank Antonio Ribichini, who assisted them in the research and elaboration of a previous version of this paper, José Ryb, who helped in the editing of a version for the Seminar held in April 2016, Francisco Rodriguez Abinal, who helped in the checking of sources for the last version, and María Victoria Gama, for her valuable comments.

[1] International Covenant on Economic, Social and Cultural Rights (opened for signature 16 December 1966, entered into force 3 January 1976) 993 UNTS 3.

[2] For a full list of ratifications and accessions, see United Nations Treaty Collection <https://treaties.un.org/Pages/ViewDetails.aspx?src=IND&mtdsg_no=IV-3&chapter=4&clang=_en> accessed 27 March 2016.

into litigation concerning ESCR; (d) in relation to the Optional Protocol to the ICESCR,[3] there is nearly no international case law in the region because of its recent entry into force. In spite of this, the regional system relies on the Covenant as a source of rights and as the instrument providing the *pro persona* interpretation of the scope of certain rights; (e) poverty plays a crucial role in the field of ESCR because it deepens the structural inequalities and exclusions present in the region. It has led to a variety of approaches in domestic legislation, but should also lead to political changes and public policy developments aiming to reduce it; (f) all of these developments have evoked important debates on the scope of ESCR and on the capabilities and roles of enforcement agencies.

In order to address these issues, the chapter is divided into six sections. First, we will depict the particularities of the constitutional framework in Latin American countries and their relationship with international human rights instruments. Second, we will analyse the trajectory followed by the judiciary in determining the justiciability of ESCR. Third, we will present examples of how the jurisprudence of national courts has helped shape the impact of the ICESCR. Fourth, we will enlarge upon the impact that the ICESCR has had on regional mechanisms and jurisprudence. Fifth, we will consider the central role of poverty and inequality as the causes of violations of ESCR and their political impact in Latin America and, lastly, we will expand on the by-products of the justiciability of ESCR in the region.

As a caveat, we need to underline that the chapter suggests traces left by the ICESCR at different levels of the domestic and regional systems, but does not pretend to show that the ICESCR was a variable acting independently from others at the time of incorporating ESCR nationally. In fact, the influence of the Covenant coexists and interacts with the influence of other factors and variables (ie political reforms, social movements and civil society actions, economic crisis, the changing social understanding of local constitutions and constitutional reforms, the changing degree of judicial independence, the influence of other international human rights treaties, some of which also deal with ESCR, and the role of academia, among many others), which makes it improper to take the ICESCR as an isolated variable.

For that reason, we take the ICESCR as one relevant variable among several others which interact with each other, causing changes and progress in the domestic legal systems. In some cases, the traces of the ICESCR are explicit (eg when judges cite the ICESCR in their decisions, or when the Covenant is referred to in States' constitutions); in others the influence is implicit (eg when judges do not cite the ICESCR in their decisions, but decide based on ESCR that are recognized in the Covenant, while at the same time granting the Covenant a high hierarchical position in the domestic field).

Also, due to space constraints, it would not have been possible to analyse the influence of the ICESCR on all dimensions of the domestic systems of all the States included in the region. In this light, for Section II, we opted to analyse a number

[3] Optional Protocol to the International Covenant on Economic, Social and Cultural Rights ('Optional Protocol') (10 December 2008) United Nations General Assembly (UNGA) Resolution (Res) 63/117.

of countries which share certain characteristics, such as being members of the continental law tradition, being receptive to international human rights treaties, and having recognized ESCR in recent constitutional reforms, and a selection of countries in which courts have adjudicated social rights cases (in which the influence of the ICESCR may be traced either explicitly or implicitly), including Argentina and Colombia, which play a leading role in the adjudication of structural cases involving social rights. The selection of countries could have included others or replaced some of the ones on the list, but the chapter's conclusions would not have varied significantly.

II. The Region's Constitutional Frameworks and Their Approach to International Human Rights Instruments

Decolonization in America developed at two different points in time, namely in the early nineteenth century, when the great majority of Spanish colonies emancipated and became nation states, and in the second half of the twentieth century, when the British possessions in the region declared their independence and became part of the British Commonwealth of Nations.[4] These two processes shaped much of the constitutional life of Latin American States. They also made room for some distinctive differences between States.

Because of the Enlightenment's influence on Spain, the constitutions of its former colonies include chapters dealing with civil liberties. At the same time, the constitutional framework adopted by the United States was also a reference for other countries deciding on their emancipation.[5] Even though the United Kingdom was a forerunner in recognizing civil liberties, its former colonies kept much of the—eventually outdated—British legal infrastructure upon independence, and changes came a long time after the United Kingdom itself had changed its position in these areas.[6]

Latin American constitutions started embodying ESCR early in the twentieth century, beginning with the 1917 Mexican Constitution.[7] Argentina incorporated all of these rights into a Constitution adopted in 1949 by the Peronist government

[4] The first movement developed early in the nineteenth century, mainly after Napoleon's invasion of Spain, and the second started with the twentieth century decolonization period, after the adoption of the General Assembly Declaration on the Granting of Independence to Colonial Countries and Peoples (UNGA Res 1514 (XV) (14 December 1960).

[5] See Mónica Pinto, 'Droits humanitaires et droits de l'homme en Amérique latine' in Jean-René Garcia, Denis Rolland, and Patrice Vermeren (eds), *Les Amériques, des constitutions aux démocraties* (Éditions de la Maison des sciences de l'homme 2015) 353.

[6] The death penalty is a good illustration. While the United Kingdom progressively abolished it for different crimes (in 1965, 1973, 1998, and 2004), some of its former colonies kept it longer. See Amnesty International, 'Death Sentences and Executions 2016' (2017) Global Report ACT 50/5740/2017, 43, listing as 'retentionists' the following former colonies in the region: Antigua and Barbuda, Bahamas, Barbados, Belize, Guyana, Jamaica, Saint Kitts and Nevis, Saint Lucia, Saint Vincent and the Grenadines, and Trinidad and Tobago.

[7] See Political *Constitution* of Mexico, 1917.

and, after a constitutional amendment, they became the object of a single constitutional provision that entered into force in 1957. Other constitutional texts, like the ones that entered into force in Paraguay, Brazil, and Ecuador in 1967, included chapters dealing with social and economic order and the rights to education and culture, among others.[8] This historical background provides some explanation as to the rationale of the processes of reception of international human rights treaties in national contexts and their elevated position in the hierarchical order.

In Latin America, constitutional rules are supreme in the great majority of States. There are, however, some differences regarding the relationship between domestic law and international human rights instruments. Some constitutions place international treaties on the same footing as the constitutional text, while others assign them higher ranking over domestic legislation, and still others are silent on this point. Some specific examples of these practices are worth analysing in detail, especially in light of the concluding observations of the Committee on Economic, Social and Cultural Rights (CESCR) relating to the periodic reports submitted by States Parties, wherein it has highlighted the need to make ESCR justiciable without using deference to domestic legal hierarchies as an excuse.

A. Argentina

In Argentina, the amendment of the Constitution in 1994 brought two major innovations: new social rights were added and a number of international human rights instruments were given a status on par with or directly below the Constitution and above domestic law. One of the particularities of the Argentine Constitution is that it makes a distinction between some human rights instruments and other treaties. In force since 24 August 1994, it provides a constitutional-level hierarchical position to eleven international instruments—nine treaties, including the two international covenants, and two declarations—'in the full force of their provisions'.[9] By this wording, the Constitutional Assembly meant that these instruments are binding together with the reservations and declarations made at the time of accession, and that they are not to be understood as repealing any section of the First Part of the Constitution, but as complementing the rights and guarantees therein.[10] The Constitution also provides that Congress, by a special majority, may award the same hierarchical position to other international human rights treaties. Three other treaties have accordingly joined those named in the Constitution.[11] As a result of

[8] Constitution of the Republic of Paraguay, 1967; Political Constitution of Brazil, 1967; Constitution of the Republic of Ecuador, 1967. All three texts later underwent amendments resulting in the Constitutions of 1992, 1988, and 2008, respectively.

[9] See Constitution of the Nation of Argentina, 1994, ss 75(22) and (23), 41, 42, and 75(17).

[10] ibid.

[11] Convention on the Rights of Persons with Disabilities (opened for signature 13 December 2006, entered into force 3 May 2008) 2515 UNTS 3; Inter-American Convention on Forced Disappearance of Persons (opened for signature 9 June 1994, entered into force 28 March 1996); A-60 Organization of American States (OAS) Treaty Series; Convention on the Non-Applicability of Statutory Limitations to War Crimes and Crimes Against Humanity (opened for signature 26 November 1968, entered into force 11 November 1970) 754 UNTS 73.

this provision, international human rights obligations in Argentina have thus become constitutionalized.

B. Brazil

When Brazil adopted a new Constitution, in 1988, after more than twenty years of authoritarian rule, it placed human dignity in a position of privilege at the instrument's centre, as an interpretive guide to be followed in order to determine the meaning of other domestic legal provisions.

The 1988 Constitution consolidated fundamental rights and guarantees, incorporating new provisions and international human rights treaties. ESCR were strategically placed with other fundamental rights[12] so that the principles of indivisibility and interdependence were reinforced. The Constitution sets out the duties of the government, which must shape its programs, policies, and goals towards the full protection of these social priorities. In order to fulfil this objective, new, enforceable guarantees were added and mechanisms set up to prompt State action.[13]

The Brazilian Constitution of 1988 establishes the precedence of human rights—*prevalência dos direitos humanos*—as one of the cardinal principles guiding the international relations of the State.[14] Accordingly, it has been said that it cemented Brazilian engagement concerning the international protection of human rights.[15] At the same time, the Constitution states that the rights protected by it do not exclude others whose source is to be found in international law, and that international treaties on human rights, once approved by three-fifths of Congress, have equivalent status to constitutional amendments.[16] Legal authorities agree that the constitutional status of international treaties has therefore been established.[17]

C. Chile

In the case of Chile, the Constitution of 1980, as amended in 2005, establishes a State duty to respect and promote fundamental rights, as guaranteed by the Constitution and by the international treaties ratified by Chile.[18] In this context, it

[12] Constitution of the Federal Republic of Brazil, 1988, chs I and II.

[13] See Flavia Piovesan, 'Brazil' in Malcolm Langford (ed), *Social Rights Jurisprudence: Emerging Trends in International and Comparative Law* (CUP 2008) 182, 184.

[14] Constitution of the Federal Republic of Brazil, 1988, s 4(II).

[15] See Nadia de Araujo and Inés da Matta Andreiuolo, 'A internalização dos Tratados no Brasil e os Direitos Humanos' in Carlos Eduardo de Abreu Boucault and Nadia de Araujo (eds), *Os direitos humanos e o direito internacional* (Renovar 1999) 63, 102, supported by comments and statements by Pedro Dallari and Flavia Piovesan.

[16] Constitution of the Federal Republic of Brazil (n 14) ss 5, 2, and 3.

[17] See Antônio A Cançado Trindade, 'Direito Internacional e Direito Interno: Sua Interação na Proteção dos Direitos Humanos' (1996) <http://egov.ufsc.br/portal/sites/default/files/anexos/22361-22363-1-PB.pdf> accessed 23 March 2016; Flavia Piovesan, 'Direitos Humanos e o Dereito Constitucional Internacional' (Caderno de Direito Constitucional / Escola da Magistratura do Tribunal Regional Federal da 4a Região, 2006) <www.dhnet.org.br/direitos/militantes/flaviapiovesan/piovesan_dh_direito_constitucional.pdf> accessed 23 March 2016.

[18] See the Political Constitution of the Republic of Chile, 1980, s 5 (amended on 26 August 2005).

is crucial to keep in mind the self-executing nature of international human rights law as a *iuris tantum* presumption.

D. Paraguay

In Paraguay, the Constitution of 1992 recognized the superior rank of international treaties over all domestic legislation except the Constitution. In this sense, the Constitution is the supreme law of the Republic. The Constitution, international treaties, conventions, and agreements that have been approved and ratified by Congress, the laws dictated by Congress, and other related legal provisions of lesser rank make up the national legal system, in descending order of pre-eminence.[19]

E. Uruguay

The Uruguayan Constitution in force since 1997 makes no mention of the hierarchy of international instruments. However, it has been claimed that it recognizes the predominance of international law.[20] It provides, furthermore, for the application of 'implicit' rights. This means that constitutional provisions dealing with the rights of individuals should not be prevented from application on the grounds that the respective rules have not yet been adopted.[21]

F. Venezuela

Some Latin American States have enacted constitutional amendments in light of new popular movements. These texts are usually very detailed and complete. The 1999 Bolivarian Constitution of Venezuela is an example, and one that provides for the constitutional footing of treaties, pacts, and conventions relating to human rights. As a result, human rights treaties precede domestic rules when they embody more favourable standards than those in the Constitution and the national legislation, and they are immediately and directly applicable by courts and other public organs.[22]

G. Ecuador

In the same vein, the 2008 Constitution of Ecuador proclaims that international human rights instruments recognizing more favourable rights than those contained

[19] Constitution of the Republic of Paraguay, 1992, s 137(1).

[20] Article 85(7) of the Constitution of the Eastern Republic of Uruguay, 1967, as last amended in 2004: 'A la Asamblea General compete: Decretar la guerra y aprobar o reprobar por mayoría absoluta de votos del total de componentes de cada Cámara, los tratados de paz, alianza, comercio y las convenciones o contratos de cualquier naturaleza que celebre el Poder Ejecutivo con potencias extranjeras.' See Eduardo Jiménez de Aréchaga, 'La Convención Americana de Derechos Humanos como derecho interno' (1988) 7 Revista del Instituto Interamericano de Derechos Humanos 25.

[21] Constitution of the Eastern Republic of Uruguay, 1967, as last amended in 2004, s 85(7).

[22] Constitution of the Bolivarian Republic of Venezuela, 1999, as last amended in 2009, art 23.

in the Constitution will prevail over any other norm or legal rule. At the same time, it states that, as a general rule, the Constitution enjoys pre-eminence over international treaties.[23]

H. Bolivia

The 2009 Constitution of the Plurinational State of Bolivia states that international treaties protecting human rights and prohibiting limitations during states of emergency, where ratified by the legislature and Plurinational Assembly, have priority in the domestic legal order. In addition, the Constitution should be interpreted in conformity with the human rights treaties ratified by Bolivia.[24]

I. Interim conclusion

On the one hand, the influence of the Covenant may be traced to the incorporation of several economic, social, and cultural rights into the domestic constitutions of the States under study. At the same time, the ICESCR's relevance in the domestic legal orders of several countries in the region becomes clear when analysing the constitutional provisions that determine how human rights treaties operate internally and the normative hierarchy that each State gives to such instruments. Further, these constitutional clauses provide the necessary framework for courts to interpret both the Constitution and treaties under the lens of a more *pro persona* or expansive view of human rights in the resolution of particular cases.

III. Justiciability of Economic, Social, and Cultural Rights

A. The road to justiciability

We understand justiciability as the capability of a right to be the object of a claim that can be adjudicated by a court of law.[25] In order for that to happen, the right needs to be recognized by the domestic legal order in a certain way so that courts can order its enforcement by the political authorities.

By contrast, non-justiciability encompasses both the situation in which the non-recognition of the right impedes the possibility of making that right enforceable and, independently or because of that, the lack of immediate applicability. In that sense, the CESCR has a long tradition of deploring the non-justiciability of ESCR in given national contexts, for example finding that it 'regrets that laws incorporating

[23] Constitution of the Republic of Ecuador, 2008, ss 424 and 425.

[24] Political Constitution of the Plurinational State of Bolivia, 2009, s 13(IV).

[25] CESCR, 'General Comment 3' in 'Note by the Secretariat, Compilation of General Comments and General Recommendations Adopted by Human Rights Treaty Bodies' (2003) UN Doc HRI/GEN/1/Rev.6, para 5.

the Covenant into Bolivia's domestic legal system have not yet been adopted';[26] expressing concern about the fact that 'some economic, social and cultural rights, including the right to housing, are not considered justiciable in [Chile, while noting] the scarcity of case law in which the rights of the Covenant have been invoked before and directly applied by domestic courts';[27] regretting 'that legislation aimed at the incorporation of the Covenant directly into Panama's domestic legal system has not been adopted and that as a result the Covenant cannot be invoked before the internal authorities';[28] and noting 'that, under the 1993 [Peruvian] Constitution, international human rights instruments are on the same level as domestic laws and that a recent decision of the Supreme Court of Justice stated that the provisions of those instruments do not have constitutional status'.[29]

Traditionally, ESCR have been viewed as unenforceable, non-justiciable, and to be fulfilled 'progressively' over time,[30] as opposed to their more popular siblings, civil and political rights (CPR).[31] As Craig Scott points out, States understood the difference between ESCR and CPR as based on 'implementation-based reasons', among others.[32] According to this reasoning, the two categories of rights were seen as different in nature and, hence, each of them required different methods of implementation. The source for these conclusions derived from the Covenants themselves, as the International Covenant on Civil and Political Rights (ICCPR) establishes obligations 'to respect and ensure',[33] whereas the ICESCR requires State parties to 'undertake to take steps ... to the maximum of [their] available resources, with a view to achieving progressively the full realization of the rights'[34] recognized by the Covenant. When drafting the Covenants, it was believed that CPR required merely non-interference by the State and the adoption solely of legislation and administrative measures. On the contrary, ESCR required positive State action depending on the level of economic resources of the State and thus, their implementation was deemed to be gradual.

Slowly but surely, the discussion about the progressive versus immediate character of the obligations derived from the ICESCR shifted into the understanding that ESCR, like any rights, require the adoption of legal rules and public policies so

[26] CESCR, 'Consideration of Bolivia's Initial Periodic Report' (21 May 2001) UN Doc E/C.12/1/Add.60, para 11.

[27] CESCR, 'Consideration of Chile's Third Periodic Report' (1 December 2004) UN Doc E/C.12/1/Add.105, para 12.

[28] CESCR, 'Consideration of Panama's Second Periodic Report' (24 September 2001) UN Doc E/C.12/1/Add.64, para 9.

[29] CESCR, 'Consideration of Peru's Initial Periodic Report' (20 May 1997) UN Doc E/C.12/1/Add.14, para 13.

[30] See Magdalena Sepúlveda, *Nature of the Obligations under the International Covenant on Economic, Social and Cultural Rights* (Intersentia 2003) 117.

[31] See CESCR, 'Fact Sheet No 16 (Rev. 1)' s 2 <www.ohchr.org/Documents/Publications/FactSheet16rev.1en.pdf> accessed 23 March 2016.

[32] See Craig Scott, 'The Interdependence and Permeability of Human Rights Norms: Towards a Partial Fusion of the International Covenant on Human Rights' (1989) 27 Osgoode Hall Law Journal 769, 791, 794–95.

[33] International Covenant on Civil and Political Rights (opened for signature 16 December 1966, entered into force 23 March 1976) 999 UNTS 171, art 2(1).

[34] ICESCR art 2(1).

that individuals can exercise said rights and, if needed, demand their enforcement through legal action. The fact that CPR also require legal rules, public policies, and resources to be fulfilled became clear in the discussion. Also, the growing shared understanding that progressivity does not imply the absence of immediate obligations (and creates certain immediate duties to adopt measures, for example) created room for the intervention of courts and tribunals. At the same time, the interpretations created by those courts and tribunals exert a great influence on the content of the obligations imposed on the State in relation to ESCR. The CESCR's General Comment 3[35] has been a crucial tool to advance this discussion.

As stated above, the non-justiciability of ESCR and claims about their programmatic nature have long been excused because of the use of the expression 'progressively' in article 2 of the Covenant. This is not a valid conclusion in light of the fact that the provision must be interpreted in good faith: that is, according to the rules of interpretation embodied in article 31 of the Vienna Convention on the Law of Treaties.[36] Any other result would be arbitrary and contrary to the interdependence and indivisibility of human rights. CESCR, General Comment 3 sheds some light on the expression by understanding that:

> full realization of all economic, social and cultural rights will generally not be able to be achieved in a short period of time. ... Nevertheless, the fact that realization over time, or in other words, progressively, is foreseen under the Covenant should not be misinterpreted as depriving the obligation of all meaningful content. ... It thus imposes an obligation to move as expeditiously and effectively as possible towards that goal [the full realization of the rights in question].

General Comment 3 further informs this understanding by providing that 'any deliberately retrogressive measures in that regard would require the most careful consideration and would need to be fully justified by reference to the totality of the rights provided for in the Covenant and in the context of the full use of the maximum available resources'.[37]

Following this interpretation, when the Organization of American States' General Assembly adopted the 'Standards for the Preparation of Periodic Reports Pursuant to Article 19 of the Protocol of San Salvador', it decided that progressiveness means 'gradual advancement in the creation of the conditions necessary to ensure the exercise of an economic, social and cultural right',[38] thus pushing for the enforceability of the protected rights. At the same time, the CESCR has constantly submitted that some provisions of the Covenant, including articles 3, 7(a)(i), 8, 10(3), 13(2)(a),

[35] See CESCR, 'General Comment 3' (n 25). In this General Comment, the Committee states that the Covenant 'imposes various obligations which are of immediate effect' including '"undertaking to guarantee" that relevant rights "will be exercised without discrimination"' and 'undertaking in article 2(1) "to take steps" ... within a reasonably short time after the Covenant's entry into force for the States concerned' to fulfil the obligations established in it.

[36] Philip Alston, 'U.S. Ratification of the Covenant on Economic, Social and Cultural Rights: The Need for an Entirely New Strategy' (1990) 84 American J of Intl L 365, 391.

[37] CESCR, 'Fact Sheet' (n 31) para 9.

[38] OAS (General Assembly), 'Standards for the Preparation of Periodic Reports Pursuant to Article 19 of the Protocol of San Salvador' (7 June 2005) AG/RES. 2074 (XXXV-O/05) para 5(1).

(3), and (4), and 15(3), would seem to be capable of immediate application by judicial and other organs in many national legal systems.[39]

The justiciability of ESCR has also been supported by some of the most well-known legal authorities in the Americas, who have written numerous pages devoted to analysing ESCR and the clauses of the Covenant. Current trends in academia and among the judiciary seem to prove that there is a growing consensus on their justiciability.[40] According to César Rodríguez, two angles of analysis have dominated this perspective. On the one hand, there have been many contributions that have concentrated on making a theoretical case for the justiciability of ESCR in light of the demands of democratic theory and the reality of social contexts marked by deep economic and political inequalities. On the other, a number of contributions have focused on a doctrinal human rights perspective, which has given greater precision to judicial standards for upholding ESCR and boosted the utilization of these rights by judicial organs and supervisory bodies at both the national and international level.[41]

Further, some of the judges at the Inter-American Court of Human Rights, including Antonio Cançado Trindade (in a paper published in 1994)[42] and later on Sergio García Ramírez (in 2003)[43] and Manuel Ventura Robles (in 2004),[44] have produced legal literature on ESCR and on the ICESCR. Other well-known specialists dealing with this set of rights and their normative sources have joined their number, including Ligia Bolívar,[45] Víctor Abramovich and Christian Courtis,[46] Julieta Rossi,[47] César Rodríguez-Garavito,[48] and Rodrigo Uprimny Yepes,[49] among others.

[39] See CESCR, 'Fact Sheet' (n 31) para 5.

[40] Malcolm Langford, 'The Justiciability of Social Rights: From Practice to Theory' in Malcolm Langford (ed), *Social Rights Jurisprudence: Emerging Trends in International and Comparative Law* (CUP 2008) 3, 45.

[41] César Rodríguez-Garavito, 'Beyond the Courtroom: The Impact of Judicial Activism on Socioeconomic Rights in Latin America' (2011) 89 Texas L Rev 1669.

[42] Antonio A Cançado Trindade, 'La protección internacional de los derechos económicos, sociales y culturales' (1994) 1 Estudios Básicos de Derechos Humanos 39.

[43] Sergio García Ramírez, 'Protección jurisdiccional internacional de los derechos económicos, sociales y culturales' (2003) 9 Cuestiones Constitucionales 127.

[44] Manuel E Ventura Robles, 'Jurisprudencia de la Corte Interamericana de Derechos Humanos en materia de derechos económicos, sociales y culturales' (2004) 40 Revista Instituto Interamericano de Derechos Humanos 87.

[45] Ligia Bolívar, 'Derechos económicos, sociales y culturales: derribar mitos, enfrentar retos, tender puentes—Una visión desde la (in)experiencia de América Latina' in Sonia Picado Sotela, Antônio A Cançado Trindade, and Roberto Cuéllar (comps), *Estudios Básicos de Derechos Humanos*, vol V (Instituto Interamericano de Derechos Humanos 1996) 85.

[46] Víctor Abramovich and Christian Courtis, 'Hacia la exigibilidad de los derechos económicos, sociales y culturales: Estándares internacionales y criterios de aplicación ante los tribunales locales' in Martín Abregú and Christian Courtis (comps), *La aplicación de los tratados sobre derechos humanos por los tribunales locales* (Editores el Puerto / CELS 1997) 283.

[47] See Julieta Rossi, 'Mecanismos internacionales de protección de los derechos económicos, sociales y culturales' in Víctor Abramovich, María José Añón, and Christian Courtis (comps), *Derechos sociales: instrucciones de uso* (Fontamara 2003) 355; Julieta Rossi and Victor Abramovich, 'La tutela de los derechos económicos, sociales y culturales en el artículo 26 de la Convención Americana sobre Derechos Humanos' (2007) 9 Revista Estudios Socio-Jurídicos 34.

[48] eg see Rodríguez-Garavito, 'Beyond the Courtroom' (n 41) among other works. For a complete list of the author's publications, see <http://cesarrodriguez.net/files/cvingles.pdf> accessed 10 March 2017.

[49] Rodrigo Uprimny Yepes, 'Should Courts Enforce Social Rights? The Experience of the Colombian Constitutional Court' in Fons Coomans (ed), *Justiciability of Economic and Social Rights: Experiences*

B. A new form of litigation

The incorporation of human rights treaties guaranteeing ESCR into the domestic systems of the countries in the region added to the acceptance of the justiciability of such rights and created the need to redesign the country-level litigation and procedural rules so that they would be able to process rights claims of a collective nature (like those involving ESCR). For example, social rights have a collective dimension, and therefore the violation of such rights tends to imply the violation not only of individual rights, but also of those of groups or communities. Also, violations derived from public policies, which often exclude marginalized groups or communities in a region with very high levels of inequality, tend to have a structural nature that may only be challenged through collective litigation seeking collective and structural remedies. This led the Inter-American Commission on Human Rights to state that a central requirement for the enforceability of ESCR is to design and implement collective proceedings that allow for collective claims. Furthermore, the Commission claimed that the possibility of filing collective claims in representation of vulnerable groups that may suffer a violation of their ESCR is a requirement of the right to have effective recourse to justice.[50]

The collective dimension of certain violations of ESCR has also been identified by the Inter-American Court of Human Rights, for example, in a case concerning indigenous peoples' right to their ancestral lands, in which it stated that the communal property rights characteristic of these communities imply that there is no one single individual who may claim ownership, since such ownership belongs to the group and its community.[51] The same idea was asserted, invoking General Comment 14 of the CESCR, in the *Yakye Axa v Paraguay* case.[52]

Also, as emerges from the cases mentioned in the following section, the requirement for collective proceedings may respond to the practical impossibility facing members of a given collective in filing an individual claim in court. This may be due to the particular situation of vulnerability of such individuals, which constitutes an empirical barrier to carrying out all of the steps necessary to file a judicial case, or to the structural nature of the situation that produces the rights violation in question,

from Domestic Systems (Intersentia 2006) 355. For a complete list of this author's publications, see <https://uprimnyrodrigoenglish.wordpress.com/publications> accessed 10 March 2017.

[50] See Inter-American Commission on Human Rights (IACHR) 'El acceso a la justicia como garantía de los derechos económicos sociales y culturales: Estudio de los estandares fijados por el sistema interamericano de derechos humanos' (7 September 2007) OEA/Ser.L/V/II.129 Doc 4, paras 268–75.

[51] *Case of the Mayagna (Sumo) Awas Tigni Community v Nicaragua*, Judgment (Merits, Reparations and Costs) Inter-American Court of Human Rights Series C No 79 (31 August 2001) paras 146 and 149. All of the IACtHR's jurisprudence is available online at <www.corteidh.or.cr/index.php/en/jurisprudencia> (last visited 10 March 2017).

[52] *Case of the Yakye Axa Indigenous Community v Paraguay*, Judgment (Merits, Reparations and Costs) Inter-American Court of Human Rights Series C No 125 (17 June 2005) para 166.

which therefore requires a structural remedy (eg cases in which prison system reform is required to change inhuman conditions of detention).

This collective nature of ESCR led countries to progressively recognize collective proceedings for filing claims for their protection. These proceedings adopted different forms in different jurisdictions, examples of which are the *acción de amparo colectivo* (in Argentina), *acción de tutela* (in Colombia), and the *mandados de segurança* (in Brazil), among others. As time passed, different types of civil society organizations, indigenous peoples, public defence institutions, and ombudspersons exerted societal oversight of public policies using a human rights approach, making the region a leader in human rights strategic litigation experiences. These types of proceedings propelled cases which promoted public discussions on policies such as guidelines for social security reform, mass pension and wage reduction programs, HIV/AIDS drugs provision policy, education quota systems for Afro-descendant populations, distribution of public education budget appropriations, exclusion of social sectors from food assistance programs, discriminatory practices against immigrants in access to social services and housing schemes, and non-fulfilment of social policy for displaced persons in armed conflicts. These remedies have also contributed to the monitoring of companies that provide public services, in order to protect the rights of users, or private groups and companies that engage in economic activities that have an environmental impact. They have also served to secure the disclosure of information and demand participation mechanisms in processes prior to the design of a policy or the award of concessions for potentially harmful economic activities.[53]

IV. Influence of the ICESCR on the Jurisprudence of National Courts

As the present section will show, the ICESCR and the 'decisions' (understood as General Comments, Views, concluding observations, reports, and provisional measures) issued by the CESCR have a strong presence in the decisions of most national courts in cases related to ESCR. According to Julieta Rossi and Leonardo G Filippini, this fact is explained by at least four conditions. The first is the availability of these documents as relevant normative material for the resolution of a specific case in the local domain. The second is the higher precision and sophistication of the international human rights rules and 'decisions' in delineating the scope of human rights obligations, as a consequence of the activity of specialized treaty bodies (ie the CESCR). The third is the massive judicialization of politics, which implied that, as of the 1990s in Latin America, the judiciary became an avenue for political participation, activism, and contesting issues which were once discussed in the political domain but are now claimed in court through a rights-based approach. The last factor is the robust presence of invocations of international law in judicial decisions, which may be explained by the fact that, as a consequence of the incorporation of international obligations into domestic legal systems, litigants are invoking international

[53] IACHR, 'El acceso a la justicia' (n 50) para 238.

treaties and decisions in court.[54] The ways in which States have implemented their Covenant obligations have become the set of criteria through which the courts find that positive obligations exist and that States have to enforce them.

As stated in the introduction to this chapter, domestic courts have found different ways of addressing issues regulated under the ICESCR, and it is difficult to isolate the influence of the Covenant from the influence of other factors that may have impacted the courts' decisions—such as the recognition of certain rights by the domestic Constitution and references to other international human rights treaties or to other countries' judicial decisions. The following are some examples in which rights that emerge from the ICESCR have been adjudicated by national courts in countries that have ratified the Covenant. As explained in the previous section, constitutions throughout the region grant a high hierarchical position to treaty provisions in the domestic legal system. Also, as emerges from the following decisions, the influence of the ICESCR on the judicial system is explicit in some cases, with courts citing the CESCR, or implicit in others. In the latter case, even if the ICESCR is not cited, the rights which are the basis for the decisions are rights recognized by the ICESCR and by the internal legal orders, which assign international human rights treaties a high position in the normative hierarchy.

A. Argentina

The Argentine Supreme Court applies ESCR contained in international human rights treaties, including the ICESCR, either directly or in complement to constitutional provisions. It has done so across the board, including in a variety of fields such as the right to health, the right to social security, labour rights, and children's rights, in a progressive and non-regressive fashion. The Court has also based its rulings on the CESCR's General Comments and the decisions and advisory opinions of the Inter-American Court of Human Rights.[55]

In *Campodónico de Beviacqua,* the Court delivered a seminal decision regarding the right to health.[56] The case revolved around the obligation of the federal government to continue assisting in the treatment of a child with disabilities. The State had discontinued the provision of medication to the affected child, affirming that this was compatible with its human rights obligations. It argued that it had previously provided the medication not out of legal duty but for 'humanitarian reasons'. An appellate court found against the State and ordered the re-establishment of the

[54] Julieta Rossi and Leonardo G Filippini, 'El derecho internacional en la judiciabilidad de los derechos sociales: El caso de Latinoamérica' in Pilar Arcidiácono, Nicolás Espejo Yaksic, and César Rodríguez-Garavito (eds), *Derechos sociales: Justicia, política y economía en América Latina* (Siglo del Hombre, Uniandes, CELS, and Universidad Diego Portales 2010) 193.

[55] Víctor Abramovich, Alberto Bovino, and Christian Courtis (eds), *La aplicación de los tratados sobre derechos humanos en el ámbito local: La experiencia de una decada* (CELS 2007).

[56] See Supreme Court (Argentina) No C.823.XXXV.RHE, *Campodónico de Beviacqua, Ana Carina c/ Ministerio de Salud y Acción Social—Secretaría de Programas de Salud y Banco de Drogas Neoplásicas,* 24 October 2000. All Argentine Supreme Court decisions are available online at <www.csjn.gov.ar/sentencias-acordadas-y-resoluciones> accessed 10 March 2017.

benefit, and the Supreme Court confirmed the decision. In doing so, the Court stated that the right to health is constitutionally protected and that it is the duty of the federal State to implement positive action in order to guarantee it. The judges also pointed out that international human rights treaties protect children's right to life and health and cited article 12 of the ICESCR. They then affirmed that States parties to the Covenant 'must take steps to the maximum of their available resources, with a view to achieving, progressively, the full realization of the rights recognized in the Covenant.' They also based their decision on articles 23, 24, and 26 of the Convention on the Rights of the Child.[57] Based on this, the Supreme Court affirmed that the Argentine government could not validly refuse to comply with its international duties to promote and facilitate the health treatment required by children. More so, the involvement of other public or private entities did not preclude participation by the State, especially when the best interests of the child were at stake.

In another important decision, *Asociación Benghalensis*, the Supreme Court ordered the federal government to guarantee the provision of HIV-related medicine to public hospitals, in compliance with a federal statute, as the result of an injunction that had been filed by a non-governmental organization (NGO).[58] The Court upheld the judgment of the appellate court and confirmed the arguments advanced by the attorney general. The judges stated that the right to health is recognized in article 12(c) of the ICESCR, articles 4(1) and 5 of the American Convention on Human Rights,[59] and article 6 of the ICCPR.[60] Consequently, it is up to the government not only to 'abstain from interfering in the exercise of individual rights' but also to 'perform positive actions, without which the exercise of rights would be illusory'. Further, this was the first case in which the Court recognized the collective standing of an NGO.

More recently, the Federal Supreme Court ruled in a right to housing case wherein it explicitly argued for the State's obligation to guarantee the rights recognized in the Constitution and international human rights treaties.[61] In doing so, the Court heavily relied on and even quoted the CESCR's General Comment 5, and reiterated that the Committee is the authorized interpreter of the ICESCR and that, for that reason, its interpretation of the Covenant should be taken into account by the Court.[62] Further, the Court directly relied on the standards established by

[57] Convention on the Rights of the Child (opened for signature 20 November 1989, entered into force 2 September 1990) 1577 UNTS 3.

[58] Supreme Court (Argentina) No A.186.XXXIV.REX, *Asociación Benghalensis y otros c/ Ministerio de Salud y Acción Social—Estado Nacional s/ amparo ley 16.986*, 1 June 2000, 22.

[59] See arts 4(1) and 5 of the American Convention on Human Rights (ACHR) (opened for signature 22 November 1969, entered into force 18 July 1978) 36 OAS Treaty Series, 1144 UNTS 123.

[60] ICCPR art 6.

[61] Supreme Court (Argentina) No Q.64.XLVI, *Q. C., S. Y. c/ Gobierno de la Ciudad Autónoma de Buenos Aires s/ amparo*, 24 April 2012 (cita Fallos: 335:452) <www.cij.gov.ar/nota-9003-Derecho-a-la-vivienda--la-Corte-ordeno-a-la-Ciudad-poner-fin-a-la-situacion-de-calle-de-una-madre-y-su-hijo-discapacitado.html> accessed 10 March 2017.

[62] ibid para 10, referring to CESCR, 'General Comment 5' in 'Compilation of General Comments' (2003) (n 25) 24.

the Committee on how to understand the obligation under the Optional Protocol to adopt measures using the maximum available resources, stating that even if the availability of resources may condition the obligation to adopt measures (or take steps), it does not alter the immediate nature of this obligation; it also rejected the scarcity of resources as an argument to justify not having adopted any measures.[63] The Court went on to adopt the Committee's approach to analysing the objective criteria to be considered in cases in which the State invokes the lack of resources or limited resources.[64]

At the provincial level, the settlement agreement between the government of the City of Buenos Aires and the non-governmental association ACIJ (Civil Association for Equality and Justice) helped to clarify the content and scope of the State's obligations with regards to the right to education. The injunction filed by ACIJ demanded that the government allocate enough resources to properly finance the education system and execute budgetary allocations to the fullest. After a positive decision by an appellate court, which included as a central argument that the government had not respected the obligation imposed by the ICESCR to adopt measures using the maximum available resources,[65] the government and ACIJ reached an agreement containing provisions for the building of adequate facilities and the implementation of a control and audit mechanism. Still in progress today, this precedent proved to be a milestone in the litigation of ESCR and an important guideline for the State in the execution of public policy.[66]

B. Brazil

As concerns the right to health care, the Brazilian courts have stated that this right stems from the right to life and is, as such, its inseparable consequence. In *Diná Rosa Vieira v Município de Porto Alegre*, the Superior Federal Tribunal affirmed that it was the responsibility of the State to design its public policies so as to guarantee equal access to medical, hospital, and pharmaceutical assistance. The judges stressed that the government cannot transform constitutional rules into an empty constitutional promise and that the right to health 'imposes upon the government a positive duty to provide the means for it, which will only be fulfilled by government bodies when they adopt measures designed to promote, in full, effective compliance with the determinations contained in the constitutional text'.[67] The same tribunal has also

[63] ibid para 14, citing CESCR, 'Statement of Evaluation of the Obligation to Take Steps to the "Maximum of Available Resources" under an Optional Protocol to the Covenant' (21 September 2007) E/C.12/2007/1, para 10.

[64] ibid para 14.

[65] *Asociación Civil por la Igualdad y la Justicia c/ GCBA s/ amparo (art 14 CCABA)* No 23360/0 (19 March 2008) <http://campusvirtual.justiciacordoba.gob.ar/moodle/pluginfile.php/2799/mod_folder/content/0/CCAyT%20ACIJ%20Educacion%20Inicial.pdf?forcedownload=1> accessed 10 March 2017, s A.5.

[66] See the *Acta de Acuerdo* between the government of the City of Buenos Aires and ACIJ (9 February 2011) <http://acij.org.ar/wp-content/uploads/ACTA_ACUERDO_4_de_febrero.pdf> accessed 23 March 2016.

[67] See Supreme Federal Court (Brazil), RE-AgR 271286 RS, *Diná Rosa Vieira c/ Município de Porto Alegre*, 12 September 2000.

affirmed that those in need are entitled not just to any sort of treatment, but to the most suitable and effective kind. This, in turn, provides the patient 'with the greatest dignity and least amount of suffering'.[68]

Regarding the right to education, the courts have stressed the right to elementary schooling, deriving it from the general duty of the State in this matter. In this line, domestic judges have emphasized the importance of verifying compliance beyond any economic restraints. In other rulings, they have established the obligation of the public authorities to provide vacancies in day-care centres for children of up to six years of age. As for higher education, rulings point to the duty of the State to sustain its provision even when students are behind on the payment of fees.[69]

It can be pointed out that, with an exception for the right to health, Brazilian courts have not dealt with as many cases concerning ESCR as other States in the region, and that direct citations of the ICESCR are not commonly found in their decisions, reflecting the country's traditional reticence towards international law. Such lack of explicit reliance may also be explained by the normative structure for the domestic enactment of rights. As explained by Octavio Luiz Motta Ferraz in his analysis of Brazilian right to health litigation, such enactment is very detailed and specific and does not even contain references to the limitation of the State's duty based on the availability of resources, which may explain the different approaches to adjudication taken in comparison with other jurisdictions.[70]

However, there is an increasing trend to litigate ESCR, which reveals the potential to fully ensure compliance with the relevant international human rights instruments.

C. Colombia

Colombia's Constitutional Court plays a leading role in the protection of ESCR and in promoting their effectiveness. The Court has done so through the so-called *acción de tutela*—one of the judicial remedies available before it—as well as through its review of laws. The Court has stated that, although ESCR are defined by their progressive realization, it is an inalienable duty of the State to develop a plan for their implementation, as well as to commit not to adopt retrogressive measures, neither in legislation nor in the allocation of resources.[71]

As for the right to health, the Court has generally considered that ESCR should be progressively realized, except for the cases in which the right in question is linked

[68] See Supreme Federal Court (Brazil), RMS 17903, *Kátia Mendes Campos c/ Estado de Minas Gerais*, 10 August 2004.

[69] See Piovesan, 'Brazil' (n 13) 188–89.

[70] Octavio Luiz Motta Ferraz, 'Between Usurpation and Abdication? The Right to Health in the Courts of Brazil and South Africa' in Oscar Vilhena, Upendra Baxi, and Frans Viljoen (eds), *Transformative Constitutionalism: Comparing the Apex Courts of Brazil, India, and South Africa* (Pretoria University Law Press 2013) 375.

[71] Magdalena Sepúlveda, 'Colombia: The Constitutional Court's Role in Addressing Social Injustice' in Malcolm Langford (ed), *Social Rights Jurisprudence: Emerging Trends in International and Comparative Law* (CUP 2008) 144, 147.

to another fundamental right. In the case of children, the Constitution establishes that it is a fundamental right on its own and is, thus, directly applicable.[72] In that vein, in a high-profile decision, the Court ordered the State to implement a free vaccination program for children in one of the poorest districts of Bogotá. More than four hundred parents filed an injunction against the government requesting assistance from the State and denouncing the violation of their children's right to health. They argued that they lacked the resources to provide for their families and that the children were in a high-risk situation. In its ruling, the Court stressed that the lack of a vaccination plan affected the core content of the right to health—as protected by local laws, the Constitution, and international human rights treaties ratified by Colombia (which include the ICESCR)—and, hence, superseded any concerns about a violation of the principle of separation of powers.[73] The judges also required that treatments be provided to children even when these were excluded from the coverage of the compulsory health plan, including, in some instances, when these interventions needed to take place overseas.[74] The Court has made an effort to place human dignity at the centre of its decisions and, in doing so, has eschewed utilitarian considerations. Further, the influence of the ICESCR may be traced not only to the recognition of ESCR rights by the Constitution and courts, but also to the direct citation of and recourse to certain doctrines related to the Covenant. For example, in a recent case concerning the right to health of an imprisoned person, the Constitutional Court strongly relied on the CESCR's General Comment 14 to define the scope of such a right;[75] in a case related to employment stability and labour rights, the Court based its decision on ICESCR article 10(2).[76]

With regards to the right to education, the Constitution recognizes it as a fundamental right and, as such, as directly enforceable. The Constitutional Court has affirmed that it is an inalienable duty of the State to make sure that access to educational institutions is guaranteed, and supported its position by citing General Comment 13 of the CESCR. In this sense, it has found that this right is violated when public or private schools deny access to children without adequate justification.[77] In another case, the Court analysed the principle of progressive realization and non-retrogression, citing General Observation 3 of the CESCR in deciding that the State had an obligation to provide access to primary education to adults.[78]

[72] Political Constitution of Colombia, 1991, s 44.

[73] Colombian Constitutional Court, Judgment SU225-98, *Sandra Clemencia Perez Calderon y otros c. Ministerio de Salud y la Alcaldía de Santa Fe de Bogota*, 20 May 1998.

[74] ibid.

[75] Colombian Constitutional Court, No T-020/17, *Yeison Fabian Arciniegas Omaña c. el Centro Penitenciario y Carcelario de Cúcuta y el Instituto Nacional Penitenciario y Carcelario (INPEC)* 20 January 2017.

[76] Colombian Constitutional Court, No C-005/17, *Demanda de inconstitucionalidad c. el numeral 1 del artículo 239 y el numeral 1 del artículo 240 del Decreto Ley 2663 de 1950 (Código Sustantivo del Trabajo)* 18 January 2017.

[77] Colombian Constitutional Court, No T-533/09, *Luis Alberto Lozano y otros c. el Municipio de Ibagué y otros*, 6 August 2009.

[78] Colombian Constitutional Court, No T-428/12, *Carlos Armando Orbes Benavides y otros c. la Secretaría de Educación Departamental de Nariño y el Ministerio de Educación Nacional*, 8 June 2012.

The Colombian Constitutional Court delivered its most structural and ambitious judgment in this regard—to date—in 2004. Judgment T-025 was the result of the accumulation of over 1,000 complaints filed by displaced families by way of *acción de tutela*, and declared that the humanitarian emergency caused by forced displacement constituted an 'unconstitutional state of affairs'; that is, a massive human rights violation associated with systemic failures in State action.[79] The desperate situation of displaced families coexisted with the lack of an articulated State policy for providing emergency aid and the absence of reliable information on the number of displaced people or the conditions in which they lived. As part of the lack of adequate policies, the State was not devoting sufficient resources to tackling this situation. As César Rodríguez-Garavito has explained, Judgment T-025 was not the Court's first structural decision declaring an unconstitutional state of affairs.[80] The Court has handed down judgments of this kind in diverse situations including non-compliance with the State's obligation to affiliate numerous public officials to the social security system, massive prison overcrowding, lack of protection for human rights defenders, and failure to announce an open call for public notary nominations. In other cases, the Court has aggregated different *tutela* actions and ordered long-term structural remedies without formally declaring an unconstitutional state of affairs. It did so most recently in its Judgment T-76014 of 2008, which resolved twenty-two complaints about systemic failures in the health care system.[81]

The basis for all this jurisprudential development is the Constitution of 1991.[82] This instrument, which defines Colombia as a 'social State', contains an extensive catalogue of ESCR—as a corollary to the aforementioned principle—and establishes that international human rights treaties take precedence over domestic law. Further, the Constitutional Court has developed the concepts of progressivity and non-retrogression established in the Constitution following the ICESCR standards and the jurisprudence of the CESCR on those issues, and has recurred to decisions and reports of the universal treaty bodies, including the CESCR, to interpret the human rights norms included in international instruments or the Colombian Constitution.[83]

D. Venezuela

Venezuela's 1999 Constitution places respect for human rights at its core. This new instrument includes a comprehensive list of human rights and guarantees for their

[79] Colombian Constitutional Court, No T-025/04, *Abel Antonio Jaramillo y otros c. la Red de Solidaridad Social y otros*, 22 January 2004.

[80] Rodríguez-Garavito, 'Beyond the Courtroom' (n 41).

[81] ibid; Sepúlveda, 'Colombia' (n 71) 147.

[82] For a more detailed description of the evolution of the arguments used by the Constitutional Court to enforce ESCR rights, see Rodrigo Uprimny Yepes, 'La justiciabilidad de los DESC en Colombia en perspectiva comparada' in Magdalena Cervantes Alcayde and others (eds), ¿Hay justicia para los derechos económicos, sociales y culturales?: debate abierto a propósito de la reforma constitucional en materia de derechos humanos' (Instituto de Investigaciones Jurídicas 2014) 65.

[83] See Rossi and Filippini, 'Derecho internacional' (n 54).

realization, as well as proclaiming Venezuela to be a democratic 'social State of law and justice'.[84]

Along with proclaiming justice, equality, and human rights as superior values, the Constitution's catalogue of ESCR encompasses more than fifty prerogatives ranging from policy goals to justiciable guarantees. The Constitution also includes participatory mechanisms to encourage the active involvement of citizens in the design and management of public social services and policies, as well as the right to act before the courts in defence of collective and diffuse interests.

Scholars claim that the justiciability of ESCR has been significantly advanced under the new Constitution.[85] However, the courts have yet to reach a point of maturity, and their findings are contradictory at times. Nevertheless, the Supreme Tribunal of Justice has consistently affirmed that constitutional rights possess a normative nature and are therefore immediately enforceable by the courts. Also, the Constitution recognizes, in its article 23, that human rights treaties have constitutional hierarchy and prevail over local laws as long as they provide stronger rights protection.

With regard to the right to health, the Supreme Tribunal of Justice has enforced decisions allowing HIV-positive patients to access medication from the Social Security Agency. The judges extended the effects of the decision to all rights-bearers, giving their holding a collective nature and stressing that people need to attain the 'ideal health care' necessary to safeguard their 'mental, social and environmental integrity'.[86] The Court also stated that the Social Security Agency could not justify non-compliance on the basis of a lack of resources. This case was filed by plaintiffs invoking violations of the ICESCR.[87]

In another landmark decision, the Tribunal ordered the Social Security Agency to reverse the closure of the emergency service and night shift in one of its health centres.[88] In still another ruling, it affirmed that the right to health is enforceable and that the State must not only intervene as appropriate to create the conditions necessary for the enjoyment of this right, but also to remove the obstacles to its exercise.[89]

Finally, in a more recent ruling concerning a case filed by an NGO invoking—among other treaties—the State's obligations under the ICESCR, the Supreme Tribunal found that the National Assembly's failure to institute an unemployment benefit scheme violated the right to social security and to worker protection and was inconsistent with the progressiveness of social rights in the Constitution and the

[84] Constitution of the Bolivarian Republic of Venezuela, 1999, art 2.

[85] See Enrique González, 'Venezuela: A Distinct Path Towards Social Justice' in Malcolm Langford (ed), *Social Rights Jurisprudence: Emerging Trends in International and Comparative Law* (CUP 2008) 192, 196.

[86] Supreme Tribunal of Justice (Venezuela) No 00-1343, *López, Glenda y otros c. Instituto Venezolano de los Seguros Sociales (IVSS) s/ acción de amparo*, 2 December 2002.

[87] ibid.

[88] Supreme Tribunal of Justice (Venezuela) No 00-2305, *Peña Linares y otros c. Instituto Venezolano de los Seguros Sociales (IVSS)* 12 June 2001.

[89] Supreme Tribunal of Justice (Venezuela) No 01-2832, *Balza Meza, Maza de Balza y otros c. Ministro de la Defensa y el Comandante General del Ejército*, 12 June 2001.

international human rights obligations assumed by Venezuela. The judges ordered the government to take action and pass a law on the matter or to implement a temporary remedy to satisfy the plaintiffs.[90]

E. Other countries' experiences

Other countries' courts also exhibit an influence of the ICESCR in their decisions. In Costa Rica, for example, the Supreme Court decided a case related to the right to health and access to HIV medications by directly citing ICESCR article 12(2).[91] The Supreme Court also considered that not allowing a pregnant adolescent access to education would violate ICESCR article 13(3).[92]

In Peru, the Constitutional Tribunal ruled in favour of the protection of the right to health of a patient with HIV, invoking the doctrine of progressive realization and use of maximum available resources under ICESCR article 2(1).[93] Further, in a right to education case in which access was denied to a child, the Tribunal stated that local laws should be interpreted according to the obligations stemming from the human rights treaties ratified by Peru (among which the ICESCR can be found).[94]

The Supreme Court of Justice of Mexico relied on the ICESCR to obligate the State to finish the construction of a health services facility in order to guarantee the right to health. The decision relied on the ICESCR and the guidance of the CESCR. On the one hand, the Court defined the scope of the right to health by citing ICESCR article 12 and the CESCR's General Comment 14. On the other hand, the Court analysed the CESCR's General Comment 3 and stated that it was mandatory for Mexico to adopt measures up to the maximum available resources and also that the State had certain obligations of immediate effect.[95] In a more recent case, even though the Court dismissed a claim from a group of neighbours that demanded the construction of an arts building, it analysed the right to culture under the CESCR's General Comment 21 and defined the international obligations of Mexico regarding this right according to ICESCR article 2.[96]

[90] Supreme Tribunal of Justice (Venezuela) No 03-1100, *Demanda de inconstitucionalidad por omisión de la Asamblea Nacional al promulgar la Ley Orgánica de Seguridad Social*, 2 March 2005.

[91] Supreme Court of Costa Rica, No 06096-1997, *Luis Murillo Rodríguez c. el Presidente Ejecutivo de la Caja Costarricense de Seguro Social*, 26 September 1997. See Nash Rojas, Claudio, 'Los derechos económicos, sociales y culturales y la justicia constitucional latinoamericana: tendencias jurisprudenciales' (2011) 9 Estudios Constitucionales 65.

[92] Supreme Court of Costa Rica, No 05316-2003, *Ligia Agüero Hernández c. directora del Centro Educativo Nuestra Señora de Desamparados*, 20 June 2003; Nash Rojas, 'Tendencias jurisprudenciales' (n 91).

[93] Constitutional Tribunal of Peru, No 2945-2003-AA, *Azanca Alhelí Meza García c. la sentencia de la Tercera Sala Civil de la Corte Superior de Justicia de Lima*, 20 April 2004; Nash Rojas, 'Tendencias jurisprudenciales' (n 91).

[94] Constitutional Tribunal of Peru, No 00052-2004-AA, *Martha Elena Cueva Morales c. la resolución de la Primera Sala Civil de la Corte Superior de Justicia del Callao*, 1 September 2004; Nash Rojas, 'Tendencias jurisprudenciales' (n 91).

[95] Supreme Court of Justice of Mexico, No 378/2014, 15 October 2014.

[96] Supreme Court of Justice of Mexico, No 566/2015, 15 February 2017.

V. Influence of the ICESCR on the Regional Human Rights System

A. The San Salvador Protocol

Notwithstanding the confirmed justiciability of ESCR, a question remains unanswered: are the ICESCR obligations of States fulfilled by the mere adoption of measures ordered by regional treaties which create obligations along the same lines as the ICESCR? The Inter-American Court of Human Rights has attempted to provide an answer to this question, stating that simply fulfilling the obligation to adopt treaty measures is not enough. The Court has stressed that '[t]he obligation to ensure the free and full exercise of human rights is not fulfilled by the existence of a legal system designed to make it possible to comply with this obligation—it also requires the government to conduct itself so as to effectively ensure the free and full exercise of human rights.'[97] In the same vein, the CESCR has traditionally asked States parties to submit practical and empirical information in their periodic reports together with information on normative structures and, therefore, its General Comments contain detailed information on the requirements in such fields.[98]

The adoption of adequate measures is one of the issues to be measured through the progress indicators adopted under the Additional Protocol to the American Convention on Human Rights in the Area of Economic, Social and Cultural Rights, or Protocol of San Salvador,[99] in order to implement the duty to submit periodic reports.[100] The Protocol of San Salvador took nearly eleven years to enter into force and only binds sixteen States,[101] all of which are States parties to the Covenant. The objective of the Protocol is to complement the ACHR, whose article 26 is the only provision in its chapter III dealing with ESCR. This provision, under the title of Progressive Development, states that the parties are bound to:

> undertake to adopt measures, both internally and through international cooperation, especially those of an economic and technical nature, with a view to achieving progressively, by legislation or other appropriate means, the full realization of the rights implicit in the economic, social, educational, scientific, and cultural standards set forth in the Charter of the Organization of American States as amended by the Protocol of Buenos Aires.[102]

It is common wisdom in the Inter-American system of human rights that the ESCR referred to in article 26 are those mentioned in the OAS Charter and those embodied

[97] See *Velásquez Rodríguez v Honduras*, Judgment (Merits) Inter-American Court of Human Rights Series C No 4 (29 July 1988) para 167.

[98] See CESCR, 'General Comment 1' in 'Compilation of General Comments' (2003) (n 25) para 7.

[99] Additional Protocol to the American Convention on Human Rights in the Area of Economic, Social and Cultural Rights ('Protocol of San Salvador') (opened for signature 17 November 1988, entered into force 16 November 1999) OAS Treaty Series 69.

[100] See OAS (Executive Secretariat for Integral Development), *Progress Indicators for Measuring Rights under the Protocol of San Salvador* (OEA/Ser.D/XXVI.11, 2nd edn, OAS 2015) 21.

[101] For the full list of ratifications and accessions regarding the Protocol of San Salvador, see <www.oas.org/juridico/english/sigs/a-52.html> accessed 13 March 2016.

[102] ACHR art 26 (n 59).

in the American Declaration of the Rights and Duties of Man. This provision has been considered a suitable entry point for this set of rights in the strategies for the justiciability of ESCR at the regional level.[103]

The relationship between the ICESCR and the Protocol of San Salvador is close in substance because the two instruments deal with almost the same rights, but the wording and the legislative techniques employed are quite different. Aiming to supersede the gap between the East and the West in the international arena, the drafters of the Protocol decided to conceive of the protected rights as entitlements similar to CPR. The protection system ultimately established by the Protocol is half-way between the ICESCR and the ICCPR, as it provides that complaints relating to rights protected in its articles 8 and 13 (trade union rights and the right to education) can be lodged with the Inter-American Commission on Human Rights (IACHR), and therefore with the IACtHR, and that reports should be submitted relating to all protected rights even though the specificities of such a reporting system remain open in the text.

B. Measuring progress

It was only in 2005 that the rules governing the periodic reports that States should submit according to article 19 of the Protocol were adopted by the OAS General Assembly on the grounds of the above-mentioned indicators of progress.[104] Such measurement of progress is conducted with quantitative and qualitative indicators and analysed under certain categories that are transversal to all rights. At all stages, a human rights perspective is adopted.[105]

The institutional decision to establish a specific method of analysis to assess compliance with ESCR through the construction of periodic reports as a set of progressive indicators led specialists to intensely deal with these rights and to produce relevant legal writings, for example the articles written by Flavia Piovesan and Laura Pautassi, two experts assigned with the task of building the indicators.[106]

A specific Working Group was created in 2010, which divided the rights into two groups, namely (i) health, social security, and education, and (ii) labour rights and trade-union rights, the right to food, and environmental and cultural rights. The Working Group has now concluded the evaluation process of the first group.

While this reporting system is relatively new, the failure to adopt adequate measures as well as the adoption of inadequate ones has been a central argument in ESCR adjudication throughout the region.

[103] See *Acevedo Buendía et al v Perú*, Judgment (Preliminary Objection, Merits, Reparations and Costs) Inter-American Court of Human Rights Series C No 198 (1 July 2009) para 100.

[104] See OAS, 'Standards' (n 38).

[105] OAS, *Progress Indicators* (n 100).

[106] ibid; Laura Pautassi, 'Monitoreo del acceso a la información desde los indicadores de derechos humanos' (2013) 10 Sur—Revista Internacional de Derechos Humanos 57.

C. Incorporating ESCR into the regional case law

By contrast to the universal and other regional systems, the evolution of the Inter-American system is the result of many factors not necessarily linked to the normative process. The normative structure embodied in the treaties evolved due to the continuous updating of the rules by both the Commission and the Court. The scope of the protected rights increased because of the integration of many human rights rules into the Inter-American system. Based on the provision authorizing the Court to adopt advisory opinions on 'other treaties concerning the protection of human rights in the American states'[107] and on the *pro homine / persona* principle of interpretation,[108] both the Commission and the Court are used to bringing other international human rights rules that are binding on the States into the system by means of their decisions.

Whenever the scope of a given protected right is broader in another instrument binding a State, the Court relies on article 29 of the ACHR to apply the broader obligation to the State.[109] That is the case with the ICESCR, too. In a case dealing with an indigenous community's property, the IACtHR noted the absence of a national rule but, based on the CESCR's interpretation of ICESCR article 1 as applicable to indigenous peoples, declared that '[a]ccording to Article 29(b) of the American Convention, this Court is unable to interpret the provisions of Article 21 of this instrument in a sense that would limit the enjoyment and exercise of the rights recognized by Suriname in these Conventions.'[110] The Court has based many of its decisions on the broader interpretations contained in the General Comments of the CESCR on different rights protected under both systems, or even applied the CESCR's argumentation to its interpretation of rights protected under the regional system.[111]

In the case of *Five Pensioners*, the IACtHR adopted, without further discussion, a development produced by the jurisprudence of the CESCR and ruled on this basis that

> [the] progressive development [of ESCR], about which the United Nations Committee on Economic, Social and Cultural Rights has already ruled [quoting General Comment 3 of the CESCR], should be measured in function of the growing coverage of economic, social and cultural rights in general, and of the right to social security and to a pension in particular, of the entire population, bearing in mind the imperatives of social equity, and not in function

107 See art 64(1) ACHR (n 59). 108 See art 29 ACHR (n 59).

109 ibid. The original text states: '[n]o provision of this Convention shall be interpreted as: ... b. restricting the enjoyment or exercise of any right or freedom recognized by virtue of the laws of any State Party or by virtue of another convention to which one of the said states is a party'.

110 *The Kaliña and Lokono Peoples v Suriname*, Judgment (Merits, Reparations and Costs) Inter-American Court of Human Rights Series C No 309 (25 November 2015) para 122.

111 See eg *Suarez Peralta v Ecuador*, Judgment (Preliminary objections, Merits, Reparations and Costs) Inter-American Court of Human Rights Series C No 261 (21 May 2013) paras 130, 131, 134, 150, and 152. See also *Gonzales Lluy et al v Ecuador*, Judgment (Preliminary objections, Merits, Reparations and Costs) Inter-American Court of Human Rights Series C No 298 (1 September 2015) paras 159, 173, 234, 235, and 262. See also *Ximenes Lopes v Brazil*, Judgment (Preliminary objections, Merits, Reparations and Costs) Inter-American Court of Human Rights Series C No 149 (4 July 2006) para 51.

of the circumstances of a very limited group of pensioners, who do not necessarily represent the prevailing situation.[112]

Later on, in the *Acevedo Buendía* case, which concerned the payment of pensions in Peru, the IACtHR stressed the interdependence of rights, the absence of hierarchies between ESCR and CPR, and the enforceability of all rights, citing the *Airey* judgment of the European Court of Human Rights.[113] The Court made its clearest statement to date regarding how the State duty to adopt measures should be analysed by citing the CESCR. Among other concepts, the Court expressed that even if the fulfilment of ESCR requires time and flexibility according to the practical reality of each country, the State essentially (though not exclusively) has an obligation to adopt measures and provide resources to fulfil the requirements of ESCR to the extent of its available resources. The Court went on to underline that the progressive implementation of the relevant measures is subject to control and accountability, and that the State's fulfilment of its obligations may be enforced by any institution devoted to human rights protection. Furthermore, it underlined the prohibition of adopting retrogressive measures in ESCR-related areas.[114]

In addition, the IACtHR has invoked the concept of a life in dignity under the obligations stemming from ACHR art 4, stating for example that the fundamental right to life includes the right of every human being not to be deprived of life arbitrarily, but also the right to have access to conditions that grant an existence in dignity.

In other cases involving ESCR, the IACtHR resolved the issues at hand without dealing with ACHR article 26 or the progressivity concept. In the *Yakye Axa v Paraguay* case, the Court considered that the State had not adopted the necessary measures to grant essential conditions for a life in dignity, since it had not guaranteed the provision of water, food, health, or education, among others.[115] In the same vein, and in relation to children in prisons, the Court considered that the protection of the life of the child requires that the State take special care concerning the conditions of detention, specifying that the State has, regarding children in prison, an obligation to provide them with health assistance and education in order to guarantee that their detention will not destroy their future life projects.[116]

[112] *'Five Pensioners' v Peru*, Judgment (Merits, Reparations and Costs) Inter-American Court of Human Rights Series C No 98 (28 February 2003) para 147. This decision was criticized for the difficulty implied, for a single litigant by the need to produce evidence concerning the situation of an entire population instead of only his or her own. In this regard, see for example Christian Courtis, 'Luces y sombras: La exigibilidad de los derechos económicos sociales y culturales en la sentencia Cinco Pensionistas de la Corte Interamericana de Derechos Humanos' (2004) 6 Revista Mexicana de Derecho Público, ITAM, Departamento de Derecho (2004) 37–67.

[113] IACtHR, *Acevedo Buendía* (n 103) paras 99–103, citing *Airey v Ireland* App no 6289/73 (ECtHR, 9 October 1979) para 26.

[114] IACtHR, *Acevedo Buendía* (n 103) para 102. Also, it should be noted that, despite adopting such a clear position in favour of the justiciability of ESCR, the court decided the case based on arts 25 (judicial protection) and 21 (property) of the American Convention, and not on progressivity.

[115] *Yakye Aya v Paraguay* (n 52) paras 161–62.

[116] *Instituto de Reeducación del Menor v Paraguay*, Judgment (Preliminary Exceptions, Merits, Reparations and Costs) Inter-American Court of Human Rights Series C No 112 (2 September 2004) paras 156–61.

VI. Political Impact, Poverty, and Social Rights Violations: The CESCR and the IACHR

The Optional Protocol to the ICESCR is in force in six Latin American States (Argentina, the Plurinational State of Bolivia, Costa Rica, Ecuador, El Salvador, and Uruguay) and was signed by another three States (Guatemala, Paraguay, and Venezuela). However, there has not been, as of yet, any jurisprudence of the CESCR dealing with Latin American States.

Latin America—mainly through the examination of periodic reports—provided a good testing field for the CESCR, which did not hesitate to criticize States' policies on the adjustment of public debt and the liberalization of national economies, which were understood as an obstacle for the reasonable enforcement of the Covenant.[117] The region also allowed the Committee to recommend that the obligations undertaken under the Covenant have to be taken into account by States Parties during their negotiations with international financial institutions.[118]

Moreover, the CESCR first objected to States' recurrent arguments concerning the lack of resources as a justification for their non-compliance with the obligations deriving from the Covenant. Some States were accustomed to invoking their poverty as an excuse for their failure to fulfil their Covenant obligations. Instead of accepting these arguments, the CESCR blamed States and international organizations for these situations, and took the lead in considering poverty to be a denial of human rights.[119]

Eschewing a strictly economic definition, the Committee has asserted that poverty can be more accurately defined as the lack of basic capabilities required to live in dignity.[120] This means that it encompasses hunger, poor education, discrimination, vulnerability, and social exclusion. It has found that:

> In light of the International Bill of Rights, poverty may be defined as a human condition characterized by sustained or chronic deprivation of the resources, capabilities, choices, security and power necessary for the enjoyment of an adequate standard of living and other civil, cultural, economic, political and social rights.[121]

Consequently, enforcing ESCR is a fundamental step in the eradication of poverty.

The IACHR has followed the path created by the CESCR and has built on its own vision, as expressed in a 2011 country report where it suggested that poverty is, overall, a major human rights concern in the Americas and a phenomenon that

[117] See CESCR, 'Consideration of Argentina's Second Periodic Report' (8 December 1999) UN Doc E/C.12/1/Add.38, para 10; CESCR 'Consideration of Honduras's Initial Periodic Report' (21 May 2001) E/C.12/1/Add.57, paras 9–10; CESCR, 'Consideration of Colombia's Fourth Periodic Report' (6 December 2001) E/C.12/1/Add.74, para 9.

[118] See CESCR, 'Consideration of Argentina's Second Periodic Report' (8 December 1999) UN Doc E/C.12/1/Add.38, para 28.

[119] See CESCR, 'Substantive Issues Arising in the Implementation of the International Covenant on Economic, Social and Cultural Rights: Poverty and the International Covenant on Economic, Social and Cultural Rights' (10 May 2001) UN Doc E/C.12/2001/10, para 1.

[120] ibid para 7.

[121] ibid para 8.

constitutes an across-the-board violation of all human rights: civil, political, social, economic, and cultural.[122] In 2016 the IACHR produced a Preliminary Report on Poverty, Extreme Poverty and Human Rights in the Americas,[123] in which it now submits that:

> poverty constitutes a human rights problem manifested in obstacles to the enjoyment and exercise of human rights on a genuinely equal basis by the persons, groups and communities experiencing it. Under certain circumstances, it also involves violations of human rights for which the State may bear international responsibility. At the same time, extreme poverty constitutes a serious human rights issues [*sic*] because of the intensity with which it undermines the enjoyment and exercise of human rights.[124]

This report was coordinated by a special Unit on ESCR created by the OAS in 2012 and operating within the IACHR. It clearly stresses the importance of tackling poverty from a human rights perspective, which involves considering human beings as rights holders who may actively participate in decision-making processes relating to them, who require protection, and who demand accountability.

The influence of the ICESCR and the CESCR over the regional system is clear in this report. In fact, the report cites the CESCR's ideas on how to understand discrimination;[125] on the links between the discrimination of vulnerable groups and poverty;[126] on the interpretation and understanding of the obligation to adopt measures;[127] and on the understanding of the acceptability and quality of health care provisions presented in General Comment 14,[128] among others.

Also, it emerges as exceedingly clear from the report that the region faces a context of structural poverty that is intimately related to a persistent situation of inequality, exclusion, and discrimination. Under these conditions, the structural violation of ESCR in the region is widespread and especially impacts people living in poverty, specifically certain groups who have historically suffered discrimination.[129] Furthermore, the Commission has stressed the deeper impact created by intersectional discrimination.[130] It specifically pointed out how the IACtHR has identified the effects of such intersectionality in the context of its discrimination analysis in a

[122] See IACHR, 'Third Report on the Situation of Human Rights in Paraguay' (9 March 2001) OEA/Ser.L/V/II.110 Doc 52, ch II, para 8, and ch V, paras 8–9, citing United Nations Development Programme, *Human Development Report 2000* (OUP 2000) Foreword and 6, 42.

[123] See IACHR, 'Preliminary Report on Poverty, Extreme Poverty and Human Rights in the Americas' (2016) <www.oas.org/es/cidh/desc/docs/Pobreza-DDHH-InformePreliminar-2016-en.pdf> accessed 10 March 2017.

[124] ibid para 2.

[125] ibid para 95, citing CESCR, 'General Comment 20' (25 May 2009) UN Doc E/C.12/GC/20.

[126] IACHR, 'Preliminary Report on Poverty' (n 123) para 98, citing CESCR, 'Substantive Issues' (n 119) para 11.

[127] IACHR, 'Preliminary Report on Poverty' (n 123) paras 143, 155–57.

[128] ibid para 170, referring to CESCR, 'General Comment 14' in 'Compilation of General Comments' (2003) (n 25) 85.

[129] IACHR, 'Preliminary Report on Poverty' (n 123) paras 18 and 88.

[130] ibid para 106.

case in which the victim was a girl living in a situation of poverty and with HIV.[131] The Court argued that the various discrimination-related factors interacted with one another: poverty impacted the applicant's access to adequate health care, which ended up causing her to become infected with the HIV virus when she was three years old, but it also impacted her right to access the education system and to find adequate housing.[132]

The numbers concerning the gravity of poverty and inequality in the region, and showing how certain groups are especially affected in their access to rights, are telling. These numbers show a different side of the impact of the ICESCR in the region. Whereas, as shown, the Covenant has had a significant influence on domestic legal systems and local adjudication bodies, such influence coexists with a desolate state of affairs in terms of poverty and inequality. The increasing recognition of ESCR in domestic constitutions and by courts has not been paired with adequate public policies to fulfil the goals of the Covenant in terms of real access to ESCR.

The following will present only a brief selection of data as a sample for the whole region. According to the Economic Commission for Latin America and the Caribbean (ECLAC),[133] in 2014, the number of people living in poverty in the region reached 168 million (70 million in extreme poverty), and this figure grew again in 2015, reaching 175 million (of whom 75 million are indigent). Furthermore, Latin America and the Caribbean continues to be the most unequal region in the world, with an economic inequality gap that strengthens social inequalities, despite economic growth during the last decade. According to ECLAC, in 2014, 10 per cent of the population owned 71 per cent of the existing wealth in the region, while 50 per cent of the population owned 3.2 per cent. The richest 1 per cent owned 40 per cent of wealth. In certain Caribbean states, the rates of people living in poverty are even higher, with Haiti (77 per cent), Belize (41.3 per cent), Grenada (37.7 per cent), and Guyana (36.1 per cent) representing the worst examples.

The report clearly shows how poverty directly impacts access to basic ESCR, and how deprivation is more acute for certain vulnerable groups. Though the report thoroughly analyses the situation of women, migrants, imprisoned or detained persons, persons with disabilities, and LGBTI persons, we will focus—due to space constraints—on the situation of children as an example. In this regard, the report notes, first, that around 80 million children live in poverty in Latin America and the Caribbean, which implies that over 45 per cent of the population under eighteen years of age lives in such conditions. Of these, 32 million live in extreme poverty. This gets worse in the case of indigenous communities (wherein one out of three children live in poverty) and Afro-descendants (whereof two out of four children live in poverty). Second, malnutrition affects 2.3 million children aged 0-4, which

[131] ibid paras 108–09, referring to *Gonzales Lluy et al v Ecuador*, Judgment (Preliminary Exceptions, Merits, Reparations and Costs) Inter-American Court of Human Rights Series C No 298 (1 September 2015).

[132] IACHR, 'Preliminary Report on Poverty' (n 123) citing *Gonzales Lluy et al v Ecuador* (n 131) para 290.

[133] ECLAC, 'Social Panorama of Latin America 2015' <http://repositorio.cepal.org/bitstream/handle/11362/39964/1/S1600226_en.pdf> accessed 10 March 2017, 7.

represents 4.5 per cent of the children in this group, and 8.8 million children are affected by chronic malnutrition. In other words, this affects 16 per cent of children in the region. If this average is disaggregated, it emerges that certain countries will be closer to a 3.5 per cent child malnutrition rate,[134] and others closer to 10 per cent.[135] Third, 5.7 million children work under the legal age, many of them in risky activities such as mining, dumps, domestic work, fishery, and so on. Fourth, even if advances have been registered, 1.4 million children never attend school, and in certain countries this number rises to 2–4 per cent of school-aged children.[136] Fifth, 5.6 per cent of children (10 million) have abandoned school. This number rises to 10 per cent in certain countries.[137] These numbers get even worse in indigenous communities and regarding Afro-Americans,[138] who exhibit higher rates of malnutrition (eg in Colombia, 5.9 per cent of children under five years old had had at least one day of fasting during the week previous to the 2005 Census).[139]

This situation of extreme and structural inequality has had an impact on the regional bodies' way of understanding equal protection. In effect, the regional system employs an idea of formal equality focused on demanding objective and reasonable criteria to trace distinctions. This view is complemented by an idea of structural or material equality, which implies and accepts the need to adopt a policy of affirmative action to level the situation of certain groups, and makes States responsible for omitting to adopt such policies.[140]

Dealing with structural inequality and discrimination seems to be the most urgent mission of the Inter-American human rights system given the dramatic circumstances described above. Victor Abramovich has clearly described the evolution of the system's role in the region through the last decades, as well as the requirements of the current historical moment for the agenda of the Court and Commission. During the period of dictatorships and State terrorism in the region, the role of the Inter-American system was that of a last resort for victims who could not find local courts to address human rights violations. Human rights bodies clearly contributed to eroding the legitimacy of the dictatorships by producing information, buffering local situations, and contributing to the creation of international pressure on illegitimate governments. Later on, during the 1980s and 1990s, the system played a relevant role in the transition to democracy, playing a part in the discussions on how to

[134] This is true for Argentina, Chile, Brazil, Jamaica, Mexico, Paraguay, and the Dominican Republic. See IACHR, 'Preliminary Report on Poverty' (n 123) para 291.

[135] This applies for Guatemala, Haiti, Honduras, Guyana, and Suriname (ibid).

[136] Specifically in El Salvador, Guatemala, Honduras, and Nicaragua (ibid paras 292–94).

[137] Namely in Peru, Guatemala, Honduras, and Nicaragua (ibid para 294).

[138] See IACHR, 'Informe sobre la situación de personas afrodescendientes en las Americas' (15 December 2011) OEA/Ser.L/V/II. Doc 62 <www.oas.org/es/cidh/afrodescendientes/docs/pdf/afros_2011_esp.pdf> accessed 10 March 2017.

[139] Mortality rates during childhood are also higher, country by country, for Afro-descendant children vis-à-vis white children (ibid paras 18, 68).

[140] IACHR, 'Preliminary Report on Poverty' (n 123) para 110, citing the IACtHR in the case of *Ximenes Lopes v Brazil*, Judgment (Preliminary objections, Merits, Reparations and Costs) Inter-American Court of Human Rights Series C No 149 (4 July 2006) paras 104 and 106, citing *Caso Comunidad Indígena Xákmok Kásek v Paraguay*, Judgment (Merits, Reparations and Costs) Inter-American Court of Human Rights Series C No 214 (24 August 2010) paras 270–71.

deal with past authoritarian regimes. During that period, the system contributed to delineating the standards for transitional justice, established limits on the legitimacy of amnesties, helped expand free speech protection, ruled against military tribunals to decide on human rights issues, and focused on the establishment of adequate standards to strengthen local mechanisms of human rights protection. Today, the challenge for the regional system is to contribute to improving structural conditions to enable effective enjoyment of rights in a context of huge inequality, poverty, and rights violations vis-à-vis groups and communities systematically excluded from access to fundamental rights.[141]

VII. The By-products of ESCR's Justiciability in the Region

As shown, the Covenant and the work of the CESCR, together with the Inter-American system, have contributed to the justiciability of ESCR being widely accepted in Latin America. Thus, judges have started hearing claims and reaching decisions that establish control over public policies that disregard or ignore ESCR. These interventions, taken in many countries and by different judges at various levels, have provoked important debates.

Such discussions have revolved around reshaping the role of judges as auditors of public policy, namely their technical capacity and their democratic legitimacy to do so. Several important discussions on the implementation of complex judicial decisions were provoked by ESCR-related judgments. Concerns related to the impact on the separation of powers implied by the judiciary's involvement in the review of public policies promoted discussions leading to different ways of conceiving interactions between the judiciary and the executive.[142] There resulted a shift from a more rigid conception of the division of powers to a more dialogical one,[143] in which judges show deference to the executive's power to design policies, but at the same time provide remedies, establish limits, and maintain oversight and the final word on the adequacy of a remedy in a given case.

Furthermore, as a result of the justiciability and adjudication of ESCR-related cases, new evidence of the absence of institutional infrastructure as a cause of ESCR violations arose. The lack of coordination between agencies, the failure to produce information that would allow for the design of public policies that are respectful of ESCR or to monitor progressive implementation, and deficiencies in the use of public resources (inefficiency and lack of effective use of resources, among others) were all shown to contribute to the violation of ESCR.

141 See Victor Abramovich, 'De las violaciones masivas a los patrones estructurales: Nuevos enfoques y clásicas tensiones en el sistema Interamericano de derechos humanos' (2009) 63 Derecho PUCP (Revista de la Facultad de Derecho de la Pontificia Universidad Católica de Perú) 95.

142 Rodríguez-Garavito, 'Beyond the Courtroom' (n 41).

143 See Roberto Gargarella (comp), *Por una justicia dialógica: El poder judicial como promotor de la deliberación democrática* (Ediciones Siglo Veintiuno 2014).

Accepting ESCR as enforceable rights required addressing and defining certain concepts: the scope of the rights that might be enforced, that is, the individualization of the core obligations; the relationship between the scarcity of resources and the correct fulfilment of rights, that is, which delays by the State might be justified due to a lack of resources; the precise meaning of concepts such as the obligation to use the maximum available resources established by article 2 of the Covenant and the CESCR's General Comment 3; and the interpretation of the notion of progressiveness. Addressing and resolving these issues required interaction between the law and other fields, such as the social sciences, economics, or public finance. At the same time, strategies to enforce ESCR turned to important quantitative tools, like indicators and measurement strategies, to be able to produce evidence on the violation of these rights. Legal education started focusing on ESCR, and seminars, workshops, and legal materials helped law schools to have a decisive influence on the legal profession and to make lawyers familiar with ESCR litigation strategies, with the periodic reporting mechanism, and with the relevant indicators themselves. In addition, the Inter-American Institute on Human Rights has not only promoted the study of ESCR and the various relevant treaties from the standpoint of specific rights (such as education, housing, etc), but also from the standpoint of poverty.[144]

Along the same lines, this movement and reflection contributed to developing the approach that understands ESCR as collective rights. In turn, as mentioned above, this gave rise to new collective procedures (similar to class actions) that did not previously exist in the region, in turn evoking an intense debate on procedural rules.[145] In addition, new actors started to emerge through the growth of NGOs specialized in ESCR, which resorted to novel strategies such as (strategic) litigation and the drafting of shadow reports.

VIII. Concluding Remarks

Jurisprudential trends in Latin America point to a growing consensus on the full justiciability of ESCR. The Covenant plays a fundamental role in this regard. On the one hand, its progressive incorporation into domestic law and its implementation provides judges with the opportunity to address situations that have thus far been out of reach and marginalized by the traditionalist constitutions of the region, which are characterized by their liberal underpinnings. On the other hand, together with the General Comments published by the Committee, the Covenant helps judges by setting standards of interpretation. These are of central importance to judges across the continent and have proven to be an invaluable tool in the implementation, application, and enforcement of international human rights law.

[144] See Mónica Pinto, 'Los derechos humanos desde la dimensión de la pobreza' (2008) 48 Revista Instituto Interamericano de Derechos Humanos 43; Mónica Pinto, 'Poverty and Constitutional Rights' (2010) 28 Penn State Intl L Rev 477.

[145] Martin Sigal, Julieta Rossi, and Diego Morales, 'Argentina: Implementation of Collective Cases' in Malcolm Langford, César Rodríguez-Garavito, and Julieta Rossi (eds), *Social Rights Judgments and the Politics of Compliance: Making It Stick* (CUP 2017) 140.

Discussions about justiciability have also contributed to the progressive development of international human rights law in the field of ESCR. These discussions have given rise to new debates and new reactions about institutional frameworks and legal approaches aimed at giving us, the persons entitled to these rights, the possibility to better and more fully enjoy and exercise them.

Justiciability needs public policy as a companion. People must be in a position to exercise their ESCR without having to knock down the doors of judges. In this regard, there is—as the abovementioned numbers from the IACHR's report, based on ECLAC's data on poverty, show—unfortunately still a lot to be done.

Bibliography

Abramovich, Victor, 'De las violaciones masivas a los patrones estructurales: Nuevos enfoques y clásicas tensiones en el sistema Interamericano de derechos humanos' (2009) 63 Derecho PUCP (Revista de la Facultad de Derecho de la Pontificia Universidad Católica de Perú) 95

Abramovich, Victor, and Courtis, Christian, 'Hacia la exigibilidad de los derechos económicos, sociales y culturales: Estándares internacionales y criterios de aplicación ante los tribunales locales' in Martín Abregú and Christian Courtis (comps), *La aplicación de los tratados sobre derechos humanos por los tribunales locales* (Editores el Puerto / CELS 1997)

Abramovich, Victor, Bovino, Alberto, and Courtis, Christian (eds), *La aplicación de los tratados sobre derechos humanos en el ámbito local: La experiencia de una decada* (CELS 2007)

Alston, Philip, 'U.S. Ratification of the Covenant on Economic, Social and Cultural Rights: The Need for an Entirely New Strategy' (1990) 84 The American Journal of International Law 365

Bolívar, Ligia, 'Derechos económicos, sociales y culturales: Derribar mitos, enfrentar retos, tender puentes—Una visión desde la (in)experiencia de América Latina' in Sonia Picado Sotela, Antônio A Cançado Trindade, and Roberto Cuéllar (comps), *Estudios básicos de derechos humanos*, vol V (Instituto Interamericano de Derechos Humanos 1996)

Cançado Trindade, Antônio A, 'Direito Internacional e Direito Interno: Sua Interação na Proteção dos Direitos Humanos' (1996) <http://egov.ufsc.br/portal/sites/default/files/anexos/22361-22363-1-PB.pdf> accessed 23 March 2016

Cançado Trindade, Antonio A, 'La protección internacional de los derechos económicos, sociales y culturales' (1994) 1 Estudios Básicos de Derechos Humanos 39

Courtis, Christian, 'Luces y sombras: La exigibilidad de los derechos económicos, sociales y culturales en la sentencia Cinco Pensionistas de la Corte Interamericana de Derechos Humanos' (2004) 6 Revista Mexicana de Derecho Público 37

de Araujo, Nadia, and da Matta Andreiuolo, Inés, 'A internalização dos Tratados no Brasil e os Direitos Humanos' in Carlos Eduardo de Abreu Boucault and Nadia de Araujo (eds), *Os direitos humanos e o direito internacional* (Renovar 1999)

Ferraz, Octavio Luiz Motta, 'Between Usurpation and Abdication? The Right to Health in the Courts of Brazil and South Africa' in Oscar Vilhena, Upendra Baxi, and Frans Viljoen (eds), *Transformative Constitutionalism: Comparing the Apex Courts of Brazil, India, and South Africa* (Pretoria University Law Press 2013)

García Ramírez, Sergio, 'Protección jurisdiccional internacional de los derechos económicos, sociales y culturales' (2003) 9 Cuestiones Constitucionales 127

Gargarella, Roberto (comp), *Por una justicia dialógica: El poder judicial como promotor de la deliberación democrática* (Ediciones Siglo Veintiuno 2014)

González, Enrique, 'Venezuela: A Distinct Path Towards Social Justice' in Malcolm Langford (ed), *Social Rights Jurisprudence: Emerging Trends in International and Comparative Law* (CUP 2008)

Jiménez de Aréchaga, Eduardo, 'La Convención Americana de Derechos Humanos como derecho interno' (1988) 7 Revista del Instituto Interamericano de Derechos Humanos 25

Langford, Malcolm, 'The Justiciability of Social Rights: From Practice to Theory' in Malcolm Langford (ed), *Social Rights Jurisprudence: Emerging Trends in International and Comparative Law* (CUP 2008)

Nash Rojas, Claudio, 'Los derechos económicos, sociales y culturales y la justicia constitucional latinoamericana: tendencias jurisprudenciales' (2011) 9 Estudios Constitucionales 65

Pautassi, Laura, 'Monitoreo del acceso a la información desde los indicadores de derechos humanos' (2013) 10 Sur—Revista Internacional de Derechos Humanos 57

Pinto, Mónica, 'Droits humanitaires et droits de l'homme en Amérique Latine' in Jean-René Garcia, Denis Rolland, and Patrice Vermeren (eds), *Les Amériques, des constitutions aux démocraties* (Éditions de la Maison des sciences de l'homme 2015)

Pinto, Mónica, 'Los derechos humanos desde la dimensión de la pobreza' (2008) 48 Revista Instituto Interamericano de Derechos Humanos 43

Pinto, Mónica, 'Poverty and Constitutional Rights' (2010) 28 Penn State Intl L Rev 477

Piovesan, Flavia, 'Brazil' in Malcolm Langford (ed), *Social Rights Jurisprudence: Emerging Trends in International and Comparative Law* (CUP 2008)

Piovesan, Flavia, 'Direitos Humanos e o Dereito Constitucional Internacional' (Caderno de Direito Constitucional/Escola da Magistratura do Tribunal Regional Federal da 4a Região, 2006) <www.dhnet.org.br/direitos/militantes/flaviapiovesan/piovesan_dh_direito_constitucional.pdf> accessed 23 March 2016

Rodríguez-Garavito, César, 'Beyond the Courtroom: The Impact of Judicial Activism on Socioeconomic Rights in Latin America' (2011) 89 Texas L Rev 1669

Rossi, Julieta and Abramovich, Victor, 'La tutela de los derechos económicos, sociales y culturales en el artículo 26 de la Convención Americana sobre Derechos Humanos' (2007) 9 Revista Estudios Socio-Jurídicos 34

Rossi, Julieta and Filippini, Leonardo G, 'El derecho internacional en la judiciabilidad de los derechos sociales: El caso de Latinoamérica' in Pilar Arcidiácono, Nicolás Espejo Yaksic, and César Rodríguez-Garavito (eds), *Derechos sociales: Justicia, política y economía en América Latina* (Siglo del Hombre, Uniandes, CELS, and Universidad Diego Portales 2010)

Rossi, Julieta, 'Mecanismos internacionales de protección de los derechos económicos, sociales y culturales' in Víctor Abramovich, María José Añón, and Christian Courtis (comps), *Derechos sociales: Instrucciones de uso* (Fontamara 2003)

Scott, Craig, 'The Interdependence and Permeability of Human Rights Norms: Towards a Partial Fusion of the International Covenant on Human Rights' (1989) 27 Osgoode Hall Law Journal 769

Sepúlveda, Magdalena, 'Colombia: The Constitutional Court's Role in Addressing Social Injustice' in Malcolm Langford (ed), *Social Rights Jurisprudence: Emerging Trends in International and Comparative Law* (CUP 2008)

Sepúlveda, Magdalena, *Nature of the Obligations under the International Covenant on Economic, Social and Cultural Rights* (18 School of Human Rights Research Series, Intersentia 2003)

Sigal, Martin, Rossi, Julieta, and Morales, Diego, 'Argentina: Implementation of Collective Cases' in Malcolm Langford, César Rodríguez-Garavito, and Julieta Rossi (eds), *Social Rights Judgments and the Politics of Compliance: Making It Stick* (CUP 2017)

United Nations Development Programme, *Human Development Report 2000* (OUP 2000)

Uprimny Yepes, Rodrigo, 'Should Courts Enforce Social Rights? The Experience of the Colombian Constitutional Court' in Fons Coomans (ed), *Justiciability of Economic and Social Rights: Experiences from Domestic Systems* (Intersentia 2006)

Uprimny Yepes, Rodrigo, 'La justiciabilidad de los DESC en Colombia en perspectiva comparada' in Magdalena Cervantes Alcayde and others (eds), ¿Hay justicia para los derechos económicos, sociales y culturales?: debate abierto a propósito de la reforma constitucional en materia de derechos humanos' (Instituto de Investigaciones Jurídicas 2014)

Ventura Robles, Manuel E, 'Jurisprudencia de la Corte Interamericana de Derechos Humanos en materia de derechos económicos, sociales y culturales' (2004) 40 Revista Instituto Interamericano de Derechos Humanos 87

9

Influence of the ICCPR in Asia

*Yogesh Tyagi**

I. Introduction

At the concluding stage of its drafting, the International Covenant on Civil and Political Rights (ICCPR)[1] was considered to be 'the most important legal instrument in the hierarchy of international agreements'.[2] Today, it is a basic pillar of the International Bill of Rights, one of 'the core human rights treaties' of the UN system, and the constituent instrument of the Human Rights Committee (HRC). Since it contains certain rich normative standards, the ICCPR merits attention on account of its influence on domestic law and practice. Being the largest continent, with more than half of the world's population, Asia is a natural choice for the study of its engagement with the ICCPR. Considering that the current century has been projected as the Asian century, implying Asian predominance in shaping the destiny of humankind, the influence of the ICCPR in the most populous continent is a matter of compulsive curiosity.

This chapter begins with a few preliminary observations about its subject matter and then outlines a theoretical framework for studying that subject. The analysis seeks to assess the influence of the ICCPR in the selected States on a number of grounds. It then offers a few concluding remarks about the status of the ICCPR in Asia, draws attention to the influence of the Covenant in Asia in the foreseeable future, and suggests an agenda for further research in this field. The absence of adequate data does not encourage a law and society approach, which could help measure the impact of the ICCPR in Asia in terms of compliance at the grassroots level.

* The author gratefully acknowledges the help of Xiaohua Chen (China), Naoko Maeda (Japan), Deepika Udagama (Sri Lanka), and several students of South Asian University.

[1] International Covenant on Civil and Political Rights (adopted 16 December 1966, entered into force 23 March 1976) 999 UNTS 171.

[2] Evgeny Nasinovsky (USSR) in United Nations General Assembly (UNGA) 'Third Committee Records' (24 November 1966) 1433rd meeting, agenda item 62 UN Doc A/C.3/SR.1375–1464, para 35.

II. Preliminary Observations

It is useful to preface the analysis of the ICCPR's impact in Asia with a number of preliminary observations. First, it should be noted that, since religion and culture play a crucial role in the lives of a large majority of people in Asia, cultural relativism has a strong presence in the field of human rights in this region.

Second, owing to their socio-economic realities, most Asian States seek to accord primacy to economic, social, and cultural rights over civil and political rights. This implies that the principle of the interdependence and inseparability of civil and political rights on the one hand, and economic, social, and cultural rights on the other, has its limitations in Asian State practice.

Third, there is no agreement on what exactly constitutes Asia. Some States, such as Cyprus, Russia, and Turkey, have more than one regional identity, namely both an Asian and a European one. Dual regional identity may create doubts about the selection of States relevant for conducting a region-specific study and also about the accuracy of conclusions drawn therefrom. Therefore, the present chapter excludes those 'Asian' States from its purview that have dual regional identity and are parties to the ICCPR as well as the African Charter on Human and Peoples' Rights (ACHPR) or the European Convention on Human Rights (ECHR). It also excludes the States of the Middle East because this region is the subject of a separate chapter.[3] Thus, it adopts a rather narrow definition of 'Asian' States. The selection of States was made so as to assess the influence of the ICCPR in those States that have distinguished themselves on the following grounds:

(i) the region's largest democracy (India);
(ii) the first Asian State to participate in the international community (Japan);
(iii) the last Asian State party to the ICCPR (Pakistan);
(iv) the State with the latest constitution (Nepal);
(v) the most isolated State (North Korea);
(vi) the frontline of the 'war on terror' (Afghanistan);
(vii) one of the least developed States (Bangladesh);
(viii) a civil war-affected State (Sri Lanka);
(ix) the most populous State that has signed—but not ratified—the ICCPR (China); and
(x) a unique entity (Hong Kong), which is a party to the ICCPR but remains part of a State non-party to the Covenant (China).

Malaysia, once the champion of Asian values, with considerable influence on the international human rights discourse during the 1990s, finds a brief mention in this study to illustrate the impact of the ICCPR on those Asian States that are still

[3] Başak Çali, 'Influence of the ICCPR in the Middle East', Chapter 7 in this volume.

struggling with the question of adhering to the Covenant. Thus, the selected States fairly represent 'the different forms of civilization and of the principal legal systems'[4] which are a basic feature of the international legal system.

III. Theoretical Framework

The influence of an international legal instrument like the ICCPR in a domestic legal system depends, inter alia, on the relationship between international law and the domestic legal system, the willingness of the domestic courts of the State concerned to employ the applicable international law provisions in the functioning of the system, the intensity of interaction between the system and the international bodies in the given field, and the impact of the related international legal instruments that have some substantive norms in common with the Covenant. One may have a glimpse of the influence of an international legal instrument in a domestic legal system by examining the participation of the State concerned in the drafting of the relevant instrument. The signing and ratification of, or accession to, an international legal instrument indicates its acceptance at the domestic level. Generally, declarations and/or reservations to an international legal instrument point out its limits in the State concerned. Whether a State has adopted enabling legislation or incorporated an international legal instrument into domestic law demonstrates the degree of its preparedness to respect the instrument.

The status of international legal instruments under domestic law reflects their domestic reception. Institutionalization of the implementation of an international legal instrument at the domestic level testifies to the seriousness of the State concerned in respect of the instrument. The willingness of a State to subject itself to international accountability and its compliance with the outcome of implementation procedures indicate the self-confidence of the State and the influence of the instrument. Follow-up to the assessment of national compliance with an international legal instrument demonstrates the degree of respect attached to the instrument. The existence and effectiveness of a regional and/or parallel regime dealing with the same subject matter also have a bearing on the influence of the instrument. The availability of the relevant documents in the local languages and the accessibility of these documents reflect the seriousness of the State's level of commitment towards equipping its subjects to seek enforcement of their human rights.

Although consideration of these criteria does not ensure a comprehensive assessment of the influence of an international legal instrument in a domestic legal system, they cover the most important aspects of State practice in respect of a given instrument. They therefore constitute the basis for the assessment of the influence of the ICCPR in the aforementioned selected States in the following section.

[4] UNGA Resolution (Res) 64/173 (24 March 2010) UN Doc A/RES/64/173.

IV. Assessment of the Influence of the ICCPR

A. Participation in the drafting of the ICCPR

Not many Asian States were independent when the former UN Commission on Human Rights began drafting the International Covenants on Human Rights in the late 1940s. Therefore, the draft ICCPR, as produced by the Commission in 1954, benefitted from only a modest contribution by Asian States. During the discussions of the draft ICCPR in the Third Committee of the UN General Assembly (UNGA), however, some Asian States—such as India and Pakistan—participated and helped shape its content.[5]

The drafting of the ICCPR took place during the period of the Cold War. When the East–West differences in respect of human rights appeared to be insurmountable, a group of Asian and African States introduced the Afro–Asian amendments to overcome those differences. The amendments paved the way for the adoption of the ICCPR and the first Optional Protocol thereto, along with the International Covenant on Economic, Social and Cultural Rights (ICESCR), in 1966.[6] Among the thirteen powers involved were India and Pakistan.[7] A number of other Asian States did not participate in this process at all, however: Japan played little role in the drafting of the ICCPR, China could not participate owing to a dispute over its representation at the UN, North Korea was absent because it was not a member of the organization, Bangladesh was not even in existence at that time, and Malaysia had not yet emerged as a champion of Asian values.

Altogether, a handful of Asian States contributed considerably to formulating the provisions concerning implementation of the ICCPR and the first Optional Protocol thereto. Sceptical of strong international implementation measures, these States did not want the ICCPR to imitate the European model of implementation. Owing to the colonial past, there was some distrust towards any international machinery for the implementation of the ICCPR. While Asian States had an affinity with Western States in respect of the substantive provisions of the ICCPR, they were closer to socialist States regarding the implementation provisions of the Covenant. Since they successfully advocated for the optional nature of both the individual and inter-State communications procedures, the ICCPR and the first Optional Protocol thereto envisage modest international machinery for monitoring the implementation of the Covenant.[8]

[5] UNGA, 'Amendments submitted by India, Iran, Iraq, Libya, Mauritania, Nigeria, Pakistan, Senegal, Sierra Leone, Sudan, Tunisia, the United Arab Republic, and Upper Volta' (4–7 November 1966) UN Doc A/C.3/L.1373 and Add.1 and Add.1/Corr.1 (hereafter 'The Afro–Asian amendments').

[6] Egon Schwelb, 'The International Measures of Implementation of the International Covenant on Civil and Political Rights and of the Optional Protocol' (1977) 12 Texas Intl L J 141, 148 (fn 36).

[7] The Afro–Asian amendments (n 5).

[8] For a summary of the drafting history of the international measures of implementation of the ICCPR and the Optional Protocol thereto, see Yogesh Tyagi, *The UN Human Rights Committee: Practice and Procedure* (CUP 2011) 153–56, 326–34, and 389–96.

B. Acceptance of the ICCPR

In spite of the campaign for universal adherence to the ICCPR, several Asian States (namely Malaysia, Myanmar, and Singapore) have not yet signed the Covenant. Had there been no emergency during 1975–77, even India would not have acceded to the ICCPR in 1979. The Philippines was the first Asian State to sign the ICCPR in 1966, and Pakistan became the latest in 2008. While the chronology of accession to or ratification of the ICCPR does not establish that the Asian democracies are more enthusiastic adherents to the Covenant, the strength of adherence proves that democracies are more Covenant-friendly than States with other forms of government.

Like Hong Kong, Macao became a party to the ICCPR without signing it. While the ratification of the ICCPR by the United Kingdom made the Covenant applicable to Hong Kong in 1976, Portugal sought to accomplish the same task in respect of Macao in 1978. China assumed responsibility as a party to the ICCPR in respect of both Hong Kong and Macao since regaining sovereignty over these cities in 1997 and 1999 respectively. China signed the ICCPR in 1998, but has yet to ratify it. The Chinese Ministry of Foreign Affairs set up an inter-ministerial working group on the ratification of the ICCPR in November 2003.[9] According to its current national human rights action plan, China 'shall continue to advance related legal preparations and pave the way for ratification of the International Covenant on Civil and Political Rights'.[10] Some unofficial news suggests that China will ratify the ICCPR soon, but not many share this optimism. The prospects of China ratifying the ICCPR in the near future are not good because the Covenant and the current system in China seem to give differing answers regarding various big political questions, and also because the interpretation of the Covenant by the HRC is considered alarming by the Chinese ruling class, which is concerned about whether it can exercise any measure of control over the HRC's interpretive activities.

Comparatively, Asia has the largest number of States *not* parties to the ICCPR[11]—even more than the Middle East.[12] This deficit is striking in the absence of any regional regime for the promotion and protection of human rights in Asia. Further, Asian States have a rather poor rate of subscription to the ICCPR article 41 procedure[13] as well as the Optional Protocol procedure.[14] Furthermore, the Asian States

[9] Björn Ahl, 'Exploring Ways of Implementing International Human Rights Treaties in China' (2010) 28 Netherlands Q of Human Rights 361, 363.

[10] Information Office of the State Council of China, 'National Human Rights Action Plan of China (2016–20)', pt V ('Fulfillment of Obligations to Human Rights Conventions, and International Exchanges and Cooperation in the Field of Human Rights') <http://english.gov.cn/archive/publications/2016/09/29/content_281475454482622.htm> accessed 16 April 2017.

[11] Twenty-one Asian States are parties to the ICCPR, whereas the following six are not: Brunei, China, Bhutan, Malaysia, Myanmar, and Singapore.

[12] The following five Middle Eastern States are not parties to the ICCPR: Oman, Qatar, Saudi Arabia, South Sudan, and the United Arab Emirates.

[13] Only three Asian States—the Philippines, the Republic of Korea, and Sri Lanka—have accepted the article 41 procedure.

[14] Of the twenty-seven Asian States, the following eleven have subscribed to the Optional Protocol procedure: Kazakhstan, Kyrgyzstan, the Maldives, Mongolia, Nepal, the Philippines, the Republic

parties to the ICCPR maintain a large number of reservations and declarations. Also, while a number of the Asian States parties to the ICCPR have faced emergency situations, only three of them (Nepal, Sri Lanka, and Thailand) have made notifications under article 4(3) of the Covenant; the rest of them have occasionally exercised emergency powers without such a notification. Moreover, Asia hosts the various 'forms of civilization and of the principal legal systems' without adequate representation on the HRC. Since the HRC plays an important role in the implementation of the ICCPR, the inadequate representation of the Asian civilizations and legal systems on the said body reflects their inadequate contribution to the development of Covenant standards.

This gives an impression that Asia is the least enthusiastic region when it comes to ICCPR adherence, although most Asian States proclaim their strong commitment to civil and political rights. For instance, without making any commitment to accede to the ICCPR, Singapore submitted the following statement to the Human Rights Council: '[w]e are fully committed to the protection and promotion of the human rights of our citizens. We take a practical, not an ideological approach to the realisation of human rights.'[15] In other words, accession to the ICCPR is not considered necessary for adherence to civil and political rights by some Asian States.

C. Reservations and declarations

A majority of the Asian State signatories or parties to the ICCPR have made reservations and/or declarations in respect of the Covenant. There are three most common reservations/declarations, each of which has been made by at least three Asian States. First, China, India, Indonesia, and Thailand have made declarations regarding ICCPR article 1, thus restricting the application of the right of self-determination.[16] Secondly, almost half of the Islamic States parties reserve the right of Islamic Sharia to govern personal status laws: some directly (eg Pakistan[17]) and a few indirectly (eg the Maldives[18]). Thirdly, unlike many Islamic States of the Middle East (eg Iraq,

of Korea, Sri Lanka, Tajikistan, Turkmenistan, and Uzbekistan. Cambodia has signed the Optional Protocol, but has not yet ratified it.

[15] UNGA, 'National Report Submitted in Accordance with Paragraph 5 of the Annex to Human Rights Council Resolution 16/21: Singapore' (28 October 2015) UN Doc A/HRC/WG.6/24/SGP/1, para 4.

[16] China does not want the right of self-determination to affect the status of Macao as defined in the Basic Law and the Joint Declaration of the Government of the Portuguese Republic and the Government of the People's Republic of China on the Question of Macau, signed on 13 April 1987. India, Indonesia, and Thailand confine the right of self-determination only to the peoples under foreign domination, not to a section of people within a sovereign independent State. UN, 'Multilateral Treaties Deposited with the Secretary-General', chapter IV.4 <https://treaties.un.org/pages/ViewDetails.aspx?src=TREATY&mtdsg_no=IV-4&chapter=4&clang=_en> accessed 2 April 2017.

[17] ibid.

[18] ibid. The Maldives ratified the ICCPR with the understanding that '[t]he application of the principles set out in Article 18 of the Covenant shall be without prejudice to the Constitution of the Republic of Maldives', and article 10 of the Constitution of the Maldives, 2008, proclaims: (a) '[t]he religion of the State of the Maldives is Islam. Islam shall be the one of the basis of all the laws of the Maldives'; and (b) '[n]o law contrary to any tenet of Islam shall be enacted in the Maldives.'

Libya, Syria, and Yemen), there are several Islamic States in Asia (eg Bangladesh, Indonesia, the Maldives, and Pakistan) that have refrained from making reservations against the recognition of Israel as a State. In addition, the participation of Hong Kong in the ICCPR is subject to reservations entered by both China and the United Kingdom.[19] Lastly, Pakistan made reservations to articles 3, 6, 7, 12, 13, 18, 19, 25, and 40 of the ICCPR at the time of its ratification of the Covenant but subsequently withdrew most of them under international pressure.

Some of the Asian States parties to the ICCPR have adduced reasons for their respective reservations or declarations. Incompatibility between domestic law and the ICCPR has been the most-cited reason. A few Asian States have also argued on the basis of financial and logistical constraints (this is true, for example, for Bangladesh's declaration in respect of ICCPR article 10(3)). Both Bangladesh and India have made declarations regarding the right to compensation, although for different reasons and in respect of different provisions of the ICCPR.[20]

1. *Objections to reservations and declarations*

Except for Pakistan's objection to India's declaration (which is construed as a 'reservation' by Pakistan) in respect of ICCPR article 1, no Asian State party to the Covenant has made any objection against any declaration or reservation of any other Asian State party. Instead, criticism tends to come from outside of the region: Pakistan's reservations to the ICCPR have been the target of the largest number of objections from the Western world, including from the United States, which rarely makes such objections.[21] The most objectionable reservation of Pakistan concerned ICCPR article 40, which envisages the compulsory reporting procedure for monitoring the implementation of the Covenant. In response, the European Parliament passed a resolution calling on Pakistan to reconsider its blanket reservation to several provisions of the ICCPR.[22] It also asked the European External Action Service (EEAS) to take into account the human rights position in Pakistan 'during the examination of a possible application of the GSP+ scheme to Pakistan from 2013 onwards'.[23] The HRC also immediately issued a statement regarding Pakistan's reservation to article 40. The HRC made it clear that its competence to consider State reports under article 40 was of 'critical importance for the performance of the Committee's monitoring functions and essential to the *raison d'être* of the Covenant'.[24] The HRC asked Pakistan to submit its initial report pursuant to the requirements of article 40(1)(a),[25] and the State submitted its report more than four years later.[26] In effect,

[19] ibid. [20] ibid. [21] ibid.

[22] European Parliament Resolution P7_TA(2011)0098 of 10 March 2011 on Pakistan, in particular the murder of Shahbaz Bhatti, OJ 2012/C 199 E/21, para 20.

[23] ibid.

[24] UNGA, 'Report of the Human Rights Committee' (2011) UN Doc A/66/40 (vol I) 10–11, para 49.

[25] ibid paras 48–49.

[26] HRC, 'Initial Periodic Report of Pakistan' (24 November 2015) UN Doc CCPR/C/PAK/1.

therefore, the HRC had declared the article 40 reservation incompatible with the object and purpose of the ICCPR, and this finding delivered its results in due course.

In its concluding observations on State reports, the HRC has invariably asked the Asian States parties to review, reconsider, and withdraw their respective reservations and declarations in respect of the ICCPR.[27] Apparently, the objective is the eventual withdrawal of reservations and declarations in general, even if these are not considered incompatible with the object and purpose of the ICCPR.

2. *Withdrawal of reservations and declarations*

Japan, Pakistan, and South Korea are among those exceptional States that have withdrawn some of their declarations or reservations to the ICCPR. It has been argued that Pakistan's withdrawal of some of its reservations was 'not prompted by a change of attitude towards human rights, but by economic pressure from the EU, the biggest market for Pakistan's exports', and aimed to serve political ends only.[28] This seems to ignore ignores the influence of State objections to Pakistan's reservations[29] as well as the importance of the HRC's statement regarding those reservations.[30]

Although India has not formally withdrawn any of its declarations or reservations, its higher judiciary and the human rights commissions have rendered the article 9-related declaration practically ineffective by awarding compensation to victims of illegal detention or certain other human rights violations in a number of cases.[31] This means that the judicial and/or quasi-judicial neutralization of an ICCPR reservation or declaration is not necessarily dependent on any treaty action in this regard and that the number of withdrawn or neutralized reservations or declarations is higher than what the official records of the HRC or the UN show.

D. Status of treaties under domestic law

States follow different approaches in respect of treaties. Some States consider treaties as part of their domestic law; others require domestic legislation to incorporate treaties into their domestic legal system; some consider treaties equal to their basic law; some place treaties at a higher level; and some deny treaties of one kind any

[27] eg HRC, 'Concluding Observations on the Third Periodic Report of Hong Kong, China' (29 April 2013) UN Doc CCPR/C/CHN-HKG/CO/3.

[28] Lorenz Langer, *Religious Offence and Human Rights: The Implications of Defamation of Religions* (CUP 2014) 364.

[29] The following States made objections against the reservations of Pakistan: Australia, Austria, Belgium, Canada, the Czech Republic, Denmark, Estonia, Finland, France, Germany, Greece, Hungary, Ireland, Italy, Latvia, the Netherlands, Norway, Poland, Portugal, the Slovak Republic, Spain, Sweden, Switzerland, the United Kingdom, the United States, and Uruguay. See UN, 'Multilateral Treaties Deposited with the Secretary-General' (n 16).

[30] HRC, 'Statement on the Reservation of Pakistan to Article 40' (30 March 2011); UNGA, 'Report of the Human Rights Committee' (2011) UN Doc A/66/40 (vol I) 10–11.

[31] See the following series of rulings by the Supreme Court of India: *Rudul Sah v State of Bihar*, AIR 1983 SC 1086; *Nilibati Behra v State of Orissa*, AIR 1993 SC 1960; *N Sengodan v Secretary to Government, Home (Prohibition and Excise) Department, Chennai and Ors* (2013) 8 SCC 664.

space in their domestic law while giving a preferential position to treaties of other kinds. One distinction is between those States that place treaties on a constitutional rank and those that position treaties below their respective constitutions. Some of the Asian constitutions specifically mention multilateral treaties such as the UN Charter,[32] thus distinguishing them from other treaties.[33]

Those States that rank treaties below their respective constitutions may be divided further into those that accord supremacy to treaties over legislation (for example, Japan[34] and Nepal[35]) and those that do not (for example, Bangladesh, India, Malaysia, Sri Lanka, and Pakistan). For example, treaties in China 'acquire prevailing force over domestic law only when the relevant domestic law includes an explicit stipulation to that effect'.[36] Otherwise, the general domestic adoption of human rights treaties is denied on the grounds that the scope of domestic provisions referring to international treaties is confined to legal relationships in private or economic law, and does not extend to the relations between individuals and the State. Further, unlike article 39 of the Basic Law of Hong Kong, no provision in the domestic law of China refers explicitly to human rights treaties.[37]

In some States, treaties in compliance with certain procedural requirements have the authority of law. For example, in the absence of any prescribed legal status for treaties in China, some commentators consider that if the concluded treaty has been authorized by the Standing Committee of the National People's Congress, it has the same rank as laws enacted by the same body.[38] Another example stems from the Japanese context. Being the supreme law of the land, the Constitution of Japan supersedes the ICCPR in domestic effect. However, the Japanese government claims that 'since the Constitution can be interpreted as covering the same range of human rights' as the ICCPR, 'there can be no conflict between the Constitution and the Covenant'.[39]

Only a few States, such as Nepal and North Korea, have separate legislation dealing with the nuances related to treaty-making and the obligations flowing therefrom.[40] North Korea has the Treaty Law of 18 December 1998, which describes inter alia the relationship between the treaties to which it is a party and domestic law.[41] In some

[32] Charter of the United Nations (opened for signature 26 June 1945, entered into force 24 October 1945) 1 UNTS XVI.

[33] eg art 25 of the Constitution of Bangladesh, 1972; Preamble and art 7 of the Constitution of Afghanistan, 2004; art 51(m) of the Constitution of Nepal, 2015.

[34] Meryll Dean, *Japanese Legal System* (2nd edn, Routledge-Cavendish 2002) 166, noting that, in the *Jewellery Smuggling* case, the Kobe district court stated that 'the principle of faithful observance of treaties ... is understood to proclaim superiority of treaties [over domestic law]'.

[35] Nepal Treaty Act, 1990, s 9.

[36] Hanqin Xue and Qian Jin, 'International Treaties in the Chinese Domestic Legal System' (2009) 8 Chinese J of Intl L 299, 305.

[37] Ahl, 'Exploring' (n 9) 366–67.

[38] Björn Ahl, 'Chinese Law and International Treaties' (2009) 39 Hong Kong L J 737, 738.

[39] HRC, 'Fourth Periodic Report of Japan, Addendum' (1 October 1997) UN Doc CCPR/C/115/Add.3, para 11.

[40] Nepal Treaty Act, 1990; and North Korea's Treaty Law, 1998.

[41] HRC, 'Second Periodic Report of North Korea' (4 May 2000) UN Doc CCPR/C/PRK/2000/2, para 12.

States, the reference to status is conspicuously missing (for example, in Sri Lanka). In some other States, such as India, the written domestic law on treaties remains unchanged but judicial practice in respect of human rights treaties has gone through a transformation without comparable effects on other kinds of treaties. In yet other States, the constitution has simply referred to international law as non-enforceable and non-binding (in a positive law sense).[42]

Interpretations provided by national courts have played an important role in most of the States under study. Most of the domestic case law points towards a harmonious construction of statutes and treaties.[43] In some cases, indeed, the domestic courts have even tried to fill in gaps whenever legislation is absent.[44]

There are various methods of implementation of treaties, depending on the domestic legal system. Most Asian States selected for the present study are dualist (for example, Bangladesh, India, Sri Lanka, and Pakistan) or partly dualist (for example, Hong Kong).[45] Like several other dualist States, Malaysia practices the 'doctrine of transformation' as evidenced in *Public Prosecutor v Narongne Sookpavit and Others*.[46] Thus, even if a treaty is binding on Malaysia under international law, it has no domestic legal effect unless a law is adopted by the legislature giving effect to that treaty. If there is a conflict between a statute and a treaty, the general rule is that the statute shall prevail.[47]

Japan follows a monist approach, signifying that ratified treaties are automatically accepted into domestic law from the time of promulgation in the Official Gazette (*kampō*).[48] Faithful implementation of treaties concluded by Japan is a matter of constitutional obligation.[49]

Some States, such as China, have underlined the difference between self-executing and non-self-executing treaties.[50] In Hong Kong, implementing legislation is not required where the relevant provisions of the international agreement relate to matters of principle, or to matters that are already dealt with under existing legislation, or where the international obligations can be implemented by administrative means, or 'where the international agreement purely concerns an international matter which has no relevance in the domestic context'—for example, the 1969 Vienna Convention on the Law of Treaties.[51]

[42] eg for the Indian Constitution, 1950, see art 51(c), pt IV, ie Directive Principles of State Policy. See also the Preamble to the Constitution of Afghanistan, 2004; art 25 of the Constitution of Bangladesh, 1972; art 55 of the Constitution of Nepal, 2015.

[43] eg Gujarat High Court, *Ktaer Abbas Habib Al Qutaifi v Union of India*, 1999 Cri LJ 919.

[44] Supreme Court of India, *Vishaka v State of Rajasthan*, 1997 (6) SCC 241.

[45] Anthony Aust, *Modern Treaty Law and Practice* (3rd edn, CUP 2013) 191.

[46] *Public Prosecutor v Narongne Sookpavit* [1987] 2 MLJ 100.

[47] Illustrated in Supreme Court of the Federated Malay States, *PP v Wah Ah Jee* (1919) 2 FMSLR 193.

[48] Yuji Iwasawa, 'Effectuation of International Law in the Municipal Legal Order of Japan' in Ko Swan Sik, M Christopher W Pinto, and JJG Syatauw (eds), *Asian Yearbook of International Law*, vol 4 (Kluwer 1994) 143, 148.

[49] The Constitution of Japan, 1947, art 98(2).

[50] Xue and Jin, 'International Treaties' (n 36) 305.

[51] LegCo Panel on Administration of Justice and Legal Services, 'Implementation of International Agreements in the Hong Kong SAR' (No CB(2)1398/06-07(04), 26 March 2007) paras 3–4.

In the case of India, generally, treaties require domestic legislation to become enforceable.[52] Judicial trends in India show that some treaties need specific legislation, including in cases that imply a heavy financial burden on the exchequer,[53] an infringement of private rights,[54] or a cessation of territories,[55] and where the treaty itself stipulates it.[56] In the case of human rights treaties, however, various judgments show the application of some of those treaties even in the absence of enabling legislation.[57]

In North Korea, article 17 of the Treaty Law 1998 provides that '[a]n institution that has concluded a treaty ought to fulfill without fail the obligation under the treaty.' International human rights instruments are given effect through their 'incorporation into domestic laws and regulations or through direct invocation of the provisions of the instruments'.[58] North Korea claims that the necessary changes have been made to the Constitution and statutes after the ratification of international human rights instruments in order to reflect the 'requirements of the instruments'.[59] It has also been claimed that North Korea:

> maintains the policy of steadily promoting the human rights which are recognized or existing by national legislation or custom in step with the development of the State and social system, without restriction or derogation for the reason that they are not indicated in the Covenant.[60]

According to North Korea, it does not accept any interpretation that curtails the rights and freedoms enshrined in the ICCPR.[61] However, according to Amnesty International, fundamental rights and freedoms embodied in the Universal Declaration of Human Rights (UDHR) and the treaties to which North Korea is a party 'remain largely unprotected by domestic legislation'.[62] The HRC observes that, although the ICCPR has 'the same status as domestic law' in North Korea, it remains doubtful 'whether the Covenant would have primacy over domestic law if the latter is in conflict with Covenant provisions'.[63]

[52] P Chandrasekhara Rao, *The Indian Constitution and International Law* (Martinus Nijhoff 1993).

[53] Calcutta High Court, *Union of India v Manmull Jain*, AIR 1954 Cal. 615.

[54] Supreme Court of India, *Ram Jawaya Kapur v State of Punjab*, AIR 1955 SC 549, para 19.

[55] Supreme Court of India, *Maganbhai Ishwarbhai Patel v Union of India*, (1969) 3 SCR 254, 299.

[56] The Rights of Persons with Disabilities Act, 2016, was enacted to give effect to the 2006 Convention on the Rights of Persons with Disabilities (adopted 13 December 2006, entered into force 3 May 2008) 2515 UNTS 3 .

[57] Supreme Court of India, *NALSA v Union of India* (2014) 5 SCC 438.

[58] HRC, 'National Report Submitted in Accordance with Paragraph 15(A) of the Annex to Human Rights Council Resolution 5/1 by North Korea' (27 August 2009) UN Doc A/HRC/WG.6/6/PRK/1, para 28.

[59] UN, 'Core Document Forming Part of the Reports of States Parties, North Korea' (16 July 2002) UN Doc HRI/CORE/1/Add.108/Rev.1, paras 49–56. See also HRC, 'Second Periodic Report of North Korea' (n 41) para 2; CEDAW Committee, 'Consideration of the Initial Periodic Report by North Korea' (11 September 2002) UN Doc CEDAW/C/PRK/1, para 56; CRC Committee, 'Consideration of the Combined Third and Fourth Periodic Reports by North Korea' (15 January 2008) UN Doc CRC/C/PRK/4, paras 6–30.

[60] HRC, 'Second Periodic Report of North Korea' (n 41) para 27.

[61] ibid para 26.

[62] Amnesty International, 'Democratic People's Republic of Korea: Submission to the UN Universal Periodic Review (November–December 2009)' <www.amnesty.org/download/Documents/44000/asa240082009en.pdf> accessed 2 April 2017.

[63] HRC, 'Concluding Observations on the Second Periodic Report of North Korea' (27 August 2001) UN Doc CCPR/CO/72/PRK, para 9.

E. Influence of the ICCPR on domestic law

Among the Asian States parties to the ICCPR, Hong Kong's legal system displays the most conspicuous influence of the Covenant on domestic law. Article 39 of the Basic Law of Hong Kong grants a special status to the ICCPR, as a result of which any legislation inconsistent with the Covenant may be challenged before a court of law. In India, the Protection of Human Rights Act, 1993 defines the term 'human rights' with reference to 'the International Covenants'.[64] Bangladesh witnessed the influence of the ICCPR over its domestic law even before signing the Covenant. In the case of *The Chief Prosecutor v Abdul Quader Molla*, for instance, M Amir-Ul Islam, the counsel of the aggrieved party who was also the author of the 1971 Declaration of Independence and a member of the Constituent Assembly of Bangladesh, submitted that the International Crimes (Tribunals) Act, 1973 'included important fair-trial and due-process rights enshrined in the International Covenant for Civil and Political Rights, which was not yet in force when the ICT Act 1973 was enacted'.[65] The Tribunal apparently endorsed this observation by stating that 'the provisions of the ICTA 1973 and the Rules framed there under offer adequate compatibility with the rights of the accused enshrined under Article 14 of the ICCPR'.[66]

Since the Constitution of Afghanistan refers to the UDHR, one may read a number of the provisions of the ICCPR into the Constitution where the two international instruments have a common normative content. Sri Lanka has passed the ICCPR Act, 2007 to give effect to certain provisions of the Covenant. However, some ambiguity exists about the status of those Covenant provisions that are not mentioned in the ICCPR Act.

There is a view that, although the annually issued government report on *Progress in China's Human Rights* induced the development of national legislation in China concerning those human rights that are enshrined in the ICCPR, it is difficult to conclude that the Covenant has influence over national legislation. Some scholars think that 'the Chinese government looks to national instruments and mechanisms for guidance in making international legal commitments, rather than looking to international instruments and mechanisms for guidance in formulating national law'.[67] This means that, in China, the consideration of national policy and domestic demand are more important than international human rights treaties.

[64] Article 2(d).

[65] *Government of Peoples' Republic of Bangladesh v Abdul Quader Molla*, Criminal Appeal No 24 of 2013 and *Abdul Quader Molla v Government of Peoples' Republic of Bangladesh*, Criminal Appeal No 25 of 2013, ICT-BD Case No 02 of 2012, 546.

[66] ibid 515.

[67] Friedrich Ebert Foundation (ed), *The Universal Declaration of Human Rights at 50: Progress and Challenges* (Friedrich Ebert Foundation 1999) 9.

F. Influence of the ICCPR on domestic courts

The influence of the ICCPR on the domestic courts of the Asian States under study is not fully known. While decisions of the apex courts of most Asian States are available, thus enabling an assessment of the influence of the ICCPR on those courts, it is difficult to evaluate the impact of the Covenant on the courts of a State like Afghanistan that does not publish the entire judgments even of its Supreme Court, or *Stera Mahkama*.[68]

1. Influence of the draft ICCPR

The draft ICCPR had modest influence on the domestic courts of India. In *Francis Manjooran and Ors v Government of India*,[69] for instance, Justice PT Raman Nair, in a separate opinion, referred to article 12 of the draft ICCPR to hold that article 21 of the Constitution of India entails a wide interpretation of the freedom to travel. In the absence of the requisite information, it is difficult to assess the influence of the draft ICCPR in other Asian States.

2. Influence of the ICCPR before States' ratification or accession

Information relating to the influence of the ICCPR prior to its ratification is not available in respect of most of the Asian States. The ICCPR had some influence on the domestic courts of India even before the State's accession to the Covenant. Indian courts treated the ICCPR as a book of knowledge, from which various concepts were taken and applied without any reference to the instrument. If a court did apply the ICCPR to give a judgment directly, the appellate court would overturn it.[70] A significant development in this regard came in the case of *Jolly George Verghese v Bank of Cochin*,[71] for instance, where the Supreme Court of India made an apparently conflicting but essentially complementary observation. While holding that the ICCPR was not binding on India, as it had not ratified it at the time, the Court cleverly read article 11 of the Covenant into article 21 of the Constitution and thereby sought to harmonize the pertinent provision for civil prison in the Civil Procedure Code of India, 1908 (section 51) with article 51 of the Constitution of India and ICCPR article 11.

[68] Eli Sugarman and others, *An Introduction to the Law of Afghanistan* (3rd edn, Stanford Law School Afghanistan Legal Education Project (ALEP) 2011) 53–54.

[69] Kerala High Court, *Francis Manjooran and Ors v Government of India*, AIR 1966 Ker. 20, para 13.

[70] *Padam Singh and others v Superintendent of Police, Agra and others*, MANU/UP/0259/1969; *The Superintendent of Police and Ors v Padam Singh and Ors*, 1977 AWC 515 (All.).

[71] Supreme Court of India, *Jolly George Verghese v Bank of Cochin*, MANU/SC/0014/1980.

3. *Influence of the ICCPR on the domestic courts of the States parties*

The domestic courts of several Asian States parties to the ICCPR accept a varying degree of influence of the Covenant on their jurisprudence. This is true even in those States that have not incorporated the ICCPR into their domestic law.

In *Prem Shankar Shukla v Delhi Administration*, for instance, the Supreme Court of India used the ICCPR as guidance to pronounce its judgment.[72] Transforming the use of the ICCPR from a guiding force to an understanding of the presence of a State obligation to implement the Covenant, in *Dilip K Basu v State of West Bengal*,[73] the Supreme Court emphasized that the ICCPR formulated 'legally enforceable rights of the individuals' and that the Covenant is binding on the parties.[74] Subsequently, while deciding on the application of the ICCPR in Indian courts,[75] the Supreme Court held that since India has acceded to the Covenant, this instrument 'can be used by the municipal courts as an aid to the interpretation of statutes by applying the Doctrine of Harmonization'.[76] The Court went to the extent of observing that 'if the Indian law is not in conflict with the International Covenants, particularly pertaining to human rights, to which India is a party, the domestic court can apply those principles in the Indian conditions'.[77] The HRC has welcomed the 'frequent references to provisions of international human rights instruments by the courts, in particular the Supreme Court [of India]'.[78]

Like the domestic courts of India, courts in Bangladesh have referred to the provisions of the ICCPR in several cases.[79] In Japan, judges tend to prioritize national legislation or their own precedents rather than international human rights law. Even in the government's view, the status of the jurisprudence on the ICCPR is not uniform. For example, the Ministry of Justice insisted that the ICCPR was not self-executing because article 2(2) of the Covenant requires the States parties to take the necessary steps to adopt such legislative or other measures as may be necessary to give effect to the rights recognized in the Covenant.[80]

Lately, however, there have been some cases in which judges have taken into account the ICCPR and its jurisprudence.[81] In Pakistan, a single-judge bench of the Peshawar High Court referred to ICCPR article 6(1) in order to hold that 'the drone

[72] Supreme Court of India, *Prem Shankar Shukla v Delhi Administration*, AIR 1980 SC 1535.

[73] Supreme Court of India, *Dilip K Basu v State of West Bengal*, MANU/SC/0799/2015.

[74] ibid para 7.

[75] Supreme Court of India, *NALSA v Union of India*, MANU/SC/0309/2014, paras 47–53.

[76] ibid para 51. [77] ibid.

[78] HRC, 'Concluding Observations on the Third Periodic Report of India' (4 August 1997) UN Doc CCPR/C/79/Add.81, para 6.

[79] *BNWLA v Government of Bangladesh and others*, 14 BLC (2009) (HCD) 703, para 45; *Bangladesh and another v Hasina and another*, 60 DLR (AD) (2008) 90, para 86.

[80] Yuji Iwasawa, *International Law, Human Rights and Japanese Law: The Impact of International Law on Japanese Law* (Clarendon Press 1998) 49–56.

[81] eg in a case questioning the constitutionality of art 900(4) of the Civil Code before the Supreme Court of Japan, the plaintiffs invoked articles of the ICCPR and the Convention on the Rights of the Child (CRC) (opened for signature 20 November 1989, in force 2 September 1990) 1577 UNTS 3, to claim a right to non-discrimination against children born out of wedlock with respect to their statutory inheritance share (Supreme Court (Grand Bench), Decision of 4 September 2013, *Hanrei Taimuzu* [Law Times Reports], No 1393, 64; *Japanese YB of Intl L*, vol 57 (International Law Association of Japan 2014) 480–81).

strikes in Pakistan is blatant breach of absolute right to life (*sic*)'.[82] Likewise, a single-judge bench of the Lahore High Court made use of ICCPR articles 11, 13, and 23 to pronounce that gender discrimination in granting citizenship was contrary to article 25 of the Constitution of Pakistan, 1973.[83] In Sri Lanka, while the *Singarasa* judgment presented a pessimistic view of the first Optional Protocol to the ICCPR,[84] the Advisory Opinion of the Supreme Court on the ICCPR Act suggested a positive influence of the Covenant on domestic courts.[85] Again in *Visuvalingam v Liyanage*,[86] the Sri Lankan Supreme Court, alluding to ICCPR article 19, recognized the need to broadly interpret the free expression clause of the Constitution of 1978 to include the right to receive information. The trend is towards greater cognizance of the ICCPR in domestic judicial practice, although judges are constantly inhibited owing to the doctrine of dualism.

G. Influence of the ICCPR on legal scholarship

Since its adoption in 1966, the ICCPR has been a focus of attention, though more in Europe than in Asia. There has been a varying degree of scholarship on the Covenant in Asian States, although this assessment is largely confined to the availability of literature in the English language. In Afghanistan, for instance, although some commentators have made passing references to the ICCPR,[87] it is hard to find publications that deal in any detail with its implementation.[88] By contrast, a major study has been done on Bangladesh's compliance with the ICCPR[89] and a number of articles make references to the Covenant in relation to that State.[90]

A few commentators have published work on the implementation of the ICCPR in India.[91] Some Indian scholars have relied upon ICCPR provisions while

[82] *Advocate F M Sabir & Others v Federation of Pakistan*, Writ Petition No 1551-P/2012, para 12.

[83] *Mst Rukhsana Bibi, etc v Government of Pakistan, etc* (Writ Petition No 5939 of 2006) Lahore High Court, Multan Bench (18 May 2016) paras 15 and 16 <http://sys.lhc.gov.pk/appjudgments/2016LHC2281.pdf> accessed 17 April 2017.

[84] Sri Lankan Supreme Court, *Singarasa v Attorney General* SC Spl (LA) No 182/99 (2006).

[85] Sri Lankan Supreme Court, Advisory Opinion on the ICCPR Act, SC Ref No 01/2008.

[86] Sri Lankan Supreme Court, *Visuvalingam v Liyanage* [1984] 2 Sri LR 123.

[87] eg Mandana Knust Rassekh Afshar, 'The Case of an Afghan Apostate: The Right to a Fair Trial Between Islamic Law and Human Rights in the Afghan Constitution' in Armin von Bogdandy and Rüdiger Wolfrum (eds), *Max Planck United Nations Yearbook*, vol 10 (Brill 2006) 591.

[88] eg Alexandra Hilal Guhr and others, 'Max Planck Manual on Fair Trial Standards in the Afghan Constitution, the Afghan Interim Criminal Code for Courts, the Afghan Penal Code and other Afghan Laws as well as in the International Covenant on Civil and Political Rights' (4th edn, Max Planck Institute for Comparative Public Law and International Law 2009).

[89] Mohammad Shahabuddin, 'The International Covenant on Civil and Political Rights: A Study on Bangladesh Compliance' (National Human Rights Commission of Bangladesh 2013).

[90] Mohammad Ershadul Karim, 'Health as Human Rights under National and International Legal Framework: Bangladesh Perspective' (2010) 3 J of East Asia and Intl L 337.

[91] eg Abdulrahim P Vijapur, 'Domestic Application of the International Covenant on Civil and Political Rights – With Special Reference to Rights of Minorities in India' in Krishan P Saksena (ed), *Human Rights and the Constitution: Vision and Reality* (Gyan Publishing House 2003); Hari Om Agarwal, *Implementation of Human Rights Covenants: With Special Reference to India* (Kitab Mahal 1983); Brij Kishore Sharma, *Human Rights Covenants and Indian Law* (PHI Learning 2010).

substantiating their arguments concerning diverse issues.[92] ICCPR-related issues have also been subject to research interest at some universities in India.[93]

There is rich literature on the implementation of the ICCPR in Japan.[94] Besides the legal literature, quite a few activities to promote the ICCPR take place in that country. For instance, the Japanese Society of International Law held its annual meeting focusing on the fiftieth anniversary of the ICCPR in September 2016, and the *Japanese Yearbook of International Law* published half a dozen articles on 'Half a Century with the International Covenants on Human Rights: Long-Term Impacts on the World'.[95]

There is a small amount of literature on the implementation of the ICCPR in Nepal,[96] with passing references to the provisions of the Covenant made in discussions about specific issues.[97] Similarly, just a few scholarly writings deal with the implementation of the ICCPR in Sri Lanka.[98] North Korea once drew the attention of the international community by attempting to withdraw from the ICCPR, and Elizabeth Evatt's article on the subject is one of the most-cited scholarly works relating to that State.[99] Non-North Korean commentators have contributed more scholarly works on the ICCPR obligations of North Korea than domestic scholars.[100]

With regard to Pakistan, three main issues have been widely discussed in relation to that State's obligations under the ICCPR: blasphemy,[101] minority

[92] International Human Rights Law Clinic, 'The Right to a Remedy for Enforced Disappearances in India: A Legal Analysis of International and Domestic Law Relating to Victims of Enforced Disappearances' (2014) Berkeley School of Law Working Paper Series 1 <www.law.berkeley.edu/wp-content/uploads/2015/04/Working-Paper-1-India-Right-to-a-Remedy-151027.pdf> accessed 13 March 2017; Arthur Mark Weisburd, 'Customary International Law and Torture: The Case of India' (2006) 2 Chicago J Intl L 81.

[93] eg Ravender Kumar, 'India, the International Covenant on Civil and Political Rights, and its Implementation Machinery' (PhD dissertation, Jawaharlal Nehru University 1991).

[94] Timothy Webster, 'International Human Rights in Japan: The View at Thirty' (2010) 23 Columbia J of Asian L 241; Yuji Iwasawa, 'International Human Rights Adjudication in Japan' in Benedetto Conforti and Francesco Francioni (eds), *Enforcing International Human Rights in Domestic Courts* (Martinus Nijhoff 1997) 223.

[95] Koichi Morikawa (ed), 'Half a Century with the International Covenants on Human Rights: Long-Term Impacts on the World (Part I)' *Japanese YB of Intl L*, vol 59 (International Law Association of Japan 2016).

[96] eg National Human Rights Commission of Nepal, 'A Study of the Domestication Status of International Covenant on Civil and Political Rights in Nepal' (August 2007) Report No 32/82/2064; Padma Prasad Khatiwada, 'Nepal: Domestication of Treaties—What about Implementation?' (2012) Human Rights Alliance Review Report <https://reliefweb.int/sites/reliefweb.int/files/resources/Domestication%20of%20Major%20International%20Treaties%20in%20Nepal%20Problems%20and%20Prospects.%202012.pdf> accessed 22 January 2018.

[97] Hemang Sharma, 'Rights against Torture in Nepal: Commitment and Reality' (2015) 4 Intl Human Rights L Rev 104.

[98] eg Deepika Udagama, 'The Politics of Domestic Implementation of International Human Rights Law: A Case Study of Sri Lanka' (2015) 16 Asia-Pacific J on Human Rights & L 104.

[99] Elizabeth Evatt, 'Democratic People's Republic of Korea and the ICCPR: Denunciation as an Exercise of the Right of Self-defence?' (1998) 5 Australian J of Human Rights 215.

[100] Danielle Chubb, 'North Korean Human Rights and the International Community: Responding to the UN Commission of Inquiry' (2014) 15 Asia-Pacific J on Human Rights & L 51.

[101] Richard Lombardi, 'The Influence of the International Covenant on Civil and Political Rights on Anti-Blasphemy Laws' (2013) Law School Student Scholarship Paper 158 <http://scholarship.shu.edu/student_scholarship/158/> accessed 2 April 2017.

rights[102] and the status of the Ahmediya community,[103] and the death penalty.[104] Though Pakistan's reservations to certain provisions of the ICCPR and withdrawal of some of those reservations have attracted attention from several quarters, very little on the subject has appeared in the legal literature.[105]

As concerns China, human rights law scholars regard the ICCPR as an important instrument for improving the state of human rights. A number of Chinese as well as Western scholars have done work on the ICCPR in relation to the country.[106] They have referred to ICCPR provisions in respect of some burning issues, such as the death penalty,[107] media freedom and digital oppression,[108] and national security.[109] Some literature on Taiwan's obligations under the ICCPR is also available,[110] but the non-assumption of those obligations by China remains unexplored. On the other hand, a number of scholarly writings on Hong Kong and the ICCPR appeared in the 1990s, upon the transfer of the island's sovereignty to China.[111] Post-2000 writings have focused on issues such as immigration and refugee protection,[112] the interface between domestic and international human rights law,[113] environmental issues,[114] and adult suffrage.[115]

[102] Abbas Kassar, 'Pakistan Unwilling to Protect Religious Minorities Rights under ICCPR' *The Pioneer* (Hyderabad, 14 July 2014) <http://thepioneer.com.pk/pakistan-unwilling-to-protect-religious-minorities-rights-under-iccpr/> accessed 2 April 2017.

[103] Qasim Rashid, 'Pakistan's Failed Commitment: How Pakistan's Institutionalized Persecution of the Ahmadiyya Muslim Community Violates the International Covenant on Civil and Political Rights' (2011) 11 Richmond J of Global L & Business 1.

[104] Shagufta Omar, *Abolition of Death Penalty with Special Reference to Pakistan* (Women Aid Trust Pakistan 2012).

[105] Aistė Akstinienė, 'Reservations to Human Rights Treaties: Problematic Aspects Related to Gender Issues' (2013) 20 Jurisprudencija 451.

[106] eg Na Jiang, *China and International Human Rights: Harsh Punishments in the Context of the International Covenant on Civil and Political Rights* (Springer 2014); Eric Kolodner, 'Religious Rights in China: A Comparison of International Human Rights Law and Chinese Domestic Legislation' (1994) 16 Human Rights Q 455; Shiyan Sun, 'Understanding and Interpretation of the ICCPR in the Context of China's Possible Ratification' (2007) 6 Chinese J Intl L 17.

[107] Roger Hood, 'Abolition of the Death Penalty: China in World Perspective' (2009) 1 City U of Hong Kong L Rev 1.

[108] Katharine M Villalobos, 'Digital Oppression in Cuba and China: A Comparative Study of ICCPR Violations' (2014–15) 24 J of Transnational L & Policy 161.

[109] Kelly A Thomas, 'Falun Gong: An Analysis of China's National Security Concerns' (2001) 10 Pacific Rim L and Policy J 471.

[110] Mark L Shope, 'Adoption and Function of International Instruments: Thoughts on Taiwan's Enactment of the Act to Implement the ICCPR and the ICESCR' (2012) 22 Indiana Intl & Comparative L Rev 159.

[111] Johannes Chan, 'State Succession to Human Rights Treaties: Hong Kong and the International Covenant on Civil and Political Rights' (1996) 45 Intl & Comparative L Q 928.

[112] Michael Ramsden, 'Reviewing the United Kingdom's ICCPR Immigration Reservation in Hong Kong Courts' (2014) 63 Intl & Comparative L Q 635.

[113] Albert HY Chen, 'International Human Rights Law and Domestic Constitutional Law: Internationalization of Constitutional Law in Hong Kong' (2009) 4 National Taiwan U L Rev 237.

[114] Heather R Croshaw, 'The "Right To Health" and "Right To Life": Positive Obligations for Controlling Air Pollution in Hong Kong in Clean Air Foundation v. HKSAR' (2014) 15 Vermont J of Environmental L 450.

[115] Michael C Davis, 'Basic Law, Universal Suffrage and the Rule of Law in Hong Kong' (2015) 38 Hastings Intl & Comparative L Rev 275.

In brief, the total amount of literature relating to the ICCPR in Asia is very limited; Japan is the subject of the largest amount of literature, whereas North Korea remains the least researched State. Notably, the quantity of literature is much less than the intensity of interest in the ICCPR in Asia. The contribution of legal scholarship is quite modest, but various civil society reports have had some influence on State practice. Therefore, it is possible to establish, interestingly, that civil society reports have more influence on the human rights situations in the selected Asian countries than the scholarly literature on the subject.

H. Influence of national human rights institutions

National human rights institutions (NHRIs) may act as local foot soldiers for the HRC in respect of the ICCPR. That is why the HRC invariably recommends the establishment of NHRIs in those States that do not have such an institution. NHRIs can take various forms, ranging from human rights commissions or ombudsmen to human rights institutes or centres.

Most of the Asian States parties to the ICCPR have NHRIs. Among the selected States, India was the first to establish the National Human Rights Commission (NHRC) in 1993, and Pakistan was the latest, establishing its NHRI in 2015. China, Japan, and North Korea do not have NHRIs. Not many of the Asian NHRIs meet the test of the Paris Principles relating to the Status of National Institutions.[116] Yet, a majority of the NHRIs have sought to overcome their respective limitations by expanding their functional orbits and by improving their public images. Since the Universal Periodic Review (UPR) in 2009, for instance, Bangladesh has prioritized transforming its NHRC into the primary institution that oversees human rights implementation in the country.

Since Japan does not have an NHRI, the Human Rights Organs of the Ministry of Justice carry out human rights protection activities there. In September 2012, the Cabinet adopted a decision confirming the content of a bill to establish an independent human rights commission compliant with the Paris Principles and a bill to partially amend the Human Rights Volunteers Act; however, these measures were later scrapped.[117]

[116] eg the appointment of a member of the NHRC was challenged before the Supreme Court of India on the grounds of non-compliance with the Paris Principles (Supreme Court of India, *People's Union for Civil Liberties v Union of India (UOI) and Anr*, MANU/SC/0039/2005; and Supreme Court of India, *Anupriya Nagori v Union of India, Thr its Secretary and Ors*, MANU/SCOR/00058/2017). Because of the questionable selection and appointment process of the NHRC, in particular, the Global Alliance for National Human Rights Institutions (GA-NHRI) deferred the accreditation of the NHRC until late 2017, thus barring the commission from representing India in the UN Human Rights Council and the UNGA (Saurav Datta, 'Major Setback, Embarrassment to National Human Rights Commission' *National Herald* (New Delhi, 9 February 2017) <www.nationalheraldindia.com/institution/setback-embarrassment-to-national-human-rights-commission-report-un-recommends-accreditation-deferred-till-nov-2017> accessed 30 March 2018.

[117] Silvia Atanassova Croydon, 'A National Human Rights Commission for Japan: Domestic and Regional Implications' (30 May 2013) Nordic Association of Japanese and Korean Studies <www.najaks.org/?p=1032> accessed 11 April 2017; Asia-Pacific Human Rights Information Centre, 'Japanese National Human Rights Commission' (2002) 28 Human Rights Forum 21 <www.hurights.

Nepal established its National Human Rights Commission in 2000. Like the Constitution of Afghanistan, the Constitution of Nepal of 2015 embodies the mandate of the Human Rights Commission. Among other things, the Constitution empowers the Commission to monitor the implementation of those human rights treaties to which Nepal is a party and to make recommendations to the government regarding the ratification of those treaties to which Nepal is not a party. Pursuant to the Human Rights Commission Act 1997, Nepal defines 'human rights' in broader terms than its larger neighbour India.[118]

North Korea claims that its people's committees at all levels have 'direct responsibility' for the promotion of human rights and that '[p]rocuratorial, judicial, and people's security organs also discharge important functions of protecting human rights'.[119] Since its establishment in April 2015, the National Committee for the Implementation of International Human Rights Treaties (NCIIHRT) provides 'unified coordination for the implementation of all the treaties' to which North Korea is a State party.[120]

Pakistan set up a National Commission for Human Rights (NCHR) in June 2012; however, the members of the Commission were appointed only three years later. The NCHR has a mandate to make recommendations for the implementation of international human rights treaties. However, like the Indian NHRC, the NCHR of Pakistan is only authorized to seek reports from the government and make recommendations in cases of allegations against the armed forces.[121] The HRC has asked India to remove restrictions on the mandate of the NHRC,[122] and Pakistan is likely to receive a similar recommendation in respect of the NCHR.

In 1996, Sri Lanka adopted legislation to establish the Human Rights Commission of Sri Lanka (HRCSL). The HRCSL is empowered to advise the government of Sri Lanka on the ratification of human rights treaties and also on bringing legislation and administrative practices and procedures into line with international human rights norms and standards. Prior to the establishment of the

or.jp/archives/focus/section2/2002/06/japanese-national-human-rights-commission.html> accessed 11 April 2017.

118 While the definition of human rights pursuant to the 1993 Indian Protection of Human Rights Act covers the rights embodied in the ICCPR and ICESCR (Republic of India, The Protection of Human Rights Act, 1993, Act No 10 of 1994 <http://nhrc.nic.in/documents/Publications/TheProtectionofHumanRightsAct1993_Eng.pdf> accessed 20 June 2017), the definition of human rights according to the 1997 Nepalese Human Rights Commission Act extends to the rights enshrined in the human rights treaties to which Nepal is a party (Kingdom of Nepal, The Human Rights Commission Act, 2053 (1997) <www.asiapacificforum.net/media/resource_file/Human_Rights_Commission_Act_1997.pdf> accessed 20 June 2017).

119 UNGA, 'National Report by North Korea' (27 August 2009) UN Doc A/HRC/WG.6/6/PRK/1, para 23.

120 CRC Committee, 'Fifth Periodic Report of North Korea' (25 October 2016) UN Doc CRC/C/PRK/5, para 22.

121 Indian Protection of Human Rights Act, 1993, s 19 (<http://nhrc.nic.in/documents/Publications/TheProtectionofHumanRightsAct1993_Eng.pdf> accessed 13 April 2016); and Pakistani National Commission for Human Rights Act, 2012 s 14 (<http://pgil.pk/wp-content/uploads/2014/06/National-Commission-for-Human-Rights-Act-2012.pdf> accessed 13 April 2017).

122 HRC, 'Concluding Observations on the Third Periodic Report of India' (4 August 1997) UN Doc CCPR/C/79/Add.81, para 22.

HRCSL, two institutions existed under emergency regulations: the Human Rights Task Force (HRTF) to prevent illegal arrest and detention, and the Commission for Eliminating Discrimination and Monitoring of Human Rights (CEDMHR) to prevent discrimination.

On 27 March 2013, the Chinese Ministry of Foreign Affairs and the Australian Human Rights Commission jointly organized a seminar in Beijing in which topics such as the function, role, and future development of an NHRI and an analysis of the feasibility of establishing such an institution in China were discussed in depth. Yet, China—along with Japan and North Korea—has not established an NHRI to date.

The National Human Rights Commission of Malaysia (Suruhanjaya Hak Asasi Manusia) (SUHAKAM) was established under the Human Rights Commission of Malaysia Act 1999. Like the NHRC of India, the SUHAKAM has advocated for the ratification of the Convention against Torture (UNCAT).[123] It has done considerable work in respect of CEDAW,[124] which elaborates the rights of women as partly recognized in the ICCPR, and its work consequently has an indirect bearing on the Covenant. However, the Malaysian government has failed to take its findings and recommendations seriously. The Parliament of Malaysia has not discussed the annual reports of SUHAKAM.

This survey of Asian States' NHRIs gives rise to a few impressions. First, developed legal systems do not necessarily feature developed NHRIs as well (as is shown by the examples of Hong Kong and Japan). Secondly, the presence of an NHRI does not always ensure a satisfactory state of human rights protection in the State concerned (as is the case eg in India and Pakistan). Thirdly, the ranking of an NHRI does not necessarily represent its performance in respect of human rights (for example, in Afghanistan). Finally, compliance with the Paris Principles does not *ipso facto* guarantee ICCPR standards (eg, again, in Afghanistan); however, an NHRI in compliance with those principles is better situated to improve the human rights situation in a country, including adherence to ICCPR standards; and a compromised NHRI dramatically dilutes the possibility of compliance.

I. Reporting record

ICCPR article 40 envisages a compulsory monitoring procedure, and its article 41 concerns the optional competence of the HRC to receive inter-State communications. Pursuant to article 40, State reports constitute the basis of constructive discussions between the HRC and the States parties concerned. The international monitoring of the implementation of the ICCPR critically depends on the timely submission of reports by States parties. Unlike most European States, most Asian States do not submit their respective reports within the stipulated deadlines. Some

[123] Convention against Torture and Other Cruel, Inhuman or Degrading Treatment or Punishment (opened for signature 10 December 1984, entered into force 26 June 1987) 1465 UNTS 85.

[124] Convention on the Elimination of All Forms of Discrimination against Women (opened for signature 18 December 1979, entered into force 3 September 1981) 1249 UNTS 13.

Asian States, such as Afghanistan, have not submitted their periodic reports for as long as twenty years;[125] India's fourth periodic report is more than fifteen years overdue.[126] Bangladesh had not submitted its initial report for fourteen years, thus forcing the HRC to initiate the review procedure to examine the country situation[127] that prompted the State to submit its initial report without further delay.[128] By its reservation to article 40, Pakistan unsuccessfully sought to escape from submitting any report to the HRC. Thus, generally, the Asian States have been reluctant communicators with the Committee.

Since delays in the submission of State reports constitute a violation of the reporting obligations under ICCPR article 40, several measures have been developed to persuade States parties to comply with those obligations in a timely manner. At least four measures have an Asian imprint.

First, in 1997, when the former UN Sub-Commission on Prevention of Discrimination and Protection of Minorities noted that North Korea had not submitted its second periodic report in the preceding ten years, it deplored the delay and requested the State to delay no longer and to extend its cooperation with the reporting procedure. Annoyed with this admonition, North Korea declared its withdrawal from the ICCPR. While Asian States kept quiet over the purported withdrawal by North Korea, certain Nordic States denounced this move.[129] In response, the HRC disapproved the purported withdrawal and adopted General Comment 26 on the continuity of human rights obligations, stating that no State party to the ICCPR was entitled to withdraw from the Covenant.[130] Partly as a result of General Comment 26, North Korea resumed its reporting under ICCPR article 40 in 2000.

Second, when a State party to the ICCPR fails to submit its report under article 40 of the Covenant for more than five years, the HRC may place that State on the list of serious defaulters of reporting obligations. Since its inception in 1994, the annual list of defaulters has always included some Asian States parties. Figure 9.1 below shows an increasing number of Asian States parties appearing in the list of defaulters over the years.

Third, when a State party fails to submit its report for a long time in spite of repeated reminders, the HRC may serve notice on the State concerned that it intends to consider the measures adopted by that State to give effect to the provisions of the Covenant, even in the absence of a report. Since April 2001, the HRC has applied this procedure in respect of more than a dozen States.

Fourth, the increasing reporting burden on the States parties to the UN human rights treaties and the failure of a number of those States to submit their respective reports without delay have led to a set of procedural reforms.[131] Accordingly, a

[125] UNGA, 'Report of the Human Rights Committee' (2017) UN Doc A/72/40, 18.
[126] ibid.
[127] UNGA, 'Report of the Human Rights Committee' (2015) UN Doc A/70/40 (vol I) paras 73–74.
[128] HRC, 'Initial Periodic Report of Bangladesh' (3 September 2015) UN Doc CCPR/C/BGD/1.
[129] Hans Klingenberg, 'Elements of Nordic Practice 1998: Denmark' (1999) 68 Nordic J of Intl L 163.
[130] HRC, 'General Comment 26' (1997) UN Doc CCPR/C/21/Rev.1/Add.8/Rev.1.
[131] UNGA Res 68/268 (21 April 2014) UN Doc A/RES/68/268.

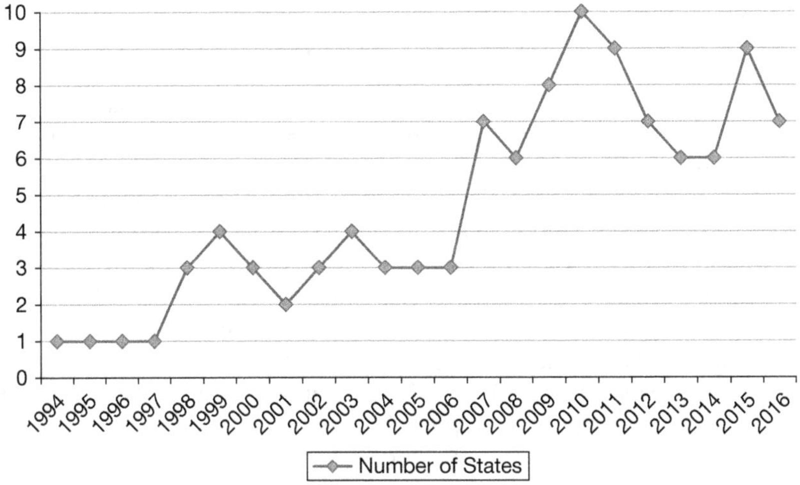

Figure 9.1 Number of Asian States which failed to file reports under article 40 of the ICCPR

number of States parties to the ICCPR, including Afghanistan and Japan, have accepted the new optional procedure of focused reports based on replies to the list of issues provided prior to reporting (LOIPR).[132]

J. Influence of General Comments and concluding observations

General Comments of the HRC on the provisions of the ICCPR constitute its universalist guidance to States. Although the reporting guidelines of the HRC require the States parties to the ICCPR to take its General Comments into account while submitting their respective reports under article 40 of the Covenant, the Asian States parties hardly do the needful in this regard. As for the use of General Comments in domestic legal processes, for instance, the Supreme Court of Bangladesh referred to General Comment 7 on ICCPR article 7 but refused to enforce the Covenant in the absence of its incorporation into municipal legislation.[133]

In Japan, General Comments are paid considerable attention and treated as significant standards for the promotion and protection of human rights. Several Japanese scholars and practitioners translate General Comments into the Japanese language for the purpose of dissemination and the formulation of critical reviews of the Japanese courts' practice. It has been found that plaintiffs' representatives have asserted human rights protection arguments built on General Comments

[132] UNGA, 'Report of the Human Rights Committee' (2014) UN Doc A/69/40 (vol I) 9–10; 'Report of the Human Rights Committee' (2017) UN Doc A/72/40, 23.

[133] *Bangladesh Legal Aid and Services Trust v Bangladesh*, Writ Petition Nos 5863 of 2009, 754 of 2010, and 4275 of 2010.

in legal proceedings before national courts in a number of cases.[134] In such cases, the defendants (namely the government, including local authorities) argue against the applicability of General Comments as legal norms in Japan. They insist that General Comments have no binding force, neither at the international level nor at the national level. It is rather difficult to find cases where judges relied upon General Comments in their reasoning.[135]

North Korea has indirectly admitted the influence of HRC, General Comment 6 on ICCPR article 6 (the right to life)[136] by stating that it 'considers an aggressive war, especially thermonuclear war, as the most serious threat to the life of mankind and resolutely rejects it'.[137] However, North Korea's nuclear threats against its arch-enemies expose the limits of the influence of General Comment 6.

As for the HRC's concluding observations on State reports, the Special Rapporteur for Follow-Up on Concluding Observations monitors their implementation by the States parties concerned. Official records reveal a mixed response in this regard. In response to the concluding observations on its report, for instance, Japan conveyed its inability to respect the observations relating to the death penalty but expressed its intention to solve the problem of comfort women. In fact, in December 2015, Japan entered into an agreement with South Korea to redress the grievances of comfort women.[138] Similarly, in its follow-up to the concluding observations on its fifth periodic report,[139] Sri Lanka highlighted that it has taken steps to comply with some of those observations. Thus, in comparison to General Comments, concluding observations have greater influence on the Asian States parties.

K. Influence of Views

Following the submission of individual complaints under the Optional Protocol procedure, a number of the target States have administered remedies to the victims of ICCPR violations, sometimes even before the HRC's adoption of its Views on the merits of those cases. Since not many Asian States are parties to the first Optional Protocol,[140] only a relatively small number of cases have been submitted

[134] Among more than 100 cases are: Supreme Court (1st Bench), Judgment, 14 January 2002, Hanrei Taimuzu [Law Times Reports], vol 1085, 169; Supreme Court (1st Bench), Judgment, 21 January 1999, Hanrei Taimuzu [Law Times Reports], vol 1002, 94.

[135] Kimio Yakushiji, 'Domestic Implementation of Human Rights Conventions and Judicial Remedies in Japan' (2003) 46 Japanese Ann Intl L 1, 27–37.

[136] HRC, 'General Comment 6' in 'Note by the Secretariat, Compilation of General Comments and General Recommendations Adopted by Human Rights Treaty Bodies' (27 May 2008) HRI/GEN/1/Rev.9 (vol I) 176–78.

[137] HRC, 'Second Periodic Report of North Korea' (n 41) para 32.

[138] Kwanwoo Jun and Alexander Martin, 'Japan, South Korea Agree to Aid for "Comfort Women"' *Wall Street Journal* (28 December 2015) <www.wsj.com/articles/japan-south-korea-reach-comfort-women-agreement-1451286347> accessed 13 March 2017.

[139] Government of Sri Lanka, 'Update to the Fifth Periodic Report of Sri Lanka under the ICCPR' (16 October 2015) <http://tbinternet.ohchr.org/Treaties/CCPR/Shared%20Documents/LKA/INT_CCPR_FCO_LKA_22048_E.docx> accessed 13 March 2017.

[140] Only eleven Asian States are parties to the Optional Protocol.

to the HRC[141] and one does not find many illustrations of the positive influence of the Views on the Asian States parties, whereas some of the worst cases of non-compliance with the Views and interim measures of the Committee have taken place in Asia.[142]

Among the States selected for the present study, only Nepal and Sri Lanka are parties to the first Optional Protocol. The HRC has found ICCPR violations in all those cases against Nepal and in all except for one case against Sri Lanka in which it expressed its Views on the merits, thus warranting follow-up action on the part of these States. As for Nepal, the Views adopted in the cases of *Sharma*,[143] *Giri*,[144] *Maharjan*,[145] and *Sedhai*[146] have been a subject of discussion in the report of the Special Rapporteur for Follow-Up on Views for a long time,[147] and the follow-up dialogues on these cases are still going on.[148] Similarly, referring to the *Weerawansa* case involving Sri Lanka,[149] the HRC stated that its decision had not been implemented and sought observations from the State party in this regard.[150] Also, when the government of Sri Lanka failed to respect the interim measures of protection in the case of *Fernando v Sri Lanka*, the HRC reiterated those measures.[151] In the *Singarasa* case, instead of implementing the HRC's Views, the Supreme Court of Sri Lanka found the State's accession to the first Optional Protocol unconstitutional.[152] All of these cases underline the limitations of the ICCPR and the first Optional Protocol thereto and consequently convey that Asia is still not well prepared to comply with the Views of the HRC.

L. Influence of the Universal Periodic Review

UPR seeks to reinforce the implementation of human rights irrespective of a State's accession to or ratification of the ICCPR. In the absence of HRC monitoring of the States not parties to the ICCPR, UPR assumes even greater importance.

[141] As of March 2016, the HRC had registered 2756 cases against 115 States parties to the Optional Protocol. Only 490 cases (18 per cent) were against the 11 Asian States parties.

[142] eg *Ruzmetov v Uzbekistan* (2006) HRC Communication No 915/2000, UN Doc CCPR/C/86/D/915/2000, paras 1.2, 5.1, and 8.

[143] *Sharma v Nepal* (2008) HRC Communication No 1469/2006, UN Doc CCPR/C/94/D/1469/2006.

[144] *Giri v Nepal* (2011) HRC Communication No 1761/2008, UN Doc CCPR/C/101/D/1761/2008.

[145] *Maharjan v Nepal* (2012) HRC Communication No 1863/2009, UN Doc CCPR/C/105/D/1863/2009.

[146] *Sedhai v Nepal* (2013) HRC Communication No 1865/2009, UN Doc CCPR/C/108/D/1865/2009.

[147] eg HRC, 'Follow-up Progress Report on Individual Communications Received and Processed Between June 2014 and January 2015' (29 June 2015) UN Doc CCPR/C/113/3.

[148] ibid 16.

[149] *Weerawansa v Sri Lanka* (2009) HRC Communication No 1406/2005, UN Doc CCPR/C/95/D/1406/2005.

[150] UNGA, 'Report of the Human Rights Committee' (2014) UN Doc A/69/40 (vol I) 215–16.

[151] *Fernando v Sri Lanka* (2005) HRC Communication No 1189/2003, UN Doc CCPR/C/83/D/1189/2003, para 5.6.

[152] *Singarasa v Attorney General of Sri Lanka*, SC Spl (LA) No 182/99 (September 2006).

During their respective UPRs, the Asian States under study pointed out the measures they had taken for the promotion and protection of human rights; some other States, including quite a few Asian ones, made certain recommendations; and most target States gave a mixed response. For instance, Pakistan was asked to withdraw remaining reservations to the ICCPR, review and align its legislation with the rights to freedom of religion and belief and freedom of expression as stipulated in the Covenant, and sign the Second Optional Protocol to the Covenant.[153] Similarly, Sri Lanka was asked to ratify the Second Optional Protocol;[154] China was recommended to speed up the process of ratification of the Covenant;[155] and Malaysia was asked to expedite the process of accession to the Covenant.[156] In spite of the fact that most of these recommendations remain unimplemented, UPRs contribute to enhancing the influence of the ICCPR in Asian States even if that influence is currently far from satisfactory. Since several Asian States make recommendations to other States in the region,[157] UPRs also contribute to the development of human rights diplomacy among those Asian States.

M. Availability of human rights documents in local languages and their accessibility

The literacy rate in most of the selected Asian States is very low in comparison to the global literacy rate. This underlines the limitations on the influence of the availability of human rights documents in local languages. In addition, international human rights instruments are not available in all the languages of the Asian States parties. For instance, the ICCPR and several other human rights treaties were published in only one official language of Afghanistan—Dari—and some of these instruments, including the Covenant, were translated into the other official language—Pashto—rather late. Likewise, although India has Hindi and English as its official languages and also twenty-two languages listed in the Eighth Schedule of the Constitution of India, the ICCPR is available in Bengali, English, Hindi, and Malayalam, while other language versions of the Covenant are difficult to find. A strong attachment to the local languages in India has shaped the boundaries of several states in this country, but it is surprising that linguistic loyalties do not get reflected in the availability of the ICCPR and other human rights instruments in all these languages.

The government of Japan makes Japanese translation of a treaty a prerequisite for seeking ratification of the treaty from the Diet. After ratification, the Japanese text is disseminated in the *Kampo* (official announcements) to the public. The government

[153] UNGA, 'Universal Periodic Review of Pakistan' (26 December 2012) UN Doc A/HRC/22/12.

[154] UNGA, 'Universal Periodic Review of Sri Lanka' (18 December 2012) UN Doc A/HRC/22/16.

[155] UNGA, 'Universal Periodic Review of China' (4 December 2013) UN Doc A/HRC/25/5.

[156] UNGA, 'Universal Periodic Review of Malaysia' (4 December 2013) UN Doc A/HRC/25/10.

[157] During the second Universal Periodic Review of India in 2012, for instance, the following Asian States made recommendations: Indonesia, Japan, Kyrgyzstan, Laos, Malaysia, the Maldives, Myanmar, Nepal, Singapore, South Korea, Sri Lanka, Thailand, Timor-Leste, and Viet Nam (OHCHR, 'Universal Periodic Review Second Cycle: India' <www.lan.ohchr.org/EN/HRBodies/UPR/Pages/INSession13.aspx> accessed 16 February 2018).

also provides treaty collections on an official website. As a result, all human rights treaties to which Japan is a party are available in the Japanese language. Several Japanese universities offer courses that include human rights. In North Korea, the texts of human rights instruments 'have been translated into Korean and disseminated to the people's power organs, judicial, procuratorial and people's security organs, economic and cultural organs and public organizations, and are taught in the regular higher educational institutions'.[158] There are no independent sources to reaffirm this claim of human rights teaching in North Korea.

N. General support

Besides the necessary legal architecture, powerful forces such as business communities, corporate entities, educational institutions, religious bodies, social media, and political parties have a significant role to play in ensuring respect for human rights. In particular, religious institutions and religious leaders shape the psyche of people in those societies where people have religious beliefs and sometimes prejudices, too. This is the case with most of the States selected for the present study.

In a politically organized society, political parties set the political agenda and influence the state of human rights. Further, the lack of political will generally affects the implementation of international human rights instruments. Political institutions are important tools for awakening political consciousness, which is a vital process for the true realization of human rights. The lack of political will, commonly cited as a ground for not assuming human rights obligations, has its origins in the political parties that form the government in a country. For example, owing to the lack of political will, the ratification of the UNCAT by India remains an ambition of human rights activists and an expectation of UPR participants. Similarly, one of the reasons for the lack of an NHRI in Japan is the lack of political will: the ruling Liberal Democratic Party has long opposed an NHRI. Likewise, both of the leading political parties in Bangladesh were reluctant to establish an NHRI, and it was a non-party caretaker government that created the country's NHRC in response to repeated calls and pressure from the international community and donors. The manner in which war criminals are being tried in Bangladesh is again an exhibition of the required political will, which actually is the result of the ideology of the present ruling party.

V. Concluding Remarks

Since Asia is the most diverse region in the world, it is difficult to identify a single Asian perspective on human rights, and any generalization about the influence of the ICCPR in this region is bound to be unsafe. This insecurity is aggravated

[158] UN, 'Core Document Forming Part of the Reports of States Parties: North Korea' (16 July 2002) UN Doc HRI/CORE/1/Add.108/Rev.1, para 57.

by the fact that a majority of Asian States lack satisfactory human rights databases. There is intolerable indifference towards the systematic collation and dissemination of information relating to human rights in Asia. It is not easy to obtain information about those aspects of Asian States' practice concerning the ICCPR that are essential for a scientific study of the subject. Only a few civil society actors in Asia attach importance to the development of human rights databases or to the submission of parallel or shadow reports following the respective State reports to the HRC under ICCPR article 40.

The HRC has had inadequate 'constructive discussions' with the Asian States parties to the ICCPR because a number of these States have not submitted their respective reports within the stipulated periods, becoming persistent defaulters of their respective reporting obligations, and most of those States that submitted their respective reports failed to provide all of the necessary information and disaggregated data. The inadequate 'constructive discussions' between the Asian States and the HRC have constrained an in-depth understanding of the ICCPR practice of these States. Since the first Optional Protocol to the ICCPR has the least adherents in the most populous continent, only a small number of individuals from Asia have been able to invoke the individual communication procedure of the HRC, and therefore a relatively smaller number of opportunities arises for the Committee to examine and appreciate the engagement with the Covenant in the domestic law of the Asian States. While some of the Asian States played a decisive role in the finalization and adoption of the ICCPR, these States have not played an equally effective role in determining the interpretation of the Covenant. Except for a few experts, not many members of the HRC from Asia have distinguished themselves as active members of the Committee. Similarly, not a single Asian State (except Pakistan) made a statement during the negotiation of the April 2014 Resolution of the UNGA regarding the reform of human rights treaty implementation procedures.[159] Even Pakistan did not make a direct statement (the Russian Federation spoke on behalf of a cross-regional group that includes Pakistan). Also, Asia witnesses the largest number of death sentences in the world, and this explains why only a small number of Asian States have become parties to the Second Optional Protocol to the ICCPR on the abolition of the death penalty[160] and one of them (the Philippines) has tried to reintroduce the death penalty and leave the ICC.[161]

The ICCPR has had varied influence on the domestic law, judicial decisions, and institutional practices of the Asian States parties to the Covenant. While Hong Kong, India, and Japan are encouraging examples, although not fully satisfactory, Pakistan needs to do more and Afghanistan remains extremely vulnerable. Bangladesh, Nepal, and Sri Lanka face considerable internal challenges to welcoming the ICCPR within their respective jurisdictions. North Korea continues to challenge the efficacy

[159] UNGA, Res 68/268 (21 April 2014) UN Doc A/RES/68/268.

[160] These are Kyrgyzstan, Mongolia, Nepal, the Philippines, Timor-Leste, Turkmenistan, and Uzbekistan.

[161] Open ended letter dated 27 March 2017 by the HRC Chairperson to the Philippines <www.ohchr.org/Documents/HRBodies/CCPR/NV_from_HRC_ThePhilippines_28March2017.pdf> accessed 15 February 2018.

of diplomacy, and the ICCPR is no panacea in this regard. China wants to take time to ratify the ICCPR, with uncertain prospects of greater openness in its socialist legal system, and Malaysia remains shy of the Covenant even after de-escalating its advocacy of Asian values.

The development of systemic databases is essential to understanding and appreciating the influence of the ICCPR in Asia. Both governmental and non-governmental bodies, especially educational institutions and NHRIs, ought to do justice to their obligations and potential in this regard. They are expected to conduct meticulous studies on the compatibility between the domestic law of every Asian State and the provisions of the ICCPR, the General Comments, and the applicable concluding observations of the HRC. They are also expected to investigate the factors and difficulties, if any, in the implementation of the ICCPR in every Asian State party. Further, every Asian State party's report to the HRC and its resulting concluding observations ought to be subjects of discussions at the domestic level. All the General Comments and concluding observations ought to be distributed by NHRIs or other civil society actors in local languages, with efforts to bring them to the attention of law enforcement officials and judges in particular. To comply with the Views of the HRC on the merits of the Asian cases submitted under the Optional Protocol, the Asian States parties ought to develop response mechanisms with the help of their respective NHRIs.

Asia as a whole is unlikely to have a regional human rights body in the foreseeable future, but Southeast Asia has already made some progress in this regard,[162] and South Asia has the potential to develop some limited human rights regimes to reinforce the ICCPR. The way the regional human rights treaties have enhanced compliance with civil and political rights in other regions ought to be a source of envy for those who are delighted with the projection of the current century as the Asian century.

Asia has already emerged as the leader of economic growth in the world. Most probably, Asia will become a hub of technological and military power in the years to come. This is bound to liberate the world from Eurocentrism. However, there is no comparable confidence that Asia will also do justice to its rich cultural heritage or that the growing economic, technological, and military power of Asian States will go along with a strengthening of the humanitarian values of the Asian people. Their cultural heritage, especially its collective moral dimension, is also a reminder of the importance of universal value pluralism, and hence the HRC should be aware of the same. The history of international law shows that besides law and morality, power and hegemony have had an impact on the formulation and application of international legal instruments. By the same logic, the anticipated Asian dominance in the world is likely to influence the formulation and interpretation of human rights instruments. Material growth without moral strength is not an Asian value, and the Asian century ought to combine the two by safeguarding and enriching the content

[162] In 2009, the Association of Southeast Asian Nations (ASEAN) established the Intergovernmental Commission of Human Rights (AICHR) as an 'overarching human rights body (...) with a cross-cutting mandate' <http://aichr.org/> accessed 2 April 2017.

and principles inherent in the concept of human rights that finds an eloquent expression in the ICCPR.

Bibliography

Agarwal, Hari Om, *Implementation of Human Rights Covenants: With Special Reference to India* (Kitab Mahal 1983)

Ahl, Björn, 'Chinese Law and International Treaties' (2009) 39 Hong Kong L J 737

Ahl, Björn, 'Exploring Ways of Implementing International Human Rights Treaties in China' (2010) 28 Netherlands Q of Human Rights 361

Akstinienė, Aistė, 'Reservations to Human Rights Treaties: Problematic Aspects Related to Gender Issues' (2013) 20 Jurisprudencija 451

Asia-Pacific Human Rights Information Centre, 'Japanese National Human Rights Commission' (2002) 28 Human Rights Forum 21 <www.hurights.or.jp/archives/focus/section2/2002/06/japanese-national-human-rights-commission.html> accessed 11 April 2017

Aust, Anthony, *Modern Treaty Law and Practice* (3rd edn, CUP 2013)

Chan, Johannes, 'State Succession to Human Rights Treaties: Hong Kong and the International Covenant on Civil and Political Rights' (1996) 45 Intl & Comparative L Q 928

Chen, Albert HY, 'International Human Rights Law and Domestic Constitutional Law: Internationalization of Constitutional Law in Hong Kong' (2009) 4 National Taiwan U L Rev 237

Chubb, Danielle, 'North Korean Human Rights and the International Community: Responding to the UN Commission of Inquiry' (2014) 15 Asia-Pacific J on Human Rights & L 51

Croshaw, Heather R, 'The "Right To Health" and "Right To Life": Positive Obligations for Controlling Air Pollution in Hong Kong in Clean Air Foundation v. HKSAR' (2014) 15 Vermont J of Environmental L 450

Croydon, Silvia Atanassova, 'A National Human Rights Commission for Japan: Domestic and Regional Implications' (30 May 2013) Nordic Association of Japanese and Korean Studies <www.najaks.org/?p=1032> accessed 11 April 2017

Datta, Saurav, 'Major Setback, Embarrassment to National Human Rights Commission' *National Herald* (New Delhi, 9 February 2017) <www.nationalheraldindia.com/institution/setback-embarrassment-to-national-human-rights-commission-report-un-recommends-accreditation-deferred-till-nov-2017> accessed 30 March 2018

Davis, Michael C, 'Basic Law, Universal Suffrage and the Rule of Law in Hong Kong' (2015) 38 Hastings Intl & Comparative L Rev 275

Dean, Meryll, *Japanese Legal System* (2nd edn, Routledge-Cavendish 2002)

Evatt, Elizabeth, 'Democratic People's Republic of Korea and the ICCPR: Denunciation as an Exercise of the Right of Self-defence?' (1998) 5 Australian J of Human Rights 215

Friedrich Ebert Foundation (ed), *The Universal Declaration of Human Rights at 50: Progress and Challenges* (Friedrich Ebert Foundation 1999)

Guhr, Alexandra H, and others, 'Max Planck Manual on Fair Trial Standards in the Afghan Constitution, the Afghan Interim Criminal Code for Courts, the Afghan Penal Code and other Afghan Laws as well as in the International Covenant on Civil and Political Rights' (4th edn, Max Planck Institute for Comparative Public Law and International Law 2009)

Hood, Roger, 'Abolition of the Death Penalty: China in World Perspective' (2009) 1 City U of Hong Kong L Rev 1

International Human Rights Law Clinic, 'The Right to a Remedy for Enforced Disappearances in India: A Legal Analysis of International and Domestic Law Relating to Victims of Enforced Disappearances' (2014) Berkeley School of Law Working Paper Series 1 <www.law.berkeley.edu/wp-content/uploads/2015/04/Working-Paper-1-India-Right-to-a-Remedy-151027.pdf> accessed 13 March 2017

Iwasawa, Yuji, 'Effectuation of International Law in the Municipal Legal Order of Japan' in Ko Swan Sik, M Christopher W Pinto, and JJG Syatauw (eds), *Asian Yearbook of International Law*, vol 4 (Kluwer 1994)

Iwasawa, Yuji, 'International Human Rights Adjudication in Japan' in Benedetto Conforti and Francesco Francioni (eds), *Enforcing International Human Rights in Domestic Courts* (Martinus Nijhoff 1997)

Iwasawa, Yuji, *International Law, Human Rights and Japanese Law: The Impact of International Law on Japanese Law* (Clarendon Press 1998)

Jiang, Na, *China and International Human Rights: Harsh Punishments in the Context of the International Covenant on Civil and Political Rights* (Springer 2014)

Jun, Kwanwoo, and Martin, Alexander, 'Japan, South Korea Agree to Aid for "Comfort Women"' *Wall Street Journal* (28 December 2015) <www.wsj.com/articles/japan-south-korea-reach-comfort-women-agreement-1451286347> accessed 13 March 2017

Karim, Mohammad Ershadul, 'Health as Human Rights under National and International Legal Framework: Bangladesh Perspective' (2010) 3 J of East Asia and Intl L 337

Kassar, Abbas, 'Pakistan Unwilling to Protect Religious Minorities Rights under ICCPR' *The Pioneer* (Hyderabad, 14 July 2014) <http://thepioneer.com.pk/pakistan-unwilling-to-protect-religious-minorities-rights-under-iccpr/> accessed 2 April 2017

Khatiwada, Padma P, *Nepal: Domestication of Treaties—What about Implementation?* (Human Rights Alliance 2012)

Kitamura, Yasuzo, 'The Influence of the International Covenant on Civil and Political Rights on Prisoners' Rights and Criminal Justice in Contemporary Japan' *Japanese YB of Intl L*, vol 59 (International Law Association of Japan 2016)

Klingenberg, Hans, 'Elements of Nordic Practice 1998: Denmark' (1999) 68 Nordic J of Intl L 163

Knust Rassekh Afshar, Mandana, 'The Case of an Afghan Apostate: The Right to a Fair Trial Between Islamic Law and Human Rights in the Afghan Constitution' in Armin von Bogdandy and Rüdiger Wolfrum (eds), *Max Planck United Nations Yearbook*, vol 10 (Brill 2006)

Kolodner, Eric, 'Religious Rights in China: A Comparison of International Human Rights Law and Chinese Domestic Legislation' (1994) 16 Human Rights Q 455

Kumar, Ravender, 'India, the International Covenant on Civil and Political Rights, and its Implementation Machinery' (PhD dissertation, Jawaharlal Nehru University 1991)

Langer, Lorenz, *Religious Offence and Human Rights: The Implications of Defamation of Religions* (CUP 2014)

Lombardi, Richard, 'The Influence of the International Covenant on Civil and Political Rights on Anti-Blasphemy Laws' (2013) Law School Student Scholarship Paper 158 <http://scholarship.shu.edu/student_scholarship/158> accessed 2 April 2017

Morikawa, Koichi (ed), 'Half a Century with the International Covenants on Human Rights: Long-Term Impacts on the World (Part I)' *Japanese YB of Intl L*, vol 59 (International Law Association of Japan 2016)

National Human Rights Commission of Nepal, *A Study of the Domestication Status of International Covenant on Civil and Political Rights in Nepal* (National Human Rights Commission 2007)

Omar, Shagufta, *Abolition of Death Penalty with Special Reference to Pakistan* (Women Aid Trust Pakistan 2012)

Ramsden, Michael, 'Reviewing the United Kingdom's ICCPR Immigration Reservation in Hong Kong Courts' (2014) 63 Intl & Comparative L Q 635

Rao, P Chandrasekhara, *The Indian Constitution and International Law* (Martinus Nijhoff 1993)

Rashid, Qasim, 'Pakistan's Failed Commitment: How Pakistan's Institutionalized Persecution of the Ahmadiyya Muslim Community Violates the International Covenant on Civil and Political Rights' (2011) 11 Richmond J of Global L & Business 1

Schwelb, Egon, 'The International Measures of Implementation of the International Covenant on Civil and Political Rights and of the Optional Protocol' (1977) 12 Texas Intl L J 141

Shahabuddin, Mohammad, 'The International Covenant on Civil and Political Rights: A Study on Bangladesh Compliance' (National Human Rights Commission of Bangladesh 2013)

Sharma, Brij Kishore, *Human Rights Covenants and Indian Law* (PHI Learning 2010)

Sharma, Hemang, 'Rights against Torture in Nepal: Commitment and Reality' (2015) 4 Intl Human Rights L Rev 104

Shope, Mark L, 'Adoption and Function of International Instruments: Thoughts on Taiwan's Enactment of the Act to Implement the ICCPR and the ICESCR' (2012) 22 Indiana Intl & Comparative L Rev 159

Smith, Adam M, 'Making Itself at Home: Understanding Foreign Law in Domestic Jurisprudence: The Indian Case' (2006) 24 Berkeley J Intl L 218

Sugarman, Eli, and others, *An Introduction to the Law of Afghanistan* (3rd edn, Stanford Law School Afghanistan Legal Education Project (ALEP), Stanford Law School, 2011)

Sun, Shiyan, 'Understanding and Interpretation of the ICCPR in the Context of China's Possible Ratification' (2007) 6 Chinese J Intl L 17

Thomas, Kelly A, 'Falun Gong: An Analysis of China's National Security Concerns' (2001) 10 Pacific Rim L and Policy J 471

Tyagi, Yogesh, *The UN Human Rights Committee: Practice and Procedure* (CUP 2011)

Udagama, Deepika, 'The Politics of Domestic Implementation of International Human Rights Law: A Case Study of Sri Lanka' (2015) 16 Asia-Pacific J on Human Rights & L 104

Villalobos, Katharine M, 'Digital Oppression in Cuba and China: A Comparative Study of ICCPR Violations' (2014–15) 24 J of Transnational L & Policy 161

Vijapur, Abdulrahim P, 'Domestic Application of the International Covenant on Civil and Political Rights – With Special Reference to Rights of Minorities in India' in Krishan P Saksena (ed), *Human Rights and the Constitution: Vision and Reality* (Gyan Publishing House 2003)

Webster, Timothy, 'International Human Rights in Japan: The View at Thirty' (2010) 23 Columbia J of Asian L 241

Weisburd, Arthur Mark, 'Customary International Law and Torture: The Case of India' (2006) 2 Chicago J Intl L 81

Xue, Hanqin, and Jin, Qian, 'International Treaties in the Chinese Domestic Legal System' (2009) 8 Chinese J of Intl L 299

Yakushiji, Kimio, 'Domestic Implementation of Human Rights Conventions and Judicial Remedies in Japan' (2003) 46 Japanese Ann Intl L 1

10

Influence of the ICESCR in Europe

*Amrei Müller**

I. Introduction

Studies evaluating the legal influence of the ICESCR[1] and the work of the Committee on Economic, Social and Cultural Rights (CESCR or the Committee) in European States are few and far between. Those that exist have often found that this influence has been limited,[2] while others have gone as far as to announce the 'death of socio-economic rights'[3] in an era of neo-liberal globalization affecting Europe and the rest of the world, suggesting a vanishingly low influence at best.

On the occasion of the fiftieth anniversary of the ICESCR in 2016, it is timely to (re-)examine the influence that the ICESCR has had in Europe. The focus is on analysing the positive and negative influence of Covenant law (comprising both the ICESCR and its interpretation by the CESCR) on domestic law, both on legal processes and outcomes.[4] The scope of this chapter precludes tracing this influence in all of the European States,[5] virtually all of which ratified the ICESCR early

* The author would like to thank Aslan Abashidze, Ed Bates, Virginia Bras-Gomes, Colm O'Cinneide, Aleksandra Koneva, Claudia Mahler, Isabel Maillo, and Maksim Usynin, who generously helped with finding relevant information about the ICESCR's influence in the four countries studied. Many thanks to Samantha Besson, Andreas Føllesdal, and Geir Ulfstein for their very helpful comments on earlier versions of this contribution. All remaining errors are of course my own. I would also like to thank the Geneva Academy for International Humanitarian Law and Human Rights for hosting me as a visiting fellow while I conducted the research for this chapter, and the Research Council of Norway for the financial support provided through its Centres of Excellence Funding Scheme, 'PluriCourts: The Legitimacy of the International Judiciary' (project number 223274).

1 International Covenant on Economic, Social and Cultural Rights (opened for signature 16 December 1966, entered into force 3 January 1976) 993 UNTS 3 (ICESCR or Covenant).

2 eg Jasper Krommendijk, *The Domestic Impact and Effectiveness of the Process of State Reporting under UN Human Rights Treaties in the Netherlands, New Zealand and Finland: Paper-Pushing or Policy Prompting?* (Intersentia 2014) 143–63; Christof Heyns and Frans Viljoen, *The Impact of the United Nations Human Rights Treaties on the Domestic Level* (Martinus Nijhoff 2002).

3 Paul O'Connell, 'The Death of Socio-Economic Rights' (2011) 74 Modern L Rev 532.

4 For a more detailed definition of 'legal influence' that also underlies the analysis in the present chapter, and for a distinction of 'influence' from other concepts (eg 'compliance', 'reception', and 'effectiveness'), see the contribution by Samantha Besson in this volume.

5 For the purpose of the present chapter, the forty-seven member States of the Council of Europe and Belarus are counted as European States.

The Human Rights Covenants at 50: Their Past, Present, and Future. Daniel Moeckli, Helen Keller, and Corina Heri. Published 2018 by Oxford University Press.

on.[6] The chapter therefore concentrates on four representative countries (Germany, Russia, Spain, and the United Kingdom)[7] and on three broader questions that help to uncover the wider trends and challenges of the ICESCR's influence. First, it asks whether the direct effects of the ICESCR (and of domestic economic, social, and cultural rights (ESCR)) are now widely recognized in the four countries (Section II.A). In other words, are ESCR today accepted as individual rights that create binding obligations and can thus have practical implications for government policy, law-making, domestic jurisprudence, and the distribution of resources within a State, and can they be enforced (usually by a domestic, regional, or international judiciary)[8] similarly to the civil and political rights set out in the International Covenant on Civil and Political Rights (ICCPR)[9] and the European Convention on Human Rights (ECHR)?[10] This question is examined against the background of the well-known circumstance that the impact of the ICESCR has been hampered in many States by the fact that its direct effect has been questioned, an attitude which is often reflected in statements that qualify the ICESCR's provisions (and domestic ESCR) as mere 'aspirations' guiding social policies, and thus reject their status as individual rights that create binding obligations. Relatedly, the chapter investigates whether we can still observe a difference in the approach to ESCR in Eastern and Western European States, a holdover from the East–West confrontation during which the Eastern bloc championed ESCR while the West promoted civil and political rights (Section II.B).[11] Second, the chapter discusses the extent to which particularities of the political and legal systems in the four countries have determined and shaped the legal influence that the ICESCR has had (Section III). Third, it considers whether the recent financial and economic crises, which have led to far-reaching interferences with ESCR in Europe and elsewhere[12] and thus attest a limited influence of

[6] All European States have ratified the ICESCR, with the exception of Andorra.

[7] The criteria for the selection of these countries were: their geographical distribution, their degree of scepticism towards ESCR (reflecting also the former East–West divide), the way in which the country in question has been affected by the recent global financial and economic crises, and the author's languages abilities.

[8] For a more comprehensive discussion of the notion of 'direct effect' and the relationship between international and domestic human rights underlying this article's analysis, see Samantha Besson's contribution to this volume (Samantha Besson, 'The Influence of the Two Covenants on States Parties across Regions: Lessons for the Role of Comparative Law and of Regions in International Human Rights Law').

[9] International Covenant on Civil and Political Rights (ICCPR) (opened for signature 16 December 1966, entered into force 23 March 1976) 999 UNTS 171.

[10] Convention for the Protection of Human Rights and Fundamental Freedoms (European Convention on Human Rights, as amended) (ECHR).

[11] For a summary of the main arguments and the relevant literature, see Olivier De Schutter, *International Human Rights Law* (1st edn, CUP 2010) 740–42. These arguments have been discussed extensively and refuted by many, eg in Asbjørn Eide, Catarina Krause, and Allan Rosas (eds), *Economic, Social and Cultural Rights: A Textbook* (2nd edn, Martinus Nijhoff 2001); David Bilchitz, *Poverty and Fundamental Rights: The Justification and Enforcement of Socio-Economic Rights* (OUP 2007).

[12] As established by the CESCR's first View adopted under the Optional Protocol to the ICESCR (OP-ICESCR) (opened for signature 10 December 2008, entered into force 5 May 2016) UN Doc A/RES/63/117, 48 ILM 256 (2009)), namely in *IDG v Spain* CESCR Communication No 2/2014 (13 October 2015) UN Doc E/C.12/55/D/2/2014, as discussed in many contributions, including in Aoife Nolan (ed), *Economic and Social Rights after the Financial Crisis* (CUP 2014), and Aoife Nolan, 'Not Fit

the ICESCR, could nonetheless increase awareness for the ICESCR after a long period of decline of a 'social Europe' and the steady downsizing of social protection systems in many European States, which can be traced back to the ideological shifts of the 1980s (Section IV).[13] It is submitted that such awareness, and thus a stronger influence of the ICESCR, is highly desirable to ensure a 'decent life' for everyone, including socio-economically disadvantaged individuals,[14] and given the fundamental connection between the protection of human rights, equality, and the functioning of inclusionary and emancipatory democratic systems[15]—a connection that calls for levelling out undue socio-economic inequalities within a polity (and among polities).[16]

To paint a comprehensive picture of the various aspects of the broader trends and challenges characterizing the ICESCR's legal influence in the four countries, the chapter conducts comparative research on the four States' participation in the CESCR's reporting process, the influence of the ICESCR and the CESCR's General Comments and concluding observations on domestic legislation, legislative processes, and policies, on national courts' jurisprudence, and on civil society's engagement with and media coverage of the ICESCR and the CESCR's work.[17] Where indicated, but without any claim of exhaustiveness, the influence of the ICESCR is compared to the influence of the ICCPR, the ECHR, or other international or European human rights treaties protecting ESCR.[18] Some of the influence of the

for Purpose? Human Rights in Times of Financial and Economic Crisis' (2015) 4 European Human Rights L Rev 360.

[13] Colm O'Cinneide, 'Austerity and the Faded Dream of a "Social Europe"' in Nolan, *ESCR* (n 12) 169, 170.

[14] For a thorough analysis of the normative foundation of ESCR see Bilchitz, *Poverty and Fundamental Rights* (n 11).

[15] Richard Burchill, 'Democracy and the Promotion and Protection of Socio-Economic Rights' in Mashood Baderin and Robert McCorquodale (eds) *Economic, Social and Cultural Rights in Action* (OUP 2007) 361, 366, noting that an understanding of democracy that embraces ESCR would reject a neo-liberal understanding that sees 'democracy as limited to a process of choosing leaders, and [letting] competitive free-market systems dominate the organisation of all other aspects of the economy and society.' Instead, as noted by Susan Marks, it is necessary to establish an understanding that represents 'an on-going call to enlarge the opportunities for popular participation in political processes and end social practices that systematically marginalise some citizens while empowering others' (Susan Marks, *The Riddle of All Constitutions: International Law, Democracy and the Critique of Ideology* (OUP 2000) 109); also David Beetham, *Democracy and Human Rights* (Polity 1999) chapter 6.

[16] See Burchill, 'Democracy' (n 15) 379; CESCR, 'General Comment 20' (2 June 2009) UN Doc E/C.12/GC/20, paras 8–9 and 39.

[17] Due to space constraints, not all components of the grid for comparative analysis of Covenant law influence on domestic law identified in Samantha Besson's contribution to this volume could be covered. Moreover, not all examples and evidence collected to identify this influence in Europe can be presented here.

[18] ie Convention on the Elimination of All Forms of Discrimination against Women (CEDAW) (opened for signature 18 December 1979, entered into force 3 September 1981) 1249 UNTS 13; Convention on the Rights of the Child (CRC) (opened for signature 20 November 1989, entered into force 2 September 1990) 1577 UNTS 3; Convention on the Rights of Persons with Disabilities (CRPD) (opened for signature 13 December 2006, entered into force 3 May 2008) 2515 UNTS 3; and the (Revised) European Social Charter ((R)ESCh) (opened for signature 3 May 1996, entered into force 1 July 1999), European Treaty Series (ETS) No 163, which revised the European Social Charter (ESCh) (opened for signature 18 October 1961, entered into force 26 February 1965) ETS No 35.

ICESCR on the Council of Europe (CoE) and the European Union (EU), in particular the jurisprudence of the European Court of Human Rights (ECtHR), the European Committee of Social Rights (ECSR), and the Court of Justice of the European Union (CJEU), is also traced.

II. Influence of the ICESCR by Acceptance of ESCRs' Direct Effect?

Through its General Comments and 'constructive dialogue' with the States parties to the ICESCR, the CESCR has worked over the years to counter the aforementioned assumption that the Covenant has no direct effect. In this section, six developments that indicate an enhanced significance and recognition of ICESCR rights as individual rights in the four States shall be discussed, pointing towards an increased influence of the ICESCR (II.A), before giving four examples that highlight the fact that there is still a certain way to go in order to achieve full recognition of these rights as human rights on an equal level with the civil and political rights set out in the ICCPR and the ECHR (II.B).[19]

A. Signs of increased legal influence

As the first sign of the influence of ICESCR rights, it can be observed that Germany, Russia, Spain, and the United Kingdom ratified the ICESCR early on,[20] and actively participated in the reporting process to the CESCR and its predecessor—a Working Group of the Economic and Social Council (ECOSOC)—from the time when it was set up in 1979. This ratification and participation is on par with the States' ratification of the ICCPR and their participation in the reporting process before the UN Human Rights Committee (HRC). In all four States, comprehensive reports are prepared by a lead ministry that pools information from other relevant ministries and governmental agencies, and reports are submitted on time.[21] All four States regularly send high-level delegations composed of experts from relevant ministries and governmental agencies to Geneva, and the CESCR recognizes this—and the high quality of the reports—as a positive feature in its concluding observations.[22]

[19] Note that Russia is an exception when it comes to recognizing the direct effect of ESCR. Whilst there are of course numerous problems with the implementation of ESCR in Russia, it does have a far-reaching constitutional ESCR catalogue. ECSR can be invoked before domestic courts, and Russia (and its predecessor the USSR) has never questioned that ESCR constitute judicially enforceable human rights.

[20] The Federal Republic of Germany, the German Democratic Republic, and the Soviet Union ratified the ICESCR in 1973; Spain did so in 1977, and the United Kingdom in 1976.

[21] All four States have so far submitted five or six periodic reports.

[22] eg CESCR, 'Concluding Observations on the Fifth Periodic Report of Germany' (12 July 2011) UN Doc E/C.12/DEU/CO/5, paras 2–3; CESCR, 'Concluding Observations on the Fifth Periodic Report of Russia' (1 June 2011) UN Doc E/C.12/RUS/CO/5, para 2; CESCR, 'Concluding Observations on the Fifth Periodic Report of Spain' (6 June 2012) UN Doc E/C.12/ESP/CO/5, paras 2–3; CESCR, 'Concluding Observations on the Combined Fourth and Fifth Periodic Report of the United Kingdom of Great Britain and Northern Ireland' (12 June 2009) UN Doc E/C.12/GBR/CO/5, para 2.

Second, with the exception of the United Kingdom, where these issues still evoke considerable discussions with the CESCR,[23] Germany, Russia, and Spain no longer question the character of ESCR as human rights or their enforceability (at least not openly), and they recognize the minimum core approach as an important concept guiding the progressive realization of ESCR.[24]

Third, all States have given the Covenant a place in their legal order that is largely equal to that of the ICCPR and the ECHR[25]—even if this place varies depending on the degree of openness of the respective domestic legal order to international law. Formally, Russia affords the ICESCR the strongest position, whereas it remains very weak in the United Kingdom. The 1993 Russian Constitution declares that international treaties are a component part of the Russian legal system,[26] and establishes that 'if an international treaty of the Russian Federation stipulates other rules than those stipulated by the law, the rules of the international treaty shall apply'.[27] Based on this provision, the primacy of international human rights treaties (including the ICESCR) in relation to ordinary laws has been confirmed by the Russian Supreme Court (RSC), which has also endorsed the direct effect of the ICESCR's provisions.[28] In addition, the Russian Constitution contains an extensive catalogue of ESCR, the drafting of which has been influenced by the ICESCR.[29] In Germany, the ICESCR was transformed into domestic law by means of federal legislation,[30] and has the rank of an ordinary federal law.[31] The provisions of the ICESCR have direct effect in Germany: they are binding on all governmental institutions at federal and *Länder* level,[32] and can in principle be invoked before domestic courts. Similarly, in Spain, as a duly concluded and officially published treaty, the ICESCR is part of the Spanish legal order.[33] Even in the United Kingdom, where the ICESCR has not been transformed into the domestic legal order, and thus cannot be invoked before domestic courts, the Covenant nonetheless has some influence on legislative processes, policies, and jurisprudence, as will be discussed further below. The position of ESCR more generally in the domestic legal orders is also strengthened by the fact that other regional and international treaties containing ESCR have been

[23] As will be argued further on in this chapter (n 93).

[24] Based on the CESCR's concluding observations on the respective States (n 22) and the author's conversations with CESCR members.

[25] Note that, among the countries studied, the United Kingdom is the only one that formally gives the ECHR a much stronger position in its legal order than the ICCPR and the ECHR.

[26] Gennady M Danilenko, 'The New Russian Constitution and International Law' (1994) 88 AJIL 451.

[27] Russian Constitution, 1993, art 15(4), also confirmed by arts 17(1) and 55(1).

[28] Resolution of the Plenum of the RSC of 10 October 2003, No 5, paras 1, 4, and 8; Resolution of the Plenum of the RSC of 5 March 2013, No 4, para 2. This is also in line with the Federal Law on international treaties of 15 July 1995, No 101-FS, paras 3 and 5(3).

[29] Danileko, 'The New Russian Constitution' (n 26) 467; Heyns and Viljoen, *Impact* (n 2) 503. In addition, the drafting was influenced by the ESCR catalogue of the Soviet Constitution.

[30] Bundesgesetzblatt (BGBl) II 1973/428, 1570.

[31] German Constitution, 1949, art 59(2).

[32] In accordance with art 20(3) of the German Constitution, 1949; confirmed by the FCC, 2 BvR 2125/01, 19 September 2006, para 52.

[33] Spanish Constitution, 1978, art 96(1).

transformed into the respective domestic legal orders of three of the States under study with direct effect,[34] with the United Kingdom being the exception.

Fourth, domestic courts in all four countries have engaged with the ICESCR, even though the extent and effect of this engagement varies once more. The Russian Constitutional Court (RCC) referred to the ICESCR fifty-eight times between 1992 and December 2016,[35] and the Spanish Constitutional Court (SCC) had done so on fifty-one occasions by December 2016, with the first reference appearing in 1981.[36] In the jurisprudence of the German Federal Constitutional Court (FCC) and the UK Supreme Court (UKSC) and its predecessor, the House of Lords (HL), references to the ICESCR are hardly found. From the ICESCR's entry into force for both countries in 1976 until December 2016, the FCC mentioned the ICESCR only five times,[37] and the UKSC/HL referred to the ICESCR only in four cases,[38] two of which included this reference only because they cited other material that contained it.[39] References to the (R)ESCh, CEDAW, CRC, and CRPD are also found in the work of all four apex courts,[40] confirming domestic courts' readiness to enforce ESCR more broadly.[41] In parallel, at the European level, the reporting process before the ECSR has gathered momentum and more collective complaints about alleged violations of the (R)ESCh have been submitted.[42] At the same time,

[34] The (R)ESCh, CEDAW, CPED, and CRC have been transformed into German, Russian, and Spanish law in a similar way as the ICESCR.

[35] Search conducted at <http://ksportal.garant.ru:8081/SESSION/PILOT/main.htm> accessed 30 March 2017. No research was conducted on the influence of the ICESCR on the jurisprudence of the Supreme Court of the Soviet Union, which ceased to exist in 1992.

[36] Search conducted at <http://hj.tribunalconstitucional.es/es-ES/Resolucion/List> accessed 30 March 2017.

[37] Search conducted at <www.bundesverfassungsgericht.de/SiteGlobals/Forms/Suche/Entscheidungensuche_Formular.html?language_=de> accessed 30 March 2017.

[38] Search conducted at <www.bailii.org> accessed 30 March 2017.

[39] *AA v Secretary of State for the Home Department* [2013] UKSC 49; *A & Ors v Secretary of State for the Home Department* [2004] UKHL 56, para 62.

[40] By December 2016, the FCC had referred to the CRC three times (since 1992 [note: this and the following dates refer to the year in which the respective treaties entered into force for the respective country]); six times to the CRPD (since 2009); never to the CEDAW (since 1985); and only twice to the ESCh (since 1965). The RCC referred to the CRC seventy-seven times (since 1990); three times to the CRPD (since 2012); three times to the CEDAW (since 1981); and eleven times to the (R)ESCh (since 2009). The SCC referred to the CRC twenty times (since 1990); four times to the CRPD (since 2007); twice to the CEDAW (since 1984); and forty-eight times to the ESCh (since 1980). The UKHL/SC referred to the CRC forty-one times (since 1991); five times to the CRPD (since 2009); five times to the CEDAW (since 1986); and never to the ESCh (since 1962).

[41] More frequent references to the CRC and CRPD than to the ICESCR are likely due to the fact that these instruments contain more specific provisions than the ICESCR and that NGOs specifically promoting the rights of children and persons with disabilities actively invoke these Conventions before domestic courts.

[42] See the overview in the ECSR's 'Activity Report 2015' (2016) <https://rm.coe.int/CoERMPublicCommonSearchServices/DisplayDCTMContent?documentId=09000016805ab9c7> accessed 30 March 2017; and the analysis by Holly Cullen, 'The Collective Complaints System of the European Social Charter: Interpretative Methods of the European Committee of Social Rights' (2009) 9 Human Rights L Rev 61. Note, however, that none of the four States analysed here have ratified the Additional Protocol to the ESCh providing for a System of Collective Complaints (opened for signature 9 September 1995, entered into force 1 July 1998) ETS No 158.

the number of references to the ICESCR in the work of the ECSR and the ECtHR has increased.

There are some judgments in which the respective courts engaged with the substance of the ICESCR and where this had an influence on the outcome of the case. For example, in March 2015, the RCC declared parts of a Russian law that provided for the deportation of HIV-positive foreigners or stateless persons legally residing in Russia with the aim of protecting public health to be unconstitutional. The RCC relied inter alia on the ICESCR's non-discrimination clause,[43] and observed that the CESCR, in its General Comment 20, had unambiguously established that among the prohibited grounds for discrimination under 'other status' was an individual's health status, explicitly including people suffering from HIV/AIDS.[44] Another example is a 2012 judgment of the FCC wherein the FCC concretized the scope and content of an autonomous fundamental right to a dignified minimum existence under the German Constitution.[45] The judgment concerned the unconstitutionality of the Asylum Seekers Benefits Act's provisions on cash benefits, and the FCC relied on the ICESCR to further substantiate the existence of this constitutional right.[46] Both dimensions of the right—the individual right to have one's physical existence secured as well as the right to maintain interpersonal relationships and a minimum of participation in social, cultural, and political life—were reinforced with references to ICESCR articles 9 and 15(1)(a).[47]

Fifth, in all four countries, the ICESCR and the CESCR's output have had some influence on ordinary legislation, legislative processes, and policies, even if this influence might not extend so far as to affect the ultimate content of a certain piece of legislation or the outcome of a legislative process. In addition, this influence can take many different routes. Influence on ordinary legislation has been noted in Russia and, more recently, on legislation adopted by regional parliaments in Spain.

Concerning Russia, the CESCR observed that the revision process of the Russian Labour Code, which was amended throughout the 1990s and adopted in 2001, was inspired by the ICESCR.[48] In addition, many ordinary Russian laws refer to international human rights law in general in their preambles or operative paragraphs. An example is the federal framework law on health care for Russian citizens of November 2011.[49] Article 5 of the framework law sets out that 'health interventions should be conducted based on the recognition, observance and protection of

[43] ICESCR art 2(2).

[44] Judgment of the RCC of 12 March 2015, No 4-P, paras 2.1 and 4.

[45] FCC, 1 BvL 10/10, 18 July 2012.

[46] ibid para 75.

[47] ibid para 70. Surprisingly, in a 2010 judgment (1 BvL 1/09, 9 February 2010) wherein the FCC concretized the scope of the right to a dignified minimum existence, it did not refer to the ICESCR.

[48] Labour Code of the Russian Federation of 30 December 2001, N 197-FS; CESCR, 'Concluding Observations on the Third Periodic Report of Russia' (20 May 1997) UN Doc E/C.12/1/Add.13, para 5; and CESCR, 'Concluding Observations on the Fourth Periodic Report of Russia' (12 December 2003) UN Doc E/C.12/1/Add.94, para 7.

[49] Documents relating to the drafting history of the law do not, however, reveal that the ICESCR or any document issued by the CESCR was referred to during this process. However, references to the right to health under the Russian Constitution were made (see <http://asozd2.duma.gov.ru/main.nsf/(Spravka)?OpenAgent&RN=534829-5&02> accessed 30 March 2017).

human rights and in accordance with universally recognized principles and norms of international law,'[50] and contains a strong anti-discrimination clause.[51] The law furthermore establishes the priority of patients' interests in the provision of health care as a fundamental principle,[52] something the CESCR's 2003 concluding observations on the Russian State report had recommended.[53]

In Spain, regional parliaments adopted legislation that qualifies ESCR as 'subjective rights' and gives individuals the right to invoke them before domestic courts. These legislative acts have been supported with references to the ICESCR in their preambles.[54] They concern the right to housing and include provisions that recognize a right to occupy dwellings on the part of those who live in them but who do not have the resources to buy (their) homes or pay their mortgages, and are not provided with alternative housing by the authorities.[55]

The influence of the ICESCR on legislative processes can be observed in all four countries under study. In some instances, legislation has been adopted that establishes a concrete and measurable mechanism for the progressive realization of obligations under the ICESCR. An example is the 2010 UK Child Poverty Act.[56] While human rights language had been absent in the government-initiated Child Poverty Bill,[57] the UK Parliament's Joint Committee on Human Rights (JCHR) brought in this language in its legislative scrutiny report.[58] The Act enshrined the government's commitment to eradicating child poverty by 2020 in law, and thus constituted a mechanism to measure concrete steps towards the progressive realization of the UK's obligations under ICESCR articles 2(1) and 11 as well as CRC article 27.[59] To some extent, this has been repeated in the UK Equality Act (2010),

[50] Federal Law of 21 November 2011, N 323-FS, art 5(1). [51] ibid arts 5(2) and (3).

[52] ibid art 6.

[53] CESCR, 'Concluding Observations: Fourth Report of Russia' (n 48) paras 32 and 60.

[54] See eg Ley 3/2015, 18 June 2015, de Vivienda; Ley 4/2013, 1 October 2013, de medidas para asegurar el cumplimiento de la función social de la vivienda, Comunidad Autónoma de Andalucía; and Ley 24/2015, 29 July 2015, de medidas urgentes para afrontar la emergencia en el ámbito de la vivienda y la pobreza energética, Comunidad Autónoma de Cataluña.

[55] Generally, see the analysis by Emilio José Gómez Ciriano, 'La protección de los derechos económicos, sociales y culturales desde una perspectiva diacrónica y comparada: Estudio en cinco países europeos', VII Informe sobre exclusión y desarrollo social en España 2014, documento de trabajo 8.4 <www.foessa2014.es/informe/uploaded/documentos_trabajo/15102014153319_5781.pdf> accessed 30 March 2017.

[56] Child Poverty Act (2010) (ch 9). Other prominent examples are the Equality Act (2010) and the Apprenticeships, Skills, Children and Learning Act (2009).

[57] Ellie Palmer, 'The Child Poverty Act 2010: Holding Government to Account for Promises in a Recessionary Climate?' (2010) 3 European Human Rights L Rev 305, 307.

[58] JCHR, 'Legislative Scrutiny: Child Poverty Bill', HL Paper No 183, HC 1114 (28th report of session 2008–09) para 1.22; Murray Hunt, 'Enhancing Parliament's Role in Relation to Economic and Social Rights' (2010) 3 European Human Rights L Rev 242.

[59] For a critical analysis, also in light of the UK's obligations under the ICESCR, see Palmer, 'Child Poverty Act' (n 57) 307, 310, and 314. Regrettably, the UK government repealed the duty to meet time-bound targets on child poverty in 2016. The CESCR has expressed concerns about this measure; see CESCR, 'Concluding Observations on the Sixth Periodic Report of the United Kingdom of Great Britain and Northern Ireland' (14 July 2016) UN Doc E/C.12/GBR/CO/6, paras 47–48.

which establishes a public sector duty to reduce inequalities resulting from socio-economic disadvantage.[60]

In Russia, the influence of the ICESCR on legislation, policies, and legislative processes comes via the work of the High Commissioner for Human Rights in the Russian Federation and of the Council for Civil Society and Human Rights under the President of the Russian Federation. Both entities have been tasked with ensuring that Russian legislation conforms to the ICESCR and other international human rights treaties. Even though they prefer to base their arguments on the ESCR contained in the Russian Constitution, and thus rarely expressly refer to the ICESCR or the CESCR's concluding observations, both entities have urged the adoption of legislative and other measures that would contribute to the implementation of ICESCR law. For example, the 2014 report of the High Commissioner reveals that she has taken many initiatives to enhance peoples' ability to enjoy their rights to health, education, housing, and social security,[61] and has called on the government to increase minimum wages to address the growing number of the 'working poor'.[62] The Council for Civil Society and Human Rights, a consultative body to the President, has a permanent commission on social rights which is involved in improving peoples' access to health care in Russia, also in regard to many issues that the CESCR flagged in its 2011 concluding observations.[63] Currently, the Council also has a temporary Working Group on the Realization of Citizens' Right to Affordable Housing,[64] which deals with many issues concerning access to housing, in particular access by vulnerable groups, and has issued recommendations to change the Housing Act.[65] Like the recommendations of the JCHR to the UK Parliament and government, the suggestions of the Russian High Commissioner and the Council have recommendatory character only. It is difficult to assess their exact influence without conducting a more detailed and systematic study. However, due to the fact that the issues related to the implementation of ESCR are relatively less controversial than many other human rights questions in the current Russian political climate,[66]

[60] Equality Act (2010) s 1(1) and s 149. For a comprehensive discussion see Sandra Fredman, 'Positive Duties and Socio-economic Disadvantage: Bringing Disadvantage onto the Equality Agenda' (2010) 3 European Human Rights L Rev 290.

[61] High Commissioner for Human Rights in the Russian Federation, '2014 Report' <http://ombudsmanrf.org/www/upload/files/docs/appeals/doklad2014.pdf> accessed 30 March 2017, 27–29, 60, 67–72, 94, 104 (health); 30–31, 87–88, 104 (education); 28, 73, 75, 78–82 (housing); 72, 104 (social security).

[62] ibid 76–77.

[63] 'Совет при Президенте Российской Федерации по развитию гражданского общества и правам человека, Постоянные комиссии Совета, ПК 2—по социальным правам' <http://president-sovet.ru/about/comissions/permanent/read/2/> accessed 30 March 2017, also listing the relevant documents issued by the commission.

[64] 'Совет при Президенте Российской Федерации по развитию гражданского общества и правам человека, Временная рабочая группа по реализации права граждан на доступное жилье' <http://president-sovet.ru/about/comissions/temporary/read/3/> accessed 30 March 2017.

[65] Рекомендации по итогам специального заседания 'Проблемы реализации прав граждан на доступное жилье и пути преодоления социальной исключенности' (30 May 2014) <http://president-sovet.ru/documents/read/211/> accessed 30 March 2017).

[66] Thus, despite continuing efforts to this end, neither the High Commissioner nor the Council succeeded in preventing the adoption of laws unduly restricting civil and political rights, eg laws classifying NGOs receiving funding from abroad and involved in 'political activities' as 'foreign agents', the

it seems that the recommendations in this area have a slightly greater chance of being taken on by the State Duma, the relevant ministries, or the President.[67]

In Germany, the ICESCR and the CESCR's concluding observations and General Comments have featured in the activities of opposition parties. These parties have initiated bills directly relating to the ICESCR, or requested the government to prepare relevant bills. Among many examples are a bill introduced by the Green Party on the ratification of the OP-ICESCR in 2012[68] and a 2009 bill introduced by the party *Die Linke* calling for the inclusion of ESCR in the German Constitution.[69] Opposition parties have furthermore put critical questions to the government concerning the implementation of the ICESCR and the CESCR's concluding observations in Germany,[70] the relevance of the obligations and responsibilities flowing from the Covenant for governmental acts and omissions beyond German borders, and the activity of Germany as a member of international organisations. This has happened, for instance, in regard to development cooperation[71] and in the context of austerity policies at the EU level, which have been strongly promoted by the German government in concert with the International Monetary Fund (IMF).[72]

Also in Spain, the ICESCR has been (re-)discovered by opposition parties: in preparation for the general elections in December 2015, the then recently-established political party *Podemos* presented an initiative on the right to housing with reference to ICESCR article 11, the aim of which was to ensure that people without sufficient economic resources to pay their mortgages would be protected from eviction and provided with affordable housing.[73] In addition, the situation in Spain reveals

controversial laws prohibiting 'gay propaganda', laws that unduly limit the right to freedom of assembly, laws that legalize (excessive) use of force by the police, and laws that tighten the State's control over the Internet. On this, see the interviews with the chairman of the Council, Mikhail Fedotov, in Александр Мельман, 'Михаил Федотов: "Я знаю людей, которые звали себя демократами, а были ворьем"', *Московский комсомолец* (Moscow, 18 September 2014), and Елена Мухаметшина, 'Россия не имеет права на новую гражданскую войну', *Ведомости* (Moscow, 30 March 2015).

[67] This is confirmed, in regard to some ESCR-related activities, in the 2014 report of the High Commissioner (n 61) 28–29, 49, 68–69, 76, 82, and 94.

[68] Entwurf eines Gesetzes zum Fakultativprotokoll zum Internationalen Pakt über wirtschaftliche, soziale und kulturelle Rechte, Initiative der Fraktion Bündnis 90/Die Grünen, Drucksache des Bundestages (BT) 18/8452, 24 January 2012; see also Entwurf eines Gesetzes zur Gewährleistung der Wahrnehmung sozialer Rechte von Menschen ohne Aufenthaltsstatus, Initiative der Fraktion Bündnis 90/Die Grünen, Drucksache BT 18/6278, 8 October 2015, III.

[69] Entwurf eines Gesetzes zur Änderung des Grundgesetzes (Aufnahme sozialer Grundrechte in das Grundgesetz), Initiative der Fraktion Die Linke, Drucksache BT 16/13791, 14 July 2009.

[70] Antrag der Fraktion Die Linke, 'Konkrete Maßnahmen zur Stärkung wirtschaftlicher, sozialer und kultureller Rechte ergreifen', Drucksache BT 14/8502, 13 March 2002; Antrag der Fraktion Die Linke, 'Vom Anspruch zur Wirklichkeit: Menschenrechte in Deutschland schützen, respektieren und gewährleisten', Drucksache BT 17/5390, 6 April 2011; and Große Anfrage der Fraktion Die Linke, 'Abschließende Bemerkungen der UN zum Staatenbericht an den Ausschuss für wirtschaftliche, soziale und kulturelle Rechte', Drucksache BT 17/8966, 9 March 2012.

[71] Antrag der Fraktion Bündnis 90/Die Grünen, 'Für eine kohärente Politikstrategie zur Überwindung des Hungers', Drucksache BT 17/13492, 15 May 2013; Antrag der Fraktion Bündnis 90/Die Grünen, 'Aktionsplan Soziale Sicherung: Ein Beitrag zur weltweiten sozialen Wende', Drucksache BT 17/11665, 28 November 2012.

[72] Antrag der Fraktion Die Linke, 'Kürzungspolitik beenden - Soziale Errungenschaften verteidigen - Soziales Europa schaffen', Drucksache BT 18/1116, 9 April 2014.

[73] cf the *Podemos* party programme <http://podemos.info/wp-content/uploads/2015/05/prog_marco_12.pdf> accessed 30 March 2017.

another way in which the ICESCR and the CESCR's concluding observations and General Comments can influence domestic legislation and policies: it is likely that they influenced Spain's national human rights plan, which was approved by the Spanish parliament in 2008, at a time when the Socialist Party (PSOE) was in government. Of the 172 measures suggested in the plan, around fifty-two related to the promotion and protection of ESCR.[74] In addition, measure number 5 of the plan recommended the elaboration of a strategy to enhance compliance with the recommendations of various UN human rights treaty bodies.[75] Spain's ratification of the OP-ICESCR is a result of the plan's implementation.

Sixth, in all four countries, civil society engagement with Covenant law has increased in recent years.[76] This is complemented by growing engagement with other international human rights treaties containing ESCR, in particular the CRC and the CRPD, which are often promoted by strong networks of non-governmental organizations (NGOs) advocating children's rights and the rights of persons with disabilities.[77]

Whilst these examples hint at an increased influence of the ICESCR, including an increased recognition of the direct effect of ESCR, there are other developments that show that this influence and recognition do not yet compare to the level enjoyed by the ICCPR and the ECHR.

B. Signs revealing the limits of legal influence

There are a number of signs indicating the limits of the ICESCR's legal influence. First, the CESCR's periodic concluding observations concerning all four States reveal a number of repeated recommendations to take legislative measures toward improving the protection of ESCR. To name but one example among many per country, the Committee has repeatedly called on Germany to remove the domestic law prohibition on public servants' right to strike;[78] on Russia to adopt legislative measures that would unequivocally decouple the enjoyment of many ESCR and benefits from the requirement of valid residence registration;[79] on Spain to enhance the protection of migrants' ESCR;[80] and on the United Kingdom to address the

[74] Spain's national human rights plan of 2008 <www.ohchr.org/Documents/Issues/NHRA/Spain_NHRAP.pdf> accessed 30 March 2017.

[75] ibid 11 (medida 5).

[76] As discussed in Section IV.

[77] See the (alternative) submissions of NGOs and charities in the reporting processes before the respective treaty bodies <www.ohchr.org/EN/Countries/Pages/HumanRightsintheWorld.aspx> accessed 30 March 2017.

[78] CESCR, 'Concluding Observations on the Third Periodic Report of Germany' (4 December 1998) UN Doc E/C.12/1/Add.29, paras 19 and 31; CESCR, 'Concluding Observations on the Fourth Periodic Report of Germany' (24 September 2001) UN Doc E/C.12/1/Add.68, para 22; CESCR, 'Concluding Observations: Fifth Report of Germany' (n 22) para 20.

[79] CESCR, 'Concluding Observations: Fifth Report of Russia' (n 22) para 8; CESCR, 'Concluding Observations: Fourth Report of Russia' (n 48) para 12.

[80] CESCR, 'Concluding Observations: Fifth Report of Spain' (n 22) paras 11 and 19; Concluding Observations—Spain, UN Doc E/C.12/1/Add.99, 7 June 2004, paras 7 and 24; CESCR, 'Concluding Observations on the Third Periodic Report of Spain' (28 May 1996) UN Doc E/C.12/1/Add.2, para 17.

high domestic levels of poverty, including through legislative measures.[81] This tentatively indicates that none of the four States systematically implements the CESCR's concluding observations[82] or uses the process of preparing the periodic reports to examine domestic law and policies for their compatibility with the ICESCR and its principles, in particular the principle of 'progressive realization' in line with 'maximum available resources'.[83]

Second, with the exception of Russia, the number of ESCR in the respective domestic constitutions remains limited, and not all ICESCR rights are effectively protected by ordinary laws. It is in this area where the greatest difference between the influence of the ICESCR and the ICCPR (or the ECHR) can be noted, as Germany's, Spain's, and even the UK's constitutional laws include judicially enforceable civil and political rights. Also at the regional European level, the legal protection of ESCR remains weaker than that of civil and political rights,[84] including when it comes to their judicial enforcement.[85] Moreover, while all four States ratified the OP-ICCPR,[86] only Spain is party to the OP-ICESCR, and none of the four States has ratified the 1995 Additional Protocol to the (R)ESCh providing for a system of collective complaints before the ECSR—facts that reflect lasting scepticism towards accepting ESCR as enforceable human rights.

In addition, in Spain and the United Kingdom, the direct effect of the ICESCR and domestic ESCR continues to be challenged—including when compared to the ICCPR, the ECHR, and domestic civil and political rights—due to the way in which the Covenant is incorporated and/or the way in which its position in domestic law is understood by the respective apex courts. For example, the Spanish Constitution establishes that its text should be interpreted in conformity with international human

[81] CESCR, 'Concluding Observations: Fourth and Fifth Report of the UK' (n 22) para 28; CESCR, 'Concluding Observations on the Fourth Periodic Report of the United Kingdom' (5 June 2002) UN Doc E/C.12/1/Add.79, paras 18 and 37; CESCR, 'Concluding Observations on the Third Periodic Report of the United Kingdom' (12 December 1997) UN Doc E/C.12/1/Add.19, paras 9 and 22.

[82] Concerning the United Kingdom, see Ed Bates, 'The United Kingdom and the International Covenant on Economic, Social and Cultural Rights' in Mashood Baderin and Robert McCorquodale (eds), *Economic, Social and Cultural Rights in Action* (OUP 2007) 258, 272–82. The author's conversations with CESCR members also support this assumption.

[83] ICESCR, art 2(1), and also the objectives of the reporting process identified by the CESCR in its 'General Comment 1' in 'Compilation of General Comments and General Recommendations Adopted by Human Rights Treaty Bodies' (2003) UN Doc HRI/GEN/1/Rev.6, 8, para 2.

[84] See eg the EU Fundamental Rights Charter (Charter of Fundamental Rights of the European Union, OJ C 326, 26 October 2012, 391–407), which, in contrast with the treatment of civil and political rights, classifies some ESCR not as fundamental (individual) rights but as principles (art 52(2) of the Charter). Note, however, that the difference between rights and principles remains unclear. For an analysis, see Jasper Krommendijk, 'Principled Silence or Mere Silence on Principles? The Role of the EU Charter's Principles in the Case Law of the Court of Justice' (2015) 11 European Constitutional L Rev 321. While the (R)ESCh establishes ESCR as individual rights, it allows parties to pick and choose the provisions to which they wish to be bound. The hope that States would opt in to more provisions over time has not yet materialized. Of the States analysed here, only Russia has ratified the (R)ESCh.

[85] In contrast to the individual complaint procedure under the ECHR, the 1995 complaint system under the (R)ESCh does not permit individual complaints to the ECSR, but only collective complaints by some NGOs.

[86] First Optional Protocol to the ICCPR (opened for signature 16 December 1966, entered into force 23 March 1971) 999 UNTS 171.

rights treaties.[87] The SCC has, however, maintained that this does not give constitutional individual rights status to the rights set out in these treaties, but that they only serve to complement the provisions found in the Spanish Constitution itself.[88] The ESCR provisions in the Spanish Constitution are established as guiding principles of social and economic policy, and not as individual rights.[89] The ESCR in the Spanish Constitution and the ICESCR therefore only inform substantive legislation and judicial practice as general principles, but cannot be invoked before domestic courts as self-standing individual rights.[90]

In the United Kingdom, due to a strict dualist tradition, non-transformed international treaties are not considered part of the UK legal system.[91] While some human rights treaties containing primarily civil and political rights have been transformed into UK law, the ICESCR is not among them. On the contrary, as expressed in its reports to the CESCR and reiterated in the 'constructive dialogue' with the Committee, the government has no intention of doing so any time soon.[92] In its submissions to the CESCR, the UK government also maintains that the provisions of the Covenant 'constitute principles and programmatic objectives rather than legal obligations',[93] and cannot therefore be enforced by domestic courts or other authorities. Moreover, when the civil and political rights of the ECHR were 'constitutionalized' in the UK legal order through the adoption of the Human Rights Act 1998, doing the same for the rights set out in the ICESCR or (R)ESCh was not even considered.[94]

Third, overall and despite the aforementioned increase in references to the ICESCR by domestic apex courts, engagement with the actual substance of Covenant law remains very limited and the outcome of a case is rarely influenced by this engagement. Most of the time, the ICESCR is mentioned only in passing. In many cases decided by the RCC (and the RSC), the ICESCR is only listed together with other relevant international human rights treaties.[95] This is usually done

[87] Spanish Constitution, art 10(2). [88] SCC, judgment 36/1991, 14 February 1991.

[89] Spanish Constitution, arts 53(3) and 39–52.

[90] Spanish Constitution, art 53(3), as confirmed by the SCC, judgment 247/2007, 12 December 2007. See also the detailed discussion of ESCR under Spanish constitutional law as complemented by the ICESCR in María José Añón and Gerardo Pisarello, 'The Protection of Social Rights in the Spanish Constitutional System', in Fons Coomans (ed), *Justiciability of Economic and Social Rights* (Intersentia 2006) 67.

[91] Bharat Malkani, 'Human Rights Treaties in the English Legal System' [2011] Public Law 554, 554–55.

[92] See the most recent report of the UK government, which the Committee examined in its 58th session in June 2016 (CESCR, 'Sixth Periodic Report of Great Britain' (25 September 2014) UN Doc E/C.12/GBR.6, para 11).

[93] The Committee has strongly criticized this position. cf CESCR, Concluding Observations: Third Periodic Report of the United Kingdom' (n 81) paras 10 and 21; Concluding Observations: Fourth Periodic Report of the United Kingdom' (n 81) paras 11 and 24; Concluding Observations: Fourth and Fifth Periodic Report of the United Kingdom (n 22) para 13; 'Concluding Observations: Sixth Periodic Report of the United Kingdom' (n 59) paras 5 and 6.

[94] As pointed out by Bates, 'The UK and the ICESCR' (n 82) 266.

[95] eg judgment of the RCC of 17 January 2013, No 1-P, para 2; judgment of the RCC of 24 October 2013, No 22-P, para 2; and the analysis by Александра Конева 'Комитет по экономическим, социальным и культурным правам о статусе Международного пакта об экономических, социальных

to confirm the findings that are made on the basis of the ESCR contained in the Russian Constitution.[96] This can also be observed in Germany[97] and Spain.[98] In the two judgments in which the UKSC/HL referred to the ICESCR, findings based on international treaties that have been incorporated into UK law—the ECHR and the UN Refugee Convention[99]—were confirmed through these references.[100] The very few express references made to the CESCR's General Comments by domestic courts also reflect this limited influence on domestic jurisprudence. Only two such references each were found in the FCC's jurisprudence,[101] that of the RCC,[102] and that of the SCC,[103] respectively, and none in that of the UKSC/HL. The RSC has further pointed out the recommendatory character of General Comments,[104] and the SCC has observed that, under the Spanish Constitution, it is only required to interpret Spanish law in conformity with 'international treaties' ratified by Spain that create binding obligations. General Comments do not, it has held, generate such obligations.[105] Overall, one can observe that domestic courts in all four countries do not review in detail whether an interpretation of domestic law in light of the relevant articles of the ICESCR and their interpretation by the CESCR would lead to a different outcome than their own interpretation based primarily on domestic sources. Thus, the Covenant has no noticeable influence on the outcome of the courts' decisions. Similar patterns can be observed when it comes to domestic courts' engagement with the CEDAW, CRC, CRPD, and (R)ESCh or with the guidance of the relevant international and European monitoring bodies.[106] By contrast, engagement with

и культурных правах 1976 г. в национальных правовых системах применительно к Российской Федерации' (2015) 12–13 (unpublished, on file with author) (hereafter Koneva, 'CESCR').

[96] See eg ruling of the RCC of 5 November 2003, No 343-O, para 3; judgment of the RCC of 24 January 2002, No 3-P, para 2.1; ruling of the RCC of 8 June 2010, No 13-P, para 2; ruling of the RCC of 2 July 2015, No 1539-O, para 3; Koneva, 'CESCR' (n 95) 12–13.

[97] FCC, 2 BvL 1/03, 26 January 2005, para 72; FCC, 1 BvL 1/08, 8 May 2013.

[98] eg SCC, judgment 10/2014, 27 January 2014; SCC, judgment 188/2013, 4 November 2013; SCC, judgment 247/2007, 12 December 2007.

[99] Convention relating to the Status of Refugees (opened for signature 28 July 1951, entered into force 22 April 1954) 189 UNTS 137.

[100] *Quila & Anor v Secretary of State for the Home Department* [2011] UKSC 45, as per Lady Hale, para 66; *Januzi v Secretary of State for the Home Department & Ors* [2006] UKHL 5.

[101] FCC, 1 BvL 1/08, 8 May 2013, para 43, mentioning CESCR, 'General Comment 13' in 'Compilation of General Comments' (2003) (n 83) 70; FCC, 1 BvR 1842/11, 23 October 2013, para 88, referring to CESCR, 'General Comment 17' (2006) UN Doc E/C.12/GC/17.

[102] Judgment of the RCC of 12 March 2015, No 4-P/2015, para 2(1); ruling of the RCC of 20 October 2016, No 20-P/2016, para 2.

[103] SCC, judgment 247/2007, 12 December 2007; SCC, judgment 110/2011, 22 June 2011.

[104] Resolution of the Plenum of the RSC of 10 December 2003, No 5, para 16. In another document, summarizing the relevant Views of UN human rights treaty bodies that issue decisions on individual complaints, the RSC has referred to these Views as subsequent practice under art 31(3)(b) of the Vienna Convention on the Law Treaties (opened for signature 23 May 1969, entered into force 27 January 1980) 1155 UNTS 331) that should be taken into account by Russian courts, see RSC, Правовые позиции Комитета ООН по правам человека, Комитета ООН по ликвидации расовой дискриминации, Комитета ООН по ликвидации дискриминации в отношении женщин, Комитета ООН по правам инвалидов и практика их реализации при рассмотрении конкретных сообщений <www.vsrf.ru/Show_pdf.php?Id=8853> accessed 30 March 2017.

[105] SCC, judgment 247/2007, 12 December 2007.

[106] A great majority of the references to the CEDAW, CRC, CRPD, and (R)ESCh in the decisions counted in this chapter (n 40) are made in passing. Very few references to the General Comments of the

the ECHR and the ECtHR's jurisprudence is more extensive, and their influence on the outcome of the respective domestic courts' decisions is much stronger.[107] Additionally, despite the existence of the ECHR and the ECtHR, the influence of the ICCPR on domestic courts in the four countries seems to be greater than that of the ICESCR.[108] This is also observable in regard to the ECHR's influence on the jurisprudence of the CJEU.[109]

Furthermore, in some lower courts' decisions in Germany and the United Kingdom, doubts about the suitability of ICESCR rights for judicial enforcement are still prevalent. In Germany, some lower courts reject applying the ICESCR due to its perceived vagueness or due to the fact that it has not been incorporated also at the level of the *Länder* through legislation adopted by the respective *Länder* parliaments,[110] even though these positions contradict the pronouncements of the FCC.[111] In the United Kingdom, a few judgments of Courts of Appeal, High Courts, and Immigration Tribunals refer to the ICESCR. Some reiterate that the ICESCR does not form part of the UK legal order and thus cannot be applied by UK courts;[112] in other judgments, the UK courts deny that the provisions of the ICESCR establish individual rights.[113]

Fourth, the positive influence of the ICESCR on domestic legislation, legislative processes, and policies remains limited. For example, the influence of opposition parties' aforementioned engagement with the ICESCR and the CESCR's General Comments and concluding observations in the German *Bundestag* are marginal at best. While the government gives oral or written answers to these ICESCR-related

CRC Committee were found in the decisions of the FCC (one) and the UKHL/SC (six); one reference was found to the General Comments of the CRPD Committee in the jurisprudence of the FCC (none in that of the other three apex courts); no references to General Comments of the CEDAW Committee were found in any of the four apex courts.

[107] For a comprehensive study, see Helen Keller and Alec Stone Sweet, *A Europe of Rights: The Impact of the ECHR on National Legal Systems* (OUP 2008).

[108] All four of the apex courts under consideration have referred to the ICCPR more frequently than to the ICESCR in the same timespan (cf Section II.A): FCC (sixteen references to the ICCPR), RCC (425 such references), SCC (382 such references), and UKHL/SC (fifteen such references). Ten references to the HRC's General Comments have also been found in the UKHL/SC, and two in the RCC.

[109] While the CJEU engages with the ECHR and ECtHR jurisprudence, it very rarely refers to the ICESCR, the ICCPR, or the (R)ESCh. For details, see Sarah Schadendorf, 'Die UN-Menschenrechtsverträge im Grundrechtsgefüge der Europäischen Union' (2015) 1 Europarecht 28. Note, however, that the EU has been a party to the CRPD since 2010. This has led to some decisions in which the CJEU adapted EU law provisions to the higher protection offered under the CPRD (see ibid 31).

[110] eg Higher Administrative Court of Nordrhein-Westfalen, 15 A 1596/07, 9 October 2007; Administrative Court of Ansbach, AN 2 K 07.00603, 7 August 2008.

[111] See the German Constitution, art 20(3), as confirmed by the FCC, 2 BvR 2125/01, 19 September 2006, para 52, and the discussion by Valentin Aichele, 'Die UN-Behindertenrechtskonvention in der gerichtlichen Praxis' (2011) 10 Anwaltsblatt 727, 730; Claudia Mahler, 'Wirtschaftliche, soziale und kulturelle Rechte sind einklagbar!' (2013) 4 Anwaltsblatt 245, 247.

[112] cf *'B' & Ors v Secretary of State for the Foreign & Commonwealth Office* [2004] EWCA Civ 1344, para 90; *R (Hurley and Moore) v Secretary of State for Business Innovation & Skills* [2012] EWHC 201 (Admin) paras 43–44; *The Ministry of Justice v Prison Officers Association (POA)* [2008] EWHC 239 (QB) para 50.

[113] eg *Whaley & Another v Lord Advocate* [2003] Scottish Court of Session (ScotCS) 178, para 33; and *Hurley and Moore* (n 112) paras 43–44.

questions posed by the opposition, their influence on the actual outcome of government policies is in all likelihood very limited,[114] and bills tabled by opposition parties aiming to improve the protection of ESCR in German law are regularly rejected and thus have not had any positive influence on the legislation in force. Similarly, in Spain, the implementation of the human rights plan mentioned above lost momentum with the change of government and the adoption of austerity policies in 2011.[115] As mentioned, recommendations made by the Russian High Commissioner for Human Rights, the Russian Council for Civil Society and Human Rights under the President, and the JCHR in the UK parliament are recommendations only, and are often not taken on by the authorities to which they are addressed.

Furthermore, analysis based on the ICESCR or ESCR more generally has, so far, not positively influenced legislative measures related to budget decisions, taxation, and economic policies in the States analysed or at EU level,[116] something which has once more become clear from the reactions to the financial and economic crises. In other words, principled policy and law-making that explicitly reflect the provisions of the ICESCR, set targets, and establish appropriate priorities in domestic and EU law, focusing on the most vulnerable and marginalized in line with the CESCR's suggestions in many of its General Comments, so far remain a rare exception in the countries studied.[117] This includes laws and policies that affect the enjoyment of ESCR outside of a respective State's jurisdiction, for example through (neo-liberal) economic policies promoted through the EU or the IMF. This is evident in the Spanish central government's reaction to the aforementioned regional legislation that qualifies ESCR as 'subjective rights'. As these regional laws collide with the austerity policies adopted by the central government since 2010, the central government has challenged their constitutionality before the SCC. This challenge is based on the argument that a (limited) right to lawfully occupy uninhabited houses to mitigate the social consequences of the mortgage crisis would 'put the stability of the economic and financial system at risk', given that most of the properties affected

[114] See eg 'Antwort der Bundesregierung auf die Große Anfrage der Abgeordneten Diana Golze, Matthias W Birkwald, Heidrun Bluhm, weiterer Abgeordneter und der Fraktion Die Linke—Abschließende Bemerkungen der Vereinten Nationen zum Staatenbericht an den Ausschuss für wirtschaftliche, soziale und kulturelle Rechte', Drucksache BT 17/11265, 31 October 2012.

[115] While the government agreed, in 2013, to approve an updated human rights plan (II), little has been done so far; see Miguel Ángel Vázquez, 'Sin noticias del plan nacional de derechos humanos' *El País* (Madrid, 11 July 2014).

[116] Concerning austerity policies promoted by the EU and ESCR, see Andreas Fischer-Lescano, 'Human Rights in Times of Austerity Policy: The EU Institutions and the Conclusion of Memoranda of Understanding' (Legal Opinion commissioned by the Vienna Chamber of Labour, 2014).

[117] eg Nicholas Lusiani, 'Rationalising the Right to Health: Is Spain's Austere Response to the Economic Crisis Impermissible under International Human Right Law?' in Nolan, *ESCR* (n 12) 202–33, discussing human rights-centred fiscal alternatives to the austerity policies and laws adopted by the Spanish government. See also the suggestions for human rights-centred tax law and policies in the 'Report of the UN Special Rapporteur on Extreme Poverty and Human Rights, Ms. Maria Magdalena Sepúlveda Carmona, on Taxation and Human Rights' (22 May 2014) UN Doc A/HRC/26/28; more generally on human rights-based economic analysis, see Radhika Balakrishnan and others, *Maximum Available Resources and Human Rights* (Center for Women's Global Leadership 2011).

are owned by banking institutions.[118] In addition, in its submissions to the SCC, the central government held that it is under an obligation under the Memorandum of Understanding of Financial-Sector Policy Conditionality of 20 July 2012 to consult ex-ante with the European Commission and the European Central Bank and to solicit technical advice from the IMF on the adoption of any financial measure that could have an impact on the achievement of the objectives of the programme, namely to regain financial stability through the restructuring of the financial sector. The government also referred to a letter from the European Commission in support of its arguments, in which the Commission expressed its concern that the measures taken by the region of Andalucía compromise the reforms introduced into the Spanish mortgage sector.[119] In its judgment of 14 May 2015,[120] the SCC agreed with the government. It held that the regional legislation interfered with the constitutional competence of the central government to plan and coordinate economic policies,[121] and thus declared the legislation unconstitutional. The SCC emphasized the importance of the general objective pursued by the government to ensure the stability of the financial system, backing its arguments with a reference to the aforementioned Memorandum of Understanding between Spain and the EU that, it observed, afforded Spain financial assistance precisely to strengthen the solvency of troubled credit institutions.[122] The SCC referred neither to the ICESCR, nor to any other international treaty containing ESCR, nor to the fact that the regional legislation had been enacted with reference to the Covenant. Moreover, it remained silent on the question of how Spain's obligations under the ICESCR could potentially be reconciled with the obligations under the Memorandum of Understanding.

III. Particularities of Domestic Systems

To further assess the broader influence of Covenant law in the four European States, and in particular the relevant variations between States, this section will highlight some of the particularities of the respective domestic legal and political systems that shape this influence, as well as the challenges faced in this regard.

In the United Kingdom, where the doctrine of 'parliamentary sovereignty' reiterates that it is primarily the parliament that is responsible for ensuring the implementation of the ICESCR, we can observe that the ICESCR has had considerable influence on the work of the JCHR, which has a mandate to scrutinize every government bill for its compatibility with human rights. This scrutiny also involves considering whether bills present an opportunity to improve human rights protection.

[118] 'El Gobierno acusa a la ley andaluza de vivienda de aumentar la prima de riesgo' *El País* (Sevilla, 29 January 2012).

[119] See the central government's submissions to the SSC <www.juntadeandalucia.es/fomentoyvivienda/estaticas/sites/consejeria/contenidos/noticias/documentos/recurso_contra_ley_vivienda.pdf> accessed 30 March 2017, including the letter from the European Commission (124–25).

[120] SCC, judgment 93/2015, 14 May 2015.

[121] Spanish Constitution, s 149.

[122] SCC, judgment 93/2015, 14 May 2015, s II, para 17.

The JCHR has taken on some of these opportunities,[123] and, in particular since 2010, has worked to alleviate the retrogressive effects on the enjoyment of socio-economic rights caused by the government's far-reaching austerity policies. Three examples of the JCHR's work in relation to the ICESCR shall be given here. First, in 2003, recognizing that the UK parliament had never engaged with the ICESCR, the JCHR conducted an inquiry into the implementation of the ICESCR in the United Kingdom, including the government's reporting to the CESCR and its follow-up of the CESCR's concluding observations.[124] The JCHR pointed out that there were gaps or inadequacies in the protection of ESCR through ordinary legislation, and that, therefore, the domestic legal system could not always provide redress for violations of Covenant rights.[125] It rejected the government's claim that ESCR were inherently non-justiciable (and thus non-enforceable by domestic courts) and recommended a better incorporation of the ICESCR into UK law.[126] Second, the JCHR succeeded in improving several pieces of draft legislation with references to the ICESCR.[127] The aforementioned 2010 Child Poverty Act is a prominent example. Third, and more recently, the JCHR has concentrated on alleviating regressive effects on people's ability to enjoy their socio-economic rights in a context of austerity policies and laws adopted to downsize the UK's welfare system in a sustained manner. One example[128] is the numerous concerns that the JCHR voiced in a legislative scrutiny report on the Welfare Reform Bill under debate in 2011. The Bill (and the 2012 Welfare Reform Act eventually adopted) introduced a new welfare benefit (universal credit), reformed the housing benefit, introduced a benefit cap limiting the total amount of money available to individuals, and changed the support schemes for persons with disabilities.[129] Reviewing the Bill, the JCHR reminded the government of its obligations under the ICESCR, including the obligation to take steps to progressively realize the right to an adequate standard of living and social security, and to thoroughly evaluate any retrogressive measures in line with the criteria set out in the CESCR's General Comments.[130] It voiced its concerns about the potentially discriminatory effect of these measures on persons with disabilities, single mothers, large families, children in poorer households, and ethnic minorities,[131] and criticized the retrogressive character of the measures affecting these groups in particular,[132] which are difficult to justify

[123] For an overview of this work in 2001–10, see Hunt, 'Parliament's Role' (n 58).

[124] JCHR, 'The International Covenant on Economic, Social and Cultural Rights', HL Paper No 183, HC 1188 (21st report of session 2003–04).

[125] ibid para 73. [126] ibid para 73; Bates, 'The UK and the ICESCR' (n 82) 272–82.

[127] Hunt, 'Parliament's Role' (n 58) 245–49.

[128] Others are eg JCHR, 'Implementation of the Right of Disabled People to Independent Living', HL Paper No 257, HC 1074 (23rd report of session 2010–12); JCHR, 'Legislative Scrutiny: Legal Aid, Sentencing and Punishment of Offenders Bill', HL Paper No 237, HC 1717 (22nd report of session 2010–12); JCHR, 'The Implications for Access to Justice of the Government's Proposals to Reform Judicial Review', HL Paper No 147, HC 868 (13th report of session 2013–14); JCHR, 'Legal Aid: Children and the Residence Test', HL Paper No 14, HC 234 (1st report of session 2014–15).

[129] Welfare Reform Act 2012 (ch 5).

[130] JCHR, 'Legislative Scrutiny: Welfare Reform Bill', HL Paper No 233, HC 1704 (21st report of session 2010–12) paras 1.27–1.32.

[131] ibid paras 1.51–52, 1.60–1.62, 1.64; 1.58, 1.56, and 1.57, respectively.

[132] ibid paras 1.71 and 1.76–1.79.

from a human rights and equality perspective.[133] The government, specifically the parliament, did not follow the JCHR's recommendations. The fact that many of the JCHR's concerns were justified has been confirmed inter alia by the 2016 Concluding Observations on the UK's sixth report to the Committee,[134] the 2015 shadow report to the CESCR of the Equality and Human Rights Commission (one of the UK's national human rights institutions (NHRIs)) on this sixth State report,[135] by statistics collected by the government itself,[136] by NGO reports,[137] and by academic research.[138] This also reveals a weakness of the purely recommendatory character of the JCHR's reports, which, without reinforcement through binding judicial review based on socio-economic rights, cannot prevent retrogressive measures leading to violations of these rights in situations where such measures are part of the political-ideological agenda of a parliamentary majority. The reluctance of UK courts to engage with the ICESCR aggravates this outcome: in recent decisions concerning the far-reaching domestic welfare reforms, no references to the ICESCR were made.[139] The UK courts decided these cases (and earlier ones[140]) based solely on ECHR articles 3 and 8, resulting in a low level of protection of socio-economic rights.[141]

[133] As clearly noted in ibid para 1.82.

[134] CESCR, 'Concluding Observations: Sixth Periodic Report of the United Kingdom' (n 59) paras 16–19, 40–41, 47–54, 59–60, and 63–64.

[135] EHRC, 'Socio-Economic Rights in the UK: Equality and Human Rights Commission Submission to the United Nations Committee on Economic, Social and Cultural Rights on the United Kingdom's Implementation of the International Covenant on Economic, Social and Cultural Rights' (2015) UN Doc INT/CESCR/IFL/GBR/21491.

[136] See eg the statistics finding that 63 per cent of capped households under the benefit cap constituted a single parent with one or more dependent child (Department for Work and Pensions, 'Benefit Cap Quarterly Statistics: GB households capped to February 2015' <www.gov.uk/government/uploads/system/uploads/attachment_data/file/426846/benefit-cap-statistics-to-feb-2015.pdf> accessed 31 March 2017).

[137] David Webster, 'Independent Review of Jobseeker's Allowance (JSA) Sanctions for Claimants Failing to Take Part in Back to Work Schemes: Evidence Submitted by Dr David Webster' (Child Poverty Action Group, 2014) <www.cpag.org.uk/sites/default/files/uploads/CPAG-David-Webster-submission-Oakley-review-Jan-14_0.pdf> accessed 31 March 2017; and the welfare reform impact assessments by *Citizens Advice* (2015) <www.citizensadvice.org.uk/about-us/policy/policy-research-topics/welfare-policy-research-surveys-and-consultation-responses/welfare-policy-research/welfare-reform-impact-assessments/> accessed 31 March 2017.

[138] Among many, see Rachel Loopstra and others, 'Austerity, Sanctions, and the Rise of Food Banks in the UK' (2015) 350 British Medical Journal 1880.

[139] eg *McDonald v Royal Borough of Kensington and Chelsea* [2011] UKSC 33; *MA & Ors v The Secretary of State for Work and Pensions* [2014] EWCA Civ 13; *Rutherford & Ors v Secretary of State for Work and Pensions (Rev 1)* [2014] EWHC 1631 (Admin); *Condliff v North Staffordshire Primary Care Trust* [2011] EWCA Civ 910; *SG & Ors (Previously JS & Ors) v The Secretary of State for Work and Pensions* [2014] EWCA Civ 156.

[140] eg *Anufrijeva v London Borough of Southwark* [2003] EWCA Civ 1406; *Limbuela v Secretary of State for the Home Department* [2005] UKHL 66.

[141] eg in *Limbuela* (n 140) the House of Lords held that a general public duty 'to house the homeless and provide for the destitute cannot be spelled out of Article 3' (para 7 *per* Lord Bingham and para 66 *per* Lord Scott). For more details, see Merris Amos, 'The Second Division in Human Rights Adjudication: Social Rights Claims under the Human Rights Act 1998' (2015) 15 Human Rights L Rev 549.

In Germany, changes made to the Asylum Seekers Benefits Act by the parliament in 2014,[142] in reaction to a judgment of the FCC of 2012, reveal that judicial review based on socio-economic rights can have protection-enhancing effects in a system where strong judicial review is widely accepted. In the aforementioned judgment of 2012, the FCC declared sections of the Asylum Seekers Benefits Act unconstitutional (and incompatible with the ICESCR). The 2014 changes made to the Act brought it into line with the FCC's requirement that benefits provided to asylum seekers need to be consistent with the constitutional right to a dignified minimum existence, a right also supported by the ICESCR.[143] In addition, the German system exhibits a stronger role for the executive to ensure compliance with the ICESCR. Every piece of draft legislation that is discussed and adopted by the legislature is checked for its compatibility with the German Constitution and EU and international law, including the ICESCR, usually by the Ministry of Justice and Consumer Protection and its Human Rights Section. Most bills that are introduced before parliament thus contain a section that explains their compatibility with EU and international law. It is very rare, however, that these sections expressly refer to the ICESCR.[144] In most cases, this section is limited to a general statement that the bill in question does not conflict with EU or international law.[145]

In Russia, one can observe that civil society organizations working in the area of ESCR often attempt to directly address the President, and less frequently the State Duma or the ministries. Recent examples are the Moscow Helsinki Group's call for President Putin to change legislation that allows for the eviction of unregistered families without ensuring the availability of alternative accommodation and to develop a comprehensive housing policy along the lines of suggestions made by the Council for Civil Society and Human Rights,[146] as well as the Andrey Rylkov Foundation for

142 Gesetz zur Änderung des Asylbewerberleistungsgesetzes und des Sozialgerichtsgesetzes of 10 December 2014, BGBl I 2014/59, 2187.

143 Whilst no direct references to the ICESCR were made in the parliamentary processes amending the Asylum Seeker Benefits Act, some members of the opposition criticized the amendments for failing to give asylum seekers adequate access to health care in violation of their right to health during the debate in the *Bundestag* (see <http://dipbt.bundestag.de/extrakt/ba/WP18/620/62000.html> accessed 31 March 2017). See also Markus Kaltenborn, arguing that further changes based on a thorough compatibility analysis with the ICESCR could have avoided the changed law still interfering with asylum seekers' right to health: Markus Kaltenborn, 'Die Neufassung des Asylbewerberleistungsgesetzes und das Recht auf Gesundheit' (2015) 5 Zeitschrift für Sozialrecht 161.

144 One of these rare examples is the recently adopted Law on Equal Participation of Women and Men in Leadership Positions in the Private and Public Sectors (Gesetz für die gleichberechtigte Teilhabe von Frauen und Männern an Führungspositionen in der Privatwirtschaft und im öffentlichen Dienst of 24 April 2015, BGBl I 2015/17, 642). The government's draft law indicated that one of the aims was to further Germany's international obligations to promote gender equality, flowing inter alia from the ICESCR (Entwurf eines Gesetzes für die gleichberechtigte Teilhabe von Frauen und Männern an Führungspositionen in der Privatwirtschaft und im öffentlichen Dienst, Initiative der Bundesregierung, Drucksache BT 18/3784, 20 January 2015, s A.6.2.).

145 One of many examples is the Entwurf eines Gesetzes zur Reform des Wohngeldrechts und zur Änderung des Wohnraumförderungsgesetzes (WoGRefG), Initiative der Bundesregierung, Drucksache BT 18/4897, 13 May 2015, s V.

146 Moscow Helsinki Group, 'Почему детям негде жить в самой большой стране мира?, Президенту РФ В.В. Путину' (16 April 2015) <http://mhg-main.org/news/pochemu-detyam-negde-zhit-v-samoy-bolshoy-strane-mira> accessed 31 March 2017.

Health and Social Justice's call on (then) President Medvedev to change the highly controversial Russian policies concerning drug users, in line with the CESCR's 2011 concluding observations.[147] This could be a reflection of the limited trust that civil society organizations have in the ability of the State Duma and the ministries to act without the direct approval of the President in the Russian political system, which is characterized as a 'competitive authoritarian' one today.[148] This is confirmed by the fact that many individual members of civil society organizations remain members of the Council for Civil Society and Human Rights under the President,[149] and are thus involved in the Council's above-discussed advisory work concerning the implementation of ESCR, despite the fact that some of the participating organizations have had to scale back their activities considerably after being classified as 'foreign agents'. For many civil society organizations, the Council remains the *only* mechanism for influencing executive decisions (if only marginally) in areas that affect the protection of human rights.[150]

IV. The Financial and Economic Crises as a Chance for Reinforced Engagement with the ICESCR in Europe?

So far, the issues discussed in regard to the financial and economic crises and the ICESCR have revealed the limited influence of the ICESCR in Europe. This last section highlights broader reactions to the legislative and policy measures undertaken in response to these crises, which can be interpreted as signs that the financial and economic crises could also offer tentative opportunities to strengthen the influence of the ICESCR in Europe in the future.

The increased civil society engagement with the ICESCR in Spain and the United Kingdom in response to the respective governments' austerity policies can be seen as one such opportunity. Among the many examples from Spain are, first, a letter from 2013 signed by a group of more than 500 lawyers, judges, public prosecutors, and law professors, which deplored the devastating social consequences of eviction procedures in Spain and requested a legislative change that would allow individuals

147 Фонд содействия защите здоровьяи социальной справедливостиимени Андрея Рылькова, 'Обращение ФАР к Президенту РФ Медведеву Д.А. по поводу исполнения РФ рекомендаций Международного Комитета по экономическим, социальным и культурным правам касательно реализации программ обмена шприцев и заместительной терапии' (24 October 2011) <http://rylkov-fond.org/blog/prava-cheloveka/pravo-na-zdorovie/icescr/> accessed 31 March 2017.

148 Steven Levitsky and Lucan A Way, *Competitive Authoritarianism: Hybrid Regimes after the Cold War* (CUP 2010); Alfred Evans, 'The Failure of Democratization in Russia: A Comparative Perspective' (2011) 2 Journal of Eurasian Studies 40.

149 Many of the sixty-one members of the Council are representatives of civil society organizations.

150 See eg the comments by Igor Kalyapin—head of the NGO 'Committee Against Torture', which was classified as a 'foreign agent' by the Russian Ministry of Justice in July 2015, but who remains a member of the Council—on the annual meeting of the Council with President Putin in October 2015 in Дмитриева, Ольга and Елагина, Александрина, 'Минута президентского внимания' *Новое Время* (Moscow, 13 October 2015), and statements by several civil society members of the Council in Gabrielle Tetrault-Farber, 'Russian Human Rights Council: Toothless but not Worthless' *The Moscow Times* (Moscow, 16 June 2015).

to cover mortgage loans by giving their properties back to the bank. The letter made reference to the ICESCR provision on housing and Spain's obligations flowing from it.[151] A second example of a civil society organization's renewed use of the ICESCR in the current context is the practice of *Plataforma de Afectados por la Hipoteca*. In submissions to Spanish courts on behalf of people affected by eviction procedures, the *Plataforma* requests the courts to suspend these procedures. It substantiates its requests with references to the right to adequate housing in the ICESCR, as well as to the CESCR's General Comment 7 on forced evictions.[152] A third example is an instance of social mobilization that successfully prevented the privatization of public hospitals in Madrid in 2014. Among other things, human rights organizations argued that the privatization process was contrary to the right to health under the Spanish Constitution and ICESCR article 12.[153]

In the United Kingdom, the most prominent example is the establishment of *Just Fair*, a consortium of more than eighty national charities and local community groups committed to building a fairer society, which introduces itself on its website as 'leading the [ESCR] movement that is beginning to emerge in England'.[154] *Just Fair* concentrates explicitly on the promotion of the rights set out in the ICESCR.[155]

In addition to NGOs, NHRIs in the United Kingdom and Spain have stepped up their work on the ICESCR and ESCR in general. The ICESCR and CESCR documents have featured in the work of all three UK NHRIs: the Equality and Human Rights Commission (EHRC), the Northern Ireland Human Rights Commission (NIHRC), and the Scottish Human Rights Commission (SCHR). For example, the EHRC's/SCHR's Human Rights Measurement Framework is built inter alia on the ICESCR and CESCR documents.[156] The NIHRC has conducted several human rights inquiries related to ESCR and subsequently issued reports referring directly to Covenant law,[157] and recommended the inclusion of ESCR into a future Bill of Rights for Northern Ireland.[158] The ICESCR also figures strongly in many areas of work of the SCHR, for example in Scotland's National Human Rights Action Plan and the SCHR's activities on poverty reduction.[159] Thus, while UK courts remain

[151] Anabel Díez, 'Los antidesahucios quieren retirar la iniciativa legislativa el día de su votación' *El País* (Madrid, 18 April 2013).

[152] See *Plataforma de Afectados por la Hipoteca*, 'Documentos útiles' <http://afectadosporlahipoteca.com/documentos-utiles/> accessed 10 May 2017.

[153] Olivia Muñoz-Rojas, 'Hablemos de Madrid' *El País* (Madrid, 7 February 2014).

[154] Just Fair <www.just-fair.co.uk> accessed 31 March 2017.

[155] See Just Fair, 'About Us' <www.just-fair.co.uk/#!about_us/csgz> accessed 31 March 2017, and the reports that Just Fair has produced in 2014 and 2015.

[156] EHRC, Human Rights Measurement Framework <www.equalityhumanrights.com/en/our-research/human-rights-measurement-framework> accessed 10 May 2017.

[157] eg NIHRC, 'Human Rights Inquiry: Emergency Health Care' (2015) <www.nihrc.org/Publication/detail/human-rights-inquiry-emergency-healthcare> accessed 10 May 2017; and NIHRC, 'Education Reform in Northern Ireland: A Human Rights Review' (2013) <http://www.nihrc.org/publication/detail/education-reform-in-northern-ireland> accessed 10 May 2017.

[158] NIHRC, 'A Bill of Rights for Northern Ireland: Advice to the Secretary of State for Northern Ireland', 10 December 2008 (<http://www.nihrc.org/publication/detail/advice-to-the-secretary-of-state-for-northern-ireland> accessed 10 May 2017).

[159] SCHR, 'Scotland's National Action Plan for Human Rights 2013–2017' <http://www.snaprights.info/wp-content/uploads/2016/01/SNAPpdfWeb.pdf> accessed 23 June 2017; and

reluctant to challenge the government's retrogressive measures on the basis of the ICESCR or other international human rights treaties containing ESCR,[160] awareness of these rights could grow further among civil society actors faced with the devastating social consequences that these measures have for individuals. In Spain, the Ombudsman (*Defensor del Pueblo*) has been involved in activities concerning the protection of the rights to housing, education, social security, and health, primarily through the consideration of individual complaints,[161] and has issued a special report on the economic crisis and mortgage debtors.[162] Space constraints preclude discussing these examples in detail.

In Russia and Germany, no such increased civil society and NHRI engagement with the ICESCR can be observed.[163] However, the link between the protection of ESCR, German foreign (economic) policy, and the conduct of German enterprises abroad has become a focus of some NGOs in recent years.[164] In addition, the German Institute for Human Rights (Germany's NHRI) is working towards sensitizing NGOs, charities, and trade unions to the ESCR dimension of their activities, is running several projects to enhance the protection of ESCR in Germany, and has repeatedly called for the ratification of the OP-ICESCR.[165] In Russia, the falling oil price, sanctions, and the prioritization of military spending, among other things, have led to cuts in the health and education budgets in recent years.[166] Whilst this has been criticized[167] and the All-Russian Union of Patients and the National Medical Chamber have called for protecting the health budget from further cuts to prevent tragic consequences,[168] it is not clear to what extent this will lead to

overview of the SHCR's work on poverty and the ICESCR <http://www.scottishhumanrights.com/poverty/economic-social-cultural-rights/> accessed 10 May 2017.

160 Exceptions are the dissenting judgments of Lady Hale and Lord Kerr in *R (SG and Others) v Secretary of State for Work and Pensions* [2015] UKSC 16.

161 See the website of the *Defensor del Pueblo* <www.defensordelpueblo.es> accessed 31 March 2017.

162 *Defensor del Pueblo*, Report on 'Crisis económica y deudores hipotecarios: actuaciones y propuestas del Defensor del Pueblo' ('Economic Crisis and Mortgage Debtors: Actions and Propositions by the *Defensor del Pueblo*') (January 2012) <www.defensordelpueblo.es/wp-content/uploads/2015/05/2012-01-Crisis-econ%C3%B3mica-y-deudores-hipotecarios-actuaciones-y-propuestas-del-Defensor-del-Pueblo.pdf> accessed 31 March 2017.

163 An exception is the Eberhard-Schultz-Stiftung für soziale Menschenrechte und Partizipation founded in 2011 (<www.sozialemenschenrechtsstiftung.org/> accessed 31 March 2017).

164 eg the work of the FoodFirst Information and Action Network (FIAN) (<www.fian.de> accessed 31 March 2017) and the working group on 'Development and Economy' of Forum Menschenrechte, a network of more than fifty German NGOs (<www.forum-menschenrechte.de/1/arbeitsgruppen/entwicklung-und-wirtschaft/> accessed 31 March 2017).

165 Based on the German Institute for Human Rights' website (<www.institut-fuer-menschenrechte.de/themen/wirtschaftliche-soziale-und-kulturelle-rechte/> accessed 31 March 2017) and the author's personal correspondence with the Institute.

166 For an overview, see Елена Малышева, 'Здравоохранение в минусе—Расходы на здравоохранение в России сократятся на 20%', *Газета.ru* (Moscow, 17 November 2015); Арнольд Хачатуров, 'Резервы растают к 2019 году – Правительство представило в Госдуму проект трехлетнего бюджета. Что важно?' *Новая газета* (Moscow, 28 October 2016).

167 eg Сергей Гуриев, 'Чем высокие военные расходы вредят экономике России', *Forbes.ru* (18 May 2015); Наталья Чернова, 'Теперь уже без иллюзий', *Новая газета* (Moscow, 19 October 2016).

168 'Здравоохранение в опасности', *Российский медицинский сервер*, 25 November 2015, <http://rusmedserver.com/?p=3003> accessed 31 March 2017.

increased civil society engagement with the ICESCR in a country where civil society organizations are under growing pressure from the government.[169]

Increased media attention to the ICESCR and the Committee's work can also be observed in the United Kingdom and Spain concerning the unfolding effects of austerity policies. This could be another opportunity to raise lasting awareness for ESCR in these and other European States. While the consideration of the Spanish and UK periodic reports in 2004 and 2009 respectively did not attract much media attention,[170] this has changed in regard to most recent reviews. Media reports on the CESCR's 2012 concluding observations on Spain reveal a positive attitude towards the recommendations, with the media sharing the Committee's concerns about the negative impact of austerity measures on the protection of ESCR.[171] The adoption of the Committee's first View on a Spanish citizen's individual complaint under the OP-ICESCR in September 2015 has also been reported on positively in Spanish media, which commended the applicant for winning a difficult case by using this new and innovative international instrument to mitigate the negative effects of the government's austerity policies.[172] In the United Kingdom, due to the increasingly negative social effects of the welfare reforms implemented over the last years, media coverage on ESCR in general has risen. Headings like 'UK "Breaching Human Rights" Over Housing',[173] 'Disabled Failed by Savage Cuts: Coalition Treatment is an Attack on Their Human Rights'[174] and 'Food Poverty "puts UK's International Human Rights Obligations in Danger"'[175] can be found in various UK media outlets. Moreover, the Committee's review of the UK's sixth periodic report to the CESCR in June 2016 achieved broad media coverage despite the fact that it coincided with the Brexit referendum.[176]

[169] The Russian Ministry of Justice is working to widen the scope of the law on 'foreign agents' to also cover NGOs that work in the social sector and receive foreign funding, see Екатерина Шульман, 'Удар по ребрам' *Новое Время* (Moscow, 01 March 2016) and 'Просто больше будет бедных и больных', *Российский медицинский сервер* (21 February 2016) <http://rusmedserver.com/?p=3122> accessed 31 March 2017.

[170] Regarding the United Kingdom, see Bates, 'The UK and the ICESCR' (n 82) 11.

[171] Olga R Sanmartín, 'Una veintena de ONG denuncia ante la ONU los recortes sociales del gobierno' *El Mundo* (Madrid, 6 May 2012); 'Naciones Unidas pide revisar las medidas de austeridad', *Compromiso Empresarial* (1 August 2012) <www.compromisoempresarial.com/rsc/2012/08/naciones-unidas-pide-revisar-las-medidas-de-austeridad/> accessed 25 June 2017.

[172] 'La ONU acusa a España de violar el derecho a la vivienda de una mujer desahuciada', *Público* (Madrid, 18 September 2015) <http://www.publico.es/sociedad/onu-acusa-espana-violar-derecho.html> accessed 28 June 2017; 'España violó el derecho de una mujer desahuciada', *JerezSinFronteras.es* (21 September 2015) <http://www.jerezsinfronteras.es/onu-dictamina-espana-violo-derecho-vivienda-mujer-desahuciada/> accessed 26 June 2017.

[173] Afua Hirsch, 'UK "Breaching Human Rights" Over Housing' *Sky News* (London, 14 October 2015) <http://news.sky.com/story/uk-breaching-human-rights-over-housing-10343185> accessed 28 June 2017.

[174] James Lyons, 'Disabled Failed by Savage Cuts: Coalition Treatment is an Attack on Their Human Rights' *The Mirror* (London, 7 July 2014).

[175] Patrick Butler, 'Food Poverty "Puts UK's International Human Rights Obligations in Danger"' *The Guardian* (London, 18 February 2013).

[176] eg Ros Wynne Jones, 'Brexit Has Left the Poor up the Creek without a Paddle as "Rats Leave a Sinking Ship"' *The Mirror* (London, 7 July 2016); Anna Leszkiewicz, 'The UN Declares the UK's Austerity Policies in Breach of International Human Rights Obligations' *New Statesman* (London, 29

V. Concluding Remarks

Overall, this chapter confirms that the influence of the ICESCR in the four European States under examination has been limited. The absence of human rights language in European (and global) responses to the financial and economic crises and the fact that the rights set out in the ICESCR did not serve as an effective tool for social protection during these crises makes this very clear.[177] This is unlikely to change as long as it is not recognized that the ICESCR has 'a lot to say about the parameters and impacts of economic decision making [and related law making]'[178] and the ICESCR is not used to challenge the prevailing economic paradigm of anti-statist, unregulated free market liberalism that has been reinforced by the response to the crises (through mass socialization of debt by rescuing the financial markets with taxpayer money).[179] This goes hand-in-hand with the fact that, in the constitutional orders of Western European States, in EU law, and in the legal instruments of the CoE, ICESCR rights have still not attained a place as enforceable individual rights on an equal basis with the civil and political rights enshrined in the ECHR and the ICCPR, including as concerns the degree to which they can be enforced by national and European courts or the ECSR. By contrast, in Russia, the influence of the ICESCR is not hampered by the fact that the direct effect of ESCR is questioned, something that might also be observed in other Eastern European States that have included ESCR in their constitutions.[180] However, there are other considerable obstacles that a competitive authoritarian regime like Russia imposes on the influence of the ICESCR, among them the staggeringly high level of corruption,[181] deficits in the rule of law, a strong focus on executive action, a decreasing number of mechanisms for citizen and civil society engagement with State institutions,[182] and a growing scepticism towards international human rights law in general.[183]

To end on a positive note, the analysis has also revealed that, in all four States, there are governmental and non-governmental actors that have increased their activities related to the ICESCR over the years, hinting towards a growing legal influence of the Covenant. Together with the increased activity of the ECSR[184]

June 2016); 'UK's Austerity Policy a Breach of International Human Rights, Says UN Report' *Belfast Telegraph* (Belfast, 29 June 2016).

177 Nolan, *ESCR* (n 12).

178 ibid 370–71, and Balakrishnan and others, *Maximum Available Resources* (n 117).

179 For more details and further references, see Nolan, *ESCR* (n 12).

180 For an overview, see Wojciech Sadurski, *Rights before Courts: A Study of Constitutional Courts in Postcommunist States of Central and Eastern Europe* (Springer 2014) ch 7.

181 See Transparency International, 'Corruption Perceptions Index 2016' <http://www.transparency.org/news/feature/corruption_perceptions_index_2016> accessed 10 May 2017 (wherein Russia was ranked 131st, together with Iran, Kazakhstan, Nepal, and Ukraine).

182 High Commissioner for Human Rights in the Russian Federation, '2014 Report' (n 61) 103–04.

183 Ruling of the RCC of 14 July 2015, No 21-P/2015; judgment of the RCC of 19 April 2016, No 12-P/2016; judgment of the RCC of 19 January 2017, No 1-P/2017; Federal Law 'On Changes to the Federal Constitutional Law "About the Constitutional Court of the Russian Federation"' of 14 December 2015, N 7-FKS.

184 The ECSR's cautious but increasing engagement with the ICESCR (ECSR 'Activity Report 2015' (n 42)) might also lead to better reinforcement of ICESCR law.

and the enhanced quality and specificity of the CESCR's concluding observations and General Comments, if persistent, these developments could pave the way for a steadily growing legal influence of the ICESCR in Europe, eventually extending also to economic policy and law-making.

Bibliography

'El Gobierno acusa a la ley andaluza de vivienda de aumentar la prima de riesgo' *El País* (Sevilla, 29 January 2012)

'España violó el derecho de una mujer desahuciada', *JerezSinFronteras.es* (21 September 2015) <http://www.jerezsinfronteras.es/onu-dictamina-espana-violo-derecho-vivienda-mujer-desahuciada/> accessed 26 June 2017

'La ONU acusa a España de violar el derecho a la vivienda de una mujer desahuciada', *Público* (Madrid, 18 September 2015) <http://www.publico.es/sociedad/onu-acusa-espana-violar-derecho.html> accessed 28 June 2017

'UK's Austerity Policy a Breach of International Human Rights, Says UN Report' *Belfast Telegraph* (Belfast, 29 June 2016)

'Здравоохранение в опасности', *Российский медицинский сервер*, 25 November 2015 <http://rusmedserver.com/?p=3003> accessed 31 March 2017

'Просто больше будет бедных и больных', *Российский медицинский сервер* (21 February 2016) <http://rusmedserver.com/?p=3122> accessed 31 March 2017

Aichele, Valentin, 'Die UN-Behindertenrechtskonvention in der gerichtlichen Praxis' (2011) 10 Anwaltsblatt 727

Amos, Merris, 'The Second Division in Human Rights Adjudication: Social Rights Claims under the Human Rights Act 1998' (2015) 15 Human Rights L Rev 549

Añón, María José, and Pisarello, Gerardo, 'The Protection of Social Rights in the Spanish Constitutional System', in Fons Coomans (ed), *Justiciability of Economic and Social Rights* (Intersentia 2006)

Balakrishnan, Radhika and others, *Maximum Available Resources and Human Rights* (Center for Women's Global Leadership 2011)

Bates, Ed, 'The United Kingdom and the International Covenant on Economic, Social and Cultural Rights' in Mashood Baderin and Robert McCorquodale (eds) *Economic, Social and Cultural Rights in Action* (OUP 2007)

Beetham, David, *Democracy and Human Rights* (Polity 1999)

Bilchitz, David, *Poverty and Fundamental Rights: The Justification and Enforcement of Socio-Economic Rights* (OUP 2007)

Burchill, Richard, 'Democracy and the Promotion and Protection of Socio-Economic Rights' in Mashood Baderin and Robert McCorquodale (eds) *Economic, Social and Cultural Rights in Action* (OUP 2007)

Butler, Patrick, 'Food Poverty "Puts UK's International Human Rights Obligations in Danger"' *The Guardian* (London, 18 February 2013)

Cullen, Holly, 'The Collective Complaints System of the European Social Charter: Interpretative Methods of the European Committee of Social Rights' (2009) 9 Human Rights L Rev 61

Danilenko, Gennady M, 'The New Russian Constitution and International Law' (1994) 88 AJIL 451

De Schutter, Olivier, *International Human Rights Law* (1st edn, CUP 2010)

Díez, Anabel, 'Los antidesahucios quieren retirar la iniciativa legislativa el día de su votación' *El País* (Madrid, 18 April 2013)

Eide, Asbjørn, Krause, Catarina, and Rosas, Allan (eds), *Economic, Social and Cultural Rights: A Textbook* (2nd edn, Martinus Nijhoff 2001)

Evans, Alfred, 'The Failure of Democratization in Russia: A Comparative Perspective' (2011) 2 Journal of Eurasian Studies 40

Fischer-Lescano, Andreas, 'Human Rights in Times of Austerity Policy: The EU Institutions and the Conclusion of Memoranda of Understanding' (Legal Opinion commissioned by the Vienna Chamber of Labour, 2014)

Fredman, Sandra, 'Positive Duties and Socio-economic Disadvantage: Bringing Disadvantage onto the Equality Agenda' (2010) 3 European Human Rights L Rev 290

Gómez Ciriano, Emilio José, 'La protección de los derechos económicos, sociales y culturales desde una perspectiva diacrónica y comparada: Estudio en cinco países europeos', VII Informe sobre exclusión y desarrollo social en España 2014, documento de trabajo 8.4 <www.foessa2014.es/informe/uploaded/documentos_trabajo/15102014153319_5781.pdf> accessed 30 March 2017

Heyns, Christof, and Viljoen, Frans, *The Impact of the United Nations Human Rights Treaties on the Domestic Level* (Martinus Nijhoff 2002)

Hirsch, Afua, 'UK "Breaching Human Rights" Over Housing' *Sky News* (London, 14 October 2015) <http://news.sky.com/story/uk-breaching-human-rights-over-housing-10343185> accessed 28 June 2017

Hunt, Murray, 'Enhancing Parliament's Role in Relation to Economic and Social Rights' (2010) 3 European Human Rights L Rev 242

Kaltenborn, Markus, 'Die Neufassung des Asylbewerberleistungsgesetzes und das Recht auf Gesundheit' (2015) 5 Zeitschrift für Sozialrecht 161

Keller, Helen, and Stone Sweet, Alec, *A Europe of Rights: The Impact of the ECHR on National Legal Systems* (OUP 2008)

Krommendijk, Jasper, *The Domestic Impact and Effectiveness of the Process of State Reporting under UN Human Rights Treaties in the Netherlands, New Zealand and Finland: Paper-Pushing or Policy Prompting?* (Intersentia 2014)

Krommendijk, Jasper, 'Principled Silence or Mere Silence on Principles? The Role of the EU Charter's Principles in the Case Law of the Court of Justice' (2015) 11 European Constitutional L Rev 321

Leszkiewicz, Anna, 'The UN Declares the UK's Austerity Policies in Breach of International Human Rights Obligations' *New Statesman* (London, 29 June 2016)

Levitsky, Steven, and Way, Lucan A, *Competitive Authoritarianism: Hybrid Regimes after the Cold War* (CUP 2010)

Loopstra, Rachel, and others, 'Austerity, Sanctions, and the Rise of Food Banks in the UK' (2015) 350 British Medical Journal h1880

Lusiani, Nicholas, 'Rationalising the Right to Health: Is Spain's Austere Response to the Economic Crisis Impermissible under International Human Right Law?' in Aoife Nolan (ed), *Economic and Social Rights after the Financial Crisis* (CUP 2014)

Lyons, James, 'Disabled Failed by Savage Cuts: Coalition Treatment is an Attack on Their Human Rights' *The Mirror* (London, 7 July 2014)

Mahler, Claudia, 'Wirtschaftliche, soziale und kulturelle Rechte sind einklagbar!' (2013) 4 Anwaltsblatt 245

Malkani, Bharat, 'Human Rights Treaties in the English Legal System' [2011] Public Law 554

Marks, Susan, *The Riddle of All Constitutions: International Law, Democracy and the Critique of Ideology* (OUP 2000)

Muñoz-Rojas, Olivia, 'Hablemos de Madrid' *El País* (Madrid, 7 February 2014)

Nolan, Aoife (ed), *Economic and Social Rights after the Financial Crisis* (CUP 2014)

Nolan, Aoife, 'Not Fit for Purpose? Human Rights in Times of Financial and Economic Crisis' (2015) 4 European Human Rights L Rev 360

O'Cinneide, Colm, 'Austerity and the Faded Dream of a "Social Europe"' in Aoife Nolan (ed), *Economic and Social Rights after the Financial Crisis* (CUP 2014)

O'Connell, Paul, 'The Death of Socio-Economic Rights' (2011) 74 Modern L Rev 532

Palmer, Ellie, 'The Child Poverty Act 2010: Holding Government to Account for Promises in a Recessionary Climate?' (2010) 3 European Human Rights L Rev 305

Sadurski, Wojciech, *Rights before Courts: A Study of Constitutional Courts in Postcommunist States of Central and Eastern Europe* (Springer 2014)

Sanmartín, Olga R, 'Una veintena de ONG denuncia ante la ONU los recortes sociales del gobierno' *El Mundo* (Madrid, 6 May 2012)

Schadendorf, Sarah, 'Die UN-Menschenrechtsverträge im Grundrechtsgefüge der Europäischen Union' (2015) 1 Europarecht 28

Tetrault-Farber, Gabrielle, 'Russian Human Rights Council: Toothless but not Worthless' *The Moscow Times* (Moscow, 16 June 2015)

Vázquez, Miguel Ángel, 'Sin noticias del plan nacional de derechos humanos' *El País* (Madrid, 11 July 2014)

Webster, David, 'Independent Review of Jobseeker's Allowance (JSA) Sanctions for Claimants Failing to Take Part in Back to Work Schemes: Evidence Submitted by Dr David Webster' (Child Poverty Action Group, 2014) <www.cpag.org.uk/sites/default/files/uploads/CPAG-David-Webster-submission-Oakley-review-Jan-14_0.pdf> accessed 31 March 2017

Wynne Jones, Ros, 'Brexit Has Left the Poor up the Creek without a Paddle as "Rats Leave a Sinking Ship"' *The Mirror* (London, 7 July 2016)

Гуриев, Сергей, 'Чем высокие военные расходы вредят экономике России', *Forbes.ru* (18 May 2015)

Дмитриева, Ольга and Елагина, Александрина, 'Минута президентского внимания' *Новое Время* (Moscow, 13 October 2015)

Конева, Александра, 'Комитет по экономическим, социальным и культурным правам о статусе Международного пакта об экономических, социальных и культурных правах 1976 г. в национальных правовых системах применительно к Российской Федерации' (2015) (unpublished, on file with author)

Малышева, Елена, 'Здравоохранение в минусе – Расходы на здравоохранение в России сократятся на 20%', *Газета.ru* (Moscow, 17 November 2015)

Мельман, Александр, 'Михаил Федотов: "Я знаю людей, которые звали себя демократами, а были ворьем"', *Московский комсомолец* (Moscow, 18 September 2014)

Мухаметшина, Елена, 'Россия не имеет права на новую гражданскую войну', *Ведомости* (Moscow, 30 March 2015)

Хачатуров, Арнольд, 'Резервы растают к 2019 году – Правительство представило в Госдуму проект трехлетнего бюджета. Что важно?' *Новая газета* (Moscow, 28 October 2016)

Чернова, Наталья, 'Теперь уже без иллюзий', *Новая газета* (Moscow, 19 October 2016)

Шульман, Екатерина, 'Удар по ребрам' *Новое Время* (Moscow, 1 March 2016)

11

The Influence of the Two Covenants on States Parties Across Regions

Lessons for the Role of Comparative Law and of Regions in International Human Rights Law

Samantha Besson

I. Introduction

To celebrate the fiftieth anniversary of the adoption of the International Covenant on Civil and Political Rights (ICCPR)[1] and the International Covenant on Economic, Social and Cultural Rights (ICESCR),[2] the organizers of the present volume commissioned five comparative legal studies of the influence of the two Covenants in the (States parties belonging to) five regions of the world: Africa, Asia, Europe, Latin America, and the Middle East.

This is a welcome contribution to the new and fast-growing field of comparative international human rights law,[3] but also a novel way to celebrate the coming of age of the two Covenants. It departs from the approach to Covenant law used in most commentaries,[4] which barely mention domestic law and domestic practice concerning the Covenants, but also, more generally, from many international human rights lawyers' top-down treatment of domestic compliance with Covenant law.[5]

[1] International Covenant on Civil and Political Rights (ICCPR) (opened for signature 16 December 1966, entered into force 23 March 1976) 999 UNTS 171.

[2] International Covenant on Economic, Social and Cultural Rights (ICESCR) (opened for signature 16 December 1966, entered into force 3 January 1976) 993 UNTS 3.

[3] See eg Christopher McCrudden, 'Why Do National Court Judges Refer to Human Rights Treaties?: A Comparative International Law Analysis of CEDAW' (2015) 109 AJIL 534; Christopher McCrudden, 'Comparative International Law and Human Rights: A Value-Added Approach' in Anthea Roberts and others (eds), *Comparative International Law* (OUP 2018) 439.

[4] See eg Sarah Joseph and Melissa Castan, *The International Covenant on Civil and Political Rights: Cases, Materials and Commentary* (3rd edn, OUP 2013); Ben Saul, David Kinley, and Jacqueline Mowbray, *The International Covenant on Economic, Social and Cultural Rights: Commentary, Cases, and Materials* (OUP 2014).

[5] See eg Benedetto Conforti and Francesco Francioni (eds), *Enforcing International Human Rights in Domestic Courts* (Brill 1997); Helen Keller and Geir Ulfstein (eds), *UN Human Rights Treaty Bodies: Law and Legitimacy* (CUP 2012).

The Human Rights Covenants at 50: Their Past, Present, and Future. Daniel Moeckli, Helen Keller, and Corina Heri. Published 2018 by Oxford University Press.

Actually, even from a comparative international human rights law perspective, the present project is unprecedented in its global scope, its broad focus, and its comparative legal method.

Scope-wise, first of all, while comparative international human rights studies have lately become common on the regional plane, either for a given regional human rights instrument[6] or among them,[7] they have been much rarer with respect to universal human rights instruments. Moreover, the latter studies have not focused on the two Covenants in a comparative fashion,[8] but have either encompassed all international human rights treaties[9] or, in a more recent and more nuanced vein,[10] addressed one of them only, like the ICCPR[11] or the Convention on the Elimination of All Forms of Discrimination against Women (CEDAW)[12] in particular. On the domestic law side of the comparison, most of the existing studies have started by selecting the States compared according to a preliminary assessment of the effectiveness of international human rights law's protection domestically in order to reach a more fine-grained understanding of the causes of its 'success'.[13] This has often led these studies to privilege democratic and unitary States and leave aside, as a result, States, or even entire regions, where the human rights record has not been so good. This is not a criterion of selection used by the reports in this project, which cover all kinds of States in each region. In terms of focus, secondly, existing studies have often concentrated only, on the one hand, on the influence of the Committees' guidance in general (ie their concluding observations, Views, General Comments, and provisional measures) or of some types of guidance only,[14] or, on the other hand, on their influence on some domestic institutions only, such as courts in particular.[15] The five reports discussed here, by contrast, address the entire range of Covenant law, from

[6] See eg Helen Keller and Alec Stone Sweet (eds), *A Europe of Rights: The Impact of the ECHR on National Legal Systems* (OUP 2008).

[7] See eg Gerald L Neuman, 'Import, Export, and Regional Consent in the Inter-American Court of Human Rights' (2008) 19 EJIL 101; Gerald L Neuman, 'The External Reception of Inter-American Human Rights Law' [2011] Quebec J of Intl L 99.

[8] As a matter of fact, none of the regional reports in this project have done so comparatively either.

[9] See eg Helen Keller and Geir Ulfstein, *Treaty Bodies* (n 5).

[10] See Daniel W Hill, 'Estimating the Effects of Human Rights Treaties on State Behavior' (2010) 72 J of Politics 1161, 1172; McCrudden, 'National Judges' (n 3) 549.

[11] See eg Christopher Harland, 'The Status of the International Covenant on Civil and Political Rights (ICCPR) in the Domestic Law of States Parties: An Initial Global Survey Through UN Human Rights Committee Documents' (2000) 22 Human Rights Q 187.

[12] See eg Christopher McCrudden, 'CEDAW in National Courts: A Case Study in Operationalizing Comparative International Law Analysis in a Human Rights Context' in Anthea Roberts and others (eds), *Comparative International Law* (OUP 2018) 459.

[13] See Başak Çali, 'Influence of the ICCPR in the Middle East', Chapter 7 in this volume. See also Jasper Krommendijk, 'The Domestic Effectiveness of International Human Rights Monitoring in Established Democracies: The Case of the UN Human Rights Treaty Bodies' (2015) 10 Rev of International Organizations 489.

[14] See eg Rosanne van Alebeek and André Nollkaemper, 'The Legal Status of Decisions by Human Rights Treaty Bodies in National Law' in Keller and Ulfstein, *Treaty Bodies* (n 5) 356; Helen Keller and Leena Grover, 'General Comments of the Human Rights Committee and their legitimacy' in Keller and Ulfstein, *Treaty Bodies* (n 5) 116.

[15] See eg Gábor Halmai, 'Domestic Courts and International Human Rights' in Anja Mihr and Mark Gibney (eds), *The SAGE Handbook of Human Rights* (SAGE 2014) 749.

treaties through the Committees' concluding observations or Views to their General Comments, and their influence on all dimensions of State practice, including legislative or administrative aspects of domestic law. Finally, from a methodological perspective, existing comparative international human rights studies have been either conducted by international human rights organizations, non-governmental organizations, or professional associations,[16] or single-authored by academics.[17] The five reports discussed here, by contrast, have been drafted separately by individual human rights specialists from each region and are compared to one another in the present chapter. Moreover, most of the existing comparative studies have endorsed quantitative methods[18] and actually stem from political science or international relations scholars.[19] The reports discussed here are, but for one exception, written by human rights lawyers resorting to comparative human rights law methodology (in all its variety).

In all of these respects, in contrast to past comparative international human rights studies, the five reports discussed here provide the first opportunity for a global or universal comparison of the influence of the two Covenants in domestic law. As a companion to these five reports, this chapter has a double aim: first, to bring the comparison one rung up, to the regional level, in order to assess the influence of the Covenants on domestic law across regions and identify emerging trends; and, second, to develop a pattern of analysis comprising the set of (international and) domestic institutions, procedures, and mechanisms that can affect how any international human rights law instrument influences domestic law.[20] The study should therefore be read as much as a study in comparative international human rights law as a contribution to its methodology.

The study's structure is four-pronged. Section II—after this introduction—clarifies the aim, object, and method of the proposed comparison. Section III presents a comparative assessment of the domestic influence of the Covenants across regions and, to do so, develops a grid of comparative analysis. Section IV addresses the classical issue of the authority of the Committees' interpretations of the Covenants, albeit from a bottom-up approach and relying on a comparative law

[16] See eg International Law Association (ILA), Committee on International Human Rights Law and Practice, 'Final Report on the Impact of Findings of the United Nations Human Rights Treaty Bodies' (ILA 2004); David C Baluarte and Christian de Vos, 'From Judgment to Justice: Implementing International and Regional Human Rights Decisions' (Open Society Justice Initiative 2010); Venice Commission, 'Report on the Implementation of International Human Rights Treaties in Domestic Law and the Role of Courts' (8 December 2014) Doc No CDL-AD (2014) 036.

[17] See eg Christof Heyns and Frans Viljoen, 'The Impact of the United Nations Human Rights Treaties on the Domestic Level' (2001) 23 Human Rights Quarterly 483; Krommendijk, 'Domestic Effectiveness' (n 13).

[18] Universal datasets pertaining to international law in domestic legal settings remain too general in focus (eg Oxford Reports on International Law in Domestic Courts <http://opil.ouplaw.com/page/ILDC/oxford-reports-on-international-law-in-domestic-courts> accessed 3 June 2016).

[19] See eg Hill, 'State Behavior' (n 10); Heyns and Viljoen, 'The Impact' (n 17); Krommendijk, 'Domestic Effectiveness' (n 13); Mila Versteeg, 'Law versus Norms: The Impact of Human Rights Treaties on Constitutional Rights' (2015) 171 J of Institutional and Theoretical Economics 87.

[20] For a regional example, see Keller and Stone Sweet, *Europe of Rights* (n 6). For a universal example, see Venice Commission, 'Implementation' (n 16).

argument. Finally, Section VI discusses the role of human rights comparison and of regional human rights law in enhancing the legitimacy of the Committees' future interpretations.

II. A Framework for the Proposed Regional Human Rights Comparison

Comparative law studies differ significantly in their aims (why compare?), objects (what is compared?), and methods (how is it compared?).[21] Comparative international human rights studies are no exception, and it is therefore important to clarify the present chapter's comparative framework.

The *aim* of the comparison, first of all, is the assessment, through a region-by-region comparison, of the extent to which the Covenants—and their interpretation by the Committees—have influenced domestic law, and the identification of the institutions, procedures, and other mechanisms that have contributed to that influence. The main characteristic of the analysis is that it amounts to a 'comparison of a comparison': it compares the influence of the Covenants on domestic law across regions, but relies on a first-level State-by-State comparison of that influence in each region. Even if the interest in a State-by-State comparison under comparative international human rights law is beyond question (after all, States are the duty-bearers of international human rights law), one may wonder about the relevance of the regional unit of reference and, accordingly, about the interest in a regional comparison in this respect.

The notion and role of regions in international human rights law have rarely been addressed as such.[22] Regions are not the subjects of rights or duties under international human rights law. More generally, they do not amount to an explicit legal concept in international human rights treaties and practice. At the same time, it is clear that they are much more than a scholarly reconstruction of geographical vicinity; they sometimes match the boundaries of regional legal communities or organizations pursuing political or economic integration or those of a common legal culture or system. Importantly, these regions may be either vindicated by States

[21] See Christopher McCrudden, 'What Does Comparing (Law) Mean and What Should It Mean?' in Samantha Besson, Lukas Heckendorn Urscheler, and Samuel Jubé (eds), *Comparing Comparative Law* (Schulthess 2017) 61.

[22] With some exceptions (eg Christof Heyns and Magnus Killander, 'Universality and the Growth of Regional Systems' in Dinah Shelton (ed), *The Oxford Handbook of International Human Rights Law* (OUP 2013) 670), most discussions have focused on human rights regionalism as yet another case of fragmentation in international human rights law. See eg Eva Brems, 'Should Pluriform Human Rights Become One?: Exploring the Benefits of Human Rights Integration / Intégrer le droit des droits de l'homme: une exploration' (2014) 4 Journal européen des droits de l'homme / European J of Human Rights 447; Mehrdad Payandeh, 'Fragmentation within International Human Rights Law' in Mads Andenas and Eirik Bjorge (eds), *A Farewell to Fragmentation: Reassertion and Convergence in International Law* (CUP 2015) 297; Yuval Shany, 'International Human Rights Bodies and the Little-Realized Threat of Fragmentation' (2016) Hebrew University of Jerusalem Legal Research Paper 16/06 <https://papers.ssrn.com/sol3/papers.cfm?abstract_id=2722663> accessed 31 March 2017.

situated within them or labelled as such from the outside.[23] Some States in different regions may also share commonalities, but without belonging to a third common region as a result.[24]

What international human rights lawyers know about regions, however, is, first, that there are regional human rights treaties (and bodies) in Africa, the Americas, Europe, and the Middle East, but not in Asia,[25] and, second, that the United Nations (UN) human rights system is organized (especially with respect to membership and representation in human rights treaty bodies or at the Human Rights Council) according to the five UN regional groups. The latter regions are different from the former: they regroup African States, Asian-Pacific States, Eastern European States, Latin American and Caribbean States, and Western European and Other States.[26] While there are overlaps between the two sets of regions applicable under international human rights law, the most striking mismatches are that, in the latter set, the Middle East is divided between Asia and Eastern Europe and Europe is divided into two regions.[27]

The tensions between the two understandings of regions applicable under international human rights law can be sensed in the UN General Assembly's Resolution 64/173,[28] wherein the 'five regional groups established by the General Assembly' (para 4(a)) are mentioned for membership purposes, but reference is also made 'to equitable geographical distribution of membership and to the representation of the different forms of civilizations and of the principal legal systems' (para 1).[29] Unsurprisingly, therefore, UN regional groups have been reorganized a few times since 1945 to reflect changes in UN membership, but also political realignments; the latest regrouping dates back to May 2014. There are many other causes for discontent with the UN regions, and one may mention the lack of proportionate demographic representation, but also of proportionate representation of cultural diversity. Attempts to sidestep the UN regional division in the Human Rights Council and in other UN human rights treaty bodies have failed, however. This may be due to the sheer difficulty of finding a consensual replacement unit—these groupings being necessary for practical political reasons—and in particular for fear of the other, necessarily more diverse and especially fluctuating ways of regrouping State interests in the world (eg along religious lines, such as in the Organisation of Islamic Cooperation).[30] The first set of human rights regions persists, moreover, because of

[23] See Çali, 'Middle East' (n 13).

[24] See eg the common law tradition and the Commonwealth, which includes States in Europe, Asia, and the Middle East. See especially the Asian report (Yogesh Tyagi, 'Influence of the ICCPR in Asia', Chapter 9 in this volume).

[25] See Tyagi, 'Asia' (n 24).

[26] See eg UNGA (United Nations General Assembly) Res 60/251 (3 April 2006) UN Doc A/RES/60/251, para 7; UNGA Res 64/173 (24 March 2010) UN Doc A/RES/64/173, para 4.

[27] See Tyagi, 'Asia' (n 24) and Çali, 'Middle East' (n 13), which feature a discussion of their respective geographical boundaries. See also the European report (Amrei Müller, 'The Influence of the ICESCR in Europe', Chapter 10 in this volume) on the East–West divide.

[28] UNGA Res 64/173 (n 26).

[29] See also ICCPR art 31(2).

[30] See Richard Gowan and Franziska Brantner, 'Regionalism and Human Rights at the UN' in Philippe Lombaerde, Francis Baert, and Tânia Felicio (eds), *The United Nations and the Regions: Third World Report on Regional Integration* (Springer 2012) 243, 246–48.

existing regional human rights instruments and the many political and legal implications of these regional forms of human rights integration in the corresponding areas. Of course, these are contingent arguments that beg the question of the actual role of regions in international human rights law and of the justification of a region-based approach given the universal scope of international human rights law. The chapter will come back to these questions in Section V.C.

Secondly, the *object* of this study in comparative international human rights law is the influence of Covenant law on domestic law. The chapter is not interested in how other non-legal features of the Covenants influence States in the non-legal dimensions of their domestic orders. Even within these legal boundaries, it is important to specify further what (i) 'Covenant law', (ii) 'domestic law', and (iii) 'influence' actually mean.

The 'Covenants', first, refers to the two actual international human rights treaties, but also to their interpretation by their respective Committees. The latter may be found in concluding observations, Views, General Comments, or provisional measures. In order to contribute to the discussion of their authority in Section IV, it is important to assess how much respect they are actually granted in domestic law, independently from their claim to bind. What is meant by Covenant 'law' in this study is therefore quite loose; it entails binding as much as non-binding decisions by the two Committees.

Second, the 'influence' of the Covenants on States is assessed only by reference to their influence on States' legal structure and institutions, that is, 'domestic law', and not domestic politics, culture, or society more generally. This assessment includes any kind of domestic law and the interpretation thereof, but also any kind of domestic legal institutions and procedures, such as legislation, administration, or adjudication. Importantly, legal influence may be formal, as in legislation or adjudication, but it may also be material, as in administrative practice or governmental policy. This way, the study hopes to escape the referential blind spot that makes comparatists assume that there is no influence when there is no textual or formal reference to Covenant law to point to as evidence.[31] This should also prevent us, conversely, from taking the formal recognition and implementation of Covenant rights in domestic law as necessarily meaning that they have some impact in practice.[32]

The Covenants' 'influence' on domestic law, third, is understood in many ways, even by comparative international human rights lawyers. The term is often used interchangeably with 'impact',[33] but also sometimes with 'compliance', 'reception',[34] or 'effectiveness'.[35] Some authors have even used it together with other distinct notions, such as 'authority' or 'persuasiveness'. In this study, influence is understood as any form of 'impact' (on domestic law). It is something that can be described to the extent that impact on a normative practice like law can be. The notion of influence covers positive or 'successful' impacts (what may be referred to as the 'effectiveness'

[31] See McCrudden, 'National Judges' (n 3).
[32] See Çali, 'Middle East' (n 13).
[33] See Heyns and Viljoen, 'The Impact' (n 17) 485.
[34] See Keller and Stone Sweet, *Europe of Rights* (n 6).
[35] See Krommendijk, 'Domestic Effectiveness' (n 13) 491–92.

of international human rights law, whether it is intentional and stems from 'compliance' or not) as much as negative ones.[36] To that extent, this study should not be confused with an assessment of domestic law's compliance with States parties' duties under the Covenants. The notion of influence captures processes as much as their outcomes (when these outcomes are positive, they are sometimes also referred to as 'reception'). Importantly, and *a fortiori*, influence should not be conflated with 'authority', even *de facto*; Covenant law influence may be explained through reasons other than coercion and even through reasons other than *de jure* authority, and this whether Covenant law's claim to bind is justified or not. As a result, the Covenants and their interpretation may exercise a legal influence without being legally binding and even without that authority being justified or legitimate.

Finally, the *method* chosen for this comparative international human rights study is legal. As a matter of fact, the proposed region-by-region comparison relies on the State-by-State legal comparison conducted within each region by the five reports discussed.

Because comparative international human rights law is a new field in comparative human rights law, a few methodological remarks are called for.[37] This field should be conflated neither with a comparison of *international human rights law*, which concerns competing universal and/or regional international human rights law regimes and the interactions between their monitoring bodies without reference to their reception in domestic law,[38] nor with a comparison of *domestic constitutional or human rights law* without reference to international (universal or regional) human rights law in domestic law.[39] Instead, comparative international human rights law is best approached as a combination of both fields, to the extent that domestic and international human rights law are difficult to separate from one another in practice, as the five reports demonstrate. This is also why it would be wrong to consider comparative international human rights law as yet another area of comparative international law. Unlike what applies in other areas of international law and their interpretation and enforcement under domestic law, domestic human rights law cannot be reduced to the implementation of international human rights law, but is constitutive thereof. This mutual constitution between domestic and international human rights law occurs through the transnational comparison of domestic human rights law and the identification of a transnational consensus.[40] As a result, and as the present chapter will argue, human rights comparison amounts to much more

[36] *Contra* Heyns and Viljoen, 'The Impact' (n 17).

[37] See McCrudden, 'CEDAW in National Courts' (n 12).

[38] See eg Burns H Weston, Robin Ann Lukes, and Kelly M Hnatt, 'Regional Human Rights Regimes: A Comparison and Appraisal' (1987) 20 Vanderbilt J of Transnational L 585.

[39] See eg Vicky C Jackson and Mark Tushnet, *Comparative Constitutional Law* (3rd edn, Foundation 2014).

[40] See Samantha Besson, 'Human Rights and Constitutional Law: Mutual Validation and Legitimation' in Rowan Cruft, S Matthew Liao, and Massimo Renzo (eds), *Philosophical Foundations of Human Rights* (OUP 2015) 279; Samantha Besson, 'Human Rights as Transnational Constitutional Law' in Anthony F Lang and Antje Wiener (eds), *Handbook on Global Constitutionalism* (Edward Elgar 2017) 234.

than a scholarly exercise, and is a central part of the practice of international human rights law (Section V).

Last but not least, a caveat is in order. The chapter assumes, for practical reasons, that the proposed framework of comparison is shared by the five regional reports and that, accordingly, the proposed region-by-region comparison (of State-by-State comparisons in each region) actually relies on 'comparable' reports. Of course, there are important variations between them. To start with, their aims are very different: some test hypotheses or answer questions,[41] while others describe various types and degrees of influence,[42] and yet another group makes a normative argument on that basis.[43] Two reports focus on the ICCPR,[44] while the other three concern the ICESCR.[45] They understand 'influence' differently: for some of them, it is a form of impact, whether negative or positive and hence whether 'successful' or not,[46] while most of them understand the concept as a form of positive compliance and in fact discuss the extent to which States conform to their duties under the Covenants.[47] Some look at all the States in their respective region,[48] while others focus only on a selection of States, although they select them on different grounds.[49] Some overlap regarding States whose regional belonging is controversial,[50] while some States, like the United States, are not addressed by any of the reports. Some of the reports focus on the Covenants' influence on domestic law only,[51] while others include politics and society more broadly.[52] One report endorses a political science and more quantitative approach,[53] while the others are more legal. While all this diversity may be seen as a problem, the present study tries to make a virtue of a necessity and turns some of the reports' specificities into characteristics of the influence of the Covenant in the respective regions.[54]

[41] See Çali, 'Middle East' (n 13).

[42] See the African report (Manisuli Ssenyonjo, 'Influence of the ICESCR in Africa', Chapter 6 in this volume), the Latin American report (Mónica Pinto and Martín Sigal, 'Influence of the ICESCR in Latin America', Chapter 8 in this volume), and Tyagi, 'Asia' (n 24).

[43] See Müller, 'Europe' (n 27).

[44] See eg Çali, 'Middle East' (n 13) and Tyagi, 'Asia' (n 24).

[45] See eg Müller, 'Europe' (n 27), Ssenyonjo, 'Africa' (n 42), and Pinto and Sigal, 'Latin America' (n 42).

[46] See Müller, 'Europe' (n 27) and Tyagi, 'Asia' (n 24).

[47] See eg Çali, 'Middle East' (n 13), Ssenyonjo, 'Africa' (n 42), and Pinto and Sigal, 'Latin America' (n 42).

[48] See Pinto and Sigal, 'Latin America' (n 42).

[49] See Müller, 'Europe' (n 27), Çali, 'Middle East' (n 13), and Tyagi, 'Asia' (n 24).

[50] See the African and Middle Eastern reports (Ssenyonjo, 'Africa' (n 42) and Çali, 'Middle East' (n 13)).

[51] See Ssenyonjo, 'Africa' (n 42) and Pinto and Sigal, 'Latin America' (n 42).

[52] See Müller, 'Europe' (n 27), Çali, 'Middle East' (n 13), and Tyagi, 'Asia' (n 24).

[53] See Müller, 'Europe' (n 27).

[54] For instance, the fact that some reports focus more on the influence of the Covenants on the regional human rights instruments than on domestic law (eg in Africa and, although to a lesser extent, in Latin America) is an indicator of a regional specificity.

III. Comparative Analysis of the Regional Influence of the Two Covenants

This section develops a grid or pattern for comparative analysis articulating the different institutions, procedures, and mechanisms that affect how the Covenants can influence domestic law (III.A). The pattern of analysis consolidates the different dimensions identified by the five reports and adds on some more so as to constitute an instrument of use for future comparative international human rights law studies. The section concludes with an overall comparative assessment and identifies some trends (III.B).

Four caveats are in order regarding the structure of the analysis. First of all, all of these comparative dimensions should be read in combination and can either reinforce or weaken one another. For instance, the ratification of the two Covenants' Optional Protocols on their respective individual complaint mechanisms[55] affects the influence that existing domestic judicial remedies for the violation of domestic human rights law can have on Covenant rights' protection through domestic courts.[56] Another example is the overlap between the Covenants' regime and those of applicable regional human rights law instruments, and how the former may be enhanced through the latter's influence on domestic law.[57] A third type of interaction to be noted is the relationship of mutual reinforcement between the existence of domestic judicial remedies and domestic enabling legislation, on the one hand, and regional human rights monitoring, on the other; without the former, the latter may not always be able to secure a domestic influence, not to mention an impact on the Covenants' influence domestically.[58] Secondly, some of these dimensions can change over time, including under the influence of the Covenants and international human rights law in general. This may contribute to undermining the distinction between the causes and outcomes of influence. For instance, the kind of separation of powers in place domestically or the relationship between domestic and international law are two dimensions of domestic law that have evolved in certain States under the influence of the Covenants.[59]

Thirdly, some of the features of the comparative analysis are actually requirements of Covenant law and international human rights law more generally. For instance, having a democratic regime, respecting the independence of the judiciary, and providing judicial remedies in case of human rights violations are all dimensions of a

[55] First Optional Protocol to the ICCPR (opened for signature 16 December 1966, entered into force 23 March 1971) 999 UNTS 171; Optional Protocol to the ICESCR (opened for signature 10 December 2008, entered into force 5 May 2016) UN Doc A/RES/63/117, 48 ILM 256 (2009) (OP-ICESCR).

[56] See eg Pinto and Sigal, 'Latin America' (n 42) and, *a contrario*, Çali, 'Middle East' (n 13) and Tyagi, 'Asia' (n 24).

[57] See eg Müller, 'Europe' (n 27) and Ssenyonjo, 'Africa' (n 42) and, *a contrario*, Çali, 'Middle East' (n 13).

[58] See Ssenyonjo, 'Africa' (n 42).

[59] See Pinto and Sigal, 'Latin America' (n 42) and Tyagi, 'Asia' (n 24).

general positive duty to set up a given institutional regime under Covenant law. It is no surprise, therefore, that the positive influence of the Covenants in domestic law is enhanced by the display of these features.[60] This may also explain why, at times, the comparative analysis comes close to an assessment of comparative compliance with Covenant duties. Finally, comparing (international) human rights law is not only a scholarly activity, but also amounts to an integral part of domestic (and international) human rights reasoning, thereby instilling a comparative regress in the analysis. For instance, domestic courts may resort to the comparison of their domestic human rights law with that of other States, including other domestic judicial decisions pertaining to the Committees' decisions and/or to other universal or regional human rights bodies' decisions, themselves potentially including comparisons amongst themselves and/or with the Committees' decisions.[61]

A. Comparative analysis

The present section identifies five dimensions that may affect how Covenant law influences domestic law: its international law status (Section III.A.1), its 'domestic international law' status (Section III.A.2), the domestic constitutional order (Section III.A.3), domestic institutions (Section III.A.4), and other domestic actors (Section III.A.5).

1. *International law status*

There are many ways in which States *qua* subjects of international law can relate to the Covenants on the international plane. The various dimensions of that relationship explain variations in the influence of the Covenants in domestic law.

First of all, States' relationships to the two *Covenants* themselves *qua* human rights treaties need to be considered. The Covenants' influence on domestic law indeed reflects the degree of States' involvement during their negotiation and drafting, if applicable. Another relevant dimension is whether the two Covenants were signed and then ratified in a short period of time, and, if not, how long it took for them to be ratified and why. If the two Covenants were not signed and/or ratified at the same time, it may be interesting to wonder why, as this may affect their influence domestically. Another important factor is whether the Covenants were signed and ratified at the same time as other international and regional human rights instruments. The national historical context of signature and ratification matters as well. It is important to know especially whether ratification was motivated by internal (eg decolonization, democratization) or external (eg human rights conditionality, occupation) factors, and of what kind.[62] Another relevant question is how many States in the region have ratified one or both Covenants, and on what grounds.[63]

[60] See Çali, 'Middle East' (n 13) *a contrario*.

[61] See Ssenyonjo, 'Africa' (n 42) and Pinto and Sigal, 'Latin America' (n 42).

[62] See Çali, 'Middle East' (n 13).

[63] There is an important difference in this respect between Europe, Latin America, and Africa on the one hand, and the Middle East and Asia on the other.

Once the Covenants have been ratified, the next question is whether and which of the (material and/or procedural) Optional Protocols[64] have been ratified, whether this occurred at the same time or later on, and why. Reservations and interpretative declarations matter too. Besides their content (eg restrictions to the personal, material, or territorial scope of some rights; religious exceptions; federal clauses), it is important to know whether they have been controversial, domestically and on the international plane. They may have been invalidated by the Committees because they objected to them, could have been withdrawn, or may have grown obsolete in the meantime through contrary domestic practice. Finally, the level of implication of States in the UN General Assembly or the Human Rights Council, and, more specifically, in the Office of the UN High Commissioner for Human Rights (OHCHR) context (eg reform,[65] finances, etc) also matters.

Secondly, States' relationships to the two *Committees* need to be considered. A first factor of variation pertains to the procedures ratified by States, and in particular whether the Committees may hear inter-State and/or individual complaints against them in addition to reacting to their submissions in the periodic reporting procedure. When one or both of these complaint mechanisms applies to given States, it matters how they relate to other international and regional individual human rights complaint mechanisms that these States may have ratified, whether they are used regularly, and whether States comply with the resulting Views or provisional measures. Regarding periodic reports, it is important to establish how regularly States' reports have been submitted, what kind of information States have provided (eg merely formal or substantial), whether they have adopted the simplified reporting procedure (based on the List of Issues), and how they have behaved in the follow-up procedures and in the dialogue with the Committees following concluding observations, but also, if applicable, in the various default procedures.[66] More generally, it is interesting to know how many members of the Committees there have been for each State since it ratified the Covenants, how these individuals were selected, and how involved they have been in the Committees' daily work (and, accordingly, in their reform process) and especially their interpretations of the Covenants.[67] Other issues in States' relations with the Committees also need to be considered, in particular potential notices of derogation in case of national emergency[68] or retrogressive measures and their follow-up by the Committee.

A third relevant feature is the interaction with *other international (universal or regional) human rights instruments* applicable to the States concerned and the

[64] On the ratification of the OP-ICESCR, contrast Çali, 'Middle East' (n 13) and Tyagi, 'Asia' (n 24) with Pinto and Sigal, 'Latin America' (n 42).

[65] See the discussion of the adoption of UNGA Res 68/268 (21 April 2014) UN Doc A/RES/68/268 in Tyagi, 'Asia' (n 24).

[66] See the Asian and Middle Eastern reports (Tyagi, 'Asia' (n 24) and Çali, 'Middle East' (n 13)) for the consequences of the non-submission or of irregularities in the submission of reports for the lack of integration of regional specificities into the Committees' interpretations.

[67] See Tyagi, 'Asia' (n 24), for the consequences of the lack of representation in the Committees for the integration of regional specificities into the Committees' interpretations.

[68] See Çali, 'Middle East' (n 13).

procedures open before their *corresponding bodies or courts*. To assess how the influence of the Covenants may be tied to that of other international human rights instruments, first of all, issues of timing (ratification and entry into force) and the scope of the respective rights (material, personal, or territorial) need to be explored. Starting with the other universal human rights instruments, first, many of them have fewer States parties than the Covenants, but their procedures are often more advanced and may be used to promote the Covenants domestically. The potential overlaps between their respective rights and complementarity between their interpretations by their respective general and specific treaty bodies are worth considering too. With respect to regional human rights instruments, second, some of them refer expressly to the Covenants.[69] As a matter of fact, some regional human rights bodies have made it a practice to include interpretations by the Committees in their own interpretations of their respective instruments.[70] Still other regional human rights instruments were actually drafted on the model of one of the two Covenants. This steers their interpretation by the corresponding regional human rights bodies even more towards a parallel with that of the relevant Covenant.[71] All of this affects the overall influence of the Covenants in domestic law, especially when one of these international human rights bodies issues binding judicial decisions.[72] Other benefits to the Covenants' influence stemming from their coexistence with regional human rights instruments may be the individuation of remedies or the application of indicators in the context of economic and social rights.[73] Of course, the coexistence of the Covenants and other international (universal or regional) human rights instruments may not only give rise to mutual reinforcements, but also to jurisprudential contradictions and even conflicts and, accordingly, to the limitation of the influence of Covenant law in domestic law.[74] Various principles and methods apply to the resolution of these conflicts under general international law (eg systemic interpretation), as we will see (Section V). Moreover, it may be the case that regional human rights instruments have worked or still work as quasi-constitutions in certain States, thereby benefitting from a privileged position in the domestic legal order.[75] This may either favour the influence of other international human rights treaties domestically or, on the contrary, signal their difference to domestic authorities.

Finally, another interesting international law feature is the *relationship to other international bodies and courts* whose practice includes or emulates the Covenants. One may think of the Human Rights Council, whose special procedures, individual complaint mechanism, or universal periodic review (UPR) may include the monitoring of Covenant rights for their States parties. Another relevant body may be the

[69] See Ssenyonjo, 'Africa' (n 42) on art 60 of the African Charter on Human and Peoples' Rights (African Charter or ACHPR) (adopted 27 June 1981, entered into force 21 October 1986) (1982) 21 ILM 58).

[70] See Pinto and Sigal, 'Latin America' (n 42) on art 29(b) of the American Convention of Human Rights (ACHR) (opened for signature 22 November 1969, entered into force 18 July 1978) 36 OAS Treaty Series, 1144 UNTS 123.

[71] See Ssenyonjo, 'Africa' (n 42), on the African Charter.

[72] See *a contrario* Çali, 'Middle East' (n 13) and Tyagi, 'Asia' (n 24).

[73] See Pinto and Sigal, 'Latin America' (n 42).

[74] See Müller, 'Europe' (n 27).

[75] See Pinto and Sigal, 'Latin America' (n 42).

International Court of Justice (ICJ), whose case law has contributed to reinforcing the authority of the Committees' interpretations of the Covenants.[76]

2. *'Domestic international law' status*

Domestic law entails rules pertaining to the relationship between domestic and international law, ie domestic foreign relations law or 'domestic international law'. These rules affect the influence of the Covenants on domestic law.

First of all, it is interesting to start by looking at the *domestic procedures of approval* that precede the Covenants' ratification. The existence of a procedure of parliamentary approval, or even of a popular referendum on the Covenants, matters for their democratic legitimacy domestically and hence for their influence. Generally, the issue of the domestic law 'pedigree' (eg constitutional or legislative) of the Covenants, where they are enacted as a piece of domestic legislation, is relevant as it may, later on, condition the rank of the Covenants in the domestic legal order. The same may be said about the existence of a procedure of pre-approval abstract judicial review of international human rights treaties, including of the Covenants. Such a procedure may indeed lead to the amendment of domestic legislation and/or constitutional law prior to ratification.

A second dimension pertains to potential *domestic reforms* occurring prior to or at the time of the entry into force of the Covenants. Some States wait until the entry into force to proceed with reforms, or do not plan any systematic reforms at all, while others organize them and postpone international treaties' entry into force until the completion of the required domestic reforms. It is in this context, too, that the question of the integration of Covenant rights into the domestic bill of rights (whether it is constitutional or not) or into another form of domestic legislation is to be considered. In dualist countries, this takes the shape of incorporation legislation, but some monist countries are also known to integrate (some) Covenant rights into their bill of rights or legislation. Independently from general reforms or from the actual integration of Covenant rights into domestic law, or in addition to them, some States, although this is rare in practice, have adopted enabling legislation to help enforce the Covenants alone, and sometimes also the Committees' concluding observations, Views, or General Comments, in domestic law. Enabling laws vary greatly in content: some only pertain to domestic adjudication, while others even foresee special domestic remedies and reparations for violations of the Covenants established by the Committees in their Views.

Once the Covenants are in force, a third relevant issue is the *relationship between domestic and international law*. This relationship is organized around questions of validity, rank, and effects, and the same applies to international human rights law and the Covenants—although one may interestingly observe a certain level of uncertainty or even overlaps between these categories in regions other than Europe.

[76] See eg *Ahmadou Sadio Diallo* (*Republic of Guinea v Democratic Republic of the Congo*) (Merits) [2010] ICJ Rep 639, 664.

In certain States, international human rights law behaves like international law in general, but, in others, it has a special status, both in terms of validity (usually immediate) and rank (usually supra-legislative). Some constitutions even entail a clause establishing what rank international human rights law, including the Covenants, should have in domestic law.[77] With respect to validity, some States are monist and recognize the immediate validity of the Covenants, while others are dualist and have to incorporate them, either into their domestic bill of rights or in a separate piece of legislation, for them to have any form of validity and effect in domestic law. Regarding the rank granted to the Covenants in domestic law, States vary significantly: some grant them legislative rank, while others give them supra-legislative, constitutional, or even supra-constitutional value. With respect to the Covenants' effects, States usually give individual rights under the Covenants direct effect (whether it is through their justiciability or not, depending on how judicialized domestic human rights protection is in general). The rights under the ICESCR are often treated differently in this respect, depending in particular on the extent to which the direct effect of economic and social rights is recognized under domestic law in general. Note that dualist legal orders usually address issues of the rank and effects of the Covenants in their incorporating legislation. Finally, some States distinguish between Covenant rights and their interpretations by the Committees' decisions, and do not grant the latter the same validity, rank, and effects. Some regard the latter as binding, while others do not (see Section IV).

Fourthly, another ground of variation pertains to the *relationship between domestic and Covenant rights*. The first question to ask is whether the State has a domestic bill of rights (constitutional or not) and whether that bill includes all rights protected under the two Covenants (maybe with differences between economic and social rights and civil and political rights), as this may affect the significance of the Covenants domestically.[78] What matters in the latter case is whether the inclusion or 'internalization'[79] of Covenant rights pre-existed the ratification of the Covenants or is a consequence thereof. The domestic bill of rights' degree of constitutional entrenchment and its relationship to domestic legislation matter also by comparison to the entrenchment of the Covenants in domestic law. The relationship between the domestic bill of rights and the Covenants in case of conflict between their respective interpretations, and especially their ranking, also needs to be explored. In some States, domestic and international human rights are subsumed in the context of special judicial human rights remedies or, at least, in regular domestic courts' human rights reasoning. This may, in the long run, lead to the levelling-up or the levelling-down of the protection of Covenant rights domestically, through mutual influence between domestic human rights law and the Covenants with respect to various features of human rights reasoning (eg jurisdiction and applicability; personal, material, and territorial scope, such as horizontal effect; positive and/or negative duties;

[77] See especially Pinto and Sigal, 'Latin America' (n 42).

[78] See Pinto and Sigal, 'Latin America' (n 42).

[79] See Versteeg, 'Law versus Norms' (n 19). See also Çali, 'Middle East' (n 13).

procedural obligations; restriction justifications, such as proportionality; rights' inner core; and constitutionality/conventionality review).

Finally, the *relationship between the Covenants and other international (universal or regional) human rights instruments* (and, more accurately, their interpretations by their respective bodies/courts) can affect the influence of the former in domestic law. This relationship can be approached from an international law perspective (eg conflict rules, systemic interpretation), as in the previous section, but it may also be affected by domestic law's approaches to these instruments. Domestic law may expressly or tacitly rank certain instruments (usually regional ones, with a regional court monitoring them) higher than others.[80] It may also provide some instruments with more effective judicial remedies domestically after an adverse decision by these other international human rights bodies. Depending on whether other international human rights instruments, and their monitoring bodies' interpretations, refer to the Covenants and their interpretations, therefore, the former's privileged position in domestic law may enhance the influence of the Covenants.

3. *Domestic constitutional order*

Various other background or constitutional factors in domestic law affect the influence of the Covenants domestically.

This is the case, first of all, of the *constitutional order* itself. The influence of the Covenants can vary considerably depending on whether there is a formal constitution domestically, whether it is entrenched, whether it includes a bill of rights, and whether it is monitored by a constitutional court and through constitutional review of legislation.

Secondly, other more general features of the domestic *legal order* may also affect the influence of the Covenants domestically. One should mention in particular the recognition of legal pluralism (religious or not) or of other forms of legal devolution and special legal regimes within the domestic legal order. Despite the State's international responsibility under the Covenants, the latter may not be applied in the same way in all parts of the domestic legal order. Issues of rank and effect, in particular, may be addressed differently in each of them. One should also enquire about the role of the predominant legal theories or cultures in the legal order, and in particular legal realism, legal formalism, or jusnaturalism.[81]

A third influential feature is the *political organization* of the State. This includes primarily the question of its federal organization, with the implications this may have on the ranking and effects of the Covenants in domestic law. The issue of (allocation of and potential centralization of) competences in federal States often interferes with the implementation of international human rights law in practice and can have a chilling effect on compliance.[82] Other related questions, such as

[80] Contrast Ssenyonjo, 'Africa' (n 42) with Pinto and Sigal, 'Latin America' (n 42).

[81] See Çali, 'Middle East' (n 13) on the former and Pinto and Sigal, 'Latin America' (n 42) on the latter.

[82] See eg Krommendijk, 'Domestic Effectiveness' (n 13).

political inequalities among citizens (eg under a caste system or a personal status system under Sharia[83]) can affect the Covenants' influence by discriminating between groups of right-holders.

A fourth and related feature pertains to the *political regime* applicable domestically. When it is democratic,[84] as it should be according to the political requirements imposed by the Covenants, it is important to know whether it is parliamentary or not, whether it grants direct democratic rights, and whether it adheres to a majoritarian or consociational system, for all these features may modulate the Covenants' influence in practice. Other features of the political regime can also affect the Covenants' interpretation domestically, in particular predominant political ideologies like liberalism, communism,[85] or socialism.[86] One should also consider cultural characteristics of domestic politics, such as their relationship to religion or other forms of social morality. Thus, the existence of collective moralities tends to affect the influence of individual rights, and hence of the Covenants, in practice.[87]

A fifth background or constitutional dimension that may affect the Covenants' influence is the *supranational or international integration* of States. One may think of various forms of integration of States, be they economic or political (eg the European Union, the African Union, the Economic Community of West African States, the Arab League, or the Organization of American States). Some have a human rights dimension, as discussed before, that may also affect the influence of the Covenants, usually with a positive effect. When these integrated communities of States do not have their own human rights regimes and do not refer to one, their secondary law (eg on trade-related matters) may affect the international legal duties of States, including those arising under the Covenants, thereby raising issues of the fragmentation of international law.

Finally, one should mention the role played by *structural difficulties*. One may think of migration, poverty,[88] literacy,[89] corruption, climatic hardship, armed conflict (international or not),[90] epidemics, or financial and economic crisis.[91] These difficulties all hamper, in one way or another, the capacity of States to comply with their international human rights duties, and hence with the Covenants.

4. *Domestic institutions*

Domestic institutions and their respective organization also affect the influence of the Covenants domestically.

This is the case, first of all, of the *separation of powers*. The first thing to ask is whether the domestic institutional order employs that principle and how it

[83] See Çali, 'Middle East' (n 13).

[84] On authoritarian regimes, compare Müller, 'Europe' (n 27), Tyagi, 'Asia' (n 24), and Çali, 'Middle East' (n 13).

[85] See Müller, 'Europe' (n 27), on the Russian and Eastern European exception.

[86] See Pinto and Sigal, 'Latin America' (n 42).

[87] See Tyagi, 'Asia' (n 24) and Çali, 'Middle East' (n 13).

[88] See Ssenyonjo, 'Africa' (n 42).

[89] See Tyagi, 'Asia' (n 24).

[90] See Çali, 'Middle East' (n 13).

[91] See Müller, 'Europe' (n 27).

understands it. It is important to know, in particular, whether the legislative, executive, and judicial powers exercise mutual checks on one another or whether some have supremacy (eg due to parliamentary sovereignty) over others, and how. Given the close relationship between international human rights law and the Covenants, on the one hand, and domestic courts and judicial remedies, on the other, situating judicial power in relationship to the other two domestic powers, and in particular the parliament and the administration, is key.[92] The situation of judicial power may affect other fundamental considerations, such as the existence of constitutional and/or, at least, 'conventional' review (based on international human rights treaties like the Covenants) and the scope of the judicial remedies that can be ordered. It is also important to know whether that constitutional review can be abstract and thus pertain to legislation or even constitutional changes.

Secondly, the existence and scope of *pre-legislative human rights scrutiny* can also affect the influence of the Covenants domestically. Its role is to scrutinize any proposed legislation for its compatibility with human rights law. It is important to ascertain whether its scope is restricted to domestic human rights law or whether it extends to international human rights law and the Covenants, and to which extent it encompasses the latter's interpretations by the Committees' concluding observations, Views, or General Comments.[93]

Thirdly, the existence and scope of *executive human rights monitoring* is another factor affecting the influence of the Covenants in domestic law. More and more States have established an ombudsman or a national human rights commission of some kind. Some of these have as their mandate to monitor domestic human rights protection, but most expand it to include international human rights law and the Covenants.[94] Establishing a national human rights institution (NHRI) has become a requirement for governments and administrations under international human rights law and the Paris Principles, and this duty has been monitored through the Human Rights Council's UPR in particular.

Finally, the scope and organization of *domestic human rights adjudication* can affect how the Covenants influence domestic law. The first variation factor is whether domestic courts can review legislation on human rights grounds, adjudicate individual cases of human rights violations, and/or even interpret domestic legislation in the light of the Covenants (eg in order to fill gaps). It is also important to know which courts can do so (only federal ones, or local ones too; only constitutional or highest courts, or all of them). Regarding individual human rights complaints, it is important to identify whether there are specific judicial remedies for human rights violations. Another relevant feature is whether these remedies are open to violations of domestic and international human rights law (including the Covenants) alike.[95] Another question is whether Covenant rights are applied as such or in light of their interpretation in the Committees' concluding observations, Views, or General Comments and, in the latter case, whether these interpretations are only referred to

92 See Pinto and Sigal, 'Latin America' (n 42).
93 See Müller, 'Europe' (n 27).
94 ibid.
95 Contrast Ssenyonjo, 'Africa' (n 42) and Pinto and Sigal, 'Latin America' (n 42) in this respect.

when they pertain to the State in question or to any State (so-called *erga omnes* effect). The question of 'judicial' or 'quasi-judicial' dialogue between domestic courts and the Committees may be raised in this context. Regarding domestic courts' reasoning, it may be interesting to assess how comparative it is, whether across domestic human rights law or between international (universal and/or regional) human rights law and domestic human rights law. As explained previously, it is relevant to identify whether domestic courts merge domestic and Covenant rights in their reasoning, and what this leads to with respect to various issues such as jurisdiction, scope, restrictions, or remedies. More generally, it is interesting to ascertain what areas of domestic human rights adjudication are most influenced by Covenant rights and their interpretations.

Interestingly, some States have introduced special remedies that apply following a violation of Covenant rights (usually as established in adverse Views by the Committees), often in their domestic legislation incorporating the Covenants or facilitating their enforcement in domestic law. These remedies may be prescribed specifically, such as, for instance, to order the reopening of the domestic judicial procedure that led to the violation or to fast-track remedial orders when the violation stems from domestic legislation. In most cases, however, it is up to domestic judges to remedy the situation within the constraints of the separation of powers and the domestic constitutional order. Pre-existing domestic judicial remedies of this kind help compensate for the lack of binding nature of the Committees' Views. The absence of such remedies in domestic law explains, for instance, why the most that victims can expect from governments after adverse Views of the Committees are often *ex gratia* payments.

5. *Other domestic actors*

The role of other domestic actors also affects the influence of the Covenants domestically.

A first set of such actors are *political parties* and *lobbies*. Some have placed international human rights law, and the Covenants, at the core of their political mandate and project. This is often the case of opposition parties,[96] but not only.

A second group of relevant domestic actors are *non-governmental organizations* (NGOs). Some are national, while others are regional or even universal in scope. NGOs may contribute to the influence of international human rights law and the Covenants, both in domestic and international institutions and procedures, but also through sensibilization work with civil society.[97] Their contribution may be felt in the legislature, but also in the judicial process through representation, fact-finding, or third-party interventions. The Committees have long associated NGOs with the follow-up process and the reporting procedure in general, and this has

[96] See Müller, 'Europe' (n 27).

[97] See Tyagi, 'Asia' (n 24); Patrick Mutzenberg, 'NGOs: Essential Actors for Embedding the Covenants in the National Context', Chapter 5 in this volume.

contributed, when these NGOs also have a strong foothold domestically, to enhancing the Covenants' influence in domestic law.

A third relevant domestic actor for the influence of the Covenants in domestic law is *academia or scholarship*. Its influence can occur through research and publications, but also through teaching, professional training, and academic conferences. All of these avenues can potentially include Covenant law and contribute to its dissemination in the domestic legal order.[98] Other important factors are the translation of the Committees' decisions into local languages or the development of databases pertaining to Covenant law, as these are often academic projects. One may also mention other kinds of advanced training in Covenant law, be they organized together with the bar or other professional associations.

Finally, the role of the *media* on the influence of the Covenants in domestic law needs to be assessed in each State. Regular coverage of Views or General Comments can help remind domestic lawyers and human rights-holders about the Covenants.[99]

B. An overall assessment: Four trends and five needs

There are four trends that emerge clearly from the comparative analysis of the influence of the Covenants in domestic law across the five regions examined.

First of all, the existence of preventive *domestic legislation* and/or remedial *judicial remedies* enforcing Covenant rights enhances their domestic influence. In that context, what matters especially is the relationship between the legislature (and/or administration) and the judiciary, and especially the existence of a separation of powers and mutual checks between them. This is confirmed by all reports, either positively in Europe and Latin America[100] or negatively in Africa.[101] Importantly, ratification of the two Optional Protocols on the individual complaint mechanism enhances the influence that existing judicial remedies for the violation of domestic human rights law can have on Covenant rights protection through domestic courts. This is echoed in the reports' findings on Latin America[102] and, *a contrario*, on the Middle East and Asia.[103]

Secondly, the overlap between the Covenants and *regional human rights law instruments*, and their monitoring bodies, enhances the former's influence in domestic law. The reports confirm this in Europe and Latin America,[104] but also, *a contrario*, in Asia and the Middle East.[105] Interestingly, however, in the absence of domestic enabling legislation and judicial remedies specifically dedicated to the Covenants, the existence of a regional human rights monitoring system, including a system that includes the Committees' interpretations into its regional body's own

98 Tyagi, 'Asia' (n 24).
99 See Müller, 'Europe' (n 27).
100 See Müller, 'Europe' (n 27) and Pinto and Sigal, 'Latin America' (n 42).
101 See Ssenyonjo, 'Africa' (n 42).
102 See Pinto and Sigal, 'Latin America' (n 42).
103 See Çali, 'Middle East' (n 13) and Tyagi, 'Asia' (n 24).
104 See Müller, 'Europe' (n 27) and Pinto and Sigal, 'Latin America' (n 42).
105 See Tyagi, 'Asia' (n 24) and Çali, 'Middle East' (n 13).

interpretations, does not necessarily suffice to secure domestic influence, as confirmed in the African report.[106]

Thirdly, the Covenant's influence in domestic law depends to a great extent on *political (and judicial) culture*. It requires more than *pro forma* legal protection of Covenant rights, in other words.[107] All of the reports confirm this, but especially the Asian and Middle Eastern ones,[108] which emphasize the lack of political will in some of the States in these regions and hence also the lack of constructive interaction with the Committees.

Finally, the Covenants' influence in domestic law is enhanced when the *political and institutional requirements* that stem from general positive duties arising under Covenant rights are fulfilled. All reports confirm the importance of democracy, constitutionalism, and judicial review for the Covenants' influence. This is especially true in Latin America,[109] but the same conclusion may also be drawn from the Middle Eastern report *a contrario*.[110]

Generally, among the main directions for future reform that one may identify from the reports, one should mention the following five.

A first set of needs includes human rights *education and information* and, more specifically, the development of *databases* pertaining to Covenant law domestically and regionally.[111] A second common concern is the need for heightened sensitivity to *moral (and religious) pluralism*, and the legal diversity that stems from it across regions, at the risk of otherwise alienating some States from the Covenants and the Committees.[112] Thirdly, there is a need for more (demographic or cultural) *proportionate representation* in the Committees.[113] A fourth concern pertains to the need for new *means of constructive dialogue and/or pressure* by the Committees on States that do not provide information or only do so *pro forma*.[114] Finally, and more generally, there is a call for more *resources* as the price of better human rights protection.[115]

IV. A Comparative Law Argument for the Authority of the Committees' Interpretations

The (legal) authority or binding nature of the Committees' interpretations of the two Covenants (concluding observations, Views, and General Comments) has long been controversial. Instead of approaching the issue in the traditional way and top-down as a compliance problem, that is, from the perspective of the Committees, whose authority to settle the question is as controversial as their authority to interpret the Covenants in the first place, comparative international human rights law

[106] See Ssenyonjo, 'Africa' (n 42). [107] ibid.

[108] See Tyagi, 'Asia' (n 24) and Çali, 'Middle East' (n 13).

[109] See Pinto and Sigal, 'Latin America' (n 42). [110] See Çali, 'Middle East' (n 13).

[111] See Ssenyonjo, 'Africa' (n 42), Tyagi, 'Asia' (n 24), and Çali, 'Middle East' (n 13).

[112] See Tyagi, 'Asia' (n 24). [113] ibid.

[114] See Tyagi, 'Asia' (n 24) and Çali, 'Middle East' (n 13).

[115] See Ssenyonjo, 'Africa' (n 42), Pinto and Sigal, 'Latin America' (n 42), and Müller, 'Europe' (n 27).

provides an opportunity to look at it differently, that is, bottom-up and from the perspective of States.

As a matter of fact, most of the decisive arguments advanced in the discussions to date stem from general international law, and in particular from the international law on sources and on responsibility. Interestingly, these customary rules and general principles arise from State practice. It is the very kind of topic in international law, therefore, regarding which comparative international law can amount to an essential resource: it enables us to map State practice and identify a transnational consensus on the matter.

This comparative approach fits the issue of authority very well. It is a question whose treatment, as legal philosophers have long realized, should bridge the sociological and normative realms.[116] It suffices to stress how difficult it is to distinguish the duty to obey from the practice of obeying, or the claim to authority from the exercise of authority, and, more generally, to decide what comes first: the claim or the practice.[117] Given that the kind of sociological data required to settle this question cannot but be domestic, since international human rights law binds States to individuals under their jurisdiction, the comparison of domestic human rights law and practice has to be central to the elucidation of the authority of the Committees' interpretations of the Covenants.

Scope precludes rehearsing the debate pertaining to the authority of the Committees' interpretations of the Covenants.[118] In short, like any other international treaty, the two Covenants are binding international law. The problem is that the interpretations of the treaties given by the two Committees were expressly considered as non-binding by the two treaties. This is evidenced by the terms used, such as 'views', 'observations', 'comments', or 'recommendations'.

Unsurprisingly, the Committees have distanced themselves from this starting point by referring to the good faith obligations of States parties and, more generally, to their interpretations' 'authority'.[119] As a result, they have relied on their past interpretations of the Covenants as if they were binding. The ICJ itself considered that the Committees' interpretations should be ascribed 'great weight' in the *Diallo* case. The reasons it gave were that the States parties have established independent bodies to interpret the Covenants on the one hand, and that granting their interpretations special weight would serve the goals of 'clarity', 'consistency', and 'legal security' on the other.[120] It is difficult, however, to see how the latter could amount to an argument in the absence of the former: it is the interpretative authority of the Committees that seems to be key. Curiously, however, no argument to that effect is to be found in the ICJ's decision.

116 See eg Nicole Roughan, 'From Authority to Authorities: Bridging the Normative/Sociological Divide', in Roger Cotterrell and Maksymilian Del Mar (eds), *Authority in Transnational Legal Theory: Theorising across Disciplines* (Edward Elgar 2016) 280.

117 See Joseph Raz, *The Morality of Freedom* (OUP 1986) 65.

118 See eg Gerald L Neuman, 'Giving Meaning and Effect to Human Rights: The Contributions of Human Rights Committee Members', Chapter 3 in this volume.

119 See HRC, 'General Comment 33' (2009) UN Doc CCPR/C/GC/33, para 13–14.

120 See ICJ, *Diallo* (n 76) 664.

Among the international law arguments brought so far in favour of the binding nature of the Committees' interpretations, one could mention the responsibility argument (under ICCPR article 2(2) and (3)) and the 'quasi-judiciality' argument. The former begs the question of why the Committees' interpretation of the secondary duties of responsibility, which arise for States anyway, actually binds, and the latter begs the question of what makes a finding a 'judgment', and thus binding, in the first place. A third argument put forward is that of States' 'subsequent practice', whether it is validated *qua* interpretation of the Covenants under the conditions of article 31(3)(b) of the Vienna Convention on the Law of Treaties (VCLT)[121] or arises *qua* customary international law norm. This is not an argument for the binding nature of the Committees' interpretations, however; it merely grounds the separate authority of the latter's content in another source of law: States' consensual practice or custom.[122] The question of the authority of the Committees and their interpretations remains open as a result.

It is here that comparative international human rights law can help us map State practice and identify the existence of a potential transnational consensus in that practice that is sufficiently common to become either a ground for an evolutive interpretation of the treaty or a new custom pertaining to the binding nature of the Committees' interpretations. What the five reports show is that the Committees' interpretations are increasingly treated as part of Covenant law (and not only when these interpretations are grounded in States' subsequent practice or custom, as explained above), and that this applies particularly to concluding observations and Views. This is especially the case in States that have ratified regional human rights instruments and acceded to the jurisdiction of their respective courts, since the latter systematically include the Committees' interpretations in their interpretations of their own respective instruments.

V. Three Proposals for Enhancing the Legitimacy of the Committees' Interpretations

If the argument proposed in the previous section is correct, and the Committees' interpretations can bind, their practice needs to change also with respect to legitimacy. Indeed, establishing the authority of the Committees' interpretations and their binding nature under international law does not yet imply that their authority is justified and hence legitimate. Of course, because the Committees lacked authority for a long time, their concern for legitimacy was limited. This has even arguably led to the converse paradox: it is because the Committees did not care enough about

[121] Vienna Convention on the Law of Treaties (VCLT) (opened for signature 23 May 1969, entered into force 27 January 1980) 1155 UNTS 331.

[122] This may explain the confusion of the Committee on Economic, Social and Cultural Rights (CESCR) pertaining to *whose* subsequent practice should matter under VCLT art 31(3)(b): its own or States'. See eg CESCR, 'General Comment 19' (2008) UN Doc E/C.12/GC/19, para 53a; Daniel Moeckli, 'Interpretation of the ICESCR: Between Morality and State Consent', Chapter 4 in this volume.

justifying (the authority of) their interpretations that these were not considered as binding by States until recently. As a result, the time has come to think about justifying the Committees' interpretations, and the present comparative study of the influence of the Covenants, with its transregional focus, is a good opportunity to do so.

This section makes three interrelated proposals regarding the Committees' future practice in this respect: it should take subsidiarity more seriously (V.A); in order to do so, it should resort to comparison to identify a transnational human rights consensus on Covenant law (V.B); and, finally, it should make the most of regional mechanisms for the identification of that consensus (V.C).

A. The role of subsidiarity in Covenant law

A way to justify the authority of the Committees' interpretations of the Covenants could be to respect a core principle of international human rights law: human rights subsidiarity.

A descriptive survey of international human rights law shows that subsidiarity is usually approached as a two-sided principle: States have the primary responsibility to secure human rights protection, including through judicial review, and international human rights bodies or courts have a complementary review power in cases where international minimal standards are not effectively protected domestically.[123] More specifically, the survey reveals three types of human rights subsidiarity: 'procedural', when it pertains to the actual power of the international human rights court or body to review (eg exhaustion of domestic remedies); 'substantive', when it qualifies the intensity of that review (eg the fourth instance doctrine, the margin of appreciation, or the principle of favour); and 'remedial', when it pertains to the scope of review (eg the *restitutio in integrum* principle).[124]

If the principle of subsidiarity so described is very much at the core of regional international human rights regimes, the same cannot yet be said about the Covenants and the Committees' practice. Interestingly, it is within judicialized international human rights law regimes, and hence the regional ones, like the 1950 European Convention on Human Rights (ECHR), with its Court, the European Court of Human Rights (ECtHR), or the 1969 American Convention on Human Rights, with its Court, the Inter-American Court of Human Rights (IACtHR), that one encounters all three types of human rights subsidiarity. In the universal international human rights regimes, by contrast, the rule seems to be, first of all, that the less institutionalized they are, the less frequently subsidiarity is invoked and respected. Thus, while some forms of subsidiarity may be identified in the practice of UN human rights treaty bodies, very few subsidiarity requirements subsist in the individual

[123] See eg the prevailing approach under the law of the European Convention on Human Rights law (ECtHR, 'Subsidiarity: A Two-Sided Coin?' (2015) ECtHR Background paper <www.echr.coe.int/Documents/Seminar_background_paper_2015_ENG.pdf> accessed 1 April 2017, 1).

[124] For a full argument, see Samantha Besson, 'Subsidiarity in International Human Rights Law: What is Subsidiary about Human Rights?' (2016) 61 American J of Jurisprudence 69.

procedures before the Human Rights Council. A second observation is that, even before human rights treaty bodies like the two Committees, if procedural subsidiarity is usually respected, this is not the case for substantive subsidiarity, or then only in a very limited fashion to the extent that there is no clear reference to the notion of 'margin of appreciation';[125] this is also not the case for remedial subsidiarity given the frequent prescription of individual or general measures as remedies.

Claiming authority for the Committees' interpretations comes at a price, however: they should endeavour to respect the principle of human rights subsidiarity in order to justify the authority of their interpretations and secure their legitimacy. In international human rights law, subsidiarity amounts to the justification for the complementary review and interpretation power of international human rights bodies or courts.[126]

Justifications of human rights subsidiarity itself are two-fold: epistemic and democratic. This has been confirmed by the ECtHR, which refers to domestic authorities' being 'better placed than an international court to evaluate local needs and conditions', on the one hand, and to reasonable disagreement and the special weight that should be given to the democratically-elected domestic policy-maker, on the other.[127] The epistemic justification of subsidiarity is to be found in the concrete nature of human rights duties, whose content can only be specified by reference to threats existing in domestic circumstances. The democratic justification of human rights subsidiarity is egalitarian and pertains to the protection of the political equality of individuals in the specification of their respective human rights and duties through domestic democracy.[128]

If the Committees are to develop a more rigorous practice of substantive subsidiarity, they will need a test to apply in this regard. In regional human rights law, the test used for human rights subsidiarity is the effectiveness of domestic protection of the minimal international standard of human rights. The ECtHR and the IACtHR have developed the criteria of transnational consensus, 'common ground', or 'converging approach' to identify what constitutes that minimal standard of human rights protection across the States parties and to determine the corresponding degree of scrutiny applicable to a given domestic measure. Regrettably, this is not the sole test at play in these courts' reasoning when setting the margin of appreciation, however, and its application remains largely unpredictable as a result. Nevertheless, there are ways for the transnational consensus test to be streamlined and generalized as a test for substantive subsidiarity in international human rights law.

Referring to democratic consensus as constitutive of a minimal standard of human rights protection ties into the democratic justification of human rights subsidiarity. Importantly, however, the existence or absence of democratic consensus should only

[125] See eg HRC, 'General Comment 34' (2011) UN Doc CCPR/C/GC/34, para 36.

[126] See eg David Szymczak, 'Rapport introductif: Le principe de subsidiarité dans tous ses états' in Frédéric Sudre (ed), *Le principe de subsidiarité au sens du droit de la Convention européenne des droits de l'homme* (Anthémis 2014) 15, 27.

[127] See ECtHR, *SAS v France*, App no 43835/11, 1 July 2014, para 129.

[128] See Samantha Besson, 'The Egalitarian Dimension of Human Rights' (2012) 136 Archiv für Sozial- und Rechtsphilosophie Beiheft 19.

work as a test for the margin of appreciation within the limits of the democratic justification of subsidiarity itself, that is, provided non-discrimination rights and the fundamental core of human rights are not infringed.

Of course, some may object that not all States parties to the Covenants are democratic, and that this jeopardizes the democratic argument for applying human rights subsidiarity to the Committees' power of review and to the latter's intensity and scope. This democratic objection applies from the perspective of both non-democratic States and democratic States.

With respect to the former, this is a false problem given that, under international human rights law, all States have to be democratic as much as they have to respect human rights. It is unclear, therefore, why the lack of democratic legitimacy of minimal international democratic and human rights standards should worry the people of a non-democratic State that is not yet abiding by either of these standards. Secondly, regarding the impact on democratic States and their populations, the concern may also be put aside. When a State has not ensured sufficient democratic deliberation in a given human rights case, its margin of appreciation should be limited and subsidiarity sidestepped because the conditions for the latter, that is, domestic deliberation and reason-giving, are not fulfilled.[129] Non-democratic States should not be allowed to contribute further, for instance through the consolidation of their respective human rights practice into the transnational human rights consensus, to the development of the minimal international human rights standard that also amounts to a minimal democratic standard constraining democratic States parties in return.[130]

B. The role of comparison and transnational consensus in Covenant law

If transnational human rights consensus is to become the test for substantive subsidiarity, and for States' margin of appreciation under Covenant law, the Committees should generalize their recourse to comparative international human rights law. Comparison is the main method available to international human rights bodies and courts in order to identify a common ground or consensus in States' human rights practice.

The importance of comparison in international human rights law becomes clear once the duality of the domestic-international regime of human rights law is fully understood.[131] One of human rights law's features, indeed, is the transnational

[129] See also Andreas Føllesdal, 'Appreciating the Margin of Appreciation' in Adam Etinson (ed), *Human Rights: Moral or Political?* (OUP 2018).

[130] For a full argument, see Besson, 'Transnational Constitutional Law' (n 40). It would be paradoxical indeed to insist, on the one hand, on participatory grounds, that all non-democratic States should be included in the determination of international human rights law and hence in the transnational human rights consensus, while, on the other, refusing at a later stage to take that consensus seriously because it is dominated or tainted by so-called 'pretenders' and could impose parochial conceptions of human rights. See also Heyns and Killander, 'Universality' (n 22) 673–74.

[131] See also Gerald L Neuman 'Human Rights and Constitutional Rights: Harmony and Dissonance' (2003) 55 Stanford L Rev 1863.

nature of its sources, be they international or domestic.[132] Domestic and international legal norms protecting human rights relate in a way that is uncommon in international law: they are not only situated in a relationship of top-down enforcement of an international standard in domestic law, but also in a relationship of bottom-up international recognition of the common law stemming from different domestic legal orders and of its progressive consolidation into a minimal international human rights standard. Because this transnational minimal standard, once it has been entrenched, requires the same level of transnational commonality to evolve one way or the other, levelling-down is rare in practice. Moreover, as explained before, only the domestic human rights practices regarded as minimally democratic according to the common standards entrenched in international human rights law may and should be considered in the further transnational development of this minimal international human rights standard.

Again, justifications for this transnational process of human rights law-making are both democratic and epistemic. The moral epistemology of human rights is social and reflexive,[133] and this requires that human rights first be identified in the socio-political context in which they are already protected in substance, that is, domestically and democratically, followed by international recognition to protect and entrench these epistemic egalitarian constraints.

Of course, some may object to this justification of transnational human rights law-making on grounds of the universality of (minimal) international human rights law. The problem is that international human rights law itself may be criticized for its lack of universality. The parochialism objection is indeed usually raised in opposition to the claimed universality of international human rights law and based on what it regards as the largely parochial conceptions of these rights stemming from one dominant culture and imposed on others in the name of universality.[134] In reply to this objection, one may therefore argue that the transnational making of human rights law actually amounts to a way of preventing parochial conceptions from being too quickly entrenched into international human rights law. Starting from many distinct domestic human rights interpretations and comparing them on a transnational scale in order to identify common ground can contribute to questioning the future international human rights standard and hence to making it less parochial. This is not to say that there are no epistemic qualities in existing international human rights institutions, such as for example their inclusiveness, representativeness, or deliberativeness,[135] but only that the latter are actually best understood as complementary and transnational in their functioning rather than unilateral and top-down.

[132] For a full argument, see Besson, 'Transnational Constitutional Law' (n 40).

[133] See Allen Buchanan, 'The Reflexive Social Moral Epistemology of Human Rights' in Miranda Fricker (ed), *Social Epistemology* (2018) forthcoming.

[134] See Samantha Besson, 'Justifications' in Daniel Moeckli, Sangeeta Shah, and Sandesh Sivakumaran (eds), *International Human Rights Law* (3rd edn, OUP 2017) 22.

[135] See Allen Buchanan, 'Human Rights and the Legitimacy of the International Order' (2008) 14 Legal Theory 39.

The transnationality of human rights law, thus understood and justified, explains the specific function comparative law plays or should play in domestic[136] and international human rights reasoning, a role very different from that of scholarly comparisons or one-to-one judicial references.[137] If there is comparison in the contemporary dual human rights regime, it is because human rights law claims to be transnational and hence universal and shares a common ground. It is not merely because it is interesting, or even strategic, to compare domestic practices, for instance to clarify certain constitutional concepts.

What this means for the Committees is that they should resort more systematically to comparative international human rights reasoning by comparing the various domestic practices pertaining to Covenant rights and try, more regularly, to identify a transnational consensus.[138] Arguably, this is already the way in which State practice becomes consolidated into Covenant law as subsequent State practice in the Committees' concluding observations[139] and then reimposed as such onto States thanks to the perpetuation of this transnational human rights law-making cycle over time.[140] To that extent, the way in which the Covenants' interpretation is developed is already truly transnational. It is important, however, to make this process even more comparative, and in particular to extend that human rights comparison into the other procedures whereby Covenant law is interpreted, such as General Comments and individual Views.

Resorting to human rights comparison would enable the Committees to comply more strictly with the conditions of VCLT article 31(3)(b) when they interpret the Covenants by reference to subsequent State practice; this method implies substantiating State practice and assessing whether it reveals a new agreement. The fact that domestic institutions, and especially domestic courts, increasingly resort to comparative human rights law (across domestic human rights law rules, but also between the various universal and regional regimes of human rights law) could, of course, be of great help to the Committees in this comparative endeavour and should be encouraged on the same grounds.

C. The role of regions and regional human rights regimes under Covenant law

Pursuing human rights comparison, and especially identifying a transnational consensus on that basis, may be more difficult on the Covenants' universal scale than on the regional level. This may explain why the minimal human rights standard under Covenant law has overall been thinner in scope than under regional human rights

136 See Jeremy Waldron, 'Rights and the Citation of Foreign Law' in Tom Campbell, KD Ewing, and Adam Tomkins (eds), *The Legal Protection of Human Rights: Sceptical Essays* (OUP 2011) 410, 423.

137 See eg Christopher McCrudden, 'Common Law of Human Rights? Transnational Judicial Conversations on Constitutional Rights' (2000) 20 OJLS 499.

138 See Pinto and Sigal, 'Latin America' (n 42), on the use of the term 'consensus'.

139 See eg CESCR 'Report on the Seventh Session' (23 November–11 December 1992) UN Doc E/1993/22, para 32 and 49.

140 See also Moeckli, 'Interpretation' (n 122).

regimes. Clearly, however, identifying such a universal transnational human rights consensus is not impossible. As a matter of fact, comparing human rights practice across regions rather than States may ease the process. Looking for regional human rights consensuses may be a good way to promote, at an intermediary level, the consolidation of a universal consensus around interpretations of Covenant rights.

Various *general* arguments for the beneficial role of regional human rights law regarding the influence of the Covenants in domestic law have been mentioned in this study, including the supranational judicial remedies available under these regimes and their integration rules (Section III). These benefits were confirmed by the regional reports corresponding to the four regions, out of the five studied, that have regional human rights instruments in place. From a broader perspective, and to quote Gerald L Neuman, one may make three arguments for the adoption of regional human rights regimes: trust, effectiveness, and expertise.[141] Regional human rights bodies staffed by neighbour States' nationals are more likely to be trusted in adjudicating and interpreting human rights than universal ones like the Committees, more likely to be effective in the authority they claim and in enforcing human rights, and likely to know better how to interpret human rights in domestic circumstances. The Asian report actually emphasizes Asian States' distrust of the distant universal human rights machinery in charge of monitoring conformity with the ICCPR.[142] As a matter of fact, some developments towards the establishment of a new regional human rights regime are now observed in that region too.[143]

Importantly, nothing in these arguments for the development of regional human rights instruments should be interpreted to mean that universal human rights instruments like the Covenants and their monitoring by the Committees would be dispensable, provided regional instruments were in place universally and inclusive of all States in every region.

Of course, for the reasons mentioned above, regional human rights instruments and especially regional human rights bodies have been easier to set up and sustain. History confirms that regional regimes were put in place first or, at least, to a greater institutional depth, and especially that they were the first ones to be judicialized. This affects the comparative advantages of both systems today and how they have grown to coexist through that differentiation. One may mention, for instance, the differences between the kinds of human rights they protect, between the thickness of the minimal consensus they reveal on these rights, and, finally, between the kinds of international remedies they provide, and especially whether these remedies are general and political (eg State reporting) and/or individual and judicial (eg individual applications).

All the same, contemporary fears that regional human rights systems could displace the universal human rights system, or at least undermine it, are wrong.[144]

141 See Neuman, 'Import, Export, and Regional Consent' (n 7) 106; Heyns and Killander, 'Universality' (n 22) 673.

142 See Tyagi, 'Asia' (n 24).

143 ibid. See Heyns and Killander, 'Universality' (n 22) 691ff.

144 See, however, Heyns and Killander, 'Universality' (n 22) 674, 695.

With respect to the former concern, one should stress that (domestic and regional) human rights law's claim to universality implies the coexistence of a (minimal) universal international human rights standard, at least *qua* general principles or customary law. As a result, there could be no regional human rights law without a universal human rights regime. A confirmation of this form of epistemic discipline generated by the universality of international human rights law may be found in regional human rights courts' interpretations. The second concern may also be set aside to the extent that, based on the arguments put forward earlier in this chapter, it is unclear why regional human rights law and institutions should necessarily be less democratic and more epistemically parochial than universal ones. Even if they were, the inherent democratic and egalitarian limitations placed on States' margin of appreciation, the international entrenchment of the minimal transnational human rights standard that requires an equivalent universal transnational human rights consensus to be amended, and, finally, the reflexive benefits of transnational human rights comparison within a region would all prevent a regional human rights system whose guarantees allegedly fall below the threshold of the minimal international human rights standard from being invoked to derogate from the latter and to level it down.

Among the *specific* arguments one may give for the contribution of regional human rights regimes to the identification of a regional human rights consensus and, accordingly, to the consolidation of a universal consensus on Covenant rights, one should, of course, mention the evidence that stems from the existing regimes.[145] What the four regional reports show is that regional human rights regimes have led to the development, over time, of common political or constitutional traits[146] in domestic human rights practice. As a matter of fact, the Asian report confirms that commonalities can also be identified in Asia despite the absence of a regional human rights instrument.[147]

Accordingly, the Committees should encourage regional human rights protection and interpretations, and, in regions where these are not present, require States to resort more regularly to regional comparisons and to the identification of a regional consensus. This could, in turn, enable the Committees, in their own reasoning, to distinguish the claims before them from those addressed by regional courts and, when available, to rely on one or more regional consensuses. This could then facilitate the identification of a transnational consensus on Covenant rights based on commonalities between regional human rights consensuses. This comparison and search for consensus should, of course, be done in an inclusive and universal way to avoid privileging some States or some regions over others and developing a parochial interpretation of the Covenants.[148] From an institutional perspective, this may imply restructuring the Committees to create regional rapporteurs, to devolve some

[145] See Neuman, 'Import, Export, and Regional Consent' (n 7).

[146] See Pinto and Sigal, 'Latin America' (n 42).

[147] See Tyagi, 'Asia' (n 24).

[148] See eg Gerald L Neuman, 'Standing Alone or Together: The Human Rights Committee's Decision in *AP v Russian Federation*' in Eva Brems and Ellen Desmet (eds), *Integrated Human Rights in Practice: Rewriting Human Rights Decisions* (Edward Elgar 2017).

of their work to regional sub-committees, or, at least, to hold regional meetings.[149] In this respect, an important contribution of better consideration of regional human rights law in the Committees' deliberations could be to compensate for the lack of proportionate representation of the regions in the Committees' membership.

Provided they can identify a transregional consensus on a given Covenant right through comparison, the Committees should demonstrate some deference to that consensus and enforce it through their interpretations of States' duties. In other cases, they should grant States parties a broad margin of appreciation. Importantly, within these boundaries, the existence of a transnational human rights consensus would not pre-empt the Committees' power to review and interpret Covenant rights.[150]

A separate and difficult question pertains to the relationship, in case of contradiction, between distinct regional human rights 'consensuses', on the one hand, and between (some of) them and the universal human rights consensus, on the other. In circumstances of reasonable disagreement, one should expect that the respective consensuses could diverge.

Regarding the former kind of conflict, first of all, the democratic and epistemic justifications of transnational human rights law point to the priority of the common ground identified in the relevant region. The existence of these contradictions should, however, remind regional human rights courts of the importance of subjecting their interpretations to comparative revision and of their necessary corrigibility. Such conflicts should not be all too common, however.[151] Indeed, existing regional human rights regimes have adopted a universalizing approach to the identification of their respective regional human rights consensuses.[152] From the perspective of the Committees, the identification of such conflicts between regional human rights consensuses should be taken as a signal in the identification of a potential universal and transnational human rights consensus.

With respect to the conflict between regional and universal human rights consensuses, second, priorities are more difficult to draw. Of course, much of the time, regional consensuses are thicker than the universal one and, if conflicts arise, they fall within the thinner scope of the latter only. However, even in that context, such conflicts should not be all too common. Indeed, as explained, existing regional human rights regimes have adopted a universalizing discipline in the identification of their regional human rights consensuses, and have integrated the Committees' interpretations of the Covenants into the interpretation of the American, African, and

149 See Heyns and Viljoen, 'The Impact' (n 17) 513.

150 Comparing human rights and identifying a transnational human rights consensus should not, therefore, be equated with requiring the Committees to adopt the lowest minimal common standard shared by States across regions. For a full argument for the authority of comparative human rights law and especially of the transnational and transregional human rights consensus, see Samantha Besson, 'Comparative Law and Human Rights' in Mathias Reimann and Reinhard Zimmermann (eds), *Oxford Handbook on Comparative Law* (2nd edn, OUP 2018) forthcoming.

151 See Heyns and Killander, 'Universality' (n 22) 688ff.

152 See eg *Demir and Baykara v Turkey* App no 34503/97 (ECtHR, 12 November 2008) para 85.

even European instruments.[153] The Committees have also shown a lot of deference to regional human rights consensus, especially when it is transregional[154]—albeit not always by referring expressly to its comparative sources or distinguishing between them.[155] Of course, there are many other reasons for convergence between the Committees and regional human rights courts.[156]

In the rare cases in which conflicts between regional and universal consensuses arise, however, the relationship between the respective consensuses cannot be one of subsidiarity; subsidiarity is justified on democratic grounds and only applies between domestic democratic and international human rights law. This is why the favour clause cannot apply either.[157] Some human rights scholars have criticized this lack of coherence in international human rights law.[158] This risk of fragmentation is usually addressed by reference to international law's rules on conflicts, and in particular to the idea of systemic interpretation (VCLT article 31(3)(c)).[159] In the case of conflicts between regional and universal human rights interpretations, one should add that they share a common universality in the human rights duties they impose; this is what should guide their respective interpretations.

VI. Conclusions

The transregional scope of this study has provided a unique opportunity to confirm the role of regional human rights instruments and bodies in international human rights law descriptively, but also to argue normatively for their justification from the perspective of the universality of human rights. It has also shown why comparative international human rights law amounts to much more than a scholarly project and should become a more integral part of the practice of international human rights law, including in the Committees' reasoning.

Bibliography

Baluarte, David C, and de Vos, Christian, 'From Judgment to Justice: Implementing International and Regional Human Rights Decisions' (Open Society Justice Initiative 2010)

Besson, Samantha, 'The Egalitarian Dimension of Human Rights' (2012) 136 Archiv für Sozial- und Rechtsphilosophie Beiheft 19

[153] See Pinto and Sigal, 'Latin America' (n 42), Ssenyonjo, 'Africa' (n 42), and Müller, 'Europe' (n 27).

[154] See Heyns and Killander, 'Universality' (n 22) 688ff, 695.

[155] See Neuman, 'Standing Alone or Together' (n 148).

[156] See Shany, 'Fragmentation' (n 22).

[157] *Contra* Adamantia Rachovitsa, 'Treaty Clauses and Fragmentation of International Law: Applying the More Favourable Protection Clause in Human Rights Treaties' (2016) 16 Human Rights L Rev 77.

[158] See eg Brems, 'Integration' (n 22); Payandeh, 'Fragmentation' (n 22).

[159] See Neuman, 'Meaning and Effect' (n 118).

Besson, Samantha, 'Human Rights and Constitutional Law: Mutual Validation and Legitimation' in Rowan Cruft, S Matthew Liao, and Massimo Renzo (eds), *Philosophical Foundations of Human Rights* (OUP 2015)

Besson, Samantha, 'Subsidiarity in International Human Rights Law: What is Subsidiary about Human Rights?' (2016) 61 American J of Jurisprudence 69

Besson, Samantha, 'Human Rights as Transnational Constitutional Law' in Anthony F Lang and Antje Wiener (eds), *Handbook on Global Constitutionalism* (Edward Elgar 2017)

Besson, Samantha, 'Justifications' in Daniel Moeckli, Sangeeta Shah, and Sandesh Sivakumaran (eds), *International Human Rights Law* (3rd edn, OUP 2017)

Besson, Samantha, 'Comparative Law and Human Rights' in Mathias Reimann and Reinhard Zimmermann (eds), *Oxford Handbook on Comparative Law* (2nd edn, OUP 2018) forthcoming

Brems, Eva, 'Should Pluriform Human Rights Become One?: Exploring the Benefits of Human Rights Integration / Intégrer le droit des droits de l'homme: une exploration' (2014) 4 Journal européen des droits de l'homme / European J of Human Rights 447

Buchanan, Allen, 'Human Rights and the Legitimacy of the International Order' (2008) 14 Legal Theory 39

Buchanan, Allen, 'The Reflexive Social Moral Epistemology of Human Rights' in Miranda Fricker (ed), *Social Epistemology* (2018) forthcoming

Conforti, Benedetto, and Francioni, Francesco (eds), *Enforcing International Human Rights in Domestic Courts* (Brill 1997)

Føllesdal, Andreas, 'Appreciating the Margin of Appreciation' in Adam Etinson (ed), *Human Rights: Moral or Political?* (OUP 2018)

Gowan, Richard, and Brantner, Franziska, 'Regionalism and Human Rights at the UN' in Philippe Lombaerde, Francis Baert, and Tânia Felicio (eds), *The United Nations and the Regions: Third World Report on Regional Integration* (Springer 2012)

Halmai, Gábor, 'Domestic Courts and International Human Rights' in Anja Mihr and Mark Gibney (eds), *The SAGE Handbook of Human Rights* (SAGE 2014)

Harland, Christopher, 'The Status of the International Covenant on Civil and Political Rights (ICCPR) in the Domestic Law of States Parties: An Initial Global Survey Through UN Human Rights Committee Documents' (2000) 22 Human Rights Q 187

Heyns, Christof, and Killander, Magnus, 'Universality and the Growth of Regional Systems' in Dinah Shelton (ed), *The Oxford Handbook of International Human Rights Law* (OUP 2013)

Heyns, Christof, and Viljoen, Frans, 'The Impact of the United Nations Human Rights Treaties on the Domestic Level' (2001) 23 Human Rights Quarterly 483

Hill, Daniel W, 'Estimating the Effects of Human Rights Treaties on State Behavior' (2010) 72 J of Politics 1161

Jackson, Vicky C, and Tushnet, Mark, *Comparative Constitutional Law* (3rd edn, Foundation 2014)

Joseph, Sarah, and Castan, Melissa, *The International Covenant on Civil and Political Rights: Cases, Materials and Commentary* (3rd edn, OUP 2013)

Keller, Helen, and Grover, Leena, 'General Comments of the Human Rights Committee and their legitimacy' in Helen Keller and Geir Ulfstein (eds), *UN Human Rights Treaty Bodies: Law and Legitimacy* (CUP 2012)

Keller, Helen, and Stone Sweet, Alec (eds), *A Europe of Rights: The Impact of the ECHR on National Legal Systems* (OUP 2008)

Keller, Helen, and Ulfstein, Geir (eds), *UN Human Rights Treaty Bodies: Law and Legitimacy* (CUP 2012)

Krommendijk, Jasper, 'The Domestic Effectiveness of International Human Rights Monitoring in Established Democracies: The Case of the UN Human Rights Treaty Bodies' (2015) 10 Rev of International Organizations 489

McCrudden, Christopher, 'Common Law of Human Rights? Transnational Judicial Conversations on Constitutional Rights' (2000) 20 OJLS 499

McCrudden, Christopher, 'Why Do National Court Judges Refer to Human Rights Treaties? A Comparative International Law Analysis of CEDAW' (2015) 109 AJIL 534

McCrudden, Christopher, 'What Does Comparing (Law) Mean and What Should It Mean?' in Samantha Besson, Lukas Heckendorn Urscheler, and Samuel Jubé (eds), *Comparing Comparative Law* (Schulthess 2017)

McCrudden, Christopher, 'CEDAW in National Courts: A Case Study in Operationalizing Comparative International Law Analysis in a Human Rights Context' in Anthea Roberts and others (eds), *Comparative International Law* (OUP 2018)

McCrudden, Christopher, 'Comparative International Law and Human Rights: A Value-Added Approach' in Anthea Roberts and others (eds), *Comparative International Law* (OUP 2018)

Neuman, Gerald L, 'Human Rights and Constitutional Rights: Harmony and Dissonance' (2003) 55 Stanford L Rev 1863

Neuman, Gerald L, 'Import, Export, and Regional Consent in the Inter-American Court of Human Rights' (2008) 19 EJIL 101

Neuman, Gerald L, 'Standing Alone or Together: The Human Rights Committee's Decision in *AP v Russian Federation*' in Eva Brems and Ellen Desmet (eds), *Integrated Human Rights in Practice: Rewriting Human Rights Decisions* (Edward Elgar 2017)

Neuman, Gerald L, 'The External Reception of Inter-American Human Rights Law' [2011] Quebec J of Intl L 99

Payandeh, Mehrdad, 'Fragmentation within International Human Rights Law' in Mads Andenas and Eirik Bjorge (eds), *A Farewell to Fragmentation: Reassertion and Convergence in International Law* (CUP 2015)

Rachovitsa, Adamantia, 'Treaty Clauses and Fragmentation of International Law: Applying the More Favourable Protection Clause in Human Rights Treaties' (2016) 16 Human Rights L Rev 77

Raz, Joseph, *The Morality of Freedom* (OUP 1986)

Roughan, Nicole, 'From Authority to Authorities: Bridging the Normative/Sociological Divide' in Roger Cotterrell and Maksymilian Del Mar (eds), *Authority in Transnational Legal Theory: Theorising across Disciplines* (Edward Elgar 2016)

Saul, Ben, Kinley, David, and Mowbray, Jacqueline, *The International Covenant on Economic, Social and Cultural Rights: Commentary, Cases, and Materials* (OUP 2014)

Shany, Yuval, 'International Human Rights Bodies and the Little-Realized Threat of Fragmentation' (2016) Hebrew University of Jerusalem Legal Research Paper 16/06 <https://papers.ssrn.com/sol3/papers.cfm?abstract_id=2722663> accessed 31 March 2017

Szymczak, David, 'Rapport introductif: Le principe de subsidiarité dans tous ses états' in Frédéric Sudre (ed), *Le principe de subsidiarité au sens du droit de la Convention européenne des droits de l'homme* (Anthémis 2014)

van Alebeek, Rosanne, and Nollkaemper, André, 'The Legal Status of Decisions by Human Rights Treaty Bodies in National Law' in Helen Keller and Geir Ulfstein (eds), *UN Human Rights Treaty Bodies: Law and Legitimacy* (CUP 2012)

Versteeg, Mila, 'Law versus Norms: The Impact of Human Rights Treaties on Constitutional Rights' (2015) 171 J of Institutional and Theoretical Economics 87

Waldron, Jeremy, 'Rights and the Citation of Foreign Law' in Tom Campbell, KD Ewing, and Adam Tomkins (eds), *The Legal Protection of Human Rights: Sceptical Essays* (OUP 2011)

Weston, Burns H, Lukes, Robin Ann, and Hnatt, Kelly M, 'Regional Human Rights Regimes: A Comparison and Appraisal' (1987) 20 Vanderbilt J of Transnational L 585

PART III

THE FUTURE

What Should Become of the Covenants?

12

The Covenants in the Light of Anthropogenic Climate Change

*Stephen Humphreys**

I. Introduction

A mere dozen years after the two principal human rights Covenants[1] entered into force in 1976, the Intergovernmental Panel on Climate Change (IPCC) was convened to assess the accumulating reports that human activity was altering the world's climate system. Among other things, the IPCC's exhaustive first report concluded, in 1990, that climate change was likely dramatically to undermine access to basic public goods—food, water, healthcare, and shelter—for many millions of persons.[2] From this report came the United Nations (UN) Framework Convention on Climate Change (UNFCCC), signed in 1992 and entering into force in 1994.[3]

These events straddle the 1993 Vienna World Conference on Human Rights, a pivotal moment in revisiting and reactivating the Covenants for a post-Cold War world. Curiously perhaps, the Vienna Declaration and Programme of Action—although it cites the Rio conference at which the UNFCCC was signed—makes no mention of climate change.[4] In retrospect, this may seem an extraordinary omission.[5] But it has also been, if not actually determinative of subsequent developments,

* This paper has benefitted immensely from review by Prof Olivier de Schutter. I signal his contributions where they arise below.

[1] The International Covenant on Civil and Political Rights (ICCPR) (opened for signature 16 December 1966, entered into force 23 March 1976) 999 UNTS 171, and the International Covenant on Economic, Social and Cultural Rights (ICESCR) (opened for signature 16 December 1966, entered into force 3 January 1976) 993 UNTS 3.

[2] See IPCC, *First Assessment Report* (1990) <www.ipcc.ch/ipccreports/far/wg_I/ipcc_far_wg_I_full_report.pdf> accessed 3 April 2017, overview chapter, 54–56.

[3] UN Framework Convention on Climate Change (UNFCCC) (opened for signature 9 May 1992, entered into force 21 March 1994) 1771 UNTS 107.

[4] World Conference on Human Rights, Vienna Declaration and Programme of Action (25 June 1993) para 36. See also paras 10 and 11. Given these references, it seems likely climate change was at least raised in preparatory discussions.

[5] The now-extensive literature on the human rights dimensions of climate change emerged only after the unsuccessful 'Inuit case' of 2005. See the petition to the Inter-American Commission on Human Rights seeking relief from violations resulting from global warming caused by acts and omissions of the United States submitted by Sheila Watt-Cloutier, with the support of the Inuit Circumpolar

The Human Rights Covenants at 50: Their Past, Present, and Future. Daniel Moeckli, Helen Keller, and Corina Heri. Published 2018 by Oxford University Press.

at least predictive of them: the concerns climate change raises for our human rights system can appear to be overwhelming and, perhaps, like looking directly at the sun, best avoided.

In this chapter, I try not to be blinded by the likelihood that climate change, and phenomena associated with it, pose a catastrophe not merely for the human rights of millions of individuals (however we understand them), but also for the international machinery nominally charged with protecting those rights. I examine the future of the Covenants in light of human-induced climate change by reference to the provisions of the Covenants themselves. The Covenants—and human rights law more broadly—are undoubtedly (and increasingly) relevant to our management, or mismanagement, of climate change. Nevertheless, I will suggest that the human rights dimensions of climate change are most pronounced in precisely those areas of international human rights law which have traditionally been most ambiguous and contested—notably social and economic rights, extraterritorial harms, and inter-State obligations. There is little doubt that climate change raises authentic human rights concerns—but, I will suggest, these largely escape international human rights law as it has developed since 1948. This fact has to do as much with other key elements of the international legal framework (such as trade and investment law) as with human rights law. In the present chapter, however, I restrict myself to the latter.

It seems fair to project one of three possible futures for the Covenants in light of climate change:[6] root-and-branch reform (or new treaty obligations) to render the human rights regime capable of taking account of the conditions giving rise to vastly unequal access to human rights protections in conditions of climate change (unlikely); 'business as usual' in which climate change takes its place next to, or indeed running through, a series of 'issues'—business, poverty, trade, tax, finance, 'development'—that engender perennial angst for a human rights regime constitutionally incapable of digesting them (more likely); or the Covenants' gradual delegitimation as felt and extensive human rights harms undermine their relevance (likely—but avoidable, given the significant institutional anchors securing what is by now a burgeoning human rights industry).

In what follows, I take a number of rhetorical stances that need flagging up front.

The first is to decouple the *existence* of 'human rights' from the institutional and legal machinery that protects them. This is a counter-realist move, insofar as I am setting aside the *ubi ius* maxim (with which I am essentially sympathetic) that a 'right' without a remedy is an immaterial abstraction, so much ideological bluster.[7] I avoid this stance here for three reasons. First, the Covenants themselves—the master texts

Conference, on behalf of all Inuit of the Arctic regions of the United States and Canada (7 December 2005) <http://tinyurl.com/zl37fpq> accessed 28 June 2016.

[6] See Stephen Humphreys, 'Climate Change Pathways and the Future of Human Rights' in Nehal Bhuta (ed), *The Futures of Human Rights: Collected Courses of the Academy of European Law* (OUP 2018) forthcoming.

[7] The debate does not need recounting here. A recent and coherent account of the view I am here calling 'realist', though the author is not 'realist' in the usual sense, is Joseph Raz, 'Human Rights Without Foundations' in Samantha Besson and John Tasoulias (eds), *The Philosophy of International Law* (OUP 2010) 321.

in the present inquiry—do not approach the *existence* of rights in this way: rights are explicitly affirmed as inherent and universal, rather than a consequence of formal law. That is to say, if we must adhere to formal readings of the law to discover 'human rights', our positive source texts themselves point up a non-positivist source for the rights they ultimately aim to secure. The human rights of the Covenants pre-exist them not as a matter of empirical fact, but as a matter of performative self-definition. Second, although the hard law of the Covenants falls some way short of fulfilling the promise of their own preambles, it nevertheless adopts a normative, rather than a descriptive, approach to the *ubi ius* principle: a lack of remedy indicates not a lack of right but rather an imperative to institute remedy. This imperative is explicit in the Covenants and has long driven the 'human rights movement'. From this perspective, all rights are, in the Covenants, 'progressively realized'. Third, in the particular context of climate change, to take such a 'realist' approach to human rights would largely miss the point. This is because the risk climate change poses for human rights is precisely that *nominal* abstract rights—rights said to exist even while awaiting a legal apparatus to 'fulfil' them—seem at risk of disappearing altogether due to the increasing intractability of the remedial deficit. In conditions of climate change, we can, in short, expect very many human rights to enter a trajectory of *progressive deterioration*, becoming ever less concrete or realizable. The fact that this deterioration takes place in such a way that our legal apparatus struggles even to notice formal 'rights violations' is less important than the substantive shrinkage of the space of human rights. For this reason we might regard climate change as an existential challenge to our existing human rights imaginary.

My second rhetorical stance follows the first: climate change affects—that is, 'impacts upon'—nominal human rights, understood in this sense. This *is* a matter of empirical fact: phenomena associated with man-made ('anthropogenic') climate change have and will have material impacts on millions of people's daily lives. Extensive basic goods are at risk for very many people—food, water, shelter, health, livelihoods, and even life itself—due both to extreme weather events, such as hurricanes, floods, and heat waves, and to more gradual changes to local environments, such as sea-level rise, coastal erosion, increases in the numbers or range of vector-disease carrying insects, and the disappearance of staple crops.[8] At the present rate at which world greenhouse gas (GHG) emissions are increasing—as they continue to do year on year—the world will have warmed by more than 4°C above preindustrial temperatures well before 2100.[9] At that temperature, according to reports published

[8] In climate literature, these two types of event are known as 'sudden-onset' and 'slow-onset', respectively. For detailed accounts, see 'Summaries, Frequently Asked Questions, and Cross-Chapter Boxes, A Contribution of Working Group II to the Fifth Assessment Report of the Intergovernmental Panel on Climate Change' in Christopher B Field and others (eds), *Climate Change 2014: Impacts, Adaptation and Vulnerability* (IPCC 2015) (hereafter Field, *AR5*). See also the series of reports commissioned by the World Bank and authored by the Potsdam Institute for Climate Impact Research and Climate Analytics (hereafter Potsdam Institute) entitled *Turn Down the Heat* (<www.worldbank.org/en/topic/climatechange/publication/turn-down-the-heat> accessed 14 November 2015) (hereafter the *Turn Down the Heat* series).

[9] Potsdam Institute, *Turn Down the Heat: Confronting the New Climate Normal* (vol 3, 2014) <https://openknowledge.worldbank.org/bitstream/handle/10986/20595/9781464804373.

by the World Bank, the world—and particularly the tropics—will regularly undergo heat-waves of a frequency, magnitude, and duration beyond anything experienced to date.[10] This expected outcome would barely be dented if all the climate policies currently tabled by the world's governments were to be fulfilled.[11] The formal Paris targets of 1.5–2°C are, in the meantime, extremely ambitious, given growing world populations and the scale of developmental needs (themselves re-describable as human rights) that must be met even as greenhouse emissions are sharply cut.[12] It is worth pointing out that, at time of writing, it is not known whether this can be done—the required technologies remain unproven.[13] Climate change thus presents much of the world with an invidious choice between the horrors of extreme climate impacts as against locked-in conditions of poverty and economic inequity. The first of these are already being felt. The second too, of course—the threat of climate change is that the horizon of eventual relief may now be receding.

These shocks are tangible whether or not we articulate them as 'human rights'-related. They can be articulated in human rights terms in part because they are ascribable to human activities (as opposed to being mere effects of 'nature').[14] This is not straightforward, of course. But if we accept the articulation of human rights found in the Covenants, we are constrained, I think, to accept this basic point: phenomena associated with climate change affect the enjoyment of the human rights enumerated in the Covenants. This is already happening and it will get much worse.

Third, climate change is, in a literal sense, a 'global' problem, one that in certain important respects is unimpressed by the territorial borders of the world. In the particular case of climate change, the (natural) borderlessness of the world is especially invidious: climate change is not typical of 'transboundary harm' as we have come to

pdf?sequence=3&isAllowed=y> accessed 4 April 2017, 4–5. This is based on a sample of 114 scenarios, collectively predicting 'a warming of 4.0–5.2°C above pre-industrial levels by 2100' (4), with most expecting 4°C by the 2080s (5).

[10] 'Projections for a 4°C world show a dramatic increase in the intensity and frequency of high-temperature extremes. Recent extreme heat waves such as in Russia in 2010 [killing 10,000 persons] are likely to become the new normal summer in a 4°C world. Tropical South America, central Africa, and all tropical islands in the Pacific are likely to regularly experience heat waves of unprecedented magnitude and duration. . . . In regions such as the Mediterranean, North Africa, the Middle East, and the Tibetan plateau, almost all summer months are likely to be warmer than the most extreme heat waves presently experienced' Potsdam Institute, *Turn Down the Heat: Why a 4°C Warmer World Must Be Avoided* (vol 1, 2012) <http://documents.worldbank.org/curated/en/865571468149107611/pdf/NonAsciiFileName0.pdf> accessed 3 April 2017, xv.

[11] Climate Action Tracker predicts a rise of 3.6°C were current policies (as opposed to promises) fulfilled. See Louise Jeffery and others, 'Climate Action Tracker Update: 2.7°C is Not Enough: We Can Get Lower' (Climate Action Tracker 2015) <http://tinyurl.com/zuzzqgl> accessed 27 June 2016, 6.

[12] Detlef P van Vuuren and others, 'RCP2.6: Exploring the Possibility to Keep Global Mean Temperature Increase Below 2°C' (2011) 109 Climatic Change 95–116.

[13] ibid.

[14] See the discussion in Judith N Shklar, *Faces of Injustice* (Yale University Press 1994) 2–3, where she notes that human responsibility also arises where there is a mere failure to predict, or protect against, natural disasters. Arguably, in conditions of climate change, the distinction between 'nature' and 'the human' assumed by Shklar has become increasingly fuzzy: earthquakes and tsunamis aside, the destructive force of very many natural phenomena (floods, storms, droughts, and hurricanes) are partly attributable to human activity. See Christopher B Field and others (eds), *Managing the Risks of Extreme Events and Disasters to Advance Climate Change Adaptation: Special Report of the IPCC* (CUP 2012).

understand the term; nor is it an obvious exercise of (executive) extraterritorial jurisdiction. It does not conform straightforwardly to the model of actions undertaken in or by one State with consequences in or for another. The causal chain is rather more complex than that familiar model implies: acts undertaken by myriad individuals in lots of States alter gas concentration levels at atmospheric (and so planetary) level, which in turn result in local-level changes that vary according to conditions that are—politically and legally, at least—quite unrelated to the locus of any particular emission of gases.[15] We can probably bracket much of this complexity for purposes of what is sometimes called 'general international law', but the problem is of particular relevance to international human rights law. The transboundary locus of climate change has generally been articulated as raising issues of extraterritorial jurisdiction under human rights law, but this may not be the most sensible, or accurate, way to approach it. I will discuss this too presently; for now it is enough to flag its centrality to any attempt to think through the relevance of the Covenants to climate change.

Those three moves in view, following this introduction (Section I), I will undertake to examine the language of the Covenants in the light of climate change, with a particular focus on the framing language of the preambles (Section II), the notion of 'self-determination' in common article 1 (Section III), the notion of jurisdiction in respective articles 2 (Section IV), and the question of derogation and limitation in respective articles 4 and common article 5 (Section V). In the light of this discussion, I will then pose the question of the relevance of the Covenants to climate change more broadly in my conclusion (Section VI).

II. Preambles to the Covenants

Although the preambles of the two Covenants are not identical, most of the text of each is common to both. Relevant excerpts follow:

Considering that … recognition of … the equal and inalienable rights of all members of the human family is the foundation of freedom, justice and peace in the world …

… these rights derive from the inherent dignity of the human person …

… the ideal of free human beings enjoying [civil and political freedom and][16] *freedom from fear and want can only be achieved if conditions are created whereby everyone may enjoy his [civil and political rights, as well as his economic, social and cultural rights]*[17] …

Considering the obligation of States under the Charter of the United Nations to promote universal respect for, and observance of, human rights and freedoms,

[15] The most succinct and authoritative account of climate science is provided in the Summary for Policymakers of successive IPCC reports, the most recent being Rajendra K Pachauri and others, *Climate Change 2014: Synthesis Report, Contribution of Working Groups I, II and III to the Fifth Assessment Report of the Intergovernmental Panel on Climate Change* (IPCC 2014) (especially the 'Summary for Policymakers', 2 ff).

[16] This clause is absent from the ICESCR.

[17] This clause is reversed in the ICESCR.

> *... the individual, having duties to other individuals and to the community to which he belongs, is under a responsibility to strive for the promotion and observance of the rights recognized in the present Covenant ...*

In the grounding register of contemporary human rights, they are 'equal' and 'inalienable' and derive from the 'inherent dignity' of the human person. These words are so familiar, indeed, that it is easy to forget how odd is the claim put forward here. Human rights are said to pre-exist the legal or institutional machinery required to frame or fulfil them. They are pre-political (equality), pre-economic (inalienable), and pre-personal (inherent). Most surprisingly of all, they are ahistorical. Human rights, as proclaimed in the Covenants, have not been won or earned. They are a prize neither of political struggle nor of what, a mere decade earlier, would still have been called, without embarrassment, the 'progress of civilization'. They owe their existence neither to the evolution of political institutions nor to any particular legal culture. They are simply there, 'natural': rights inherent to an entity found in nature, within whom they were, presumably, discovered.

There is, I think, only a mild irony in noticing that this ahistoricism and apoliticism were symptomatic of the particular time in which the Covenants were drafted and signed. At the height of the Cold War, and with colonialism collapsing apace, reference to *any* history—not to mention a politics, a 'civilization', a legal 'culture', global or local—could not have achieved universal assent. The preambles amounted to a great statement of global agreement, despite discord on just about everything else. In the particular (that is, historically contingent) context of the Covenants, the ahistoricism and apoliticism of human rights is thus, presumably, neither conjecture, conclusion, nor error, but strategy. Procedurally—and in this the Covenants repeat the war-superseding strategies of the Universal Declaration of Human Rights (UDHR)[18] and indeed the UN Charter itself[19]—they aim to achieve universalism by fiat: here are some basics on which we can all agree, even in a divided world; we *recognize* them as universal *because* we have proclaimed it so. Substantively, this universalism appears intended as a bulwark *against* history and politics. In history, in politics, human rights are frequently, repeatedly, rescinded or put into doubt. It is the point of the Covenants to stand against the tide of history and remove any doubt: human rights *are* equal, inalienable, inherent. This is a heroic effort at legislation: determining not merely what the law is to be, but what the human subject of the law too is—as a matter of simple (albeit legislated) fact.

(In climate change law, by contrast, many of these elements appear in inverse. Climate change itself is, of course, a historical, a political, an economic, possibly even a cultural phenomenon. But it is also a social error, a market failure. It is, in fact, just the sort of development the Covenants might have been designed to anticipate—a historical event that threatens ahistorical rights. In consequence, the universalism of climate change law is profoundly contingent—a series of steps and

[18] Universal Declaration of Human Rights (UDHR) (adopted 10 December 1948) UNGA (United Nations General Assembly) Res 217 A(III).

[19] Charter of the United Nations and Statute of the International Court of Justice (UN Charter) (opened for signature 26 June 1945, entered into force 24 October 1945) 1 UNTS XVI.

targets and ratchets designed to move us (all humanity!) from contagious instability into a mode of 'stabilization'. Climate change affects everyone everywhere, but not equally. In climate law, humanity appears rather as survivors on a life-raft, learning how to overcome the consequences of our hubris, than autonomous carriers of the noble 'human' spirit.)

That presumed noble human spirit drives the Covenants, however, whose preambles, like the UDHR itself, 'found' 'freedom, justice and peace' in the world on 'recognition' of this fact—that is, of the inherent equality and inalienability of human rights. The whole construction is very much more abstract than the frankly concrete statement of purpose opening the UN Charter: 'to save succeeding generations from the scourge of war, which twice in our lifetime has brought untold sorrow to mankind'. At the same time, it is difficult to understand broad appeals to 'social progress' and 'development' in the Charter and in countless subsequent international instruments—including, for that matter, the UNFCCC ('social and economic development and poverty eradication')—without an appeal to something like an inherent and universal equality of humankind. It is presumably this bald claim to a foundational status that gives the UDHR and the Covenants their privileged place in the rhetoric of international law. Similar demands have come to litter UN documents; and while they are not always articulated as human rights claims, there exists an undeniable consonance—or even identity—between 'progress', 'development', and 'human rights'. In the rhetorical universe of the United Nations, the pursuit of these goals characterizes the legitimate State.

Human 'freedom', according to the Covenants, will 'only be achieved' if 'conditions are created whereby everyone may enjoy' their rights. This looks like a restatement of article 28 of the UDHR: 'Everyone is entitled to a social and international order in which [their] rights and freedoms ... can be fully realized.' Like article 28, the preambular language looks beyond the autonomous territorial State, apparently to a community of States in the service of a universal human subject. The preambles apparently assume an obligation on States proactively to 'create' conditions for the flourishing of human rights. And yet, the only obligation concretely stated therein repeats the Charter's own mild exhortation to 'promote universal respect for, and observance of, human rights and freedoms'. The term 'universal' works hard in this formula to return some of the heft apparently abandoned by the word 'promote'. But still, it is thin gruel.

It may therefore seem reasonable to read the preambles as assuming, at a minimum, a *negative* obligation on States not to disrupt the international 'conditions' in which substantive human rights can be 'enjoyed' by 'everyone'. By the same token, should something disturb the 'equality' of rights (by rendering one person's rights more vulnerable than another's) or their inalienability (by removing a right altogether, or rendering it removable) it must also presumably alter the conditions of possibility of human rights protection. Anthropogenic climate change would then seem to be the sort of thing States are expected, even required, to avoid.

However, it is hard not to conclude, especially in light of the substantive provisions in Part III of both Covenants, that these preambles mark a shift *away* from the 'social and international order' language of the UDHR. They say nothing about what international 'conditions' for the enjoyment of human rights might be or how they might be established. This gap is of course familiar across a range of international problems: 'global poverty'; the externalities (to adopt a widely used euphemism) of international trade and of financial speculation; and 'business and human rights'. How to iron out the often-remarked mismatch between soaring global rhetoric and its persistent flouting?

Climate change revives this problem in even starker terms: the 'international conditions' for the fulfilment of human rights are worsening. Many millions are finding their human rights less available for 'enjoyment'. And some are more vulnerable than others to human rights threats or to their loss altogether.

III. Common Article 1 (Self-determination)

> *1. All peoples have the right of self-determination. By virtue of that right they freely determine their political status and freely pursue their economic, social and cultural development.*
>
> *2. All peoples may, for their own ends, freely dispose of their natural wealth and resources without prejudice to any obligations arising out of international economic co-operation, based upon the principle of mutual benefit, and international law. In no case may a people be deprived of its own means of subsistence.*

The notion of 'self-determination' in international law has undergone significant evolution since the Covenants were signed, in well-known developments that began long before their signature.[20] Legal discussion of self-determination has mainly had to do with decolonization and the preservation of borders.[21] It is interesting to notice, however, that the specific articulation of this 'right' in the Covenants has relatively little to say about either. Of much greater importance to the drafters, apparently, was the question of control over 'natural wealth and resources' as well as 'economic, social and cultural development'—elements that have received much less attention in the literature.[22]

[20] 'Self-determination' in international law is of course traceable back to the League of Nations and reappears as one of the 'purposes' of the UN Charter, art 1(2). The key development—the UN Declaration on the Granting of Independence to Colonial Countries and Peoples, UNGA Res 1514 (XV) (14 December 1960) (adopted by eighty-nine votes to none; nine abstentions)—triggered an evolution that takes place in parallel to, and certainly informs, that of the Covenants. See in particular Karen Knop, *Diversity and Self-Determination in International Law* (CUP 2008) chs 1–3.

[21] The key case law comprises the ICJ opinions on Western Sahara (*Western Sahara* (Advisory Opinion) [1975] ICJ Rep 12); the Palestinian Wall (*Legal Consequences of the Construction of a Wall in the Occupied Palestinian Territory* (Advisory Opinion) [2004] ICJ Rep 136); South Africa/Namibia (*Legal Consequences for States of the Continued Presence of South Africa in Namibia (South West Africa), notwithstanding Security Council Resolution 276 (1970)* (Advisory Opinion) [1971] ICJ Rep 12); and Kosovo (*Accordance with International Law of the Unilateral Declaration of Independence in Respect of Kosovo* (Advisory Opinion) [2010] ICJ Rep 403); and the ICJ's rulings in a number of boundary disputes.

[22] So, eg two recent major contributions on the topic essentially restrict discussion to the 'political' issues of secession and border control, largely avoiding or ignoring the questions of 'economic' self-determination. See the contributions to Fernando R Tesón (ed), *The Theory of Self-Determination* (CUP 2016) and Jörg Fisch, *The Right of Self-Determination of Peoples: The Domestication of an Illusion* (CUP 2015). The question is also raised with regard to indigenous rights and also the new prevalence

It is true that self-determination in this domain—as in the case of 'political status'—might amount to no more than the absence of 'alien subjugation, domination and exploitation' (as it is put elsewhere)[23] or to the presence of some basic institutional mechanisms of public consultation, such as democratic elections, public 'consultation' or 'participation', or 'free, prior and informed consent'.[24] But the insistence of article 1(2), in particular, would seem to point beyond this reading. '*[F]or their own ends*', 'their natural wealth and resources', a people's 'own means of subsistence': this persistent language of *ownership* is unmistakably consonant with the various expressions of 'permanent sovereignty over natural resources' (PSNR) that flourished over this same period.[25] That language was concerned not primarily with the mechanics of freedom from colonial rule itself, but with the political realities of *post*-colonial independence. The various declarations and statements about 'permanent sovereignty' rarely innovate legally, but rather—at a time (the 1950s) when the old Powers repeatedly intervened, politically and militarily (in Iran, in Egypt), to preserve privileged access to the world's natural resources—they reassert the legalist principle of sovereignty in a realist post-colonial context.[26]

The references to 'international economic cooperation' and 'mutual benefit' further emphasise this point: at issue here is the relationship between international demand for primary commodities, on which many postcolonial states were dependent, on one hand, and local needs (or 'ends'), on the other. But at what point would foreign acquisition of a people's 'natural wealth' constitute breach? The answer must presumably lie in indicators as to whether the 'people' in question 'freely disposed' of it. What might constitute such indicators? Endemic poverty? Chronic energy shortages? Whether the proceeds from exported natural resources remain solely or primarily in private hands? Whether they were inadequately taxed or contributed little to local revenues? These are in fact the sorts of questions the Committee on

of 'land-grabs', notably in Africa (itself in part a policy response to climate change). See eg Olivier De Schutter, Special Rapporteur on the Right to Adequate Food, 'Large-scale Land Acquisitions and Leases: A Set of Core Principles and Measures to Address the Human Rights Challenge' (11 June 2009) 12. See too Leif Wenar, *Blood Oil* (OUP 2016).

[23] UN Declaration on the Granting of Independence (n 20) para 1: 'The subjection of peoples to alien subjugation, domination and exploitation constitutes a denial of fundamental human rights'. See, for a later iteration, Protocol Additional to the Geneva Conventions of 12 August 1949, and Relating to the Protection of Victims of International Armed Conflicts (Protocol I) (opened for signature 8 June 1977, entered into force 7 December 1978) 1125 UNTS 3, art 1(4), bestowing legitimacy on armed conflicts against 'colonial domination and alien occupation and against racist régimes in the exercise of [the] right of self-determination'.

[24] ICCPR art 21, and the UN Declaration on the Rights of Indigenous Peoples (UNGA Res 61/295 (13 September 2007) UN Doc A/RES/61/295), respectively. See the discussion in the *Quebec* case (Supreme Court of Canada, *Reference re Secession of Quebec*, 37 ILM 1340 (1998)).

[25] See UNGA, 'Recommendations Concerning International Respect for the Rights of Peoples and Nations to Self-determination' UN GAOR 9th Session Supp No 18 UN Doc A/4090 (1954) 27: 'the right of peoples and nations to self-determination as affirmed in the two draft Covenants completed by the Commission on Human Rights includes "permanent sovereignty over their natural wealth and resources"'. See also Nico Schrijver, *Sovereignty over Natural Resources: Balancing Rights and Duties* (CUP 2008) especially 49–56 and 134–42.

[26] See the contributions to the special issue 6(1) of *Humanity* journal (2015) on the New International Economic Order.

Economic, Social and Cultural Rights might pose to States.[27] In practice, however, poverty, energy shortages, and capital flight remain common in many resource-rich developing countries—whereas violation of the right of self-determination is rarely invoked (indeed, the precise wording of article 1(2) is slippery on just this point).[28]

Revisited from the perspective of climate change, further wrinkles arise. It turns out that, under colonialism, the old powers were not merely helping themselves to the world's resource wealth; they were also exhausting the world's carbon dump.[29] Only as it has gradually become clear that the global capacity to absorb carbon is sharply limited has the global carbon dump itself become cognizable as a 'natural resource'. Indeed, it is arguably the quintessential natural resource—for, absent significant technological progress not yet seen, it remains the basic requisite for 'social and economic development'. 'Free disposition' over a notional 'national' carbon dump is, of course, precisely what is at stake in the discussions seeking reduction of greenhouse gas emissions under the UNFCCC.[30] But absent strong universal binding targets that preserve sufficient carbon space for all (an unlikely scenario), the developmental space—the carbon dump—of very many countries in the world is currently being swallowed up by a handful of high-emitting States.[31]

Moreover, a direct result of this over-ingestion of the natural resources supposedly belonging to certain 'peoples' (for that is the implication of articles 1(2) and 1(3)), is that many of those same peoples are beginning to suffer the effects of climate change: the floods, droughts, conflicts, and myriad other harms that attend it. That is, the 'peoples' in much of the world are losing the capacity to predict, much less control, the environment in which they live and work. For this reason, control over the carbon dump may be thought of as a *sine qua non* of any right of self-determination, whether conceived in the sense of actually 'disposing' over one's 'national' wealth, or in the much weaker sense of simply being able to predict the conditions in which life will be lived in the foreseeable future. Here the UNFCCC's distinction between 'developed' and 'developing' countries bites, for a principal marker of a 'developed' country is its greater resource-ability to predict and adapt to phenomena such as those associated with climate change.

As a general matter, to agree—for the purposes of managing climate change—not to dispose of certain resources at all (such as forests, coal, or oil), would look like a

[27] My thanks to Olivier de Schutter for clarifying this point.

[28] A breach may be more evident in the context of other, more quantifiable, human rights harms, such as a 'people' dwelling in proximity to a source of 'natural wealth' who experience systematic violations of human rights associated with its extraction. See African Commission on Human and Peoples' Rights, *The Social and Economic Rights Action Center and the Center for Economic and Social Rights v Nigeria*, Communication 155/96, 27 May 2002, paras 55–59.

[29] I take the term 'global carbon dump' from Larry Lohmann, *Carbon Trading: A Critical Conversation on Climate Change, Privatisation and Power* (CornerHouse 2006).

[30] An early articulation of the relevant stakes is provided in Henry Shue, 'Subsistence Emissions and Luxury Emissions' (1993) 15 L & Policy 39.

[31] Again, the point was clarified early on: Anil Agarwal and Sunita Narain, *Global Warming in an Unequal World: A Case of Environmental Colonialism* (Centre for Science and Environment 1990). For recent comparative figures of per capita greenhouse gas emissions by country, see World Resources Institute, 'CAIT Country Greenhouse Gas Emissions Data' <www.wri.org/resources/data-sets/cait-country-greenhouse-gas-emissions-data> accessed 29 January 2016.

voluntary abrogation of the right of self-determination ('inalienable' though it may remain).[32] That in view, the right to 'freely dispose' of one's natural resources 'for [one's] own ends' presumably dovetails with the principle of 'common but differentiated responsibilities' (CBDR) found in the UNFCCC (art 3(1)).[33] On this principle, 'developing countries' have lesser obligations to address climate change than 'developed' countries—although the criteria for distinguishing between these two groups are increasingly unclear.[34] So if the relevant people's 'ends' were especially pressing—and this is of course the whole point of the term 'developing country'—the Covenants' article 1(2) would presumably buttress CBDR and cognate elements of the climate regime.[35] Indeed, with their reference to the 'free disposal' of natural resources, the Covenants arguably add a more explicitly political dimension to the UNFCCC's technocratic and developmentalist language.

Although no claim based on article 1(2) has (to my knowledge) been raised in the climate context (whereas the broader question of self-determination has been discussed),[36] it seems correct to assume that its PSNR charge may exert a certain magnetism over the final shape of the climate regime. The UNFCCC itself hints at this in its preamble, in which it is 'recalled' that 'States have, in accordance with the Charter of the United Nations and the principles of international law, the sovereign right to exploit their own resources pursuant to their own environmental and developmental policies'. This 'right' is coupled, in the same paragraph, with 'the responsibility to ensure that activities within their jurisdiction or control do not cause damage to the environment of other States or of areas beyond the limits of national jurisdiction'. That this coupling takes the form of a balancing of rights and responsibilities seems

[32] Such agreements inform the 'nationally determined contributions' States must submit in accordance with the 2015 Paris Agreement (opened for signature 12 December 2015, entered into force 4 November 2016) art 4.

[33] This key principle ensured that only wealthy countries took on binding targets in the UNFCCC's Kyoto Protocol (Kyoto Protocol to the United Nations Framework Convention on Climate Change (11 December 1997, entered into force 16 February 2005) 2303 UNTS 162). Despite coming under attack, the principle remains in the Paris Agreement, signed in December 2015. All countries now undertake to act on climate change (through 'nationally determined contributions' (NDCs)), but the Agreement recognises developing countries' special need for continued development space.

[34] The UNFCCC itself and the Kyoto Protocol both included Annexes listing putative 'developed' countries—though the residual status of 'developing countries' was not altogether clear. The Paris Agreement includes no annexes; though the term remains central to the Agreement, its precise scope is speculative.

[35] Such as UNFCCC art 4(7), which recognizes that 'economic and social development and poverty eradication are the first and overriding priorities of the developing country Parties'. Though this language is not repeated in the Paris Agreement, it is honoured to a degree in repeated references to 'sustainable development and poverty eradication' (not that this is any clearer).

[36] See eg 'Understanding Human Rights and Climate Change, Submission of the Office of the High Commissioner for Human Rights to the 21st Conference of the Parties to the United Nations Framework Convention on Climate Change' (26 November 2015) <www.ohchr.org/Documents/Issues/ClimateChange/COP21.pdf> accessed 30 June 2016, 14. Self-determination in the context of climate change has been raised in reports and statements of the Office of High Commissioner for Human Rights and of its Special Procedures since about 2008, but the emphasis has generally remained on the 'political' question, particularly in light of sinking island States. See too, in this context, Susannah Willcox, 'A Rising Tide: The Implications of Climate Change Inundation for Human Rights and State Sovereignty' (2012) 9 Essex Human Rights Rev 1–19.

self-evident in the early formulation from which the UNFCCC language is lifted (Principle 21 of the 1972 Stockholm Declaration on the Human Environment).[37] However, in the context of climate change, it is far from obvious that 'balancing' is likely to be at issue here. Fossil fuels—which are far and away the primary driver of climate change—trade as international commodities, so the locus of 'belonging' in the PSNR sense and the locus of any harm-doing (ie where oil and coal are actually burned and emit carbon) are not necessarily, or even generally, the same. The 'right' and the 'responsibility' bifurcate. (Deforestation presents a less stark example of this same phenomenon insofar as much timber is produced primarily for export markets). Indeed, for the great majority of developing States voluntarily relinquishing their art 1(2) PSNR rights in the Paris context (by agreeing to mitigation measures) there is in fact no balancing 'responsibility' that would require them to do so. To this day, the world's forty-eight 'least developed countries' are not net contributors to climate change.[38] One would therefore expect art 1(2) to support a stronger form of CBDR than that found in the Paris Agreement.

A final interesting element of common article 1, from a climate perspective, is the proviso that '[i]n no case may a people be deprived of its own means of subsistence.' Much hangs on the word 'own' in this sentence. The article seems to articulate an assumption that 'peoples' actively 'own' their means of subsistence, but of course this is generally not the case. Common ownership—which this would seem to imply—is exceedingly rare, especially for resources needed for 'subsistence', such as forests, soil, food, and water.[39] Insofar as there is 'public' (rather than common) ownership in these resources (such as forests, rivers, and parks), they are generally off bounds for 'subsistence' (though not always). For the most part, however, 'means of subsistence' today refers to participation in a labour force providing the wherewithal to buy essentials on an open market—that is, from other owners, who need not be 'the people' and may well be (and often are in fact) foreign.

Still, however we understand it, climate change impinges directly on this element of the right of self-determination. To take the obvious point first: species extinction, drought, or the disappearance of locally-adapted crops: each of these would appear to pose a loss of the means of subsistence for some, whether or not the means reside in some form of communal ownership or are obtained through wage labour. The loss would presumably be, in many cases, to a 'people', because effects of this nature will tend to impact upon regions, rather than localities. The loss will amount to a

[37] Declaration of the UN Conference on the Human Environment (16 June 1972) UN Doc A/Conf.48/14/Rev.1, 11 ILM 1416 (1972).

[38] A thorough account of the relative contribution of different countries is provided in Paul Baer and others, *Greenhouse Development Rights: The Right to Development in a Climate Constrained World* (2nd edn, Heinrich Böll Foundation and others 2009). More recent, though less nuanced, information can be found on the website of the Climate Action Tracker (<http://climateactiontracker.org/countries.html> accessed 20 June 2016).

[39] Jona Razzaque, 'Natural Resources in the Global Environmental Order' in Elena Blanco and Jona Razzaque (eds), *Natural Resources and the Green Economy* (Martinus Nijhoff 2012) 82–111, 87–90; Emeka Duruigbo, 'Realizing the People's Right to Natural Resources' (2011) 12 Whitehead J of Diplomatic & International Relations 111; Emeka Diruigbo, 'Permanent Sovereignty and Peoples' Ownership of Natural Resources' (2006) 38 The George Washington Intl L Rev 33.

'deprivation' because it presumably would not have happened had the major GHG emitters desisted from the actions causing these outcomes. By the same token, their right of self-determination has been arguably violated.[40] This will also be the case where forest-dwelling peoples, for example, may be prohibited the use of forests in order to preserve them through REDD+ programmes.[41] The difficulty with each of these apparently self-evident positions is that there has been neither case law supporting claims of this sort since the Covenants' entry into force, nor much evidence of a State practice interpreting article 1 in a way that would assume that 'peoples' dispose of 'their' natural resources in this manner. Where there is such State practice, as in the case of Norway's sovereign fund for managing its oil wealth, there is little sign that it derives from an understanding of Covenant obligations.

IV. Jurisdiction (Articles 2)

The two Covenants feature differing articles 2. I will take them in turn, with the ICCPR followed by the ICESCR and then by a comparative note.

A. Article 2 of the ICCPR

ICCPR Article 2 raises a number of flags from the perspective of climate change. First, and perhaps most important, is the jurisdictional clause. Each State is to guarantee the rights recognized in the ICCPR to 'all individuals within its territory and subject to its jurisdiction' (art 2(1)). The immediate and obvious point is that, where excess GHG emissions in one State contribute to harms experienced in a second State, individuals affected in the second State cannot expect, on the wording of the Covenant, that their affected human rights are protected by the emitting State, as they are neither 'within its territory' nor 'subject to its jurisdiction'.

This would not be the case were we to interpret the actual effect of excess GHG emission to be a form of 'subjecting' individuals to the jurisdiction of the emitting State. At its extreme, such a position would amount, in effect, to asserting that excess GHG emissions in any given State subject everyone everywhere to the jurisdiction of the emitting State.[42] In a more modest form, it might be claimed that individuals

[40] The point is addressed explicitly in the 2009 report of the UN High Commissioner for Human Rights on human rights and climate change (UNGA 'Report of the Office of the United Nations High Commissioner for Human Rights on the Relationship between Climate Change and Human Rights' (15 January 2009) UN Doc A/HRC/10/61, para 40) (my thanks to Olivier de Schutter for reminding me of this source).

[41] United Nations Programme on Reducing Emissions from Deforestation and Forest Degradation (UN-REDD Programme) 'Guidelines on Free, Prior and Informed Consent' (January 2013) <www.unccleearn.org/sites/default/files/inventory/un-redd05.pdf> accessed 4 April 2017. See too UNGA 'Report of the Special Rapporteur on Extreme Poverty and Human Rights, Magdalena Sepulveda Carmona' (22 May 2014) UN Doc A/HRC/26/28, para 18.

[42] This is because specific emissions, rather than contributing in a linear manner to specific climate related events, contribute to the overarching phenomenon of climate change itself, which does, of course, affect everyone everywhere.

are subjected to the State's jurisdiction (let us say the State's 'executive jurisdiction') only insofar as they are actually *harmed* by climate change related phenomena, attributable in turn to (excess) emissions from within a given State. Since not all States are equally responsible for harmful emissions, this would imply a hierarchy of responsibility. Such an assertion throws up a number of challenges.[43] Focusing on jurisdiction, for the moment, the claim is a version of the 'authority and control' reasoning contained in some jurisprudence produced by the Inter-American and European human rights institutions from the mid-1990s, which implies that someone affected by the actions of a given State comes within its 'authority and control' (and so is subject to its jurisdiction) for that reason alone.[44]

An argument in essentially this form was famously rejected by the Grand Chamber of the European Court of Human Rights in the 2001 *Banković* case, at the admissibility phase, where it held that 'the applicants' submission is tantamount to arguing that anyone adversely affected by an act imputable to a Contracting State, wherever in the world that act may have been committed or its consequences felt, is thereby brought within the jurisdiction of that State'.[45] The statement (which does not characterize the *Banković* situation at all well) could have been tailored to the climate problem. At issue in *Banković* was whether NATO States had human rights obligations towards individuals killed when missiles were fired on a radio tower in Belgrade. The *Banković* ruling relied in part on the notion that the European Convention on Human Rights (ECHR)[46] only applied within a specific '*éspace juridique*'—the territory of signatory parties (not including Serbia)—within which alone Convention rights extended.[47] This is an idea that the Court appears to have rejected or at least de-emphasized in its subsequent jurisprudence, notably *Al-Skeini v United Kingdom*.[48] In that case, the Court ruled that States enjoy human rights

[43] Two principal challenges present themselves. First, such a test requires a threshold of 'excess' emissions, which could only be arrived at on a State-by-State basis. However, this is no longer excessively complex, given the state of climate science. A Dutch court, in the *Urgenda* ruling, turned to the authority of the IPCC to establish a desirable minimum rate of emission reduction (*Urgenda Foundation v the State of the Netherlands*, C/09/456689/HA ZA 13-1396, Judgment of 24 June 2015). A somewhat similar approach had been adopted by the European Committee on Social Rights (ECSR) in 2006, which found against Greece on the basis that its own national plans expected lower emission reductions than Greece's commitments under the Kyoto Protocol required (see ECSR, *Marangopoulos Foundation for Human Rights v Greece*, Collective Complaint No 30/2005, 6 December 2006 (my thanks to Olivier de Schutter for drawing my attention to this case)). Second, there is the need to establish a causal link between the harms suffered by an individual and the emissions of a State.

[44] *Coard v United States*, Inter-American Commission on Human Rights Report No 109/99 (29 September 1999); *Alejandro v Cuba*, Inter-American Commission on Human Rights Report No 86/99 (29 September 1999) para 25; *Loizidou v Turkey* (Preliminary Objections) App no 15318/89 (ECtHR, 23 March 1995); *Issa and Others v Turkey* App no 31821/96 (ECtHR, 16 November 2004).

[45] Decision as to the admissibility in the case of *Banković and Others v Belgium and 16 Other Contracting States* App no 52207/99 (ECtHR, 12 December 2001) para 75. See also para 52. According to the Court, 'the text of Article 1 [the equivalent of ICCPR art 2(1)] does not accommodate such an approach to "jurisdiction".'

[46] Convention for the Protection of Human Rights and Fundamental Freedoms (European Convention on Human Rights, as amended) (ECHR).

[47] *Banković v Belgium* (n 45) para 80. The idea is first mooted in *Loizidou v Turkey* (n 44) para 78.

[48] *Al-Skeini and Others v United Kingdom* App no 55721/07 (ECtHR, Judgment of 7 July 2011) para 142.

jurisdiction wherever they exercise 'public powers', a notion that appears to indicate effective control over affected persons or spaces—in situations of occupation or detention, for example—regardless of specific geographical locus.[49] Climate change harms may take place abroad without, of course, any assumption of 'public powers' or 'effective control' in the territories in question. Given the similarity to ICCPR article 2(1) of the relevant jurisdictional language in the ECHR (art 1), it is difficult not to imagine that the same reasoning must apply, *mutatis mutandis*, to the ICCPR.[50] This would also be in keeping with the Human Rights Committee's General Comment on the topic.[51]

It is, then, difficult to argue that the ICCPR expects a given State to 'respect' and 'ensure' the enumerated human rights to individuals who are not on its territory or 'subject to its jurisdiction'—meaning physically present in a space (such as a city, boat, airplane, prison, or camp) over which the State exercises control.[52] Pending further development in the law, the fact that a person in one State suffers or dies due to climate-related events that result in part from the failure of another State to curtail emissions—emissions that unquestionably take place on its territory—seems unlikely in itself to qualify that person as 'subject' to the State's jurisdiction. This does not, of course, imply that State responsibility cannot attach, under international law, for harms caused extraterritorially by emissions on its territory.[53] Nor, equally obviously, does it mean that a State might not have human rights obligations towards individuals on *its own* territory relating to GHG emissions.[54] It simply means that it appears difficult, at present, to conclude that any international law obligations States may have to rein in excess emissions derive from the *Covenant* rights of affected persons in third States.

Ironically, however, the controversial notion of an *éspace juridique*, were it to be applied in the case of the Covenants, *would* presumably extend such protection—since the *éspace juridique* of the Covenants is, in principle, the world as a whole.[55]

[49] ibid para 149.

[50] ECHR art 1: '[t]he High Contracting Parties shall secure to everyone within their jurisdiction the rights and freedoms defined in Section I of this Convention'. In the *travaux*, the words 'to all persons residing in their territory' were replaced with 'to everyone within their jurisdiction' precisely to widen the application from 'residents' to all those present on territory. See *Banković v Belgium* (n 45) para 19.

[51] HRC, 'General Comment 31' in 'Note by the Secretariat, Compilation of General Comments and General Recommendations Adopted by Human Rights Treaty Bodies' (2004) UN Doc HRI/GEN/1/Rev.9 (vol I) para 11.

[52] *Al-Skeini and Others v United Kingdom* (n 48) paras 136–37.

[53] Obvious potential sources of such an obligation are the 'no harm' principle under international environmental law and the UNFCCC itself. See Andrew Strauss, 'Climate Change Litigation: Opening the Door to the International Court of Justice' in William C G Burns and Hari M Osofsky (eds), *Adjudicating Climate Change: State, National, and International Approaches* (CUP 2009); Christina Voigt, 'State Responsibility for Climate Change Damages' (2008) 77 Nordic J of Int L 1.

[54] *Urgenda* (n 43). The human rights claim in this case failed because the Urgenda Foundation, being a legal rather than a natural person, could not itself be a 'victim' of climate harms. See Jolene Lin, 'The First Successful Climate Negligence Case: A Comment on *Urgenda Foundation v The State of the Netherlands*' (2015) University of Hong Kong Faculty of Law Research Paper 2015/021.

[55] See *Banković v Belgium* (n 45) para 80: '[t]he Convention was not designed to be applied throughout the world, even in respect of the conduct of Contracting States'.

I rehearse this well-known debate here because—as that last observation illustrates—it seems plausible that climate change reframes the old question of 'extraterritoriality' in a new light. The harms occasioned by phenomena (whether slow- or rapid-onset) ultimately attributable to climate change are no doubt less immediate and direct than the ill-treatment visited on Iraqi detainees in Basra at issue in the *Al-Skeini* case or the *Banković* missiles. But they are arguably *very much more concrete, foreseeable, and direct* than the harms attributable to, for example, international trade policy or the effects of an apparently uncontrolled and unintended financial crisis.[56] Moreover, while it may seem far-fetched to argue in the abstract that each State has human rights obligations towards 'anyone adversely affected by an act imputable' to that State, it is surely much less far-fetched to seek to end, on human rights grounds, activities within a State that have concrete and traceable human rights effects for thousands or indeed millions of persons. The activities that give rise to climate change have been known to cause harm for at least a quarter of a century—during which time they have actually increased in most States. The harms are concrete. The causal chain, though complex, is uncontroversial. This looks like an open space for judicial activism.[57]

B. Article 2 of the ICESCR

The absence of language in ICESCR article 2 identifying either territorial or jurisdictional scope of application or requiring 'effective remedy' has been extensively discussed.[58] And yet, climate change adds an intriguing dimension to this debate, dovetailing with the apparent requirement of article 2(1) of coordinated 'international assistance and co-operation, especially economic and technical' to achieve 'progressively' the human rights of everyone everywhere.[59] Precisely this emphasis on the inherently *global* nature of the obligation is salient in the context

[56] For an example of the former, see Thomas Pogge, 'Recognized and Violated by International Law: The Human Rights of the Global Poor' (2005) 18 Leiden J of Intl L 717. For an example of the latter, see the discussion at the Office of the High Commissioner for Human Rights <www.ohchr.org/EN/Issues/Development/Pages/PromotingHRbasedfinancialregulationmacroeconomicpolicies.aspx> accessed 1 April 2016.

[57] Various arguments have been raised, relevant to ICCPR art 2(3), as to whether climate change harms are justiciable at all. It is argued, on one hand, that courts are inappropriate fora for policy on issues of such complexity (see eg US District Court for the Ninth Circuit, *Native Village of Kivalina and City of Kivalina v ExxonMobil Corporation et al*, 663 F.Supp.2d 863 (2009), upheld on appeal), and, on the other, that the causal chain from specific emissions to specific harms is too complex and non-linear for the attribution of responsibility. Neither issue has proved insurmountable in practice. See eg US Supreme Court, *Massachusetts et al v Environmental Protection Agency*, 127 S.Ct. 1438, and the Dutch *Urgenda* case (*Urgenda* (n 43)).

[58] UN Doc E/1991/23, CESCR, 'General Comment 3' in 'Note by the Secretariat, Compilation of General Comments and General Recommendations Adopted by Human Rights Treaty Bodies' (1991) HRI/GEN/1/Rev.9 (vol I); Matthew Craven, 'The Domestic Application of the International Covenant on Economic, Social and Cultural Rights' (1993) 40 Netherlands Intl L Rev 367.

[59] Among recent texts raising this question: Olivier De Schutter and others, 'Commentary to the Maastricht Principles on Extraterritorial Obligations of States in the Area of Economic, Social and Cultural Rights' (2012) 34 Human Rights Q 1084; Fons Coomans and Rolf Künnemann (eds), *Cases and Concepts on Extraterritorial Obligations in the Area of Economic, Social and Cultural Rights* (Intersentia 2012); UNGA 'Final Draft of the Guiding Principles on Extreme Poverty and Human Rights, Submitted by the Special Rapporteur on Extreme Poverty and Human Rights, Magdalena

of climate change. It is not alone that the ineluctably transnational nature of climate change—a 'global problem requiring a global solution'—provides an excellent match for the internationalist language of the ICESCR; it is also because ICESCR article 2(1) remarkably echoes language already found in the climate regime, notably the UNFCCC, itself.

In particular, ICESCR article 2(1) fits snugly next to UNFCCC article 4(7), which reads as follows:

> The extent to which developing country Parties will effectively implement their commitments under the Convention will depend on the effective implementation by developed country Parties of their commitments under the Convention related to financial resources and transfer of technology and will take fully into account that economic and social development and poverty eradication are the first and overriding priorities of the developing country Parties.

That article offers concrete examples of 'international assistance and cooperation', citing obligations to provide financial resources and access to technologies, while at the same time prioritizing social and economic rights under a different rubric ('economic and social development and poverty eradication'). Moreover, the UNFCCC distinguishes between rights-bearers ('developing country Parties') and duty-bearers ('developed country Parties'). This has long been a sticking point in the vaguer language of the ICESCR, in which it is far from clear that the reference to 'international assistance and cooperation' creates any rights- or duty-bearers at all.[60]

That said, UNFCCC article 4(7) is hardly crystal clear on this matter. Indeed, one of the striking aspects of the UNFCCC is how many different terms are brought in to qualify States in terms of varying obligations. As well as the defined lists of States in Annexes I and II (and so, by corollary, the implied list of 'non-Annex I' signatories), we also find the terms 'developed', 'developing', and 'least developed' countries. UNFCCC article 4(5)—which is the source of the obligation referred to in article 4(7)—adopts a remarkably slippery formula for the duty-bearers: 'the developed country Parties and other developed Parties included in Annex II'.[61] This appears, on one hand, to draw a distinction between 'developed country parties' and the States listed in Annex II (Annex II lists the countries of Western Europe, the United States, Canada, Japan, Australia, and New Zealand), while, on the other, apparently denying that all Annex II countries are, at a minimum, 'developed'.[62] It

Sepúlveda Carmona' (18 July 2012) UN Doc A/HRC/21/39. Thanks to Olivier de Schutter for reminding me of these developments.

60 CESCR, 'General Comment 3' (n 58) paras 13–14. Also UN Doc. E/1990/23, CESCR, 'General Comment 2' in 'Note by the Secretariat, Compilation of General Comments and General Recommendations Adopted by Human Rights Treaty Bodies' (1990) HRI/GEN/1/Rev.9 (vol II); Sigrun Skogly and Mark Gibney, 'Transnational Human Rights Obligations' (2002) 24(3) Human Rights Q 781.

61 UNFCCC art 4(5): '[t]he developed country Parties and other developed Parties included in Annex II shall take all practicable steps to promote, facilitate and finance, as appropriate, the transfer of, or access to, environmentally sound technologies and know-how to other Parties, particularly developing country Parties.'

62 At the time of signature (1992), a number of Annex II countries were relatively poor: Greece, Ireland, Portugal, and Spain. However, as a signatory in its own right, the wealthy European Economic

seems fair to assume, however, that all Annex II countries are in fact covered, and others may also be, should they be, or become, 'developed'. By the same token, 'developing country parties' is an open-ended formula that creates real difficulties for classifying formally 'developing' States with large internationally-pivoted economies, such as China or Brazil (and India too, though its per capita emissions remain relatively tiny). However, the term must include 'least developed' States at a minimum. The upshot would appear to be a core group of rights-bearers (the forty-seven countries listed by the UN as 'least developed')[63] and of duty-bearers (the twenty-four countries listed in Annex II, plus the European Union).

Naturally, one cannot simply transpose a group of rights- and duty-bearers from one treaty (the UNFCCC) over to another (the ICESCR), reading an obligation into the latter where there is none in the text. Less far-fetched, however, is the suggestion that one might read the language of 'social and economic development and poverty eradication' in the UNFCCC in light of the obligations taken on by the same States in the ICESCR (all parties to the latter are parties to the former, though not vice versa). On one hand, the detailed rights listed in the ICESCR can without difficulty be read as fleshing out the oblique clause in UNFCCC article 4(7). On the other, there is a straightforward confluence between the achievement of these rights as an obligation on all countries (in the ICESCR) and as the 'first and over-riding priority' of developing countries (in the UNFCCC). The obligation in the ICESCR would thereby be grounded within the territory of certain countries, at least when the human rights dimensions of climate change are at issue, rather than abstracted around the world as a whole. And finally, the obligation on 'developed countries' in the UNFCCC to 'promote, facilitate and finance access to and transfer of environmentally sound technologies' arguably fleshes out the reference to 'international assistance and cooperation' in the UNFCCC—being essentially a rare concrete formulation of such assistance in the form of an obligation.

V. Limitation/Derogation (Articles 4 and 5)

A. Common article 4 of the ICCPR and ICESCR

The Covenants' fourth articles differ significantly. The ICCPR famously, if obscurely, invokes threats to 'the life of the nation' as a basis for a 'right of derogation' from certain human rights obligations. The right is circumscribed: derogation must not be inconsistent with 'other obligations under international law', it must not be applied in a discriminatory manner, it may only apply to some among the Covenant's enumerated rights, and the commencement and end of the derogatory

Community might presumably have absorbed the obligations of these member States (this is effectively what happened under the Kyoto Protocol).

63 The list is available online (<https://www.un.org/development/desa/dpad/least-developed-country-category/ldcs-at-a-glance.html > accessed 19 February 2018).

period must be demarcated through notifications to the UN Secretary General.[64] The ICESCR does not speak of derogation at all, but of limitations, which must be 'determined by law', 'compatible with the nature of [the] rights', and 'solely for the purpose of promoting the general welfare in a democratic society'. So far so familiar.

The general notion of derogation and limitation of rights is relevant to climate change for at least three reasons. First, climate change is already increasing the frequency and intensity of weather events which may rise to the level of public emergencies.[65] Second, climate change-related factors (such as resource shortages and mass movements of populations) are extremely likely to give rise to conflict—indeed, on many accounts, they have already contributed significantly to at least one, namely the ongoing war in Syria.[66] Third, it is not unimaginable that climate change policies may need, at some point, to be pushed through in the face of significant resistance by affected parties—a state of affairs that, were it to arise, would raise parallels with, for example, the turn to emergency legislation by the US administration under Franklin D Roosevelt in the 1930s to put the New Deal in place.[67] It is already the case that climate regulation has, in some countries, relied on executive action in the teeth of opposition from the legislature.[68]

In addition to the likelihood that States may formally limit the availability of certain human rights in order to address climate change (most likely relevant to certain rights listed in the ICCPR), climate change itself is likely to prove a limiting factor to the achievement of human rights. This is particularly so in the case of the ICESCR. It may be assumed that, for many countries, climate change limits the availability of economic, social, and cultural rights in three interrelated ways. First, it impacts directly upon the resources needed to sustain rights (food, water, shelter, and so on). Second, it requires the use of scarce public funds to deal with emergencies (such as hurricanes, floods, and so on) or climate adaptation policies that might otherwise have been used to 'progressively realize' social and economic rights. Third, it redirects resources towards cleaner energy sources and other forms of mitigation that might have been used to achieve these rights. In such circumstances, the onus of a given State to 'take steps' to 'progressively realize' the right would presumably be discharged merely by slowing down the rate of deterioration, in turn requiring meaningful 'international assistance and cooperation'. Should that not be forthcoming, however, to an extent that achieves 'progressive realization' of rights in the face of progressive climate change, the result will presumably be, once again, another

[64] HRC, 'General Comment 29' in 'Note by the Secretariat, Compilation of General Comments and General Recommendations Adopted by Human Rights Treaty Bodies' (2001) HRI/GEN/1/Rev.9 (vol I).

[65] See, for detail, the *Turn Down the Heat* series (n 8).

[66] Peter H Gleick, 'Water, Drought, Climate Change, and Conflict in Syria' (2014) 6 Weather, Climate, and Society 331; Colin P Kelley and others, 'Climate Change in the Fertile Crescent and Implications of the Recent Syrian Drought' (2015) 112 Proceedings of the National Academy of Science of the USA 3241. More broadly, see W Neil Adger and others, 'Chapter 12: Human Security' in Field, *AR5* (n 8) 755.

[67] Giorgio Agamben, *State of Exception* (University of Chicago Press 2005) Chapter 1.

[68] See eg the executive measures undertaken by the Obama administration to address climate change <www.whitehouse.gov/climate-change> accessed 14 November 2015.

wedge driven between the Covenant's utopian preambular language and its substantive provisions.

B. Common article 5 of the ICCPR and ICESCR

> *1. Nothing in the present Covenant may be interpreted as implying for any State, group or person any right to engage in any activity or to perform any act aimed at the destruction of any of the rights or freedoms recognized herein, or at their limitation to a greater extent than is provided for in the present Covenant.*
>
> *2. No restriction upon or derogation from any of the fundamental human rights recognized or existing in any country in virtue of law, conventions, regulations or custom shall be admitted on the pretext that the present Covenant does not recognize such rights or that it recognizes them to a lesser extent.*

Both elements of common article 5 are relevant to the specific circumstances of climate change. Article 5(1) might be thought pertinent insofar as States might rely on the jurisdictional clause in ICCPR article 2(1) to avoid responsibility for human rights harms in third countries stemming from a failure to limit GHG emissions in their own. But even should such a scenario amount to an 'interpretation of the Covenant', it would still be difficult to maintain that the emission of GHG was 'aimed at' the destruction of human rights, no matter how well understood the likelihood of that outcome was.

Article 5(2) is conceivably relevant to the forty-five or so States that include some form of fundamental right to a clean and healthy environment—or similar—in their laws or constitutions.[69] Such a right might be expected to bolster climate change policy; article 5(2) might be expected to bite should cases arise of an overbroad adherence to, for example, freedom of speech, resulting in policy paralysis. One can imagine tension between potential derogations—a derogatory battle—in such cases. Article 5(1) may therefore, presumably, favour effective action in countries with environmental rights legislation over and above those lacking such legislation. But this is highly speculative and context-dependent.

VI. Conclusion

Human-induced climate change will disrupt, indeed devastate, the protection of Covenant rights for many millions of persons. This is true in the simple sense that for the very many people for whom these rights—to food, health, water, shelter, and life—already appear barely protected *in practice*, they will be the more impaired as climate change hits harder. It is also true in a more fundamental sense: the institutions that have sprung up to meet the demands of the Covenants' substantive provisions are simply not equipped to deal with the inescapable transnational dimensions

[69] UNGA, 'Report of the Independent Expert on the Issue of Human Rights Obligations Relating to the Enjoyment of a Safe, Clean, Healthy and Sustainable Environment, John H Knox' (30 December 2013) UN Doc A/HRC/25/53, para 18–19.

of climate change. This gap may be understood in terms of normative developments, positive limits, or simple pragmatic resource constraints. However it is understood, it appears in the gap between the idealism of the Covenant preambles—their utopian globalism and normative idealism—and the pragmatism of their substantive provisions. It is a gap that has often seemed bridgeable in the past, but may seem less so today.

The existing literature on the substantive human rights threats presented by climate change is uneven. Some Covenant rights—perhaps most notably the right to 'adequate food' (ICESCR art 11) and the derived right to 'clean water and sanitation' as well as the right to health (ICESCR art 12)—have attracted considerable attention.[70] Other rights that seem equally likely to be affected by climate change—such as the rights to life (ICCPR art 2) and housing (ICESCR art 11)—have attracted some commentary, but comparatively less. Beyond these are Covenant rights that seem clearly relevant to climate change policies but have so far remained relatively unexplored: ICCPR article 19 guaranteeing freedom of speech and information and ICESCR article 15 guaranteeing the rights to 'take part in cultural life' (threatened in particular where island States or other dwelling places risk disappearance) and to 'enjoy the benefits of scientific progress and its applications' (presumably relevant to the question of technology transfer in the UNFCCC). A large literature by now addresses climate change migration, some of which refers to the human rights of internally displaced persons or cross-border migrants, but so far debate has centred largely on the status of 'environmental migrants' (to choose a less controversial wording); there is, in practice, relatively little in this literature addressing the Covenant rights specifically in light of climate change.[71] There is also a burgeoning literature on the relevance of human rights to certain specific climate policies—most noticeably REDD+ (in relation to indigenous peoples' rights) and the Clean Development Mechanism—and on the 'mainstreaming' of human rights into adaptation funding and programming. In general, the literature approaches the human rights threats attributable to climate change-related phenomena using a 'human rights-based approach' that initially evolved in the context of international development policy, and primarily through UN institutions.[72]

There has, at the same time, been an immense awakening of interest in the human rights dimensions of climate change within various human rights bodies, notably at the UN, but increasingly also within the NGO-centred 'human rights movement'. The move has been strongest within the Charter-based mechanisms. The Human

[70] The richest source on the right to food is undoubtedly the collected research of the former Special Rapporteur on the Right to Adequate Food, Prof Olivier de Schutter <www.srfood.org/en/climate-change-2> accessed 14 November 2015. On the right to health, see the analytical study of the OHCHR <www.ohchr.org/EN/Issues/HRAndClimateChange/Pages/StudyImpact.aspx> accessed 30 June 2016; Paul Hunt and Rajat Khosla, 'Climate Change and the Right to the Highest Attainable Standard of Health' in Stephen Humphreys (ed), *Human Rights and Climate Change* (CUP 2010) 238–56.

[71] The key text is Jane McAdam, *Climate Change, Forced Migration, and International Law* (OUP 2012).

[72] A good account is Martti Koskenniemi, 'Human Rights Mainstreaming as a Strategy for Institutional Power' (2010) 1 Humanity 47.

Rights Council has held several sessions devoted to climate change and produced five resolutions on the matter to date.[73] A preponderant number of special procedures now attend to climate change in their reporting, and there have been joint statements and open letters signed by twenty-eight special procedures.[74] And of course climate change has its own special procedure in the form of the Special Rapporteur on Human Rights and the Environment. Climate change has featured in a number of questions and reports within the Universal Periodic Review. The Treaty-based mechanisms have also been apprised, notably the Committee on Economic, Social and Cultural Rights, which has had a number of review meetings devoted to climate change and has begun regularly to question what countries have been doing to safeguard ICESCR rights in this context in their reporting requirements. All this work and activity is no doubt significant. It has, for example, contributed to the introduction of human rights language within the UNFCCC process—and ultimately in the preamble of the Paris Agreement—which may prove somewhat influential.[75]

I have largely set these developments aside in this chapter in order to focus on the specific challenges raised by the phenomenon of anthropogenic climate change for human rights as set out in the Covenants. My conclusion is that—the increasing volume of activity notwithstanding—climate change, and the various concrete phenomena associated with it, poses, and will increasingly pose, an immense, indeed possibly insurmountable, challenge to the claim of the Covenants to represent and protect 'human rights', understood as universal, inherent, equal, and inalienable as per the Covenants themselves. This is because the human harms climate change poses are concrete, universal, and progressive, and are likely cumulatively to drive a wedge between the broad aspirational language of the preambles (and the UDHR) and the narrower language of the Covenants' operative provisions. Nothing about the wording of the Covenants themselves inherently undermines the promise of the preambles and of the UDHR. Nor does the existence of the threat of climate change significantly alter how the Covenants will be 'operationalized'. However, the cumulative failure of States to attempt, through the Covenants, to achieve a 'social and international order in which the rights' of the UDHR might be 'fully realized' has, over time, instituted a legal approach to human rights that is, in practice, wholly inadequate to the challenge climate change poses. Climate change is not the cause of the gap between promise and practice that has emerged in the Covenants. It is merely the occasion to confirm that the gap is no longer bridgeable.

[73] See <www.ohchr.org/EN/Issues/HRAndClimateChange/Pages/HRCAction.aspx> accessed 14 November 2015.

[74] ibid.

[75] UNFCCC, 'The Cancun Agreements: Outcome of the Work of the Ad Hoc Working Group on Long-term Cooperative Action under the Convention' Decision 1/CP.16 (11 March 2011) UN Doc FCCC/CP/2010/7/Add.1, Preamble and art 8. The preamble to the Paris Agreement states that: 'Parties should, when taking action to address climate change, respect, promote and consider their respective obligations on human rights, the right to health, the rights of indigenous peoples, local communities, migrants, children, persons with disabilities and people in vulnerable situations and the right to development, as well as gender equality, empowerment of women and intergenerational equity'.

Bibliography

'Summaries, Frequently Asked Questions, and Cross-Chapter Boxes, A Contribution of Working Group II to the Fifth Assessment Report of the Intergovernmental Panel on Climate Change' in Christopher B Field and others (eds), *Climate Change 2014: Impacts, Adaptation and Vulnerability* (IPCC 2015)

Adger, W Neil, and others, 'Chapter 12: Human Security' in Christopher B Field and others (eds), *Climate Change 2014: Impacts, Adaptation and Vulnerability* (IPCC 2015)

Agamben, Giorgio, *State of Exception* (University of Chicago Press 2005)

Agarwal, Anil, and Narain, Sunita, *Global Warming in an Unequal World: A Case of Environmental Colonialism* (Centre for Science and Environment 1990)

Baer, Paul, and others, *Greenhouse Development Rights: The Right to Development in a Climate Constrained World* (2nd edn, Heinrich Böll Foundation and others 2008)

Coomans, Fons, and Künnemann, Rolf (eds), *Cases and Concepts on Extraterritorial Obligations in the Area of Economic, Social and Cultural Rights* (Intersentia 2012)

Craven, Matthew, 'The Domestic Application of the International Covenant on Economic, Social and Cultural Rights' (1993) 40 Netherlands Intl L Rev 367

De Schutter, Olivier, and others, 'Commentary to the Maastricht Principles on Extraterritorial Obligations of States in the Area of Economic, Social and Cultural Rights' (2012) 34 Human Rights Q 1084

Diruigbo, Emeka, 'Permanent Sovereignty and Peoples' Ownership of Natural Resources' (2006) 38 The George Washington Intl L Rev 33

Duruigbo, Emeka 'Realizing the People's Right to Natural Resources' (2011) 12 Whitehead J of Diplomatic & International Relations 111

Field, Christopher B, and others (eds), *Managing the Risks of Extreme Events and Disasters to Advance Climate Change Adaptation: Special Report of the IPCC* (CUP 2012)

Fisch, Jörg, *The Right of Self-Determination of Peoples: The Domestication of an Illusion* (CUP 2015)

Gleick, Peter H, 'Water, Drought, Climate Change, and Conflict in Syria' (2014) 6 Weather, Climate, and Society 331

Humphreys, Stephen, 'Climate Change Pathways and the Future of Human Rights' in Nehal Bhuta (ed), *The Futures of Human Rights: Collected Courses of the Academy of European Law* (OUP 2018) forthcoming

Hunt, Paul, and Khosla, Rajat, 'Climate Change and the Right to the Highest Attainable Standard of Health' in Stephen Humphreys (ed), *Human Rights and Climate Change* (CUP 2010)

Jeffery, Louise, and others, 'Climate Action Tracker Update: 2.7°C is Not Enough: We Can Get Lower' (Climate Action Tracker, 2015) <http://tinyurl.com/zuzzqgl> accessed 27 June 2016

Kelley, Colin P, and others, 'Climate Change in the Fertile Crescent and Implications of the Recent Syrian Drought' (2015) 112 Proceedings of the National Academy of Science of the USA 3241–47

Knop, Karen, *Diversity and Self-Determination in International Law* (CUP 2008)

Koskenniemi, Martti, 'Human Rights Mainstreaming as a Strategy for Institutional Power' (2010) 1 Humanity 47

Lin, Jolene, 'The First Successful Climate Negligence Case: A Comment on *Urgenda Foundation v The State of the Netherlands*' (2015) University of Hong Kong Faculty of Law Research Paper 2015/021

Lohmann, Larry, *Carbon Trading: A Critical Conversation on Climate Change, Privatisation and Power* (CornerHouse 2006)

McAdam, Jane, *Climate Change, Forced Migration, and International Law* (OUP 2012)

Pachauri, Rajendra K, and others, *Climate Change 2014: Synthesis Report, Contribution of Working Groups I, II and III to the Fifth Assessment Report of the Intergovernmental Panel on Climate Change* (IPCC 2014)

Pogge, Thomas, 'Recognized and Violated by International Law: The Human Rights of the Global Poor' (2005) 18 Leiden J of Intl L 717

Raz, Joseph, 'Human Rights Without Foundations' in Samantha Besson and John Tasoulias (eds), *The Philosophy of International Law* (OUP 2010)

Razzaque, Jona, 'Natural Resources in the Global Environmental Order' in Elena Blanco and Jona Razzaque (eds), *Natural Resources and the Green Economy* (Martinus Nijhoff 2012)

Schrijver, Nico, *Sovereignty over Natural Resources: Balancing Rights and Duties* (CUP 2008)

Shklar, Judith N, *Faces of Injustice* (Yale University Press 1994)

Shue, Henry, 'Subsistence Emissions and Luxury Emissions' (1993) 15 Law & Policy 39

Skogly, Sigrun, and Gibney, Mark, 'Transnational Human Rights Obligations' (2002) 24(3) Human Rights Q 781

Strauss, Andrew, 'Climate Change Litigation: Opening the Door to the International Court of Justice' in William C G Burns and Hari M Osofsky (eds), *Adjudicating Climate Change: State, National, and International Approaches* (CUP 2009)

Tesón, Fernando R (ed), *The Theory of Self-Determination* (CUP 2016)

van Vuuren, Detlef P, and others, 'RCP2.6: Exploring the Possibility to Keep Global Mean Temperature Increase Below 2°C' (2011) 109 Climatic Change 95

Voigt, Christina, 'State Responsibility for Climate Change Damages' (2008) 77 Nordic J of Intl L 1

Wenar, Leif, *Blood Oil* (OUP 2016)

Willcox, Susannah 'A Rising Tide: The Implications of Climate Change Inundation for Human Rights and State Sovereignty' (2012) 9 Essex Human Rights Rev 1

13

The Covenants and Financial Crises

*Christine Kaufmann**

I. Introduction

Financial crises come in different shapes and sizes and involve a variety of actors, both with regard to triggering a crisis and the responsibilities entailed. Depending on the type of financial crisis—currency, balance of payments, or debt crisis—States, private actors such as investors or banks, and international and regional organizations assume different roles. Technological progress and globalisation facilitate and accelerate financial crises' expansion in terms of their geographical scope and their severity. As a result, financial crises' detrimental effects go beyond the economy and affect society at large. In light of the fiftieth anniversary of the United Nations (UN) Covenants on Civil and Political Rights (ICCPR)[1] and Economic, Social and Cultural Rights (ICESCR)[2] and the series of financial crises that has taken place since the late 1990s,[3] the time has come to explore the potential of such crises as an 'equal opportunity menace'[4] for the implementation of the UN Covenants.

Since the early stages of the discussion,[5] the relationship between financial crises and human rights has, to a large extent, been conceptualized as a one way-street, with human rights not playing an active role but instead falling victim to the (side) effects of financial crises. This chapter suggests a different approach by exploring the role of the UN Covenants in financial crises from three perspectives: people, process, and paradigm. A first focus lies on *people* as rights-holders and the role of the Covenants in ensuring a human rights-based approach of the relevant actors during

* I am grateful to Samantha Besson, Moshe Hirsch, Helen Keller, Daniel Moeckli, Yuval Shany, and Joseph HH Weiler for their comments and suggestions and to Fabienne Bretscher for her excellent research assistance.

[1] International Covenant on Civil and Political Rights (opened for signature 16 December 1966, entered into force 23 March 1976) 999 UNTS 171.

[2] International Covenant on Economic, Social and Cultural Rights (opened for signature 16 December 1966, entered into force 3 January 1976) 993 UNTS 3.

[3] Starting with the East Asia Crisis in 1997. For a detailed account, see Stephen Haggard, *The Political Economy of the Asian Financial Crisis* (Peterson Institute for International Economics 2000).

[4] Carmen M Reinhart and Kenneth S Rogoff, 'Banking Crises: An Equal Opportunity Menace' (2013) 37 J of Banking and Finance 4557, 4559–60.

[5] See, for an example of an early analysis, Giovanni A Cornia, Richard Jolly, and Frances Stewart (eds), *Adjustment with a Human Face*, 2 vols (OUP 1987).

and in the aftermath of a financial crisis. The second focus is on *process*, including coherence and context, and will explore human rights responsibilities in the context of international financial institutions (IFIs). Thirdly, a shift in *paradigm* for emancipating the Covenants and establishing an *interface* to overcome the conceptual gap between human rights on the one hand and financial regulation on the other will be suggested.

For this purpose, Section II will—from a rights-holder perspective (*people*)—explore the anatomy of different types of financial crises with a view to identifying their actors and mechanics and to specifying their potential impacts on human rights, followed by an account of States' human rights obligations (Section III). Based on these findings, the focus will then be expanded from people to *process and coherence* with an analysis of the human-rights related responsibilities of IFIs and their members (Section IV). In an attempt to bridge the identified conceptual gaps and conflicting interests, and to pave the way for entrusting the Covenants with a more active role, translational human rights will be suggested as a new *paradigm* or interface (Section V).

II. Anatomy of Financial Crises: Who, How, and What?

A. Typologies of an 'equal opportunity menace': Currency, balance of payments, and debt and banking crises

Financial crises—described by Reinhart and Rogoff as *'an equal opportunity menace'*[6]—do not follow a unique pattern or model, but are often an amalgam of events triggered by a variety of factors involving private, public, domestic, and international actors.[7] The major groups of financial crises that have been identified in the economic literature are summarized in Table 13.1.[8]

A first group comprises crises that affect a country's *currency* (1) or *balance of payments* (2). Such crises will often involve speculative attacks on a currency by private and public investors, either as a trigger or as a reaction to a tumbling currency. Reactions will typically take place at a macroeconomic level—monetary policy, fiscal policy, and regulatory measures—and involve devaluation and austerity programmes.[9] Examples are the late crises in Mexico, East Asia, Russia, and Brazil in the 1990s.[10] Austerity programmes can originally be traced back to the so-called 'Washington Consensus' reached by the governors of the International Monetary

[6] Reinhart and Rogoff, 'Banking Crises' (n 4) 4559–60.

[7] Stijn Claessens and Ayhan Kose, 'Financial Crises: Explanations, Types, and Implications' in Stijn Claessens and others (eds), *Financial Crises: Causes, Consequences, and Policy Responses* (International Monetary Fund 2014) 3, 4. With a focus on the Euro: Markus K Brunnermeier, Harold James, and Jean-Pierre Landau, *The Euro and the Battle of Ideas* (Princeton University Press 2016) 175–84.

[8] For a comprehensive discussion, see Claessens and Kose, 'Financial Crises' (n 7) 15–26.

[9] Brunnermeier, James, and Landau, *The Euro* (n 7) 185–206.

[10] Carmen M Reinhart and Kenneth S Rogoff, *This Time is Different: Eight Centuries of Financial Folly* (Princeton University Press 2009) 189.

Table 13.1 Typologies and impacts of financial crises

	(1) Currency crises	(2) Balance of payments crises	(3) Debt crises		(4) Systemic banking crises
			Domestic public debt	Foreign debt	
Key features	Speculative attack on currency; result of debt crisis	Large, unexpected decline in international capital inflow	Country does not honour its domestic fiscal obligations	Country is unable or unwilling to service its foreign debt	Bank run (actual or potential) due to real or feared lack of liquidity; changes in asset prices
Main actors in triggering crisis	Private investors, governments, IFIs	Private investors, governments, IFIs	Governments, private and public creditors	Governments, private and public creditors	Commercial banks, investors, clients
Economic results	Devaluation, depreciation, rising interest rates, etc; contagion/spread to other countries; recession	Devaluation, depreciation, rising interest rates, etc	Default, inflation, recession	Higher costs for loans; less foreign investment; recession; default	Lack of liquidity; loss of deposits/ investments; need for government intervention; contagion
Typical reactions	Austerity programmes, devaluation		Austerity programmes	Economic reform programmes required by international organizations (IMF, EU) and/or creditors	New financial regulation; orchestrated bankruptcy of financial institutions
Main potential human rights implications	Loss of income and savings; unemployment; reduced public services ⇨ ICESCR: arts 6–8 (right to work), art 9 (right to social security), art 11 (adequate housing) ⇨ ICCPR: art 26 (equality and non-discrimination)		Unemployment; reduced public services (health, education, etc) ⇨ ICESCR: arts 6–8 (right to work), art 9 (right to social security), art 11 (adequate housing), art 12 (right to health), art 13 (right to education) ⇨ ICCPR: art 14 (access to justice), arts 19, 21, 22 (freedom of opinion, expression, assembly, and association), art 25 (public participation), art 26 (equality and non-discrimination)		Limited access to savings; limited choice of economic activities; limited access to housing ⇨ ICESCR: arts 6–8 (right to work), art 9 (right to social security), art 11 (adequate housing) ⇨ ICCPR: art 25 (public participation)
Main actors involved in mitigating the consequences	States, central banks, international organizations		States	International organizations, States	States, central banks, international organisations

Fund (IMF) in 1989 and consequently applied as a condition for IMF loans.[11] In their contemporary form, they typically involve a reduction of public deficits by lowering expenses, in particular through wage reductions, cutting social benefits such as pensions, and decreasing expenditures on public services such as health and education.[12]

Debt crises (3) may occur when a country is not able or willing to honour its *foreign debt* obligations and there is a lack of collateral (sovereign lending) from other countries. These crises are thus primarily triggered by governments and reinforced by private and public creditors. The resulting decrease in foreign investment and the related higher costs for loans will then turn an originally external crisis into a domestic problem. Typically, IFIs will prescribe austerity measures, that is, cuts on public spending, to address the lack of liquidity. This will often lead to reducing public services, such as healthcare and education. Consequently, individual expenses for these services, which are no longer paid for by the State, will increase while—at the same time—incomes tend to decrease due to a reduced government demand for private goods and services, higher unemployment, and reforms on the labour market. In absolute economic terms, debt crises are the most costly for an economy.[13] *Domestic public debt crises* may follow a foreign debt crisis or develop independently. They are often the result of high inflation caused by a government's abuse of its monopoly to increase the money supply,[14] with potential human rights implications similar to foreign debt crises. A recent example in this regard is Venezuela.[15]

Unlike most debt crises, the origin of *banking crises* (4) can typically be traced to activities by *private actors*, such as investors or commercial banks. Banking crises have the potential to quickly spread from a single institution to the whole banking sector (contagion) and turn into a systemic crisis which puts the whole financial system at risk.[16] The collapse of the financial service provider Lehman Brothers in 2008 and its repercussions on global financial stability are a drastic example for such a development.[17] From an individual perspective, limited access to savings and loans will particularly affect choices regarding economic activities as well as access to housing.

When a currency crisis—such as the recent Euro crisis and the related economic slow-down, as experienced for example in Greece—coincides with the high costs of

[11] The concept aimed at raising Gross Domestic Product (GDP) by improving resource allocation through trade liberalization, privatization, and stabilization. See Christine Kaufmann, *Globalisation and Labour Rights: The Conflict between Core Labour Rights and International Economic Law* (Hart 2007) 102, with further references.

[12] Markus Krajewski, 'Human Rights and Austerity Programmes' in Thomas Cottier, Rosa M Lastra, and Christian Tietje (eds), *The Rule of Law in Monetary Affairs* (CUP 2014) 490, 493–95.

[13] Claessens and Kose, 'Financial Crises' (n 7) 37.

[14] Reinhart and Rogoff, *This Time is Different* (n 10) 180–93.

[15] IMF, *World Economic Outlook, April 2017: Gaining Momentum*? (IMF 2017) 48, projecting 720 per cent inflation for 2017 (up from 254 per cent in 2016); Office of the United Nations High Commissioner for Human Rights (OHCHR) 'Human Rights Violations and Abuses in the Context of Protests in the Bolivarian Republic of Venezuela from 1 April to 31 July 2017' (Geneva 2017) 2.

[16] Brunnermeier, James, and Landau, *The Euro* (n 7) 180.

[17] Reinhart and Rogoff, *This Time is Different* (n 10) 204–22.

restructuring the financial system in the aftermath of a banking crisis, public debt will inevitably increase. The result is a *triplex crisis* which combines the detrimental effects of a currency, debt, and banking crisis.[18]

B. Human rights impacts of financial crises

The severe repercussions of financial crises on society at large are undisputed. The strong language used in comparing the recent financial crisis to a 'tsunami' (by Alan Greenspan, former chair of the Board of Governors of the US Federal Reserve System), an 'infectious disease' (by the IMF), or the 'sinking of the Titanic' (by former Brazilian President Ignacio Lula da Silva)[19] therefore seems appropriate. Yet, despite the strong rhetoric, political discussions in the aftermath of the crisis focused primarily on the resulting *economic* costs and effects, which could be measured through mainly quantitative indicators.[20]

While there is ample data on the economic consequences of a financial crisis, research on such a crisis's impacts on human rights is still in its infancy. This holds true particularly for the identification of *specific* human rights put at risk by austerity measures.[21] As the following sections will show, these impacts vary according to the nature of the crisis.

Before engaging in a detailed analysis of specific human rights, two general observations can be made. First, the crisis scenarios described in Section II.A above do not automatically imply human rights violations, in other words not every negative impact of a financial crisis on peoples' lives will constitute a violation of their human rights. This being said, a commonality of all financial crisis scenarios is that the related severe cuts on government expenditures and the related *lack of available resources* (ICESCR art 2(1)) carry the *risk* of infringing on human rights if the provision of essential public services such as health, education, housing, and the like can no longer be secured.

Second, all financial crises, and particularly banking crises, will go hand in hand with a lack of credit from banks and other institutions. This limited *access* to credit and loans may make it more difficult for individuals to, for instance, obtain mortgages or pay them back, with the related risk of eviction from their homes. Particular challenges arise for subsistence farmers and small-scale or micro entrepreneurs seeking to obtain loans for engaging in activities of their own *choice*.[22]

[18] Carmen M Reinhart and Kenneth S Rogoff, 'From Financial Crash to Debt Crisis' (2011) 101 American Economic Review 1676; Brunnermeier, James, and Landau, *The Euro* (n 7) 185.

[19] Matt Peterson and Christian Barry, 'Who Must Pay for the Damage of the Global Financial Crisis?' in Ned Dobos, Christian Barry, and Thomas Pogge (eds), *Global Financial Crisis: The Ethical Issues* (Springer 2011) 158, 159.

[20] For a summary, see Claessens and Kose, 'Financial Crises' (n 7) 34–41; Brunnermeier, James, and Landau, *The Euro* (n 7) 306–12.

[21] Aoife Nolan, 'Not Fit For Purpose? Human Rights in Times of Financial and Economic Crisis' (2015) 21 European Human Rights L Rev 358.

[22] Peer Stein, Oya Pinar Ardic, and Martin Hommes, 'Closing the Credit Gap for Formal and Informal Micro, Small, and Medium Enterprises' (International Finance Corporation 2013).

1. *Economic, social, and cultural rights*

Among economic, social, and cultural rights (ESCR), labour rights, the right to an adequate standard of living, the right to health and social security, the right to education, and the right to housing are particularly at risk in financial crises.[23]

All types of financial crises transmit their effects to the life of individuals primarily via labour market impacts and thus have the potential to infringe on the right to work as guaranteed in ICESCR articles 6–8.[24] The most obvious effect is an increased unemployment or underemployment rate, in particular among young people and women, as was highlighted by some of the reporting procedures with regard to the financial crises in Argentina and Greece.[25] Governmental reforms of the labour market to increase 'employer flexibility' as part of the remedies suggested by IFIs may include reductions of the minimum wage or limitations of labour unions' rights.[26] For instance, during the 1983–2001 financial crisis in Argentina, a labour law reform allowed for the modification of labour contracts, including the restriction of labour rights as mentioned in ICESCR articles 6–8, as a measure to secure the economic stability of private businesses.[27]

Additionally, children are more at risk during and after financial crises because they may drop out of school in order to support their families and engage in work which may be hazardous to their health. Such developments would result in a violation of ICESCR article 10(3).[28]

Typical austerity measures and the related unemployment and salary reductions will increase the number of people depending on social programmes, which may affect the right to social security (ICESCR article 9). In times of financial crisis, social protection is an important means to reduce and alleviate poverty as well as to prevent social exclusion.[29] Yet, when financial resources are scarce, particularly

[23] Council of Europe, 'Safeguarding Human Rights in Times of Economic Crisis: Issue Paper' (2013) <https://rm.coe.int/16806daa3f> accessed 18 May 2017, 17–20; OHCHR, 'Report on Austerity Measures and Economic and Social Rights' (7 May 2013) UN Doc E/2013/82, paras 12–14; Jernej Letnar Černič, 'State Obligations Concerning Socio-Economic Rights in Times of the European Financial Crisis' (2015) 11 Intl L and Management Rev 125, 128–31; Lisa Ginsborg, 'The Impact of the Economic Crisis on Human Rights in Europe and the Accountability of International Institutions' (2017) 1 Global Campus Human Rights J 97, 101–03.

[24] World Bank, The Jobs Crisis: Household and Government Responses to the Great Recession in Eastern Europe and Central Asia (World Bank 2011) 13.

[25] See Section II.C.

[26] Kerry Rittich, 'Labour Market Governance in Wake of the Crisis: Reflections and Possibilities' in Christian Joerges and Carola Glinski (eds), *The European Crisis and the Transformation of Transnational Governance* (Hart 2014) 123, 127–28; Philomila Tsoukala, 'Euro Zone Crisis Management and the New Social Europe' (2013) 20 Columbia J for European L 31, 59–61. See also eg the structural reform intended for Greece: European Commission, *The Economic Adjustment Programme for Greece*, Occasional Papers 61 (May 2010) 68.

[27] IMF, 'Memorandum of Economic Policies of the Government of Argentina' (14 February 2000) <www.imf.org/external/np/loi/2000/arg/01/> accessed 31 May 2017, para 23.

[28] See eg CRC, 'Concluding Observations on the Second Periodic Report of Argentina' (9 October 2002) UN Doc CRC/C/15/Add.187, para 58.

[29] CESCR, 'General Comment 19' in 'Note by the Secretariat, Compilation of General Comments and General Recommendations Adopted by Human Rights Treaty Bodies' (2008) UN Doc HRI/GEN/1/Rev.9 (vol I) para 3.

in debt crises,[30] expenses for social security are one of the first to be cut, either by reducing coverage or the level of benefits.[31] An example is Greece, which, according to the European Committee on Social Rights (ECSR), violated the right to social security because of the 'cumulative effect' of the different restrictions imposed.[32] Cutting social benefits during economic restructuring may also affect the right to an adequate standard of living in ICESCR article 11. In addressing this concern, the Argentine government decided to suspend mortgage foreclosures on family homes, because many people were at risk of losing their properties during the financial crisis.[33] Furthermore, the right to the highest attainable standard of physical and mental health (ICESCR article 12) may be affected, as the rise in the number of suicides, mental illnesses, and infectious diseases that was observed in Europe after the 2008 financial crisis indicates.[34] A further right potentially affected by austerity measures following debt and currency crises is the right to education (ICESCR article 13). Cuts in public spending for education could, in fact, reverse the progress made in school enrolment over the last decade.[35]

2. *Civil and political rights*

Although these impacts are not obvious at first glance, civil and political rights may also be at risk in times of financial crises.[36] In the course of its programme to reduce government spending, Greece increased not only taxes but also costs for litigation 'in order to prevent the abusive lodging of legal remedies'.[37] This measure raised concerns about its compatibility with Greece's obligation to guarantee access to justice (ICCPR article 14).[38] Moreover, the rights to freedom of opinion, expression, assembly, and association (ICCPR articles 19, 21, and 22) are at risk of being impaired during financial crises when protests and demonstrations against the government

[30] See Section II.A, Table 13.1, scenario (3).

[31] See eg HRC, 'Report of the Independent Expert on the Question of Human Rights and Extreme Poverty' (17 March 2011) UN Doc A/HRC/17/34, para 43.

[32] ECSR, *Federation of Employed Pensioners of Greece (IKA-ETAM) v Greece* (7 December 2012), Complaint No 76/2012, para 78.

[33] Larry Rohter, 'The Homes of Argentines Are at Risk in I.M.F. Talks' *The New York Times* (New York, 23 June 2003). For recent measures to support vulnerable defaulting households in Europe, see Alice Pittini and others, 'The State of Housing in the EU 2015' (Housing Europe 2015) 23.

[34] Marina Karanikolos and others, 'Financial Crisis, Austerity, and Health in Europe' (2013) 381 The Lancet 1323.

[35] UNGA, 'Report of the Independent Expert on the Question of Human Rights and Extreme Poverty' (11 August 2009) UN Doc A/64/279, para 35.

[36] See eg UNHCHR, 'Report on Austerity Measures and Economic and Social Rights' (7 May 2013) UN Doc E/2013/82; Parliamentary Assembly of the Council of Europe (PACE), 'Austerity Measures: A Danger for Democracy and Social Rights' (26 June 2012) PACE Res 1884 (2012); UNGA, 'Report on Extreme Poverty' (n 35) paras 52–53; Ginsborg, 'Impact' (n 23) 103–04.

[37] HRC, 'List of Issues in Relation to the Second Periodic Report of Greece, Addendum: Replies of Greece to the List of Issues' (24 August 2015) UN Doc CCPR/C/GRC/Q/2/Add.1, para 81.

[38] Greek National Commission for Human Rights, 'Written Information on the Second Periodic Report of the Hellenic Republic for the implementation of the ICCPR' (22 December 2014) <www.nchr.gr/images/English_Site/EllinikesEktheseis/ICCPR_list_of_issues.pdf> accessed 7 October 2015, 20–22.

are unduly restricted. Such protests will often occur as a reaction to domestic policy measures in the aftermath of debt crises or to regulatory measures adopted in response to banking crises.[39] Examples in this regard include the alleged human rights violations by US authorities vis-à-vis members of the 'Occupy Wall Street' movement.[40] A similar development could be observed with the Spanish anti-austerity movement, which expressed its discontent by means of various demonstrations and occupations of public places. According to the Council of Europe Commissioner for Human Rights, Spanish authorities used force in a disproportionate way in order to dissolve these manifestations of opinion.[41] The—at least partial—lack of popular support for austerity measures which was expressed through these protests touches on the right to public participation (ICCPR article 25), which gives effect to an aspect of the basic principles of democracy. The question arises whether the decision-making process at the national and international level regarding measures to address financial crises jeopardizes these principles.[42]

3. *Equality and non-discrimination*

Both Covenants guarantee the right to equality and non-discrimination (ICCPR articles 2(1), 3, and 26, ICESCR articles 2(2) and 3), which is of relevance in conjunction with nearly each of the above-presented guarantees. Measures adopted by countries during financial crises often have a disparate effect on vulnerable groups. This can be exemplified by the measures adopted by Greece to raise its fiscal revenues: Greece has been accused of targeting the 'easy-to-tax salaried employees and pensioners' instead of taking action to increase overall payment discipline.[43] As a consequence, the burden of adjustment is allocated in a disproportionate manner, continuing to leave the wealthier 'outside the tax-net'.[44] In fact, the Greek government acknowledged the disparate effect of the measures taken on vulnerable groups, not just in tax matters, but also in other sectors.[45] Among these vulnerable groups are older persons, pensioners, younger people, women, children, people with disabilities, and immigrants.[46] Finally, the domestic legal framework, particularly for

[39] See Section II.A, Table 13.1, scenarios (3) and (4).

[40] Protest and Assembly Law Project, 'Suppressing Protest: Human Rights Violations in the U.S. Response to Occupy Wall Street' (2012) <www.chrgj.org/wp-content/uploads/2012/10/suppressingprotest.pdf> accessed 7 October 2015.

[41] Council of Europe (CoE) Commissioner for Human Rights, 'Report Following the Visit to Spain from 3 to 7 June' (9 October 2013) CoE Doc CommDH(2013)18, paras 112–30.

[42] See eg PACE, 'Austerity' (n 36) para 10.1. A similar argument was made by the complainants in *Mamatas and Others v Greece* App nos 63066/14 and 66106/14 (ECtHR, 21 July 2016), but rejected by the ECtHR with reference to the necessity and proportionality of the contested collective action clauses (paras 115–16).

[43] IMF, 'Greece: Selected Issues' (June 2013) Country Report No 13/155, 18; see also HRC, 'Report of the Independent Expert on the Effects of Foreign Debt and other Related International Financial Obligations of States on the Full Enjoyment of All Human Rights, Particularly Economic, Social and Cultural Rights, Mission to Greece' (27 March 2014) UN Doc A/HRC/25/50/Add.1, para 42.

[44] IMF, 'Report on Greece' (n 43) 18; see also HRC, 'Report on Extreme Poverty' (n 31) paras 49–51.

[45] HRC, 'Second Periodic Report of Greece' (26 February 2014) UN Doc CCPR/C/GRC/2, para 4.

[46] HRC, 'Report on Foreign Debt: Greece' (n 43) para 42; on women, see CEDAW, 'Concluding Observations on the Sixth Periodic Report of Spain' (7 August 2009) UN Doc CEDAW/C/ESP/CO/

social security, may distinguish between benefits based on (human) rights on the one hand and benefits depending on available financial resources on the other. In a recent decision, the European Court of Human Rights (ECtHR) held that such differences may justify a different treatment of beneficiaries in the two groups.[47]

C. Human rights in times of financial crises: Two case studies

In order to gain an understanding of the two treaty bodies' approaches to addressing the role of the Covenants in the context of financial crises, two examples are particularly illustrative: Argentina and Greece.

1. *Argentina*

a) 1983–2001: A crisis unfolds

When Argentina re-established a democratic regime in 1983, the new government faced not only a fiscal deficit, high inflation, and a foreign debt burden, but also a history of grave human rights violations.[48] Confronted with severe debt and currency crises, Argentina entered a series of standby agreements with the IMF in order to stabilize the economy. In these agreements, the IMF insisted inter alia on targets for reducing inflation, limits on wage increases, devaluation, and reductions in government expenditures.[49] Despite these strict conditions, the economic results were not sustainable.[50] In addition, there were substantial negative impacts on specific human rights, particularly workers' and subsistence rights.[51] Accordingly, during the consideration of Argentina's second periodic report to the Committee on Economic, Social and Cultural Rights (CESCR) in 1994, the Committee acknowledged some economic progress but at the same time voiced concerns that 'the implementation of the structural adjustment programme may harm certain social groups'[52] and that the effects of such measures on ESCR were not adequately monitored by the country.[53] The role of the IMF and the applied conditionality were not addressed by the Committee.

Between 1998 and 2002, the country entered into a severe recession.[54] As before, the IMF granted financial support depending on structural reform and fiscal

6, paras 23–24; on younger people, see PACE, 'The Young Generation Sacrificed: Social, Economic and Political Implications of the Financial Crisis' (26 June 2012) PACE Res 1885; on immigrants, see CERD, 'General Recommendation 33' (29 September 2009) UN Doc CERD/C/GC/33, para I.f).

47 *Mockienė v Lithuania* App no 75916/13 (ECtHR, 4 July 2017), paras 53–54.

48 See CESCR, 'Report on the Fourth Session, Supplement no 3' (15 January–2 February 1990) UN Doc E/C.12/1990/3, paras 235–54.

49 Margaret Conklin and Daphne Davidson, 'The I.M.F. and Economic and Social Human Rights: A Case Study of Argentina 1958–1985' (1986) 8 Human Rights Q 227, 230–44.

50 Roberto Frenkel, 'Argentina: A Decade of the Convertibility Regime' (2002) 45 Challenge 41, 42–44; Andreas F Lowenfeld, *International Economic Law* (2nd edn, OUP 2008) 720.

51 Conklin and Davidson, 'The I.M.F.' (n 49) 248–57.

52 CESCR, 'Concluding Observations on the [First] Periodic Report of Argentina' (19 December 1994) UN Doc E/C.12/1994/14, paras 6 and 11.

53 ibid para 22.

54 IMF, *Evaluation Report: The IMF and Argentina*, 1991–2001 (IMF 2004) 20.

austerity, which particularly affected the public health and social security system.[55] Following Argentina's report to the CESCR in 1997, the Committee criticized the adopted measures more specifically than in 1994 and urged Argentina to comply with its obligations under the ICESCR in negotiations with IFIs.[56] The Committee was particularly concerned about a labour law reform to stabilize private enterprises at the cost of labour rights.[57] As a consequence, it recommended the withdrawal of the labour market legislation, yet did not address the fact that such a measure explicitly conflicted with Argentina's obligations in its arrangements with the IMF.[58]

By 2001, the situation had further deteriorated. After the introduction of a new 'zero deficit law' with substantial cuts in wages and pensions and strict limitations of cash withdrawals,[59] it culminated in social unrest, the president's resignation, and Argentina declaring default on its public debt.[60]

From a human rights perspective, it is interesting to note that it was IMF staff who expressed concerns about the social consequences of the zero deficit law at a very early stage and to some extent even predicted the ensuing social unrest. What had been a 'simple' debt crisis in the beginning was now a triple *debt, currency, and banking crisis* with detrimental effects on human rights.

b) 2002–14: Any lessons learnt?

Only with the arrival of a new government and after the IMF's critical review of its own actions during the crisis was it possible to work towards economic recovery.[61] Unlike previous regimes, and in close cooperation with the World Bank, the new government made social spending a priority[62] in order to reduce—in the words of the IMF—the 'traumatic' impact of the crisis on people.[63] Measures included, for example, the already-mentioned suspension of mortgage foreclosures on family

[55] IMF, 'Memorandum: Argentina' (n 27) para 8.

[56] CESCR, 'Concluding Observations on the Second Periodic Report of Argentina' (8 December 1999) UN Doc E/C.12/1/Add.38, para 28. The HRC mentioned the economic situation neither in HRC, 'Report of the Human Rights Committee' (3 October 1995) UN Doc A/50/40, paras 144–65, nor in HRC, 'Concluding Observations on the Third Periodic Report of Argentina' (15 November 2000) UN Doc CCPR/CO/70/ARG; see also Jason Morgan-Foster, 'The Relationship of IMF Structural Adjustment Programs to Economic, Social, and Cultural Rights: The Argentine Case Revisited' (2003) 24 Michigan J of Intl L 577, 595–96.

[57] IMF, 'Memorandum: Argentina' (n 27).

[58] IMF, *Evaluation Report: Argentina* (n 54) 83.

[59] The so-called 'corralito'. See Lowenfeld, *International Economic Law* (n 50) 726. This measure was later declared unconstitutional by the Argentine Supreme Court (*Smith v Poder Ejecutivo o Estado Nacional*, [2002-I] JA 237, 1 February 2002). For more information regarding the Supreme Court's approach during and after the financial crisis, see Gustavo Maurino and Ezequiel Nino, 'Economic and Social Rights and the Supreme Court of Argentina in the Decade Following the 2001–2003 Crisis' in Aoife Nolan (ed), *Economic and Social Rights after the Global Financial Crisis* (CUP 2014) 299.

[60] Lowenfeld, *International Economic Law* (n 50) 726–29.

[61] IMF, *Evaluation Report: Argentina* (n 54).

[62] World Bank, 'Argentina: Overview' (22 September 2016) <www.worldbank.org/en/country/argentina/overview#1> accessed 19 May 2017; HRC, 'Report of the Independent Expert on the Effects of Foreign Debt and Other Related International Financial Obligations of States on the Full Enjoyment of All Human Rights, Particularly Economic, Social and Cultural Rights, Mission to Argentina' (2 April 2014) UN Doc A/HRC/25/50/Add.3.

[63] IMF, *Evaluation Report: Argentina* (n 54) 58.

homes, and thus supported the right to housing.[64] With this strategy, Argentina managed to withstand the global financial crisis of 2008 quite well.[65]

Unfortunately, hopes that the lessons learnt from the Argentine crisis in 2001 would result in a more coherent approach for reconciling human rights and economic policies in times of financial crisis did not materialize.[66] Despite first signs of the IMF's and the World Bank's readiness to take human rights into consideration when tailoring their programmes, neither the UN Human Rights Committee (HRC)[67] nor the CESCR seized the opportunity to discuss coherence during the reporting procedures with Argentina in 2010 and 2011.[68] In fact, in 2011, the CESCR again ignored the regulatory context in which Argentina was acting and asked for changes in labour legislation without addressing its relationship to the conditional structural adjustment programme.[69] In the light of the rising awareness of financial crises' impact on human rights, it is difficult to understand why the two treaty bodies would let this opportunity to start a discourse on coherent human rights and financial obligations go by.

In 2014, the UN Independent Expert on the effects of foreign debt praised Argentina's progress in reducing unemployment and poverty rates and increasing pension coverage, health services, and primary school enrolment from an economic and quantitative perspective, but did not situate these findings in a specific human rights context. In rather general terms, he highlighted several shortcomings of the adopted measures, namely the uneven distribution of resources, the lack of adequate housing, and the exclusion of marginalized groups from social benefits, yet he did not clearly link his observations to the rights enshrined in the UN Covenants.[70] Despite these shortcomings in applying a rights-based approach, the report contains an important section from a *procedural* point of view because it calls on Argentina to address its debt problem in a way that respects human rights by ensuring the participation of affected people, acting transparently, and closely monitoring the effects of the debt restructuring measures on human rights.[71] In addition, the report emphasizes the role of international creditors in this scenario.[72] In sum, the report

[64] Rohter, 'Homes of Argentines' (n 33); see, for the CESCR's recommendation on the same issue in the context of Portugal, CESCR, 'Concluding Observations on the Fourth Periodic Report of Portugal' (8 December 2014) UN Doc E/C.12/PRT/CO/4, para 16.

[65] World Bank, 'Globalized, Resilient, Dynamic: The New Face of Latin America and the Caribbean' (Report No 78498 by the Chief Economist for LAC, Augusto de la Torre, 6 October 2010) inter alia 17.

[66] See eg Morgan-Foster, 'IMF Structural Adjustment' (n 56); Stephany Griffith-Jones, 'From Austerity to Growth in Europe: Some Lessons from Latin America' in Joseph E Stiglitz and Daniel Heymann (eds), *Life After Debt: The Origins and Resolutions of Debt Crisis* (International Economic Association 2014) 145.

[67] HRC, 'Concluding Observations on the Fourth Periodic Report of Argentina' (31 March 2010) UN Doc CCPR/C/ARG/CO/4.

[68] CESCR, 'Concluding Observations on the Third Periodic Report of Argentina' (14 December 2011) UN Doc E/C.12/ARG/CO/3.

[69] ibid para 15.

[70] HRC, 'IE Foreign Debt, Mission to Argentina' (n 62) paras 49–74.

[71] ibid paras 75–82.

[72] ibid paras 83, 86.

offers *procedural* suggestions for reaching coherence between human rights and economic interests.[73]

2. Greece

In October 2009, Greece announced that it had understated its deficit information for years. Since this announcement coincided with the peak of the 2008 financial crisis, the markets reacted quickly, which led to the exclusion of Greece from access to credit facilities. As a result, Greece was faced with a *debt crisis*[74] followed by a severe recession. The country's default could only be avoided with support from European and international financial institutions, which started in 2010.[75] After difficult discussions among the Euro-area Member States, an agreement was reached. It contained a package that combined bilateral governmental loans to Greece with support from the IMF.[76] As in Argentina, a set of austerity measures, including fiscal reform and restructuring the labour and product market as well as the financial sector, were set as conditions for financial support.[77] The support mechanism was first set up as the temporary European Financial Stability Facility (EFSF). However, it quickly became apparent that this arrangement would not be sufficient to overcome the legal constraints for bailing out members of the Euro area. Therefore, based on an amendment of Article 136 of the Treaty on the Functioning of the European Union,[78] a new, permanent crisis-resolution institution, the European Stability Mechanism (ESM), was established to replace the EFSF in 2011.[79]

At the time of writing, despite some progress, sustainable economic recovery is not yet in sight and the effects on individuals are severe, with very high unemployment rates[80] and a substantial part of the population at risk of poverty or social exclusion.[81] Various reports criticize the negative impact of the economic rescue

[73] See also Aoife Nolan, Nicholas J Lusiani, and Christian Courtis, 'Two Steps Forward, No Steps Back?: Evolving Criteria on the Prohibition of Retrogression in Economic and Social Rights' in Aoife Nolan (ed), *Economic and Social Rights after the Global Financial Crisis* (CUP 2014) 121, 126–27.

[74] See Section II.A, Table 13.1, scenario (3).

[75] For an excellent account of the different stages, see Olivier De Schutter and Margot E Salomon, 'Economic Policy Conditionality, Socio-Economic Rights and International Legal Responsibility: The Case of Greece 2010–2015' (legal brief prepared for the Special Committee of the Hellenic Parliament on the Audit of the Greek Debt (Debt Truth Committee), 15 June 2015; European Commission, *Economic Adjustment: Greece* (n 26).

[76] Brunnermeier, James, and Landau, *The Euro* (n 7) 20–24.

[77] European Commission, *Economic Adjustment: Greece* (n 26); it however needs to be emphasized that the negotiations between Greece and its international lenders are ongoing and thus constantly changing.

[78] European Council Decision 2011/199/EU of 25 March 2011 amending Article 136 of the Treaty on the Functioning of the European Union with regard to a stability mechanism for Member States whose currency is the euro [2011] OJ L 911.

[79] Treaty Establishing the European Stability Mechanism (signed on 2 February 2012, entered into force 27 September 2012) <www.esm.europa.eu> accessed 11 July 2017; Brunnermeier, James, and Landau, *The Euro* (n 7) 24–27.

[80] Eurostat, 'Unemployment Statistics' (June 2017) <http://ec.europa.eu/eurostat/statistics-explained/index.php/Unemployment_statistics> accessed 18 May 2017.

[81] Eurostat, 'People at Risk of Poverty or Social Exclusion' (December 2016) <http://ec.europa.eu/eurostat/statistics-explained/index.php/People_at_risk_of_poverty_or_social_exclusion> accessed 18

package on economic and social rights in general and the health system in particular.[82] In addition, as is quite common in debt crises,[83] the closure of the State-owned public broadcasting company ERN negatively affected media freedom. While the Greek government argued that the shutdown was necessary to reduce the number of public employees and therefore a required element of the rescue package, the European Commission, in its reply to a related question of a member of the European Parliament, did not mention human rights but seemed to hide behind rather technical language:

> While the Commission cannot prescribe Member States how to organise their public service broadcaster, the Commission highlights the role of a dual system of public and commercial service in promoting European values in all economic circumstances.[84]

In the reporting procedure before the CESCR, in 2015, Greece emphasized the international dimension of the implemented austerity measures, and particularly the roles of European and international financial institutions as well as the lack of a human rights dimension in austerity programmes:[85]

> It is clear that the international community and its institutions have not been able to design and implement a human rights-based response to debt crises. It has widely been acknowledged that economic, social and cultural rights have not been systematically integrated into the relevant policies and programs, while no comprehensive assessment of the impact of austerity measures on the promotion, protection and respect of economic, social and cultural rights has been conducted.

While Greece had unsuccessfully tried to justify restrictions of the right to social security before the ECSR by referring to its obligations towards IFIs,[86] it mentioned specific domestic measures taken to mitigate negative human rights impacts, but did not provide a clear view of the role the government should play for systematically integrating human rights into the rescue scenarios.[87]

In its List of Issues, the CESCR first asked the Greek authorities to provide a human rights impact assessment of the austerity programme and to present the

May 2017; Greek National Commission for Human Rights, 'Urgent Statement on Labour and Social Security Rights in Greece' (28 April 2017) <www.nchr.gr> accessed 30 July 2017.

[82] For a summary, see De Schutter and Salomon, 'Economic Policy Conditionality' (n 75); CESCR, 'List of Issues in Relation to the Second Periodic Report of Greece, Addendum: Replies of Greece to the List of Issues' (22 July 2015) UN Doc E/C.12/GRC/Q/2/Add.1, paras 5–8; Alexander Kentikelenis and others, 'Greece's Health Crisis: from Austerity to Denialism' (2014) 383 The Lancet 748, and the authors' reply to critical comments in Alexander Kentikelenis and others, 'Austerity and Health in Greece: Authors' Reply' (2014) 383 The Lancet 1544–45.

[83] See Section II.A, Table 13.1 scenario (3).

[84] Question for written answer E-007274/13 to the Commission by Inês Cristina Zuber (GUE/NGL) (20 June 2013) and joint answer given by Mr Rehn on behalf of the Commission (2 August 2013), [2014] OJ C48 E, 297-98. See also Afroditi Marketou, 'Greece: Constitutional Deconstruction and the Loss of National Sovereignty' in Thomas Beukers, Bruno de Witte, and Claire Kilpatrick (eds), *Constitutional Change through Euro-Crisis Law* (Cambridge University Press 2017) 179, 184–85.

[85] CESCR, 'Greek Replies 2015' (n 82) paras 2 and 10.

[86] ECSR, *Federation of Employed Pensioners of Greece (IKA-ETAM) v Greece* (n 32).

[87] CESCR, 'Greek Replies 2015' (n 82) paras 3–11.

principles on which the measures taken were based.[88] Following this line of reasoning, it then declared the human rights effects of the financial crisis a principal subject of concern in the Concluding Observations and reminded Greece to review the adopted austerity measures, including the programmes under the Memoranda of Understanding with the European Commission.[89] It called on the country to 'ensure that its obligations under the Covenant are duly taken into account when negotiating financial assistance projects and programmes, including with international financial institutions'.[90] Yet, no complimentary statement with regard to IFIs—at least those that are part of the UN system, ie the IMF and the World Bank—was issued.

Overall, the CESCR scrutinized the measures adopted by Greece more thoroughly than in its observations on Argentina, but it again failed to provide a thorough analysis of which ICESCR rights were affected. Accordingly, it did not take a more active role in promoting the rights enshrined in the Covenant across the whole UN system.

Similar discussions took place in the HRC when Greece presented its second periodic report. Unemployment and its effects on human rights were one of the main topics. Greece emphasized the profound adverse impact of the financial crisis on vulnerable groups and its intention to distribute the burden in a fair manner respectful of human rights.[91] Unlike the CESCR, the HRC did not issue a specific recommendation to include human rights into negotiations with IFIs, but in a rather general way expressed its concern about the impact of the financial crisis on women and disabled people.[92]

A more comprehensive analysis was conducted by the UN Independent Expert on the effects of foreign debt. He confirmed that the measures implemented by Greece in the course of the financial crisis 'have had the overall effect of compromising the living standards of the population and the enjoyment of human rights' and that the burden of the adjustment was not allocated in a fair manner among the whole population, but disproportionately affected the most vulnerable, such as the poor, older persons, pensioners, women, children, people with disabilities, and immigrants.[93] He thus complemented the IMF's identical economic findings with an at least partially human rights-based analysis.[94]

Finally, from a procedural perspective, the Independent Expert made a first small step towards a more holistic approach to implementing human rights in times of economic constraints by also including the obligations of Greece's international

[88] CESCR, 'List of Issues in Relation to the Second Periodic Report of Greece' (1 April 2015) UN Doc E/C.12/GRC/Q/2, para 2.

[89] CESCR, 'Concluding Observations on the Second Periodic Report of Greece' (9 October 2015) UN Doc E/C.12/GRC/CO/2, para 8, expressing specific concerns about the impacts of reduced social benefits and the cuts in staff and expenditures in the health sector (paras 23–24 and 35–36).

[90] ibid para 8.

[91] HRC, 'Second Periodic Report of Greece' (26 February 2014) UN Doc CCPR/C/GRC/2, para 4.

[92] HRC, 'Concluding Observations on the Second Periodic Report of Greece' (3 November 2015) UN Doc CCPR/C/GRC/CO/2, para 7.

[93] HRC, 'Report on Foreign Debt: Greece' (n 43) paras 41 and 42.

[94] IMF, 'Report on Greece' (n 43) 18.

lenders in his report.[95] Still, a more active, coherence-driven role of the treaty bodies will be decisive for advancing this agenda. Such an approach should include a systematic assessment of economic recovery programmes' impacts on human rights and—where available—relate to human rights commitments issued by IFIs. With resolution 34/3, the Human Rights Council requested the Independent Expert to develop guiding principles for human rights impact assessments for economic reform policies.[96] Such principles could serve as a starting point for the holistic approach mentioned afore. Another interesting recent development in this regard is the decision of the European Council on the revised macroeconomic adjustment programme for Greece under the ESM:[97]

> (10) Any form of financial assistance received by Greece to help it implement the policies under its Programme should be in line with the legal requirements and policies of the Union, in particular the Union's economic governance framework and the Charter of Fundamental Rights of the European Union ('the Charter'). To the extent that any of the measures envisaged in the macroeconomic adjustment programme limit the exercise of the rights and freedoms recognised by the Charter, those limitations *are*[98] in conformity with Article 52(1) thereof. Any intervention in support of financial institutions should be carried out in accordance with the Union's rules on competition. The commission should ensure that any measures laid down in a Memorandum of Understanding in the context of requested ESM financial assistance is fully consistent with this Decision.

In sum, the CESCR's call on Greece to ensure the Memorandum of Understanding's compliance with its obligations under the Covenant is still far from being fully implemented, but ongoing work by the Independent Expert on guiding principles for human rights impacts assessments for economic reform policies and the European Council's decision are first steps in this direction.

III. States' Human Rights Obligations in Times of Financial Crises

The two case studies illustrate the findings made in Section II.A, namely that, during a financial crisis, and particularly when implementing austerity measures, States face a complex web of actors, obligations, and responsibilities. This section will look at the different roles of States in different contexts for ensuring a human-rights based approach in addressing financial crises: States as duty-bearers under the UN Covenants (Section III.A), States acting as members of IFIs or participants in rescue

[95] HRC, 'Report of the Independent Expert on the Effects of Foreign Debt' (n 62) paras 12–16.

[96] HRC, 'Mandate of the Independent Expert on the Effects of Foreign Debt' (6 April 2017) UN Doc A/HRC/RES/34/3, 6 April 2017.

[97] Council Implementing Decision (EU) 2017/1226 of 30 June 2017 amending Implementing Decision (EU) 2016/544 approving the macroeconomic adjustment programme of Greece (2015/1411), [2017] OJ L174, 22, 23. Emphasis added by the author.

[98] Emphasis added. The wording 'are in conformity' implies a statement rather than a call on the responsible actors to make sure that measures are in line with art 52(1). The same wording can be found in other versions of the Decision, for instance in German ('ist vereinbar'), French ('est conforme'), Italian ('sono in conformità'), but interestingly enough not in the Greek text. The Greek text uses the word 'πρέπει' and thereby correctly holds that the measures 'should' comply with art 52(1).

programmes (Section III.B), and States' responsibilities with regard to private actors (Section III.C).

A. States' obligations as parties to the UN Covenants

State parties to the UN Covenants remain bound by them in financial crises.[99]

The nature of States' obligations under the ICESCR is essentially determined by its article 2(1), by which each State commits to 'take steps … to the maximum of its available resources, with a view to achieving progressively the full realization' of the Covenant rights. For the present purpose, two features of this concept are of particular relevance: first, the principle of progressive realization (as opposed to the immediate obligation contained in ICCPR article 2) obliges States 'to move as expeditiously and effectively as possible'[100] towards the full realization of ESCR.[101] This also entails that any deliberately retrogressive measure 'would require the most careful consideration'.[102] Second, the maximum of available resources must be made available, which according to the CESCR also refers to resources available from the international community.[103] Furthermore, in case of limited resources, priority has to be given to the so-called minimum core obligations, that is, the minimum essential levels of all Covenant rights,[104] which are 'crucial to securing an adequate standard of living through basic subsistence, essential primary health care, basic shelter and housing, and basic forms of education for all members of society'.[105] Additionally, limitations of the Covenant rights need to be determined by law and pursue the purpose of promoting general welfare in a democratic society.[106]

As a result, economic constraints will—first—not dispense States from their obligation to dedicate the maximum of available resources to ensuring the realization of human rights for everyone. It is thus decisive how scarce resources are allocated and whether basic human rights are made a priority.[107] Second, measures which lead to

[99] ICESCR art 2; ICCPR art 2.

[100] CESCR, 'General Comment 3' in 'Compilation of General Comments' (2008) (vol I) (n 29) para 9.

[101] See, for a more detailed assessment, Philip Alston and Gerard Quinn, 'The Nature and Scope of States Parties' Obligations under the International Covenant on Economic, Social and Cultural Rights' (1987) 9 Human Rights Q 156, 172–77.

[102] CESCR, 'General Comment 3' (n 100) para 9.

[103] ibid para 13; see also Alston and Quinn, 'States' Obligations' (n 101) 177–81.

[104] CESCR, 'General Comment 3' (n 100) para 10; see for example, with regard to art 12 ICESCR, CESCR, 'General Comment 14' in 'Compilation of General Comments' (2008) (vol I) (n 29) paras 43–48.

[105] HRC, 'Report on Extreme Poverty' (n 31) para 15.

[106] ICESCR art 4; see Alston and Quinn, 'States' Obligations' (n 101) 192–205.

[107] CESCR, 'Letter to States Parties from the Chairperson of the CESCR, Ariranga G Pillay' (16 May 2012) UN Doc CESCR/48th/SP/MAB/SW. The OHCHR adds more criteria to this list: OHCHR, 'Report on Austerity Measures' (n 23) paras 15–21; see also CESCR, 'General Comment 19' (n 29) para 42. These criteria were reaffirmed eg in CESCR, 'Concluding Observations: Fourth Portuguese Report' (n 64) para 6. See also HRC 'Report on Extreme Poverty' (n 31) para 14; OHCHR, 'Report of the High Commissioner for Human Rights on Implementation of Economic, Social and Cultural Rights' (8 June 2009) UN Doc E/2009/90, paras 44–54; Aoife Nolan, 'Budget Analysis and Economic and Social Rights' in Eibe Riedel, Gilles Giacca, and Christophe Golay, *Economic, Social, and Cultural Rights in International Law: Contemporary Issues and Challenges* (OUP 2014) 370.

a lowering of previously achieved human rights standards, as may be the case in the context of austerity programmes, are subject to heightened scrutiny and can only be considered consistent with the ICESCR under special conditions.[108] Both principles have recently been applied to financial crises by the CESCR.[109] In addition, the Committee confirmed that positive obligations under the Covenant are also applicable in times of financial crisis and may, for instance, require State measures 'to combat the disproportionate impact of the economic crisis ... on women's right to work'.[110]

According to ICCPR article 2(1), civil and political rights can only be restricted when the measure is necessary and 'proportionate to the pursuance of legitimate aims in order to ensure continuous and effective protection of Covenant rights'.[111] So far, little guidance exists on what these requirements entail in times of economic crises. At least with regard to the obligation to take steps to give effect to Covenant rights,[112] the HRC has clarified that non-compliance cannot be justified by reference to economic considerations, as would be common during financial crises.[113]

Unfortunately, in its Concluding Observations on Greece,[114] the HRC does not seize the opportunity to clarify whether resource constraints can justify restrictions of civil and political rights, and if so, to what extent.

Lastly, it is worth mentioning that, contrary to the ICESCR,[115] the ICCPR in its article 4 provides for the possibility of derogation from the Covenant in times of an officially proclaimed public emergency.[116] Until now, no State has invoked this clause in order to justify human rights derogations as a financial crisis-related public emergency.[117]

108 See CESCR, 'Statement: An Evaluation of the Obligations to Take Steps to the 'Maximum of Available Resources' under an Optional Protocol to the Covenant' (10 May 2007) UN Doc E/C.12/2007/1; CESCR, 'General Comment 19' (n 29) para 42. For a more detailed examination of retrogressive measures in the context of financial crises, see Nolan, Lusiani, and Courtis, 'Two Steps Forward' (n 73).

109 CESCR, 'Concluding Observations on the Fifth Periodic Report of Italy' (28 October 2015) UN Doc E/C.12/ITA/CO/5, paras 8–9, 34–35, and 38–39; CESCR, 'Concluding Observations on the Third Periodic Report of New Zealand' (31 May 2012) UN Doc E/C.12/NZL/CO/3, para 17; CESCR, 'Concluding Observations on the Fourth Periodic Report of Iceland' (11 December 2012) UN Doc E/C.12/ISL/CO/4, paras 6 and 16–18. However, in the first case addressed by the CESCR under the Optional Protocol to the ICESCR ((opened for signature 10 December 2008, entered into force 5 May 2016) UN Doc A/RES/63/117, 48 ILM 256 (2009)), which concerned the protection of homeowners in Spain in procedures for mortgage collection, it did not address the potential impacts of the financial crisis (*IDG v Spain* CESCR Communication No 2/2014 (13 October 2015) UN Doc E/C.12/55/D/2/2014).

110 CESCR, 'LOI Greece 2015' (n 88) para 8. Similarly, see the HRC 'Report on Extreme Poverty' (n 31) para 56.

111 See also HRC, 'General Comment 31' in 'Compilation of General Comments' (2008) (vol I) (n 29) paras 5–6.

112 ICCPR art 2(2).

113 See also HRC, 'General Comment 31' (n 111) para 14.

114 HRC, 'Concluding Observations: Second Greek Report' (n 92).

115 See Alston and Quinn, 'States' Obligations' (n 101) 216–19.

116 HRC, 'General Comment 29' in 'Compilation of General Comments' (2008) (vol I) (n 29) para 2.

117 After declaring a public emergency in 2001, Argentina unsuccessfully tried to justify its non-compliance with international investment agreements through their negative impact on human rights. See eg International Centre for Settlement of Investment Disputes (ICSID), *CMS Gas Transmission Company v the Argentine Republic* (award), 12 May 2005, ICSID case no ARB/01/8, paras 99 and

B. State responsibilities as members of IFIs or participants in rescue programmes

States may be indirectly involved in financial crises by their participation in assistance or recovery programmes. Based on their obligations to cooperate internationally according to ICESCR article 2(1) and its more general counterpart in articles 55 and 56 of the UN Charter, they are nevertheless required to contribute to mitigating a crisis's effects on human rights.[118] Such obligations have also been reaffirmed by the CESCR in its General Comment 2.[119]

A State that engages in bilateral rescue measures with other States or participates in crisis-related decisions in international fora, such as IFIs, therefore needs to ensure that the realization of ESCR is not obstructed or hindered.[120]

Whether this could be interpreted as adding an extraterritorial layer to this obligation remains controversial, however, as the negotiations on the Optional Protocol to the ICESCR revealed.[121] Yet, the undisputed substantial State obligations in the ICESCR, together with the obligation to cooperate according to article 2(1) and the obligation to fulfil international treaties in good faith, lead to the conclusion that States must refrain from any measures that impair the ability of another State to comply with its obligations regarding ESCR. The fact that States engage in international rescue measures or act in international fora does not change their responsibilities as parties to the Covenant. In particular, the obligation to cooperate does not entail obligations vis-à-vis rights-holders in other countries, but rather forms part of a country's responsibilities towards the international community. This finding corresponds with the judgment of the ECtHR in *Matthews*.[122]

The CESCR shows, in its practice, that it is conscious of the role of IFIs, as it, for instance, has recommended that Argentina should include its international human

114; for critics of the ICSID's approach to these cases, see David Schneidermann, 'Compensating for Democracy's 'Defects': The Case of International Investment Law' in Christian Joerges and Carola Glinski (eds), *The European Crisis and the Transformation of Transnational Governance: Authoritarian Managerialism versus Democratic Governance* (Hart 2014) 47, 54–58.

[118] See eg OHCHR, 'Draft Background Paper on Rights-based Approaches to Financial Regulation: Macroeconomic Policies and Economic Recovery' (2013) <www.ohchr.org/Documents/Issues/Development/RightsCrisis/OHCHR_Background_Paper.doc> accessed 31 May 2017, 9.

[119] CESCR, 'General Comment 2' in 'Compilation of General Comments' (2008) (vol I) (n 29). See also CESCR, 'General Comment 3' (n 100) para 14.

[120] See, with regard to the right to water, CESCR, 'General Comment 15' in 'Compilation of General' (2008) (vol I) (n 29) para 31; M Magdalena Sepúlveda, *The Nature of the Obligations under the International Covenant on Economic, Social and Cultural Rights* (Intersentia 2003) 218–22, 237–38.

[121] See ESC, 'Report of the Open-ended Working Group to Consider Options Regarding the Elaboration of an Optional Protocol to the International Covenant on Economic, Social and Cultural Rights on its Third Session' (14 March 2006) UN Doc E/CN.4/2006/47, paras 77–86; Fons Coomans, 'The Extraterritorial Scope of the International Covenant on Economic, Social and Cultural Rights in the Work of the United Nations Committee on Economic, Social and Cultural Rights' (2011) 11 Human Rights L Rev 1, 17.

[122] *Matthews v the United Kingdom* App no 24833/94 (ECtHR, 18 February 1999) para 32. For the context of labour rights, see Kaufmann, *Globalisation and Labour Rights* (n 11) 280–81.

rights obligations in the negotiations with these institutions.[123] It does not, however, see only the State in crisis as responsible for preventing adverse impacts of the practices of such institutions on the human rights of its population, but also reminds other member States of their obligations in this regard.[124] For example, in 2000 and 2001, reflecting the effects of the Asian and Argentine financial crises, it encouraged several countries in their capacity as members of the IMF and the World Bank ' ... to do all [they] can to ensure that the policies and decisions of those organizations are in conformity with the obligations of States parties to the Covenant, in particular the obligations contained in article 2.1 concerning international assistance and cooperation'.[125]

Although this recommendation was not repeated in following years,[126] the Committee confirmed its approach in an open letter to the States parties.[127] In sum, States cannot free themselves from their human rights responsibilities by transferring competences to international organizations, which are seen as collectives of States.[128] This may require a clear framework for coordinating different policies at the government level, as for instance developed by Austria.[129]

[123] CESCR, 'Concluding Observations: Second Argentine Report 1999' (n 56) para 28; see also CESCR, 'Concluding Observations on the Second Periodic Report of Morocco' (1 December 2000) UN Doc E/C.12/1/Add. 55, para 38.

[124] Coomans, 'Extraterritorial Scope' (n 121) 24–29.

[125] See eg CESCR, 'Concluding Observations on the Second Periodic Report of Belgium' (1 December 2000) UN Doc E/C.12/1/Add.54, para 31; CESCR, 'Concluding Observations on the Third Periodic Report of Italy' (23 May 2000) UN Doc E/C.12/1/Add. 43, para 20; CESCR, 'Concluding Observations on the Second Periodic Report of France' (30 November 2001) UN Doc E/C.12/1/Add.72, para 32; CESCR, 'Concluding Observations on the Fourth Periodic Report of Sweden' (30 November 2001) UN Doc E/C.12/1/Add.70, para 24; CESCR, 'Concluding Observations on the Second Periodic Report of Japan' (24 September 2001) UN Doc E/C.12/1/Add.67, para 37; CESCR, 'Concluding Observations on the Fourth Periodic Report of the United Kingdom' (5 June 2002) UN Doc E/C.12/1/Add.79, para 26; CESCR, 'Concluding Observations on the Fourth Periodic Report of Germany' (24 September 2001) UN Doc E/C.12/1/Add.68, para 31; CESCR, 'Concluding Observations on the Fourth Periodic Report of Finland' (1 December 2000) UN Doc E/C.12/1/Add.52, para 24.

[126] See eg CESCR, 'Concluding Observations on the Third Periodic Report of Belgium' (4 January 2008) UN Doc E/C.12/BEL/CO/3; CESCR 'Concluding Observations on the Fourth Periodic Report of Belgium' (23 December 2013) UN Doc E/C.12/BEL/CO/4.

[127] CESCR, 'Letter from Chairperson Pillay' (n 107); see, for a different interpretation by the former General Counsel and Director of the Legal Department of the IMF, François Gianviti, 'Economic, Social and Cultural Rights and the International Monetary Fund' (2001) <www.imf.org/external/np/leg/sem/2002/cdmfl/eng/gianv3.pdf> accessed 27 October 2015, paras 26–27; see also Mac Darrow, *Between Light and Shadow: The World Bank, The International Monetary Fund and International Human Rights Law* (Hart 2003) 133–38.

[128] See also CESCR, 'General Comment 2' (n 119) para 9; HRC, 'Guiding Principles on Foreign Debt and Human Rights' (10 April 2010) UN Doc A/HRC/20/23; Maastricht Guidelines on Violations of Economic, Social and Cultural Rights (22–26 January 1997) UN Doc E/C.12/2000/13, para 19; Magdalena Sepúlveda Carmona, 'The Obligations of "International Assistance and Cooperation" under the International Covenant on Economic, Social and Cultural Rights: A Possible Entry Point to a Human Rights Based Approach to Millennium Development Goal 8' (2009) 13 The Intl J of Human Rights 86, 91–92.

[129] Austrian Federal Ministry of Finance, 'Strategic Guidelines of the Austrian Federal Ministry of Finance for International Financial Institutions' (August 2015) <https://www.bmf.gv.at/wirtschaftspolitik/int-finanzinstitutionen/Strategischer_Leitfaden_IFI_EN_.pdf?5s3q7u> accessed 19 May 2017, 9.

In their reports to the CESCR, States are explicitly required to indicate the mechanisms in place to ensure that their obligations under the Covenant will feed into their actions as members of international organizations and IFIs.[130] So far, no corresponding guidelines have been established by the HRC and no clear benchmarks for reconciling the different levels of obligations from a human rights perspective have been developed by the treaty bodies.

C. Obligations of States with regard to private actors

The horizontal obligation of States to protect human rights from violations by private actors is accepted in international human rights law and confirmed in the first pillar of the UN Guiding Principles on Business and Human Rights (UNGP).[131] In the context of financial crises, this obligation is particularly relevant given the role that commercial banks and investors play in financial markets.[132] Accordingly, their contribution to financial crises can be substantial, as the 2008 crisis clearly indicates. At the same time, regulatory failures and inadequate supervision of financial market actors are undisputed potential triggers for financial crises.[133]

In the aftermath of the recent financial crisis, the lack of adequate regulation and supervision has been extensively discussed by national legislators and in IFIs. Where regulatory measures were adopted, they would generally focus on financial market regulation and corporate law. Little has been undertaken to include the negative impact of corporate behaviour on human rights in these regulatory processes. One avenue for clarifying the scope of State obligations to regulate corporate behaviour could be a binding treaty. In 2014, the Human Rights Council established an Intergovernmental Working Group with the mandate 'to elaborate an international legally-binding instrument to regulate, in international human rights law, the activities of transnational corporations and other business enterprises'.[134] Since this process is still in its early stages and its outcome uncertain given that there is no clear

[130] CESCR, 'Guidelines on Treaty-specific Documents to be Submitted by States Parties under Articles 16 and 17 ICESCR' (24 March 2009) UN Doc E/C.12/2008/2, para 3(c).

[131] HRC, 'Guiding Principles on Business and Human Rights: Implementing the United Nations "Protect, Respect and Remedy" Framework: Report of the Special Representative of the Secretary-General on the Issue of Human Rights and Transnational Corporations and Other Business Enterprises' (21 March 2011) UN Doc A/HRC/17/31, adopted by HRC resolution 17/4 (16 June 2011) UN Doc A/HRC/17/4, para 9; HRC, 'Report on Extreme Poverty' (n 31) paras 82–85; see also Christine Kaufmann, 'International Law in Recession? The Role of International Law When Crisis Hits: Food, Finance and Climate Change' in Ulrich Fastenrath and others (eds), *From Bilateralism to Community Interest: Essays in Honour of Bruno Simma* (OUP 2011) 1189, 1205; Olivier De Schutter, 'Towards a New Treaty on Business and Human Rights' (2016) 1 Business and Human Rights J 41, 44, with further references.

[132] HRC, 'Report on Extreme Poverty' (n 31) paras 82–85.

[133] See, for the United States, National Commission on the Causes of the Financial and Economic Crisis in the United States, 'The Financial Crisis Inquiry Report' (January 2011) <http://fcic.law.stanford.edu/report> accessed 31 May 2017.

[134] HRC, 'Elaboration of an International Legally Binding Instrument on Transnational Corporations and Other Business Enterprises with Respect to Human Rights' (26 June 2014) A/HRC Res 26/9, para 9; De Schutter, 'A New Treaty' (n 131) 41–44.

objective on what such a treaty should focus on,[135] it is even more important to use existing instruments. The UN treaty bodies, and in particular the CESCR, could contribute to creating an adequate legal and institutional framework 'which enables markets to live up to their potential to contribute to the well-being of society and the realization of human rights for everyone'.[136]

IV. Human Rights Obligations and Responsibilities of IFIs and Their Members

A. Obligations and responsibilities

Discussions on the legal role of international organizations, including IFIs, in safeguarding human rights often neglect to distinguish between the respective *obligations* and *responsibilities.* The result is a flawed reflection of the complex relationships between the individual human rights-holders, States, and non-State actors, as described at the outset of this chapter, or in the words of Samantha Besson a 'conflation of global justice and human rights'.[137] The main reason for this 'conflation' is the absence of human rights-holders from the equation: legal obligations are obligations *to* somebody, so they by definition require a rights-holder as a counterpart. In contrast, *responsibilities* are not framed as duties owed to rights-holders but as responsibilities *for* something which may include different actors, both private and public. In the following, human rights obligations to rights-holders and broader human rights-related responsibilities are treated separately.

B. IFIs' human rights obligations—Much ado about nothing?

Already in 1949, the International Court of Justice (ICJ) held that the scope of international organizations' obligations needs to be defined in relationship with the constituent treaty of the organization concerned.[138] In the context of a dispute between Egypt and the World Health Organization (WHO) on the establishment of a regional office in Alexandria, the Court seized the opportunity to clarify that, as subjects of international law, international organizations 'are bound by any obligations incumbent upon them under general rules of international law, under their constitutions or under international agreements to which they are parties'.[139]

135 See the critical comments by John Ruggie, 'Life in the Global Public Domain: Response to Commentaries on the UN Guiding Principles and the Proposed Treaty on Business and Human Rights' (23 January 2015) <http://ssrn.com/abstract=2554726> accessed 19 August 2017.

136 HRC, 'Report of the Office of the United Nations High Commissioner for Human Rights on the Impact of the Global Economic and Financial Crises on the Realization of All Human Rights and on Possible Actions to Alleviate It' (18 February 2010) UN Doc A/HRC/13/38, paras 30–31.

137 Samantha Besson, 'The Bearers of Human Rights' Duties and Responsibilities for Human Rights: A Quiet (R)Evolution?' (2015) 32 Social Philosophy and Policy 244, 246.

138 *Reparation for Injuries Suffered in the Service of the United Nations* (Advisory Opinion) [1949] ICJ Reports 174, 179.

139 *Interpretation of the Agreement of 25 March 1951 between the WHO and Egypt* (Advisory Opinion) [1980] ICJ Reports 73, 89–90, para 37. For an extensive discussion, see Jan Klabbers, 'The EJIL

Although it is easy to agree that international organizations should be bound to respect human rights, establishing corresponding legal obligations is rather difficult: First, the two UN Covenants are only open to States for ratification.[140] In addition, international organizations, including IFIs, are generally not parties to a substantial number of international treaties apart from host State agreements. Second, with the exception of the European Union (EU), no other international organization has established its own human rights regime.[141]

As a result, IFIs are not legally required to comply with the ICESCR and the ICCPR, neither under international treaty law nor under their own constitutions.[142] This leaves us with the third potential legal source for international organizations' duties mentioned by the ICJ, namely 'general international law'.

This then raises the question of the extent to which the human rights enshrined in the two Covenants can be considered customary international law or general principles of international law.[143]

With regard to human rights, the discussion focuses on the legal status of the Universal Declaration of Human Rights (UDHR).[144] So far, there is no broad consensus on which specific rights enshrined in the UDHR can be considered customary international law, and the ICJ has not issued a respective decision.[145]

Framing the consensus that was reached with the adoption of the UDHR as acceptance of human rights as general principles of international law therefore seems more promising.[146] Such an argument can be based on recent activities by States and IFIs as well as the jurisprudence of the ICJ.[147] A milestone in this development is the unanimous adoption of the UNGP by the Human Rights Council in 2011. The UNGP explicitly refer to 'internationally recognized human rights—understood, at a minimum, as those expressed in the International Bill of Human Rights and the principles concerning fundamental rights set out in the International Labour Organization's Declaration on Fundamental Principles and Rights at Work'.[148] The International Bill of Human Rights includes the UDHR.[149] A number of

Foreword: The Transformation of International Organizations Law' (2015) 26 European J of Intl L 9, 59–63.

[140] ICESCR art 26 and ICCPR art 48.

[141] TEU art 6(1); Besson, 'Quiet (R)Evolution' (n 137) 257.

[142] For a detailed discussion of the IMF and the World Bank, see Kaufmann, *Globalisation and Labour Rights* (n 11) 123–27.

[143] ibid 133.

[144] Universal Declaration of Human Rights (adopted 10 December 1948) UNGA Res 217 A(III).

[145] Olivier De Schutter, 'Human Rights and the Rise of International Organisations: The Logic of Sliding Scales in the Law of International Responsibility' in Jan Wouters and others (eds), *Accountability for Human Rights Violations by International Organizations* (Intersentia 2011) 55.

[146] Bruno Simma and Philip Alston, 'The Sources of Human Rights Law: Custom, Jus Cogens, and General Principles' (1989) 12 Australian YB of Intl L 82, 107.

[147] *United States Diplomatic and Consular Staff in Tehran* [1980] ICJ Rep 3, 42, para 91; Hurst Hannum, 'The Status of the Universal Declaration of Human Rights in National and International Law' (1995-96) 25 Georgia J of Intl and Comparative L 287, 292–312, and 351–52. For the EU: Andreas Fischer-Lescano, *Human Rights in Times of Austerity Policy: The EU Institutions and the Conclusion of Memoranda of Understanding* (Nomos 2014) 35.

[148] HRC, 'UN Guiding Principles' (n 131) para 12.

[149] ibid commentary to para 12.

international economic and financial institutions have adopted this approach; among them are the Organisation for Economic Co-operation and Development (OECD),[150] the International Finance Corporation (IFC),[151] and the World Bank.[152] Similar developments can be found in the EU[153] and at the State level.[154] All of these instruments recognize the relevance of the UDHR in a business context. Finally, the Leaders' declaration at the G7 summit in June 2015 endorsed the UNGP and the OECD Guidelines and the G20 Leaders' Declaration of July 2017 commits to fostering the implementation of labour, social, and environmental standards as contained in the UNGP and other internationally recognized instruments to achieve sustainable global supply chains.[155]

While it can therefore safely be stated that the human rights contained in the UDHR are broadly recognized as general principles of international law today, this does not—as proposed by some authors[156]—imply that the UDHR may serve as a legal basis for deriving human rights obligations of IFIs towards individual rights-holders. Instead, the UDHR will play an important role in framing IFIs' responsibilities. The recent Decision of the European Council to approve the revised adjustment programme for Greece, which refers to the Charter of Fundamental Rights of the EU, may be a first (small) step in this direction.[157] In fact, according to the European Court of Justice (ECJ)'s jurisprudence, the Charter's obligations do not apply to member States in the context of the ESM because they do not implement EU law in this context.[158] However, the Charter is binding on EU institutions, also when they act outside the EU legal framework. As a result, the European Commission, when acting on behalf of the ESM, has a legal obligation to ensure that a memorandum of understanding is consistent with the rights enshrined in the Charter.[159] In addition, the ECJ's reasoning could be interpreted as mirroring the unclear position of the ESM with regard to the EU and its fundamental values, particularly human rights. In other words, the technical legal arrangements to establish

[150] OECD, 'OECD Guidelines on Multinational Enterprises' (2011) Chapter IV: Human Rights.

[151] IFC, 'Sustainability Framework' (2012 edition) <www.ifc.org/wps/wcm/connect/topics_ext_content/ifc_external_corporate_site/ifc+sustainability/our+approach/risk+management/ifcsustainabilityframework_2012> accessed 18 May 2017.

[152] The current state of the World Bank's implementation of its new environmental and social framework is available at < http://www.worldbank.org/en/programs/environmental-and-social-policies-for-projects/brief/the-environmental-and-social-framework-esf > accessed 8 February 2018.

[153] European Commission, 'A Renewed EU Strategy 2011–14 for Corporate Social Responsibility' (25 October 2011) COM/2011/0681 final; for an update see European Commission, 'Commission Staff Working Document on Implementing the UN Guiding Principles on Business and Human Rights: State of Play' (14 July 2015) SWD(2015) 44 final.

[154] A list of national action plans to implement the UNGP can be found here: <www.ohchr.org/EN/Issues/Business/Pages/NationalActionPlans.aspx> accessed 31 May 2017.

[155] G7, 'Leaders' Declaration G7 Summit' G7 Summit (Elmau 7–8 June 2015) 6; G20, 'Leaders' Declaration: Shaping an Interconnected World' G20 Summit (Hamburg 7–8 July 2017) para 7.

[156] eg De Schutter and Salomon, 'Economic Policy Conditionality' (n 75) 12.

[157] Council Implementing Decision (EU) 2017/1226 (n 97).

[158] ECJ, Case C-370-12 *Pringle v Government of Ireland* [2012] EU:C:2012:756, paras 178–81. However, member States remain bound by their obligations under the ECHR and the UN Covenants; Fischer-Lescano, *Human Rights* (n 147) 23–26.

[159] ECJ, Joined Cases C-8/15 P to C-10/15 P *Ledra Advertising Ltd and others v European Commission and European Central Bank* [2016] EU:C:2016:701, para 67.

the ESM as an independent institution do not adequately address the underlying identity question, but add to existing regulatory fragmentation.[160]

C. Human rights-related responsibilities of IFIs?

As outlined above, under current international law, States are the primary duty-bearers with regard to human rights, and clear-cut legally binding human rights obligations of international institutions vis-à-vis rights-holders, as they can be found in the EU system, are a rare exception. While this result may—at least partially—be traced to the insufficiencies of functionalism as a conceptual underpinning of the law of international organizations,[161] rejecting the role of human rights law for IFIs altogether and deploring the supremacy of politics overlooks the *twofold role of States* as duty-bearers vis-à-vis individuals within their jurisdiction, on the one hand, and their responsibilities as members of international organizations and IFIs, on the other.[162]

Today, all members of the IMF have ratified at least one of the two UN Covenants. These obligations do not end at the doorstep to the IMF's or any other IFI's board-room, but include—as stated by the ECtHR in *Matthews*[163]—an obligation of States to ensure that IFIs of which they are members do not infringe on their obligation to protect, respect, and fulfil human rights.

While States are responsible for acting in a human rights-compatible manner in their capacity as members of an IFI, IFIs as collective organizations comprised of States have a responsibility not to jeopardize States' obligations to comply with the two Covenants.

However, it seems that this concept was somewhat turned on its head when Greece was required to provide legal evidence of the compatibility of its package of fiscal measures as requested by the ESM.[164] Accordingly, the Greek government submitted a legal opinion that, in the view of the European Commission, confirms that the pension reform is in line with the Greek Constitution, the Charter of

[160] For an excellent account of the role identity plays in a EU context, see Moshe Hirsch, *Invitation to the Sociology of International Law* (OUP 2015) 109–14.

[161] Klabbers, 'The EJIL Foreword' (n 139).

[162] For a similar argument, see André Nollkaemper, 'Saving the Scarecrow' (2015) 26 European J of Intl L 957, 962.

[163] *Matthews v the United Kingdom* (n 122) para 32.

[164] 'Supplemental Memorandum of Understanding (second addendum to the Memorandum of Understanding) between the European Commission Acting on Behalf of the European Stability Mechanism and the Hellenic Republic and the Bank of Greece' (5 July 2017) para 2.1.1: 'The authorities will provide a written independent legal opinion confirming that the contingent nature of both the income tax reform and the expansionary package to be enshrined in legislation is feasible under the Greek Constitution. The authorities will provide a legal opinion that the pension reform is in line with the Greek Constitution and the Charter of Fundamental rights. The authorities will also provide a detailed quantitative assessment of the redistributive impact of pension reforms.' Another legal opinion was required on the role of arbitration in collective bargaining in para 4.1. See also the Greek government's statement in its letter of intent to the IMF of 7 July 2017: IMF, 'Greece: Request for Stand-By Arrangement', IMF Country Report 17/229, Staff Report, Appendix I: Letter of Intent, footnotes 1 and 2.

Fundamental Rights of the EU, and the European Convention on Human Rights (ECHR). The legal opinion, which has not been published so far, concludes that the proposed reform rescues the core of the pension rights at stake by making the minimum possible necessary cuts, and is therefore in line with the Greek constitution and the ECHR.[165]

D. The role of the UN human rights bodies

The two Covenants do not operate in clinical isolation from financial crises, but need to be situated in a country's specific legal *context*. The treaty bodies must therefore consider the anatomy of a financial crisis as well as the respective State obligations under international rescue programmes when evaluating compliance with the Covenants. Understanding the specific features of a financial crisis will lead to a more thorough assessment of the related human rights impacts by the Committees. Most importantly, it will allow the Committees to engage in a substantive debate on how to reconcile economic rescue programmes with existing human rights obligations. Such a debate will be facilitated by the two Committees' relatively broad scope of examination possibilities in the reporting procedures.

In the case studies, a development in the approach of the CESCR can be observed: while, at first, it only voiced general concern about the adopted structural reform,[166] it subsequently started to criticize the modifications more specifically. The Committee referred, for example, to the Argentine legislation with regard to provisions of collective agreements, and doubted its conformity with the ICESCR.[167] Similar concerns were expressed regarding Greece.[168] Due to their specificity, the recommendations serve as an important argument in negotiations with IFIs. This significant role could be strengthened with more explicit references to the fact that these legislative changes were part of a broader structural reform influenced by several players, such as other States, international institutions, and private actors.[169] Ignoring such constraints can lead to recommendations that are difficult to implement and will eventually undermine the legitimacy and credibility of the reporting process and the treaty bodies. It is thus essential to address financial crises' human rights impacts not only in recommendations to directly affected States but also to States in their capacity as members of IFIs or as home or host States to influential private financial actors and institutions. This does not shift the responsibility for complying with the Covenants from States to international institutions,[170]

165 European Commission, 'Compliance Report: The Third Economic Adjustment Programme for Greece, Second Review June 2017' (16 June 2017) 10–11.

166 CESCR, 'Concluding Observations: First Argentine Report 1994' (n 52).

167 CESCR, 'Concluding Observations: Second Argentine Report 1999' (n 56) para 31.

168 CESCR, 'LOI Greece 2015' (n 88) para 14.

169 See also Nolan, Lusiani, and Courtis, 'Two Steps Forward' (n 73) 129–30. Steps in this direction can be found in HRC, 'Report on Foreign Debt: Greece' (n 43); HRC, 'IE Foreign Debt, Mission to Argentina' (n 62); and HRC, 'Guiding Principles on Foreign Debt' (n 128).

170 See also Magdalena Sepúlveda Carmona, 'Alternatives to Austerity: A Human Rights Framework for Economic Recovery' in Aoife Nolan (ed), *Economic and Social Rights after the Global Financial Crisis* (CUP 2014) 23, 40.

but will produce recommendations that can contribute to ensuring human rights-compatible responses to financial crises.

V. Conclusion: People, Process, and Paradigm

States that are parties to the ICCPR and the ICESCR are bound by them also in times of financial crisis. This chapter has, first, shown that financial crises and related recovery programmes, particularly austerity measures, may result in human rights violations, with already vulnerable groups being at higher risk. While all financial crises share some common features, their triggers, involved actors, and effects may vary substantially and lead to a complex web of actors, relationships, and responsibilities as well as a fragmented body of norms.

This chapter identifies three key elements for effectively implementing the Covenants in times of financial crisis: a people-oriented, rights-based perspective, a process to foster coherence, and a new paradigm for bridging the gap between human rights and international financial regulations.

A. People-oriented, rights-based perspective

Under a people-oriented, rights-based perspective, human rights play an active role instead of being banned to the sidelines and addressed as collateral damage. By expanding the focus from economic and financial facts to the impact of a financial crisis on people, conducting a human rights and equality impact assessment becomes a natural component of financial crisis management and recovery programmes. A step in this direction was undertaken at a rather late stage by Greece when its Parliament installed a Debt Truth Committee to look into the negative impact of macroeconomic adjustment measures since 2010.[171]

Parties to the ICESCR that are not immediately faced with a financial crisis will be required to integrate a human rights perspective into assistance or recovery programmes in which they participate based on their obligation to cooperate internationally. This obligation holds true for both unilateral as well as multilateral programmes, and regardless of whether such programmes are established in the framework of an international (financial) organization or outside of one. Participation in rescue plans such as the programmes concerning Greece established by the ESM therefore comes with the corresponding obligation to assess and consider such programmes' effects on the human rights enshrined in the Covenants.[172]

Contracting States' obligation to protect also extends to *private actors*, particularly commercial banks and investors, in the sense that States have to take measures to prevent or at least mitigate negative human rights impacts caused by private actors' activities. This obligation has been specified by the UNGP, which call on States to

[171] De Schutter and Salomon, 'Economic Policy Conditionality' (n 75).

[172] For a detailed discussion of the Rescue Plans for Greece, see De Schutter and Salomon, 'Economic Policy Conditionality' (n 75) 4–9.

'set out clearly the expectation that all business enterprises domiciled in their territory and/or jurisdiction respect human rights throughout their operations'.[173] As seen in the Argentine case, this obligation may become particularly relevant in the aftermath of a financial crisis, when debt restructuring packages are tailored.

B. Processes for ensuring coherence

The second element is establishing a *process* to provide for coherence among different bodies of law and different institutions. This calls on international institutions, both in the realm of human rights and international finance, to include a country's regulatory context into their considerations. While IFIs are not parties as such to the UN Covenants, they are nevertheless required to apply a human rights-based approach when addressing financial crises. This conclusion is based on the UDHR, which, as this chapter suggests, can be understood as a consensus on a set of general principles of international law, and on the fact that the vast majority of IFIs' members have ratified at least one of the UN Covenants. In other words, member States' obligation not to engage in activities in IFIs that would jeopardize their human rights obligations under the Covenants translates into a corresponding responsibility of IFIs not to impede their members' human rights compliance. Given their broad acceptance, the two Covenants can play an important role, particularly in financial crises, because they not only allow but—especially in the context of the ICESCR—require a dialogue between human rights and economic theory. On the one hand, it is undisputed and confirmed both empirically and in economic studies that financial crises have a negative impact on human rights. On the other hand, human rights and economic recovery are clearly mutually beneficial. Strikingly, a look at the Atlantic Charter, which paved the way for the institutional post-war order, including the establishment of the UN as well as the IMF and the World Bank, reveals that such considerations were already seen as the very fabric of a coherent institutional framework for a peaceful world order in 1941.[174] Finally, it is important to note that EU institutions are legally bound by the EU Charter of Fundamental Rights when acting in the context of economic recovery programmes such as the ESM, and therefore have to ensure that any measures taken will not jeopardize the rights enshrined in the Charter. This obligation also extends to cooperation with the IMF in the context of the ESM.

C. Paradigm reloaded: Emancipation and translational human rights

The result of these two elements, a people-oriented, rights-based approach and the need for coherent processes, is a call for a fresh *paradigm*. It entails *emancipating* the Covenants and the respective treaty bodies from their role as handling the 'clean-up' during and after a financial crisis so they can become actors on equal footing with

[173] HRC, 'UN Guiding Principles' (n 131) Guiding Principle 2.

[174] Reprinted in Samuel I Rosenmann (ed), *The Public Papers and Addresses of Franklin D Roosevelt* (Macmillan 1938) 314.

the principles of international economic law and the respective institutions, particularly IFIs. This will require additional knowledge and expertise in all institutions involved, and accordingly an institutionalized dialogue between the treaty bodies and the relevant IFIs.

However, this will not be sufficient to keep the Covenants alive in future crises. Therefore, an interface to bridge the conceptual gap between human rights and financial regulations needs to be developed. In borrowing a term from the medical sciences, I call this interface *translational human rights*. The objective of translational medicine is to transfer results from basic research into medical treatment from which patients can benefit. With regard to human rights, recent developments concerning the UNGP and the related OECD Guidelines for Multinational Enterprises are important steps in this direction, as they translate human rights into business language and principles that can be operationalized in a business context. Yet, at this stage, they still lack an important element which links to the first point about emancipating the Covenants and the treaty bodies: any translational instruments need to be firmly anchored in sound normative principles which give the Covenants and the treaty bodies a key if not leading role in actively shaping and defining the specific content of what human rights mean in a financial crisis. While the CESCR seems to have undertaken first steps in this direction, these attempts are still far from complying with the prerequisites for a legitimate and transparent normative process. Thus, in order for translational human rights law to perform its function as an interface between different regulatory worlds and the respective roles and responsibilities of the different actors involved in triggering and cleaning up a crisis, further work is necessary. In this sense, this chapter serves as a first step on a road to discovery beyond the traditional human rights discourse. It may not lead to exotic destinations but it will certainly offer new perspectives once we are ready to leave our comfort zone and engage with other—yet unfamiliar—concepts and disciplines: '[o]n ne peut découvrir de nouvelles terres sans consentir à perdre de vue le rivage pendant une longue période.'[175]

Bibliography

Alston, Philip, and Quinn, Gerard, 'The Nature and Scope of States Parties' Obligations under the International Covenant on Economic, Social and Cultural Rights' (1987) 9 Human Rights Q 156

Besson, Samantha, 'The Bearers of Human Rights' Duties and Responsibilities for Human Rights: A Quiet (R)Evolution?' (2015) 32 Social Philosophy and Policy 244

Brunnermeier, Markus K, James, Harold, and Landau, Jean-Pierre, *The Euro and the Battle of Ideas* (Princeton University Press 2016)

[175] 'One cannot discover new lands without consenting to lose sight of the shore for a very long time' (André Gide, *Journal des faux-monnayeurs* (Paris Gallimard Foliplus classique) 376, translation by the author).

Claessens, Stijn, and Kose, Ayhan, 'Financial Crises: Explanations, Types, and Implications' in Stijn Claessens and others (eds), *Financial Crises: Causes, Consequences, and Policy Responses* (International Monetary Fund 2014)

Conklin, Margaret, and Davidson, Daphne, 'The I.M.F. and Economic and Social Human Rights: A Case Study of Argentina 1958–1985' (1986) 8 Human Rights Q 227

Coomans, Fons, 'The Extraterritorial Scope of the International Covenant on Economic, Social and Cultural Rights in the Work of the United Nations Committee on Economic, Social and Cultural Rights' (2011) 11 Human Rights L Rev 1

Cornia, Giovanni A, Jolly, Richard, and Stewart, Frances (eds), *Adjustment with a Human Face* (2 vols, OUP 1987)

Darrow, Mac, *Between Light and Shadow: The World Bank, The International Monetary Fund and International Human Rights Law* (Hart 2003)

De Schutter, Olivier, 'Human Rights and the Rise of International Organisations: The Logic of Sliding Scales in the Law of International Responsibility' in Jan Wouters and others (eds), *Accountability for Human Rights Violations by International Organizations* (Intersentia 2011)

De Schutter, Olivier, 'Towards a New Treaty on Business and Human Rights' (2016) 1 Business and Human Rights J 41

De Schutter, Olivier, and Salomon, Margot E, 'Economic Policy Conditionality, Socio-Economic Rights and International Legal Responsibility: The Case of Greece 2010-2015' (legal brief prepared for the Special Committee of the Hellenic Parliament on the Audit of the Greek Debt (Debt Truth Committee) 15 June 2015)

Fischer-Lescano, Andreas, *Human Rights in Times of Austerity Policy: The EU Institutions and the Conclusion of Memoranda of Understanding* (Nomos 2014)

Frenkel, Roberto, 'Argentina: A Decade of the Convertibility Regime' (2002) 45 Challenge 41

Gide, André, *Journal des faux-monnayeurs* (Paris Gallimard Folioplus classique 1925/2008)

Ginsborg, Lisa, 'The Impact of the Economic Crisis on Human Rights in Europe and the Accountability of International Institutions' (2017) 1 Global Campus Human Rights J 97

Greek National Commission for Human Rights, 'Urgent Statement on Labour and Social Security Rights in Greece' (28 April 2017) <www.nchr.gr> accessed 30 July 2017

Griffith-Jones, Stephany, 'From Austerity to Growth in Europe: Some Lessons from Latin America' in Joseph E Stiglitz and Daniel Heymann (eds), *Life After Debt: The Origins and Resolutions of Debt Crisis* (International Economic Association 2014)

Haggard, Stephen, *The Political Economy of the Asian Financial Crisis* (Peterson Institute for International Economics 2000)

Hannum, Hurst, 'The Status of the Universal Declaration of Human Rights in National and International Law' (1995-96) 25 Georgia J of Intl and Comparative L 287

Hirsch, Mosche, *Invitation to the Sociology of International Law* (OUP 2015)

Karanikolos, Marina, and others, 'Financial Crisis, Austerity, and Health in Europe' (2013) 381 The Lancet 1323

Kaufmann, Christine, 'International Law in Recession? The Role of International Law When Crisis Hits: Food, Finance and Climate Change' in Ulrich Fastenrath and others (eds), *From Bilateralism to Community Interest: Essays in Honour of Bruno Simma* (OUP 2011)

Kaufmann, Christine, Globalisation and Labour Rights: The Conflict between Core Labour Rights and International Economic Law (Hart 2007)

Kentikelenis, Alexander, and others, 'Austerity and Health in Greece: Authors' Reply' (2014) 383 The Lancet 1544

Kentikelenis, Alexander, and others, 'Greece's Health Crisis: from Austerity to Denialism' (2014) 383 The Lancet 748

Klabbers, Jan, 'The EJIL Foreword: The Transformation of International Organizations Law' (2015) 26 European J of Intl L 9

Krajewski, Markus, 'Human Rights and Austerity Programmes' in Thomas Cottier, Rosa M Lastra, and Christian Tietje (eds), *The Rule of Law in Monetary Affairs* (CUP 2014)

Letnar Černič, Jernej, 'State Obligations Concerning Socio-Economic Rights in Times of the European Financial Crisis' (2015) 11 Intl L and Management Rev 125

Lowenfeld, Andreas F, *International Economic Law* (2nd edn, OUP 2008)

Marketou, Afroditi, 'Greece: Constitutional Deconstruction and the Loss of National Sovereignty' in Thomas Beukers, Bruno de Witte, and Claire Kilpatrick (eds), *Constitutional Change through Euro-Crisis Law* (CUP 2017)

Maurino, Gustavo, and Nino, Ezequiel, 'Economic and Social Rights and the Supreme Court of Argentina in the Decade Following the 2001–2003 Crisis' in Aoife Nolan (ed), *Economic and Social Rights after the Global Financial Crisis* (CUP 2014)

Morgan-Foster, Jason, 'The Relationship of IMF Structural Adjustment Programs to Economic, Social, and Cultural Rights: The Argentine Case Revisited' (2003) 24 Michigan J of Intl L 577

Nolan, Aoife, 'Budget Analysis and Economic and Social Rights' in Eibe Riedel, Gilles Giacca, and Christophe Golay, *Economic, Social, and Cultural Rights in International Law: Contemporary Issues and Challenges* (OUP 2014)

Nolan, Aoife, 'Not Fit For Purpose? Human Rights in Times of Financial and Economic Crisis' (2015) 21 European Human Rights L Rev 358

Nolan, Aoife, Lusiani, Nicholas J, and Courtis, Christian, 'Two Steps Forward, No Steps Back?: Evolving Criteria on the Prohibition of Retrogression in Economic and Social Rights' in Aoife Nolan (ed), *Economic and Social Rights after the Global Financial Crisis* (CUP 2014)

Nollkaemper, André, 'Saving the Scarecrow' (2015) 26 European J of Intl L 957

Peterson, Matt, and Barry, Christian, 'Who Must Pay for the Damage of the Global Financial Crisis?' in Ned Dobos, Christian Barry, and Thomas Pogge (eds), *Global Financial Crisis: The Ethical Issues* (Springer 2011)

Pittini, Alice, and others, 'The State of Housing in the EU 2015' (Housing Europe 2015)

Protest and Assembly Law Project, 'Suppressing Protest: Human Rights Violations in the U.S. Response to Occupy Wall Street' (2012) <www.chrgj.org/wp-content/uploads/2012/10/suppressingprotest.pdf> accessed 7 October 2015

Reinhart, Carmen M, and Rogoff, Kenneth S, 'Banking Crises: An Equal Opportunity Menace' (2013) 37 J of Banking and Finance 4557

Reinhart, Carmen M, and Rogoff, Kenneth S, 'From Financial Crash to Debt Crisis' (2011) 101 American Economic Review 1676

Reinhart, Carmen M, and Rogoff, Kenneth S, *This Time is Different: Eight Centuries of Financial Folly* (Princeton University Press 2009)

Rittich, Kerry, 'Labour Market Governance in Wake of the Crisis: Reflections and Possibilities' in Christian Joerges and Carola Glinski (eds), *The European Crisis and the Transformation of Transnational Governance* (Hart 2014)

Rohter, Larry, 'The Homes of Argentines Are at Risk in I.M.F. Talks' *The New York Times* (New York, 23 June 2003)

Rosenmann, Samuel I (ed), *The Public Papers and Addresses of Franklin D Roosevelt* (Macmillan 1938)

Ruggie, John, 'Life in the Global Public Domain: Response to Commentaries on the UN Guiding Principles and the Proposed Treaty on Business and Human Rights' (23 January 2015) <http://ssrn.com/abstract=2554726> accessed 19 August 2017

Schneidermann, David, 'Compensating for Democracy's 'Defects': The Case of International Investment Law' in Christian Joerges and Carola Glinski (eds), *The European Crisis and the Transformation of Transnational Governance: Authoritarian Managerialism versus Democratic Governance* (Hart 2014)

Sepúlveda Carmona, Magdalena, 'The Obligations of "International Assistance and Cooperation" under the International Covenant on Economic, Social and Cultural Rights: A Possible Entry Point to a Human Rights Based Approach to Millennium Development Goal 8' (2009) 13 The Intl J of Human Rights 86

Sepúlveda, Carmona Magdalena, 'Alternatives to Austerity: A Human Rights Framework for Economic Recovery' in Aoife Nolan (ed), *Economic and Social Rights after the Global Financial Crisis* (CUP 2014)

Sepúlveda, M Magdalena, *The Nature of the Obligations under the International Covenant on Economic, Social and Cultural Rights* (Intersentia 2003)

Simma, Bruno, and Alston, Philip, 'The Sources of Human Rights Law: Custom, Jus Cogens, and General Principles' (1989) 12 Australian YB of Intl L 82

Stein, Peer, Ardic, Oya Pinar, and Hommes, Martin, *Closing the Credit Gap for Formal and Informal Micro, Small, and Medium Enterprises* (International Finance Corporation 2013)

Tsoukala, Philomila, 'Euro Zone Crisis Management and the New Social Europe' (2013) 20 Columbia J for European L 31

14

The Institutional Future of the Covenants

A World Court for Human Rights?

*Felice D Gaer**

> The vision I have grounded in the treaties themselves, is nothing less than the operationalization of the principles of the universality and the indivisibility of human rights as well as the States' primary responsibility to ensure the implementation of these principles. This requires that States ratify treaties, but, more importantly, implement them.[1]

I. Introduction

At a March 2016 panel discussion commemorating the fiftieth anniversary of the two overarching UN human rights Covenants[2] at the United Nations (UN) Human Rights Council, Choi Kyonglim, its President, suggested that 'ensuring the justiciability' of all human rights could strengthen their implementation.[3] Exploration of better ways to implement human rights treaty norms has received attention over the years as an increasing number of human rights treaties have come into force. Yet proposals for institutional reform, such as President Choi's call for consolidation of the two Covenant committees into a single body, or a proposal to create a 'world court of human rights', have rarely addressed the substantive issues involved in such integration, focusing instead on a series of procedural concerns.

* All views expressed are the author's and do not represent those of the Committee against Torture.

[1] Navanethem Pillay, 'Strengthening the UN Human Rights Treaty Body System' (June 2012) <www2.ohchr.org/english/bodies/HRTD/docs/HCReportTBStrengthening.pdf> accessed 7 April 2017, 12.

[2] The International Covenant on Civil and Political Rights (opened for signature 16 December 1966, entered into force 23 March 1976) 999 UNTS 171, and the International Covenant on Economic, Social and Cultural Rights (opened for signature 16 December 1966, entered into force 3 January 1976) 993 UNTS 3.

[3] 'Human Rights Council Holds High-level Panel Discussion Marking the Fiftieth Anniversary of the Two Human Rights Covenants' (1 March 2016) <www.ohchr.org/EN/NewsEvents/Pages/DisplayNews.aspx?NewsID=17114&LangID=E> accessed 7 April 2017.

'Human rights is the idea of our time,' Professor Louis Henkin reminded us in introducing his 1981 volume on the International Covenant on Civil and Political Rights (ICCPR).[4] Yet, despite the appeal of the 'rights' idea, it took eighteen years for UN diplomats to move from approving the Universal Declaration of Human Rights (UDHR) in 1948[5] to adoption of the Covenants in 1966. A key reason, as Henkin explained, was that none of the negotiating States wanted a Covenant that would later reveal 'their behavior . . . to be wanting'.[6]

Ever since, constructing effective oversight of the implementation of the Covenants has been a focus of attention for policy makers and human rights experts at the UN and its human rights programmes. Some advocates have focused on substance (ie whether the treaties should have greater judicial authority), while others have focused on procedure (whether the treaty monitoring bodies could do a better job through consolidation, harmonization, or otherwise tinkering with their powers). Some of the ideas proposed have been grand ones, such as the proposal of High Commissioner for Human Rights Louise Arbour to create a single unified standing treaty body.[7] Other proposals have been modest, raising procedural points about consolidating State reports, or aimed at reducing operational costs, such as whether and how to limit document length and the languages into which committee reviews of periodic reports are translated.[8]

Most observers begin with the assumption that the treaty bodies can indeed be effective, reasoning that (1) they supervise binding agreements—authoritative instruments adopted by the members of the UN, a global body; (2) the treaties are ratified freely by States parties, which knowingly incur legal obligations through the ratification processes; and (3) the ratification of instruments by a large number of States parties implies the States themselves will demand proper levels of compliance by their fellow States. However, as pointed out in 2006 by the UN Secretariat, '[t]he system . . . faces challenges because many states accept the human rights treaty system on a formal level, but do not engage with it, or do so in a superficial way, either as a result of lack of capacity or lack of political will.'[9]

Other concerns abound, including: (1) issues of duplication (due to the overlap of provisions and competencies in the various treaties), (2) growth of ratifications,

[4] Louis Henkin (ed), *The International Bill of Human Rights: The Covenant on Civil and Political Rights* (Columbia University Press 1981) 1.

[5] Universal Declaration of Human Rights (adopted 10 December 1948) UNGA Res 217 A(III).

[6] ibid 9.

[7] See HRI (UN International Human Rights Instruments), 'Concept Paper on the High Commissioner's Proposal for a Unified Standing Treaty Body' (22 March 2006) UN Doc HRI/MC/2006/2.

[8] See eg the reports of the Annual Meetings of Chairpersons of the Human Rights Treaty Bodies <http://www.ohchr.org/EN/HRBodies/AnnualMeeting/Pages/MeetingChairpersons.aspx > accessed 4 July 2017 or the first report by Philip Alston prepared for the UN General Assembly (Philip Alston, 'Effective Implementation of International Instruments on Human Rights, Including Reporting Obligations Under International Instruments on Human Rights' (8 November 1989) UN Doc A/44/668.

[9] HRI, 'Concept Paper (n 7) para 16.

reports, complaints, and resource requirements, (3) low public awareness of the treaty bodies, (4) uneven levels of expertise and competence of treaty body members, (5) inadequate coordination among the treaty bodies and the risk of conflicting jurisprudence, (6) inadequacies in the State reports, and insufficient information available to the treaty body members to assess these reports appropriately and prepare concise concluding recommendations to States, (7) substantial backlogs in reviewing reports and complaints, and (8) the absence of adequate follow-up mechanisms regarding concluding observations and decisions on individual cases.[10]

Manfred Nowak and Martin Scheinin, both academics based in Europe who have served as UN special procedure mandate holders in human rights, have proposed a 'world court of human rights' as the solution to the problem of non-enforcement of UN treaty norms by the UN machinery, which they argue is the single most important problem.[11] Manfred Nowak reminds us that the 'weaknesses of this system . . . are well known,' citing delayed reports, slow handling of individual complaints 'leading to non-legally binding' decisions by 'quasi-judicial bodies', and a lack of will by States parties to comply with these decisions.[12] Nowak and Scheinin argue that a 'world court', on the other hand, would ensure an effective remedy for individuals suffering violations of rights.

As this chapter will explain, this proposal is not altogether new. It is merely the latest variation on a longstanding proposal to create a stronger petition mechanism by consolidating all of the optional procedures for individual complaints into a single body. The idea of breaking off individual petitions from the nine relevant treaty bodies has surfaced from time to time as one of the ways of restructuring the system. This proposal has rightfully focused attention on the option of consolidating the treaty bodies into a single entity, but the potential impact of such restructuring has not been fully explicated. Moreover, the focus on non-enforcement may be over-emphasized in comparison to other reform efforts needed to maintain compliance with the human rights obligations of the States parties.

Before rushing to adopt something shiny and new, we should carefully consider what has been tried with respect to reform and evaluate how best to ensure that the human rights treaty system effectively upholds the hard-won and well-established rights guaranteed in the treaties themselves.

[10] ibid and Michael O'Flaherty, 'The High Commissioner and the Treaty Bodies' in Felice D Gaer and Christen L Broecker (eds), *The United Nations High Commissioner for Human Rights: Conscience for the World* (Brill 2014) 111–12.

[11] See Manfred Nowak, 'The Need for a World Court of Human Rights' (2007) 7 Human Rights L Rev 251, 251–52, and Martin Scheinin, 'Towards a World Court of Human Rights' (2009) Swiss Initiative to Commemorate the 60th Anniversary of the UDHR <www.enlazandoalternativas.org/IMG/pdf/hrCourt_scheinin0609.pdf> accessed 9 May 2017, 63.

[12] Manfred Nowak, 'It's Time for a World Court of Human Rights' in M Cherif Bassiouni and William A Schabas (eds), *New Challenges for the UN Human Rights Machinery: What Future for the UN Treaty Body System and the Human Rights Council Procedures?* (Intersentia 2011) 17, 21.

II. Human Rights Treaty Implementation and the Covenants

In the dozen years between the drafting of the ICCPR and the International Covenant on Economic, Social and Cultural Rights (ICESCR) (1954) and their adoption (1966), the shape of a body to monitor implementation of the two treaties became a considerable point of contention, and has remained so ever since.[13] The composition of the committees established to oversee compliance with the Covenants, their functions, as well as the nomination and selection processes were changed multiple times during the drafting process. As finalized, the ICCPR was to be monitored by an independent committee of eighteen State-nominated experts authorized to receive reports and to request additional ones, if needed; the ICESCR would be monitored by the members of the UN's Economic and Social Council (ECOSOC), a key UN body composed of State representatives. This meant that, for economic and social rights, serving diplomats, rather than independent experts, were initially designated as the persons to conduct the 'oversight' of compliance. Later, in 1985, ECOSOC would establish a separate eighteen-member monitoring committee for this purpose, on which persons elected by ECOSOC would serve in their personal capacities. Some have been independent scholars and experts, others have been serving or former diplomats.

Other treaty monitoring mechanisms, on the model of the independent committee, have been established since then. In all, there are now ten treaty bodies monitoring nine core human rights treaties and their optional protocols.[14] This proliferation of normative instruments and monitoring bodies has drawn attention to whether the system of implementation established is effective, efficient, or sensible.

[13] AH Robertson, 'The Implementation System: International Measures' in Henkin, *Bill of Human Rights* (n 4) 334.

[14] The Covenants were adopted in 1966 and came into force ten years later. By then, the Convention on Elimination of Racial Discrimination had already been adopted in 1965 (Convention on the Elimination of All Forms of Racial Discrimination (opened for signature 7 March 1966, entered into force 4 January 1969) 666 UNTS 195) and there were others in relatively short order: the Women's Convention (Convention on the Elimination of All Forms of Discrimination against Women (opened for signature 18 December 1979, entered into force 3 September 1981) 1249 UNTS 13), the Convention against Torture (Convention against Torture and Other Cruel, Inhuman or Degrading Treatment or Punishment (opened for signature 10 December 1984, entered into force 26 June 1987) 1465 UNTS 85), the Convention on the Rights of the Child (Convention on the Rights of the Child (opened for signature 20 November 1989, entered into force 2 September 1990) 1577 UNTS 3), and the Convention on Migrant Workers (International Convention on the Protection of the Rights of All Migrant Workers and Members of their Families (opened for signature 18 December 1990, entered into force 1 July 2003) 2220 UNTS 3), totalling seven treaties at the time when Louise Arbour made her proposals for a unified body. These instruments were followed more recently by three others: the Convention against Disappearances (International Convention for the Protection of All Persons from Enforced Disappearance (opened for signature 20 December 2006, entered into force 23 December 2010) 2716 UNTS 3), the Convention on Rights of People with Disabilities (Convention on the Rights of Persons with Disabilities (opened for signature 13 December 2006, entered into force 3 May 2008) 2515 UNTS 3), and the Optional Protocol establishing the Subcommittee on Prevention of Torture (Optional Protocol to the Convention against Torture and Other Cruel, Inhuman or Degrading Treatment or Punishment (opened for signature 18 December 2002, entered into force 22 June 2006) 2375 UNTS 237), for a total of ten 'core' human rights treaty bodies.

It further encouraged efforts to review and revise the institutional treatment of, and monitoring by, all of these human rights entities.

Institutionally, the UN Secretariat was initially limited to providing meeting rooms and minimal secretariat services (translation etc). Financially, some treaty bodies were to be supported by the treaty-ratifying States, and others by the UN itself; later, as some countries neglected payments, a so-called temporary solution was found—for the funding to come from the UN's regular budget for all of the treaty monitoring bodies, while formally proposed amendments were circulated to States parties for adoption. (Some of these amendments, such as one for the Committee against Torture, continue in that form until the present.) It was expected, however, that the experts serving as members of the treaty bodies would do the analysis of compliance and raise any questions with States parties.[15]

III. Past Treaty Reform Efforts

Reform proposals—and criticism of the committee implementation model—have grown over the years. In 1984, in response to a request by the UN General Assembly (UNGA),[16] the UN's Human Rights Office began to facilitate meetings of the chairs of the different human rights treaty bodies to help improve coordination. In 1988, the UNGA asked for an independent expert to advise on long-term approaches to the supervision of new instruments. Australian professor Philip Alston was appointed and later submitted three reports between 1988 and 1997.[17] During and after this, numerous academic meetings and publications addressed the treaty reform issue. The UN Secretary General expressed his views on the need for reform, and two High Commissioners for Human Rights offered ideas for specific changes.[18]

A review of the literature on human rights treaties suggests that scholars and diplomats have spent a huge amount of time and space discussing how to reform or strengthen the treaty monitoring bodies. To observers, it may seem that they have spent less effort working to assess the substantive impact of the actual reviews examining compliance by specific countries with the treaty provisions, or to assess the results of individual complaint and other treaty procedures.[19] Indeed, the main issues

[15] See O'Flaherty, 'The High Commissioner' (n 10) 101, for a reflection on what was and was not considered appropriate for UN secretariat servicing of the treaty body members, and how this has changed.

[16] UNGA Res 38/117 (16 December 1983) UN Doc A/RES/38/117.

[17] Philip Alston wrote three reports for the UNGA between 1989 and 1996: Alston, '1989 Report' (n 8); 'Interim Report on Updated Study by Mr. Philip Alston' (22 April 1993) UN Doc A/Conf.157/PC/62/Add.11/Rev.1; and 'Effective Functioning of Bodies Established Pursuant to UN Human Rights System: Final Report on Enhancing the Long-term Effectiveness of the UN Human Rights Treaty System' (27 March 1996) UN Doc E/CN.4/1997/74.

[18] UNGA, 'Strengthening of the United Nations: An Agenda for Further Change—Report of the Secretary-General' (9 September 2002) UN Doc A/57/387, paras 52–54.

[19] eg the new 'Inter-Committee Meeting' (ICM) convened in June 2002 discussed State reporting and sharing of information, but did not address communications. The ICM brought together the chairs and two other members of the then six treaty bodies to discuss reform measures. See HRI, 'Report of

discussed have been various matters to simplify the reporting 'burden' on States, to strengthen the membership of the treaty bodies, to properly resource the secretariat staffing and the treaty bodies, and to decide whether or not to consolidate the multiple treaty bodies. From time to time, issues of the capacity of States to report, as well as the quality of the actual treaty body review—the questions asked, the time devoted to the review, and so on—were also raised.

IV. Recommendations for Reform by Alston, and Others

As early as 1988—when there were only four treaties in force—Philip Alston warned that the human rights treaties were at a 'critical crossroads'.[20] States complained of a reporting 'burden',[21] secretariat assistance was minimal, and there were crippling, acute funding problems.[22] He expressed serious concerns about membership, doubting that non-governmental organizations (NGOs) could maintain interest in the treaty bodies much longer due to the low quality of the diplomatic representatives then serving on the treaty bodies.

Alston pointed to four major problems with the treaty bodies: capacity, efficiency, quality, and the reporting burden. The proliferation of instruments might require more serious measures to be adopted by the General Assembly, he explained, such as a formal moratorium on new instruments, establishment of a new and separate standard-setting body, or setting priorities for any future instruments. However, he concluded, none of these seemed likely.[23] Alston also called for eliminating overlapping competences, for obtaining greater consistency between treaty bodies especially on the interpretation of norms, and for procedural standardization. With enhanced competence, he said, he hoped for greater credibility and visibility of the treaty bodies.

Alston proposed three options: to consolidate existing treaty bodies, to give new functions provided for in new treaties to existing treaty bodies, or to attach new instruments to existing treaties.[24] To a large degree these remain the options considered in most of the proposals and reform plans since. He noted that a single, consolidated committee might expand the capacity of the treaty bodies to keep up with the large quantity of reports submitted for review and individual cases requiring decisions, but would likely overlook important issues examined currently by treaty bodies, making it risky.[25]

In 1996, Alston conceded that many procedural changes had in fact been made, but found that the larger long-term issues remained. Consolidation had not been seriously considered by those treaty body members who were busy trying to make the existing system work, he noted. Changes were now urgent, he argued, but

the First Inter-Committee Meeting' (24 September 2002) UN Doc HRI/ICM/2002/3. It followed and partially overlapped with a treaty reform-focused meeting convened by Australia.

[20] This warning appeared in Alston, '1989 Report' (n 8) para 1. [21] ibid para 8.
[22] ibid paras 54–99. [23] ibid paras 150–59. [24] ibid para 178.
[25] ibid paras 181 and 183.

should not be ad hoc or reactive, and instead needed to be planned carefully and systematically.[26]

Alston examined certain ideal scenarios for reform, but in the end expressed doubts about their feasibility. Costs and budgets loomed large in his analysis. As for consolidation, he emphasized how much this depended on political will—if it was present, he called for an expert working group to begin to explore options for consolidation.

Alston made many suggestions about what needed to be done, but his recommendations ultimately tended toward the practical: addressing chronic non-reporting by introducing flexibility, including consolidation of reports; addressing documentation issues more transparently and utilizing electronic databases more effectively; ensuring better coordination among treaty bodies; and engaging the High Commissioner to bring committee experts together to develop better cooperation.[27]

V. Consolidation Ideas: Stakeholder Meetings and Beyond

The idea of a 'super-committee'—or of some form of unification or consolidation—has been a favourite in the many recommendations that were made by academics, NGOs, and other observers in the years in which Alston was examining the effectiveness of the treaty bodies and thereafter.[28]

I attended many of the treaty reform meetings, including the initial Inter-Committee meeting, Malbun I and II, and other specialized sessions that followed.[29]

[26] Alston, '1996 Report' (n 17) para 80.

[27] ibid paras 110–22.

[28] While there were many meetings and articles that discussed the impact of and reform of treaty bodies, the following were noteworthy in discussions and policy debates that followed: Anne F Bayefsky, *The UN Human Rights Treaty System: Universality at the Crossroads* (Martinus Nijhoff 2001); a collection by Anne F Bayefsky (ed), *The UN Human Rights System in the 21st Century* (Kluwer 2000); and a volume by Philip Alston and James Crawford (eds), *The Future of Human Rights Treaty Monitoring* (CUP 2000). Additionally, a lengthy article by Christof Heyns and Frans Viljoen summarized their major project, which attempted to assess the impact of the human rights treaties in many different countries (Christof Heyns and Frans Viljoen, 'The Impact of the United Nations Human Rights Treaties on the Domestic Level' (2001) 23 Human Rights Q 483).

[29] Treaty reform meetings in which I participated included six of the eleven Inter-Committee meetings (namely the 1st, 4th, 7th, 9th, 10th, and 11th ICMs: see HRI, 'Report of the First Inter-Committee Meeting' (n 19); UNGA 'Effective Implementation of International Instruments on Human Rights, Including Reporting Obligations under International Instruments on Human Rights' (19 August 2005) UN Doc A/60/278, Annex: Report on 4th Inter-committee Meeting of Human Rights Treaty Bodies, 10; UNGA, 'Report of the Chairpersons of the Human Rights Treaty Bodies on their Twentieth Meeting' (13 August 2008) UN Doc A/63/280, Annex: Report on 7th Inter-committee Meeting of Human Rights Treaty Bodies, 9; UNGA 'Report of the Chairpersons of the Human Rights Treaty Bodies on their Twenty-first Meeting' (10 August 2009) UN Doc A/64/276, Annex II: Report on 9th Inter-committee Meeting of Human Rights Treaty Bodies, 24; UNGA, 'Report of the Chairpersons of the Human Rights Treaty Bodies on their Twenty-second Meeting' (6 August 2010) UN Doc A/65/190, Annex I: Report on 10th Inter-committee Meeting of Human Rights Treaty Bodies, 11, and Annex II: Report on 11th Inter-committee Meeting of Human Rights Treaty Bodies, 24), as well as the two Malbun meetings and a variety of subsidiary working groups that focused on harmonization of guidelines, core reports, and follow-up. I also participated in the Dublin meeting, which began the treaty strengthening process, in November 2009, and a specialized inter-committee consultation on petitions.

In this capacity, I observed how earnestly the Secretariat members pressed to establish harmonized procedures and coherence in the treaty system.

In an extensive report on treaty reform produced shortly after Alston's third report, in 2000, Anne Bayefsky recommended establishing two consolidated treaty bodies, one for review of State reports and another for examining communications, interstate complaints, and inquiries.[30] She argued that the procedural requirements, concerns, and functions for handling communications sent to different treaty bodies 'are very similar and call for the same expertise' and that the substantive outcomes of the cases would be improved if staff concentrated only on communications or State reports.[31]

The UN Secretariat began to organize a new kind of treaty reform conference after this: so-called 'Inter-Committee Meetings', which consisted of the chairs of the existing human rights treaty bodies plus two other members of each committee. While ostensibly aimed at having broader discussions of reform options, Secretariat officials privately acknowledged that the Inter-Committee meetings also had the goal of breaking the stranglehold that committee chairs had had on the harmonization and reform efforts to that date.[32] Numerous interested parties were invited to weigh in with treaty reform proposals at these meetings, which began in 2002 and continued until 2011. A wide array of subsidiary meetings and discussions were also incorporated in these sessions.

In 2002, consolidation supporters picked up another influential ally in UN Secretary General Kofi Annan. Citing the 'growing complexity' of the diverse UN treaty committees and the 'burden of reporting obligations' as straining resources, Annan surprised human rights experts by calling for a simplification for States through the submission of a single comprehensive report that would, in turn, be reviewed by each relevant treaty body.[33]

After Annan's proposal for a single report, treaty reform efforts became more focused. At the invitation of Liechtenstein, in 2003, a large and high-level 'brainstorming' meeting was convened in Malbun with a wide range of stakeholders.[34] The Malbun I meeting in 2003 rejected Annan's proposal for a single report to all

[30] Bayefsky, *Universality* (n 28).

[31] ibid. Bayefsky also noted that a petitions unit had been created only a short time before her report. Indeed, the former Deputy High Commissioner for Human Rights, Bertrand Ramcharan, has explained that he considered the management consultants' recommendation to eliminate the special unit for human rights communications (including those outside the treaty system, eg under Resolution 1503 [UN Security Council Res 1503 (28 August 2003) UN Doc S/RES/1503(2003)]) to have been 'a notorious error' that he (successfully) sought to correct (Bertrand Ramcharan, *A UN High Commissioner in Defence of Human Rights* (Brill 2004)). Ramcharan has noted that a communications unit (upgraded to a 'section') existed at least from the 1970s. It was upgraded to a Communications Branch under former UN Under-Secretary-General Jan Martenson, but abolished under the management reform overseen by José Ayala Lasso, the first High Commissioner for Human Rights. As recounted in his book, Ramcharan worked successfully in 1998 to re-establish a separate petitions team during his tenure as Deputy High Commissioner.

[32] Based on confidential interviews conducted by the author on the basis of anonymity.

[33] UNGA, 'Strengthening the United Nations: An Agenda for Further Change' (9 September 2002) UN Doc A/57/387, paras 52–54.

[34] UNGA, 'Letter Dated 13 June 2003 from the Permanent Representative of Liechtenstein to the UN' (8 July 2003) UN Doc A/58/123 (hereafter 'Malbun I report').

treaty bodies, citing the difficulty both of preparing and examining a single report. Not only would it not solve the problem of non-reporting, participants concluded, it would probably make things worse by slowing down individual submissions of State reports. Participants called instead for an expanded 'core document' with basic information that could be reviewed by all the treaty bodies, and for other efforts to 'harmonize' the format of the reports submitted.[35]

In response to another, more comprehensive reform report by Secretary-General Annan, entitled 'In Larger Freedom: Towards Development, Security and Human Rights for All',[36] Louise Arbour, the new High Commissioner for Human Rights, issued a Plan of Action in which she indicated how she would expand and improve the UN's human rights programme. She affirmed that she would develop proposals for a 'unified standing treaty body' and that she would invite States parties to an intergovernmental meeting in 2006 'to consider options'.[37]

Arbour also discussed her Plan of Action with members of the Human Rights Committee (HRC), explaining that treaty body reform was then at what she termed an 'embryo stage'.[38] In a one-hour discussion, several members of the HRC mentioned the need to consider the individual petitions, or communications, as the reform proceeded, but none offered any specific suggestions for doing so. Despite earlier suggestions, the idea of a separate entity for all treaty-related petitions was not discussed at the session with Arbour. It became clear in this discussion that there was ongoing concern with preventing the loss of the specialized expertise of each of the treaty bodies while continuing to protect rights-holders.

Arbour's reform plans were discussed with lower-ranking Secretariat officials in other treaty bodies. At the Committee on the Elimination of Racial Discrimination (CERD), a Secretariat official was told that the CERD, as a whole, was not convinced that a single unified standing body was the most effective way to reform the treaties, as members were concerned that it might end up marginalizing many subjects, such as racial discrimination. It was therefore argued that alternatives to the unified body might be better. The CERD suggested that a strengthened petitions unit might speed up processing the backlog,[39] as might 'establishing a single body entrusted with considering individual communications.'[40] Only one member of the CERD actually mentioned the petitions unit, and did so solely in the context of whether it could increase visibility of petitions.[41] Other members questioned the solution offered by Arbour—the creation of a unified standing treaty body—by suggesting it was 'ill-suited' to the specific problems of the system that had been

[35] ibid paras 23–30.

[36] UNGA, 'In Larger Freedom: Towards Development, Security and Human Rights for All: Report of the Secretary-General' (21 March 2005) UN Doc A/59/2005.

[37] ibid para 147.

[38] HRC, 'Summary Record (Partial) of the 2296th Meeting' (26 July 2005) UN Doc CCPR/C/SR.2296, para 4.

[39] ibid para 6.

[40] CERD, 'Summary Record of the 1726th Meeting' (9 September 2005) UN Doc CERD/C/SR.1726.

[41] HRC, 'Summary Record of July 2005' (n 38) para 24.

outlined.[42] The Secretariat said consultations would continue as no decision had been reached yet.[43]

At the Committee on the Rights of Migrant Workers (CMW), Secretariat members also heard a variety of views, most of which also emphasized the need to maintain specific treaty bodies even as the plan for a unified body proceeded. However, one member, Ms Cubias Medina, stated that 'the only way that the treaty bodies would achieve greater political or judicial authority would be through the creation of a world court of human rights' and she asked whether this had been discussed as a possibility. She stated that the authority carried by decisions of the body were key. Other members expressed regret that no State party had yet ratified or accepted the optional individual complaint procedure as set forth in article 77 of the Migrant Workers Convention.[44]

VI. Arbour's Proposal Deferred: A Unified Standing Treaty Body

In March 2006, a Concept Paper was issued by the Secretariat, following up on High Commissioner Arbour's proposal to establish a unified standing treaty body.[45] It was aimed for consideration at the meeting of chairpersons of the human rights treaty bodies in late June and at an intergovernmental meeting to be scheduled thereafter. The Concept Paper cited a variety of by now familiar shortcomings.[46] It also brought up the issue of differing interpretations of human rights standards and inconsistent jurisprudence, and it offered a wide range of proposals for improvement—from examining reports of States parties jointly to convening joint thematic working groups and issuing joint General Comments, along with other kinds of harmonization proposals.

In the end, the Concept Paper concluded that the best way to address these challenges fully would be to create a unified standing treaty body to cover all the treaties, rights, and groups concerned. It offered several different models for such a body—from a single body that would consider every treaty provision together to one with multiple chambers, operating perhaps along the lines of each treaty, or with clustered rights, or perhaps divided along geographic lines. In addition, the Concept Paper offered assurances that the new body would take measures to ensure that 'specialized expertise' would not be lost in the new structure. Also proposed were measures to ensure the quality of the new body's members.

[42] ibid. [43] ibid.

[44] CMW, 'Summary Record of the 23rd Meeting' (19 Dec 2005) UN Doc CMW/C/SR.23, para 9.

[45] See HRI, 'Concept Paper' (n 7) 30.

[46] Such as the failure of States to submit reports or to send them in on time, the low quality of many of the reports, the uneven expertise of treaty body members, and the increased burden on the treaty body members because of the increase in ratifications and new treaties, as well as the backlog in consideration of reports and individual complaints. The lack of financial resources and meeting time was said to contribute to the low visibility of the treaty bodies and to the absence of follow-up on the recommendations of the treaty bodies.

The proposal was breath-taking not simply in its critique of shortcomings (as in prior written submissions on the treaty body system), but particularly in its proposals for change. But neither the reasoning of the Concept Paper nor the political initiatives pursued by the High Commissioner and her supporters resulted in the changes she proposed. Indeed, Arbour's proposals obtained very little support from the participants in a second 'brainstorming' meeting convened in Malbun.[47] Nearly every aspect of the proposal was criticized by one or another of the participants, who again included government representatives, treaty body members, and NGOs. However, many suggestions were proposed for further harmonization of working methods—such as the preparation of Lists of Issues for the oral dialogue with representatives of States being reviewed. Among the many suggestions voiced by participants at Malbun II was a proposal to create a separate system—an extra chamber—for individual communications lodged with any of the treaty bodies.[48] The High Commissioner recommended the designation of members to handle new complaints and authorize 'interim measures' to prohibit irreparable harm to the complainant, expedited procedures for manifestly unfounded complaints, and even giving treaty bodies the capacity to consider and decide that a violation in one case may involve provisions of more than one treaty.

Despite the absence of support for Arbour's proposed consolidation of treaty bodies, her effort was not a total failure. Participants in Malbun II and subsequent meetings engaged more actively in various 'harmonization' activities, including the preparation of guidelines for core documents, periodic reports, and greater standardization of the dialogue procedure. I participated in many of these sessions, which were often intense. These meetings would lead, once a new High Commissioner came to office in 2008, to a renewed effort to bring about reforms starting in 2009.

VII. The Dublin Statement and Treaty Body Strengthening

In November 2009, Navi Pillay, the new High Commissioner for Human Rights, began the 'treaty strengthening process' and continued it through April 2012, when she issued a major report and recommendations.[49] More than twenty consultations were convened worldwide, from Dublin (where they began) to Marrakesh, Poznan, Seoul, Pretoria, and Geneva, involving all kinds of stakeholders. Written submissions were received and posted online.[50]

Pillay reported that the treaty body 'system' doubled in size from 2004 to June 2012. During this period, four new treaty bodies came into existence, along with three new complaint procedures for other existing bodies.[51] In 2000, there were 97

[47] 'Chairperson's Summary of a Brainstorming Meeting on Reform of the Human Rights Treaty Body System', annex to UNGA, 'Letter Dated 14 September 2006 from the Permanent Representative of Liechtenstein to the UN' (18 September 2006) UN Doc A/61/351 (hereafter, 'Malbun II report').

[48] Reference was made to the CERD's proposal on this matter.

[49] Pillay, 'Strengthening' (n 1).

[50] ibid 29 (where a full list can be found).

[51] ibid 17.

experts serving on treaty bodies; in 2010 there were 125, and by 2012 there were 172.[52] Today, there are three more human rights treaties under negotiation—on multinational corporations, on the rights of 'the aging', and on the rights of peasants. Each new treaty may well establish a separate new entity to monitor its implementation. Observers have expressed concern over duplication in these treaties, as well as anxiety about differences in norms, which may create problems of consistency in interpretation and jurisprudence by the oversight bodies. A 50 per cent increase in ratifications, with the substantial backlogs in reporting and in review of individual communications remaining,[53] has created numerous pressures on the already thinly-stretched infrastructure supporting the treaty bodies.

Faced with this growth in number of instruments and of reports due, as well as the huge growth in independent experts and diverse committees monitoring compliance by States, new and huge institutional challenges for the UN and the monitoring bodies have been created. The High Commissioner's report included a bevy of recommendations developed during the many meetings and discussions convened by her. Most prominent was a proposal to develop a single five-year calendar with fixed dates for countries to report to diverse committees, which was aimed at bringing predictability to State reports.

VIII. The General Assembly Concludes the Treaty Strengthening Process

In 2012, before the High Commissioner completed her report, the UNGA intervened directly to take the process over from Geneva, eventually adopting Resolution 68/268 in April 2014.[54] Led by Russia and a 'cross-regional group' including China, Cuba, Iran, Syria, North Korea, Venezuela, and others, the Assembly's intervention seemed initially to threaten the independence of the treaty bodies, not to mention the proposals launched by Pillay. But the Resolution, after almost two more years of this process, endorsed many of the proposals made by Pillay for harmonization and simplification of working methods. Resolution 68/268 directed the UN Secretariat and the independent committees to reconsider the country-specific reporting system by adopting a simplified procedure, and suggested numerous other actions that should be taken to address institutional aspects of the system—from the languages used to the need for a training component for States burdened by numerous reports.

Although the UNGA intergovernmental process began as an effort by a group of States to instruct the treaty bodies how to conduct their affairs, it ended up technically respecting the competencies of independent treaty bodies and only 'recommended' a variety of measures, leaving it to the treaty bodies to decide whether to adopt or implement them. Its most visible output were decisions on reallocation

[52] ibid. [53] ibid.

[54] UNGA Res 68/268 (21 April 2014) UN Doc A/RES/68/268.

of financial resources, producing cost savings by curtailing the translation, interpretation, and production of documents, which account for some 65 per cent of the treaty body costs. Pocketing these savings, the UNGA authorized additional meeting time for the treaty bodies to address the reporting backlog and increase the review of reports, and allocated some five million dollars previously used for Secretariat expenses for 'capacity building' to assist States in preparing their reports to the treaty bodies.

However, a wide range of the High Commissioner's proposals were not endorsed—such as the recommendation to establish national mechanisms to coordinate with treaty bodies. Similarly, Pillay noted that the CERD recommended the creation of a joint treaty working group for communications consisting of experts from different treaty bodies whose recommendations would be presented to the plenary of the committee to which the complaint was initially directed. While she included this proposal in her 2012 report, the UNGA did not comment on it.[55]

IX. A 'World Court' for Human Rights?

Discussion of the proposal to create a 'world court' for human rights, originally made by Australia in 1947, has been revived from time to time since then by scholars.[56] The current proposal, by Manfred Nowak and Martin Scheinin, is essentially an expansion of the proposal to create a separate petition unit for treaty-based complaints by individuals.[57] The 'court' would place all treaty-related individual complaints, together with inquiries, into a new and separate unit. States would be free to designate which treaties and which rights would be subject to the binding jurisdiction of the court, and new ratification of the 'world court' statute would be all that is needed to establish such jurisdiction, they claim. Treaty bodies would continue to exist, reviewing reports on country compliance but not the individual complaints. States parties accepting the new 'world court' would thus opt out of the complaints procedures under the existing human rights treaties. Twenty-one separately selected judges would preside over the cases, which would come from all parts of the world. The proposal has gained the support of Norway, Austria, and Switzerland, and was endorsed by the Swiss Initiative for the sixtieth Anniversary of the UDHR.[58]

When participants in earlier UN treaty reform discussions addressed the matter of creating a separate body to handle all treaty-related communications, most of

[55] Pillay, 'Strengthening' (n 1) 68.

[56] Stefan Trechsel, 'A World Court for Human Rights?' (2004) 1 Northwestern J of Intl Human Rights 1, 3; Jesse Kirkpatrick, 'A Modest Proposal: A Global Court of Human Rights' (2014) 13 J of Human Rights 230.

[57] Most of the ten human rights treaties now have optional individual complaint procedures, although as many as 94 per cent of all complaints are still processed by the HRC and Committee against Torture (information obtained from the UN in response to an inquiry by the author). See also Report of the Secretary-General, Status of the Human Rights Treaty Body System, UN Doc A/71/118, Annexes VIII and IX, 18 July 2016.

[58] Scheinin, 'World Court' (n 11) 63.

those who expressed a view about such consolidation spoke positively, often citing the fact that, while States parties have obligations to give victims of violations access to an effective remedy,[59] this right remains ineffective and unenforceable at the national level. Those advocating a 'world court' seem to cite, as reasons for failure of the current system, one of two arguments: (1) the current lack of power to enforce the decisions on individual complaints under the ICCPR or other human rights treaties, or (2) the structural or organizational shortcomings of the current international supervisory system, such as the lack of visibility about decisions made and the lack of efficiency in processing cases as they come to the treaty bodies.[60]

The 'world court' proposal, its proponents argue, would correct these problems and provide victims of violations with a more effective way to pursue remedies than currently exists. Decisions on individual complaints by the treaty bodies are not binding and rarely implemented. One reason for non-implementation is that the authority of these decisions is poor,[61] in part due to low visibility, low quality of the decisions reached, and a lack of efficiency.[62] The UN devotes very minimal resources to the petition system, employing only fifteen lawyers for the unit which examines cases from all of the human rights treaties.[63]

Manfred Nowak's long list of reasons in favour of the 'world court' proposal begins by affirming the core principle that, to protect individuals, human rights must be accompanied by remedies that can be enforced. Legally binding judgements and decisions, as proposed in the 'world court', would surely be better than the current non-binding Views adopted by the HRC, Committee against Torture, and other treaty bodies. The subject matter covered in complaints to the new body could be extended to include violations by non-State actors, and the new setup could also address the matter of extraterritoriality. Nowak argues that the times have changed, as the Cold War is over and the Arab Spring has brought a new openness, and that

[59] See ICCPR art 2(3): 'Each State Party to the present Covenant undertakes: (a) To ensure that any person whose rights or freedoms as herein recognized are violated shall have an effective remedy, notwithstanding that the violation has been committed by persons acting in an official capacity; (b) To ensure that any person claiming such a remedy shall have his right thereto determined by competent judicial, administrative or legislative authorities, or by any other competent authority provided for by the legal system of the State, and to develop the possibilities of judicial remedy; (c) To ensure that the competent authorities shall enforce such remedies when granted'.

[60] See Trechsel, 'World Court' (n 56); Kirkpatrick, 'A Global Court' (n 56); Rosa Freedman, *Failing to Protect: The UN and the Politicisation of Human Rights* (OUP 2014) 141–49; and Philip Alston, 'Against a World Court for Human Rights' (2014) 28 Ethics & Intl Affairs 197. See also a simplified argument by Alston entitled 'A Truly Bad Idea: A World Court for Human Rights' (*Open Democracy*, 13 June 2014) <www.opendemocracy.net/openglobalrights-blog/philip-alston/truly-bad-idea-world-court-for-human-rights> accessed 7 April 2017.

[61] Trechsel, 'World Court' (n 56) and Freedman, *Failing to Protect* (n 60).

[62] Geir Ulfstein, 'Do We Need a World Court of Human Rights?' in Ola Engdahl and Pål Wrange (eds), *Law at War: The Law as it Was and the Law as it Should Be* (Martinus Nijhoff 2008) 261. High Commissioner Louise Arbour is associated with earlier criticism of the system for lacking accessibility and visibility to victims, and deficits in its effectiveness and authority (HRI, 'Concept Paper' (n 7) paras 21 and 27).

[63] As stated at the Oslo Conference on the Individual Communications Practice of the UN Treaty Bodies, 8–9 September 2015. The unit consists of twelve 'drafters' (P2/3 level) and three supervisors/secretaries communications procedures (P4 level). In addition, the unit was given one drafter (P3 level) on a temporary basis to help deal with the backlog.

States would more readily submit themselves to binding court decisions on a wide range of human rights issues. He points to their willingness to do this in the regional courts, whose experiences he believes would offer much insight into the new 'world court'. Enforcement of treaty body decisions could therefore be aided by actions of the Human Rights Council directly, he argues, rather than having the treaty bodies conduct their own follow-up efforts on their own decisions. A legally binding 'court' can also provide reparation to victims, pecuniary or otherwise.[64]

According to Martin Scheinin, who, together with Julia Kozma and Manfred Nowak, has developed a draft statute of the 'world court', realization of the proposal to create this new body would demonstrate the commitment of States to human rights and their universality. A 'world court' would enhance the coherence and consistency of the decisions and interpretations of norms by the committees. In this way, he argues, it would expand the binding force of the treaties worldwide.[65]

To make it happen, Nowak and Scheinin suggest that States should be free to designate which treaties, and which rights in the treaties, would be subject to the jurisdiction of the 'world court' and to its judgments, which would become binding. Nowak argues also that no treaty amendments are needed to make the institutional change to establish a 'world court' handling all petitions. A new statute, however, would need to be authorized, and a new institution, properly staffed and capable of following up on enforcement, should then be built around it.

Critics of the 'world court' cite many concerns about whether the proposed body could achieve all that it is claimed it would do to improve the binding nature of decisions on individual complaints and, more broadly, the effective implementation of human rights norms at the national level. While the visibility of the 'world court' may be its most obvious and positive added feature, there are questions whether the new body would in fact broaden the subject matter under scrutiny or, in the course of its actual development, narrow the scope of rights to those to which States subject themselves. The ability of States to pick and choose which rights in which treaties they would subject themselves to under the new 'world court' raises concerns: would this diminish existing obligations under the human rights treaties, and would it at the same time enable States to 'capture' the court's jurisprudence in ways more friendly to States than to rights-holders?[66] Similarly, it may not be feasible to assume that States would agree to have the new 'world court' cover extraterritorial acts and abuses by non-State actors.

This leads to the question whether, indeed, the times have changed in the ways Nowak suggests. Regressive trends in the former 'eastern bloc' and the collapse of the

[64] See Nowak, 'It's Time' (n 12); Manfred Nowak, 'The Right of Victims of Human Rights Violations to a Remedy: The Need for a World Court of Human Rights' (2014) 32 Nordic J of Human Rights 1, 10–11; and Nowak, 'World Court' (n 11). Non-pecuniary forms of reparation could include rehabilitative care, satisfaction, guarantees of non-repetition, etc.

[65] Scheinin, 'World Court' (n 11). See also Julia Kozma, Manfred Nowak, and Martin Scheinin, 'A World Court of Human Rights: Consolidated Draft Stature and Commentary' (2010) <www.eui.eu/Documents/DepartmentsCentres/Law/Professors/Scheinin/ConsolidatedWorldCourtStatute.pdf> accessed 7 April 2017.

[66] Alston, 'Against a World Court' (n 60).

'Arab Spring', together with a crackdown on human rights defenders and principles worldwide, may be the more relevant context in which this debate is unfolding. As for the possible role of the Human Rights Council in overseeing enforcement, the Council remains a highly political body, with a membership that is less respectful of human rights than earlier in its history.[67] Its Universal Periodic Review procedure has not, to date, developed an expert component, and it remains unlikely to take on an impartial follow-up role for treaty body decisions as proposed by Nowak.

As a practical matter, there are also serious questions about whether the new 'court' would result in greater implementation of decisions. Under the current complaints procedures of the treaty bodies, there is presently no independent fact-finding, and only a rudimentary, largely unexplored capacity for examination of witnesses and experts.[68] The authority of the treaty body decisions is in part limited because they lack a reliable means for assessing the facts. It is unclear if the will and resources exist to change this. If it is not changed, there are questions about whether national authorities are likely to implement the new 'court's' judgements when based on such procedural rules.

A large array of other practical problems with the proposed 'world court' have also been noted, ranging from whether its worldwide focus would result in an unmanageable overload of cases[69] to whether the substantial resources it would require would actually be allocated. In view of the UNGA's recent action to cut support for the treaty system following the 'treaty strengthening process',[70] the 'world court' seems likely to encounter significant resource roadblocks at its outset.

Scheinin has raised the importance of ensuring coherence and consistency of the decisions reached. Previously, advocates of a single unified treaty body questioned whether the distinct and separate treaty bodies, with differing legal instruments governing their decisions and staff dedicated to their separate entities, would maintain consistency.[71] In an important article, Geir Ulfstein has asked whether creating a separate 'world court' for complaint procedures under the treaty bodies, but separate from these bodies, might in fact fracture the movement towards the coherence of the international legal regime for human rights.[72] Nowak and Scheinin do not address this matter in their proposal.[73]

Among the factors relevant to this is whether the new 'court' would operate on a basis of deference (complementarity) with regional human rights courts, or function instead as the top of a hierarchy. It remains uncertain what authority the decisions of other treaty bodies and regional courts would have for the new 'world court' and what the screening process for taking up decisions from other courts for further review would look like. All these matters would be up for negotiation and decision in a new structure.

[67] Freedman, *Failing to Protect* (n 60) 147.
[68] Ulfstein, 'Do We Need a World Court?' (n 62) 265.
[69] ibid 263.
[70] Christen Broecker and Michael O'Flaherty, 'The Outcome of the General Assembly's Treaty Body Strengthening Process' (Universal Rights Group, June 2014) <www.universal-rights.org/wp-content/uploads/2015/02/URG_Policy_Brief_web_spread_hd.pdf> accessed 7 April 2017.
[71] HRI, 'Concept Paper' (n 7) para 42.
[72] Ulfstein, 'Do We Need a World Court?' (n 62).
[73] ibid 271.

This brings us to ask whether the 'world court' is a politically feasible option in today's world. Would States consent to broad and binding jurisdiction by such a court and would it be applicable, as well as enforceable, worldwide? Rosa Freedman recalls that a diverse set of issues—such as sexual orientation or the treatment of migrants—still divide the member States of the UN and are likely to continue to inhibit broad consent to the 'world court' decisions on controversial matters.[74] As long as adherence to the court's jurisdiction is voluntary, she questions the feasibility of enforcing human rights treaty guarantees.

Philip Alston, whose earlier work on treaty reform was so central, believes the 'world court' proposal is not merely utopian, but is actually misconceived. Citing the 'world's deep-rooted human rights dysfunctions', Alston emphasizes the need to have nationally-based legal systems in place, including national accountability mechanisms, in order to bring about implementation of human rights decisions stemming from the treaty-based complaint procedures. He further notes the weakness or absence of effective regional systems in Asia, the Pacific, and the Arab world. 'These complex challenges cannot be dealt with in a meaningful way by seeking to bypass them all and create a [world court for human rights] as if it were some magical panacea.'[75]

X. Improving Individual Communications: What Should be Done?

In considering the 'institutional future of the Covenants', the present chapter has drawn attention to the history of UN treaty reform efforts, which have been longstanding and extensive. Much attention has historically been paid to the question of reforming State reporting procedures under the treaties, and, in marked contrast, very little to the matter of how to handle individual communications (complaints) procedures that are also part of the same instruments. Despite the interest in justiciability expressed by the President of the Human Rights Council in March 2016,[76] there has been, for the most part, a dearth of serious discussion of how to examine such communications and to implement the rights guarantees of the treaties. It has only been with the proposal to create a 'world court' of human rights that the issue of effectiveness of the individual complaints procedures has gained attention, and raised questions. For this, Nowak and Scheinin deserve credit.

In general, discussions about reform of the communications procedures in the context of treaty reform have largely focused on follow-up to decisions on cases—not the admissibility, adjudication, staffing, identification of facts or evidence, standards of proof, normative consistency, or other aspects of the communications proceedings themselves. Yet these issues need attention to enable the work and decisions of any new body on complaints to ensure the availability of redress to individual complainants and the enforcement of the treaty norms.

[74] Freedman, *Failing to Protect* (n 60) 147–49.
[75] Alston, 'A Truly Bad Idea' (n 60).
[76] 'HRC High-level Panel Discussion' (n 3).

One exception to this pattern took place when the CERD raised the issue of a creating a new and separate institution to deal with communications. In 2006, the CERD had proposed that the High Commissioner create a joint body to handle *all* individual complaints submitted to all treaty bodies, arguing this would add visibility to the complaints proceedings. In October 2011, in a discussion at a small and rather narrowly-focused meeting on petitions organized by the Office of the UN High Commissioner for Human Rights (OHCHR) within the 'treaty strengthening process', the CERD suggested a different approach which would not require treaty amendment. It proposed that the joint body could be an 'Inter-Committee' working group to prepare decisions on individual cases. It would be composed of persons from each of the ten treaty bodies who would reach recommendations on the complaints and then present them, in turn, for formal approval to the plenary of the treaty body to which the complaint was initially sent.

The meeting where this idea was presented included only seven representatives from five treaty bodies. The member from the CERD, urging a holistic approach to treaty implementation, stated that the proposed joint body would offer opportunities to harmonize registration of cases and rules of procedure, and provide consistency in the application of admissibility criteria for complaints and in the interpretation of substantive norms. Key to the argument was the idea that this joint body would help bring about some cross-fertilization between treaty bodies, allowing additional expertise on the norms in question to be brought to bear by members of other treaty bodies. Later, as noted above, in 2012, the CERD formally proposed creating a joint body, and the High Commissioner endorsed the idea, though no action on it was taken by the UNGA.

There are obviously serious drawbacks that would come about if one were to consolidate all of the communications under all of the treaties into a single body, some of which were raised in the OHCHR-organized discussion in 2011. Such disadvantages could be legal, organizational, logistical, and/or financial. Because each treaty only authorizes its members to deal with that specific treaty, it is unclear whether there are legal obstacles to members of one treaty body acting to decide complaints submitted to another body. Similarly, there may be difficulty in agreeing to the optimal composition of a joint body, given that the overwhelming number and proportion of complaints presently submitted to the UN human rights treaties are directed to the HRC, with the Committee against Torture in a distant second place. Other treaty bodies have complaints procedures that have rarely if ever been employed, and they have little expertise on deliberating on complaints. This raises the question of whether membership in the proposed joint body should be weighted or not. Alternatively, there needs to be consideration of whether an equal number of members from each treaty body should routinely serve on the joint body. No one has yet examined what might be the outcome of such composition on the decisions reached, but it cannot be assumed it would constitute an ideal outcome. Since the plenary sessions of each treaty body could overrule the joint working group's decisions, there is also concern about whether such an arrangement would lessen one committee's 'ownership' of final decisions that will be taken by a different body. Additionally, there are logistical and financial matters to be sorted out to be able to convene such a body in a timely fashion, given the staggered meeting schedule of the different committees, not to mention staffing issues.

In considering the institutional future of the Covenants and the other human rights treaties more broadly, the likely size and role of individual complaints proceedings clearly needs more attention. There are already signs that the number of complaints is growing. Among other issues meriting attention are how to ensure the independence of the treaty bodies handling complaints and the impartiality of their members; whether there are inconsistent outcomes and unconvincing reasoning in cases; whether there are adequate procedural guarantees (and whether others, such as a fact-finding mechanism, should be added); whether some cases have been unduly prolonged or too expeditiously addressed; and the degree to which complainants conduct 'forum shopping' and play off international institutions against one another. Yet another area of concern is the language about complaints and remedies in the treaties themselves, which differs; the remedies in specific cases are also treated differently by the relevant treaty bodies, sometimes because of the specific and differing language of the treaties themselves. How to handle the backlog of cases remains a key concern, too. The 'world court' proposal should focus attention on whether or not there is compliance or non-compliance by ratifying States with the decisions of the treaty bodies. Clearly there is much more to be examined regarding the operation and handling of individual complaints procedures, whether by a joint entity or the original, separate committees.

Bringing together representatives of ten different treaty bodies into a special 'working group' or new committee to reach a decision on a case involving a human right in one of the treaties raises very serious questions about the likely competence and experience of the persons chosen to serve on the proposed unified body. This is a reality whether or not the new body is called a working group or a 'world court'. Most human rights complaints to the UN (74 per cent) are handled by one Committee, the HRC. The Committee against Torture, in second place, receives 20 per cent.[77] It seems inconceivable that a majority of experts deciding cases sent

[77] According to the Office of the High Commissioner for Human Rights, as of December 2016, the HRC, which first met some forty years ago, had dealt with a total of 2282 individual complaints (out of a total of 2924 received), of which 1084 had been considered inadmissible or discontinued, and 1198 had been the subject of merits decisions. By comparison, as of the end of December 2016, the Committee against Torture had dealt with a total of 623 cases (out of a total of 892 received), of which 314 were inadmissible or discontinued, and 309 had been the subject of merits decisions. The CERD—in its more than forty-five-year history—had dealt with a total of only 55 communications as of the end of December 2016, of which 21 were inadmissible or discontinued and 34 had been the subject of merits decisions. The CEDAW Committee, whose experience with complaints is much more recent, had dealt with only 67 communications in total by the end of 2016 (out of a total of 110 received), of which 42 were declared inadmissible or discontinued, and 25 have been the subject of merits decisions, 23 of which were violations. In recent years, other treaties have added complaints procedures, although not all of them are yet in force nor have all bodies adjudicated such cases. For the HRC, see 'Statistical Survey of Individual Complaints Dealt with by the Human Rights Committee under the Optional Protocol to the International Covenant on Civil and Political Rights' (March 2016) <www.ohchr.org/Documents/HRBodies/CCPR/StatisticalSurvey.xls> accessed 9 May 2017. For the Committee against Torture, see 'Status of Communications Dealt With by CAT Under Art. 22 Procedure' (15 August 2015) <www.ohchr.org/Documents/HRBodies/CAT/StatisticalSurvey.xls> accessed 9 May 2017. For the CERD, see 'Statistical Survey of Individual Complaints Dealt With by the Committee on the Elimination of Racial Discirmination (*sic*) under Article 14 of the Convention for the Elimination of all forms of Racial

to one specific treaty body would actually come from another entity, and possibly operate without substantive knowledge of the subject matter of the other treaty (or treaties)—or that they should. Yet that is one of the options that would exist if the proposal for a joint petitions body were to be implemented.

The fiftieth anniversary of adoption of the International Covenants on human rights is a fitting moment not only to ask whether the nations of the world that have ratified them are implementing the norms contained in these instruments, but also to ask whether institutional changes can bring about better compliance. While the proposal for a new 'world court' to implement the human rights guarantees in the ICCPR and other human rights treaties has drawn attention to the petition system, there remain many questions about the feasibility or desirability of such a new mechanism. Instead of arguing about the details presented in the draft statute prepared by advocates, energy and advocacy would be better devoted to examining the current system, exploring proposals developed during the treaty body strengthening process and thereafter. In searching for an institutional future, it is essential to keep in mind the need to ensure that the victims of violations have an effective remedy if the rights in the Covenants are violated. Currently, the decisions under individual petition procedures are little known and less observed by the States concerned.

When, in March 2016, the Human Rights Council's President spoke of making all rights justiciable and consolidating the two Covenant committees into a single body, he did not offer suggestions about how this might be achieved. It seems important to explore whether the different treaty bodies—the two Covenant committees as well as the other treaty monitoring committees—differ in their treatment of the normative standards they consider in individual cases.

Institutional reforms of the treaty bodies should meet several overarching concerns. In principle, any change should bring about better implementation of substantive obligations and enhance the level of protection afforded to rights-holders by States parties to the human rights treaties. Similarly, any such change should maintain, or intensify, the scrutiny of implementation of the treaty guarantees by the treaty bodies. At a minimum, any institutional changes in the future should not weaken or dilute their implementation. In recent years, a plethora of individual complaints procedures have been added to the treaties, including before the Committee on Economic, Social and Cultural Rights. New treaty bodies, such as the Committee on the Rights of Persons with Disabilities, not to mention the Committee on the Elimination of Discrimination against Women, bring new perspectives to bear on some rights issues.

Therefore, it would seem that there is room and time for another modest proposal: to explore whether there have been differences in treatment of human rights norms depending on which treaty body examines an individual complaint. One way forward might be to conduct studies to review and reassess decisions in individual

Discrimination' (May 2014) <www.ohchr.org/Documents/HRBodies/CERD/StatisticalSurvey.xls> accessed 9 May 2017. Finally, for the CEDAW Committee, see 'Status of Communications Dealt With by CEDAW Optional Protocol' <www.ohchr.org/Documents/HRBodies/CEDAW/StatisticalSurvey.xls> accessed 9 May 2017.

cases that have already been decided by the committees. Experimentation and simulations of how the cases might be decided differently by differently structured treaty bodies or joint committees could be conducted in an academic or think-tank setting. Alternatively, some model cases could be prepared and given to differently constructed joint committees to see whether each comes up with similar or different outcomes.

Similarly, there is also a need to look into the ways different States have (or have not) upheld the individual complaints decisions of the treaty monitoring committees. While the UN Secretariat has been fostering a variety of efforts aimed at harmonizing the approaches of the committees for the review of State reports, there has been little effort to examine why some States are more or less likely to comply with individual complaints decisions and proposed remedies on different topics.

It is also important to ask what will happen to the jurisprudence of the treaty bodies and to human rights more generally if the Covenant committees and/or other human rights treaty bodies are left to work solely on State reports, as the 'world court' proposal suggests they would. Would separating consideration of general compliance by a State from the consideration of individual cases lead to inconsistency and incoherence in the normative development of human rights?

To date, there has been substantial progress in adopting reforms proposed for State reporting under the human rights treaties. But there remains, by and large, a dearth of attention to the individual petition proceedings and the enforcement of their outcomes. When we look back at the treaty reform proposals that have seized reformers at the UN, very many of them concerning State reporting (including those in Alston's and Bayefsky's earlier studies) have already been implemented. This reminds us that academic proposals and subsequent advocacy have the potential to create real improvements. More attention to the individual complaints procedures could also have a substantial and institutional impact on the future efficacy of the Covenants and other human rights treaty bodies.

It seems that a proposal to abandon current human rights treaty implementation structures and start anew in favour of creating a 'world court' is based less on an analysis of what has transpired than on a desire to create the next 'big idea' in human rights in the form of a court. It also seems that questions of consolidation of staff into a single petitions unit are not based on specific data. While there are surely economies of scale to be found and expertise can be better focused in the treaty branch, it seems clear that more study is needed—the questions posed above are in need of attention, as are questions of optimal staffing requirements.

Surely the ultimate goal—to provide greater human rights protection and enforcement of decisions on individual complaints—merits exploring such approaches before forging forward too quickly with new institutional structures. Rather than rushing to tear down the treaty body system that currently exists, there is a need to do the work either to correct it or prove that it is broken beyond repair. Anything less would be a dangerous sacrifice of the institutional and legal foundations upon which the human rights treaties have been constructed. In short, there is a need for greater due diligence. Supporters of the Covenants and advocates for human rights—still the 'idea of our time'—owe it not just to ourselves but to the members of communities around the world seeking to implement the Covenants and related treaties in ways that are more effective.

Bibliography

Alston, Philip, 'A Truly Bad Idea: A World Court for Human Rights' (*Open Democracy*, 13 June 2014) <www.opendemocracy.net/openglobalrights-blog/philip-alston/truly-bad-idea-world-court-for-human-rights> accessed 7 April 2017

Alston, Philip, 'Against a World Court for Human Rights' (2014) 28 Ethics & Intl Affairs 197

Alston, Philip, and Crawford, James (eds), *The Future of Human Rights Treaty Monitoring* (CUP 2000)

Bayefsky, Anne F (ed), *The UN Human Rights System in the 21st Century* (Kluwer 2000)

Bayefsky, Anne F, *The UN Human Rights Treaty System: Universality at the Crossroads* (Martinus Nijhoff 2001)

Broecker, Christen, and O'Flaherty, Michael, 'The Outcome of the General Assembly's Treaty Body Strengthening Process' (Universal Rights Group, June 2014) <www.universal-rights.org/wp-content/uploads/2015/02/URG_Policy_Brief_web_spread_hd.pdf> accessed 7 April 2017

Freedman, Rosa, *Failing to Protect: The UN and the Politicisation of Human Rights* (OUP 2014)

Henkin, Louis (ed), *The International Bill of Human Rights: The Covenant on Civil and Political Rights* (Columbia University Press 1981)

Heyns, Christof, and Viljoen, Frans, 'The Impact of the United Nations Human Rights Treaties on the Domestic Level' (2001) 23 Human Rights Q 483

Kirkpatrick, Jesse, 'A Modest Proposal: A Global Court of Human Rights' (2014) 13 J of Human Rights 230

Kozma, Julia, Nowak, Manfred, and Scheinin, Martin, 'A World Court of Human Rights: Consolidated Draft Stature and Commentary' (2010) <www.eui.eu/Documents/DepartmentsCentres/Law/Professors/Scheinin/ConsolidatedWorldCourtStatute.pdf> accessed 7 April 2017

Nowak, Manfred, 'It's Time for a World Court of Human Rights' in M Cherif Bassiouni and William A Schabas (eds), *New Challenges for the UN Human Rights Machinery: What Future for the UN Treaty Body System and the Human Rights Council Procedures?* (Intersentia 2011)

Nowak, Manfred, 'The Need for a World Court of Human Rights' (2007) 7 Human Rights L Rev 251

Nowak, Manfred, 'The Right of Victims of Human Rights Violations to a Remedy: The Need for a World Court of Human Rights' (2014) 32 Nordic J of Human Rights 1

O'Flaherty, Michael, 'The High Commissioner and the Treaty Bodies' in Felice D Gaer and Christen L Broecker (eds), *The United Nations High Commissioner for Human Rights: Conscience for the World* (Brill 2014)

Ramcharan, Bertrand, *A UN High Commissioner in Defence of Human Rights* (Brill 2004)

Robertson, AH, 'The Implementation System: International Measures' in Louis Henkin (ed), *The International Bill of Human Rights: The Covenant on Civil and Political Rights* (Columbia University Press 1981)

Scheinin, Martin, 'Towards a World Court of Human Rights' (2009) Swiss Initiative to Commemorate the 60th Anniversary of the UDHR <www.enlazandoalternativas.org/IMG/pdf/hrCourt_scheinin0609.pdf> accessed 9 May 2017

Trechsel, Stefan, 'A World Court for Human Rights?' (2004) 1 Northwestern J of Intl Human Rights 1

Ulfstein, Geir, 'Do We Need a World Court of Human Rights?' in Ola Engdahl and Pål Wrange (eds), *Law at War: The Law as it Was and the Law as it Should Be* (Martinus Nijhoff 2008)

Index

The manufacturer's authorised representative in the EU for product safety is Oxford University Press España S.A. of el Parque Empresarial San Fernando de Henares, Avenida de Castilla, 2 – 28830 Madrid (www.oup.es/en or product.safety@oup.com). OUP España S.A. also acts as importer into Spain of products made by the manufacturer.

www.ingramcontent.com/pod-product-compliance
Lightning Source LLC
LaVergne TN
LVHW011906200926
848484LV00002B/544
* 9 7 8 0 1 9 8 8 2 5 8 9 0 *